Forbidden Grounds

Forbidden Grounds

The Case Against Employment Discrimination Laws

Richard A. Epstein

Harvard University Press
Cambridge, Massachusetts
London, England

Library of Congress Cataloging-in-Publication Data

Epstein, Richard Allen, 1943-
    Forbidden grounds: the case against employment discrimination
laws / Richard A. Epstein.
        p. cm.
    Includes index.
    ISBN 0-674-30808-5
    1. Discrimination in employment—Law and legislation—United
States. I. Title.
KF3464.E64 1992
344.73'01133—dc20
[347.3041133]

91-25250
CIP

To Eileen

For Everything

Contents

Preface

I came of age during the debates over the Civil Rights Act of 1964. My views on the subject at the time were quite conventional. I thought that the act was long overdue, that the patterns and practices of discrimination that existed in the South and around the United States were apt targets of legislative correction, and that the only hard questions about the Civil Rights Act concerned appropriate limits and techniques of implementation. In those early years I can recall only two occasions on which some of my contemporaries voiced any note of caution or uneasiness about the act itself.

For more than twenty years I did little to rethink my original position. But as the level of debate, discussion, and discord increased, my attention was drawn back into an area that was far removed from my immediate professional concerns. My original background, training, and inclination were those of a common law lawyer whose major project was to work out the correct relationships among property, contract, and tort law. I was quite content to leave questions of public law and public regulation to others, as long as I could understand the narrower domain I had carved out for myself. As my own work developed, however, I discovered that it was intellectually far more difficult than I had previously supposed to maintain the separation between private law and the grander questions of constitutional law and public regulation. Understanding common law rules required more sophisticated tools than an unflinching respect for the principle of individual autonomy on which my earlier thinking and work had rested.

In working out the exceptions to the autonomy principle in common law, especially as they related to individual actions taken by mistake or necessity (that is, imminent peril to life or property), I came, somewhat reluctantly, to the conclusion that some principle of social utility or welfare lay beneath much of the common law, and that this principle was powerful enough to account both for the areas of the common law where the autonomy principle has proved powerful and enduring and those where it has not. Dealing with the strengths and limits of the autonomy principle slowly led me to think about various questions of constitutional law, and resulted in my book *Takings: Private Power and the Power of Eminent Domain,* which was published by Harvard University Press in 1985.

As I was thinking through the radical implications of that book, my intellectual uneasiness about the New Deal and the welfare state came by degrees to be carried over to the second wave of reform legislation of Lyndon Johnson's Great Society, including the civil rights acts, at least as they applied to matters of employment discrimination. The refusal to deal for any reason lies at the root of a system of freedom of contract, itself the centerpiece of any common law order based on the autonomy principle. The employment discrimination laws represent the antithesis of freedom of contract. Yet these laws do not fit into the categories of necessity or mistake that challenge that principle. Employment markets are largely competitive and hence regulation is not justified as a means to control monopoly or to protect workers against unwise choices made under conditions of necessity. Workers and employers generally have good information about the key terms of their relationships, so that regulation is not necessary to combat mistake, especially where the issues are unrelated to health or safety. The civil rights laws cannot be justified as full disclosure laws. As I examined the matter more closely, I could not shake my own initial conviction that the employment discrimination laws were an unjustified limitation on the principle of freedom of contract, notwithstanding the overwhelming social consensus in their favor.

It also became clear to me that there was no modern (that is, post-1964), sustained treatment that either defended or attacked the employment discrimination rules. So I decided to write that study. Over the course of writing the book, as I learned more about the operation of the civil rights laws, I found that my convictions only grew stronger. There is no adequate theoretical foundation or practical justification for the employment discrimination laws. The strong national commitment to the aggressive enforcement of the antidiscrimination laws is, I believe, mistaken. I chose the title *Forbidden Grounds: The Case against Employment Discrimination Laws* to indicate my opposition to the entire complex of modern civil rights laws and their administration. In my view, the only hard questions about the employment discrimination laws concern the types and magnitudes of the social dislocations that result from their vigorous enforcement.

The political response is, quite evidently, radically different from my own. I started writing this book in the fall of 1988, before the Supreme

Court handed down its controversial decisions in a number of civil rights cases, most notably *Wards Cove Packing Co., Inc. v. Atonio,* which effectively nullified the business necessity test as it applied in disparate impact cases. Since these decisions were handed down in the spring of 1989, there has been a determined effort in Congress to reverse those decisions, in order "to restore and strengthen" the prior edifice of the civil rights laws. During that debate no one chose, or dared, to advance any of the arguments developed in this book. Instead, both the Democratic Congress and the Republican Bush administration announced themselves four-square in favor of civil rights legislation in principle, and differed only on the scope and enforcement of the civil rights effort.

For a considerable period of time the debate between the two sides focused on the issue of "quotas." The Bush Administration insisted that the proposed amendments to the civil rights statutes would introduce a system of quotas into the civil rights law, but it never could explain why it was that quotas should be regarded as a bad thing. The Congress for its part denied that there was an explicit creation of quotas, but in turn it never could explain why the strict enforcement of the civil rights laws only in favor of protected classes would not lead employers to seek the safe haven of hiring by the numbers. The struggle in Washington bore all the marks of hard-fought interest group politics. In the course of the debate, neither side addressed any of the fundamental issues about the desirability of civil rights laws as such. The dangers they pose to open markets, competitive fitness, individual freedom, equal treatment before the law, and informed public discourse were passed by in total silence.

There was an impasse at the end of 1990 when President Bush vetoed the 1990 Civil Rights Act with evident reluctance. Yet the next year when faced with a new Congress, the President backed off his earlier position after the bitter confirmation battle over Clarence Thomas's nomination to the Supreme Court. The 1991 Civil Rights Act was signed on November 21, 1991, by a reluctant President under the watchful eye of a suspicious Congress. It was a joyless occasion, immediately marred by another round of intense political infighting over the scope of affirmative action programs within the federal government. In my judgment the compromise Act represents a clear victory for the aggressive enforcement of the civil rights laws. One purpose of the statute is to "codify the concepts of 'business necessity' and 'job related' enunciated by the Supreme Court in Griggs v. Duke Power Co., 401 U.S. 424 (1971), and in other Supreme Court decisions prior to Wards Cove Packing Co. v. Atonio, 490 U.S. 642 (1989)." The criticisms of *Griggs* that are contained in chapters 11 and 12 therefore have lost none of their relevance, given the Congress's thinly veiled repudiation of *Ward's Cove*.

The 1991 Civil Rights Act also makes a number of important practical changes that should be noted in passing. Thus the Act provides that: (1) "an unlawful employment practice is established when the complaining party demonstrates that race, color, religion, sex, or national origin was a motivating factor for any employment practice, even though other factors also motivated the practice" (§703(m)(2)); where the improper motive has not influenced the employment decision, the court may grant declaratory and injunctive relief, and attorney's fees, but not damages, reinstatement, or other forms of specific relief (§706(g)(2)(B) (see pages 174-175)); (3) that race and gender norming shall be unlawful employment practices (§703(l) (see page 238)); (4) for compensatory and punitive damages, between $50,000 and $300,000, keyed to the size of the firm in cases of intentional discrimination (§1981); (5) that the statute of limitations in cases challenging seniority systems should begin to run only from the date that the violation occurred or adversely impacted upon an individual employee, whichever occurred later (§706(e)); (6) that the prevailing party can recover expert as well as attorney's fees (§706(k)); (7) that the protections of the Civil Rights Act now apply to both houses of Congress. The 1991 Act also contains an extensive codification of the extraterritorial effect of the Act; a major revision of its provisions on consent decrees (§703(n)), and a general provision that states: "Nothing in the amendments made by this title shall be construed to affect court-ordered remedies, affirmative action, or conciliation agreements, that are in accordance with law" (1991 Act, §116).

The full set of changes wrought by the 1991 legislation will doubtless give rise to difficult problems of interpretation and application. How, for example, will a court thread the delicate line between voluntary affirmative action and implicit quotas? But the issues now squarely on the judicial agenda in no way address any of the substantive themes developed in this book. To be sure, any ambiguity on Congressional intent is dispelled for the future: there is no longer any doubt that disparate impact, business necessity, and affirmative action are part of the present civil rights law. Yet the historical evolution detailed in chapters 10 and 19 still show how the Supreme Court was able under the guise of interpretation to remake the color-blind 1964 Civil Rights Act in its own image. More important, the question of justification has been assumed away in the current political climate. The fundamental challenge to the civil rights legislation is whether the centralized system of employment relations is superior to a decentralized system of market control. The White House never made these arguments; and the Congress never responded to them. I have not tried to rewrite the book in response to the most recent legislative developments, and there is no reason to do so. The strength of its arguments will have to be tested in nonpolitical markets.

In working through a book of this length and difficulty, I have incurred many debts. The first is to Francis O'Connell, Jr., who urged me to submit the original proposal to the Olin Foundation, which generously responded by funding two grants, one for the fall of 1988 and a second for the fall of 1989. These grants provided me with sufficient released time to complete the initial draft of this manuscript. The Olin Foundation has proved itself the ideal supporter of academic work, and its executive director, James Piereson, gave me constant encouragement and perfect freedom to complete a controversial project as I wanted to do it.

I am also indebted to the many people who have read and commented on various portions of the book, or some of the articles that I have written as offshoots of the project. Gary S. Becker, Penelope Brook, John Donohue, Samuel Estreicher, Abner Greene, and Richard A. Posner, as well as several referees for Harvard University Press, provided me with detailed written comments on an earlier draft of the manuscript which proved invaluable as I worked through subsequent revisions. Douglas G. Baird and Walter J. Blum made helpful oral comments, and Elizabeth Bartholet, Gerhard Casper, Douglas Ginsburg, Michael Gottesman, Daniel Greenberg, James Gwartney, Andrew Kull, Saunders Mac Lane, Ellen Frankel Paul, Stewart Schwab, Steven Shavell, Cass R. Sunstein, and Stephen F. Williams provided valuable comments, either written or oral, on specific sections or chapters of the manuscript in its earlier form. I also received useful advice and guidance about the vast literature on various aspects of the employment discrimination laws from Ian Ayres, David H. Kaye, Glenn Loury, Paul Meier, Suzanna Sherry, and Stephen Stigler. Finally, I have benefited enormously from discussions of the issues involved in these cases with Frank H. Easterbrook, Michael W. McConnell, Geoffrey P. Miller, David A. Strauss, and other stalwarts of the Chicago round table lunches. The debts that I owe to these and other scholars should be evident on each page of the manuscript.

I have also benefited from the opportunity to present all or portions of the book at workshops and lectures over the past several years. I have thus discussed ideas for this book at The University of Chicago Law School, the Department of Economics at Florida State University,

Georgetown Law School, George Washington University, Harvard Law School, McGill University Law School, New York University Law School, Northwestern Law School, the University of Illinois Law School, the University of Pennsylvania Law School, the University of Pittsburgh Law School, the University of Toledo Law School, Virginia Law School, and West Virginia Law School. I would also like to thank the American Enterprise Institute, The American Law and Economics Association, The Cato Institute, The Federalist Society, and the Social Philosophy and Policy Center at Bowling Green State University for sponsoring the conferences and debates at which I have been able to present many of the central ideas contained in this book.

At The University of Chicago, my dean and friend, Geoffrey Stone, provided full support and encouragement for the research project. I owe a large debt of gratitude to William Schwesig and Charles Ten Brink, our reference librarians, who always seemed able to track down the obscure references that I needed to pursue. I have also been blessed with three extremely able and conscientious research assistants. David Lawson, who put in too many hours on the manuscript during the 1988–89 academic year, proved indispensable in talking through the original design of the manuscript, gathering material, and editing the text, all with great insight, skill, tenacity, and dedication. Thereafter in 1989 and 1990 I had the help, first, of Ellyn Acker and then of Abigail Abrahams, both of whom provided invaluable assistance, both substantive and technical, in seeing the manuscript into its final form. Finally, my secretary, Kathy Kepchar, struggled with an unwieldy manuscript on two different word-processing systems and was always able to create order out of chaos.

A special word of thanks is also due to Michael Aronson, general editor at Harvard University Press, for his support of this project and the manuscript that emerged from it. I also thank Amanda Heller, whose expert copyediting caught and corrected innumerable mistakes of both style and substance that crept into the manuscript during its many rounds of revisions, and Lauren Osborne and Susan Wallace, who saw the book through its final stages of production.

Finally, my wife, Eileen, and my three children, Melissa, Benjamin, and Elliot, showed great patience and understanding when a distracted husband and father was trying to work through the ideas contained in this book.

Chicago
November 26, 1991

Forbidden Grounds

Introduction:
Consensus and Its Perils

The subject of this book is the proper place and scope of the antidiscrimination principle, especially as it applies to the employment relationship, in both the private and the public sector. There is little question that a broad antidiscrimination principle lies at the core of American political and intellectual understandings of a just and proper society, not only in employment but also in housing and public accommodations, medical care, education, indeed in all areas of public and private life. The consensus in favor of the principle is as wide as it is deep. Its implications profoundly influence the shape and efficiency not merely of American labor markets but also of our basic social institutions.

The cultural and historical reasons for this social consensus on discrimination provide powerful leitmotifs for the present legal discourse, especially on issues of race. The history of official and private discrimination in American life covers slavery in the South, the Civil War, Reconstruction, Jim Crow, segregation in the military, massive resistance to school desegregation, sit-ins and lunch counters, and struggles for the ballot.[1] The enormous successes in changing a misguided, and often hateful, pattern of race relations have all come through sustained government action, which often depended on the use of force. Even today frequent outbreaks of racial violence, conflict, boycotts, and demonstrations have ushered in a new spate of racial tensions greater than any that have existed in the previous twenty years. The symbolic role of an antidiscrimination statute in this context is not something that can be easily ignored or cast aside.

---

1. The relevant literature is vast. For some useful sources, see Hugh Davis Graham, *The Civil Rights Era: Origins and Development of National Policy, 1960–1972* (1990); Richard Kluger, *Simple Justice* (1976); Charles Lofgren, *The Plessy Case* (1987); Andrew Kull, *The Color-Blind Constitution* (1992); C. Vann Woodward, *The Strange Career of Jim Crow* (3rd rev. ed., 1974).

The history of sex discrimination is not as searing as that of race relations, but the transformation of the legal rights of women in both the public and private sphere has been accompanied by extensive social unrest that has often spilled over into violence. Limitations on the civil capacity for ordinary social and business transactions form a part of our nation's history, and the same is true of the long battle over women's suffrage. The full complex of women's issues is still very much in the forefront. In my judgment, feminism is the single most powerful social movement of our time, one that addresses every aspect of human and social life. But in this realm too we have not reached closure. There are continuing signs of unrest, with reports of widespread uneasiness about women in the military, and a series of incidents over such matters as whether women reporters should be barred from men's locker rooms after sporting events.

The scope of the antidiscrimination norm has its most powerful appeal in matters of race and sex, but it has been extended to other areas. When the 1964 Civil Rights Act was passed, there was little, if any, public sentiment to regulate discrimination on the basis of either age or handicap. But within a matter of a few years, protection against these forms of discrimination by analogy and extension became a dominant theme within our legal culture.

In this book I treat all four forms of discrimination in the employment market—race, sex, age, and disability—and take up the present consensus about the antidiscrimination principle as it applies to one corner of the total picture: labor markets. I argue that this consensus focuses too heavily on historical injustices, for which there is no adequate remedy, and too little on the economic and social consequences that are generated by the antidiscrimination laws, especially as they have been shaped and extended within the American political system. The future and present are being slighted in favor of the past.

In undertaking this critique of the antidiscrimination laws in employment, I have engaged in a process of relentless disaggregation by looking closely at the application of each form of law as it applies to existing employment markets. My work follows in the steps of others who have expressed uneasiness about the desirability or operation of these laws.[2] Yet several of these authors did their major work in the early period of

---

2. Gary S. Becker, *The Economics of Discrimination* (2nd ed., 1971); Harold Demsetz, "Minorities in the Market Place," 43 *N.C. L. Rev.* 271 (1965); Richard A. Posner, "An Economic Analysis of Sex Discrimination Laws," 56 *U. Chi. L. Rev.* 1311 (1989); Thomas

the civil rights movement, and none of them has urged the outright rejection of the antidiscrimination principle in private employment or the repeal of Title VII of the 1964 Civil Rights Act, as I do. I am under no illusion about the magnitude of the enterprise of seeking to undo the legal status quo, given the enormous support that it commands from the intellectual, business, and political elites in this country. The basic mood in the United States on Title VII is well captured by the opening words of President George Bush's message vetoing the proposed 1990 Civil Rights Act.

> I am today returning without my approval S. 2104, the "Civil Rights Act of 1990." I deeply regret having to take this action with respect to a bill bearing such a title, especially since it contains certain provisions that I strongly endorse.
>
> Discrimination, whether on the basis of race, national origin, sex, religion, or disability, is worse than wrong. It is a fundamental evil that tears at the fabric of our society, and one that all Americans should and must oppose. That requires rigorous enforcement of existing antidiscrimination laws. It also requires vigorously promoting new measures such as this year's Americans with Disabilities Act, which for the first time adequately protects persons with disabilities against invidious discrimination.[3]

The unchallenged social acceptance of the antidiscrimination principle has far-reaching consequences. At stake is the basic choice of legal regimes under which social life is ordered. An antidiscrimination law is the antithesis of freedom of contract, a principle that allows all persons to do business with whomever they please for good reason, bad reason, or no reason at all. Under this contractual regime, the chief job of the state is to ensure that all persons enjoy the civil capacity to own property, to contract, to sue and be sued, and to give evidence. The rights that the state thereby recognizes and protects are easily made universal, and can be held simultaneously by all persons. There is no effort to form separate codes of conduct for particular trades, professions, or businesses. There are no special status-based rules that limit the power to contract of employers, landlords, manufacturers, or suppliers of any form of goods or services. The state secures for all persons a zone of freedom against

---

Sowell, *Discrimination, Affirmative Action, and Equal Opportunity: An Economic and Social Perspective* (1982).

3. Veto message of President George Bush, October 22, 1990.

aggression and fraud in which voluntary transactions for business, personal, charitable, and religious activities of all kinds and descriptions occur. The legal system does not take it upon itself to specify the trading partners for any person or the terms and conditions under which trade takes place. Individuals themselves decide which contracts are made and on what terms.

With regard to commerce and trade, freedom of contract confines the state to functions that are both facilitative and reactive: facilitative because it provides the forms and mechanisms that allow people to exchange and trade as they please, and reactive because it enforces the trades so made. The law allows all people to enter into private agreements with the modest confidence that they will be able to enforce these agreements when the other side is in breach, but subject to the sober recognition that the power of the state will be turned against them if they themselves are in breach. Only where the state acts as an employer are there substantive limitations on the kinds of contracts that can be formed.

The antidiscrimination principle operates as a powerful brake against this view of freedom of contract and the concomitant but limited role of the state. By its nature the antidiscrimination principle is interventionist for reasons that have nothing to do with the prevention of force and fraud. Rather, the principle rests on the collective social judgment (often born out of wrenching historical experience) that some grounds for private decision are so improper that it is both immoral and illegal for the government to allow employers to use them in deciding whether to hire, retain, or promote workers.[4] The list of forbidden grounds includes race, sex, age, national origin, religious belief, handicap, and in some cases sexual orientation. Decisions made "on the merits" are allowed, but, subject to a broad and controversial exception of affirmative action, any private reliance on these socially extraneous criteria is prohibited. The defenders of the antidiscrimination principle often treat that principle as though it were a self-evident truth that certain grounds for decision should be banned for moral reasons. On other occasions they treat the principle not as a good in itself but as a means to other ends: to creating an open and equal society with full participation, or to increasing the overall wealth of society by ensuring that all productive labor may be put to its highest use.

---

4. See, for a general articulation, Paul Brest, "Foreword: In Defense of the Antidiscrimination Principle," 90 *Harv. L. Rev.* 1 (1976).

Whatever the precise rationale, the antidiscrimination principle is tenacious in labor markets. Only on rare occasions may the principle be overridden by a powerful showing of business necessity. Any person may refuse to contract for no reason at all, or even for bad reasons that lie outside the reach of the antidiscrimination principle. But refusal to deal for reasons forbidden by statute renders an employer's conduct illegal, and exposes the employer to heavy legal sanctions. Nor can an antidiscrimination statute bring about fundamental changes in labor markets if its application is confined only to refusals to deal. Employers could always make offers on terms so unattractive that they would not be accepted. Once those "terms and conditions" cases are covered by the statute, then by degrees it becomes necessary to scrutinize each and every aspect of any transaction in the employment arena.

During its 1988–89 term, the Supreme Court handed down a number of critical decisions that imposed some new limits on the reach of the antidiscrimination principle in the private sector and breathed new life into the principle in the public sector.[5] These cases have been interpreted by many in the civil rights establishment as marking a judicial retreat from two generations of unwavering support for the antidiscrimination principle. The decisions themselves are all worthy of close examination, but at the outset it is sufficient to say that none of these Supreme Court cases challenges, or even questions, the basic antidiscrimination principle, now embodied in Title VII of the 1964 Civil Rights Act. Instead, these cases are directed at collateral questions: the interaction of different statutory schemes, the proof of discrimination by statistical inference, the ability of consent decrees to bind or otherwise limit the rights of nonsigning parties, and the constitutionality of minority set-asides. At no point has the Court ever stated, or even intimated, that the basic antidiscrimination principle is not an essential part of the fabric of modern American law and social life. The debates within the Supreme Court mirror those of the larger society: they concern the reach and application of a principle that is accorded quasi-sacred status, not its essential soundness. Needless to say, under current law any constitutional attack against the antidiscrimination principle is wildly inconceivable.

Indeed, given its institutional role, the Supreme Court would be fool-

5. See *Martin v. Wilks*, 490 U.S. 755 (1989) (consent decrees); *Wards Cove Packing Co., Inc. v. Atonio*, 490 U.S. 642 (1989) (disparate impact); *City of Richmond v. J. A. Croson Co.*, 488 U.S. 469 (1989) (minority set-asides); *Patterson v. McLean Credit Union*, 491 U.S. 164 (1989) (relationship of §1981 of 1866 Civil Rights Act to the 1964 act).

hardy to take any other view on the subject, even if it were inclined to do so, which it is not. The strength of the political and intellectual consensus on behalf of the existing law is so strong, I doubt that the Court would be able to withstand the pounding that would result if it undertook a frontal assault on the basic antidiscrimination norm. Academics and scholars are not so situated or constrained, however. In this book I advance a position that is well outside the mainstream of American political thought. I develop a defense of the traditional common law approach to the regulation of labor markets. My target is the social consensus that supports one or another version of the modern antidiscrimination principle. My method is a frontal intellectual assault on that consensus.

Consensus may be indispensable for ordering political life, but it is dangerous for intellectual work. It makes intellectuals comfortable, soft, perhaps even a little bit complacent. As a consequence, the level of discussion and analysis suffers. Once everyone starts with a single common premise, there is really no reason to think hard about its soundness. If no one disagrees with the obvious conclusion, why debate it at all? Better to go on to more topical subjects on which learned and popular opinion is divided. Arguments that might otherwise be tested in the crucible of controversy are thus accepted without question as the starting point of discussions that in reality address matters of secondary intellectual and institutional importance. The skeptical probing that brings out the best in academic debate is lost. The only questions on the table are directed at how to implement some goal that all agree is just and appropriate. Issues of execution, of the relation of means to ends, dominate the discussion. The harder questions—Why is the end justified? Why are its consequences desirable?—are not asked, let alone answered. The present intellectual and political consensus imposes hidden costs on the social system by foreclosing any systematic reexamination of one very important set of rules. Serious criticism becomes oblique; serious inquiry is rendered covert.

The intellectual constructs of one generation, however, do not last forever. They depreciate over time, like buildings made of stone and mortar. Unless basic paradigms are renewed in response to challenge from without, they become weak and infirm. If the major premise about the proper scope of government action is in fact false, or even shaky, then the consequences may well turn out to be costly and unfortunate, even for the persons the law is intended to help. Proposed correctives will only be able to treat symptoms; they will not provide a cure for the basic underlying intellectual mistake. Much display will be made of the "obvious" gains that flow from acceptance of the dominant position. Scholars can insist that the principle be extended to other areas found to be irresistibly analogous to the undisputed paradigm case, just as President Bush treated discrimination based on disability as an analogue to discrimination based on race. At the same time, the awkwardness of the basic position in the core area—Is there a principled affirmative action exception for cases of race or sex discrimination?—shows that the principle no longer has unambiguous dominance even in the original area of application.

A critique of the consensus should therefore pay handsome dividends even if its only consequence is to prod defenders of the status quo to strengthen their defense of the antidiscrimination principle, complete with its exceptions. I propose to conduct such an examination in this book. The inquiry is, I believe, most timely. In doing research for this volume I have asked many people to refer me to any book or article that states in systematic terms the modern case for the antidiscrimination laws against their common law alternatives. None has been offered. Quite the opposite. The usual defenses of the antidiscrimination laws are over a generation old, and they are written in laudatory and conclusory terms, in which the soundness of the principle is taken as a given, and the only question for serious inquiry is that of political will.[6]

The time has come for reexamination. Why not test the foundations of the antidiscrimination principle using the available tools of economic and legal theory? The contemporary analysis of contract and tort remedies dates from the rise of law and economics as an academic discipline. It took its early shape in the work of, among others, Ronald Coase and Guido Calabresi in the 1960s, gained force in the 1970s, and reached a high level of technical sophistication in the 1980s. Throughout, the emphasis has been on various kinds of costs—transaction costs, information costs, agency costs, moral hazard costs, political costs—which must be minimized in order to secure a stable set of

6. See, e.g., Michael I. Sovern, *Legal Restraints on Racial Discrimination in Employment* 7–8 (1966): "Underlying this whole work is the premise that the law can and should be invoked against racial discrimination in employment. Our nation now seems irreversibly committed to this premise, and rightly so. Assessed in the light of the harm it visits upon its victims, employment discrimination is unfair, inhumane, and utterly without justification. Assessed in the light of the damage it does to our society, it is costly, wasteful and explosive." Sovern entertained little doubt about the 1964 statute; see his chapter 4, titled "Congress at Last: The Civil Rights Act of 1964." Notwithstanding its evident bias, the book provides a very accurate rendition of what the statute was intended to do, and it captures well the national mood at the time of its passage.

private and public institutions. The literature has not dogmatically favored market solutions over government solutions, but has generally sought to figure out some way to minimize the sum of abuses in both private and public activities. It has, for example, explored the collective action problems for which market responses may well be inadequate, as with the control of common resources such as air, water, and oil and gas, and lends the most powerful intellectual support to much of the modern environmental movement.

In large measure none of the insights of this modern literature have been brought systematically to bear on the subject of the antidiscrimination laws. To the contrary, there seems to be a broad separation between two intellectual cultures. With a few notable exceptions, the lawyers who work full time in the area of discrimination tend to be suspicious of the basic insights of law and economics and are, generally speaking, antilibertarian, antiutilitarian, and antimarket in their orientation. Even lawyers who defend employers and unions generally accept the basic framework of the Civil Rights Act and seek to win by showing that their clients have complied with its commands.

By contrast, lawyers with backgrounds in law and economics tend to be broadly supportive of market institutions, concentrating their efforts on issues of property, contract, tort, and procedure which are far less explosive than the basic questions raised by any antidiscrimination law. It is thus possible to find many books and articles devoted to the question of what the optimum rule is to prevent holdups in the revision of long-term contracts when circumstances change,[7] and an equal number of books and articles that debate the second-order effects of the choice between negligence and strict liability as the basic rule of tort.[8] These issues are surely important, and I have devoted a fair share of my own academic effort to taking one side or the other on various of these questions.[9] But they are all questions that are posed within a general framework that acknowledges the role of private enforcement in preventing the infliction of harm on strangers and recognizes the dominance of private

7. See, e.g., Clayton Gilette, "Commercial Relationships and Commercial Risks," 19 *J. Legal Stud.* 535 (1990); Robert E. Scott, "Conflict and Cooperation in Long-Term Contracts," 75 *Calif. L. Rev.* 2005 (1987).

8. See, e.g., Steven Shavell, *Economic Analysis of Accident Law* (1987); William M. Landes and Richard A. Posner, *The Economic Structure of Tort Law* (1987).

9. See, e.g., Richard A. Epstein, "A Theory of Strict Liability," 2 *J. Legal Stud.* 151 (1973); Richard A. Epstein, "Causation—In Context: An Afterword," 63 *Chi.-Kent L. Rev.* 653 (1987).

contracts in organizing complicated long-term business transactions. What is missing is an application of the academic work in law and economics done *after* the passage of the 1964 Civil Rights Act to the antidiscrimination question which is at the forefront of the social and political agenda. This book seeks to bridge the gap between the two cultures with respect to the antidiscrimination laws in employment relations. Because of the complex interplay of legal and historical forces, however, the study cannot be rigidly confined to one substantive area. It is necessary to speak in passing, if only by way of historical and analytical comparison, to problems of voting, public accommodations, housing, and other areas where the antidiscrimination principle has been applied.

Although the details of the analysis must wait, it is useful to set out the two parts of my basic position. First, the entire apparatus of the antidiscrimination laws in Title VII should be repealed insofar as it applies to private employers—at least (and the qualification is theoretically critical) those who operate in ordinary competitive markets without legal protection against the entry of new rivals. My view is quite categorical: it is meant to apply to criteria of race, sex, religion, national origin, age, and handicap. Second, voluntary affirmative action is perfectly acceptable by private firms but far more problematic when undertaken by government, precisely because there is no adequate theory to explain the distribution of government largess among its many eager recipients. At the level of individual employment decisions, it is difficult to stem the movement toward race-conscious or sex-conscious hiring, given the constellation of political forces that supports these practices; and it is probably fruitless to seek explicit legal restrictions on it. With regards to independent vendors to the government, the appropriate response seems clearer: for any given project, good, or service, with quality and other contract terms constant, take the lowest-price bidder—period.

The remainder of this book is devoted to fleshing out this position and its intellectual justifications. Part I consists of four chapters that rely on political and economic theory to ground an analytical assessment of the antidiscrimination norm. Chapter 1 develops a general common law theory of individual entitlements that allows all individuals to better the position they occupy in the original state of nature. Chapter 2 then argues that this general and neutral theory of individual rights and duties is incapable of generating the antidiscrimination norm on which the Civil Rights Act rests. Competitive markets with free entry offer better and more certain protection against invidious discrimination than any antidiscrimination law. Chapter 3 extends the argument to explain why some forms of explicit discrimination may be useful as a way to control the costs of governance and contract enforcement in some institutional settings. Chapter 4 takes the obverse side of the problem and indicates those circumstances in which the antidiscrimination principle serves as a counterweight for the exercise of monopoly power.

Part II switches the analysis from the theoretical to the historical perspective. Chapter 5 examines the constitutional history of race relations from *Plessy v. Ferguson*[10] to the 1937 height of the New Deal revolution. Chapter 6 takes that history forward through *Brown v. Board of Education*[11] to the passage of the Civil Rights Act of 1964. So great were the abuses of political power before 1964 that, knowing what I know today, if given an all-or-nothing choice, I should still have voted in favor of the Civil Rights Act in order to allow federal power to break the stranglehold of local government on race relations. History often leaves us with only second-best devices to combat evils that are in principle better controlled by other means.

Chapter 7 concludes Part II with a constitutional analysis of the Civil Rights Act. The Fourteenth Amendment gives Congress ample power to eliminate state-imposed segregation, and the commerce clause gives Congress the power to regulate interstate commerce, such as transportation by road, rail, sea, or air. Nonetheless, in sharp opposition to conventional wisdom and existing law, I conclude that federal power is limited to either state action or interstate commerce, narrowly conceived, and that even in those areas of interstate commerce subject to congressional regulation, the antidiscrimination laws operate as a taking of private property without just compensation.

Part III turns to an examination of the antidiscrimination laws themselves. The antidiscrimination principle has played out very differently in race, sex, age, and handicap cases. It is therefore necessary to explore the various regulatory schemes individually in order to determine whether these statutes have provided their intended beneficiaries with the promised level of protection, and if so, whether at an acceptable social cost, given the other interests that are at stake. The primary issue is whether the statutes themselves are sound instruments of social policy in light of both the historical legacy and the intellectual framework, and the subsequent expansive judicial interpretation of the congressional mandate. The examination begins with the Civil Rights Act of 1964, but it touches,

10. 163 U.S. 537 (1896).
11. 347 U.S. 483 (1954).

where appropriate, on other related statutes, such as the Equal Pay Act of 1963, the Rehabilitation Act of 1973, the Equal Opportunity in Employment Act of 1972, the Pregnancy Discrimination Act of 1978, and the Age Discrimination Act of 1986.

Chapter 8 gives a general defense of the contract at will, the legal regime that is in sharp opposition to the general antidiscrimination principle. The contract at will then becomes the foil for the more particular examination of issues that follows, both here and in subsequent sections. Chapters 9 through 12 examine the law of race discrimination. Chapter 9 analyzes the judicial approach to disparate treatment cases in connection with race. Chapter 10 traces the switch from disparate treatment to disparate impact, most notably in the decision of *Griggs v. Duke Power Co.*,[12] and the limitation on that decision in *Wards Cove Packing Co. v. Atonio.*[13] Chapter 11 contains a detailed examination of the disparate impact principle as it applies to matters of testing for employment. Finally, Chapter 12 contains a review of some of the empirical research on the impact of the civil rights law on marketplace behavior.

Part IV moves the analysis from race to sex discrimination. Chapter 13 addresses the theme of separate but equal in the context of sex discrimination, where it has far greater staying power than it does with race. Chapter 14 deals with the question of the bona fide occupational qualification applicable in sex but not in race cases. Chapter 15 addresses the problems of applying Title VII to sex-based pension systems. Chapter 16 extends the analysis to issues of pregnancy. Chapter 17 turns to the quite different problems of sexual harassment, and Chapter 18 investigates the role of disparate impact theories with respect to both wages and occupational choice.

Part V is devoted to an analysis of affirmative action by both private and government actors. The problem is addressed from the vantage point of first principle in Chapter 19 and from that of the enacted statute in Chapter 20. Part VI treats two other key forms of antidiscrimination statutes. Chapter 21 addresses the question of age discrimination, and Chapter 22 the question of handicap discrimination. A brief conclusion and overview follows in Chapter 23.

Although the particular analysis runs through many byways, the case against the antidiscrimination laws in employment arises from the proposition that labor markets raise *neither* of the two problems on which a

12. 401 U.S. 424 (1971).
13. 490 U.S. 642 (1989).

principled case for legal intervention may properly rest. There are neither the holdout, coordination, or public good problems that justify government coercion and control so long as compensation is paid to the regulated parties; nor are there the problems with externalities in the use of force or fraud against strangers that justify the use of state force without compensation. Finally, if wealth or income redistribution is regarded as a proper goal of government, the antidiscrimination laws are a clumsy, inefficient, and highly selective way to achieve these ends. The simple solution is still the best: a combination of tax and welfare systems, keyed to individual wealth, in order to achieve these goals.

PART I

Analytical Foundations

CHAPTER 1

Human Nature, Social Theory, and the Common Law

Controlling Coercion

Any examination of the desirability of the antidiscrimination principle must begin with an extended detour into basic social theory. It is, of course, very difficult to construct a social theory that accounts for all the rights and obligations that all persons hold relative to one another at all times in some original position, or what used to be called more vividly the state of nature. Nonetheless, sheer necessity leaves us with no other choice. The alternative to some theory is, quite simply, no theory; and without theory, there can be no normative limits on unbridled self-interest, no conception of antisocial behavior, and no protection of individual rights.

Within any no-holds-barred view of the world, it is easy to make somber predictions. For starters there will be no limitation on the use of force and fraud in ordinary human relations. Nor will there be any obligation to respect promises no matter how solemnly made. At this point the evolution of civil society becomes indistinguishable from the Darwinian accounts of the evolution of the species—red in tooth and claw. Every person will live by wits and brawn, and at any moment may perish at the hands of others who are more adept at their use. Long-term associations, if they can arise at all, will be mere alliances of convenience, and the betrayal of trust will be a common fact, but never a moral or legal wrong. As Hobbes so powerfully put it: "Where there is no common Power, there is not law; where no law, no Injustice. Force, and Fraud are in war the two cardinal virtues."[1] Without the restraints of any system of law,

1. Thomas Hobbes, *Leviathan*, ch. 13 (1651).

15

the worst side of human character will emerge in ways that diminish the prospects of us all.

The picture of a world without rights and duties is bleak, but not hopeless. Gainful production will, to be sure, take place even in a Hobbesian war of all against all; people who are dying of starvation do not have enough strength to fight. But some resources that might otherwise be harnessed to produce new things of value must now be diverted into guarding the few things that have already been produced. A society without the protection of laws will leave unsatisfied many desires and wants that could be met with sound social institutions. The justification for law and for the creation of some sovereign power as a means to prevent disorder is a constant theme in the works of all the writers in the social contract tradition, broadly conceived to cover Hobbes, Locke, Hume, and Blackstone. The control of force was their overriding theme. It never occurred to any of them that the private refusal to deal, for whatever reason, was any threat to the social order.

It may be objected that, however essential the control of force is to the legal and social order, this description of chaos in a world without law rests on too pessimistic a view of humanity. Its Hobbesian emphasis on the brutish side of human nature is grim, relentless, and monochromatic. It does a disservice to the large number of decent people who find the use of force abhorrent, and who are unable and unwilling to practice the fine art of deceit. As a descriptive matter this counterargument contains much truth. Surely we should not want to judge the mainstream of human conduct by looking only at the worst actions of the worst individuals. The forces of self-interest may lurk in us all, but they express themselves in different ways. For some people self-interest leads to creativity and cooperation, or it encourages them to excel at helping and not hurting. Only in a small, hardened minority does self-interest translate into the gleeful tendency to perform actions destructive of the welfare of others.

A balanced view of society, and of the role of law, requires us to recognize differences in character and temperament just as we recognize differences in height and weight. Some might sell out innocent people for a cash pittance (such was the fate of Anne Frank). So too there are others who would not betray a trust or a promise even to save their own lives; witness the heroic actions of the Dutch Resistance. The uncompromising Hobbesian view of human nature is surely overdrawn as a universal portrait. Whatever the biological origins of humankind, manifold social pressures lead to cooperation as well as conflict, to excellence as well as depravity. To portray people only in harsh tones is to develop a skewed picture of human nature that ignores the enormous variation among individuals. The model can only lead to mistaken judgments about the proper normative political order.

It is essential, however, to understand the limited political implications of this objection to Hobbesian theory. A sounder approach recognizes the wide diversity of character, talent, and inclination and then seeks to determine the set of legal rules that best promotes human happiness and welfare, given that distribution. That task is an enormous undertaking, but one critical part of the problem is to determine which segment of the overall distribution of human beings is the target of any legal rule. Here we can simplify the rich mosaic of human types by positing a single characteristic—virtue—which is the sum of all desirable human qualities. It is distributed across three groups: first, those persons who have the welfare of others close at heart; second, that great mass of persons whose character and temperament cluster at the mean—people who have, in the words of David Hume, individual self-interest tempered by a sense of "confin'd generosity" toward others;[2] and third, individuals for whom self-interest is everything, and who will stop short of theft and murder only if confronted with a force stronger than their own. Even this formula understates the level of variation, as many people will be generous toward some and hostile toward others, on either a permanent or a transient basis.

Within this framework one can see that the strength of the Hobbesian vision does not depend on a showing that everyone falls into that third category of persons moved by the most callous forms of self-interest. In making the case for political union, we put the initial emphasis not on restraining people of the first and second types but on controlling the destructive impulses of people who fall into the third group. Hobbes, in *Leviathan*,[3] asks people to reflect on their true estimate of the character of other persons by looking at the unconscious ways in which they order their own lives. After the famous passage in which he describes life without law as "worse of all continual fear, and danger of violent death; and the life of man, solitary, poor, nasty, brutish and short," he goes on to ask whether we should assent to so grim an account of mankind.

2. The full passage reads: "Here then is a proposition, which, I think, may be regarded as certain, *that 'tis only from the selfishness and confin'd generosity of men, along with the scanty provision nature has made for his wants, that justice derives its origin.*" David Hume, *A Treatise of Human Nature*, bk. 3, sec. 2 ("Of the Origin of Justice and Property") (1739).
3. Hobbes, *Leviathan*, ch. 13.

It may seem strange to some man, that has not well weighed these things; that Nature should thus dissociate, and render men apt to invade and destroy one another; and he may therefore, not trusting to this Inference, made from the Passions, desire perhaps to have the same confirmed by Experience. Let him therefore consider with himself, when taking a journey, he arms himself, and seeks to go well accompanied; when he goes to sleep, he locks his doors; when even in his house he locks his chests; and this when he knows there be laws, and public Officers, armed, to revenge all injuries shall be done him; what opinion he has of his fellow-subjects, when he rides armed; of his fellow citizens, when he locks his doors, and of his children, and servants, when he locks his chests. Does he not there as much accuse mankind by his actions, as I do by my words?[4]

Hobbes's searching inquiry is surprisingly simple: Why would people take such enormous precautions if they thought that the world was populated with virtuous individuals? A good question, and one for which there is a good answer.

The Hobbesian argument is both weaker and stronger than it appears at first blush. It is weaker because it misstates the conditions that people perceive in deciding to invest in precautions against crime and treachery. Thus an individual will find it rational to lock his house even if he thinks that 99 percent of the population would *not* steal his goods if the house were left unlocked. The possessions in his house can be stolen only once. The lock, therefore, is not put on the door because of the owner's estimate of the *average* run of humanity, which may be quite high. Rather, this decision is driven by the conduct of the *marginal,* in this case the *worst,* individuals within the group. Their willingness to violate the rules by which others live forces *everyone* to take precautions at this level, even against a single thief. The costs of crime include the costs of successfully forestalling or reducing crime. It thus follows that the fearful responses spelled out by Hobbes make perfectly good sense even if humankind, in the aggregate, contains some good people, and some bad people, with most people in between. When the issue concerns the use or threat of force, the behavior of ordinary people is quite irrelevant, and the behavior of the worst

---

4. Id. Hobbes then goes on to note that force and fraud are not wrong until there is a law that forbids them. But on this point he seems to misfire. It is because they are wrong (in terms of the consequences they generate) that we want the law to forbid them. By his logic force and fraud would be acceptable if approved by a law.

people is decisive. The conclusion is therefore a somber one. Most people avoid direct confrontations with their neighbors, but the level of vigilance that is required remains high, given the enormous harm that can be wrought by a tiny fraction of the total population.

The same argument explains why it is important to structure correctly the sanctions that are applied to criminal behavior. Most people do not know the likelihood of apprehension or the severity of the punishment for murder or theft, much less the subtle gradations in offenses and punishments. They often infer from this that the economic theory of deterrence is misplaced because of general public ignorance about the scope and application of the criminal law. But again the argument mistakes the position of the average and the marginal individual. Ordinary people really do not have to inquire closely about the enforcement of the criminal law because they would not steal or kill even if the severity of the punishment were raised or lowered by 10 percent. Their position is the same as that of the 99-plus percent of the car-buying population that will not buy a Rolls-Royce even at a year-end closeout sale.

It is a serious mistake, however, to judge the effectiveness of either a criminal system or a Rolls-Royce closeout sale by looking at its effects on the average members of the population. The critical question is what does it do for those people who are close to the line. A decrease in the price of the Rolls-Royce by 10 percent, which is of no concern to 99.99 percent of the public, may increase the number of willing buyers from 0.01 percent to 0.012 percent, which translates to a *20 percent* increase in sales for the dealer—a huge change. So too may decreasing the severity of punishment for robbery increase the pool of robbers (or the number of crimes by the same pool of robbers) by the same amount, and induce a miniature crime wave, which will then require additional precautions, public and private. Issues that are of no concern to most people in the way they lead their lives can assume enormous systemic significance because of their effects on specific subgroups. The allocative consequences of a rule can be vast even if it strikes only a tiny fraction of the total population—those people who live and work at the margin.

This basic insight—law must control the most lawless—lies behind the strong libertarian insistence on the basic rules of ordinary society. It also explains the libertarian's constant theoretical emphasis that the function of government is to control the use of force and fraud against the person and property of others.

The Determination of Ownership

Distributive and Corrective Justice

This discussion of the risks of force begins, in a sense, in medias res. To place the point in Aristotelian terms,[5] my inquiry does not start with this norm of *corrective* justice. Rather, it presupposes an answer to a prior question of *distributive* justice: Who owns any given person or thing? The answer to this question is itself not self-evident, for the institution of slavery shows clearly that it is possible to develop an elegant set of legal rules which allows persons to acquire, protect, and transfer property rights in other human beings, viewed as a cross between persons and chattels.

The standard autonomy hypothesis has as its major function ruling slavery out of bounds by making self-ownership the natural or inalienable right from which all other rights flow. Other persons cannot simply take people and make them slaves.[6] Within this framework, rules of "natural" acquisition must be developed to assign ownership of external objects—of which land and chattels are only the most obvious—to individual persons. Analogous rules then need to be fashioned to protect intangibles, as evidenced by the laws of copyright, patent, and trademark, where the task is more complicated because no person can keep exclusive possession of

5. The distinctions are set out in Aristotle, *The Nicomachean Ethics,* bk. 5, ch. 3 (distributive justice), and ch. 4 (corrective justice).

6. There remains a very hard question of whether contracts to create slavery should be allowed. On the one side it seems consistent with the autonomy principle to permit this to happen. But the issue is surely more complicated. One difficulty is with externalities: are the children of slaves to be slaves as well? Another is with the intrinsic imbalance of the exchange. If the prohibition against selling selves into slavery were lifted, how many contracts of this sort would be observed? And if there were only a few, could we say that there are good reasons to believe that most of these would be tainted with incompetence, fraud, and duress, themselves inferable from the intrinsic inequality of the terms of the exchange, just as when one sells a share of stock worth $100 for $1 in cash?

The question of inferring defects in contractual formation from major inadequacy of consideration is one that has split traditional lawyers, who have struggled inconclusively with the issue under such rubics as unconscionability and the inherent justice in exchange. For an excellent historical account of the problem, see A. W. B. Simpson, "The Horwitz Thesis and the History of Contracts," 46 *U. Chi. L. Rev.* 533 (1979), critiquing Morton Horwitz, "The Historical Foundations of Modern Contract Law," 87 *Harv. L. Rev.* 917 (1974), later reproduced as "The Triumph of Contract," in Horwitz, *The Transformation of American Law* 161–220 (1977).

the property, given the ease of imitation and copying.[7] The rules of acquisition for personal liberty and external property thus fix a set of original rights which then can be transformed and recombined through voluntary transactions. This model lies at the root of the common law and has received its most spirited philosophical justification in Robert Nozick's *Anarchy, State, and Utopia,* which follows the traditional view by speaking of the trinity of legal rules: acquisition, protection, and disposition.[8]

Although the natural rights justification has often been paramount within an ongoing social system, it is possible to give it a deeper functional justification as well.[9] Understanding how the system was put together, and how it operates, is not only important in its own right. In this context it furnishes a convenient foil against which to examine the structure and operation of an antidiscrimination law.

Rules of Self-Ownership

It is instructive to recall that the major premise of Locke's theory of property was that each person is the exclusive owner of his own labor: "Though the Earth, and all inferior Creatures be common to all Men, yet every Man has a *Property* in his own *Person.* This no Body has any Right to but himself. The *Labour* of his Body; and the *Work* of his Hands, we may say, are properly his."[10] Although that notion of ownership did not mean that every person could do exactly what he wanted, it did mean that no person could commandeer the labor of another for his own private use. The ability to use the talents of other persons depended not on coercion but rather on consent—including consent that was purchased in voluntary transactions.

7. See, generally, Wendy J. Gordon, "An Inquiry into the Merits of Copyright: The Challenges of Consistency, Consent, and Encouragement Theory," 41 *Stan. L. Rev.* 1343 (1989); William M. Landes and Richard A. Posner, "An Economic Analysis of Copyright Law," 18 *J. Legal Stud.* 325 (1989).

8. See Robert Nozick, *Anarchy, State, and Utopia,* ch. 7 (1974).

9. I develop these arguments at greater length in Richard A. Epstein, "The Utilitarian Foundations of Natural Law," 12 *Harv. J. of Law & Pub. Pol.* 713 (1989). In my book *Takings* (1985) I began with a discussion of both the natural law and the utilitarian foundations of property, which led to spirited criticism of the book; see "Symposium," 41 *Miami L. Rev.* 49–223 (1986). My own view, as stated in that symposium, was (and remains) that one cannot understand the position taken by the framers without a resort to natural law, or justify that position by a resort to natural law. Id. at 166.

10. John Locke, *The Second Treatise of Civil Government,* ch. 5, ¶27 (1690).

The functional justification for this intuitive allocation of the rights to labor becomes relatively plain when alternative initial rights structures are considered. Suppose that each person does not own his own labor even though in a physical sense he must possess it; who then does own it? One possibility is to say that the labor is not owned by anyone at all, at which point we are back in the state of nature where no person is protected against the aggression of another. This no-ownership solution thus restates the social breakdown that gave birth to social contract theory in the first place.

The other alternative is to assume that A's labor is owned by B, or perhaps by B with C, or even by A, B, and C jointly. Still more complex combinations are possible, but even the simplest system where B, however selected, is allowed to dictate the use of A's labor generates awesome bargaining complications. In order for B to use A's labor gainfully, he must either coerce A to cooperate or pay her to do so. In either case, complex and costly transactions are a prelude to any useful exchange of talent and resources. This system of divided ownership also has perverse incentives which will lead A to cut back on the labor that she generates, since she has to share its return with B. There is a conflict of interest between the two individuals, and a self-interested party will take into account only the gain he receives and not the external benefit generated for another.[11] This more complex system of ownership rights therefore not only influences the distribution of the gains, given production, but also reduces the total gain from production in the first place.

In reality these difficulties are only the tip of the iceberg. Thus, if A is subject to the claims of B to control her labor, then what about B? In order for B to enter into a transaction with A, he must obtain the consent or cooperation of some C who has an interest in B's labor. The problem does not stop with C but continues all through the alphabet, if not the telephone book. An event as simple as the birth, or the entry by immigration, of any new person raises the question of who controls his labor, and whose labor he controls. Unfortunately, there is no obvious or even plausible rule to determine who takes the role of B for each A. Each of these matters has to be determined in some arbitrary way, further adding to the

---

11. This problem of agency costs is the source of an enormous literature. See Michael C. Jensen and William H. Meckling, "The Structure of the Firm: Managerial Behavior, Agency Costs, and Ownership Structure," 3 *J. Financial Econ.* 305 (1976); for a collection of essays on the theme, see *Principals and Agents: The Structure of Business* (John W. Pratt and Richard J. Zeckhauser eds. 1985).

transactional confusion that is created by any system of divided owner-ship in human labor.

The legal system that posits the self-ownership of labor and individual talents as the initial baseline obviates all of these mind-boggling complications with a single stroke. Instead of trying to figure out how a football will bounce, we substitute a round ball in its place. The gains from simplicity are evident. Each person decides to buy and sell labor for himself. People can come into the system or leave it without undermining the prior distribution of entitlements. There is more than intuition to support the Lockean ideal of self-ownership of labor. There are powerful functional reasons to believe that the overall social consequences will be improved as well. It is as if there has been a grand initial deal that is solemnized by a hypothetical social contract. Each person will be forced to relinquish whatever rights he had to control the labor of some other individual. But in exchange each person receives the sole right to control the use of his own labor in a manner that he sees fit. The deal is hypothetical only because it is now well known in practice that it would be impossible for any voluntary contracts to overcome the holdout and bargaining problems that would exist if a system of joint ownership of labor and property were treated as the original position from which all subsequent voluntary transactions had to be made. Although it might be very possible to find someone who could profit from keeping this legal tangle alive, we would be far more likely to find hundreds and thousands of others who would be paralyzed by the fiendish intricacy of the system. Although this thought experiment is not conducted with perfect rigor, we can say that the state of the world which recognizes that each person has exclusive use of his or her own labor leaves everyone (or just about everyone) better off than an alternative system that contemplates the crisscross division of the rights over labor among individuals. No other rule comes close.

The simplicity of the Lockean position of self-ownership works, as a rough approximation, to the advantage of everyone. In making this claim one finds it possible to tie the arguments for autonomy with the modern economic definitions of social welfare (the test of Pareto superiority), which state that system A is better than system B if no one in A is *worse* off than in B and at least one person is *better* off in A than in B. Indeed, we can go one step better than that. The system of self-ownership of labor and talents seems to give major advantages to all persons simultaneously. This advantage explains why the modern attacks on the self-ownership principle, including the antidiscrimination laws, have conceded its basic soundness and have then sought to limit its scope with exceptions and qualifications. No one has ever sought to replace the autonomy principle with some wholly distinct and fully articulated alternative baseline, for example, some stated minimum wage, under which individual autonomy would then be relegated to exception status. We do not start with rules that render the use and disposition of labor presumptively illegal; quite the opposite.

Freedom of Contract and the Antidiscrimination Laws

The self-ownership of individual labor forms the cornerstone for freedom of contract in labor markets, with immediate political relevance to the antidiscrimination laws. As with the parallel rules that assign the ownership of land and chattels to their first possessor,[12] the autonomy system has one cardinal virtue: it leads to widely *decentralized* control of labor and property. All individuals own their own labor, and hence can act as both producers and consumers in a relatively competitive labor market. The distinct natural inclinations of separate individuals thus lead toward a system with many centers of property, and many centers of power. The common law, like the Lockean philosopher, knows only a *single* rule of individual ownership of labor. But it is a rule that permits all labor to be assigned to some unique owner, without incurring the enormous costs of coordination from the center—or from the top. In some natural resource markets it may be worth incurring these coordination costs, if only to prevent the premature exploitation of common pool assets such as air, water, and wild animals. But since these coordination problems simply do not arise in labor markets, it thereby strengthens the case for using the Lockean baseline of individual ownership.[13]

12. See Richard A. Epstein, "Past and Future: The Temporal Dimension in the Law of Property," 64 *Wash. U. L. Quart.* 667, 669–674 (1986); Richard A. Epstein, "Luck," 6 Soc. *Phil. & Pol.* 17; 26–28 (1988). Note that fuller development of the common law principle that ownership of land and chattels is acquired by taking first possession of them rests at bottom on functional arguments similar to those developed here to account for the ownership of labor. A detailed discussion of this issue takes us too far from labor markets, the focus of this book. But for the sake of completeness, it should be noted that an employer must have well-defined property rights in various forms of wealth in order to facilitate the formation of the complete employment contract.

13. These resources may be subject to common ownership without centralized government control. See, generally, Carol Rose, "The Comedy of the Commons: Custom, Commerce, and Inherently Public Property," 53 *U. Chi. L. Rev.* 711 (1986); and Carol Rose, "Energy and Efficiency in the Realignment of Common-Law Water Rights," 19 *J. Legal Stud.* 261 (1990).

Employment markets should be privately ordered for another reason: anyone can participate. In some contexts the operation of markets may be limited because persons with powerful needs (for emergency health care, for example) may not able to back their preferences with money. At that point the difference between utility and wealth maximization may become critical,[14] with all the advantage lying in the hands of the utilitarian. But these problems do not arise in employment situations, where even a person without assets may act as a *seller* of labor freed from the solvency constraint applicable to buyers of goods and services. The simple rules of freedom of contract therefore have far greater staying power with human labor and talents than they do with common pool resources, and in some ways even ordinary contracts for sale of goods and services. Competitive markets work well with employment, and government intervention proves to be of limited, or negative, overall social value.

Setting out the initial entitlement rules for both labor and material resources has important implications for the structure of employment markets in a world devoid of antidiscrimination laws. The basic assumption of markets is that each person is the best judge of what he or she wants and is willing to pay for it. The thing received may be property or a job. The thing surrendered may be cash or labor. But in either case the exchange is one over which each person has veto power. Once initial entitlements are secure, a system of voluntary exchange has no natural stopping point. Endowments of labor or capital are never frozen into their present condition by operation of law. As along as there is a willing buyer and a willing seller, any good can be exchanged between them, even if the rest of the world is indifferent to the exchange or opposed to it.

Similarly, the administrative demands imposed on such a legal system are relatively low, especially in comparison to a system in which motive-based inquiries are dominant. The exchange need only be monitored for the process whereby it takes place, that is, to ensure that force and fraud and incompetence are not involved. When those minimum conditions are satisfied, then the consent of both parties guarantees that the transaction works to their common benefit. Each party will surrender only as much as he is willing to give in order to obtain in exchange something he values

14. For the major defense of wealth maximization, see Richard A. Posner, "Utilitarianism, Economics, and Legal Theory," 8 *J. Legal Stud.* 103 (1979). See also, for some of the limitations of the wealth maximization theory, Herbert Hovenkamp, "Legal Policy and the Endowment Effect," 20 *J. Legal Stud.* 225 (1991).

more. There is no need to plumb the subjective valuations each party attaches to the goods or services that are obtained or transferred. It is enough to know that each party has its own reasons to be satisfied. If consent can be observed, the benefit can be inferred, even if we do not understand the reasons for the transaction ourselves. The task of external validation is far easier than the business judgment of whether or not to make an agreement.

The gains from voluntary exchange are normally not confined to the parties to the transaction, for strangers to the transaction, taken as a class and over the long haul, benefit as well. The greater post-transaction wealth of the contracting parties presents an increased opportunity for exchange that other parties can then exploit by making bargains of their own; so, in the absence of special conditions (for example, contracts to use force against third parties), the ordinary contract for the transfer of goods and services produces gains not only for the parties but also, by indirection, for the larger society as a whole. The benefits of this structure, moreover, are not confined to any single transaction or narrow set of persons. All of us are parties to many bargains and strangers to countless others. In the aggregate (virtually) no one is left worse off under this system than under a system in which all trade is prohibited, and all gains from trade are thereby extinguished.

The common law model, then, can be defended on grounds that do not rest on mere habit or convenience. It has earned the right to be called a *natural law* system not because it is prepolitical or divinely inspired, but because its simplicity and generality make it suitable for doing business in societies with widely divergent social traditions and vastly different tastes and resources. It is certainly the only set of rules that allows for trade to replace conflict between individuals of different nations, neither of which can appeal to its own special traditions in setting its relations with others.[15] Over time, place, and circumstance, rules of contracting can remain the same, even if the content of those contracts varies in response to local conditions and individual preferences.[16] There is, accordingly, a strong reason to think that the set of rights so developed at common law should exhaust the universe of rules on original entitlements, their protec-

15. Thus the rise of the *ius gentium* under Roman law. See W. W. Buckland, *A Text-Book of Roman Law* 52–55 (3rd ed., P. Stein ed. 1963).

16. See, generally, Richard A. Epstein, "The Static Conception of the Common Law," 9 *J. Legal Stud.* 253 (1980), for a defense of this proposition in connection with various aspects of Roman and common law.

tion, and their exchange. The antidiscrimination laws should be understood as an assault on the completeness of these common law rules and the intellectual foundations on which they rest. As I will demonstrate in subsequent chapters, there is no reason to believe that this antidiscrimination system generates additional benefits that exceed its costs, social or economic.

CHAPTER 2

Force, Discrimination, and Free Entry

In this chapter I develop more fully the case against the antidiscrimination laws in the private sphere. In the first part I examine the contrast between a prohibition on the use of force and a prohibition against discrimination by looking carefully at the options available to each actor under the two alternative rules. Within the framework so established I next look at the strategies and counterstrategies that are available for employees and employers in markets where entry is free and discrimination is permitted. In dealing with their behavior in open markets, I consider cases where employers both do and do not have perfect information about the characteristics of any individual worker.

The analysis of the next two chapters thus weaves together two themes central to the understanding of the antidiscrimination laws: the contrast between force and discrimination, and the opposition between markets with perfect and imperfect information. The first theme is that the anticipated economic and social consequences of allowing the private use of force and allowing private discrimination are so different that it becomes indefensible to treat ostensible wrongs in the second category as though it were akin to the former. Freedom of contract is the position that results when the employment discrimination laws are removed, and it yields vastly different results from the removal of all legal restraints on aggressive action. The second theme is that discrimination in private markets will prove more tenacious and more justifiable where information is imperfect than where it is widely available. To the extent that the antidiscrimination laws reduce the flow of permissible information to employers, they are more likely to increase the level of discrimination that is practiced in the marketplace; employers, lacking individual information about employees, will find it more necessary to resort to crude proxies to measure anticipated employee performance.

Victims of Force and Victims of Discrimination

The critical inquiry asks how markets develop within a legal system that adopts the basic common law rules of property, contract and tort set out in Chapter 1. The rules of self-ownership ensure that there is always a large number of independent suppliers of labor in the general market—and, incidentally, a large number of potential purchasers for that labor. Indeed, it is impossible to organize a labor market in a way that will improve on the world in which each person has the exclusive right to sell his or her own labor. Similarly, the rule of first possession, coupled with the right to resell property acquired by voluntary exchange, ensures large numbers of independent suppliers of goods and property. Satisfying these twin conditions makes it highly likely that competitive markets will emerge. The gains that each person can obtain in transacting with another will be limited not by any barriers created by the legal system, but only by the prospect that potential trading partners can always go elsewhere if the price exceeds what the market will bear. *Free entry* thus becomes the cardinal feature of the emergent system.

Within this framework it becomes possible to analyze the effect that private discrimination has both on the operation of the market as a whole and on the victims of discrimination. The standard modern accounts of the antidiscrimination laws in effect treat the refusal to deal on grounds of race, sex, or age as a legal wrong, that is, a wrong wholly separate from a breach of contract, and thus (at least by analogy) as some form of common law tort involving harm to strangers. One way to assess the soundness of the equation is to compare the legal prohibition against discrimination (including a refusal to deal) with the tort law's prohibition against the use of force and fraud. Just as there are victims of force, so too there are victims of discrimination, each in his own way an appealing claimant for redress. The parallel between force and discrimination has an apparent verbal seductiveness, but the differences between the two types of behavior are so profound that it is unwise to move from a condemnation of force to an equal condemnation of discrimination, at least in a system of decentralized rights over persons and things.

Recall that in dealing with force, each of us has to be concerned about the person who bears us the most ill will. That is why we lock our house even when 99 percent of our neighbors are friendly. And even if our worst enemy is bought off or placated, peace is not at hand, for another enemy virtually indistinguishable from the first may rise up to threaten us.

The case for public force to constrain aggression thus becomes over-powering because it promises (it may not deliver, but it promises) some release from what otherwise would be an endless set of violent interactions with people that each of us would rather avoid. By having no control in the selection of trading partners, all of us find our welfare bound up with the goodwill of our worst enemy. And even after that enemy is placated, there is still the necessity of dealing with the second-worst enemy, and so on.

Markets offer a radical contrast, for (with force and fraud out of bounds) each person now need look only to the other tail of the distribution—the people who make the best offers. The person who wishes to discriminate against another for any reason has it in her power only to refuse to do business with him, not to use force against him. The victim of discrimination, unlike the victim of force, keeps his initial set of entitlements—life, limb, and possession—even if he does not realize the gains from trade with a particular person.

Within that framework of property rights the counterstrategies for the victim of discrimination are clear. No resources need be devoted to self-defense because aggression is already prohibited. Instead, the victim can *unilaterally* migrate to the other tail of the distribution and seek out those persons who wish to make the most favorable transactions with him. Thus, in a world in which 90 percent of the people are opposed to doing business with me, I shall concentrate my attention on doing business with the other 10 percent, secure in the knowledge that as long as the tort law (with its prohibitions against the forceful interference with contract or prospective trading advantage) is in place,[1] my enemies are powerless to block our mutually beneficial transactions by their use of force. The universe of potential trading partners is surely smaller because some people bear me personal animus and hostility. I would prefer that everyone be willing to do business with me, even if I have no wish to do business with them. But the critical question for my welfare is not which opportunities are lost but which are retained. Even for persons who find themselves in relatively isolated minorities, the opportunities retained will not be trivial

---

1. See, e.g., *Tarleton v. M'Gawley*, Peake's N.P. 270, 170 *Eng. Rep.* 153 (1793). The protection afforded here is largely against deliberate interference with future trading. The extension to negligent or inadvertent interference raises harder questions. But for these points the details do not matter, for inadvertent intervention cannot close down markets except under rare circumstances. Deliberate intervention, of course, can close markets, and indeed has done so.

as the number of persons in society increases from the tens to the hundreds, thousands, and millions. Viable trading economies have thrived in much smaller populations.

The basic problems all involve the question of how jobs and workers should be matched. In order to get a handle on that question, it is useful to look at each side of the market separately and to ask what are the behavioral responses of both (potential) employees and employers in a market that is not constrained by any antidiscrimination law. In essence the problem is one of search, in which the question can be analogized to drawing balls from an urn. Since both sides participate in the process, let us consider cases in which first the employee and then the employer does the selection.

To the Urn

Employees

The task of a worker in finding willing trading partners has many of the characteristics of a sampling problem. Each worker puts her hand into an urn in the hope of finding a ball with a high number, that is, an employer who will make a high offer for her goods or services. She can go into the urn lots of times, in the sense that a rejection by one trading partner does not prevent her from searching for another. If there are a hundred balls in one urn and a thousand balls in the other, both drawn from some random distribution, then the relevant question is, what is the highest-numbered ball she can draw from each urn within some fixed period of time, not what is the lowest-numbered or the average-numbered ball.

The nature of her success will depend critically on the distribution of balls within each urn. In a bleak Hobbesian world in which everyone has identical tastes and selfish inclinations, the ability to search will prove of little value, for each ball in the urn has exactly the same number as all the others. And indeed those accounts that are most critical of discrimination tend to ignore or understate the variation within the class of employers and employees.[2] But let the more accurate account of some genuine

2. See, e.g., Cass R. Sunstein, "Why Markets Don't Stop Discrimination," 8 *Soc. Phil. & Pol.* 22 (1991). "Consider, for example, the case of a shopkeeper whose customers do not like dealing with blacks or women; a commercial airline whose patrons react unfavorably to female pilots; a university one of whose departments prefers to be primarily male or white; a law firm whose clients prefer not to have black lawyers; a hospital whose patients

spread in the distribution of human traits and preferences prevail, and the difference between force and discrimination becomes far more manifest and durable. In a world of free access to open markets, systematic discrimination, even by a large majority, offers little peril to the isolated minority. Unconstrained by external force, members of minority groups are free to search for jobs with those firms that do want to hire them.

Once we have acknowledged some variation in tastes and attitudes, we can speculate on the prospects of two workers, one who can draw balls from either urn, and one who knows that she is confined to the urn that contains only a tenth as many balls as the other. But if the variations in both original distributions are about the same, then the difference between the *highest* numbers in each urn is apt to be small, even if the *majority* of the desirable balls are in the larger urn. Indeed, the smaller urn is likely to offer a more favorable distribution of balls for this particular worker, because it will tend to contain balls representing the people who are most likely to be willing to do business with that individual. In many instances these will be persons of the same race, sex, age, or ethnicity, or so one might infer from the patterns of discrimination found in residential (within strong ethnic) communities and marriage (within the same race, nationality, or religion) markets. The availability of these trading partners thereby reduces the disadvantage of preferences—whether rational or arbitrary—given to the qualities that others possess. The argument here is perfectly general. It does not depend on the reasons for discrimination, the attitudes of those who would discriminate, or the cultural patterns of behavior within the system as a whole. It depends only on there being large numbers of individuals who are normally (or even widely) distributed in their talents, sentiments, tastes, and preferences.

Employers

The urn analogies are also helpful in understanding behavior on the employer side of the market, where again the constant effort to find low-cost sources of supply has powerful benefits for the victims of any form of private discrimination. Let us assume that there are two groups of

---

are uncomfortable with female doctors or black nurses." It is not accurate to generalize from the firm to the industry. There are plenty of firms and individuals whose preferences are mixed, or run the opposite way, on both race and sex, especially in an age in which diversity has become the dominant justification for race- and sex-conscious classifications.

individuals with whom a set of firms can choose to do business. One group (defined by race, sex, or age) is regarded on average as superior to the other, in the sense that each firm would rather have any employee drawn at random from the first pool than one drawn at random from the second. What strategy should the firms follow in making their employment decisions? Much depends on the ability of the employer to discriminate (that is, to determine differences) among the employees within each pool. If the employer is utterly unable to obtain any information about the worker in question, then the strategic response is relatively straightforward. The problem is the familiar one of George Akerlof's lemons,[3] which asks how markets will behave when buyers (and, by easy extension, employers) cannot differentiate superior from average products, or, in this case, workers. Here they will choose on the basis of broad statistical averages since they have no other information to go on. Sellers, and by extension employees, for their part will respond by saving costs and reducing their goods to average quality, since there is no way to internalize the gain from marketing a superior product, or a superior set of labor skills. The lack of precise information leads to a deterioration in the overall quality of both products and labor.

By analogy, if all we knew about the two urns was the expected value of any ball to be drawn from each, the decision procedure would be simple: we would pick a ball from the urn with the higher expected value, no matter what anyone else had done before us. So long as we know that the prior person can only pick at random, the quality of the pool should be no better or worse than it was before, so the basic judgment remains the same regardless of where a particular employer stands in the queue.

The theory of lemons has a direct application to the problem of discrimination in labor markets. If black and white workers were the balls in these two urns, then the employer would know only the expected rate of return for the average worker within the class, but would have no knowledge of the relative strengths of individual workers in each class. If white workers on average have higher levels of productivity (say, because they have had a better education), then the employer is better off engaging in statistical discrimination[4] because there is no way in which further investigation would allow it to identify superior black workers. Akerlof and

3. See George Akerlof, "The Market for Lemons: Quality Uncertainty and the Market Mechanism," 84 *Quart. J. Econ.* 488 (1970).

4. On statistical discrimination generally, see Edmund S. Phelps, "The Statistical Theory of Racism and Sexism," 62 *Am. Econ. Rev.* 659 (1972).

others using his basic model[5] have been able to identify some efficiency losses that follow when employers discriminate because they—by assumption—have only information about the average quality of workers within the group, and none about individual workers. This theoretical development identifies a form of economic inefficiency that is likely *even if* the preference to discriminate is taken as a legitimate subjective given and not as some illegitimate inclination which should not be registered on the social scale.

It is important, however, to stress the narrow compass of these models of statistical discrimination. First, they show only that some form of statistical discrimination is inefficient. They do not ask either of two questions: Are the sources of the inefficiency greater or smaller than the administrative costs necessary to correct them? And are the sources of market imperfection greater or smaller than anticipated efficiency losses that could result (and have resulted) from legislative interference? Second, the models presuppose that an employer can obtain no information about individual employees in either group. Yet once the market environment allows an employer to conduct an interview, ask for a reference, or require the employee to take an aptitude, skill, or psychological test, reliance on general statistical information will diminish because of the ever greater ability to individuate employees.

Let us return to our original example, in which there are two pools, with substantial variations in each group, but where the quality of the worker drawn at random in one group is known to be higher than in the other. Only now it is possible at some modest cost to determine the individual abilities of workers in each pool. It is as though the person who draws the ball from the urn can now predict the number on it with fair confidence. Initially it might be thought that the right self-interested strategy would be to concentrate one's hiring efforts exclusively on the preferred talent pool: why accept the workers one values less when it is possible to acquire workers one tends to value more?

That strategy, however, is wrong because it ignores the deterioration in average quality that follows after successive hirings from the preferred pool. Even when they confine their efforts to that pool, employers will not hire at random. To the contrary, given the variation in the quality of individuals within the pool, each firm will seek to skim off the cream of

5. See George Akerlof, "The Economics of Cast and of the Rat Race and Other Woeful Tales," in *An Economic Theorist's Book of Tales* (G. Akerlof ed. 1989). See also Stewart Schwab, "Is Statistical Discrimination Efficient?" 76 *Am. Econ. Rev.* 228 (1986).

the workers available at any set wage. Even though prospective employers have imperfect information, with a little homework they should be able to improve on a random draw. Accordingly, with wages held constant, the best workers will go first, leaving a less desirable distribution behind for subsequent hiring. At every point, therefore, employers will have to reevaluate the relative quality of the two pools, knowing that the quality in the first pool will deteriorate while the quality of the second, untouched pool remains constant. As long as there is any overlap in distribution in the two pools at the outset, then sooner or later some firms will change their hiring strategies. When the quality of the workers in the less desired pool exceeds the average quality of the remaining workers in the more desirable pool, then hiring will migrate toward the second pool, notwithstanding the original desire to remain with the preferred talent pool only.

Indeed, there is good reason to believe that the foregoing argument *understates* the willingness of employers to hire from the second pool. In principle, hiring from the second pool should begin virtually simultaneously with hiring from the first. The relative distribution of talents in both pools is known at the outset, and so too the constant process of deterioration in the first pool. Any employer who foresees the future need to switch to the second pool has a powerful incentive to beat the crowd by switching pools early in order to obtain the inside track. If one firm jumps the gun, other firms will have the incentive to follow quickly. To be sure, not all firms will search in both pools, but again it hardly matters who searches where as long as there are enough competitors in both markets to provide the workers in both pools a wide range of options. In practice the process should reach equilibrium fairly soon when many firms are in the market, each trying to find its own optimal niche in light of the strategies adopted by other firms. Viewing it as a continuous process, one should see steady hiring from both pools as firms seek the best available worker from any source.

It might be said in response that this argument presupposes that firms are rational in their behavior, which they often are not. But again there is the confusion between the competence of the marginal and the average firm. The argument works, provided there is *one* firm that understands that it is in its interest to seek gold in a new mine after the old mine has been worked out. Thus, if most firms are unaware of the way in which the quality of the pool changes as items are taken from it, then the firm that *is* aware of the shift will prosper enormously. Even if other firms are not aware of the problem at the outset, their internal feedback mechanism will tell them that their second round of new hirings is inferior to the first. Experience and example will educate where abstract calculation fails. The rationality of the market system qua system is therefore far higher than the rationality of its average participant or than the sole government bureaucrat asked to make job assignments. It is very hard to envision any state of affairs in which all firms would adopt the strategy of hiring only workers in the preferred class before taking any from the second. At the margin someone will break ranks.

The argument may be taken a step further. Let us suppose (what seems to be incorrect) that *all* the workers in the first pool are universally regarded as superior to *any* of the workers in the second pool. Will firms choose to exhaust all the workers in the first pool before they consider any in the second? Again the answer depends on other assumptions. If the wage level is kept constant for both groups, then the answer is yes, for every worker in the first pool promises the employer greater benefit than any worker in the second pool. To the extent that an antidiscrimination law requires equal wages for equal work, it will in practice encourage the very discrimination that it seeks to eliminate.[6] Relax the equal wage constraint, however, and the outcome will be different.

In a world in which all persons are masters of their own offers, the equal wage constraint does not hold, and other strategies may become viable. The workers in the less desired pool can seek to offset their perceived disadvantages by engaging in price cutting. They can provide the same services for less, so the net return to an employer from hiring these workers is the same regardless of the hiring pool. The discount, moreover, need not be permanent, for once a worker establishes performance on the job, his or her wage level will rise as other firms become willing to bid up the wages of workers with job experience, especially those with whom they have had personal contact. Here again, the success of this counterstrategy does not depend on the willingness of all firms to hire equally from both pools, given the wage differential. It is quite possible that certain firms will consider only workers from the first group, given their practical business needs or their own snobby standards. Some people will stick with a Rolls-Royce no matter how good a deal they can get on a Toyota. But the central insight—which is that with markets, only the *best* offers count for the victims of discrimination—still survives. As firms find that the alternative strategy pays, then it will be invoked.

6. See, for this point and many others, the perceptive essay by Harold Demsetz, "Minorities in the Market Place," 43 *N.C. L. Rev.* 271, 275–278 (1965).

Someone will always find it worthwhile to hire the labor from the second pool. The more some employers stay away from the pool, the greater the incentives for others to come in.

The arguments here replicate the general principles of comparative advantage outlined in standard economic texts.[7] If group A is better than group B at producing both guns and butter, it does not follow that members of group B will be left idle in the guns-and-butter economy. Group A will specialize at that task (say, guns) in which its comparative advantage is greater because its opportunity costs are lower, and workers from group B will specialize in butter. The overall output will be higher, and each side can enjoy some share of the increased pie. The model of discrimination in employment does not yield a set of outcomes in which disfavored workers are left idle because of the preferences, rational or irrational, of employers. All parties enter into the system of exchange, so in the end each person's worth is judged by the trading partner who puts the *most favorable* evaluation on what he or she does.

Thus far it has been (implicitly) assumed that a search for either employer or employee was costless in that one could look at all the balls in the urn individually before deciding which one to choose. A more realistic model assumes that in each and every case there is some cost to inspecting any ball taken from the urn. Job applicants must spend time filling out forms, attending interviews, providing references, and taking tests. Employers incur similar costs. Where both sides bear costs, then both have a need to economize on a search. With an offer in hand, a worker will seek another only if the anticipated wage increase is greater than the costs incurred to procure it. Similarly, the firm will interview the next candidate only if it thinks that the improvement in worker level will be sufficient to justify further costs of search. As these costs increase on both sides, the number of prospective contracts that can be pursued diminishes. Search costs thus can impose genuine losses on the market, given the risks of imperfect matches. A may prefer to work for Z, not Y. Z may wish to hire A over B. Nonetheless, A and Z never get together, so Z hires B and A works for Y. The social gains of the A–Z contract remain unrealized.

What, then, is the proper response? Here the answer is clear: organize institutions to minimize the costs of search. Huge portions of labor and product markets have just that goal in mind. Middlemen of all kinds and

7. See, e.g., David D. Friedman, *Price Theory—An Intermediate Text* 139 (2nd ed., 1990).

descriptions have as their function the matching of producers with ultimate buyers.[8] Their specialized knowledge of the market helps overcome the imperfect information that buyers and sellers share. In real estate transactions people typically hire brokers to expand the class of potential purchasers to include high-paying persons that the seller could not identify unassisted. Brokers cost money, but the payments are made in exchange for services worth more than their cost. The increase in selling price obtained, coupled with the reduction in seller's labor, makes brokerage a common and successful, but *not* a universal, occurrence. In some cases the owners are in a position to sell more effectively by themselves. Even where brokers are used, it is easy to recount cases in which brokers betray clients or clients take advantage of brokers. Any relationship of trust has its horror stories. But these costs can be minimized by good contract terms, by bonding, and by reputation. The difficulties of executing brokerage contracts should be understood for what they are—costs, not absolute barriers, to this form of agency relationship.

What is true in real estate markets carries over to headhunters and labor markets. People who find search expensive can reduce their costs by buying information or hiring people to find that information for them. A full-scale personnel industry, a vast array of hiring fairs and clearinghouses, exists for precisely this matching purpose. It is a mistake, therefore, to assume that search costs lock the victims of discrimination into dealing with parties who are hostile to their welfare and ambitions. The segment of the market where narrow-minded but established firms refuse to tread is the very place where the new entrepreneur can make the quickest and most dramatic inroads. Free entry does not exert its power only when entry is costless. It is also a powerful protection against being victimized by discrimination even when search and contracting costs are positive and substantial.

Notwithstanding the private mechanisms normally available to address the problem of costly search and imperfect information, a study by Paul Milgrom and Sharon Oster[9] has located in the costliness of search a theoretical explanation for the persistence of unwarranted discrimination in the marketplace. Their study advances the "invisibility hypothesis," which holds that there are certain workers whose job skills are well

8. See, e.g., Janet T. Landa, "*Hadley v. Baxendale* and the Expansion of the Middleman Economy," 16 *J. Legal Stud.* 455 (1987).

9. Paul Milgrom and Sharon Oster, "Job Discrimination, Market Forces, and the Invisibility Hypothesis," 102 *Quart. J. Econ.* 453 (1987).

known to their employers but are not observable by other persons in the marketplace. Given this asymmetry of information, Milgrom and Oster suggest that employers have an incentive to maximize their own profits by keeping some of their most productive employees in low-visibility, low-pay positions. Reduced to inferior status, the workers generate economic rents for the employer—high productivity for low wages—but they will not be bid away by rival firms, who cannot discover their personal talents and skills.

As stated, the theory of invisibility contains no necessary connection to the problem of discrimination by race or by sex. That link is supplied by two empirical assertions: first, that promotion enhances visibility, and second, that members of disadvantaged groups are more likely to be invisible. Since disadvantaged workers know that the process exists, moreover, they are discouraged from acquiring human capital, which in turn depresses wages further in the future. By stressing these two connections, Milgrom and Oster seek to undermine the conventional economic wisdom, defended here, that the least prejudiced employers will bid up the wages of disfavored groups to market levels.

As Milgrom and Oster note, this theory has the peculiar consequence of asserting that employers find it in their interest to promote their less able workers in order to keep the abler ones for themselves. That point alone should be sufficient to call into question the significance of invisibility in the ordinary operation of markets. An alternative strategy is to promote rapidly, to offer high wages to good workers to keep them from going elsewhere, and to imbue in them the culture of the firm so that they develop firm-specific human capital that is not easily transferable to a rival organization. The strategy proposed by Milgrom and Oster, moreover, does not explain how the employer keeps those coveted economic rents. The level of production for any given worker is a function of the wage that is garnered, and the prospects for promotion that are available. The highly productive invisible workers whom the employer seeks to keep secret always have the option of cutting back on their level of output, knowing that the firm has little incentive to fire them as long as the value of their output is in excess of the wage that they receive, or above the productivity of the less able replacement the firm will have to hire. The worker can take out in leisure what she cannot obtain in higher wages. Thus neither side wins, given the combination of higher wages and higher production from which both firm and employee benefit. In addition, these workers can, by speaking with friends in other firms and contacting head-hunters and employment agencies, become more visible by their own efforts instead of by those of the employer. Is it that hard to assemble and present evidence of ability and talent? The initial differences in information do not remain fixed forever in the face of the viable counterstrategies open to employees. The effort, therefore, to find any persistent large-scale source of discrimination should fail. Legal barriers to entry are in the empirical setting far more likely to account for any persistent lower wage levels by race or sex.

The view that competition tends to undermine wage differentials where entry is free is not adequately countered by pointing to statistical discrimination and imperfect information in employment markets. In addition, these models of discrimination also have, it must be stressed, clear policy implications. The strategy of the law should be to encourage employers to obtain as much individual information as possible about workers so that they can, *pro tanto,* place less reliance on broad statistical judgments. To the extent, therefore, that the present antidiscrimination law imposes enormous restrictions on the use of testing, interviews, and indeed any information that does not *perfectly* individuate workers, then by indirection it encourages the very sorts of discrimination that the law seeks to oppose.[10] Yet once the imperfect information can be taken into account, employers have private incentives to break down the stereotypes that lie at the root of effective statistical discrimination.

Even here a word of caution is in order. The introduction of evidence that allows individuation will render the accurate statistical generalization unimportant only in the case where that individual evidence is itself a certain predictor—at best a marginal case. In any other situation the proper decision procedure is to combine the specific information with information about the background distribution of probabilities in accordance with Bayes's theorem, under which the background information plays a larger role than is normally intuited.[11] The use of background

10. See discussion in Chapter 11.

11. Bayes's theorem provides as follows: $P(H/E) = [P(E/H)P(H)]/P(E)$, where $P(H/E)$ is the conditional probability of H given E; $P(E/H)$ is the conditional probability of E given H; $P(H)$ is the probability of H, and $P(E)$ is the probability of E.

The standard illustration is in Amos Tversky and Daniel Kahneman, "Causal Schemas in Judgments under Uncertainty," in *Progress in Social Psychology* 117 (Martin Fishbein ed. 1980). There are two cab companies in town, the Green Company and the Blue Company. It is known that 85 percent of the cabs are green and 15 percent are blue. One cab is involved in a hit-and-run accident, and an eyewitness reports that she is 80 percent confident that the offending cab was blue. If one looks only at the eyewitness report and disregards the background information, then there is an 80 percent probability that a blue

information will, and should, persist even when individuation is possible, even at a high degree. But the more information available, the less significant the role of baseline information on which statistical theories of discrimination rest.

These observations help explain what to some has been a puzzling empirical finding, that "it appears that blacks get more education not less than *equivalent* whites (holding other factors constant)."[12] The basic explanation for the behavior is that the education provides them, ceteris paribus, with a greater return than whites because it overcomes the willingness of employers to rely on background information. That level of investment in education would not be rational if one conceived of discrimination as placing impassable, or even powerful, barriers in the marketplace.[13] It is precisely because a significant segment of the market responds to improved information that theories of statistical discrimination are of limited use in describing any functioning employment market.

Natural Limits on Discrimination

The urn examples suggest that both employers and employees have strong, if imperfect, incentives to beat the statistical averages by engaging in search. A decision not to trade with a given person cannot be made lightly. As Gary Becker has pointed out,[14] people who decide that they do

cab was involved, more than enough to establish civil responsibility. But if we combine the background information with the eyewitness report, the accurate probability assessment is that there is only a 12/29 (or 41 percent) probability that the offending cab was blue, less than the 50 percent required under the ordinary burden-of-proof rule.

The calculation goes like this. The eyewitness would correctly identify a green cab as green 80 percent of the time, or 68 out of 85 times. The other 17 times she would call that cab blue. Similarly, she would identify the blue cab as blue 12 out of 15 times, and green the other 3. Her calling a cab blue would be correct 12 times and wrong 17 times, for a 12/29 probability (around 41 percent). On the legal implications of this rule, see David Kaye, "The Law of Probability and the Law of the Land," 47 *U. Chi. L. Rev.* 34 (1979); Jonathan J. Koehler and Daniel Shaviro, "Veridical Verdicts: Increasing Verdict Accuracy through the Use of Overtly Probabilistic Evidence and Methods," 75 *Cornell L. Rev.* 247 (1990); and sources cited in note 1.

12. See Kevin Lang, "A Language Theory of Discrimination," 101 *Quart. J. Econ.* 363, 365 (1986).

13. See, e.g., Sunstein, "Why Markets Don't Stop Discrimination," 8 *Soc. Phil. & Pol.* 22, 29 (1991), who then notes that the empirical evidence on human capital investment cuts the other way. Id. at 29–30.

14. See Gary S. Becker, *The Economics of Discrimination*, ch. 3 (2nd ed., 1971). The first edition of the book dates from 1957.

not want to trade with or hire certain people because of race, sex, or age are making a decision that has more than just external costs. They bear a large part of the costs themselves, for their decision will surely limit their own opportunities for advancement and success, even as it leaves others free to pursue alternate opportunities. The greater the class of persons who are regarded as off-limits, and the more irrational the preferences, the more the decision will hurt the people who make it, and the more numerous the options it will open to rival traders.

As I have noted, the common law system of freedom of contract allows bargains to be made for good reason, bad reason, or no reason at all. The virtue of that rule is *not* that it promotes or extols bad or pointless bargains. Quite the opposite. The rule means that the state need not expend resources to superintend the "merits" of any bargain in deciding whether to enforce it. It also means that we shall not all suffer together when the state overreaches or makes the wrong judgments as to what reasons for noncontracting are good or bad. Freedom of contract does not, however, require individual contracting parties to be indifferent among contracts that are good, bad, or pointless. Indeed, it works so well precisely because people do tend to their own interests and are sensitive to changes in costs and benefits that routinely follow from the ebb and flow of events great and small. The legal system normally has no need to superintend the wisdom of bargains when the contracting parties have strong incentives to do so for themselves. There are natural curbs against irrational contracting behavior even in a system that makes no formal condemnation of practices that others think, perhaps rightly, to be irrational.

In reaching this conclusion, one must use the term *irrational* with a certain caution because there is some disagreement between lawyers and economists about its proper application in describing human behavior. Lawyers are much freer in using the term as a form of condemnation and are routinely tempted to conclude that certain behaviors are irrational because they are known to be against one's own interests. Economists as a group tend to be more cautious; they simply chalk up the behavior to a distinctive set of subjective preferences, which are not necessarily seen as right or wrong but are simply taken as *there*.[15] The taste for discrimination is just another preference of some utility known to the actor but typically discoverable only by inference to an outsider. Within the economic per-

---

15. The model is adopted, for example, in John Donohue, "Is Title VII Efficient?" 134 *U. Pa. L. Rev.* 1411 (1986), discussed in Chapter 3 at 76–78.

spective, the relevant questions are two: From the individual point of view, what action will private persons take to maximize their welfare, given the legal, budgetary, and social constraints they face? And, from the social point of view, when they take this action, will it lead to an increase or a decrease in overall levels of social satisfaction, subjectively measured for all persons?

On balance I incline toward the economists' account, and to the theoretical rigor that it makes possible by not requiring one to ask whose preferences are legitimate and whose are not. For these purposes, though, it is not strictly necessary to decide whether to adopt the subjective view, which tends to deny that irrational behavior exists, or the objective view, which condemns it for the heavy social toll it exacts. In either case a taste for discrimination, even if not irrational, may place those who hold it at a substantial cost disadvantage relative to their competitors. Thus, consider what happens to a taste for discrimination, and the harms that it causes to its victims, when the dynamic elements of the system are taken into account. Suppose for the moment that some people refuse categorically to do business with certain other people. If their behavior is irrational, the practitioners of discrimination will find their opportunities restricted because they bear certain costs not borne by their rivals. That loss in opportunities will in turn be translated into a reduced share of wealth relative to other individuals and firms who have a better sense of what their own self-interest properly requires. It follows that where entry to markets is open, the *mix* of firms will change over time. It is therefore very risky to move from any account of the attitudes of individual employers to the structure of industries, or even entire economies.

The point is important to an understanding of the weaknesses in some defenses of the antidiscrimination law. When Kenneth Arrow, for example, seeks to give demand-side explanations for the perpetuation of discrimination in employment markets, he writes as though *all* employers had the same utility function that seeks to maximize a mix of monetary profit and minimize contact with black workers, whom they dislike:

> If we assume away productivity differences between black and white employees, the simplest explanation of the existence of wage differences is the taste of the employer. Formally, we might suppose that the employer acts so as to maximize a utility function that depends not only on profits but also on the numbers of white and black employees. Presumably, other variables being held constant, the employer has a negative marginal utility for black labor. A specific version of this hypothesis

would be that the employer's utility depends only on the ratio of black to white workers and is independent of the scale of operations of the firm.[16]

Although that profile may be true of some employers, it surely is not true of all. There is no reason to assume that all white employers have the same utility functions, or share the same distaste for dealing with black workers. And as long as there is any difference, those employers who do not dislike dealing with blacks will have a comparative advantage over those who do. Nor is there any reason to assume that all employers are white males, especially in an open market where women and blacks and other minority individuals may become employers, and have in fact increasingly assumed hiring and personnel functions in mainstream corporations. If we are to model the world accurately, Arrow's implicit assumption of employer homogeneity must be rejected. Once differences in tastes and preferences are introduced among employers, it is less possible to portray labor markets as monoliths. Instead, heterogeneity makes it evident that there is no single dominant strategy that represents the behavior of "the" employer—who may be white or black, male or female, old or young. If some employers favor white workers, then other employers will move in to take up the slack. That diversity of taste undercuts any inference from the preferences of employers to the emergence of systematic discrimination in voluntary markets. The primary risk is that some external political force will impose a uniform preference on all segments of the market, as is common today with explicit government policies that mandate affirmative action.[17]

The same conclusion holds when we deal with the preferences of employees. One assumption of Arrow's argument (like Becker's, from which it is in part derived) is that blacks uniformly prefer to be with whites, whereas whites prefer not to be with blacks. From that assumption only two possibilities emerge. First, there will be fully segregated firms because the black workers do not value working with whites as

---

16. Kenneth J. Arrow, "Models of Job Discrimination," in *Racial Discrimination in Economic Life* 83, 86 (Anthony H. Pascal ed. 1972). Arrow previously noted that supply-side explanations (e.g., differentials in human capital) could not account, according to the existing evidence, for more than about 50 or 60 percent of the wage differential. Id. at 84–85.

17. The present accreditation standards of the American Association of Law Schools, for example, state that each school must have a successful affirmative action program for minorities in order to remain accredited.

much as the whites value not working with blacks. In that case there are no successful trades that can take place between members of the two groups because blacks will not pay whites (here in the form of wage differentials) enough for them to work together. It is as if whites demand eight units of wealth to work with blacks whereas blacks are willing to pay only four units to work with whites.

The second possibility makes the reverse assumption, that whites demand four units of wealth to work with blacks whereas blacks are willing to pay eight units of wealth to work with whites. On that assumption we should expect to see whites and blacks employed within the same firm at different wages, where that wage differential (between four and eight units of wealth) represents an implicit transfer from black to white workers for the privilege of working side by side with them, such that both whites and blacks will both be better off than they are with fully segregated firms.

Becker's model *posits* the truth of the assumption of asymmetrical preferences for black and white workers, and explores its consequences for market behavior. Empirically, however, the premise itself seems false, relative to a more realistic set of assumptions, parallel to those made about employer preferences, which yields very different conclusions. If we assume that some blacks prefer to work with blacks and some whites prefer to work with whites, we should see some firms that voluntarily segregate their work forces and others that do not. But by the same token we should no longer expect to see any market differential in wages, for there are no side payments made between workers. As Becker himself has trenchantly observed:

> Many serious errors have been committed because of a failure to recognize that market segregation and market discrimination are separate concepts referring to separate phenomena. Market discrimination refers to the incomes received by different groups and ignores their distribution in employment; market segregation refers to their distribution in employment and ignores their incomes. Market segregation can occur without market discrimination . . . ; market discrimination can occur without market segregation . . . and quite often they occur together.[18]

Using Becker's terminology, one can explain why voluntary market segregation will occur as long as there is some fraction of the population that

18. Becker, *The Economics of Discrimination* 57–58.

prefers (irrationally or not) to work with persons of like kind, whether defined along racial, ethnic, religious, sexual, or age lines. Yet, by the same token, it is possible that this market is in equilibrium, because the sorting that has taken place is efficient and therefore may generate *higher* incomes than are otherwise obtainable with work forces integrated under legal mandate.[19] Each firm will make an efficient deployment of its labor resources, and so members of each group should have a wage equal to their marginal product whether they choose to work in a firm that observes voluntary segregation or one that is mixed with respect to race.

In theory, then, the persistence of voluntary segregated markets with free entry is not odious. Instead, it must be sharply distinguished from the system of government-mandated segregation on grounds of race that has been extensively practiced throughout much of the country well into this century.[20] The persistence of both market segregation and wage differentials should not be attributable to any uniform preferences of employers or employees in market settings, as Arrow and Becker presuppose.[21] Historically the conditions of free entry did not obtain in markets where the powerful hand of Jim Crow touched all aspects of southern life, and influenced many aspects of northern life as well.

The Davis-Bacon Act of 1931, for example, provided that construction workers on federally funded contracts should receive "the prevailing wage." It was passed with the explicit intention of protecting incumbent white construction workers in the North from competition with those from the South, and was largely effective in achieving its goal, especially in the period before the passage of the 1964 Civil Rights Act.[22] Elsewhere, an elaborate constellation of labor, zoning, licensing, police, and other regulations made it very clear that the official establishment was not indifferent to the behavior of firms in private markets. Private market actors should respond to the stimuli set out by the government as much as they do to the price signals that are sent out by private firms. If the state makes it more costly for a firm to hire and promote black workers, to give them

---

19. See the discussion in Chapter 4 under the heading "Monopoly and Price Discrimination."

20. See the discussion in Chapter 5.

21. There is this difference. Becker uses the assumption of asymmetrical preferences to construct a model that shows the effect on wage and employment levels. Arrow concludes that the assumption is a true description of the state of affairs (as of 1972).

22. The Davis-Bacon Act is presently codified at 40 U.S.C. §276a-c (1988). For an account, see David Bernstein, "The Davis-Bacon Act: Vestige of Jim Crow," ms., Yale Law School, on file with author.

places of public influence and prominence, then we should expect to see fewer blacks advance in labor markets. The system of direct government control injects a strong element of monopoly power in what would be competitive markets if the industry were unregulated. The dangers of government force can be compounded if private violence is used to enforce the dominant social norm. Neither supply nor demand but external regulation may account for the unexplained portion of the wage differential.[23]

Some Empirical Evidence

The arguments just advanced are all of a distinct theoretical cast. The question naturally arises as to the state of the empirical evidence in unregulated markets. That evidence is of course difficult if not impossible to find in labor markets today, given the pervasive presence of Title VII. Defenders of the antidiscrimination law therefore have sought to find evidence of persistent market discrimination based on the preferences of white employers, workers, or consumers, which could account for wage differentials that are unrelated to differences in output. In principle, as long as the alternative of voluntary sorting is available, overall wage effects of this sort should be small. Nonetheless, three recent studies have sought to show that the effects of discrimination are larger than one might have supposed. Two of these studies are directed to unregulated markets, and both lie outside the labor area. The first of these, which examines the market for baseball cards, was done by Clark Nardinelli and Curtis Simon.[24] The second study, on the level of dealer markups on staged car purchase transactions, was undertaken by Ian Ayres.[25] The last of the studies, by the Urban Institute, deals with the effects of discrimination in two selected employment markets.[26]

Nardinelli and Simon, and then Ayres, found persistent price differentials that are not easily explained by any difference in underlying cost. On one point they diverge. Nardinelli and Simon believe that the price differentials they observed with baseball cards are attributable if not to bad

23. I attend to the historical importance of these matters in Chapter 5.

24. Clark Nardinelli and Curtis Simon, "Customer Racial Discrimination in the Market for Memorabilia: The Case of Baseball," 105 *Quart. J. Econ.* 575 (1990).

25. Ian Ayres, "Fair Driving: Gender and Race Discrimination in Retail Car Negotiations," 104 *Harv. L. Rev.* 817 (1991).

26. Margery Austin Turner, Michael Fix, and Raymond J. Struyk, *Opportunities Denied, Opportunities Diminished: Discrimination in Hiring* (Urban Institute, 1991).

animus then at least to a clear preference among collectors for white players. Ayres in turn believes that the higher prices paid by black and female customers in the retail car market are best explained by statistical discrimination—a set of patterns whereby sales personnel believe that they can obtain higher prices through shrewd bargaining with blacks and women than they can with white men. A closer examination of their work, however, reveals some genuine difficulties in interpreting the available data as well as complications when the results of these studies are extended to the very different arena of the employment market.

Baseball Cards

Nardinelli and Simon sought to measure discrimination in tastes by looking at the prices at which baseball cards traded. The market for these cards is well developed and, as they remark, "has long ceased to be the domain solely of children."[27] Baseball cards can sell for thousands of dollars in an active market richly endowed with professional dealers, conventions, and clubs. In addition, Beckett's *Official Price Guide to Baseball Players* gives standard prices for cards in what has become effectively a national market. Nardinelli and Simon sought to determine by objective measures the athletic performance of various players and its relation to the price at which each player's cards are exchanged, taking into account the scarcity of the cards on the market. They eschewed any effort to measure certain exogenous variables that might influence value in individual cases, such as the success or failure of the players' teams, the size of the hometown crowds, and individual personalities, on the grounds that these factors would tend to cancel out over a large study.[28] The cards that were the subject of their study were issued in 1970 by a single monopoly supplier, the Topps Company, a factor that further eased the difficulty of value comparisons.

In order to carry out their study, Nardinelli and Simon constructed separate performance measures for hitters and for pitchers. When all the data were tallied, they concluded that for hitters, with scarcity and performance accounted for, differences in valuation emerged that were best attributable to buyer discrimination. Thus for hitters the numbers revealed that cards featuring blacks sold for 6.4 percent less than those for whites, while cards featuring Hispanics sold for some 17 percent less

27. Nardinelli and Simon, "Customer Racial Discrimination" at 577.
28. Id. at 580–582.

than those for white players. Overall, nonwhite players' cards did about 10 percent worse than those of white players.[29] For pitchers the situation was somewhat different; controlled for performance and scarcity, cards traded at 12 percent less for Hispanics than for whites and 16 percent less for blacks than for whites, or about 13 percent less for nonwhites overall.[30] Measured by standard statistical tests these variations are significant.

Notwithstanding the obvious care shown in this study, some unavoidable problems should be pointed out. First, there is no reason to expect a lockstep correspondence between lifetime performance records and the value of cards. Players with an otherwise flat record who have had a single terrific year, or even made a single famous play, may be better remembered than other players who gave a solid but inconspicuous performance over an entire season. Reggie Jackson carries the label "Mr. October" not because of his record number of strikeouts during the regular season but because of his clutch performance during the World Series. Bobby Thomson is remembered for hitting the most famous home run in baseball, and Ralph Branca for throwing that pitch. Roger Maris is remembered for sixty-one home runs in 1961 and little else, even though he was a fine ball player for several seasons. And today Bo Jackson is (or was) known far better than his raw numbers would suggest for his prodigious home runs, numerous strikeouts, and effective ad campaigns. Peaks, in other words, may have more impact than plateaus in determining market value.

Getting a good measure of these variations is difficult, but there is at least one systematic, telltale sign that the lifetime performance measures used by Nardinelli and Simon do not capture all the relevant variables that go into determining public perception of prominence. In principle there is no reason to expect a different racial ranking for hitters than for pitchers. Nor is there any reason to expect that the gaps will be different for hitters than for pitchers. Yet for hitters the order of valuation is white, black, Hispanic while for pitchers it is white, Hispanic, black. Similarly, the gradients are steeper for pitchers than for hitters, again without apparent connection to any taste for discrimination. Nor are the gaps trivial. If the 6.4 percent differential between white and black hitters is regarded as substantial, then what significance should attach to the fact that black hitters trade for 10.6 percent more than Hispanic hitters, while

29. Id. at 586–587.
30. Id. at 592.

Hispanic pitchers trade for 4 percent more than black pitchers, a total reversal of some 14.6 percent? Nardinelli and Simon's performance variables probably miss something about player appeal which undercuts their significance, although it might not eliminate it altogether. As long as there are factors other than regular season performance that can influence valuation, one must be cautious in correlating race and market value.

The second issue is perhaps more relevant: What significance would these results have for employment markets, even if they were regarded as wholly unassailable on their own terms? Nardinelli and Simon are too confident that any observable differences attributable to a taste for discrimination would be larger in an employment market than in the market for baseball cards. "Race enters only as a picture on a piece of cardboard, and should, therefore, have only minimal effect. The absence of personal contact should reduce the potential for consumer discrimination."[31] But surely the situation is more complex. The only gain a person derives from a baseball card is the pleasure of its contemplation, and if that consumption benefit is tied in any sense to race, then that pleasure can be exercised almost costlessly; nothing has to be given up in exchange. But within the employment market, personal contact and interaction may induce some form of discrimination, but in ways that need not be invidious.[32] Simultaneously it also provides a strong incentive to take into account the productive aspects of a given worker, an issue that does not arise with trading cards. It is far more costly to indulge mere personal prejudices if a loss of production is one consequence of the behavior. Again, it is easy to institute an affirmative action program in employment settings, but impossible to think what that might mean in the market for trading cards.

In sum, the differences between labor and trading card markets are so substantial and so numerous that it cannot be stated with confidence that they all cut in the same direction. It may be possible that there is, overall, less taste for discrimination in labor markets than in trading card markets. Labor markets are far more rich and diverse than baseball card markets, and the mix of employers is far more diverse than among traders of playing cards, who, given the nature and cost of the hobby, are likely to be drawn from a relatively narrow stratum of society. Finally, as will become painfully clear in the analysis of Title VII, any system of regulation that is designed to undo the effects of private discrimination is apt to

31. Id. at 594. That is, consumer discrimination that reduces the wage employers are willing to pay.
32. See Chapter 3.

be costly on the one hand and counterproductive on the other. Even if we were to accept without question all the findings of Nardinelli and Simon's study, there is no conceivable form of regulation that could eliminate the lingering effects of discrimination on the prices of these cards. Regulation is at best likely to reduce the total value of the cards with only a modest shift in their relative value. Owners with widespread portfolios would on balance suffer a loss, from which no one else would benefit.

Retail Car Sales

Ayres's study takes a very different tack. In order to determine the amount of dealer discrimination against women and blacks in the retail car market, Ayres sent a large number of student-testers into automobile showrooms with detailed instructions on how to negotiate the purchase price of certain preselected models.[33] The testers chosen were carefully controlled so as to appear to come from the same young, educated professional class living in the same appropriate neighborhoods; each buyer was instructed to express an interest in the same car, and to indicate a willingness to provide private financing. All potential buyers used the same bargaining strategy: buyers first obtained an offer from the dealer's representative and then made a counteroffer that indicated knowledge of the dealer's cost; thereafter the subject offered a price that split the difference between his or her original offer and the last offer received from the salesperson. The experiment continued until the sales representative refused to bargain or "attempted" to accept the last offer made by the subject. The results of the study indicated that on average the markup for white males was lower than those markups that were paid by white women, black women, and black males. Ayres tabulated dealer profits as follows:[34]

White male	$ 362
White female	504
Black male	783
Black female	1,283

33. Ayres, "Fair Driving" at 822ff.

34. Id. at 828. In a larger study of four hundred experiments, Ayres notes that the general results held, except that black female testers did better than black male testers. He attributes the results to the possible personal quirks of the single black female tester used in the original study, which points out how difficult it is to control for personal differences even where stringent guidelines are imposed.

The differences are for cars that list at $13,000 with a dealer cost about $3,000 lower, so the differences in overall price from top to bottom are on the order of 10 percent (from about $10,362 to $11,283), even though the percentage differences in the markups are far larger.

The critical question is how to interpret these results, given that they depend on simulation and not actual market data. Although Ayres tried to control for all relevant variables, there has to be a sense in which he failed. He notes that his subjects were instructed to say that they were able to provide independent financing; yet sales personnel continued to ask questions about car financing (most often of black females),[35] perhaps because they regarded any customer statement about financing as a ploy that could not be believed uncritically. In addition, his initial findings about the price differential for black females were not duplicated in his subsequent larger study, which suggests that some unaccounted-for feature of personality can skew the results. It is unlikely that these hidden difficulties account for all the differentials that were reported, but they may explain some portion of the overall picture.

There are other problems with the study. The first involves the strategies the testers used in the negotiations. Ayres is sensitive to the possibility that a bargaining strategy that offers to split the difference seems likely to yield very high final offers when the initial dealer offer is high, and he was able to control for this eventuality by having some testers increase their own bids by 10 percent of the markup for each additional round, without creating any significant difference in the final offers obtained by the various groups.[36] But other factors apart from pure bargaining strategies can influence the dealers' final offers. One obvious point is that in open markets customers are free to select not only their bargaining strategies but also the dealerships they visit. If blacks or women know that they are apt to get a good deal from some small fraction of the market, then they can avoid other, less receptive dealerships and their unattractive offers. How much of the differential found by Ayres would thus have disappeared is hard to say. In addition, it may be possible for a buyer to reduce the differentials even further by bringing along a friend, by eliciting a rival offer from another dealer over the telephone, or by insisting on a test drive (which was found to lower the final offer by $319).[37] These tactics are of course also open to white males, but

35. Id. at 834.
36. Id. at 830–831 and n.41.
37. Id. at 848.

given the lower bids that they are able to elicit, they are likely to yield better returns when adopted by others who anticipate that they will be offered higher prices. In any event, it seems possible to adopt some strategies that will reduce the variation to below that observed in Ayres's experimental studies.

Second, it is possible, as Ayres acknowledges, that cost-based differentials could account for some portion of the difference.[38] As I have noted, sales personnel pressed financing issues even though the testers all announced that they could pay cash. If the sellers thought that their potential buyers needed financing, they would have believed there was more of a chance that the deal would fall through, and acted accordingly. The greater risk arguably associated with black and female customers could induce sales personnel to charge higher prices to cover their own costs. Similarly, if any additional services had to be provided to customers to sell the car, say, because of differential customer knowledge, these too would be reflected in the bids elicited. No attempt to standardize testers along these different dimensions could be completely successful, for the shrewd car seller will take into account not only what individual customers say but whatever reliable background information he or she possesses about the relevant groups. Some portion of the observed differential may be cost driven.

Third, it is not clear what significance should attach to final offers. In Ayres's model all final offers were recorded whether (an unsigned) agreement was reached or not. In an ordinary market the transactions that fail are not recorded, so the observed prices for transactions need not mirror the final offers reported by Ayres. Since about 70 percent of his data comprised final offers that were rejected by his testers, this difference could prove to be substantial.[39] In particular, it is most likely that blacks and women tend to reject the worst dealer offers, so any observed price disparity is likely to be smaller than those obtained by the simulation. There are therefore a number of factors that tend to reduce the significance of the differential, although it is impossible to say by exactly how much.

Finally, one other point should be stressed. Ayres's study did not reveal any form of discrimination attributable to the prejudices of individual

38. Id. at 842–845.

39. With about 70 percent of the final offers rejected by the testers, there is a clear difference between the final offers recorded here and the market prices that would be tabulated from completed transactions. Letter from Ayres to author, April 16, 1991.

sellers. In fact, Ayres reports a set of seller-buyer interactions that confound any ordinary expectations:[40]

1. White male testers received best deals from white female sellers.
2. White female testers received best deals from black male sellers.
3. Black male testers received best deals from white female sellers.
4. Black female testers received best deals from white male sellers.

On balance, then, there seems to be some reason to believe that the level of disparity observed in any test will be greater than that found in any active market. In addition, there seems to be very little that can sensibly be done to change the basic situation. Even if one observed practice markets in which blacks and women paid higher prices than white males, each and every voluntary transaction that took place would improve the position of both buyer and seller. The only effect of discrimination here would be to change the percentage of the *surplus* from trade that is obtained by the two parties.

Any effort to achieve an equal division of surplus by race and sex by requiring an equal distribution of prices is likely to *reduce* the total amount of available gains. There are first the not inconsiderable costs of finding reliable data about the price differentials which might provide the basis for some relief, judicial or administrative; and there is the possibility that government-mandated changes in how cars are sold could increase the costs for everyone. Ayres suggests that it might be possible to require dealers to disclose to all customers the costs of acquiring inventory, and then to charge a fixed markup to all customers.[41] But a regulation of that sort would doubtless wreak havoc with the traditional system of commission compensation for car sellers, and would reduce their incentive to close sales. In addition, if there is any cost-based component to price differentials, this proposal might well freeze out of the market some of the very customers whom Ayres seeks to protect. It is not enough to show that there is some residual level of discrimination in a market to make the case for regulation. It has to be shown as well that the proposed cure can identify and isolate the evils in some cost-effective fashion. In light of the avenues of self-help that are available to all customers, it seems unlikely that regulation could ever accomplish a net social good.

40. Ayres, "Fair Driving" at 841.
41. Id. at 869.

The Urban Institute Study

The most recent examination of patterns of discrimination is the 1991 Urban Institute study, which focuses directly on labor markets. In one sense labor markets are the most difficult to monitor, since the employer is the buyer of services, who, unlike a seller of goods and services, is interested not primarily in cash return but in a complex set of inputs into an overall production process. Although the labor market is more difficult, therefore, to study by simulation, the Urban Institute study adopted an approach quite similar to that of the Ayres study. The institute used ten pairs of auditors, white and black males between nineteen and twenty-four, who were matched "by age, physical size, education, experience, and other 'human capital' characteristics, as well as such intangibles as openness, apparent energy level, and articulateness."[42] The study focused on entry-level positions in the retail and service trades, which were advertised in the local newspapers in the Washington, D.C., and Chicago markets. All cases of jobs obtained through personal contact or through direct application were excluded from the sample because they were regarded as too difficult to measure.[43] The auditors, whom the institute carefully prepared for their work, went through the entire job search process from asking for applications to interviews. The Institute sought to measure both the progress of its testers through the system and their ultimate success in receiving job offers. It recognized that its task was difficult because its own testers were in competition not only with one another, but with genuine job seekers.[44]

Whatever the methodological difficulties, the Institute was confident in its overall conclusion that in these two job markets "young black job seekers were unable to advance as far in the hiring process as their white counterparts 20 percent of the time; black testers advanced farther than their white counterparts 7 percent of the time. Blacks were denied a job that was offered to an equally qualified white 15 percent of the time; white testers were denied a job when their black counterparts received an offer in 5 percent of the audits."[45] The levels of discrimination reported in the study were markedly higher in Washington than in Chicago, notwithstanding the dominant position of the federal government as an employer

42. Turner, Fix, and Struyk, *Opportunities Denied* at 4.
43. Id. at 8–11.
44. Id. at 14.
45. Id. at 1.

in the Washington market.[46] From its audits the Institute concluded that there was little reason to be concerned with issues of reverse discrimination and strong evidence of "widespread" discrimination that supports the conclusion that "pressures to dismantle the machinery of civil rights enforcement are premature."[47]

The Institute's political conclusions far outstrip its data. The Report itself contains eleven tables, none of which set out the full data set and are easily liable to misinterpretation.[48] In fact the results of the study break down as possible. In 67 percent of the pairs neither candidate received an offer; in 13 percent of the cases both candidates received an offer; in 15 percent of the cases only the white tester received an offer, while in 5 percent of the cases only the black tester received an offer. Stating these results most strongly for the Institute, 28 percent of the white testers received offers, and only 18 percent of the black testers, a significant difference of over 50 percent in hiring rates. The critical question, however, involves the interpretation of the results. The Institute regards its results as a strong endorsement for the continued and stricter enforcement of the employment discrimination laws. The serious methodological difficulties with its study point to a very different conclusion.

An initial weakness of the Institute's study is that it covers only a small segment of the job market. To be sure, it recognizes that any overall assessment of the job markets must look at a random subset of the total population of jobs within the larger community.[49] But the decision to limit the study to jobs advertised in newspapers destroys any possibility of randomization. As the Institute itself recognizes, most of its sample was drawn from the retail and service industries, and at the entry level for men between nineteen and twenty-four. The jobs sampled and the total job market have very different configurations.[50] The differences are apt to

46. Id. at 32.

47. Id. at 33.

48. This confusion was evident in the *New Republic*'s editorial summary of the study, which concluded that "[i]n 80 percent of the job searches, both the white and the black applicants were offered equivalent jobs." In "Black and White," *New Republic*, June 10, 1991, at 7. The misreading occurred because the Institute did not clearly distinguish between cases where both testers were hired and neither tester was. In fact, the correct reading of the study was pointed out in a response to the editorial. Letter of Margery Austin Turner, Michael Fix, and Raymond Strunk, "Discriminating Evidence," *New Republic*, August 5, 1991, at 2.

49. Turner, Fix, and Struck, *Opportunities Denied* at 8.

50. Id. at table 1.

prove critical in any number of ways. The public sector is excluded from the entire sample, as are a disproportionate percentage of private firms with affirmative action programs. The Institute's finding of little reverse discrimination is not a statement about the market as a whole, but about its skewed selection of firms that never claimed to have these programs in the first place. To study affirmative action, one needs to look at firms and government entities that actively promote these programs.

A second weakness is the assumption that the differential hiring rates establish discrimination in the overall market. This conclusion depends critically on the reliability of its matching: is there only one relevant difference between the two members of each matched pair? Normally it is exceedingly difficult to control for all unintended variables, given the range of factors that might catch the eye of a careful interviewer or miss the eye of an incompetent one. Yet here there is an additional methodological problem. The ten pairs of auditors used for all 476 audits[51] were chosen and trained by the Institute, whose purpose in running the study was to find the discrimination in question. If that attitude is communicated to, or shared by, its testers, then whites and blacks can easily act in ways that confirm the Institute's predisposition. Perhaps the white testers will act confident and the blacks will act less so. "Who tests the testers?" is a new variation on an old theme. It would have been far better if the training and testing had been conducted by an independent organization with no political stake in the outcome.

The Institute also was unable to hold constant the relative cost to the firm of the two applicants. The point manifests itself in two ways. First, as will be discussed in Chapter 3, an important concern for a firm is how a given worker fits in. The ability to maintain cohesion within the firm and with a customer base may depend in part on the race of an employee. If these costs are higher in some settings for workers of one race than another, then we should expect to see some difference in hiring patterns. The differences need not all cut in the same direction, as is evident by the preferences that some black testers received in the Institute's own study. To hold, as the institute does, that the reasons for the discrimination are wholly irrelevant is to say that some costs are irrelevant as well. If the goal is to develop a set of rules for overall efficiency, then the benefits of a practice must be taken into account as well as its costs. It is not suffi-

---

51. Id. at 5. The number of auditors used creates an important difficulty for all studies of this sort. If too many are used, no standardization is possible; if too few, then any misjudgment in a single pairing could heavily skew the results.

cient to look at the impact of a given practice on a single group, wholly without regard to its impact on others. Each person counts for one and only one, is as a good rule of thumb in employment discrimination as it is in other contexts.

Second, all the employers who were tested operated not in an unregulated market but in a Title VII environment. If they perceived that it would be more difficult to fire blacks once hired, then the cost of taking a black worker would be higher than that of taking a white worker. Again, that difference in cost could easily be translated into a lower level of offers for black workers. The matter is complicated because under Title VII the cost of turning down a black applicant may also be higher, given the risk of suit. But the two effects need not be equal in magnitude in all cases, so the dispersion in outcomes could be interpreted as showing that most firms prefer to run the risk of litigation with initial hires, instead of with promotion and dismissal.

There is, moreover, a final question about how to interpret the social significance of the findings. One critical question raised by the study concerns the relative wages that we should expect to observe for blacks and whites, equally qualified, given these data. The answer is, there will not be much difference—if any at all. The Institute's study (like Ayres's study of new car markets) wholly ignores the selection effect that is so powerful in active markets. While testers apply for jobs in matched pairs, real job-seekers look for those employers who will offer them the most favorable deals. Black workers gravitate to firms that afford them a preference or to those that are indifferent to matters of race. The additional vitality of the job market should increase the total number of jobs available, so an open hiring process generates gains that are not captured in the Institute's implicit assumption that the total number of job opportunities is constant regardless of the legal regime governing hiring.

The Institute's study, then, does a poor job of determining the level and direction of discrimination in the market as it now operates under Title VII. Its policy implications largely outstrip its data, for the study adds little to the understanding of how unregulated markets work, and whether the discrimination found in these markets is a good thing or a bad thing. This last theme is the subject of the next chapter.

CHAPTER 3

Rational Discrimination in Competitive Markets

In the previous chapter I argued that free entry and multiple employers provide ample protection for all workers, even those faced with policies of overt and hostile discrimination by some employers. Where markets do not have formal barriers to entry, the victims of discrimination have effective strategies of self-protection and powerful allies whose own self-interest will operate on their behalf. Imperfections in employment markets, however, are not limited to imperfect information about employee quality. Other frictions must be taken into account as well. In this chapter I look at several problems, most notably search and governance costs, that help explain why certain forms of discrimination may be rational from the point of view of both the firm and the larger society. In a nutshell, discrimination in some contexts is a rational response to the frictions that necessarily arise out of long-term employment contracts.

The traditional conclusion, often repeated in the economic literature starting with Becker, that competitive markets will drive out all forms of discrimination should hold in a world in which transaction costs do not matter. But once the analysis turns to the world of positive transaction costs, identified with Ronald Coase,[1] that conclusion is no longer valid. It is now possible that some forms of discrimination could improve the ability of certain firms to compete. If so, then we should not expect to see all forms of discrimination driven out in unregulated markets. The arguments here are perfectly general, for they apply to employment contracts across the wide array of institutional settings. They indicate why *all* groups have some rational incentives to discriminate on the very grounds—race, creed, sex, age, religion—that Title VII prohibits. And if these cases of rational discrimination are the ones likely to persist, then the hidden costs of Title VII are higher than is

1. Ronald Coase, "The Problem of Social Cost," 3 *J. L. & Econ.* 1 (1960).

59

ordinarily supposed. In order to organize the inquiry, I examine issues associated with governance and enforcement costs; to enumerate other costs not identified here would only complicate the analysis.

Relational Contracts and Governance Costs

Formal and Informal Norms

The analysis thus far assumes implicitly that people enter only into spot contracts—those in which there is a simultaneous exchange of money for goods and services. In these contexts the incentive to discriminate on the basis of race, sex, or age is very low. One person's money is as good as the next's. As long as there is no residual ongoing relationship between the two sides, the bigot is well advised to take money from strangers he does not like and spend it in the company of his friends. The sale of goods in standard consumer markets is the prototype of this kind of arrangement. Employment contracts, however, typically lie at the opposite pole from sale arrangements. They often involve long-term relationships in which it is generally impossible to specify in detail and in advance the obligations and rights of the respective parties. My formal university contract, to the extent that I recall its terms, covers rank, salary, and tenure. Everything else—course work, committee assignments, research leave, salary increases—is informal. A large, often unwritten code of norms and conventions controls behavior among coworkers in this and countless other labor markets.

The business practice is thus not reflected in the law. The common law, for example, has generally—at least until recent years—followed the rule that all employees may quit, or be fired, at will, no questions asked. Often, however, the implicit ethics of the firm take quite the opposite point of view. Although there may be no legal protection against being fired, within the firm dismissal can only be with cause, for reasons that range from financial necessity and business repositioning to employee misconduct. The firm that violates these rules may not be subject to a lawsuit, but it will bear substantial loss of reputation. If other workers regard the dismissal as improper, they will treat it as an amendment of heir informal employment arrangement equivalent to a substantial decrease in salary. Their loyalties will diminish, and the rash employer will thus pay an implicit but real price: workers will be more willing to go elsewhere, and higher cash wages will be needed to keep them on the job.

Within this relational framework it becomes plausible to ask whether discrimination by sex, age, religion, or race is in some instances a viable firm strategy. The answer here is different from that appropriate to spot markets. In brief, it is yes—and for good reasons. The key to understanding the *useful* role of discrimination in firms is tied to the implicit norms that govern the workplace. The loose nature of the employment relationship requires that more stress be placed on firm culture than on external control. Within this framework decisions have to be made that routinely affect the welfare of the large number of persons, employers and employees, who are linked together in a common venture. The task that the group faces is to find a set of rules that satisfies all its members simultaneously. Even within the employment context this is no easy task, for the workers who are most dissatisfied with any collective solution may then give vent to their dissatisfaction with their feet—by leaving to work elsewhere.

Collective Choice within Groups

One question that every collective organization must face is how to make decisions that advance the overall welfare of the group without precipitating the defection of its key members. In the attempt to answer this question, most analytical work has been devoted to finding the kind of decision rule that best captures the sentiment of the various members of the collectivity. Does one use majority voting, or supermajority voting? Who sets the agenda? Should issues be considered separately or in bundles? Should compensation, in cash or kind, be provided to losers to keep them happy?

A second side to the inquiry, generally neglected, merits equal attention. How deep is the division of sentiment within the membership of the group in the first place? Here the answer depends critically on *who* is in the group, and on the distribution of tastes and preferences among the members. The group that can minimize differences in tastes will sometimes be ahead of the game, relative to one that has to rely on sophisticated decision rules to resolve deep-seated divisions of opinion. To see why, assume for the moment that all workers have identical preferences on all matters relevant to the employment relation. If the question is whether or not they wish to have music piped into a common work area, they all want music. If the question is what kind of music they wish to hear, the answer is classical—indeed, mostly Mozart. If the question is how loud, the agreement is perfect down to the exact decibel. In this employment utopia, decisions of collective governance are easy to make. The employer who satisfies preferences of any single worker knows that he or she has satisfied the preferences of entire work force. It takes little effort and little money to achieve the highest level of group satisfaction. The nonwage terms of collective importance can be set in ways that unambiguously promote firm harmony.

The situation is quite different once it is assumed that there is no employee homogeneity in taste within the workplace. At this point the critical questions are two: First, what is the variation in preferences among the members of the firm? And second, how does individual dissatisfaction increase with increases in the distance between individual personal preferences and the collective outcome? The general proposition is clear: as the tastes within the group start to diverge, it becomes harder to reach a decision that works for the common good. If half the workers crave classical music but loathe rock, and half like rock but disdain classical music, it is very difficult to decide whether music shall be played in the workplace at all, and if so what kind. The wider the variation in taste, the more troublesome these collective decisions are, especially if (as Kenneth Arrow himself has proved) the preferences "cycle" over three or more subgroups who have three or more choices.[2] If the level of dissatisfaction increases exponentially as the gap between private choice and collective decision increases, then the people at either tail of the distribution have additional incentives to leave the group when the decision goes against them. The re-sorting that takes place as individual workers make

2. See Kenneth Arrow, *Social Choice and Individual Values* (2nd ed., 1963).

The classic version goes like this. Assume that there are three groups of workers, each of equal size, and three choices, rock, classical music, or silence. The preferences are arrayed as follows:

Group A	Group B	Group C
Rock	Classical	Silence
Classical	Silence	Rock
Silence	Rock	Classical

Each choice has one first, one second, and one third place, so that in paired comparisons rock beats classical, classical beats silence, and silence beats rock, each by a two-to-one vote. There is no way to break the cycle except by weighting the intensity of individual preferences.

voluntary decisions to quit thus has a social function: it reduces the pressure of decision rules by increasing the homogeneity within the group.

In the simplest model, then, the greater the variance in preferences, the greater the costs to the firm. Where the decisions on collective issues have yet to be made, there will be a tendency for the interested parties at each extreme to lobby for decisions in their favor, given the importance that they attach to the ultimate decision. If there is an all-or-nothing decision, then one group must lose while the other one wins, save in the unlikely event that people's preferences are transformed (from rock to classical or the reverse) after they hear arguments addressed to the merits of the opposing choice. The firm has to bear the cost of the internal conflict as well as the dissatisfaction that remains after the decision has been made. Alternatively, it might be possible to avoid the problem of collective choice by abandoning piped-in music and allowing individuals to bring their own radios to the office. But here efficiency losses can result. With no uniform ambience on the premises, conflicts may arise between co-workers over excessive noise levels. As with the agency costs, none of these difficulties launches a fatal blow against the firm or dictates uniform or private solutions. Quite the opposite. They are only costs which, when taken into account, may deter the undertaking of some operations and reduce the success of others.

If voting procedures and internal rules are inadequate to control these problems, other methods may be explored. One way to cut these costs is to find means of reducing the level of variance in tastes among group members. Condominiums and cooperatives routinely try to do this by examining income statements to ensure that all tenants have the wherewithal to pay for the collective services (doormen, lobby decor, maintenance) that the association provides.[3] Roughly constant income levels also lead to a modest convergence in tastes, which reduces internal conflict. Most individuals do not seek out housing in places that provide amenities that are either more modest than they want or more luxurious than they can afford. A building half of whose residents are retirees living on fixed incomes and half young professionals is ripe for internal struggle.

Nonetheless, powerful disputes can emerge even if the income of association members is identical. It is necessary only for some members of the building association to have children while others do not. Who can use the swimming pool and when? Will the garden be off-limits to tricycles?

3. For a discussion, see Richard A. Epstein, "Covenants and Constitutions," 73 *Cornell L. Rev.* 906 (1988).

Worse still, the presence of children in certain common living situations presents a genuine physical threat to the health and safety of many elderly people who have difficulty getting around. The common policy adopted for many apartment buildings, condominiums, and cooperatives to either exclude or welcome children should not be regarded as a form of illicit discrimination. It should be understood as a commendable effort to reduce the variations in individual choice that complicate collective decision making. When in 1988 Congress passed a statute making it illegal for rental, condominium, and cooperative units to discriminate against families with children, it struck genuine fear into the hearts of many older residents.[4] The partition of the market into specialized and well-defined niches should increase the satisfaction of all consumers. *Any* anti-discrimination law cuts against that commendable objective.

A sobering lesson follows. Any social policy that requires that membership in a private association should be randomly drawn from a subset of the larger whole is an invitation to trouble. Even the ideal set of contrac-

4. See Fair Housing Amendment Acts of 1988, Pub. Law 100–430; 102 Stat. 1619, §805 (b), which allows discrimination on the basis of "family status," that is, against families with children under eighteen years of age, in two basic situations: in cases of sole occupation by persons over sixty-two years of age, or where 80 percent of the units are inhabited by persons fifty-five years of age or more and the structure is dedicated to housing older adults. Note that the statute relies on the explicit age categories that are regarded as impermissible under the Age Discrimination in Employment Act, discussed in Chapter 21.

Here again the regulators were unable to anticipate the movement in the market, which had developed housing projects with adult-only policies that contained far smaller percentages of older people. There is considerable dissatisfaction with the statute among older residents, noted even by defenders of the act (see the editorial "Fair Housing—for the Young Too," *New York Times*, December 6, 1989, at 30), who just do not want to have children around. Ironically, one of the effects of the statute is to force older people to move into senior citizen ghettos if they wish to have security against accidental injury; the statute thus leads to an unanticipated and inexcusable system of government-fostered segregation.

Similar legislation exists in many states. See, e.g., the Unruh Act, *California Civil Code* (1987) §§51.2, 51.3, which seeks to carve out limited exceptions for senior citizens. The Unruh Act begins with a general declaration that all persons are "free and equal" and then proceeds as though this proposition establishes that there shall be no discrimination by private parties on the basis of "sex, race, color, religion, ancestry national origin, or blindness or other physical disability." The second part does not follow from the first, for all are free and equal only when they trade on terms of mutual advantage. The ad hoc exception for senior citizens ignores the preferences of younger persons to associate freely among themselves and is in any event inconsistent with the basic nondiscrimination principle to which it is appended. For more on age discrimination statutes in employment, see Chapter 21.

tual terms can go only so far toward buffering the problems and tensions of long-term legal relationships. In many senses the single most important contractual decision is a business decision: the selection of contractual partners. Choosing the right partners reduces the stresses on any set of legal relationships. Choosing the wrong partners exacerbates them. Governance costs are a function of the level of variation within the firm.

Henry Hansmann has noted the reluctance of many law firms to take women in as part-time partners.[5] In addition to offering the conventional explanations that part-time attorneys are not at the beck and call of clients, and may not hone their legal skills, he identifies governance cost as a possible source of concern by noting:

> It appears likely that such inequalities among members of the firm are also resisted at least in part because they tend to destabilize the governance structure. A simple rule, under which everyone does essentially the same amount and kind of work, and receives the same pay, is by far the easiest to agree upon and to enforce, and these advantages are evidently often sufficient to outweigh the costs such a simple rule engenders in the form of inflexibility, poor incentives, and lack of diversification among the workforce.[6]

In a sense Hansmann's point is overstated, because it is evident that the relevant trade-offs will not be made in such stark terms. Some variation in work or pay may well be worth the additional strain it places on governance costs. But even when that correction is taken into account, the relation between firm composition and governance cost persists. For any given type of relationship, the level of investment in legal governance must increase as the power of selection of contracting partners diminishes: that is why political bodies must limp along with elaborate and extensive safeguards. Private parties have strong incentives to minimize the sum of their selection and governance costs, and hence to decide when the costs of exclusion are lower than the costs of more extensive governance. In contrast, state regulation only reinforces the false impression that any governance structure is equally effective regardless of the composition of the group or the identities of parties to the contract. If all persons have tastes that are represented by the values of either $+4$ or -4, governance will be far easier if voluntary

5. Henry Hansmann, "When Does Worker Ownership Work? ESOPs, Law Firms, Codetermination, and Economic Democracy," 99 *Yale L.J.* 1749, 1787–88 (1990).
6. Id. at 1787–88.

sorting creates two groups, each one homogeneous at its own pole. This principle, moreover, is not limited to two-point distributions; it carries over whenever there is any division in taste. Having two or more groups to choose from allows each person to gravitate to that group whose policies most closely conform to his or her own. The total level of personal dissonance is decreased by a choice among multiple organizations that take different positions on basic issues.

The problem here is more subtle than it might appear at first blush, given that disagreement over collective decisions may increase at an exponential rate. To return to our simple example, suppose again that half the people within a group have tastes at either $+4$ or -4. If the level of dissatisfaction with the collective outcome were a simple linear function of the difference between the private preference and the collective choice, then the total level of dissonance within the group would be independent of the final choice. If the collective choice was set at -1, then one group would lose 3 units of satisfaction and the other 5. More generally, for any point within the interval -4 to $+4$ the total level of dissatisfaction equals 8, or $(x - [-4] + [4 - x])$. (No choice outside the interval -4 to $+4$ is feasible because moving to either end point makes both sides better off simultaneously.)

Finding the right choice is more difficult and more important if one assumes that dissatisfaction rises at an exponential rate, say, with the square of the difference between one's preferences and the group outcome. Thus, at either corner ($+4$ or -4) the total level of dissatisfaction is 64 ($8^2 + 0$), whereas at 0 the total level of dissatisfaction is 32 ($4^2 + 4^2$). It is now far more critical not only to locate the right median point but also to determine magnitude of the variance in group composition, because the exponential effect magnifies the influence of distance from the collective solution. The question of the exact shape of people's preference functions is hard to project in the abstract, but the nonlinear models seem to capture a good deal of the truth. It is harder to do business as social distance between persons increases. It therefore becomes wise to allow a division of the total population into self-selected subgroups.

The identical set of concerns carries over to employment situations. The increase in the harmony of tastes and preferences thus works in the long-run interest of all members. To the extent, therefore, that individual tastes are grouped by race, by sex, by age, by national origin—and to some extent they are—then there is a necessary conflict between the commands of any antidiscrimination law and the smooth operation of the firm. Firms whose members have diverse and clashing views may well find it more difficult to make collective decisions than firms with a closer agreement over tastes.

Again, the point here does not lead to the prediction that all voluntary firms will organize along lines that are regarded as illegal under the antidiscrimination laws. Indeed, in the employment market other considerations can easily trouble the extension of the argument from partners to employees. Partners stand in a fiduciary duty with regard to one another; the individual financial share is intimately bound up with the governance of the firm; and the partners have joint responsibility in governance decisions. Employers and employees occupy distinct role relationships. These differences can influence the desirability of homogeneity for the success of the business. First, as Hansmann notes, the firms that are reluctant to accept part-time women partners routinely make arrangements to take part-time associates, including permanent associates.[7] As long as associates are not directly involved in firm governance, their continued participation in the firm may work to everyone's advantage. Second, an employer may be concerned that having a perfectly homogeneous work force exposes the firm to the threat of unionization or other concerted employee action that could reduce its effectiveness. It may well be that some differentiation is desirable where this threat is large, but not in instances where it is not. The ultimate question is an empirical one, but provided there are some cases in which the gains from homogenization outweigh the costs, then we should see firms (or perhaps only departments within firms) concerned about the interactive effects of workers and the composition of their work force.

Thus far it has been shown only that voluntary sorting can reduce the costs of making and enforcing group decisions. It remains to be noted that this sorting often takes place on racial, ethnic, religious, or sexual lines. The missing premise is that persons who are "the same" in some fundamental way are more likely to bring similar preferences to the workplace. In some cases the explanations are relatively benign. Workers may prefer to sort themselves out by language. It is easier and cheaper for everyone if Spanish-speaking workers work with Spanish-speaking workers and Polish-speaking workers with Polish-speaking workers, all other things held constant. Indeed, it seems quite possible that there are variations within the English language that make communication easier

7. Id. at 1787.

between blacks and other blacks than between blacks and whites.[8] These language differences tend to lead to a prediction of voluntary segregation within the workplace, the intensity of which varies as a function of the level of separation between the languages.[9]

The commonality of preferences may extend beyond language to other features of collective life: the music played in the workplace, the food that is brought in for lunch, the holidays on which the business is closed down, the banter around the coffeepot, the places chosen for firm outings, and a thousand other small details that contribute to the efficiency of the firm. "Like attracts like" is not a universal or a necessary truth; but as long as it is an empirical and a partial one, it helps explain why in unregulated markets some firms are organized along specialized lines while others are not. Indeed, there is no particular reason why every part of a large firm should be identically organized. Voluntary sorting by various characteristics could be much more common in some parts of the business than in others.

In certain cases it may be that the preferences for voluntary segregation are based on ill will or other uglier sentiments Nonetheless, the advantages of voluntary sorting cannot be ignored here either. If all persons who have a rabid hatred for members of different racial, ethnic, or other groups are concentrated within a small number of firms, then it makes governance questions easier for the remaining firms, as they do not have to contend constantly with dissidents and troublemakers. It follows, therefore, that voluntary sorting should (other skills being held constant) raise the level of satisfaction for all workers in the workplace. Not only are market segregation and market discrimination (that is, income differentials) distinct concepts, as Becker noted, but they are also variables that may be negatively correlated: real income will tend to rise for all as the level of voluntary sorting increases. To be sure, the large income differentials that exist across race and sex in the United States cannot be explained by an appeal to these variables: years of education and the basic skills brought to the workplace are surely more important. But when

8. See Kevin Lang, "A Language Theory of Discrimination," 101 *Quart. J. Econ.* 363 (1986).

9. See Kevin Lang, "A Sorting Model of Statistical Discrimination," ms., September 21, 1990. As Lang also notes, the differences lead to two other predictions as well. First, where the two language groups are of unequal size, members of the smaller group will normally have to learn the language of the larger group in order to communicate, and second, persons who can speak both languages stand to reap substantial economic rewards from their ability to bridge the two cultures.

these factors are held constant, they can explain why some voluntary sorting exists within the workplace along the very lines that are regarded as illegal under the antidiscrimination laws.

There are, however, two sides to this question. Still to be considered are the benefits of diversity. In the residential setting discussed earlier, these are likely to be relatively small, since members of the group do not have to buy and sell in many different markets simultaneously in order to prosper. But in the universe of firms, situations vary over a far wider range. If all employees are exactly alike, then the firm may find it more difficult to establish bonds with some classes of potential customers. Diversity in a sales force may provide a benefit that offsets the costs of internal divisions on collective tastes. But the opposite conclusion may hold if the firm caters to a single class of customers. The problem for the firm is to find a way to maximize its profits, taking into account its total costs, including organizational costs. In some cases the gains from diversity will be rejected as too costly. But in others, firms will choose to maintain some degree of diversity and some degree of homogeneity, and expend resources (on retreats, picnics, intramural athletics, personnel departments) to foster a spirit of cooperation. In this type of environment, moreover, workers who are content to go along with most decisions offer a valuable asset their more eccentric colleagues lack: at the very least, they do not make waves, and they may help foster a communal spirit within the firm. As organizations grow and seek to serve broad national or international markets, it is highly doubtful that the firm itself could employ only members of one race, sex, or ethnic background. But it is quite possible even for large firms to maintain segregated divisions of workers in its various subdepartments or plants.

Informal Enforcement of Promises

The informal nature of firm (and market) rules also helps explain why certain kinds of discrimination will emerge in voluntary competitive markets. Aside from the question of collective choice, market participants must be concerned about the enforcement of promises that are made in the ordinary course of business. In principle, legal enforcement may be available, but wholly apart from any legal obstacle (Was there an intention to create legal relations? Was the promise definite enough?) the simple truth, evident even to lawyers, is that business cannot be conducted if promises are kept only under the threat of lawsuits. Instead, business depends heavily on an informal set of sanctions that one market participant can bring to bear on the other. In this context, the concerns are often lumped together under the banner of reputation, that is, the ability to persuade other members of a trading community not to do business with any individual who has flouted its norms.

Generally speaking, the success of any system of informal enforcement is heavily dependent on the range of sanctions, legal and social, that can be brought to bear against wayward parties. Thus, one common complaint of tourists is that they have been cheated by local businessmen, who take advantage, for example, of their ignorance of exchange rates, general market prices, and local language and customs.[10] Where there are repeated dealings between individuals on a variety of transactions, these abuses are far less likely to occur. Similarly, informal enforcement becomes more effective when members of a firm are all drawn from the same ethnic or racial group. The party who cheats at work now knows that he faces stricter sanctions, given the strong likelihood that the information will be brought home to him at play, at church, or in other business and social settings. The complex network of human interactions thus induces persons to honor their deals. The merchant who is told by a new customer that X sent her knows that X will be the first to hear if she is cheated. The little ceremonial introductions so common in business are not idle chatter; they are an effective way to bond behavior through implicit third-party guarantees. The cost of doing business within a closely knit group should therefore, ceteris paribus, be cheaper than the costs of doing business with strangers.

The critical role played by these informal mechanisms of market has been well revealed in the highly publicized case, first reported by the columnist Mike Royko, of the Daniel Lamp Company.[11] The firm had been charged with discrimination by the numbers because of its twenty-six unskilled employees, twenty-one were Hispanic and five were black. The source of that imbalance was not random, but derived from the evolution of the firm's hiring practices. Initially its owner, Mike Welbek, hired his workers through the help-wanted ads. But once he established working relationships with two Hispanic organizations—the Spanish Coalition and the Latino Youth Organization—he passed them the word when he needed

---

10. See, e.g., Shirley Temple and Robert Young in *Stowaway* (1936), where Temple, owing to her ability to speak Chinese, meets Young when she intervenes to prevent him from being swindled by a local Chinese trader.

11. Mike Royko, "Where Good Sense Is in the Minority," *Chicago Tribune*, September 21, 1990, Zone C, at 3.

new employees, and they supplied him with the needed workers. He found this system cheaper to operate than his previous use of newspaper ads; it gave faster responses; and it gave Daniel Lamp a better chance of getting a reliable employee, because all referrals were implicitly bonded by the referring organizations who wanted to continue to be able to place their people. Necessarily, this system is both efficient on the one hand and skewed in its outcome along ethnic lines on the other.

Upon receiving a complaint from a disappointed black job applicant, the EEOC demanded that Daniel Lamp not only pay her back wages of some $340, but also that it spend $10,000 in advertisements to detect other blacks who might have answered want ads, and to pay them another $123,000 in back pay. The implicit social judgment in this administrative decision is that it would have been better for the firm never to have hired anyone than for it to have hired thirty-one workers on a disparate basis: how else can one interpret an administrative order sufficient to bankrupt the firm? But even if there had been perfect compliance with the antidiscrimination laws, the antidiscrimination principle leads to fewer jobs at lower wages by forcing employers plagued by imperfect information to adopt inferior hiring strategies. The stark choice takes this form: if the employment discrimination laws are enforced, then (in this example) twenty workers, some black and some Hispanic, will receive jobs at $5 per hour. If markets are allowed to operate, then twenty-five workers, all Hispanic, will receive jobs at $6 per hour. There is no reason to prefer the first outcome, with fewer workers at lower wages, to the second. Even the ostensible distributional consequences, which appear to favor Hispanics over blacks, are illusory. The informal bonding mechanism worked to the benefit of Hispanic workers in this case, but it could well work to the benefit of black workers in the next case. The long-term operation of the general rule should leave all workers from both groups better off than they were before. To impose sanctions on the firm's hiring practices is to say, without justification, that we prefer the world in which fewer workers receive lower wages by (if the EEOC sanction sticks) an amount sufficient to put Welbek's firm out of business.

Both the particular example and the general theory point in the same direction. The temptation to discriminate, which makes little sense in a world of spot transactions and perfect information, makes a great deal more sense in a world of continuous relationships in which the costs of the legal system are often high and sometimes prohibitive. As before, I speak here only of costs, and not of legal barriers to participation. Persons who can trade across ethnic or religious groups clearly have certain advantages that should yield them very handsome dividends. The bottom line, therefore, is the same with enforcement of promises as it is with collective choice. Ordinary labor markets should reveal some persistent levels of discrimination in the organization of firms and in the structure of employment markets.

Expanding Employment Opportunities

The actual dynamics internal to the firm are thus quite complex. There are good reasons why diversity is a strength, and others why it is a weakness. The basic complexity is difficult to measure, and perilous to regulate, from the outside. All that can be said with confidence is that the forces that tug in opposite directions need not be of the same strength across different firms, or even within different divisions of the same firm. Within voluntary markets we should expect to see, even in the long run, a wide divergence in the level of voluntary discrimination, but *not*, as it has sometimes been supposed, the total elimination of discrimination by competitive forces.[12] Some firms will practice it widely; others will find it of little value.

These natural differences in firm profile count as a strong argument against the view, so common in modern legal and political thinking, that any deviation between the composition of the firm and the larger work force should be met with hostility and suspicion. In fact, quite the opposite is true. A perfect correspondence between the firm and the market demonstrates that the gains from trade available through specialization have not been realized; the identical structure and composition of all firms is a clear sign of underdeveloped markets, and of the dangerous effects of regulation. As long as a large number of firms operate within any market, persons can sort themselves out in the environment that they like best, free of external constraint. If thousands of prospective employers are offering different associational mixes, then the probability that any employee will find the ideal work setting is far greater than if all firms have to conform to some rigid state-established classification, which is driven not by consideration of the business pressures on the firm but by some independent ethical idea which the state, by majority rule or administrative order, is prepared to impose on those who refuse to accept it.

To put things another way, it is often said that any legal policy that

12. As postulated in John J. Donohue, "Is Title VII Efficient?" 134 *U. Pa. L. Rev.* 1411 (1986), discussed later in this chapter at 76–78.

allows all persons the right to select their contracting partners offends the principle of equal opportunity: every qualified person should be allowed to compete for every job. Therefore, as long as voluntary discrimination exists, there are necessarily some jobs for which qualified individuals cannot apply. At first blush this point has its undoubted emotional force, in large part because it is parasitic on a far more powerful sense of equality of opportunity, namely that all persons should be allowed to *offer* their services to whomever they see fit, free of state prohibition. Nonetheless, despite these apparent similarities the broader conception of equal opportunity—that all firms have a duty to consider every applicant—violates that principle because it denies to firms, and to the individuals who own and manage them, the very rights of autonomy and self-control that it confers on other individuals (or the same individuals in other capacities). The ostensible effort to legitimate the antidiscrimination law by the appeal to equal opportunity (as in the name of the EEOC—Equal Employment Opportunity Commission) is fundamentally unsound because it ignores the critical role freedom plays on both sides of the market. The costs of the error are not inconsiderable.

First, it is a mistake to assume that the number of opportunities available to workers is constant regardless of the external legal rules that govern the operation of the firm. The antidiscrimination provision places powerful limitations on firm structure, and should, like any tax, be expected to *reduce* the number of firms that enter the marketplace, and hence the number of employment opportunities. Some firms at the margin will not survive in an environment in which their costs are increased by regulation. At the very least, the ideal of equal access for all workers to all firms necessarily reduces the number of opportunities available in the aggregate, to the detriment of all potential employees, such as those in Daniel Lamp's case, who are closest to the margin. The antidiscrimination law may appear to place a limitation on firms for the benefit of workers, but in reality its effect is quite the opposite. The legal liabilities may fall on the firm, but the impact of the regulation (given compliance) falls on both firms and workers alike. Any restriction on the class of offers that a firm may make necessarily narrows the class of offers that workers are able to accept. The more gains from trade are shared by firms and workers, and the more effective the antidiscrimination norm, the greater the limitation on worker freedom.

On this point there is an instructive parallel to the minimum wage law.

On its face that law forbids employers to offer positions below a certain stated rate. But where enforcement of the law is highly effective, the statute destroys opportunities for workers and employers alike. Since employers may no longer offer wages below the legal minimum,[13] then workers are deprived of the opportunity to accept them. The statute thus drives some workers (and some firms) from the market while increasing the wages garnered by the fortunate workers still able to command employment. The antidiscrimination law in essence makes it impossible for any worker in a marginal group to underbid any worker from an established group, and thus again hurts the very workers it is designed to protect. Faced with an equal wage constraint, employers will take workers whom they know well, or who promise high productivity and low risk. Only if one believes that a statute will lead employers to reevaluate the benefits received from a given worker is it possible to assume that the alternative conclusion *might* be true. Yet even here the change in preferences may work in the opposite direction (for example, it may create resentment toward workers whom the firm is forced by law to hire.) Or the effect may be dwarfed by the consequences that follow from neoclassical economic theory, namely that people minimize their losses under regulation, and that law does not change what people do or do not desire.

Second, the antidiscrimination policy, as I have noted, makes the problem of internal governance more difficult than would otherwise be the case. If workers who have strong preferences against any particular group are allowed to break off and form their own firms, it improves the value of the opportunities that other individuals enjoy in the firms that remain. If all the bigots and troublemakers are isolated in a small number of firms, other workers have a more attractive array of firms to choose from than they would if bigoted workers were distributed randomly across all firms. Thus, although the *number* of opportunities may go down, the *value* of the opportunities that do remain should increase.

Third, the argument for equal access presupposes some powerful notion of "legitimate" preferences that allows us to rule out of bounds the preferences of workers who do not have accepted or correct views on

---

13. For an explanation, see John R. Lott, Jr., and Russell D. Roberts, "Why Comply: One-Sided Enforcement of Price Controls and Victimless Crime Laws," 18 *J. Legal Stud.* 402 (1989), noting that if workers are allowed to recover twice the underpayment of wages, no firm will seek to undercut the minimum wage, except perhaps with illegal aliens who are unwilling to come forward to prosecute.

workplace arrangements.[14] At a practical level that view is dangerous because it requires us to overlook the problems of governance that arise when persons with radically different tastes are forced into the same business against their will. Theoretically, moreover, there is no obvious reason why the preferences of any individuals should be excluded in determining the desirability of public regulation. Certainly there is no standard measure of *social* welfare that says the preferences of some persons are to be counted while the preferences of others are to be systematically ignored.

This basic point is valid across the board, and extends to the core cases of illegal conduct. The standard prohibition against force and fraud does not depend on a simple assertion that killing or murder is just illegitimate. Rather, it rests on the powerful, albeit empirical, judgment that all people value their right to be free from coercion far more than they value their right to coerce others in a Hobbesian war of all against all. The prohibition ex ante is therefore thought to work to a (well-nigh) universal advantage. It is hard to think of any person who derives systematic advantage from the law of the jungle. But there are no similar universal gains from a rule that says people who have distinct and distasteful preferences cannot go their own way by working and associating only with people of similar views. We may find their tastes offensive, just as they find our tastes offensive and our actions meddlesome. But we do not have to determine the relative intensity of clashing preferences in order to make powerful social judgments. With violence the contracting process breaks down as it becomes impossible for any person to purchase peace from each person who might in turn choose to assault him. The costs of transacting within voluntary organizations, however, are normally low, so there is little reason to suppose that transactional barriers account for the organization of any firm along racial, religious, or sexual lines. Rather, there is good evidence that the preferences are so strong on both sides that no mutually acceptable gains are to be made from long-term forced amalgamation. The fallback position when the antidiscrimination norm is eliminated is not violence and anarchy; it is voluntary separation and competition. The uneasy truce between private voluntary groups can continue over the long run, for it is always possible to have spot trades between individuals who are loath to form permanent associations with one another.

In short, sound judgments about whether a given legal *rule* is good or bad cannot begin with an untested moral assumption that simply calls

---

14. See Chapter 14 at 299–309 for a discussion in connection with consumer preferences and the system of bona fide occupational qualification.

some preferences out of bounds before the discussion begins. All have to be taken into account, and when that is done, a powerful case exists for allowing persons to sort themselves voluntarily by inclination and taste. There are forms of discrimination that outsiders may find offensive, but which are rational nonetheless. It should go without saying that the rights to associate and contract belong to all persons at all times, regardless of their race, creed, sex, religion, national origin, and so on. What must be avoided is the temptation to find special reasons to justify for whites but not for blacks (or, as is more common today, vice versa) some freedom of association, which is then systematically denied to other persons.

Is Title VII Efficient?

The point of the foregoing arguments is to demonstrate the good reasons for expecting *rational* discrimination to persist in private markets. My position is at variance with some of the standard economic literature, which says that many forms of discrimination cannot survive in competitive markets. That conclusion would surely be true if we could say about race, sex, or religious discrimination that it were arbitrary, in the sense that it imposes costs on the firm without any offsetting benefits. Under those circumstances, as Gary Becker has shown, the inefficient firms would be at a systematic disadvantage relative to rival firms that did not labor under similar inhibitions. But once we recognize that firms are loose and imperfect networks of contracts, we can no longer treat firms as identical atoms at work in the same external market. The looseness in the internal structure of the firm is often better contained by informal than by formal sanctions, for discrimination has survival value which is apt to be missed if firm behavior is modeled on the more traditional, pre-Coasean pattern of homogeneous actors in a world of zero transaction costs. It follows that discrimination has benefits as well as costs and will be the low-cost solution in some circumstances but not in others. We should not, therefore, expect that in some long-run equilibrium there will be no private-market discrimination.

Ignoring the rational grounds for discrimination has, I believe, sent John J. Donohue astray in his efforts to show on traditional neoclassical assumptions (assumptions that seek to take into account all preferences, including those of employers and workers who prefer discrimination) that Title VII is nonetheless efficient, at least in the case of race. The basis of Donohue's argument is that in the long run the efficient firms will all be free of discrimination because their inability to compete means that they will eventually be driven from the market.[15] Discriminating firms, he notes, have imperfect abilities to adjust to all relevant information, and may therefore not respond to the powerful incentives on which the standard prediction rests. Title VII can thus fill a gap by speeding up a process that would otherwise take place in the absence of some regulation (for example, Jim Crow laws) that protects the market position of discriminating firms. The trade-off involved in Donohue's view is whether the costs of expediting a nondiscriminatory workplace are justified by the benefits obtained.

In light of my arguments, his conclusion cannot be accepted. The simplest point is that on any realistic assessment of the market, one cannot assume a competitive equilibrium in which it is irrational (that is, not profit maximizing) for any firm to discriminate. The problems of harmonizing tastes and enforcing informal contracts may explain why some discrimination is valuable in an imperfect world (that is, a world of high transaction costs). Title VII at its best directs us to an end position that would not be attained in the long run in any well-functioning market subject to the usual frictions and uncertainties of business. Although Donohue confines his attention to racial discrimination, the point is surely true with other forms of discrimination as well. We should expect to see many forms of discrimination on the grounds of sex, age, and handicap as well, for these are often precisely the steps that, absent regulation, allow the firm to become a low-cost producer.[16]

In addition, Donohue's argument lacks any dimension of political or public choice. Once these additional factors are taken into account, there is nothing which says that Title VII could operate with laserlike precision so as to achieve its goal and nothing more. Any model of government behavior has to ask the question of whether administrative agencies and courts will be content to follow the nondiscrimination model, or will in fact impose on firms costs that they would never agree to bear voluntarily. The imperatives of bureaucratic expansion and majoritarian politics have exerted a powerful force, for over the life of the Civil Rights Act the simple color-blind norm has yielded a massive, complex set of laws that

15. Donohue, "Is Title VII Efficient?" at 1421–22.

16. See, e.g., Victor Fuchs, *Women's Quest for Economic Equality* (1988), noting the extensive differences in occupational patterns for men and women, which he (rightly) attributes not to discrimination by employers but to the different preference structures of men and women. On differences in preferences by sex, see my discussion of *EEOC v. Sears*, 839 F.2d 302 (7th Cir. 1988), in Chapter 18 at 385–391.

has basically done two things: (1) made it permissible to discriminate at will against whites and men (especially white men), and (2) made it possible to charge race- or sex-neutral firms with discrimination on the strength of statistical techniques whose application is flawed at every critical juncture.[17] Neither of these transformations was mandated by the act itself, but they were, in a sense, made inevitable by the constellation of political forces that became identified with the civil rights movement. A familiar note of caution is again in order. It is a serious mistake to compare imperfect markets with perfect legislative systems. The dangers of excess have to be taken into account in both cases, and these are always far greater with legislation than with markets, for the state is a *single* entity that wields monopoly power, for ill as well as good.

These public choice complications figure heavily in an analysis of the current civil rights laws, but I shall postpone discussion of them until later. It is first necessary to ask whether some prohibition against discrimination can make sense in certain limited settings, even if there are situations in which discrimination is rational and not invidious or self-destructive. The key question here is not whether certain forms of discrimination are bad in themselves but whether they can yield inferior social outcomes in certain contexts, namely where entry into a market is for some reason (whether practical or legal) no longer free. That subject is the topic of the next chapter.

17. See my discussion of the disparate impact test in race cases in Chapter 10 and in sex cases in Chapter 17.

CHAPTER 4

When Entry Is Restricted: The Case of Monopoly

From Many to One

The benign conclusion of the previous two chapters—that private discrimination holds little risk of social or private peril—depends heavily on the critical assumption that there are no systematic barriers to entry in labor markets. With that assumption in place, it became possible to contrast discrimination and the refusal to deal with the use of force. With discrimination in ordinary markets, each person gets to sell his labor to the parties most favorably disposed to him, and need not transact with any other persons. With force, he risks life and limb at the hands of his worst enemy, and he secures no permanent peace by buying off that enemy if others threaten harm as well. In a world in which there is a large number of individuals, all with different tastes, temperaments, and abilities, the spread in sentiment from the most sympathetic to the most hostile is likely to be very substantial. Potential victims can adopt strategies of evasion to escape the sting of discrimination, no matter how irrational and prejudiced. It is far harder to outrun a bullet.

Nonetheless, it is evident that not all labor markets are characterized by a large number of competing firms, each constrained by the prospect of new entry. In theory it is instructive to analyze cases that lie at the opposite pole, where a single individual or firm controls all prospects of employment. A government monopoly on employment yields just that situation, which is one strong reason to fear nationalization of major industries under the British Labour party, or (to spread the blame equally) the continuation of state control over the British universities begun under Margaret Thatcher's Conservative administration. Within this context the risks and benefits of discrimination change radically. Under monopoly, especially legal monopoly, it is no longer possible for any single person to move elsewhere to escape hostile parties. The temperaments, inclinations, and biases of those with monopoly power can exert an enormous influence over every person on the opposite side of the market. In this context some antidiscrimination norm becomes an integral part of the basic legal system, where its role is necessary, powerful—and problematic.

Monopoly and Price Discrimination

Basic Economics of the Problem

In order to understand the place of an antidiscrimination norm in monopoly settings, it is useful again to leave the employment context for a moment. Assume that there is a single seller of a unique commodity. Typically all buyers will not have identical demand functions for the product.[1] Some will be prepared to pay more than others. Within the competitive market the seller will produce the good at the point where price and marginal cost are equal. There is no bargaining over price. The seller who raises prices loses all customers to rivals. The producer who lowers prices cannot cover costs or make a normal profit and remain in business. In the ideal model, competition generates all the gains from bargains without incurring any of the costs from strategic bargaining behavior. In contrast, the monopolist has systematic incentives to cut back production to some higher price in order to maximize the private profits from sale. If bound by legal constraints against price discrimination, the seller is forced to pick a single price for the commodity that she sells. In that event customers who value the good above the competitive but below the monopoly price will exit the market. Similarly, those who value the good more than the monopoly price will remain in the market, where they still will obtain from their purchases some reduced consumer surplus—the difference between the highest price they are willing to pay (the so-called reservation price) for the good and the market price of that same good.

---

1. The exposition of the problem can become quite involved where buyers purchase multiple units of a single good, some of which they demand at the monopoly price, and some not. Those complexities can be ignored, without sacrificing the central analytical point, by assuming that each consumer demands only one unit of the good for which he is prepared to pay either (a) below the competitive price, (b) between the competitive and monopoly price, or (c) above the monopoly price. Since people in group (a) are always out of the market, the analysis in the text focuses on groups (b) and (c).

The existence of these two classes of buyers suggests that price discrimination (we are inching back toward labor markets) might be a viable strategy for the seller of the good to adopt. The first part of the strategy is to reduce the price for those consumers who are not prepared to pay the monopoly price. Similarly, for those buyers who still have consumer surplus at the monopoly price, the discriminating monopolist has an incentive to raise the price to erode that surplus further. Ideally the seller will try to sell each unit of the good at a price just below that which would induce her various purchasers to leave the market entirely. In addition, the seller will try to create barriers against resale among the various purchasers which might otherwise defeat the price discrimination scheme. If this overall strategy could be executed perfectly in all cases, then the output under a pure monopoly system would be identical to that observed under perfect competition.[2] All of the possible exchanges of goods that are to the mutual benefit of buyer and seller would be made, and no others.

Any seller who tries to discriminate among her purchasers, however, faces a number of practical difficulties, all of which impose real costs without generating offsetting social benefits. The first is that the seller must be able to counteract the risk that low-demand purchasers will resell their goods on the secondary market to purchasers otherwise willing to pay a monopoly price or higher. In effect, future competition by the seller's own purchasers can defeat the operation of any price discrimination scheme. The problem here is most acute with fungible and portable goods. With labor markets, however, it is quite difficult for anyone to "resell" his job to someone who is willing to work for lower wages. Wage discrimination is for that reason easier to achieve in practice than price discrimination.

Price discrimination also requires that sellers make estimations of the reserve prices of all their customers. As long as the price payable by any consumer is a function of the private demand for the good, consumers are well advised to keep the intensity of their preferences secret so as to look like low rather than high demanders. Sellers for their part may find it worthwhile to invest funds in discovering the true preferences of their customers, or in devising pricing strategies that induce high-demand buyers to pay higher prices. This intrigue generally consumes substantial resources, which further reduces the total amount of gain available to buyer and seller from the resulting market transactions.

2. See, generally, David D. Friedman, *Price Theory* 255–263 (2nd ed., 1990).

The social implications are clear enough. Removing any legal protections or breaking up the monopoly would help drive the market back to the competitive solution, where price discrimination is no longer possible. Perfect price discrimination by a single monopolist yields the same social output as perfect competition. But once imperfect information and game playing are recognized as dominant possibilities, then competitive markets are uniformly superior to monopolistic ones, with or without price discrimination. Transaction costs again reveal their critical role in shaping the inquiry. The best solution to the monopoly problem is to break up the monopoly or remove any legal protection it obtains from the legislature. Preventing price discrimination once the monopoly is acquired is only a second-best solution to the problem.

Nonetheless, there are certain cases in which the option of knocking out the monopoly is not viable. The primary example involves the so-called natural monopoly industries, those with diminishing costs to scale (that is, the cost per unit decreases as the number of units increases).[3] In these markets a single party is the cheapest producer of the goods in question, so the introduction of competition thus requires a costly duplication of certain fixed costs.[4] Should anything be done to limit the discretion of the seller with this natural monopoly position? One regulatory option has been a restriction on the ability of sellers to discriminate (the relationship to the antidiscrimination laws should now be clear) among buyers. Like all second-best solutions, this response has both its good and its bad features. To ban discrimination by the seller creates a legal world in which those consumers who value the good between the competitive

3. See, generally, James D. Gwartney and Richard L. Stroup, *Economics: Public and Private Choice* 460–461 (4th ed., 1987). For an instructive judicial account of the takings issues implicit in the regulation of natural monopolies, see *Duquesne Light Co. v. Barasch,* 488 U.S. 299 (1989).

4. The most famous example, discussed in R. H. Coase, "The Marginal Cost Controversy," reprinted in Coase, *The Firm and the Market* 75 (1988), concerns a bridge that costs a huge sum to build and nothing to maintain. What price should consumers be charged? If they are charged marginal cost, then they should be allowed to use the bridge for free; any positive toll will result in an inefficiency because it will exclude consumers who attach a positive value to the use of the bridge that is greater than the cost of providing the service to them. Nonetheless, if no toll is collected, then it will not be possible to tell whether the bridge should have been built at all. The total demand could well exceed the costs of construction, which are funded not in the market but by taxation. One could try to adopt schemes with variable charges, but none eliminates the difficulty. Allocating the charges of a single fixed asset among competing users never yields an ideal solution. The only question is which scheme of allocation minimizes the total level of distortion from all sources.

and the monopoly price are shut out of the market. Yet to allow discrimination not only increases the price for higher demands (itself only a transfer) but also invites a new round of strategic maneuvers that dissipates the gains from productive activities.

Matters are made more complicated when the single seller faces different costs in selling to different consumers. An antidiscrimination provision that calls for a single price to all customers therefore requires that price be above cost to some customers (say, those who order in bulk) and below cost to others (say, those who do not). The outcome is an implicit cross-subsidy between consumers resulting in a market inefficiency. If it costs $10 to produce a good for which the consumer is charged $15, then that consumer will leave the market if his reservation price is between $10 and $15, thereby removing the potential payer of subsidy. The choice between single and multiple price structures becomes an inescapably close one, and countless schemes for the allocation of fixed and variable costs are designed to minimize the distortions when a single seller exerts monopoly power.

The dynamics of price discrimination require us to take into account cases in which consumers have different demands for the seller's product and also impose different costs on the seller. On the demand side, the effort to raise prices above the competitive level results in strategic bargaining and welfare losses. Yet where the costs of providing identical goods to consumers differ, price discrimination becomes necessary to prevent the costly consumers from obtaining an unwarranted subsidy from the economical ones. The hard legal question asks what set of rules can be used to distinguish between the two relevant forms of discrimination, that is, to distinguish between charging high prices to high demanders who can be served at low cost and charging high prices to persons who are intrinsically costly to serve.

Historical Solutions

The price discrimination debate first began with an analysis of the common law obligations of innkeepers and common carriers. Both classes of entrepeneurs, at least in the conditions of earlier times, enjoyed genuine elements of monopoly power. When travel was restricted to a few highways or rivers, frequently only one carrier was available, or one inn at any given location. Often the monopoly was not by virtue of position alone but also by virtue of government grant, such as a franchise from the Crown. It was understood that as an offset to the monopoly position, the innkeeper or carrier could not exclude any passenger or discriminate by price in an effort to obtain higher rates from customers at the top end of the market. In practice, the social judgment was that the danger of excluding low demanders from the market was far smaller than the alternative risk of soaking high demanders.

In many cases this general nondiscrimination obligation was coupled with a system of direct regulation of prices in an attempt to reduce the common carrier to a competitive rate of return on its original investment. The entire enterprise could be quite tricky in practice. Once it became clear that the carrier's cost was not the same for all customers, then it was necessary to distinguish between the motivations for price differentials. Where the increased rates reflected increased costs, discriminatory rates were easily justified. If it costs extra to hire a night crew for a riverboat, night travel should be more expensive than day travel. Where the price discrimination reflected a perception of high demand without change in costs, it represented a clear (and costly) effort to capture some portion of the consumer surplus. Frequently both elements could be present simultaneously, making it at best very difficult to disentangle the portions of a price increase that were cost justified from those that were not.

That system of regulation could be complex, but with the types of discrimination most relevant to the present discussion most of these difficulties dropped out. There are relatively few differences in the costs of transporting individuals on a train or of putting them up at an inn. Within these settings a strong presumption for a uniform price, subject to exceptions on proof of cause, generally made sense. Even if there were price differences, they were typically a factor of the time at which services were demanded, and not of the race or sex or age of the person who required carriage or accommodation. The formulation of the rule was that common carriers and innkeepers were obliged to "take all comers" at a uniform price, at least within broad classifications related only to the costs of providing services.

A rule of that sort creates a new risk that some of the customers will impose extra costs on the carrier or innkeeper, for example by unruly behavior. Yet here the correlation between such behavior and race, sex, age (small children could be an exception), and national origin is either weak or unknown. The concern can be addressed largely by allowing the removal of any person from the inn or carriage "for cause" after the fact and not before. Fleshing out what counts as "cause" in this context is not especially difficult. The ability to pay the standard price is one proper requirement, and one that is easy to monitor. Conformity to customary rules of behavior is another straightforward requirement: no screaming or punching, and in some establishments no drinking or smoking either. A short list of dos and don'ts can go a long way toward defining the ground rules.

These work well with carriers and inns, because virtually all of the obligations to perform are on the carrier or innkeeper. One does not have to use testing devices to see who can sleep in a bed or sit on a chair. Unlike in some private clubs, there are no strong associational bonds that might be forged by a policy of discrimination. Virtually no collective decisions are made easier to reach by reducing the heterogeneity of group members. The sensible uses of discrimination mentioned in the last chapter might be relevant in varying degrees to ordinary businesses, private clubs or intimate associations, but they do not seem strong here if we look at the matter from the position of all the participants in the market.

The use of the antidiscrimination provision, therefore, has powerful justification whenever practical or legal circumstances prevent the emergence of a competitive market. The necessity of dealing with a single seller means that going elsewhere is not a viable strategy. To be sure, the single seller does not present the customer with the same dreadful prospects associated with the use of force. There is always the option to decline to take the trip, so what is at stake is not bodily integrity but only lost opportunity. Even then the service would typically be offered at an increased price, which, owing to the monopolist's imperfect inability to discriminate, leaves some surplus for the buyer as well.

These basic differences between force and monopoly were duly reflected in the general legal rules. No one was required as a matter of law to buy liberty back from all potential aggressors. But the right to be free from the monopolist's discrimination did not give one the right to service at no cost; instead, it carried with it the correlative duty to pay a fee sufficient to cover costs and provide an appropriate return on investment.

No system of monopoly regulation, even one as simple as a general nondiscrimination provision, works as well as pure competition. But there is a credible, if not powerful, case with common carriers and innkeepers that some regulation is better than no regulation at all. The nondiscrimination norm can be enforced at low cost and thus counteract the holdout problem. That case becomes strongest when the locus of concern is discrimination by race, sex, or national origin. Age presents a harder problem. The common practice of discounts for senior citizens reflects the judgment that their demand for services is lower, so that some price break may make sense for the firm, provided its variable costs for serving its older customers are below its price. Handicap discrimination, the subject of massive regulation under the 1990 Americans with Disabilities Acts, presents far harder problems because the costs of rendering services are vastly higher than they are with ordinary consumers. There is thus a common law basis for some restricted antidiscrimination norm to control monopoly power against some classes of persons. The question is how far the monopoly rationale extends beyond inns and common carriers.

Employment Situations

The employment relation provides a far less suitable target for state regulation. In the case of innkeepers and common carriers, two features lend (or at least historically lent) credible justification for using the nondiscrimination provision. First, the norm was relatively easy to impose, given the uniform requirements for service demanded by customers. Second, the norm promised some substantial social gain by curbing the monopoly power of the innkeeper or common carrier. Both sides of the argument are far weaker in the context of employment.

First, there is much wider variation in the types of business arrangements that are subject to the general nondiscrimination rule. Employers come in all sizes and shapes. The internal demands of one firm are likely to differ considerably from those of another. Whereas passengers and hotel guests are relatively fungible, employees are not. The variety of tasks entrusted to employees is essentially infinite. For small firms that work in specialized markets, an antidiscrimination norm may be impossible to comply with, and major firms that compete in world markets may have to adopt many different strategies as they move from place to place and from function to function. Some jobs allow employees to work in the relative isolation of their own homes. Others require employees to live where they work, often away from home, at close quarters and in cramped situations. Compatibility of employees is far more critical in the second setting than it is in the first, and we should expect more racial or ethnic, and perhaps sexual, homogeneity in those contexts.[5] The range of variation is enormous, and there is no reason to expect a close fit between the voluntary norms that emerge through market behavior and the formal requirements

5. See discussion of *Wards Cove Packing Co. v. Atonio*, 490 U.S. 642, in Chapter 11 at 233–236, where one reason suggested for the strong ethnic lines of the fishermen involved in that case is that their employment was at an isolated site far removed from their homes.

of the antidiscrimination norm. One rule fits all is as bad a policy in the law of employment discrimination as it is in the law of employer liability, where there is no obvious reason to believe that systems of common law negligence are uniformly superior to, or inferior to, systems of workers' compensation. The variety of occupations resists any uniform characterization.

What, then, is the justification for imposing the costs of a nondiscrimination rule? With common carriers and innkeepers, it was to combat the dangers of monopoly power. But no private employer in any industry has anything close to the level of monopoly power that justifies the use of the antidiscrimination principle. From both points of view, therefore, the antidiscrimination norm is peculiarly unattractive in private employment contexts. The costs of its implementation are exceedingly high, and the benefits are exceedingly low. And the risks of regulation are also great. Employment markets are normally competitive, but they need not remain so if government is allowed to set terms with which all firms must comply. In the modern setting it is commonly believed that Title VII represents a benevolent government intervention. But the use of state power in the Jim Crow era shows the other face of government regulation. The next section traces the pattern of government intervention in the period that runs roughly from the rise of Jim Crow to the passage of the Civil Rights Act of 1964, some seventy or eighty years later. As we shall see, too often regulation is the problem, not the solution.

PART II

History

CHAPTER 5

Race and the Police Power: 1890 to 1937

A Morality Play

The analysis in the previous four chapters was undertaken on a blank slate where the state acted as a neutral umpire to control private aggression and enforce private contracts in accordance with their terms but otherwise did not restrict entry on either side of the market. Only where conditions of natural monopoly obtained, as with common carriers and innkeepers, did it follow that the state should impose an obligation not to discriminate among the persons who received service. In essence the legal regime of strong property rights and free contract, notwithstanding the persistent problems of high transaction costs and imperfect information, is better able to respond to the issues posed by discrimination than any comprehensive system of state regulation directed at the practice. It is not that all forms of private discrimination will disappear under this regime; they will not and should not. But there is a powerful, long-term, and impersonal test which suggests that, subject to the common carrier exception, the forms of discrimination that will survive are those that ought not to be suppressed.

Theory is, of course, one thing and practice is another. Yet the soundness of this theory is difficult to test because the initial conditions of state neutrality and faithful contractual enforcement were rarely satisfied in the long period from the end of the Civil War to the passage of the Civil Rights Act of 1964. Far from being a system of open and competitive markets, the dominant institution was Jim Crow, that set of explicit racial restrictions governing voting, marriage, economic arrangements, and schooling that permeated every important aspect of southern life under segregation.[1] Huge portions of American racial history are thus concerned not with the behavior of private markets as such but with the neutralization of the massive apparatus of state control over private behavior. That narrative, which lies at the moral core of the civil rights movement, reads much like a modern morality play. Its message is both powerful and compelling because of the ease with which it is possible to distinguish good from evil. The evil of Jim Crow and segregation in the South was a national disgrace. The critical decisions of the Supreme Court, which allowed the southern states (and to a lesser extent the northern ones) to impose this regime, were equally disgraceful.

In 1896 *Plessy v. Ferguson*,[2] written by Justice Henry Brown of Massachusetts, gave full sway to the notorious separate but equal doctrine in race relations. At the time Justice John Marshall Harlan, himself a former slave owner, wrote in lonely dissent, "In my opinion, the judgment this day rendered will, in time, prove to be quite as pernicious as the decision made by this tribunal in the *Dred Scott* case."[3] He stood alone at the time, but history has proved him right. For over sixty years this nation grappled with the legacy of *Plessy*. To be sure, *Plessy* did not introduce Jim Crow; but *Plessy* did insulate the basic structure of Jim Crow from constitutional attack by allowing segregated facilities on common carriers, school segregation, and antimiscegenation laws. Its blanket authorization of wide-scale state regulation under the police power thus dictated the agenda that governed civil rights at both the state and the national level for the next seventy years. Good came first with *Brown v. Board of Education*,[4] which undid school segregation, and then with the passage of the Civil Rights Act of 1964, which administered the final crushing blow to the old order. The bankruptcy of Jim Crow, and the system of racial segregation it spawned, legitimated the Civil Rights Act far more vividly than any argument of moral philosophy. The statute was passed as much for what it repudiated as for what it introduced.

The speed with which events moved in the United States in the 1960s,

---

1. C. Vann Woodward, *The Strange Career of Jim Crow* 7 (3rd rev. ed., 1974).

The origin of the term "Jim Crow" is lost in obscurity. Thomas D. Rice wrote a song and dance called "Jim Crow" in 1832, and the term had become an adjective by 1838. The first example of "Jim Crow law" listed by the *Dictionary of American English* is dated 1904.

See also Benno C. Schmidt, Jr., "Principle and Prejudice: The Supreme Court and Race in the Progressive Era: Part I: The Heyday of Jim Crow," 82 *Colum. L. Rev.* 467 (1982).

2. 163 U.S. 537 (1896).

3. Id. at 559.

4. *Brown v. Board of Education of Topeka*, 347 U.S. 483 (1954).

however, took its toll on the understanding of just what was wrong with Jim Crow. Too often the dominant explanations are based on racial hatred or prejudice. The response to Jim Crow was equally clear and authoritative: any practice, public or private, that drew distinctions between whites and blacks in social, economic, or political life fell outside the pale. Under the Civil Rights Act, the distinction between private and government discrimination is rendered largely, if not wholly, irrelevant. No effort was made to relate the impact of private discrimination to the structure of the market, to the role of barriers to entry, to the viability of competition, or to the threat of monopoly. The antidiscrimination principle was no longer conceived as a well-tailored antidote to the monopoly position of the innkeeper or the common carrier, or as a check on the power of the state to take from some and give to others. The experience of Jim Crow was so powerful that it pushed to one side any conceptual understanding of discrimination and its consequences in private markets. Economic analysis, game theory, and the like formed no part of the discourse. The question of civil rights was perceived first and foremost as a moral issue, as a question of simple justice,[5] which admitted only one categorical answer: any form of discrimination on grounds of race is morally wrong and ought to be illegal. It was the practice of discrimination that mattered. What was wholly irrelevant was its source, public or private.

The world view of the Civil Rights Act of 1964 is radically different from the approach that I sketched out in the earlier chapters of this book. I believe that the received wisdom, both in 1964 and today, does not grasp what was wrong with Jim Crow and segregation. The dominant evil in the pre-1964 period was not self-interest or markets, inflexible human nature, or even bigotry. It was excessive state power and the pattern of private violence, intimidation, and lynching, of which there is a painful record[6] but against which there was no effective federal remedy.[7] The explicit discrimination in the South and elsewhere was preserved by the

5. See Richard Kluger, *Simple Justice* (1976), for a history of the most important desegregation decision, *Brown v. Board of Education of Topeka*, 347 U.S. 483 (1954).

6. See, e.g., Jennifer Roback, in "Southern Labor Law in the Jim Crow Era: Exploitative or Competitive?" 51 *U. Chi. L. Rev.* 1161 (1984), reprinted in *Labor Law and the Employment Market* 217 (R. Epstein and J. Paul eds. 1985).

7. See, e.g., *Hodges v. United States*, 203 U.S. 1 (1906), with its extensive account of the private acts of violence, which fell outside the Thirteenth Amendment since individual acts of violence were not tantamount to slavery because they did not involve the total "subjection" of one person to the will of another. Id at 17. *Hodges* was overruled in *Jones v.*

use of coercion, both by state law and by private individuals (such as the Ku Klux Klan) whose activities were left unchecked by state agents. The history of failure in the South is not a history of the failure of individual character or individual will. It is not a history of the failure of markets. It does not demonstrate the need for federal intervention to eradicate the "harm" that private markets caused. To the contrary, the lessons from our history of civil rights all stem from two sources: first, the abnegation of the principles of limited government, that is, government restricted to those areas where it is required, such as taxation and law enforcement; and second, the massive state legislative regulation of private markets that was left unchecked by passive judicial action. Under Jim Crow, big government fell into the hands of the wrong people, who were able to perpetuate their stranglehold over local communities and businesses by means of a pervasive combination of public and private force. Jim Crow is best attacked from the limited-government, libertarian perspective as another illustration of Lord Acton's insight: power corrupts, and absolute power corrupts absolutely.

Who Governs?

It is necessary to return briefly to the central theme of Chapters 1 and 2. Within a well-functioning competitive market every person's wealth and livelihood depends on the attitude of that person who will make him the highest offer. Within the political context this same relationship is more difficult to establish, for legislative decisions are always a function not only of individual preference but also of the way they are aggregated into some collective decision. In a world devoid of constitutional restraint, the (bare) majority rules.

The question thus becomes who will be able to assemble a dominant coalition on matters of race. Here enormous leverage rests with the median voter, at least in any choice between two persons or positions.[8] If it is possible (as it often is not) to array all the voters within the jurisdiction along a single axis, then the individual whose preferences are in the middle will tend to dominate the tastes of persons at either extreme. The conclusion follows from the premise that self-interested voters will

---

Mayer Co., 392 U.S. 409 (1968), discussed in Chapter 7 at 134–135 under the heading "The Civil War Amendments."

8. On matters of voting theory generally, see James M. Buchanan and Gordon Tullock, *The Calculus of Consent* (1962).

choose that social alternative which is closest to their own private preferences. If the only available position (or candidate), A, is not in the middle,
then a new political entrant, B, who takes the middle position will be able
to get 50 percent of the vote (representing those who are farther from A
than B, plus some fraction of the people whose preferences lie between
the two).

Where most individuals are closely bunched toward the middle of the
distribution, the median voter theorem still holds, but the problem of
collective choice becomes tractable because very few people will perceive
any great difference between their first and second choices. Indeed, in a
world of perfectly homogeneous preferences, politics and markets yield
the same result. Thus far the analysis is identical to that of the condominium association whose members have similar tastes.[9] But for other
distributions of tastes and preferences political markets do far worse.
Thus, suppose that the voters in a community are divided into two hostile
camps, one with 51 percent of the vote and the other with 49 percent.
The median voter theorem suggests that the well-advised politician will
cater to the tastes of the majority, thereby inflicting very large losses on
the minority if unconstrained by constitutional principles. In addition, the
situation can become very unstable if the populations shift because of
differential birth rates, immigration and migration, or (in extreme cases)
by intimidation and assassination.[10] Now the minority can suddenly
become the majority, at least if the census is retaken: instability may
compound oppression. Markets are largely resistant to these problems.
Since choices are not aggregrated on an all-or-nothing basis, it is not the
case that two wholly separate and hostile groups are faced with sharply
discontinuous choices at the median. A shift in population of 2 percent
does not mean the difference between control and no control, between
domination and oppression. It means only a small difference (2 percent) in
wealth or market share.

This political market was not kind to the blacks, both in the South and
nationwide. As has been well documented, the systematic exclusion of
blacks from the electorate shifted the voting population in favor of
whites.[11] On matters of both education and employment Price Fishback

9. See Chapter 3 at 62–69, under the heading "Collective Choice within Groups."

10. See David Levy, "The Statistical Basis of Athenian-American Constitutional
Theory," 18 *J. Legal Stud.* 79 (1989).

11. As reflected in the Supreme Court decisions that struck down poll taxes, *Harper v.
Virginia Board of Elections*, 383 U.S. 663 (1966); and literacy tests, *South Carolina v.*

has provided good empirical evidence that the legislative politics were more hostile to blacks than, for example, the coal companies, which, when forced to compete strenuously in a regional labor market, assiduously courted black labor.[12] In the legislative arena racists and bigots could, and did, outvote more moderate whites. Within a market that same majority could not bind any minority, no matter how small. But in the political setting it could, by passing laws that *required* segregation, discrimination, unequal taxes, and biased enforcement of the law. The South of Jim Crow must be understood as a comprehensive network of interlocking institutions. The Supreme Court's routine willingness, prior to 1937, to defer to the political judgments of the legislatures thus allowed a virulent majority to choke off the improvements that blacks and others could have achieved among themselves, or by doing business with whites who were sympathetic to them and supportive of their aspirations. The local situation was further aggravated because the existence of hostile laws made the South a less attractive place for new entrants from outside the region who might otherwise have made substantial profits from doing business with local blacks.

It is often said that this view of the world places far too much emphasis on the legal regime and not enough on the pervasive attitudes and extensive network of social practices that dominated the society. Typical of this vein is the assertion of James Heckman and J. Hoult Verkerke that segregation in labor markets was not attributable to legal rules: "In most southern states . . . informal codes effectively regulated individual conduct and severely constrained employers' conduct."[13] But even here they recognize immediately that social pressure alone does not create the employer's refusal to deal. "The southern code was enforced primarily through social and economic pressure with the threat of private violence should less severe sanctions fail."[14] That is, the social and economic pressures could be, and doubtless were, understood as an implicit threat that violence would be used if polite measures failed. The effectiveness of that private violence in turn depended heavily on the willingness of law

Katzenbach, 383 U.S. 301 (1966), sustaining the Voting Rights Act of 1965, Pub. L. no. 89–110, 79 Stat. 437, codified at 42 *U.S.C.* §1973 et seq. (1982).

12. Price V. Fishback, "Can Competition among Employers Reduce Governmental Discrimination? Coal Companies and Segregated Schools in West Virginia in the Early 1900s," 32 *J. Law & Econ.* 311, 313, 324 (1989).

13. James J. Heckman and J. Hoult Verkerke, "Racial Disparity and Employment Discrimination Law: An Economic Perspective," 8 *Yale Law & Policy Rev.* 276, 278 (1990).

14. Id. at 278 n.9.

enforcement officials to turn a blind eye to its prosecution, or indeed to participate in it.

In order to sustain the basic position that cultural and social norms are sufficient to sustain Jim Crow, it becomes necessary to abstract away from these pervasive threats and to ask whether Jim Crow would have survived if southern whites had voluntarily relinquished their control over the ballot, the police force, the courts, and the other instruments of state domination. The prolonged fight to wrest control of these powers away from local majorities shows that they did not believe that it could. And on this point the defenders of Jim Crow were right. Once political power is gone, new entry can take place by firms willing to cater to blacks in all segments of the economy. The tighter the social cartel against blacks under Jim Crow, the larger the returns to new entry in the marketplace, notwithstanding a social consensus in the opposite direction. In speaking of the same problem in connection with litigation in Japan, J. Mark Ramseyer and Minoru Nakazato have demonstrated in the Japanese context that these community norms are fragile in the sense that a single outsider who has little to fear from ostracism can undermine them by going to court.[15] Once the first party has left the fold, then others will find it more easy to follow. Japan is regarded as a closed society, perhaps even more so than the Old South. If the single marginal entrant can change the social balance of power in the one case, then it can do so in the other.

Under Jim Crow the social fabric was as dependent on the legal regime as the legal regime was dependent on the social fabric. Behind the complex interplay of forces remains this basic truth: in politics the median voter is decisive. An antidiscrimination law has its broadest appeal when it is used to combat the sentiments of an angry and ugly majority. But that is precisely when it is least likely to pass because it will not command the support of the median voter. To understand why Jim Crow survived as long as it did, it is necessary to understand the legal rules that allowed the electoral process to dominate the market. That inquiry in turn requires that close attention be given to the dominant legal doctrines of the time, most notably the expansive use of the police power as the limitation on private property and private contract.

---

15. J. Mark Ramseyer and Minoru Nakazato, "The Rational Litigant: Settlement Amounts and Verdict Rates in Japan," 18 *J. Legal Stud.* 263, 286–287 (1989). It is noteworthy that their particular targets are the social anthropologists, such as Marshall Sahlins, *Culture and Practical Reason* (1976).

The Police Power

An Ace in the Hole

The emergent pattern of local politics took place in a system that was, at least on its face, sensitive to the risks of untrammeled popular democracy. In large measure the Civil War had been fought against the institution of slavery and white dominance. The Civil War amendments—on slavery, citizenship, voting, equal protection, due process, and privileges and immunities—were designed to decrease the scope of state power to confer ordinary common law liberties selectively on some while denying them to others. The basic structure was simple and ingenious. Specific limitations on state power that were lacking in the original Constitution were now imposed by the Civil War amendments.[16] The enforcement of a system of small state government was entrusted to the federal government.[17] With the passage of the Civil War amendments, there should have been in total less government at all levels after the Civil War than before, as no new and separate grants of power were accorded the federal government beyond its power to limit state misbehavior. In 1866 Congress did pass a civil rights statute in the wake of the Civil War amendments, but it dealt with civil capacity, not private discrimination as such.[18] The history of federal regulation before the 1964 Civil Rights Act shows very little direct federal intervention, either useful or destructive. It does show, however, a pattern of extensive state regulation, notwithstanding the limitations contained in the Civil War amendments. The states necessarily

16. The key limitations on the power of the state were two. The first was the contract clause, U.S. Const., Art. I, §10, "No State shall . . . pass . . . any Law impairing the Obligation of Contracts," which was interpreted in *Ogden v. Saunders*, 25 U.S. 213 (1827), not to reach contracts not yet formed when a statute was passed. The effect of the decision meant that only retroactive invalidation was reached by the clause, so there was no effective federal constitutional constraint on general legislation. This pattern was sharply reversed by the Civil War amendments.

Second, the privileges and immunities clause of Art. IV, §2, "The Citizens of each State shall be entitled to all Privileges and Immunities of Citizens in the Several States," only gave citizens of one state the same rights against another state as those of its own citizens. The clause did not impose any independent substantive limitations on what a state could do to its own citizens. See David P. Currie, *The Constitution in the Supreme Court: The First Hundred Years, 1788–1888* 239 n.12 (1985).

17. See U.S. Const., Amend. XIV, cl. 5: "The Congress shall have power to enforce, by appropriate legislation, the provisions of this article." Analogous language appears in the Thirteenth Amendment on slavery and the Fifteenth Amendment on voting.

18. See my discussion in Chapter 7.

held an ace in the hole, the police power, or the ability to regulate to achieve "safety, health, morals and general welfare of the public," as this power came to be construed in connection with race relations.

In order to see how the pattern unfolded, it is instructive to review some of the most notorious of the Jim Crow constitutional decisions on the police power from the perspective not of a defender of the modern civil rights legislation but of a believer in the traditional Lockean virtues of private property, individual liberty, and limited government. What approach might have been taken to race relations if the principles of substantive due process, as embodied in *Lochner v. New York*,[19] had been carried over to race relations? There is an irony here because, next only to *Plessy* itself, *Lochner* is widely regarded as the most indefensible constitutional law decision during the period between 1870 and 1937, often dubbed, misleadingly in my view, the "Lochner Era."[20] Today *Lochner* is praised for its Oliver Wendell Holmes dissent, with its famous epigram, "The Fourteenth Amendment does not enact Mr. Herbert Spencer's Social Statics."[21] Yet, whatever the soundness of Holmes's general legal position, the *Lochner* approach had and has far greater appeal on matters of race than on the questions of health and safety regulation that it directly addressed. Mr. Herbert Spencer's Social Statics is just the right antidote to Jim Crow.

The Plessy Case

Plessy v. Ferguson, decided some nine years before *Lochner,* illustrates the tension between the two approaches, one of which champions legislative power and the other judicial control. Louisiana passed a statute in 1890 which *required* that "all railway companies carrying passengers in their coaches in this State, shall provide equal but separate accommodations for the white, and colored races, by providing two or more pas-

---

19. 198 U.S. 45 (1905).

20. See Laurence H. Tribe, *American Constitutional Law* 567 (2nd ed., 1987), noting that the description should be used "with great caution," because the term *Lochnerizing* has become "so much an epithet." For criticism of *Lochner,* see Paul Murphy, *The Constitution in Crisis Times* (1972); Thomas Reed Powell, "The Judiciality of Minimum-Wage Legislation," 37 *Harv. L. Rev.* 545 (1924); Cass R. Sunstein, "Lochner's Legacy," 87 *Colum. L. Rev.* 873 (1987). I have defended *Lochner* in Richard A. Epstein, "Self-Interest and the Constitution," 37 *J. Legal Ed.* 154 (1987), and "The Mistakes of 1937," 11 *George Mason L. Rev.* 5 (1988).

21. 198 U.S. 45, 75.

senger coaches for each passenger train, or by dividing the passenger coaches by a partition so as to secure separate accommodations."[22] The statute was challenged under the Equal Protection Clause of the Constitution on the ground that the separate treatment it demanded of railroads necessarily infringed the rights of individual black citizens to the equal protection of the law. To stress the obvious, the case itself does not deal with the private, voluntary discrimination that railways might practice in their own self-interest. Government coercion required the separation of the races.

The Louisiana statute sustained in *Plessy* was one of many passed in the late 1880s and the early 1890s that mandated the practice of segregation on the rails. Prior to that time the situation was, according to a careful study by Charles Lofgren,[23] a confused mosaic. Lofgren notes that no historian to date has done the "company-by-company or perhaps route-by-route study necessary to determine the exact degree of separation by race, and of discrimination in the level of service, on public conveyances in the South during the three decades following the Civil War."[24] He then concludes with this generalization about the available sources:

> It suffices to say that in the states of the former Confederacy, from the end of the war into the late 1880s and early 1890s, segregation or discrimination existed almost everywhere to an identifiable degree; and in perhaps half these states these practices flourished to the extent that their absence was the exception. If streetcars were less segregated for fifteen or twenty years, that openness was declining by 1890; integrated travel on steamboats had always been the exception; and throughout the period, black travelers on regular railways more often than not encouraged either segregation or discrimination in quality of service—or both. Moreover, unlike other public institutions and accommodations, with which Negroes had only temporary contact (as in the case of schools) or could avoid (hotels, restaurants, and places of amusement), reliance on public conveyances was unavoidable for large numbers throughout their lives.[25]

The source of the historical difficulties lies in the tangled web of laws and practices that governed the Southern states. As Lofgren reports, Mis-

22. *Louisiana Act of 1980,* no. 111, at 152.
23. Charles A. Lofgren, *The Plessy Case: A Legal-Historical Interpretation* 7–27 (1987).
24. Id. at 17.
25. Id.

sissippi and Florida, for example, passed statutes that not only segregated blacks on trains but also excluded them from service.[26] Texas passed a measure that confined blacks to the smoking car, which was located right behind the coal tender, and was the most uncomfortable for passengers, in which they received inferior accommodations to boot.[27] Many of these statutes, in fact, were replaced by general antidiscrimination norms when the Radical Republicans took control during Reconstruction.[28] But for these purposes it is necessary to stress that statutes of this sort *do* run afoul of the general antidiscrimination norm applicable to the common carrier at common law.[29]

Here, in principle, if the demand for separation between the races is strong enough on either side, then separate accommodations can be required. Indeed, the black protests of the period were directed largely against the inequality of the accommodations, not the racial segregation iteslf.[30] In this context, moreover, separate but equal does contain powerful teeth, as long as the accommodations are kept equal in fact. The best way to ensure that result is to require that the cars be rotated randomly across various groups, a practice of which there is only a trace during the period.[31] At this point the preferences for segregated cars now

26. *Laws of Florida*, ch. 1466, §14 (1865–66); *Laws of Mississippi*, ch. 74, §6 at 231–232 (1865); Lofgren, *The Plessy Case* at 18.

27. *General Law of Texas*, ch. 52 at 97 (1866).

28. Lofgren, *The Plessy Case* at 18–19.

29. See the discussion id., ch. 6. The key case was *West Chester and Philadelphia Railroad Co. v. Miles*, 55 Pa. 209 (1867), which among other things affirmed the propriety of using so-called ladies' cars. "The ladies' car is known upon every well-regulated railroad, implies no loss of equal right on the part of the excluded sex, and its propriety is doubted by none." Id. at 211. The common law rule allowing separate but equal accommodations was repealed in Pennsylvania in 1867 by a requirement that all passengers had to be seated in the same cars. Id. at 215.

30. Lofgren, *The Plessy Case* at 16, quoting from Booker T. Washington (1885), 2 *Booker T. Washington Papers* (Louis R. Harlan ed. 1972–1988).

31. See *Railway Co. v. Brown*, 84 U.S. 445 (1873). The decision arose when a railroad received its grant under an act of Congress that provided that "no person shall be excluded from the cars on account of color," which was construed to preclude the practice of using separate cars for blacks, "though they were as good as those which they assigned exclusively for white persons, and in fact the very cars which were, at certain times, assigned exclusively to white persons." The evidence does not quite support randomization, for it is quite possible that these cars were the least desirable, and were pressed into service for white passengers only when other cars were unavailable or insufficient to satisfy the demand. The Court read the act as requiring fully integrated service and then concluded in strong language: "It was the privilege of the company to reject [the condition], but to do

come at a price that is explicitly borne by the railroad and the white customers. (Indeed, the proper procedure would require any additional costs from separation to be borne by the group that insists on it.) As the costs become clear, there is a quick progression to full integration of all compartments. On this view, the Louisiana separate-cars statute allows a political majority to force segregation on firms that have strong private incentives to integrate, notwithstanding the admitted prejudice of some of its passengers.

The passage of the Louisiana statute suggests that its railways always were—or, more likely, had become—unwilling to practice racial discrimination. In fact, some studies of the history of Jim Crow legislation in the South confirm what is evident from the statutes themselves.[32] The railroads were opposed to the requirements of the statutes and resisted their passage: "The roads are not in favor of the separate car law, owing to the expense entailed, but they fear to array themselves against it."[33] They posted the signs required by law but in practice did not enforce the ordinance,[34] and it is highly likely that they colluded in *Plessy*, for Homer Plessy himself was only one-eighth black, and his color was said to be not "discernible."[35] It would be idle to pretend that the managers and shareholders of the railway declined to enforce the law or decided to cooperate with the suit because they were persons of perfect, or even exceptional, virtue. They were ordinary businessmen, more concerned with their financial profits than with correcting any larger social injustices. Yet it is precisely that modest characterization of their motives which explains why in open markets there is so little to fear from private discrimination. Self-interested businessmen will be loath to practice discrimination when it hurts the bottom line.

Louis Martinet's statement of the railways' position reduces the issue to one word: cost. Racial segregation is expensive for the firm. The basic problem goes to how the railroad utilizes its capacity. Before the statute every space was available for any passenger. Hence the railroad could be confident that at peak hours it could fill its cars with passengers on a first-

---

this, it must reject the whole grant with which it was connected." Note that this argument is a two-edged sword, for if the condition mandated segregation, then railroads would be required to comply as well.

32. Jennifer Roback, "The Political Economy of Segregation: The Case of Segregated Streetcars," *J. Econ. Hist.* 893 (December 1986).

33. Lofgren, *The Plessy Case* at 32, quoting Louis Martinet, one of Plessy's lawyers.

34. Id. at 32.

35. Id. at 41.

come, first-served basis. Once the statute was passed, however, the railway necessarily lost revenue because of its obligation to maintain redundant and unused seating. Thus, if the railway decided to operate two cars, each with a capacity of 100 persons, it could not accommodate rush hour traffic of 120 whites and 40 blacks. In contrast, an integrated system would allow yet another 40 passengers to come on board. Nor was it possible to counter the problem by using cars of unequal size, given the problem of variable proportions: on the next run the traffic might be 40 whites and 120 blacks. Furthermore, it would have been expensive to maintain different kinds of rolling stock and to train personnel in its operation.

The second alternative open to the railroad under the Louisiana statute is little more appealing than the first. Partitions do allow for the separation of passengers within a car. But they do not respond ideally to the problem of variable proportions unless the partitions can be made movable, and then the railroad incurs the expense of shifting the partition every time the proportion of whites and blacks on the train changes. With any kind of commuter railroad this becomes an infeasible and unattractive alternative. The separate but equal requirement substantially increases the railroad's costs of serving its customers. The rule might satisfy the demands of a political market, but it is unlikely to survive in an economic market, where the locus of power moves from the legislature to the railway owner. Even whites who are prejudiced against blacks may prefer cheap transportation to segregated transportation if the price differential is steep enough. And it is surely unlikely that railways could charge higher rates to blacks under a price discrimination policy if the lower wealth were translated into a lesser willingness to pay. Even where separate but equal treatment is allowed as a matter of law, the self-interest of the railroad protects the position of a racial minority far better than appeals to republican virtue.

Understanding the Police Power

Where, then, does the state obtain the power to *require* the railway to segregate its space? In *Plessy* the challenge to the statute was premised on the equal protection clause of the Fourteenth Amendment. Within a libertarian framework, freedom of contract becomes the central issue. Here we have a private party that wants to sell its services to whites and blacks on identical terms, without discrimination. It does *not* seek to avail itself of the power to discriminate, even on reasonable terms. Why should the state be able to curtail the private party's power? Ironically, freedom of contract under the Fourteenth Amendment had been constitutionalized in another Louisiana case, *Allgeyer v. Louisiana*,[36] which dealt with the arcane mysteries of the insurance industry. If freedom of contract works for insurance companies, then railroads should be covered as well. Presumptively the statute that requires separate but equal accommodations is constitutionally infirm.

That same conclusion could be reached by way of the equal protection clause, given the coercive regulation that subordinates blacks to whites. Whenever there is state coercion, the state must justify its conduct. It is at this juncture that the police power issue intrudes itself into constitutional discourse. Does the regulation fall within the police power of the state? It is useful to recall the definition in *Lochner:*

> There are, however, certain powers existing in the sovereignty of each State in the Union, somewhat vaguely termed police powers, the exact description and limitation of which have not been attempted by the courts. Those powers, broadly stated and without, at present, any attempt at a more specific limitation, relate to the safety, health, morals and general welfare of the public."[37]

The police power, it should be stressed, is entirely a creature of judicial implication. The two words appear nowhere in the Constitution. This is not to say that judicial implication is necessarily illegitimate. The great questions of constitutional interpretation arise precisely because everyone concedes that some limitation must be grafted onto the text, but disagree as to what it should be.

The word *police* in the phrase *police power* offers one useful clue about the scope of this power: the police can restrain the use of force by private individuals. Their power is at its highest when they disarm a criminal who has perfect common law title to his gun. More generally, it was clear by the 1890s that the police power extended to wrongful actions of all kinds and descriptions, most notably those forms of conduct that were regarded as nuisances, both at common law and in ordinary English.[38]

36. 165 U.S. 578 (1897).

37. 198 U.S. 45, 53. See generally Ernst Freund, *The Police Power: Public Policy and Constitutional Rights* (1904), for the most exhaustive contemporary account of the subject. I have given my views on the subject in Richard A. Epstein, *Takings*, chs. 8 and 9 (1985).

38. See, e.g., *Fertilizing Co. v. Hyde Park,* 97 U.S. 659 (1878).

The owner of a factory did not have the right to pollute his neighbor's well or a navigable river. Where private suits to enjoin the action or to recover damages were clumsy and unwieldy, a system of state regulation was an appropriate and desired substitute. By this account the police power is closely tied to the idea of the protection of persons and property from tortious interference, as it has long been understood at common law.

The police power also had a second dimension, one that justified anti-fraud legislation. The argument is parallel to that made with respect to nuisances. Fraud is often difficult to detect and prevent. Leaving victims of fraud to the vagaries of private lawsuits is sometimes tantamount to saying that there can be no relief at all. A statute that enjoins the publication of fraudulent information, or subjects the perpetrators of fraud to fine or punishment, may well play a legitimate role under a libertarian model of the police power. To be sure, prophylatic rules are often justified when case-by-case prosecution is both costly and unreliable, subject always to the major dangers of overbreadth.

These two aspects of the police power leave considerable scope to government action on issues as diverse as environmental pollution and securities fraud. So directed, the police power does not come within a country mile of overriding Plessy's prima facie case, whether advanced on freedom of contract or on equal protection grounds. Sitting next to another passenger on a train is not the same as the commission of robbery or the creation of a common law nuisance. Nor does it involve deceit or fraud. The white passenger who does not like his black neighbor (or vice versa) can change his seat; he may not force the railroad to provide separate or partitioned carriages. The principle of freedom of contract allows the unhappy passenger not to ride the train for good reason, bad reason, or no reason at all. Even today businesses cannot sue prospective customers or employees who do not deal with them on grounds of race or sex. Those tastes, however intense, do not allow unhappy passengers (or their favorite legislators) to remake the railroad in their own image. Indeed, if the railroad had any monopoly position that justified regulation, the regulation should move in exactly the opposite direction. The railway, consistent with the common law view, would be under an obligation *not* to discriminate among its passengers unless it could show a viable cost justification. Within the libertarian framework, then, *Plessy* is an easy case, even after the elusive police power limitation on property and contract is taken into account.

Historically, however, the doctrinal development was far more muddled, for even in areas having little to do with race, the police power had already been extended far beyond the contours of common law nuisance and fraud. During the 1880s, for example, the Supreme Court, speaking through the first Justice Harlan, sustained grotesque restrictions on the sale of margarine which were designed not to prevent fraud but to suppress competition.[39] The technique that was used rested in large measure on the posture of judicial deference to legislative determinations of what counted as permissible forms of health and safety regulation. These were construed broadly where there was the tiniest risk to health and safety, as long as the statutory language nodded weakly to some ostensible health purpose. The police power was used to sustain manifestly anticompetitive measures.

As broad as these precedents were, the Court in *Plessy* could sustain the Louisiana statute only by going one step further. It had to include racial segregation among the proper ends of the police power. Thus the Court wrote:

> The object of the [Fourteenth] amendment was undoubtedly to enforce the absolute equality of the two races before the law, but in the nature of things it could not have been intended to abolish distinctions based upon color, or to enforce social, as distinguished from political equality, or a commingling of the two races upon terms unsatisfactory to either. Laws permitting, and even requiring, their separation in places where they are liable to be brought into contact do not necessarily imply the inferiority of either race to the other, and have been generally, if not universally, recognized as within the competency of the state legislatures, in the exercise of their police power. The most common instance of this is connected with the establishment of separate schools for white and colored children, which has been held to be a valid exercise of the legislative power even by courts of States where the political rights of the colored race have been longest and most earnestly enforced.[40]

39. See, e.g., *Powell v. Pennsylvania*, 127 U.S. 678 (1888) (punitive regulations against sale of margarine upheld as a "health" measure). See also *McCray v. United States*, 195 U.S. 27 (1904) (sustaining ten-cent tax on yellow oleomargarine when comparable tax on butter was one-half cent).

40. 163 U.S. at 544. The decisions cited were not only from the South; they included (at 548) *West Chester & Philadelphia Railroad Co. v. Miles* (see note 29). That decision, however, was concerned only with permitting the carrier to provide separate facilities, not with the state decision to require them—a distinction consciously blurred in the quoted passage from *Plessy*. *Miles* did rely on the argument that such separation was necessary

This passage from *Plessy* offers no account of the scope and limits of the police power, and it is written as though the statute were designed to protect the principle of freedom of association (to prevent the enforced "commingling" of the races) when its purpose and effect are the opposite: it prevents contractual freedom between the railroad and its black and/or white customers. Under the standards developed shortly thereafter in *Lochner* for economic liberties, the Louisiana statute in *Plessy* would have been doomed.

The Supreme Court in *Plessy,* however, relied on the decisions of northern state courts to justify its own position. The critical decision in this regard was *Roberts v. City of Boston,*[41] which sustained the city's operation of a system of racially segregated schools. The headnote to the opinion makes clear its scope: "The general school committee of the city of Boston have power, under the constitution and laws of this commonwealth, to make provision for the instruction of colored children, in separate schools established exclusively for them, and to prohibit their attendance upon the other schools."[42] *Roberts* predated the Civil War amendments, and Chief Justice Lemuel Shaw's opinion did not invoke the police power or the doctrine of separate but equal that grew up in its elaboration.[43] Shaw did discuss the great principle "that by the constitution and laws of Massachusetts, all persons without distinction of age or sex, birth or color, origin or condition, are equal before the law."[44] He concluded, however, that, given "the actual and various conditions of persons in society, it will not warrant the assertion, that men and women are legally clothed with the same civil and political powers, and that children and adults are legally to have the same functions and be subject to the same treatment."[45] In light of these evident difficulties, Shaw then took the line that as long as the committee deliberated honestly, anxiously, and in good faith, its decision could not be challenged in court.[46] This early set of intuitions can

---

"for the preservation of the public peace" (id. at 212), but did not pause to examine the nature or extent of the risk.

41. 59 Mass. 198 (1850). It is invoked in *Plessy,* 163 U.S. at 544.

42. 59 Mass. at 198.

43. For an exhaustive account of *Roberts,* its origins, and its consequences, see Andrew Kull, *The Color-Blind Constitution,* chs. 2 and 3 (1992). The Boston schools were desegregated by administrative action in 1855.

44. 59 Mass. at 206.

45. Id.

46. Id. at 209–210.

easily be transformed into the later pattern of constitutional adjudication. Shaw's view was that judicial deference was required in the oversight of difficult administrative decisions, and that approach fit perfectly with *Plessy*'s view that state officials were accorded broad deference under the omnipresent police power. The pattern of deference so dominant in *Plessy* had its roots in cases such as *Roberts*.

Lochner, however, points in quite a different direction. Its doctrinal significance lay in its holding that the state's police power did not allow the state to impose a maximum ten-hour workday on certain classes of bakers for the purported end of protecting their health. That ten-hour limitation on employment was held to be a "labor statute" that fell outside the permissible ends of government, and although the Court did not stress the point, the beneficiaries of the statute were not the workers but the rival bread firms (and their unions) whose employees worked shorter shifts and thus were not crimped in their operation by the statute's ten-hour-per-day limitation.

Under *Lochner,* only "labor" (that is, anticompetitive) statutes fell beyond the scope of the police power; so decisions that required railroads, for example, to bargain in good faith with majority unions were held to be outside the police power,[47] over, it must be stressed, the dissent of Justice Holmes. *Plessy* did not fall along the health-labor continuum used to organize police power cases. Rather, it assumed that race relations were, like health, proper subjects of government regulation, notwithstanding the legislation's manifest limitation on both common law rights of contract and property. *Plessy* was not a decision that celebrated vested rights under the constitutional order, nor did it enshrine or protect freedom of association. Quite the contrary. The whole area of racial relations was left to unfettered political control. The state that imposed a requirement of equal but separate accommodations could repeal that statute tomorrow. *Plessy* championed big government because it endorsed the assumption of government rectitude. *Lochner* stood for small (but not small enough) government.

Unconstitutional Conditions

Direct regulation is not the only way for a state to impose its will on its citizens. In some situations state power is exercised through grant or contract. The state owns the public railroads and may impose con-

---

47. *Adair v. United States,* 208 U.S. 161 (1908); *Coppage v. Kansas,* 236 U.S. 1 (1915).

ditions on the private parties that use them. If it has the greater power to deny the grant, then it has, or so it may be argued, the lesser power to require that the grant be accepted subject to conditions. Just that strategy had been adopted by the Court in *Railroad Co. v. Brown*[48] to explain why a railroad was required to offer integrated service to its black and white passengers. Yet the argument is in a sense too powerful for its own good, because if the state power is unfettered, then it may require as a condition of a grant that the state supply only segregated services.

Arguments of this sort had a certain credence at the turn of the century. Justice Holmes, for example, championed this analogy between private and public owners both on the Massachusetts Supreme Judicial Court[49] and on the United States Supreme Court.[50] But it has generally been rejected, usually decisively, as a matter of constitutional law, through the so-called doctrine of unconstitutional conditions.[51] Today the state, with its enormous monopoly power, does not have an absolute freedom to contract with its citizens any more than it has an absolute right to regulate them as it sees fit. In its present form this doctrine provides that the state cannot demand that individuals waive their constitutional rights in order to receive some benefit from the state.

The unconstitutional conditions doctrine was not available to protect individual rights of association after *Plessy*. To be sure, there seems to be no recorded instance after *Plessy* in which the state has enforced its segregationist policies on transportation through its power to control the use of the highways[52] or the rails. It was unnecessary to rely on a conditional grant when the general police power had clearly been made available. But the absence of a strong doctrine of unconstitutional conditions did pave the way for the state to use its control over corporate charters to impose racial segregation on private colleges. The basic rule requires all

48. 84 U.S. 445 (1873), discussed in note 31.

49. *McAuliffe v. New Bedford,* 155 Mass. 216, 29 N.E. 517 (1892).

50. *Western Union Tel. Co. v. Kansas,* 216 U.S. 1, 53 (1910) (Holmes, J., dissenting).

51. On which see generally Seth Kreimer, "Allocational Sanctions: The Problem of Negative Rights in a Positive State," 132 *U. Pa. L. Rev.* 1293 (1984). For a more detailed statement of my views, see Richard A. Epstein, "Foreword: Unconstitutional Conditions, State Power, and the Limits of Consent," 102 *Harv. L. Rev.* 4 (1988).

52. See *Frost & Frost Trucking Co. v. Railroad Commission,* 271 U.S. 583 (1926), where it was applied to limit the state power to subject a private carrier to the regulatory scheme normally applicable to a common carrier.

corporations to obtain their charters, and hence the protection of limited liability, from the state.

In *Berea College v. Kentucky*[53] the Court used the expansive view of government power over grants to crush what opposition remained to Jim Crow and segregation in the South. Berea College operated an integrated campus that offered education to black and white students on equal terms. A 1904 Kentucky statute prohibited any individual or corporation from operating an integrated campus at the same location; nonetheless, its constitutionality was sustained by the Supreme Court. As with *Plessy,* the statute in *Berea College* was a direct assault on freedom of contract and association. It was the *Lochner* line of cases, so criticized today, that was cited to the Court in an effort to strike the statute down.[54] Yet that argument foundered on two grounds. First, the ground that the police power of the state was broad enough to require separation of the races,[55] a point no more valid in this context than it was in *Plessy,* was stressed (especially in the Kentucky state proceedings). Second, it was held that the college, being in a corporate form, was dependent for its very existence on a grant from the state.[56]

In practice matters were complicated by the fact that Berea College had received its charter long before passage of the 1904 statute requiring it to maintain separate campuses for blacks and whites. Yet here the expansive "implied right" (under the police power, of course) of the state to "alter, amend or repeal" its prior charter[57] was thought sufficient to allow this regulation to be imposed "over its own corporate creatures."[58] Doctrines were championed and developed to attack large corporations, and could also be directed toward private integrated institutions. The Supreme Court thus sustained this exercise of government power against the college without addressing the question of whether the state could limit the instruction of ordinary individuals under its police power, as the Kentucky state courts had held.

As a matter of first principle that decision is surely wrong, for it wholly ignores the potential for abuse in the state exercise of its monopoly

53. 211 U.S. 45 (1908). The case is discussed in detail in Benno C. Schmidt, Jr., "Principle and Prejudice: The Supreme Court and Race in the Progressive Era," 82 *Colum. L. Rev.* 444 (1982).

54. 211 U.S. at 49 (argument for plaintiff in error).

55. Id. at 51 (argument for defendant in error).

56. Id. at 53 (argument for defendant in error).

57. Id. at 57.

58. Id. at 58.

power of incorporation. The state may decide not to incorporate anyone at all, but once the privilege of incorporation is allowed generally, it must be granted to anyone who does not abuse the corporate form.[59] The power to grant and deny incorporations should be used in ways that maximize the total value of the resources in private and public hands. To give the state the power of selective incorporation necessarily provides enormous benefits to some fortunate individuals at the expense of others who are denied the like privilege. In order, therefore, to condition the privilege, it becomes necessary to explain how the restriction in question prevents the abuse of the corporate form, much as restrictions on highway use must be justified by a showing that they prevent individual misconduct on the public highways. A statute, for example, that requires corporations to purchase insurance in order to protect tort creditors from the risk of limited liability imposes a proper condition, much like the condition that demands that all users of the roads within a state agree to be sued within that state for personal injury or property damage that occurs on its roads. The "natural law" tradition, which tends to regard corporations as voluntary associations that receive certain limited privileges from the state (for example, limited liability), speaks strongly against the massive assertion of government power that was invoked in *Berea College.*

The connection between *Berea College* and state power is revealed as well in the lone dissent of Justice Harlan, who had previously dissented in *Plessy.* In *Berea College* he saw the freedom of contract issues involved, and he knew that this case could not fall within the class of health and safety statutes. His dissent therefore relied heavily on the decision in *Allgeyer v. Louisiana,*[60] which recognized freedom of contract in the first instance, and on *Adair v. United States,*[61] which struck down a federal statute that imposed collective bargaining on the railroads and gave constitutional protection against the yellow-dog contract—an agreement by workers not to join a union as long as they worked for the employer. Once again the constitutional protections for economic liberty were invoked in a vain effort to limit the scope of the state to regulate race relations.

The internal coherence of the Harlan dissent should be contrasted with the bankrupt position of Justice Holmes. In 1881 in *The Common Law*

59. See, e.g., *First National Bank of Boston v. Bellotti,* 435 U.S. 765 (1978).
60. 165 U.S. 578 (1897).
61. 208 U.S. 161 (1908).

he had written, "The life of the law has not been logic: it has been experience."[62] But his constitutional jurisprudence revealed quite the opposite approach. His rejection of the doctrine of unconstitutional conditions rested on the dubious syllogism that since the state could grant or withhold corporate charters at will, it could grant the charter on whatever terms and conditions it saw fit. On his view it followed that there could be no obstacle to tying the use of the corporate form to the condition of ensuring racially separate instruction. With regard to the power to alter or amend existing charters, he thought it routinely within the police power of the state as well. The net effect was that he had committed himself to the side of government power on the critical issues in *Berea College*. His legal position left him no escape. Sandwiched between the decision of Justice David Brewer and the dissent of Justice Harlan was the single line: "Mr. Justice Holmes and Mr. Justice Moody concur in the result."[63]

Constitutional Counterattack and Retreat

In the period before the 1937 revolution, not all decisions gave sway to government power over race relations. Those decisions that prohibited the use of government power were of two varieties. On the one hand, some cases invalidated state rules because they did not meet the minimum guarantees of separate but equal, as when no services were provided to blacks at all. Thus, in *McCabe v. Atchison, Topeka & Santa Fe Railway*[64] an Oklahoma statute allowed the railroads to provide separate sleeping car accommodations to blacks and whites if the railroad so desired. But the statute also allowed the railroads to provide such accommodations only to whites if they did not think the demand for black cars was sufficient. This the Supreme Court struck down, and it thereby took a modest bite out of the capacity of the states to discriminate. Far from assaulting the principle of separate but equal, however, it only fortified its place within the existing constitutional order, and gave defenders of the old order a convenient way to show that the courts did not ignore blacks, who could prevail when they received no accommodations of any sort.

The more significant attack on the old regime, however, came from the perspective of strong economic liberties and private property. *Buchanan*

62. Oliver Wendell Holmes, Jr., *The Common Law* 1 (1881).
63. 211 U.S. at 58.
64. 235 U.S. 151 (1914).

v. Warley[65] involved another Kentucky- ordinance, regulating the sale of land. Under its terms black persons were forbidden to purchase or occupy homes in those blocks where the majority of houses were occupied by whites. A like restriction against sale or occupancy by whites applied to blocks where the majority of the residents were black. The case arose when a black purchaser refused to take a conveyance of property citing the ordinance, which the white seller then attacked on constitutional grounds.

Under the basic logic of the separate but equal standard, this statute should have been sustained, for there were no formal privileges accorded to whites that were not accorded to blacks as well. Nonetheless, the Court in this instance began not with the idea of parity but with the idea of property and liberty. In accordance with the analysis just outlined, the case breaks down into two parts: the prima facie violation and the state's justification under the police power. In addressing the former, the Court found that there was a taking or deprivation of property in the limitation on the owner's right to sell. The definition of property was comprehensive and covered the right "to acquire, use and dispose."[66] Those broad definitions have been compromised if not rejected under modern case law, in which the "mere regulation" of the right to dispose of property has not been regarded as a taking.

The broad definition of the property right thus forced the state to justify its restriction. In this instance the police power arguments all centered on the regulation as a means to prevent racial conflicts, to maintain racial purity, and to prevent the deterioration of property values in mixed neighborhoods. We are a long way from the control of force and fraud.

The more complex argument concerned the ostensible neutrality of the statute. Although the statute had explicit racial classification, it was "race neutral" in the sense that parallel restrictions were imposed on black and white owners and purchasers. In time the effect of the ordinance, if carried out, would have been to make every block either all black or all white. Its neutrality, however, cannot be evaluated in isolation. It was clear that the dominant political forces were white, and that the gradual separation of neighborhoods along racial lines would allow public authorities to direct money and services into white areas, to the systematic detriment of black neighborhoods. The race classifications involved were far from benevolent, and indeed had systematic insidious effects. In

65. 245 U.S. 60 (1917).
66. 245 U.S. at 74.

striking down the ordinance, the Court had to place limits on the police power and to distinguish both *Plessy* and *Berea College,* which it did. *Plessy* allowed blacks to have equal accommodation, and *Berea College* depended on the power of the state to alter or amend corporate charters. But the basic point here is far simpler. In *Buchanan* the asserted justifications of the police power are both lacking: either they address the wrong ends (for example, the maintenance of racial purity, which had previously been advanced to sustain antimiscegenation laws[67]), or they give relief far in advance of any conceivable abuse (for example, a nuisance) that might justify the police power. Arresting the occasional offender is a better way to control violence than prohibiting sales of homes to persons who have done no wrong at all. As before, the success in controlling the politics of racial domination did not required the courts to override the behavior of private individuals in markets. It was quite sufficient for them to protect markets against legislative intervention.

Notwithstanding its useful contribution, *Buchanan* could not play a dominant role in constraining local political forces intent on discriminating against blacks through public means. The decision itself reached

---

67. See *Plessy,* 163 U.S. at 545. The antimiscegenation laws were eventually struck down in *Loving v. Virginia,* 388 U.S. 1 (1967), where the Supreme Court held unanimously that statutes preventing intermarriage between white persons and persons of any other race (with an exception for the descendants of Pocahontas) violated the equal protection and the due process clauses. Unlike many of the modern Supreme Court decisions on matters of race, this case shakes out easily on *Lochner*-like lines. Marriage is a contract, and the police power justifications advanced by the state (see *Naim v. Naim,* 197 Va. 80, 87 S.E.2d 749 [1955]) are plainly worthless. The analytical difficulty in the case was that a prohibition that applies equally to whites and blacks does not appear to offend any equal protection argument. Laurence Tribe says that *Loving* spoke of a "fraudulent equality." See Tribe, *American Constitutional Law* 1480 (2nd ed., 1987). But there was surely formal, and valued, equality, and it is hard to see how there could be any disparate impact on the white and black persons who seek to marry each other.

The fuller analysis should recognize that one can understand the role of equality only against a background of substantive rights, here those to contract. The limitation on the rights may have been equal for both parties to the marriage, but the critical point is that the benefits generated were solely for strangers to the marriage contract, i.e., persons who disapprove of such marriages. There is accordingly no police power justification, rightly understood, and no just compensation for the persons so aggrieved. Hence the statute operates as an unjustified interference with contractual relations. The Supreme Court had some sense of this, for at the end of its opinion it noted that in addition to the equal protection deficiencies, the Virginia statute could be struck down for its interference with one of the "basic civil rights of man," a substantive and not an equality-based claim. See 388 U.S. at 12.

only those statutes and ordinances that contained explicit racial classifications. It did not extend to the whole range of zoning and land-use ordinances that could limit the free disposition of land in ways that prevented the development of effective low-cost housing for persons of all races. In a sense, therefore, the far more important decision for race relations was *Euclid v. Ambler Realty Co.*,[68] which on its face had nothing to do with race at all. That decision sustained a local zoning ordinance that prevented the construction of multiple-unit dwellings on large parcels of land. A consistent protection of economic liberties would have blunted the use of the zoning power in so dramatic a fashion. Zoning should be confined to the prevention of ordinary nuisances, or on limited occasion to overcoming certain collective-action problems, as with the placement of signs over public streets and sidewalks. But once the broad discretion was conferred on local governments, statutes that were facially neutral could be used to exclude vulnerable or unwelcome political groups. The modern response is to try to filter out the discriminatory uses from the legitimate ones, or to impose elaborate restrictions that require states to subsidize housing for racial groups that are systematically excluded by zoning practices.[69] Yet two wrongs do not make a right, for the unwise subsidy does not cancel out the unwise exclusion. It is far easier to control government abuse by enforcing the constitutional limitations on legislative power in the first instance.

The lesson of the early race cases should be clear. The police power exception to a wide range of constitutional protections was the vehicle that allowed local government to trample the ordinary rights of property and contract, which were as valuable to blacks as they were to whites. The pattern of abuse could not be stemmed overnight even after the early decisions were reversed. Instead, the mistakes of constitutional passivity created a situation of near-crisis proportions to which there were no obvious answers, given that it became necessary to undo past wrongs while simultaneously fashioning policy to guide future interactions. The next chapter traces the original response starting with the 1937 constitutional revolution and moving forward to the Civil Rights Act of 1964.

68. 272 U.S. 365 (1926).

69. See *Southern Burlington County NAACP v. Mount Laurel,* 67 N.J. 151, 336 A.2d 713 (1975), setting in motion a mass of litigation that is still active today.

CHAPTER 6

From the 1937 Revolution to the 1964 Civil Rights Act

The Changing Regulatory Environment
from *Carolene Products* to *Brown*

The previous chapter is intended to show the close connection between the constitutional protection of property rights and the protection of members of minority groups. Where deference to political authority was exercised under the police power, state-sponsored discrimination against blacks flourished. Where individual property rights were protected to a modest extent, discrimination was limited. Before the 1937 constitutional watershed, the Supreme Court had a dismal record on race relations: the few rays of light emanated from its property rights decisions. Yet ironically, during the early New Deal period property rights were stripped of their basic constitutional protection. The dominant criticism of the Old Court was directed not at its passive constitutional performance in the race cases but rather at its modest interventionist posture on matters of economic liberty. The first order of business under the new constitutional regime was the removal of the remaining restrictions on the scope of government power, state or federal, in economic affairs. Initially this was done by the eradication of the once critical line between health and safety on the one hand and labor statutes on the other.[1] In the Court's view, the citizens and workers who could not protect themselves by contract from health risks were held by an easy process of extension to be equally at peril with respect to economic risks. Maximum price, maximum hour, and minimum wage laws (even those that applied to women only) thus

---

1. See, e.g., *Nebbia v. New York*, 291 U.S. 502 (1934); *West Coast Hotel Co. v. Parrish*, 300 U.S. 379 (1937).

became constitutionally permissible at both the state and the federal level. Closer to home, the institution of collective bargaining, which had been struck down in the first part of the century in the yellow-dog contract cases (again at both state and federal levels),[2] was now upheld against constitutional challenges based on theories of liberty of contract.[3] The pattern of judicial deference appeared to hold across the board. As the 1937 revolution wound down, it looked as though the courts had withdrawn constitutional scrutiny from all areas of government regulation.

That hiatus proved to be a short one, however. In the next year, in its famous fourth footnote to the *Carolene Products* case,[4] the Supreme Court sought to set out the conditions under which some form of heightened scrutiny was appropriate in the judicial review of legislative action. The note made reference to the close connection between the level of judicial review and the operation of the political process. Where the political process left "discrete and insular minorities" at the mercy of legislative majorities, judicial intervention was needed to correct the imperfections of the political order. In principle the formulation in *Carolene Products* was sufficient to justify the striking down of the max-

2. *Adair v. United States,* 208 U.S. 161 (1908); *Coppage v. Kansas,* 236 U.S. 1 (1915).

3. See *National Labor Relations Board v. Jones & Laughlin Steel Corp.,* 301 U.S. 1 (1937).

4. *United States v. Carolene Products Co.,* 304 U.S. 144, 152 n.4 (1938): "There may be narrower scope for operation of the presumption of constitutionality when legislation appears on its face to be within a specific prohibition of the Constitution, such as those of the first ten amendments, which are deemed equally specific when held to be embraced within the Fourteenth . . .

"It is unnecessary to consider now whether legislation which restricts those political processes which can ordinarily be expected to bring about repeal of undesirable legislation, is to be subjected to more exacting judicial scrutiny under the general prohibitions of the Fourteenth Amendment than are most other types of legislation. On restrictions upon the right to vote, see *Nixon v. Herndon,* 273 U.S. 536; *Nixon v. Condon,* 286 U.S. 73; on restraints upon the dissemination of information, see *Near v. Minnesota,* ex rel. Olson, 283 U.S. 697; on interference with political organizations, see *Stromberg v. California,* 283 U.S. 359; on prohibition of peaceable assembly, see *De Jonge v. Oregon,* 299 U.S. 353, 365: "Nor need we enquire whether similar considerations enter into the review of statutes directed at particular religious, . . . national, . . . or racial minorities; whether prejudice against discrete and insular minorities . . . may be a special condition, which tends seriously to curtail the operation of those political processes ordinarily to be relied upon to protect minorities, and which may call for a correspondingly more searching judicial inquiry."

See generally Bruce A. Ackerman, "Beyond *Carolene Products,*" 98 *Harv. L. Rev.* 713 (1985); Geoffrey P. Miller, "The True Story of *Carolene Products,*" 1987 *Sup. Ct. Rev.* 397.

imum hour legislation in *Lochner,* which had left immigrant German bakers to the mercy of their more established unionized rivals. Modern theories of public choice were not applied, however, to the basic economic matters from which constitutional review had just been withdrawn. The core of good sense in *Carolene Products* did carry over to other areas, such as the First Amendment rights to participate in the political process. It also applied to race relations, where a substantial fraction of individuals were denied all access to the political process through state manipulation and control over the voting franchise—itself a development not attacked systematically and effectively by Congress until Title I of the 1964 Civil Rights Act.

It is unnecessary to trace in any detail the growing judicial awareness that southern political institutions could not be counted on to correct their own governmental misconduct. The white primary cases[5] and the attack on separate but equal schools have been recounted many times. The decision in *Brown v. Board of Education*[6] was the welcome culmination of a direct judicial assault on state systems of political manipulation and oppression against blacks in the South and, to a lesser extent, in the North as well. The massive intervention seemed strange to many commentators,[7] but only because they had been raised on the judicial orthodoxy of the New Deal, which held that courts should not act as "superlegislators" in reviewing state economic regulation. The difficulty judges faced in striking down the segregated school system in *Brown* would have been much reduced if they had hewed to the *Lochner* line of cases, because it would no longer have seemed aberrant for federal judges to strike down state laws.

Post–New Deal Protection of Employment Discrimination

Collective Bargaining

The 1937 constitutional watershed also left a powerful legacy in the area of racial discrimination. One direct consequence of the 1937 cases was to

---

5. See, e.g., *Nixon v. Herndon,* 273 U.S. 536 (1927) (striking down exclusion of blacks from state primary elections); *Grovey v. Townsend,* 295 U.S. 45 (1935) (upholding white primaries organized by Democratic party); *Smith v. Allwright,* 321 U.S. 649 (1944) (striking down white primaries; overruling *Grovey).*

6. 347 U.S. 483 (1954).

7. See, e.g., Herbert Wechsler, "Toward Neutral Principles of Constitutional Law," 73 *Harv. L. Rev.* 1 (1959).

legitimate minimum wage, maximum hour, and collective bargaining legislation. The theory of the collective bargaining statutes was that the government could require any employer to negotiate "in good faith" with a union chosen by a majority of the workers in any bargaining unit that had been designated by administrative procedures.[8] In essence the system makes it impossible for workers to underbid one another in the quest for jobs, and hence allows a group of like-minded workers to cartelize themselves in the effort to raise their wages above the competitive level. The system of mandatory collective bargaining had been held unconstitutional in earlier eras because of its interference with the employer's (and employees') freedom of contract in ways not justified under the police power.[9] Those decisions were, in my view, correct, for competitive markets work neither a nuisance nor a deception on the public at large, which benefits from goods produced under competitive labor conditions.[10] Collective bargaining has solidified by force of law the monopolistic position of a dominant union. By pitting union against employer, it sets the stage for extensive negotiation over the division of gains between the two sides, as well as (a critical point) the division of employee gains among the workers represented by the union.

These liberty of contract arguments against the labor statutes fell on deaf ears in the New Deal period, where the general affection for industrywide cartels carried over to labor unions as well. In particular, the early decisions of the Supreme Court in the area of labor went out of their way to emphasize the dominance that the union enjoyed as sole representative of the workers. Historically, statutory regimes for compulsory collective bargaining by majority unions were found not only in the National Labor Relations Act (NLRA)[11] but also in the earlier (1926) Railway Labor Act (RLA).[12]

8. See National Labor Relations Act, 29 *U.S.C.* §157 (1982).

9. See, e.g., *Adair v. United States,* 208 U.S. 161; *Coppage v. Kansas,* 236 U.S. 1. There is of course no objection if the employer decides to confer by contract exclusive bargaining rights on a particular union.

10. See Richard A. Epstein, "A Common Law for Labor Relations: A Critique of the New Deal Labor Legislation," 92 *Yale L. J.* 1357 (1983).

11. 29 *U.S.C.* §§151–169 (1982).

12. Railway Labor Act, 44 Stat. 577 (1926), codified and amended at 45 *U.S.C.* §§151–163 (1982). The statute continues in operation, and today governs both the railroads and (since 1936) the airlines. For a general description of its provisions, see Katherine Van Wezel Stone, "Labor Relations on the Airlines: The Railway Labor Act in an Era of Deregulation," 42 *Stan. L. Rev.* 1485, 1494–1500 (1990).

One critical question raised by both statutory schemes concerned the level of individual control over the employment contract after the union had been designated representative of the bargaining unit. In *J. I. Case Co. v. National Labor Relations Board*,[13] the Court, speaking through Justice Robert Jackson, opted squarely in favor of dominant union control over the bargaining process. The precise issue in the case was whether individual contracts negotiated between the employer and individual workers prior to the certification of a union, and which by their terms had not expired, remained enforceable after the union became the bargaining agent. The judicial answer was clear: even where the individual worker had secured a contract more favorable than those the union had bargained for, its provisions could not be enforced. The language admits little doubt: "The practice and philosophy of collective bargaining looks with suspicion on such individual advantages."[14] The Court added: "The workman is free, if he values his own bargaining position more than that of the group, to vote against representation; but the majority rules, and if it collectivizes the employment bargain, individual advantages or favors will generally in practice go in as a contribution to the collective result. We cannot except individual contracts generally from the operation of collective ones because some may be more individually advantageous."[15]

The apparent effect of *J. I. Case* was to make the union the sole and final arbiter of conflicts of interest among members of the bargaining unit. Although the opinion of Justice Jackson speaks only in terms of the individual workman, the point is especially critical when the same union contains workers from different factions, or workers drawn from different races. The very existence of a union implies that the total wage package is superior to that which the workers could obtain in a competitive market. The union therefore has some discretion in the way in which the supracompetitive element of wages will be allocated among its members. In principle, for example, the premium extracted from management could be allocated pro rata among the union members. That result is stable in the sense that no individual employee will find it in his or her interest to leave the bargaining unit for other employment. Nonetheless, if the return to some class of workers were reduced, say, to a competitive level (or perhaps even a little bit lower, given the costs of leaving), they would still be better off in keeping their present jobs than looking for

13. 321 U.S. 332 (1944).
14. Id. at 338.
15. Id. at 339.

employment elsewhere. Hence, there is no unique allocation of the monopoly gain. If, moreover, the entire industry were unionized, disappointed workers might find it even more difficult to obtain work elsewhere; thus the fraction of the total wage package that could be reallocated to a dominant faction is increased without causing defection by the disadvantaged workers. The size of the differentials at stake may seem small, but where monopoly power is pronounced, it could be very substantial indeed. Discriminatory wage schedules could not survive in competitive markets because the newer workers would force the established workers to lower their rates to keep their employment. These contracts, however, were negotiated under the union structure of restricted entry that made this pay scale possible.

The bargaining structure created by the NLRA and the RLA is one in which a monopoly organization possesses the power to discriminate in the wages it pays its members. *J. I. Case* showed that the Supreme Court did not want to oversee those intraunion disputes once the collective bargaining structure was in place. That message was quickly grasped by the Alabama Supreme Court in *Steele v. Louisville & Nashville Railroad Co.*,[16] which turned the principle of collective rule to far different ends from those originally contemplated. *Steele* arose under the collective bargaining provisions of the RLA. The designated bargaining representative for all firemen was the Brotherhood of Locomotive Firemen and Enginemen, an all-white organization which had power to bargain on behalf of the black firemen who worked for the railroad. As part of its demands in 1929, the union served notice on the employer that it wished to renegotiate the master employment agreement with a view toward eliminating all blacks from preferred positions on the line; preventing blacks from taking firemen positions, from which they could be promoted to engineers; and finally stripping black firemen who had done their work well of their desirable positions in the so-called passenger pool and replacing them with white firemen junior in terms of service and no more competent than the black firemen they would replace. The goal was to squeeze black workers by relegating them to the most marginal jobs. In a manner consistent with this strategy, the black firemen were never consulted before the contract negotiations went forward between the union and the railroad, and their loud protests once the agreement was concluded went unanswered. The Alabama Supreme Court did nothing to overturn the negotiated settlement; the United States Supreme Court set

16. 245 Ala. 113, 16 So.2d 416 (1943).

the agreement aside because of the union's breach of its duty of fair representation to its black members under the RLA. What happened and why?

The entire pattern of negotiation was driven by the most overt forms of racism, but it would be a mistake to argue that poor racial attitudes alone explained the set of union and railroad moves made under the RLA. Racial attitudes were as bad before the passage of the RLA in 1926 as they were after it, and it was also apparent that the labor unions were segregated by race. The RLA did not transform racial attitudes, but it did change the balance of power by giving the white majority total control over the choices of both black workers and the railroads. The white majority had less leverage under the system of multiple unions which was in place prior to the passage of the RLA. Before the statute, the white majority would have found it more difficult to exploit the passions and prejudices of the moment, because each worker, black or white, had the right to negotiate individual contracts on his own behalf, or to bargain through a voluntary union of his own choosing—even one whose members were of a single race. Monopoly power breathed new life into old racial prejudices, and the radical shift in the contract provisions offers unmistakable testimony on the extent to which bargaining structures determine bargaining outcomes.

The Alabama Supreme Court had no difficulty in preserving the power that the RLA conferred on the white majority. Its position was that the "custom" of the trade was to keep blacks in subordinate positions, and it then concluded that the labor contract was "a lawful contract entered into in a lawful manner."[17] This custom did not, however, operate in a void. It became the law of the bargaining agreement only in 1929, three years after the passage of the RLA. In general, custom is the most powerful evidence of efficient contracts and efficient safety rules.[18] Where the parties are silent about matters of mutual concern, courts do far better

17. Id. at 122.

18. In this connection, Learned Hand's opinion in *The T. J. Hooper,* 60 F.2d 737 (2nd Cir. 1932), famous for its aphorism "a whole calling may have unduly lagged in the adoption of new and available devices," is one of the most mischievous opinions in the tort law because it assumes that consensual judgments may routinely be inferior to the ex post judgments rendered by judges and juries. The decision thus removes a huge portion of personal injury and property damage cases from the realm of contract into the realm of tort, where they are subject to highly complex cost-benefit analyses that are difficult to understand and easy to misapply. For criticism of the new movement toward balancing tests, see Richard A. Epstein, "The Risks of Risk/Utility," 48 *Ohio St. L. J.* 469 (1987).

when they rely on the wisdom of the trade or practice instead of their own. But the limits of this principle are as important as the principle itself. Custom is an excellent criterion where the harms generated by the practice do not fall on *strangers*. But a tenacious custom among the members of group A to pollute the waters owned by group B has a wholly different status from that of a custom whereby members of group A must themselves suffer in proportion to the share of the pollution they generate. *Steele* involves customs that seek to bind strangers. That "custom" should have no effect at all.

The language quoted in *J. I. Case,* however, renders any appeal to custom quite beside the point. Its steadfast adherence to the dominance of majority rule should in principle be sufficient to justify the decision of the Alabama court, and to doom the claim of the black workers under the RLA. By the same token, if that conclusion is sustained, then the defective, and perhaps immoral, structure of the collective bargaining statute is revealed as well. Government power was not sufficient in *Buchanan v. Warley*[19] to allow majority rule to restrain the alienation of property of any single individual. That form of majority oppression fares no better when it seeks to restrain the alienation of labor. The black-white division exploited in *Steele* is the most vivid illustration of the schism that can take place within a union structure, but it is not the only one. The plaintiff's plight in *Steele* should have led the Supreme Court to reconsider its earlier decisions to allow collective bargaining as a constitutional matter. But the New Deal consensus on the curtailment of economic liberties was as solid as ever in 1944, as the Court was busy hammering out the rules of judicial deference which in general gave broad scope to the administrative state.[20] The Court therefore took some liberties with the text of the statute, which was silent on the issue of union fiduciary duties, and imported into the RLA a duty of "fair representation" (subsequently carried over to the NLRA) which prohibited discrimination between workers on the grounds of race.

> So long as a labor union assumes to act as the statutory representative
> of a craft, it cannot rightly refuse to perform the duty, which is insepa-

---

The same attack on private ordering is a necessary prerequisite to the antidiscrimination laws as well.

19. 245 U.S. 60 (1917), discussed in Chapter 5 under the heading "Constitutional Counterattack and Retreat."

20. See, e.g., *Parker v. Brown,* 317 U.S. 341 (1943); *Federal Power Commission v. Hope Natural Gas Co.,* 320 U.S. 591 (1944).

rable from the power of representation conferred upon it, to represent the entire membership of the craft. While the statute does not deny to such a bargaining labor organization the right to determine eligibility to its membership, it does require the union, in collective bargaining and in making contracts with the carrier, to represent non-union or minority union members of the craft without hostile discrimination, fairly, impartially, and in good faith.[21]

The pattern of argument is thus a familiar one. The duty against discrimination is created by deft judicial construction in order to soften the scope of government-created monopoly power. This approach offers a strictly second-best solution, but one that is absolutely necessary where the monopoly position is itself impregnable. The repeal of the RLA would return the situation to the competitive market, and in so doing would obviate the need for any duty of fair representation. This duty, though a necessary corrective for the excesses of union power, still leaves black workers far more exposed to the wishes of a hostile white majority than they would be if they could bargain free from the constraints of any collective bargaining system at all. Nothing in *Steele* required the white craft unions to open their membership to blacks, so white workers hostile to black interests could still choose the fiduciaries responsible for protecting black interests without violating their statutory duties. Black workers would not have selected those leaders voluntarily by contract. If the levers of power remain in hostile hands, disenfranchised black workers will find it difficult to protect themselves against the thousands of opportunities for decisions, small and large, public and covert, that union management could seize on to disadvantage them.

Even if the duty of fair representation prevents some of the most obvious forms of racial discrimination, many opportunities remain for ostensibly neutral rules to impose disproportionate losses on black workers, given the costs of fashioning an effective legal remedy. Unions negotiate job, seniority, and salary classifications; they press individual grievances; they make critical decisions on whether to strike and whether to fight subcontracting and plant closing. The very structure of the law confers on union leadership a substantial degree of discretion that one would want to vest only in a friendly fiduciary, for which a duty of fair representation is a poor substitute at best. Over time, racial divisions have

21. *Steele v. Louisville & Nashville Railroad*, 323 U.S 192, 204 (1944).

become less potent with the shift in union membership and changes in the external environment. Other issues (for example, foreign competition) have moved to the top of the union agenda. But as recently as the early 1950s more than a score of unions had white-only membership provisions and monopoly bargaining power vis-à-vis black workers and their employers.[22] Second-best solutions are often weak substitutes for best ones.

Is the Minimum Wage Really Neutral?

The limitations on employment markets tolerated in the aftermath of the New Deal were not limited to union operations but also included the minimum wage laws. Indeed, during the course of the debates over the 1964 Civil Rights Act, Senator Hubert H. Humphrey among others observed that the power of the Congress to regulate public accommodations and employment was beyond doubt, given its powers to impose minimum wages and mandate collective bargaining.[23] But again the irony is manifest. It is the very existence of the minimum wage law that increases the incentive of the employer to discriminate against blacks or other workers whose low skill levels leave them at the fringes of the economic market. In seeking workers whose value to the firm is above the minimum wage, the employer is likely to turn to white or other workers with more education or experience. Predictably, the minimum wage laws have a disproportionate effect on black workers, especially those at the margin. It is, moreover, highly unlikely that the antidiscrimination principle could protect the black workers from the minimum wage, even with the fitful success of *Steele,* for its adverse effects depend not on the arbitrary use of union power within the plant setting but on the foreseeable consequences of the statute itself. Defenders of the antidiscrimination laws in employment have noted the close connection between the antidiscrimination law and other forms of regulation. As Owen Fiss has

22. "He [Senator Griswold] particularly asked about discrimination on the part of unions. It happens that the Bureau of Labor Statistics made a study some years ago which they now haven't in publication, but which is available. It shows that there were 17 A.F. of L. unions which still have in their constitutions that a man must be Caucasian, white, 21 and of good character in order to be a member." Statement of Mr. Edgar G. Brown, Director, National Negro Council, Hearings before the Subcommittee on Civil Rights on S. 692 (A Bill to Prohibit Discrimination in Employment because of Race, Color, Religion, National Origin, or Ancestry).

23. 110 Cong. Rec. 4824 (1964).

written: "One irony is that the need for a fair employment law arises in part from the existence of other laws (such as minimum wage laws, laws protecting union hiring halls, laws limiting profit levels, and laws limiting entry) that impair the effectiveness of the market; by interfering with the market, these laws impair the capacity of the merit principle to protect itself."[24]

The situation as it existed before the passage of the 1964 statutes evidently did not represent the ideal competitive labor market.[25] There were extensive limitations on the ability to enter all forms of markets. Worse still, many of the statutes that were part of the general New Deal labor program were at cross-purposes with the ideal of securing higher levels of black participation in the marketplace. A neutral minimum wage law operates like a neutral zoning principle: both can have adverse effects on discrete portions of the population.[26] And both mistakes are best removed by repeal, not by the superimposition of an antidiscrimination law on top of an existing set of misguided regulations.

Public Accommodations and the Barriers to Entry

In order to understand the historical setting for the civil rights laws, it is necessary to comment as well on the public accommodations sections of the statute, which were more widely discussed both in the Congress and by the public at large.[27] There were innumerable horror stories of blacks who had to plan their trips throughout the South with the knowledge that they could find eating and sleeping accommodations only at widely distant points. One could try to attribute this pattern of exclusion and humiliation to the market, but it seems highly unlikely that so large a

24. Owen M. Fiss, "A Theory of Fair Employment Laws," 38 *U. Chi. L. Rev.* 235, 251–252 (1971).

25. For the empirical evidence against the minimum wage, see Richard B. McKenzie, *The American Job Machine* 198–217 (1988), and studies he cites (n. 19). The Davis-Bacon Act, 40 *U.S.C.* §276a-c (1988), has had a similar effect. See Chapter 2, note 22.

26. For a contemporary account, see "Where Wage-Fixing Keeps Kids Idle," *Nation's Business* 34 (July 1965). "Hopkinsville, Ky., dropped plans to put needy youngsters to work on school grounds and in cafeterias under the Administration's antipoverty program after the Labor Department insisted that they receive the federal minimum wage, above the going rate for regular employees." Id. at 34. The applicable minimum wage was $1.25. Even when the money was paid by the federal government, the programs were turned down because of their ratchet effect on noncovered workers.

27. See, for a balanced account, Leslie A. Carothers, *The Public Accommodations Law of 1964: Arguments, Issues, and Attitudes in a Legal Debate* (1968).

demand for services would have gone unsatisfied if free entry had been preserved in the hotel and restaurant businesses. Someone could have made a fortune catering solely to blacks who were kept out of the white hotels that adopted segregationist policies. Yet if one looks at the barriers to entry that existed from the strong government control over land use, labor relations, zoning, and police protection, and the full apparatus of segregation, it is possible to see why no one came forward to provide such accommodations. No firm could have entered the market in the face of the political forces that were arrayed against it. The dog that did not bark gives the best evidence of pervasive government involvement in this area.

In this context the antidiscrimination principle could work wonders as a second-best solution. The ability of the federal government to eliminate all local barriers to entry was very weak prior to the passage of Title II. The simple expedient of demanding that all public accommodations be opened to black and white alike was, and is, easy to enforce, notwithstanding the dire predictions that the law would require the establishment of an extensive police state.[28] Title II thus provided powerful protection to the mass of private firms that wanted to escape the clutches of local restrictions and local prejudices but could not. Although our most dramatic recollections about the enforcement of Title II in 1964 revolve around the few establishments that defied the law, the basic pattern was one of ready compliance from the outset. National firms were eager to shed local restrictions that were an embarrassment to them in their wider markets. The early instances of noncompliance all arose when individual firms, eager to obey the law, found themselves set upon by gangs of racists determined to shut them down by brute force.[29]

It has been suggested that civil rights statutes are necessary to overcome the prisoner's dilemma that would otherwise prevent businesses from integrating their customers. In line with the traditional pattern, the argu-

28. See, e.g., reference of Governor George Wallace to the "army of federal agents" necessary to enforce the law. United States congress, Senate Hearing on S. 1732 (civil rights), vol. 1 (1964) at 315.

29. See, e.g., *Time,* August 14, 1964 at 51, in a story called "Hoss Unhorsed," which begins: "In St. Augustine, Fla., most of the previously white-only motels and restaurants began serving Negroes as soon as the Civil Rights Act became law. The owners wanted peace; racial violence already had cut the tourist trade by 50%. Yet a few days later, most places were resegregated. An army of white racists, the owners said, had forced them to lock out Negroes once more on pain of assault or worse."

ment goes as follows: Each establishment would prefer to open its doors to black customers, but fears the loss of business from rival establishments that did not. If all these establishments could coordinate their activities, then discrimination would no longer be practiced by any of them. But since they cannot, the older patterns of doing business persist in the unregulated market.

A prisoner's dilemma problem did exist, but it had nothing to do with customers or an ostensible failure of markets. Any firm that defects from the once dominant position (that is, no integration) will make huge profits if other firms do not follow. The rigidity of its rivals gives it a critical market niche. The innovating firm need not fear its inability to coordinate its activities with others', but may well profit if its rivals decide to coordinate their decision not to follow suit. The coordination problems loom far more ominous, however, when merchants are confronted by gangs bent on violence if they break the dominant norm. Any firm that defies the convention on its own is singled out for swift retribution while the others stand passively aside.

In the Old South Title II was needed to overcome the coordination problem. But it was not a problem of the market. It was brought on by the selective use of private force to interfere with ordinary common law rights of trade. It is not surprising, therefore, that, after an initial constitutional flurry of litigation, the law of public accommodations could be described as "ancient history."[30] The deviation between what the statute requires and what people want is too small to be of any real consequence, so the levels of compliance are high

---

30. "Today, many then-controversial provisions of the Civil Rights Act of 1964—those relating to public accommodations, for example—are observed so universally that they are ancient history, of no concern to anyone in the workaday world. Title VII, in contrast, is a mighty engine that is gradually forcing the alterations of the employment practices of a nation in innumerable ways." Norbert A. Schlei, foreword to Barbara L. Schlei and Paul Grossman, *Employment Discrimination Law* xii (2nd ed., 1983).

The contemporary passions over the issue were far more heated. As one author noted: "Discrimination in public accommodations may seem to be the least important problem in the long run, when compared to the right to vote or chance at a better education and a decent job. However, the most direct confrontation of the competing interests of discriminators and Negroes has occurred in this arena. Friction between proprietors claiming the right to serve whom they please on their own premises and Negroes claiming the right to be served in a public place has led to violence and arrest." Leslie A. Carothers, *The Public Accommodations Law of 1964: Arguments, Issues, and Attitudes in a Legal Debate* xiv (1968). So much have the passions abated that virtually none of my younger colleagues knew when asked what topic was covered by Title II of the 1964 act.

without enforcement. But employment relations are quite a different story, as is evidenced by litigation that has mushroomed far beyond what anyone, friend or foe, predicted in 1964. Before we turn to the statute itself, however, let us examine the unsuccessful, indeed futile, challenges to its constitutionality which were mounted shortly after its passage.

CHAPTER 7

Constitutional Challenges to the 1964 Civil Rights Act

The Civil Rights Act of 1964 was passed against the backdrop of some lingering uncertainty about whether Congress had the power to legislate over public accommodations and employment discrimination. The conventional analysis identified two possible sources of power to support the statute. The first was the Civil War amendments, and the second was the commerce power. Each line of argument presents its own distinctive possibilities and difficulties.

The Civil War Amendments

The Thirteenth and Fourteenth Amendments were passed in the aftermath of the Civil War, and they remain one major source of federal authority over the states.[1] As drafted, however, both amendments are problematic sources of federal power to enact a general antidiscrimination law applicable to the actions of private parties. The prohibitions of both amendments are on their face directed toward actions undertaken by the states themselves. By negative implication they do not appear to reach any decisions made by private parties, whatever the grounds on

---

1. Amendment XIII, section 1: "Neither slavery nor involuntary servitude, except as a punishment for crime whereof the party shall have been duly convicted, shall exist within the United States, or any place subject to their jurisdiction."

Section 2: "Congress shall have power to enforce this article by appropriate legislation."

Amendment XIV, section 1: "All persons born or naturalized in the United States, and subject to the jurisdiction thereof, are citizens of the United States and of the State wherein they reside. No State shall make or enforce any law which shall abridge the privileges or immunities of citizens of the United States; nor shall any State deprive any person of life, liberty, or property, without due process of law; nor deny to any person within its jurisdiction the equal protection of laws."

Section 5: "The Congress shall have power to enforce, by appropriate legislation, the provisions of this article."

which those decisions rest. In some cases there may be a question of drawing the line as to whether certain decisions have been made by the state or by private parties: a state collective bargaining statute that confers on a union a legal monopoly is one such example. But as a first approximation most businesses operate not under the protection of a legal monopoly but only with the ordinary protections that are afforded by the law of property, contract, and tort. To say that the receipt of these legal protections converts private decision into state action does away with any distinction between state and private action, and thus undermines the same legal regime of private rights that the Civil War amendments sought to protect. The amendments are directed toward state enforcement, state deprivations, and state denials. The actions of private parties fall outside their scope.

It was just this state action objection that doomed the Civil Rights Act of 1875 on public accommodations, passed near the end of the Reconstruction period. That statute provided that all persons were "entitled to the full and equal enjoyment of the accommodations, advantages, facilities, and privileges of inns, public conveyances on land or water, theaters, and other places of public amusement; subject only to the conditions and limitations established by law, and applicable alike to citizens of every race and color, regardless of any previous condition of servitude."[2]

That statute was struck down in 1883 in *The Civil Rights Cases*[3] by an eight-to-one vote, with only Justice Harlan dissenting. The amendment was directed to the abuses of state actors. The legislative power conferred on Congress in the fifth section of the Fourteenth Amendment did not expand the class of permissible objects to which the first section of that amendment applied. The Congress, therefore, had only the power

> to adopt appropriate legislation for correcting the effects of such prohibited State laws and State acts, and thus to render them effectually null, void and innocuous . . . It does not invest Congress with power to legislate upon subjects which are within the domain of State legislation, or State action, of the kind referred to. It does not authorize Congress to create a code of municipal law for the regulation of private rights; but to provide modes of redress against the operation of State laws, and the

2. Act of 1875, ch. 114, §1, 18 Stat. 335.
3. 109 U.S. 3 (1883).

action of State officers executive or judicial, when these are subversive of the fundamental rights specified in the amendment.[4]

That analysis seems as correct today as the day it was written.[5] The dissent of Justice Harlan, although it contains much impassioned rhetoric, does not (in contrast to his views in *Plessy v. Ferguson*)[6] meet the textual and structural objections. Harlan, relying on the first sentence of the Fourteenth Amendment, argued that the mere fact that all persons within the jurisdiction enjoyed the rights of citizens of the United States empowered the Congress to pass any laws necessary to protect them against private discrimination. But the argument surely proves too much, if only because it renders superfluous all of the particular restrictions on state governments found in the second sentence of the same amendment, with its specific substantive guarantees.[7]

Justice Harlan also took a second line of argument: "In every material sense applicable to the practical enforcement of the Fourteenth Amendment, railroad corporations, keepers of inns, and managers of places of public amusement are agents or instrumentalities of the state, because they are charged with duties to the public and are amenable, in respect of their duties and functions, to governmental regulation."[8] But again his argument proves far too much, for state regulation of health and safety was commonplace in 1875, just as it is today. There is no reason to think that one form of state regulation is tantamount to the nationalization of the industry so regulated; this is to conflate the decisions made by the officers in charge of the regulated firm with the decisions of the state regulators. The critical question is whether the state by its regulation makes the decision to exclude blacks or other groups on grounds of race. State regulation of one area of private conduct does not transform the independent decisions of the regulated parties into state decisions, especially when, to use Justice Joseph Bradley's apt phrase, the private party proceeds "without any sanction or support from any State law or regulation."[9]

---

4. Id. at 11.
5. See, for a defense of the decision, David P. Currie, *The Constitution in the Supreme Court: The First Hundred Years, 1789–1888* 398–402 (1985); for criticism, see generally Charles Lofgren, *The Plessy Case* 70–76 (1987).
6. See Chapter 5 at 91–94, under the heading "A Morality Play."
7. See note 1.
8. *The Civil Rights Cases,* 109 U.S. at 58–59.
9. Id. at 23.

This last qualification returns us to the general issue with which this book is preoccupied, for a respectable case can be made to show such sanction and support where the state law provides formal barriers to entry which confer a substantial level of monopoly status on the railroads, inns, and places of amusement covered by the statute. The point could be fortified if it were shown that the firms so protected acted in concert with one another, so that consumers faced not a marketplace of separate suppliers but a single entrenched cordon of like-minded firms. Nonetheless, that facet of the case was not developed at all in *The Civil Rights Cases*. There was no reason to assume that all the private establishments covered by the act had received the requisite level of government protection, or that Congress sought to identify which particular institutions might have been so protected, when the rise of Jim Crow lay more than a decade in the future. Making a case of sanction and support requires digging into the facts of particular cases, and is wholly unsuited for any facial attack on (or defense of) the statute. It is easy to understand why the advocates of the Civil Rights Act would not have wanted to mount so particularistic a defense. To do so would have been to cripple the statute's across-the-board application, for then each firm could have insisted that its own decisions were self-generated, wholly without regard to any possible barriers to entry created under state law. To gain constitutional validation on so dense a factual theory is to fritter away the benefits that the universal statutory language sought to provide. It was better, perhaps, to defend the statute on its face, and fail, than to make a stronger argument that yielded so small a payoff. Harlan's comprehensive defense of the statute, then, was heroic but wrong.

Finally, Justice Harlan took the position that the first sentence of the Fourteenth Amendment gave blacks the same rights as ordinary white citizens. "Citizenship in this country necessarily imports at least equality of civil rights among citizens of every race in the same State."[10] So it does; but the proposition is perfectly consistent with the observation that every private person is entitled to deal with whomever he wants on whatever terms he sees fit. White people can discriminate against blacks, or (in the name of diversity or affirmative action) blacks can discriminate against whites if they so choose. There is nothing in a general commitment to equality before the law that compels adoption of an antidiscrimination norm applicable to both public and private persons alike. The early natural lawyers were as committed as anyone else to a free, equal, and inde-

10. Id. at 48.

pendent citizenry, but it was the universal liberty to own and contract that held their fancy, not the antidiscrimination norm of a civil rights statute.

The natural law tradition is, moreover, reflected in another general statute—the Civil Rights Act of 1866—which on any fair reading holds that blacks are entitled to the same class of civil rights as whites. All citizens of the United States "shall have the same right, in every State and Territory, to make and enforce contracts, to sue, to be parties, to give evidence, to inherit, purchase, lease, sell, hold and convey real and personal property, and to the full and equal benefit of all laws and proceedings for the security of person and property, as is enjoyed by white citizens."[11] The difference in world views between the 1866 act the 1875 act seems too vast to require much comment. The former deals with civil capacity and the latter with discrimination. Nonetheless, the Supreme Court in *Jones v. Mayer Co.*[12] performed a dubious tour de force of constitutional misconstruction in upholding the 1866 act under the Thirteenth Amendment as a proper attempt to remove all the "badges and incidents" of slavery.[13] The irony could not be more palpable, given that the antithesis of slavery is not an antidiscrimination statute but the freedom of association and choice repudiated by the Supreme Court's construction in *Jones*. Justice Potter Stewart, writing for the Court in *Jones,* is correct that the statutory language is "plain and unambiguous."[14] But he then gives us what is blatantly the wrong interpretation by treating it as a general antidiscrimination law when the statute is actually consistent with a uniform regime of free choice for all persons: as long as whites have the right to discriminate against whites or blacks, then blacks have the same right, that is, to discriminate against either whites or blacks or both. When Congress wanted to pass an antidiscrimination statute, most notably the Civil Rights Act of 1875, it knew how to draft one. In contrast the 1866 statute reads like the women's property statutes of the same period.[15] The evil to which the statute was directed was a wrong

11. Section 1 of the Civil Rights Act of 1866, 14 Stat. 27., codified at 42 *U.S.C.* §1982.

12. 392 U.S. 409 (1968). See Gerhard Casper, "*Jones v. Mayer:* Clio, Bemused and Confused Muse," 1968 *Sup. Ct. Rev.* 89, for a detailed analysis of the case.

13. *Jones,* 392 U.S. at 439–441.

14. Id. at 420.

15. See generally Richard H. Chused, "Late-Nineteenth-Century Women's Property Law: Reception of the Early Married Women's Property Acts by Courts and Legislatures," 29 *Am. J. Leg. Hist.* 3 (1985). The effect of the general statutes was summarized in Jesse Dukeminier and James Krier, *Property* (2nd ed., 1988): "These statutes removed the disabil-

committed by the state, its systematic denial of ordinary civil capacity. Its target was not private discrimination.

For better or worse, the modern Civil Rights acts patterned on the 1875 statute and not the earlier 1866 one. It follows, therefore, that they are not sustainable under either the Thirteenth or the Fourteenth Amendment, save where the actions of private parties can be brought under some rule in which state action "sanctions and supports" private discrimination, noted in *The Civil Rights Cases.* That possibility gains credibility in light of the restrictions on entry imposed by a wide network of Jim Crow statutes, especially in the Old South. But, as with its predecessors, the 1964 Civil Rights Act is surely overbroad, especially in terms of employment relations, for it applies with full force to those private firms that have made independent and autonomous decisions to exclude persons on statutorily prohibited grounds. Whatever the lure of "state sanction and support" with respect to public accommodations, that conception is far weaker in connection with employment discrimination, except again in contexts where federal (or state) statutes give certain unions exclusive rights to bargain.

The Fourteenth Amendment, then, is the wrong weapon for the federal government to use to direct its power against private discrimination in both public accommodations and employment. The legal issues of 1964 were the same as those of 1883.[16] Given the power of the majority's analysis in *The Civil Rights Cases,* it is not surprising that the Supreme Court did not want to cross swords with its own precedents. The Fourteenth Amendment relies on the sharp distinction between private and public action that the 1964 Civil Rights Act repudiates.

The Commerce Power

The commerce clause presented far more attractive opportunities for the Court, and it took full advantage of them. The text of the clause is

---

ities of covertures and gave a married woman, like a single woman, control over all her property."

16. The point was denied by supporters of the civil rights bill during the Senate hearings, but not persuasively. See, e.g., *Senate Hearings,* vol. 1 (1964) at 230, for an exchange between Senator Strom Thurmond and Assistant Attorney General Burke Marshall, where, in answer to questions about the power of the earlier decisions, Marshall could assert only that "the situation is different today, senator," without explaining why. For an exhaustive account of the legal situation, see the remarks of Senator Sam Ervin, 110 *Cong. Rec.* 8081–86 (1964).

simplicity itself: "Congress shall have Power . . . to regulate Commerce with foreign Nations, and among the several States, and with the Indian Tribes."[17] On its face the commerce clause looks like an unlikely candidate for the source of federal power for the entire range of New Deal legislation. But Article I, section 8 contains no alternative, broader grant of power to Congress; so all the pressure to expand the role of federal government fell on this frail reed, which has been transformed from a modest enumerated power to the constitutional underpinning of the welfare state, limited only by the substantive commands found in the Bill of Rights.

Matters were not always this way. If we turn the clock back to 1883, the time of *The Civil Rights Cases,* then the 1875 act would have had but limited success under the commerce clause. At that time the dominant precedent was *Gibbons v. Ogden,*[18] decided in 1824 toward the end of Chief Justice John Marshall's era. When measured against the restrictive interpretations of the commerce clause then championed by the states, *Gibbons* reads like a grand charter of national power, one that fully justifies Marshall's reputation as the judicial architect of the new nation. But context is critical. Marshall's views are expansive only in comparison with the position, urged by the states, that the federal power consisted only in the ability to regulate interstate journeys at state borders,[19] and not to follow them into the "interior" roads and waterways of any state.[20] This reading of the clause would have given the federal government the same control over commerce that school crossing guards have over education. Marshall repudiated this narrow version and held that commerce "comprehended" all navigation and interstate travel regardless of where a journey began or ended. He further held that all contracts for interstate sale and carriage were covered by the clause. As broad as his definition was, however, it excluded from its contours the control of agriculture (which, it should never be forgotten, included plantation slavery in the South)[21] and manufacturing, as well as ordinary trade and transportation

17. U.S. Const., Art. I., §8, cl. 3. I have written about the clause extensively in Richard A. Epstein, "The Proper Scope of the Commerce Power," 73 *Va. L. Rev.* 1387 (1987).

18. 22 U.S. 1 (1824).

19. See *Livingston v. Van Ingen,* 9 Johnson 506 (N.Y. 1812).

20. See, e.g., *Gibbons,* 22 U.S. at 195.

21. The Constitution contains a special provision that limited until 1808 the power of Congress to regulate "the Migration or Importation of Such Persons as any of the States now existing shall think proper to admit"—a euphemism for the slave trade. U.S. Const., Art. I, §9, cl. 1. There was no parallel limitation on the regulation of slaves once they were

within the borders of any single state, such as the railways, governed by the separate but equal ordinance in *Plessy*.[22] It was quite inconceivable in Marshall's world that Congress could pass laws regulating either public accommodations or employment, except as they related to interstate commerce as defined. The public accommodations provisions of the 1875 statute could have been sustained in 1883 if—but *only* if—they had been confined to interstate commerce as it was then understood.

The 1875 Civil Rights Act, however, was not drafted in so limited a fashion. To save it under the commerce clause, the Court would have had to construe it as applying only to those public accommodations that serve interstate commerce. Yet in all likelihood the Supreme Court would have been unwilling to truncate the statute in order to salvage it. Nor would the statute's supporters have been satisfied with a partial victory that allowed federal regulation of only a fraction of public accommodations. The supporters of the act wanted more by way of a comprehensive solution. They were right to spurn the uncertain prospect of a slice of bread and go for the whole loaf. But their efforts would have been doomed under the commerce clause of the day. The same point applies to any antidiscrimination law governing employment. Under the commerce clause this statute would allow the reach of Congress to extend to the hiring practices of the interstate railroads and airlines. But ordinary local businesses would lie beyond the scope of congressional power.

Lest it be thought that this narrow (in comparison to the current view) construction of the commerce clause is idiosyncratic, it should be noted that the expansion of federal power to cover all forms of railroad transportation was in doubt as late as the early 1920s. In 1913 *The Shreveport Rate Case* held that the power of Congress under the Interstate Commerce Act of 1887 extended to the local service of railroads whose interstate lines served the same local markets.[23] The railroads could not discriminate in favor of their interstate traffic and against their intrastate traffic. Intrastate runs that were not in competition with interstate runs

---

on the plantation because there was no basic federal power that made such a limitation constitutionally necessary. The regulation of importation is an explicit exception to the power to regulate commerce. It is quite impossible to believe that commerce was then defined to include agriculture, thus providing from the outset complete federal power to regulate the local use of slaves. The Constitution would never had been adopted in 1787 if anyone had thought then that it had the meaning attributed to it today.

22. 163 U.S. 537 (1896).

23. *Houston, East & West Texas Railway Co. v. United States* (*The Shreveport Rate Case*), 234 U.S. 342 (1914).

still fell outside the scope of the commerce power. Only ten years later, in the early 1920s, did the Court hold that Congress could regulate all railroads, whether or not their business had any interstate component—a move that was necessary to sustain the cartelized industry structure introduced by the 1920 amendments to the Interstate Commerce Acts.[24] Thereafter the 1920s saw the slow extension of federal power to the various activities so tied to the transfer of goods in interstate commerce as to be a virtual part of them: the middleman who arranged for the sale of western cattle to the Chicago Stock Yards,[25] and the sale of grain future contracts in interstate markets.[26] One sign of the universally restrictive view of Congress's commerce power was the 1926 Railway Labor Act, which introduced collective bargaining specifically into the railroads precisely because of their special status as instrumentalities of interstate commerce, and which was easily sustained on that ground.[27] Notwithstanding these incremental movements, as late as 1936 the Supreme Court could hold that issues of "local" employment were outside the scope of the federal commerce power,[28] a decision that squares completely with the understanding of Chief Justice Marshall in *Gibbons v. Ogden.*

The transformation of the commerce clause that took place in 1937 was dramatic in scope. After the 1936 election the Court, by a five-to-four majority, sustained the National Labor Relations Act, which applied to all types of businesses, wholly without regard to any special showing of their connection with interstate commerce. The decision in *National Labor Relations Board v. Jones & Laughlin Steel Corp.*[29] was in my view wrong on historical, structural, and textual grounds. But there is no reason to repeat arguments that I have set out elsewhere in detail.[30] The critical point is that once Congress can have a collective bargaining statute

24. Transportation Act, 1920, Pub. L. no. 91–152, 41 Stat. 456, sustained in *Wisconsin Railroad Commission v. Chicago, Burlington & Quincy Railroad Co.*, 257 U.S. 563 (1922).

25. Packers and Stockyards Act, 1921, Pub. L. no. 64–51, 42 Stat. 159, sustained in *Stafford v. Wallace,* 495 U.S. 517 (1922).

26. Grain Futures Act, Pub. L. no. 369–331, 42 Stat. 998 (1922), sustained in *Chicago Board of Trade v. Olsen,* 262 U.S. 1 (1923).

27. *Texas & New Orleans Railroad Co. v. Railway Clerks,* 281 U.S. 548 (1930).

28. *Carter v. Carter Coal Co.,* 298 U.S. 238 (1936) (holding that regulation of time and hours does not fall within the commerce clause).

29. 301 U.S. 1 (1937).

30. See Epstein, "The Proper Scope of the Commerce Clause," 73 *Va. L. Rev.* at 1443–1455.

that covers all forms of employment, there can be no objection to an employment discrimination statute, such as Title VII, which covers the same types of transactions. Indeed, no separate commerce clause challenge of Title VII ever reached the Supreme Court.

The public accommodation provisions of the statute were a slightly different matter. In the aftermath of *Jones & Laughlin*, the Supreme Court in *Wickard v. Filburn*[31] held that the power of Congress to regulate commerce allowed it to prohibit farmers from planting crops that were consumed on their own premises. The decision, while widely praised,[32] is manifestly erroneous, both as a matter of original textual interpretation and as an application of *Gibbons v. Ogden*. The absence of any trade or exchange keeps the conduct in *Wickard* out of all types of commerce, and necessarily out of interstate commerce. *Wickard*'s contrary conclusion rested on the false assumption that the decisive feature was the level of interdependence between the amounts of local consumption and the levels of supply and demand in an integrated market. What was consumed on the farm in one state could have been shipped in interstate commerce into another. Congress, which could determine the rules of common carriage in interstate commerce, could therefore control matters that influenced the extent of the flow, positive or negative. With so expansive a theory, there could be no conceivable stopping point for the federal commerce power. What few matters remained "local" under this definition would be the very issues that no Congress would ever choose to address.

Nonetheless, the public accommodations statute provided the acid test of the scope of the commerce clause. The 1964 term brought two public accommodations cases to the Supreme Court. The first, *Heart of Atlanta Motel v. United States*,[33] involved a large hotel located in downtown Atlanta, which catered extensively to interstate traffic. Finding that it was engaged in interstate commerce took little imagination, even under *Gibbons*. Its companion case, *Katzenbach v. McClung*,[34] which upheld the statute insofar as it applied to Ollie's Barbecue, a small local restaurant off the beaten track, is quite another story. Congressional power over Ollie's Barbecue did not rest on the fact that the restaurant served interstate travelers, or even that its decision to run a segregated business had any

31. 317 U.S. 111 (1942).

32. See Robert Stern, "The Commerce Clause and the National Economy," *59 Harv. L. Rev.* 645 (1946).

33. 379 U.S. 241 (1964).

34. Id. at 294.

effect, up or down, on the total level of goods and services that flowed in interstate commerce. Rather, it was quite sufficient that Ollie's had purchased $70,000 worth of foodstuffs from suppliers located in other states. Indeed, even if Ollie's Barbecue had not purchased meat from South Carolina, surely some of its suppliers were engaged in interstate commerce, broadly defined. The Supreme Court thus removed the last possible element of doubt on the scope of the commerce clause that remained after *Wickard*. Any court that is ingenious enough to find that Ollie's Barbecue operates within interstate commerce is ingenious enough to find that every restaurant in the land does so as well.

Historically these finely spun doctrinal arguments proffered by the Supreme Court are a manifest anomaly. Contacts with interstate commerce of this sort could have been established as easily in 1789 as they were in 1964, in which case the Founders' battle for enumerated federal powers would have been over before it had started. The Supreme Court observed that the volume of commerce was greater in 1964 than it had been 100 or 175 years before, but to what purpose? The volume did not measure the reach of the federal commerce power in 1789; nor should volume measure it in 1964 or today. Reduced to a numbers game, the matter has no logical stopping point. Ollie's Barbecue would have been subject to federal power if it had purchased even $100 worth of supplies from out of state. In truth—and it is an open secret—the case was not about the scope of the commerce power but about the perceived moral necessity of sustaining a statute, which on any less result-oriented reading of the constitutional text exceeded the permissible scope of congressional powers. The Court rested its result on the amiable fiction that the scope of the comprehensive national power was settled when *Gibbons* was decided in the 1820s.[35] But that rhetoric is only a determined effort to dress legal revolution (here a New Deal revolution) in the more respectable garments of prudent reform. Ollie's Barbecue was hardly the occasion for the Court to reimpose traditional limits on congressional power: the perceived stakes were far too high and the respectable consensus behind the Civil Rights Act too great. There is no turning back today. The Constitution is what the Supreme Court says it is, at least in cases of political moment. There is no question that the 1964 Civil Rights Act falls within the scope of the commerce power as it is currently understood, and none that it falls outside that power as it was originally written and understood.

35. Id. at 299–303.

Unconstitutional Interference

The last constitutional challenge to the Civil Rights Act of 1964 assumes that the statute falls within the affirmative powers available to Congress, and then asks whether the statute itself runs afoul of the substantive limitations protecting liberty and property found in the Bill of Rights. Here, too, the outcome of the analysis depends very heavily on the basic analytical framework. For the Supreme Court this case was an easy one. The aftermath of 1937 reduced to the vanishing point the level of protection that private property and private contract received from the government against general forms of economic regulation. By 1965 virtually all types of economic regulation were permissible under the police power as it had come to be construed. The level of scrutiny was low indeed— some, indeed any, weak rational basis was sufficient to sustain a challenged statute. The Civil Rights Act thus presented an obvious case. The end—eliminating racial discrimination—was beyond question within the power of Congress, and a statute that did just that surely picked means appropriate to the end in question. The entire discussion was brief and self-assured.[36]

And analytically unconvincing. The Court's argument in upholding the public accommodations provisions of Title II under the police power bears a haunting similarity to *Plessy v. Ferguson*,[37] which likewise took a very relaxed view of the asserted police power grounds on which state legislation could override individual claims of both liberty and property. Prior to 1937, freedom to contract was protected either as an element of ordinary personal liberty or, alternatively, as part of the right of ordinary property, namely the freedom to dispose of one's land and capital as one sees fit. These rights are necessarily infringed by a statutory command that denies the owner of property the rights to the exclusive possession and use of his own land. That is exactly what an antidiscrimination statute does by requiring the employer to hire a given worker against his will. The conflict between the civil rights statutes and ordinary constitutional freedoms of both liberty and property is far more insistent than the cavalier analysis of the Supreme Court in *Heart of Atlanta Motel* suggests.

Once rights of property and liberty are infringed by the antidiscrimination statutes, then their constitutionality again turns on the police power. But if that doctrine cannot justify the imposition of state-required sys-

36. *Heart of Atlanta Motel*, 379 U.S. at 258–261.
37. See the discussion in Chapter 5 at 99–103.

tems of segregation, how can it account for state-imposed antidiscrimination laws? The argument surely cannot turn on the motives of the legislature or any of its members, for some defenders of segregation may well have thought that those laws worked toward the common good even if they incidentally abrogated the legitimate interests of blacks. But the argument can be directed toward the proper ends of the police power, which according to the earlier analysis were confined to the prevention or control of physical harms—trespass and nuisance—and of private deception. In contrast, the prime illustration of an illegitimate use of the police power was to stifle the ordinary business activities of a competitor.

This last account of the police power meshes perfectly with the dominant libertarian account of the proper scope of government power—as a means to protect against the use or threat of force and fraud. The same account protects freedom of contract and private property as much against an antidiscrimination law as it does against a law that mandates segregation. Forced associations are in principle no better than legal prohibitions against voluntary associations. It is only when we return to the dominant theme—that legislative intervention is necessary to protect businesses that want to integrate despite threats from both local governments and private parties who would shut them down—that the police power arguments become forceful.

In this context, the argument goes, some federal presence is necessary to neutralize a consistent pattern of abuse by state and local governments and private individuals. The only way to protect any firms that wish to serve on a nondiscriminatory basis, the argument continues, is to require all firms to behave in that fashion, for it is just too costly to operate a system of freedom of choice, given the subtle but pervasive patterns of coercion, official and unofficial, that have dominated the local scene, especially in the South. There is polar opposition between mandated segregation and a pure competitive market.

This argument, however alluring, remains both contingent and partial. It does not justify the statute as a matter of first principle, that is, good as a fundamental moral norm for all times and all places. Rather, it suggests that the Civil Rights Act is justified only as a "jolt" to the system, designed to overcome the legacy of racial injustice that had worked itself into the fabric of law, where it had distorted basic social institutions. But by the same token argument suggests that over time, when the system returns to a steady state, that justification ceases. The police power argument thus bears only limited fruit in this context. It does not provide any justification for the statute in a "first-best" world without prior official and private abuse. Since no compensation, either in cash or in kind, is afforded persons who object to Title VII, the just compensation required by the Constitution for the taking of property is denied as well.[38] As long as there is a competitive equilibrium in employment markets, a statute that reduces overall levels of output cannot provide just compensation to all the parties whom it regulates.

This constitutional analysis leads to exactly the same conclusion reached by the theoretical arguments advanced earlier. The only justification for the antidiscrimination laws is to offset the barriers to entry created by legal rule or by the private use of force. Within the rigorous takings analysis that applies generally to economic liberties, the case for Title VII looks very weak indeed when it is set against a competitive economy. But, as with the commerce clause arguments, the most plausible counterarguments against the Civil Rights Act were practically (if erroneously) disposed of by the earlier doctrinal developments of 1937. Given the moral sentiment throughout the bench, the bar, and much of the country, it was simply not possible for long-discredited constitutional arguments on property and liberty to be revived selectively in the context of race. At present there is no political sentiment anywhere for a revival of the constitutional doctrine, as it relates to either race or sex, for striking down the Civil Rights Act. Practical reform is not the point of the foregoing constitutional analysis. But the points here are not unimportant, for the question of policy still remains. Title II on public accommodations has been accepted (or ignored) so completely that it should not be disturbed at all.

The application of the antidiscrimination law to employment relations is a different matter entirely. Although there has been widespread social acceptance of the basic antidiscrimination norm, there is massive disagreement on every aspect of its operation: the standards of proof for the basic violation, the class of permitted exceptions and defenses, and remedies imposed when violations have been established. The main weakness of the debate is that no one seems willing to consider the possibility that the entire argument rests on a false premise that some antidiscrimination law is necessary in the first place. It is to that larger issue that I now turn.

---

38. I address this argument in greater detail in Richard A. Epstein, "Two Conceptions of Civil Rights," 8 *Soc. Phil. & Pol.* 38 (1991).

PART III

Race Discrimination

CHAPTER 8

The Contract at Will

This chapter begins the more detailed examination of how the antidiscrimination laws operate in their current setting. The problems that arise in race cases differ in significant ways from those that involve sex, age, and handicap cases. The separate analysis for each classification is designed to capture those relevant differences. Each, however, depends on setting the proper benchmark for comparison. It makes no sense to say that some legal rule is undesirable unless it is possible to identify what alternative is superior and why. The alternative that I shall pursue here is that of the unregulated competitive market, which allows the parties to set whatever terms of employment they see fit. As should now be evident, the antidiscrimination laws impose restrictions that require employers and employees to deviate from that market standard. The question is whether that deviation leads to net benefits or net burdens for the parties involved and society as a whole. The issue can be approached in two ways. The first is to look at the preferences of both employers and employees as revealed in their market behavior. The second is to identify the reasons that make the contract at will work. I will consider them in turn.

Revealed Preferences in the Marketplace

In practice voluntary markets create countless variations on the basic employment contract, and it is surely a strike against the antidiscrimination laws that they limit the diversity of terms to which private parties may resort. A characteristic of most contracts in voluntary labor markets is that they operate under relatively fixed understandings about whether the employment relation shall continue or terminate. These rules for hiring or firing systematically avoid a rule of the "for cause" type, which requires the employer to show some good reason for any personnel decision. But it is just such a regime that is necessarily imposed under Title VII. Once it is said, for example, that workers cannot be dismissed for certain illicit motives, then the choices are dismissal for no reason, for good reason, or for bad reasons not covered by the statute, such as eye color. Courts will rightly be skeptical of any defense of a Title VII claim that says dismissal occurred for no reason at all. In some cases it might be possible to show that there was a bad but irrelevant reason. But in the typical case the best line of defense is to show that a refusal to hire or a decision to fire was made for a good cause, that is, for legitimate business reasons unrelated to race or sex.

Title VII thus works a major shift from the paradigmatic and most common version of an employment contract, the contract at will.[1] The at will contract avoids the complications of the for cause arrangement because it treats the three possibilities just mentioned equally: the employer can hire and fire for good reason, for bad reason, or indeed for no reason at all. Equally important, the employee has the same set of options, both for accepting employment and for quitting. Nothing in the common law, of course, *requires* that parties enter into contracts at will. They can enter into long-term employment contracts if they choose. They can enter into agreements that restrict the right to fire for cause, or that allow dismissal at will but require the employer to pay fixed severance damages (for instance, two weeks' wages) upon dismissal. The parties can adopt extensive internal review procedures for firing and promotion decisions, which may include some recourse to arbitration or judicial review, or which may be legally unenforceable.

Notwithstanding all these available options, the use of the at will contract is still the most frequent, perhaps even dominant, form in the United States, just as it was before the passage of the antidiscrimination laws. Its dominance is being challenged at common law by a raft of suits for "unjust dismissal" in cases where charges of discrimination play no role. But those suits, like the antidiscrimination laws, are the product not of joint consent at the time the contract is formed but of an insistence by the courts (and now increasingly the legislature) that certain "minimum

1. I have previously discussed the contract at will in Richard A. Epstein, "In Defense of the Contract at Will," 51 *U. Chi. L. Rev.* 947 (1984), and many of the arguments here are made at greater length in that article. The general legal view today is heavily in favor of abrogating the contract at will. See, for the most comprehensive statements of the modern attacks on the rule, Paul C. Weiler, *Governing the Workplace: The Future of Labor and Employment Law* 48–104 (1990) and material he cites at n.6. The first of the modern attacks on the contract at will is found in Lawrence E. Blades, "Employment at Will v. Individual Freedom: On Limiting the Abusive Exercise of Employer Power," 67 *Colum. L. Rev.* 1404 (1967).

terms" must be included in every contract regardless of the intention of the parties.[2] The question is whether any legal restrictions, judicial or legislative, on the at will (or other employment) contract make sense, both for the parties to it and for the society at large.

I think that the answer to that question is no. It is not necessary here to demonstrate that the contract at will is ideal for all persons and all circumstances. It isn't. Rather, the point of this exercise is only to show why it should be legally permitted, not why it should be legally required. There are doubtless cases for which the at will contract is inappropriate; but even if stronger contractual bonds are created, it need not follow that these must assume the contours of the antidiscrimination laws. Let us turn to the distinctive, and attractive, features of the contract at will.

The simplest, and for some the most persuasive defense is that the terms of an employment contract are the business of only the parties to it. Freedom of contract on this matter is no different from freedom of speech or freedom of action. Unless and until the contract in question poses the threat of harm to third parties (the police power again) or is procured by fraud or sharp practice, then each person is his or her own best judge both of the private costs incurred by contracting and of the private benefits obtained from that contract. Individuals have the best knowledge of their own preferences and have the strongest possible motivation to make the best deal for themselves. A desirable contract is one in which each party to the agreement regards himself or herself as better off with the agreement than without it. Armed with that knowledge of general theory, we do not have to concern ourselves further with the actual operation of the contract at will to decide that it should be legally permissible. It should be enough for judges, legislators, and commentators that the people who enter into an agreement have manifested their consent to it, either by word or by common practice. In a world of repeated dealings with literally millions of contracts at will, the odd case of fraud or sharp practice is of marginal institutional concern.

In a similar vein, it seems farfetched to assume that more complex agreements are not pursued because millions of workers and managers suffer some fundamental psychological block to their own vision which makes them unable to transcend the world of contractual arrangements commonly used at present. It has been suggested, for example, that most

2. For a defense of minimum terms, see Charles Fried, "Individual Collective Rights in Work Relations: Reflections on the Current State of Labor Law and Its Prospects," 51 *U. Chi. L. Rev.* 1012 (1984).

contracts do not call for extensive worker participation in firm governance because no models of that sort are available. Thus Cass Sunstein has written:

> Workers seem not to be willing to trade much in the way of money for self-government. But that preference may be a product of a belief that self-government in the workplace is unavailable. Were the option to be one that workers conventionally thought available, the option might be highly valued. If the preference for wages over self-government is a product of sour grapes—to be sure, a controversial proposition—there is a defect in cognitive processes that provides at least a potential justification for government action.[3]

This potential justification for government interference, however, falls far short of its goal because it makes it appear that the path never taken is the path that is so widely desired that it could justify comprehensive government regulation. Of course workers should be allowed to form cooperatives if they choose, and they are so allowed today. Nonetheless, we must resist the temptation to override any common practice, including the contract at will, on the strength of so elusive a set of psychological concerns as Sunstein posits. Even if most people did suffer such cognitive or emotional limitations, surely some (if only the critics of the contract at will) would rise above the traditional practices to envision alternative contractual arrangements, especially now that these forms have been trumpeted countless times in legal commentary and have been introduced by government fiat in collective bargaining arrangements. Every form of market innovation, from the "money-back guarantee" in retailing to time-sharing agreements for condominiums, is a deviation from the status quo. If people are not blind to some forms of innovation, then why assume that they are blind to this one if it is valuable? As long as innovation is allowed, then in the short term the innovators should have free range to experiment with alternative contract terms, including those that stipulate worker governance or a strong antidiscrimination norm. The fewer the imitators, the larger the potential gains for the innovators who first strike a responsive chord. Workers with any latent preferences for some untried system should quickly gravitate toward firms that adopt it. It can hardly be a point against the contract at will—which excludes workers from a

---

3. Cass R. Sunstein, "Legal Interference with Private Preferences," 53 *U. Chi. L. Rev.* 1129, 1148 (1986) (footnote omitted).

formal stake in governance—that huge numbers of people prefer higher wages to participation in self-government. No one would say that it was a point in favor of requiring a contract at will that no employers had adopted it. Why, then, accept the opposite argument?

We can test the durability of the contract at will in another fashion. Surely if the dominant form of contracting did call for worker participation, as in collective bargaining or socialist systems, there would be no need to mandate that employment agreements be drafted as contracts at will in order to get workers to abandon the older system. As the events in Eastern Europe in 1989 dramatically showed, any system of free entry (such as by West German companies) will induce workers to depart from a system of shared governance in droves because workers value higher compensation more than they value participation in governance. (More precisely, I suspect that workers, like limited partners, value their own participation in governance but fear that of their fellow workers. Better, therefore, that all contracts be at will than none.) Similarly, the tidal migrations of workers across borders happen because they are in search of increased freedom and higher wages, not additional formal rights of participation in state-run enterprises. First Eastern Europe and now the disintegration of the Soviet Union offer dramatic examples.

We should not make the rarity of a contractual form a sign of its hidden and unappreciated virtues. It is at best a weak psychological surmise that workers do not like what they get in the marketplace, or indeed that they cannot participate unless they have some formal right that guarantees participation. In addition, it would be very costly to force every firm to adopt some new mode of industrial organization, only to discover that it is not desired by the persons who are forced to work under it. Someone in the world has to have undistorted preferences in order for any system of government control to work. Why assume that academics have a better sense of the preferences of people in the field than those people have themselves? There is no good reason to require either firms, workers, or taxpayers to subsidize the cost of experimenting with novel contract forms that neither party wants. The patterns of existing behavior are simply inconsistent with the proposition that all ordinary contracting behavior is fundamentally flawed or misguided. To accept the argument that latent preferences will receive expression only if harnessed by government coercion is a sure way to impose unpopular and unworkable forms of business organization on the economy as a whole.

Functional Advantages of the Contract at Will

The defense of the contract at will has proceeded thus far on the grounds of caution and reaction. We allow contracts at will to be used because people want to use them, and because people generally know what they want better than others do. The virtue of this argument is that it leads to sound legal policy even if we are ignorant of the reasons why the contract at will, or indeed any contract, makes sense from the vantage point of the parties. But it is possible to go further. We can sketch the reasons why the contract at will often has the desirable property of maximizing the benefit to both employer and employee when the contract is formed.

In this discussion I assume, as before, that the set of relevant benefits is subjective to each person. But even though that is true, there are enough regularities in human tastes and preferences to make it plausible that each person is not so unique that he or she must have a special form of contract to satisfy every aspect of his or her distinctive personality. Nonetheless, differences in tastes, temperaments, and talents are critical in a number of ways. They explain why I am a law professor and not a singer, and (I suppose) why Frank Sinatra is a singer and not a law professor. Temperaments and talents have everything to do with the line of work that people undertake. But these differences do not necessarily require different contracting forms for different types of labor. The selection of lines of work and of contracting partners is typically made in response to unique subjective factors; yet self-interest and risk aversion are constant forces in human nature. Contracting partners are selected with an eye for both production and distribution. Parties wish to secure the largest overall output and a suitable fraction of the gain for themselves. It thus remains to explain why the contract at will often helps to improve production and to eliminate the risks of advantage taking that might otherwise occur.

Once parties in the employment setting have identified each other, they must must decide whether to contract, and if so on what terms. One point that must concern both sides is the extent of the commitment that each has to make at the time of contract formation. On this issue both the employer and the employee will have conflicting emotions. Thus, on the one hand, the employer (like the employee) wants a stable long-term relationship. The advantages accrue to both sides. Each party has the security of knowing the anticipated gain from the relationship, and each can organize the rest of his or her life with the knowledge that the contract reduces personal uncertainty about income and future prospects.

The worker can decide to buy a home in the vicinity of the factory or office because the job will be there next year and the year after. The firm can afford to invest in training the worker because it knows that he or she will continue to work on the job, or in the firm, for several years at least. The sense of long-term bonding therefore induces each side to increase its investment in specific capital so as to increase the gains from their ongoing trade.

But there are drawbacks to this strategy as well, for each side is concerned not only with the benefits from contracting but also with its potential risks. The worker who starts with a friendly employer wants to be able to leave if wages are reduced, working conditions deteriorate, or fringe benefits are eliminated. The employer wants to be able to fire the worker who slacks off on production or provokes discord in the workplace. A simple long-term contract which obligates both sides to a deal where X will work for Y at a certain wage for life, or for five years, does very well if these other conditions remain constant, that is, if the two sides get along just fine, and if external circumstances do not change. But at the outset who knows if this will be the case? If the relationship turns sour, if one side decides to take advantage of the contractual lock, then this long-term contract may be insufficient for the task at hand. The employee who bridles under a capricious boss cannot leave. The employer who has a good reason to dismiss a worker will not be able to do so under the terms of the agreement as drafted, or the whole matter may be sufficiently unclear as to require litigation. One way to avoid this problem is to draft more detailed agreements, but that task is itself costly and probably fruitless; and the level of legal ambiguity—not to mention psychological unease—often increases as negotiations drag on and the employment contract takes on the look of a huge corporate merger. A long-term contract may provide only a shaky foundation for a long-term employment relationship.

One possible alternative is to move to the other extreme, and to make it clear that the contract is at will on both sides. Here *at will* means just that and nothing more. Negotiation costs can be reduced drastically. There is still the risk that investments in long-term relationships cannot be made if the other side is free to back out at any time. But to counter that risk, the bonding mechanism of the contract at will, although subtle, is often quite effective. The worker's security is that the employer does not want to lose a well-trained, reliable employee. The employer's security is that the worker does not want to lose a good job. In other words, once the relationship starts to flourish, each side can obtain specific gains from keeping it alive that are greater than those obtainable by terminating the arrangement and by hiring or selling labor in the spot market. Both sides therefore have an incentive to make small, sensible marginal adjustments, and hence not to drive too hard a bargain lest the other party withdraw from the deal. Indeed, the most stable point for the contract is when the gains from trade are roughly split, for then the probability that either party will have the incentive to break off the deal is minimized.

The contract at will thus works like a gyroscope, with a strong mechanism for self-correction against personal aggrandizement. If the employer starts to get greedy, say, reducing lunch breaks and speeding up the assembly line, the worker's threat to leave becomes more credible: a competitive return for labor in the open market may now be preferable to staying. If the employee starts to sleep on the job or damage the inventory, the employer has all the more reason to look for a substitute on the open market. As long as each of the parties knows that the overall relationship must thrive if he or she is to garner some fraction of the specific (that is, supercompetitive) gains that it generates, then the deal can continue for long periods of time without any formal mechanism binding each side to the other. The low administrative costs are an additional inducement. The contract at will thus has very attractive features, not only when work is desired in the spot market but also when long-term relationships are sought.

Reputational constraints are also relevant. Ironically, on this issue there is an instructive asymmetry between the worker and the employer, which becomes more pronounced as firm size increases. The worker has less by way of reputation to lose from quitting a job than the employer has by firing a worker. In some cases references will be hard to come by (a problem that has been aggravated by the willingness to hold employers liable in defamation for negative references,[4] a development that has decreased the value of favorable references). But workers often can and do get jobs without employer references, for instance by explaining that the boss was unreasonable, or by obtaining references from prior

---

4. See, e.g., *Lewis v. Equitable Life Assur. Society,* 389 N.W.2d 876, 888 (Minn. 1986), which held that an employee could maintain an action for defamation against the employer when the employee felt compelled to disclose to a prospective employer the reasons for the original firing. Prior law had treated any publication by the plaintiff as negating any liability for defamation. The rule places an employer in a bind. If information is disclosed, then it could be used as the basis for a defamation action. If it is not disclosed, then the employer could be sued for unjust dismissal.

employers or from friends and associates. Indeed, the widespread reluctance today to give references at all makes the lack of any particular reference seem less damning. But whatever the short-term frustrations of a particular case, the employer does not occupy a strong monopoly position, if it has any monopoly power at all. Nonetheless, the employer does have to take into account the effect of the decision to fire X on all other actual and prospective employees. If those workers perceive that the dismissal is not in line with the implicit norms of the workplace, they will reevaluate their own job prospects, even in a world in which dismissals can legally be made at will. To fire capriciously, therefore, is exceedingly costly to the firm because of its effects on the morale of the remaining workers. Even those firms that reserve explicitly the right to fire at will often make it clear in their own literature that workers will receive some kind of internal hearing before they are dismissed, and courts only complicate an otherwise sensible business arrangement by aggressively reading such internal manuals as the source of a legal obligation enforceable in the courts.[5]

It is a constant weakness of academic lawyers to think that the world is divided into two domains, one of absolute liberty and the other of binding legal rules. But in truth any complex institution has norms that are far more variegated than any overly simple model contains. People expend resources to create informal agreements only because they generate returns in the form of increased predictability and output. The situations that they create are usually stable without legal intervention, but often quite unstable once every informal promise is converted by the law into one that is answerable in damages in a common law court. An employer who treats its informal promises as though they had no social force just because they have no legal force runs the risk of ruining his own business. There are always isolated instances where informal mechanisms break down; even a large firm such as IBM may occasionally mishandle a personnel matter.[6] But these aberrations must be kept in

5. See *Toussiant v. Blue Cross & Blue Shield of Michigan,* 408 Mich. 579, 292 N.W.2d 880 (1980). Most handbooks have been modified to make clear that challenges on the grounds of the at will nature of the job have proved less successful in recent years. Weiler, *Governing the Workplace* at 55 n.18.

6. See *Rulon-Miller v. International Business Machines,* 162 Cal. App.3d 241 (1984), discussed in Weiler, *Governing the Workplace* at 62 nn.31, 62, 80. The suit was brought by a woman who had been fired for dating an employee of a small competitor firm. She received $200,000 in compensatory damages and $100,000 in punitive damages. Although Weiler is opposed to the at will doctrine, he is also suspicious of common law remedies,

perspective. No system of judicial supervision is likely to work a tenth as well as IBM's internal procedures.

Arguments against the Contract at Will

Notwithstanding these arguments, the contract at will is in general retreat today. As Paul Weiler has written: "Because it has been made and reiterated by so many judges and scholars for the last decade, the case for protection against unjust dismissal now seems virtually self-evident to many sophisticated commentators."[7] But what seems self-evident is often wrong. The common arguments that are advanced in favor of limiting the contract at will by law are in my view wholly unpersuasive.

First, it is often said that the contract at will can be abused, as when an employer uses the threat of firing a worker as a way to induce the worker to violate the law.[8] This limitation on the contract at will is surely appropriate, for an employer can no more bribe a worker to perjure testimony with an offer of a cash payoff or a job promotion than it can threaten her with dismissal if she tells the truth. But there is hardly any reason to extend the limitation on freedom of contract beyond the situations that give birth to it. The entire edifice of the contract at will should not be dismantled when an area of genuine abuse can be handled by a well-tailored remedy.

---

which have given very extensive awards; he advocates a system in which bonuses are added to unemployment insurance for unjust dismissal. See Weiler, *Governing the Workplace* at 78–87. The most extensive empirical study of wrongful dismissal cases is the Rand study, James N. Dertouzas, Elaine Holland, and Patricia Ebener, *The Legal and Economic Consequences of Wrongful Termination* (1988), which looks at 120 California cases between 1980 and 1986 and reports that the average defendant paid $293,000 and the average plaintiff received $144,000, the rest being consumed in legal fees. Punitive damages were awarded in half the cases, an average of $500,000. See Weiler, *Governing the Workplace* at 80, nn.62, 63.

7. Weiler, *Governing the Workplace* at 50.

8. See, e.g., *Peterman v. Teamsters Local 396*, 174 Cal. App.2d 184 (1959) (effort to induce perjured testimony; *Frampton v. Central Indiana Gas Co.*, 297 N.E.2d 425 (Ind. 1973) (filing worker's compensation claim that would increase employer's insurance premiums); *Novosel v. Nationwide Insurance Co.*, 721 F.2d 894 (3rd Cir. 1984) (refusal to support lobbying efforts against no-fault tort reform). These cases are discussed in Weiler, *Governing the Workplace* at 49–51. Note that *Novosel* was wrongly decided even under this exception. The firm has its interest in expressing its position before legislators. It engages in a constitutionally protected activity when it lobbies. The employee may have a constitutional right to express his point of view as well, but not to require his opponent to subsidize the activity.

Second, it is commonly urged that a job should be treated like property because of the enormous value that is attached to it by workers. Empirically the claim is surely false in many cases, given the constant turnover of workers made possible by the contract at will. And analytically the claim is incomplete because it takes into account only one form of value while ignoring others. The workers who prize the security of their present position are also on the lookout for advancement elsewhere. Yet those prospects will be blocked if the law makes it more costly to dismiss current workers from their positions, or more costly to hire a worker of uncertain quality, given the legal impediments against an at will dismissal. In any event, the soundness of a contractual arrangement is not measured solely by the gains or losses of one side. The interests of the employer have to be taken into account as well, given that many managers are as devoted to their firms as workers are to their jobs. To say that workers are entitled to have property rights in their jobs is necessarily to strip property rights from managers. There is no way in the abstract to evaluate which set of desires or expectations is the more powerful, but in a setting of low transaction costs, the dominance of the at will arrangement suggests in many instances that both sides prefer legal freedom to withdraw coupled with informal security to stay. Why upset the applecart?

Third, it is often argued, as by Theodore St. Antoine, that the severe regret, and perhaps psychological depression, that some workers suffer when they are improperly dismissed is so important a considertion that it weighs in favor of eliminating the contract at will by state fiat.[9] Yet problems of this sort can also arise after a worker has been dismissed and told, whether wrongly or rightly, that the dismissal was for cause. And it would be a mistake to ignore the psychological pounding that employers and supervisors face when they are accused of wrongfully dismissing an employee. Any form of contract seems inefficient if we look only to a single set of losses that it generates in some limited class of cases. But to assess the desirability of a contract arrangement in the aggregate, we have to see how it works over the full run of cases that it governs. St. Antoine's methodology is similar to one that condemns commercial aviation by looking only at the planes that crash while ignoring those that safely reach their destination.

The prominent objections to the at will rule all suffer from a common methodological failing of special pleading: they weight heavily the objec-

9. See Theodore St. Antoine, "At-Will Employment and the Handsome American," 33, 1 *Law Quadrangle Notes: University of Michigan* 26 (Fall 1988).

tions of the individuals who lose under an at will arrangement but over-look the gains that the regime generates in the countless cases where it proceeds smoothly.[10] Only by taking a consistent ex ante perspective is it possible to get the right result. The older common law rule is as func-tional today as it ever was, provided persons can modify the basic agree-ment to suit their particular circumstances. It is therefore an appropriate baseline against which to compare the legal situation in which contracting is subject to the general caveats of the antidiscrimination principle.

10. For an illustration of the mistake, see Weiler, *Governing the Workplace* at 62 n.31, speaking of *Rulon-Miller*: "Although the employees of IBM taken as a group and viewed ex ante arguably might be better off without the right to mount a legal challenge to their possible discharge, the same could certainly not be said about Rulon-Miller herself, the actual victim of the illegitimate firing."

Disparate Treatment

Title VII: A "Moderate" Interference with the Market

Having completed the analysis of the contract at will, I now turn to Title VII itself. At the broadest level of principle my position is that Title VII should be repealed with respect to all private employers, as long as the condition of free entry, normally easily obtainable in employment contexts, holds in the marketplace. In general this view would leave some (disparate treatment) antidiscrimination provision in place with respect to unions and unionized employers, but only where mandatory collective bargaining under the National Labor Relations Act is in effect.

The basic case against Title VII rests on the superiority of private contracting over government regulation. Private forms of contract generally veer away from costly determinations of motive; as with the contract at will, they tend to adopt clear rules to govern all stages in the life of a contract, from formation to termination. Title VII necessarily injects noncontractual elements into the determinations that would otherwise take place at every stage of contractual activity. The deviations it imposes from the normal rules applicable to voluntary transactions are a rough measure of the social losses imposed.

All deviations from contractual solutions do not, however, generate identical results. The relative undesirability of a statute is a function of the type of prohibition involved: as will become clear, race, sex, and age cases often present very different issues. Thus, explicit age classifications are common in all segments of the unregulated labor market. My educated guess is that the statutes that render these classifications illegal are apt to be far more intrusive than those statutes that prohibit racial classifications, which most firms would find largely irrelevant. Sex classifications form an intermediate case; these are desirable in many occupations (nursing, heavy labor) but are usually regarded as far less relevant in others (academics, for example). The mischief worked by an antidiscrimination statute is not constant across all occupations and all grounds for discrimination.

Similarly there are vast differences between disparate treatment and disparate impact cases. The former, which involve efforts to show that the defendant's conduct was actuated by some illegitimate motive, often raise very delicate questions of procedure and proof, but these difficulties are of the sort with which the general legal system can ordinarily cope, at least at a price. The disparate impact cases, which allow courts to infer unlawful discrimination, wholly without evidence of improper motive, and solely from the (perceived) disparate consequences of certain hiring tests or procedures, represent a very different threat, one that poses intolerable and unnecessary demands on both the legal system and the affected employment markets. All deviations from standard market principles are not equally significant or dangerous. But before analyzing these various manifestations of the antidiscrimination principle, I shall examine the common threads that link these theories together.

The original conception of the civil rights statute was captured by a straightforward declaration:

> Section 703. (a)   It shall be an unlawful employment practice for any employer—
> (1) to fail or refuse to hire or to discharge any individual, or otherwise to discriminate against any individual with respect to his compensation, terms, conditions, or privileges of employment, because of such individual's race, color, religion, sex or national origin.

In the eyes of its supporters the grand injunction of this statute would not unduly interfere with the operation of markets, even if it did place restrictions on freedom of contract. Senator Thomas Kuchel, a key supporter of the bill, said, "Title VII might justly be described as a modest step forward."[1] According to its supporters, Title VII was thought to make a surgical strike against the various forms of irrational and invidious conduct that rendered markets inefficient, so that only the correct, or relevant, characteristics of workers would be taken into

1. 110 *Cong. Rec.* 6553 (1964). And he continued: "Yet it is pictured by its opponents and detractors as an intrusion of numerous Federal inspectors into our economic life." Id. at 6553.

account with regard to any aspect of the employment relation, including hiring, promotion, transfer, or firing. In some cases the effect of the statute was described very narrowly. Thus Senator Hubert Humphrey said: "Employers may hire and fire, promote and refuse to promote for any reason, good or bad, provided only that individuals may not be discriminated against because of race, religion, sex or national origin."[2] More frequently the effect of the statute was expressed in more optimistic terms: since employers would presumably not act for no reason at all, personnel decisions would be based on the merits and not on caprice or prejudice.

Senator Humphrey (who did not comment on the difference between his two formulations) spoke eloquently to the point:

> In Title VII we seek to prevent discriminatory hiring practices. We seek to give people an opportunity to be hired on the basis of merit, and to release the tremendous talents of the American people, rather than to keep their talents buried under prejudice or discrimination.[3]

The theme was picked up by others as well:

> Under Title VII, employment will be on the basis of merit, not race. This means that no quota system will be set up, no one will be forced to hire incompetent help because of race or religion, and no one will be given a vested right to demand employment for a certain job. The Title is designed to utilize to the fullest our potential workforce, to permit every worker to hold the best job for which he is qualified. This can be done by removing the hurdles that have too long been placed in the path of minority groups who seek to realize their rights and to contribute to a full society.[4]

2. 110 *Cong. Rec.* 6548 (1964). Elsewhere Senator Humphrey said that Title VII "does not limit the employer's freedom to hire, fire, promote, or demote for any reason—or no reason—so long as his action is not based on race, color, religion, national origin or sex." Id. at 5423.

3. Id. at 6549.

4. Id at 1600 (statement of Congressman Joseph Minish) The language about "removing hurdles" was carefully chosen, for the supporters of the bill were eager to avoid any charges that the statute required the implementation of quotas. Thus the remarks of Senator Humphrey: "Contrary to the allegations of some opponents of this title, there is nothing in it that will give any power to the Commission or to any court to require hiring, firing, or promotion of employees in order to meet a racial "quota" or to achieve a certain racial balance . . . Title VII is designed to encourage hiring on the basis of ability and qualifications, not race or religion." 110 *Cong. Rec.* 6549 (1964).

The antidiscrimination rules were also defended on the ground that they improved overall economic welfare:

> The failure of our society to extend job opportunities to the Negro is an economic waste. The purchasing power of the country is not being fully developed. This, in turn, acts as a brake upon the potential increases in gross national product. In addition, the country is burdened with added costs for the payment of unemployment compensation, relief, disease, and crime.[5]

Senator Joseph Clark echoed the same theme:

> "Economics is at the heart of the racial situation. The Negro has been condemned to poverty because of a lack of equal job opportunities. This poverty has kept the Negro out of the mainstream of American life. This is the issue that confronts us on the economic side.[6]

And finally, Senator Humphrey again:

> Discrimination in employment is not confined to any region—it is widespread in every part of the country. It is harmful to Negroes and to members of other minority groups. It is also harmful to the Nation as a whole. The Council of Economic Advisors has recently estimated that full utilization of the present educational attainment of non-whites in this country would add about $13 billion to our gross national product.[7]

It was quite possible to have our cake and eat it too, to admit a new form of regulation and expand the overall level of social output and production. With these broad aims in mind, the Congress evidently drafted the statute with the view to preventing any evasions: all phases of the employment relation were regulated. Given its basic design, the statute would have become largely ineffective had it regulated employment only at the entry level but left promotion, wages, and job assignments unregulated thereafter. Successful regulation of one part of the employment relationship requires regulation of all relevant particulars, including those dealing with the "compensation, terms, conditions, or privileges of employment." It is yet another instance of the pervasive

---

5. H. Rep. no. 9014, 88th Cong. 1st sess., 1963, 149 (views of additional Republican sponsors).
6. 110 *Cong. Rec.* 13080 (1964).
7. Id. at 6547.

problem of the so-called regulatory pyramid. A regulation that covers only part of an enterprise leaves open the royal road to evasion; but that road can be closed only by extending the regulation still further, until in the end virtually nothing lies outside its scope.

At the very least, the application of Title VII to all aspects of the employment relationship should have signaled that its operation was a bigger project and a more intrusive step than the supporters of the statute had believed or insisted. But realism about consequences did not characterize the early debates, all of which stressed the limited nature of the federal intervention and the desirable economic consequences that would follow.

Two Conceptions of Merit

The underlying problem with Title VII runs far deeper than it would appear at first. The Civil Rights Act necessarily involves a different conception of value and contracting from that found in market settings. The market model assumes that all elements of gain and loss are subjective, and that explicit measurement by external parties is not possible but is obtainable only by indirect inference. There is in a market exchange no objective test of merit on which any external observer can rely. There is only the subjective test of desire manifested in consent. Those things that tend to make a worker more desirable to the employer (and the employer more desirable to the worker) count as meritorious, while those that do not are not meritorious. In most cases an employer will value intelligence, initiative, honesty, reliability, and the like, so the conventional accounts of merit carry substantial weight in individual personnel decisions. It looks, therefore, as though the civil rights statutes do not limit in the slightest the ability to discriminate on the strength of those universally desirable (because universally desired) characteristics.

This distinction between qualifications and forbidden criteria was evident in the original explication of Title VII advanced by Senators Clark and Humphrey. Title VII, they wrote, "expressly protects the employer's right to insist that any prospective applicant, Negro or white, must meet the applicable job qualifications. Indeed, the very purpose of Title VII is to promote hiring on the basis of job qualifications, rather than on the basis of race or color."[8] The division between merits and irrelevant considerations has also been picked up in subsequent Supreme Court deci-

8. Id. at 7247.

sions.[9] The plurality opinion in *Price Waterhouse v. Hopkins* summarized its view of the congressional design as follows: "When an employer ignored the attributes enumerated in the statute, Congress hoped, it would naturally focus on the qualifications of the applicant or the employee.[10] Neither in 1964 nor yet today has anyone explained how the watertight distinction between qualifications or merits (I use the terms synonymously) on the one hand and irrelevant characteristics on the other can be maintained. Surely it draws no support whatsoever from the logic of markets or voluntary exchange. Let race or sex be a point of value to the employer (as, for example, when calls for race-conscious or sex-conscious hiring are made to promote "diversity"); then there is merit in the subjective sense appropriate to economic theory, although there is none under the 1964 act, with its universal color-blind norm.

The pairing of these two definitions of merit—the market and the statutory meanings—thus points to the critical distinction between objective and subjective valuation and the associated modes of social validation. Within the subjective market system, the consent of the party is the sole test of merit, the sole test of whether the restrictions and burdens assumed were less than the benefits received. Each person fashions his or her own idea of merit and acts on the strength of it. If there are regularities in human desires and perceptions, then some widespread standards may emerge, and these will often reflect considered moral or institutional judgments, not whim or caprice. But these uniformities in preferences derive from the parties to a broad series of exchanges; they are not imposed by law from without. And they can take into account a wide range of characteristics—the ability to get along, conviviality, empathy, looks, style—and a host of hard-to-measure intangibles that may help with team as well as individual production.

The idea, then, that workers are "qualified," or that only merits are taken into account, is not drawn from the theory of private contract on which the market system operates. On the contrary, these ideas all assume that there is some objective measure that can be administered by an external agent who decides which types of agreements meet some standard of social acceptability and which do not. For these purposes it does not matter whether the prohibited grounds are defined in terms of race,

9. This language was relied on first in *Griggs v. Duke Power Co.*, 401 U.S. 424, 434 (1971), discussed in Chapter 10, and then in *Price Waterhouse v. Hopkins*, 490 U.S. 228 (1990).

10. Id. at 243.

sex, eye color, or anything else. What does matter is that the government makes the effort to define those prohibited grounds at all and enforces its judgments by coercive means. The argument here is, moreover, perfectly general: there is no independent objective standard of what package of benefits is right for all workers. There are only offers that can be accepted or rejected at will, and these reveal the benefits that are desired by the parties.

Once certain grounds for judgment are ruled out of bounds, the legal system must respond to a fresh round of imperatives. How does any court or administrative tribunal decide whether a personnel decision was made on the strength of one of the prohibited criteria, such as race or sex? The obvious case is easy to state and relatively easy to control. The employer who places a sign over the entrance to the workplace reading, "No blacks, women, or Jews allowed" (or "No whites, men, or Christians [or, as lately in Chicago, Arabs] allowed"), is in violation of Title VII, without any further probing.[11] In these disparate treatment cases the stated grounds for rejection, which were unquestionably legal in the common law world, now become the paradigmatic wrong within the regulatory framework. But the system of civil rights enforcement cannot stop with the obvious violations as long as some employers treat regulation as a burden that they try to evade. If the overt forms of discrimination are prohibited, then some recalcitrant employers will go underground, at a price. Given the prior commitment to the universal antidiscrimination norm, it therefore becomes necessary, albeit costly, to impose restrictions as well upon the *covert* schemes and devices whereby employers seek by indirection the objective of the "no blacks" (or "no whites") sign. At this point the government prosecutor or aggrieved individual can no longer use a firm's public admission to establish its guilt; rather, it becomes necessary to collect the circumstantial evidence needed to justify criminal punishment or civil liability.

How does a trier of fact come by that evidence? One possible source is discarded memos or overheard discussions that indicate that decisions made on ostensibly neutral, or merit, grounds were in fact made on prohibited ones. The confidential admission is thus the "smoking gun" that takes the place of the defiant public refusal to

11. "Those who are opposed to [the bill] should realize that to hire a Negro solely because he is a Negro is racial discrimination, just as much as a 'white only' employment policy. Both forms of discrimination are prohibited by title VII of this bill." Remarks of Senator Harrison Williams of New Jersey, 110 *Cong. Rec.* at 8921.

deal. But these statements themselves are not easy to uncover, and cases of this sort are "relatively unusual."[12] Once it is clear that powerful consequences attach to using forbidden criteria, some parties will abandon them. But for others the preferred alternative will be to burrow in deeper so as to keep their true grounds concealed. Memos to the file, far from being candid, will now be phrased in language that tracks the statute. Candidate X was not hired or promoted because he or she failed on grounds related to merit and to merit only. Much of the enforcement of Title VII on race or sex would grind to a halt if explicit evidence of motive were required to show that a refusal or failure to hire or promote was made "because of race, color, religion, sex or national origin." But it should not be supposed that the statute would have no effect at all. The explicit "whites only" provisions once common in union charters would, for example, be a thing of the past, and so would the explicit affirmative action programs of such rising popularity today.

Nonetheless, a strong commitment to a color-blind system of employment requires a sustained and systematic level of interference in the business place. The demands of enforcement are such that some types of external proof are needed to show whether the employer operated with the wrong type of mental state. It then becomes necessary to ask just what form that public evidence has to take. The current literature customarily distinguishes between the disparate treatment cases mentioned earlier and the disparate impact cases, which focus on the effects of hiring practices rather than on their motivation. At one level it may appear that the distinction is overdrawn, for both sets of cases raise basically the same question: Where there is no admission, public or private, of guilt, what evidence can the plaintiff introduce in order to prevail, and what types of evidence can the defendant introduce to rebut the claim? The disparate treatment cases involve shorter chains of inference than the disparate impact cases.

Given the evolution of the legal system, however, the line between disparate treatment and disparate impact becomes the essence of the modern law. These structural similarities should not be allowed to obscure the massive differences in degree, which are often very pronounced. In practice Title VII in race relations would be a modest shadow of itself if plaintiffs were confined to the disparate treatment

---

12. See Barbara L. Schlei and Paul Grossman, *Employment Discrimination Law* 15 (2nd ed., 1983).

framework. The complexities inherent in disparate impact cases are sufficient to deserve a separate analysis of their own, in Chapters 10 and 11.

The Problems of Disparate Treatment

The Tripartite Case

The tests generally fashioned in disparate treatment cases originally stem from *McDonnell Douglas Corp. v. Green*,[13] a case in which the employer prevailed, having refused to rehire a worker who had committed acts of criminal trespass against the employer after he had been laid off. The very fact that such behavior could credibly raise antidiscrimination issues shows how quickly the case law strayed from the core instances, where race was the *sole* reason for not hiring a person. The case is important because it sets out the Supreme Court's initial view on disparate treatment:

> The complainant in a Title VII trial must carry the initial burden under the statute of establishing a prima facie case of racial discrimination. This may be done by showing (i) that he belongs to a racial minority; (ii) that he applied and was qualified for a job for which an employer was seeking applicants; (iii) that despite his qualifications, he was rejected; and (iv) that, after his rejection, the position remained open and the employer continued to seek applicants from persons of complainant's qualifications . . .
>
> The burden then must shift to the employer to articulate some legitimate, nondiscriminatory reason for the employee's rejection . . . [The Court accepted the plaintiff's criminal trespasses against the employer as a valid reason.]
>
> [The employer's] reason for rejection thus suffices to meet the prima facie case, but the inquiry does not end here. While Title VII does not, without more, compel rehiring of [the former employee], neither does it permit [the employer] to use [the employee's] conduct as a pretext for the sort of discrimination prohibited by [the statute]. On remand, [the employee] must . . . be afforded a fair opportunity to show that [the employer's] stated reason for [the employee's] rejection was in fact pretext.[14]

13. 411 U.S. 792 (1973).
14. Id. at 802–804.

The Court then stressed that the pretext inquiry depended in part on whether the employer had reacted improperly to the legitimate civil rights activities of the employees. The inquiry also turns on the employer's general views and practices on minority employment, an issue on which the use of "statistics as to [the employer's] employment policy and practice" could also be relevant. "In short, on the retrial [the employee] must be given a full and fair opportunity to demonstrate by competent evidence that the presumptively valid reasons for his rejection were in fact a coverup for a racially discriminatory decision."[15]

In essence there was a tripartite standard of prima facie case, justification, and pretext.[16] In subsequent decisions the Court has elaborated on this tripartite standard, making clear that its divisions should not be taken in any "rigid, mechanized, or ritualistic" way.[17] In addition, the ultimate burden of persuasion on the question of disparate treatment was placed on the plaintiff after all the evidence had been marshaled.[18] Given the requirements of the statute, these rules of proof for disparate treatment cases seek on balance to make a reasonable effort to give respect to the statute on the one hand while limiting its scope of application to manageable proportions on the other. I doubt that anyone could come up with a simpler set of rules that would capture the full set of relevant considerations under the statute in a clearer and more logical form than was done in *McDonnell Douglas* and its progeny. Indeed, that is just the problem; for as careful as the *McDonnell Douglas* formulation is, it shows just how wide a gulf exists between any theory of wrongful discrimination and the simple contract model of no agreement, no lawsuit. The basic disparate treatment regime calls for more extended comment.

15. Id. at 805.

16. There is an enormous case literature on the subject of pretext. See, e.g., *Grigsby v. Reynolds Metals Co.,* 821 F.2d 363 (11th Cir. 1987) (plaintiff not singled out for special treatment in reduction-in-force case); *Smith v. Papp Clinic, P.A.* 808 F.2d 1449 (11th Cir. 1987) (no pretext when supervisor who had been previously warned received heavier sanctions than other workers involved in misconduct).

17. *Furnco Construction Corp. v. Waters,* 438 U.S. 567, 577 (1978). On the subject of burdens of proof generally, see Robert Belton, "Burdens of Pleading and Proof in Discrimination Cases: Toward a Theory of Procedural Justice," 34 *Vand. L. Rev.* 1205 (1981).

18. *Texas Department of Community Affairs v. Burdine,* 450 U.S. 248 (1981).

The Joint Causation Dilemma

The tripartite pattern of argumentation in *McDonnell Douglas* is strictly necessary whenever motivation becomes the dominant test of legality. The point is not confined to the discrimination laws but carries over to any system in which liability rests on motive rather than consent. The National Labor Relations Act (NLRA), for example, includes in its catalogue of statutorily defined "unfair labor practices" one that forbids the employer to "discriminat[e] in regard to hire or tenure of employment or any term or condition of employment to encourage or discourage membership in any labor organization."[19] The theory of the section is that once union activities are protected, the employer cannot selectively fire those workers who join or support a union. No union organization could continue to operate if dismissals on the ground of union membership were freely allowed. Nonetheless, it is quite dangerous to pass any law that provides that workers who join or support a union are thereby wholly immune from dismissal, even if they refuse to work or seek to sabotage the plant.[20] The abandonment of the contract at will approach in a collective bargaining context therefore requires a legal regime that distinguishes between work-related and antiunion employer sanctions.

Only some form of motive test can do that job. The problems that this test creates are not inconsiderable, however.[21] Whether we are dealing with NLRA cases or antidiscrimination cases, the factual questions are insistent. In the simplest form the issue of motive will present an either-or case, where "*either* a legitimate *or* an illegitimate set of considerations led to the challenged decision."[22] Although many cases

---

19. National Labor Relations Act, 29 *U.S.C.* §158 (1982).

20. See, e.g., *Mount Healthy City School Distict Board of Education v. Doyle,* 429 U.S. 274 (1977), where the question concerned the dismissal of a teacher who had criticized the school board. The Supreme Court adopted a similar set of motive-based rules because it did not wish to "place an employee in a better position as a result of the exercise of a constitutionally protected conduct than he would have occupied if he had done nothing." The Court noted the close parallel of this First Amendment issue with both NLRA and Title VII issues. See *Price Waterhouse v. Hopkins,* 490 U.S. 228, 249 (1989).

21. See, e.g., *NLRB v. Transportation Management Corp.,* 462 U.S. 393 (1983). See, generally, Thomas G. S. Christensen and Andrea H. Svanoe, "Motive and Intent in the Commission of Unfair Labor Practices: The Supreme Court and the Fictive Formality," 77 *Yale L. J.* 1269 (1968); Julius G. Getman, "Section 8(a)(3) of the NLRA and the Effort to Insulate Free Employee Choice," 32 *U. Chi. L. Rev.* 735 (1965).

22. See *Price Waterhouse,* 490 U.S. at 247.

will take this form, some large fraction, perhaps a majority, will reveal mixed or dual motive, in which *both* kinds of consideration may be present.

The rules in *McDonnell Douglas* were directed toward the first and simpler pretext situation, in which the sole question is to identify the *single* motive that was the real basis for the decision to hire or fire. Again a collective bargaining comparison is instructive. Suppose a worker who has just been discovered to be engaged in union organizing activities is fired, ostensibly because he has left the keys in the ignition of a company van. That entire account can be dismissed as pretextual if leaving the keys in the ignition is standard practice for all employees.[23] In the pure either-or case the evidence on the question of pretext is designed to ferret out which motive was the exclusive one. The only relevant difficulty is that of uncertainty on the strength of the evidence. In some cases the point is easy to resolve, but where the evidence is clouded, litigation may be protracted, and the assignment of the burden of proof is often decisive.

The dual motive cases are more difficult. In these circumstances it is necessary, within the context of Title VII, or indeed any motive-based regime, to plumb the relative causal contributions of the two sets of motives to the final decision of the employer: how much incompetence and how much forbidden animus were involved in the case? The sex cases are governed by the same rules as the race cases, and in both the range of difficulties is well illustrated in the 1989 decision of *Price Waterhouse v. Hopkins*.[24] There the employee worked for an accounting firm and had a mixed record, with points of great distinction and points of genuine concern. On the plus side of her ledger were her ability to obtain large contracts from government sources and her ability to deal with people outside the firm in positions of influence and authority. On the minus side were her relations with other employees in the firm, where her conduct was often perceived as aggressive and

---

23. See, e.g., *NLRB v. Transportation Management Corp.*, 462 U.S. at 396. The Court upheld the finding of pretext by an administrative law judge when firing was not consistent with the normal practices within the firm. The Court of Appeals had taken the position that it was improper to place the burden of proof on the defendant to show that the dismissal would have taken place without taking into account the forbidden motive, *NLRB v. Transportation Management Corp.*, 674 F.2d 130 (1st Cir. 1982). The Supreme Court, however, held it appropriate for the board in its discretion to make that division of proof. *Transportation Management Corp.* 462 U.S. at 402–403.

24. 490 U.S. 228 (1989).

abrasive. There was some question as to whether these character traits were thought undesirable in a woman even though they might have been acceptable in a man. There were certain suggestions about her dress and makeup that were without doubt directed to her solely as a woman. And there was ample evidence that all these factors had been taken into account in the employment decision. The question for any court is how to sort out their relative significance.

The issue of joint causation is not new to antidiscrimination law, and it is no accident that the Court's opinion in *Price Waterhouse* contained extensive discussions of the tort law's response to the problem of joint causation.[25] Nothing could be a more powerful signal that something is very much awry in the underlying structure of the law. The basic problem within the tort context is to fashion some theory, any theory, that works in the *simplest* cases where two or more separate forces (for example, two bullets) combine to cause a single harm. There is always a myriad of possibilities as to the extent to which the two forces contributed to the basic harm, especially when either one is neither necessary nor sufficient to cause the harm. The common law has flirted with a huge number of probabilistic rules to answer the various questions of attribution and division of responsibility,[26] and academic commentators are in hopeless division over the choice from a large menu of joint and several liability or apportionment rules.[27] Yet with physical injuries these cases are usually sidestepped. Only infrequently is a single hunter struck by two bullets fired at the same instant,[28] and only rarely is an unfortunate teenager who

25. Id. at 1785–86 (plurality opinion); id. at 4479 (concurrence of Justice O'Connor); id. at 1807 (dissent of Justice Kennedy).

26. See, e.g., *Union Stock Yards Co. v. Chicago, Burlington & Quincy, R.R. Co.* 196 U.S. 217 (1905) (both defendants accountable to plaintiff, but no contribution or indemnity in cases of "like negligence"); *American Motorcycle Association v. Superior Court*, 20 Cal.3d 578, 578 P.2d 899, 146 *Cal. Rptr.* 182 (1978) (adopting general joint and several liability; finessing statutory scheme of pro rata liability).

27. See, e.g., William M. Landes and Richard A. Posner, *The Economic Structure of Tort Law*, ch. 7 (1987); Mario J. Rizzo and Frank S. Arnold, "Causal Apportionment in the Law of Torts: An Economic Theory," 80 *Colum. L. Rev.* 1399 (1980); David Kaye and Mikel Aickin, "A Comment on Causal Apportionment," 13 *J. Legal Stud.* 191 (1984); William Kruskal, "Terms of Reference: Singular Confusion about Multiple Causation," 15 *J. Legal Stud* 427 (1986); Richard W. Wright, "Allocating Liability among Multiple Responsible Causes," 21 *U. C. Davis. L. Rev.* 1141 (1987). My own skeptical views on any definitive solutions are set out in Richard A. Epstein, "Causation in Context: An Afterword," 63 *Chi.-Kent L. Rev.* 653, 670–674 (1987).

28. See *Summers v. Tice*, 33 Cal.2d 80, 199 P.2d 1 (1948).

is falling to his death over the side of a cliff electrocuted by exposed wires before he hits the ground.[29]

Joint causation is both more frequent and more complicated in disparate treatment cases, for although cases involving multiple forces are an uncommon occurrence, cases involving multiple motives are commonplace. All that is necessary for the issue to arise is for the defendant to know that the plaintiff is black, or a woman, or sixty years of age. That knowledge in itself raises a credible case that the forbidden ground alone served as a reason—perhaps a dominant reason—for the decision not to hire or to fire.

Title VII offers yet another instance where original intentions could not bind the subsequent expansion of legal rules. The original defenders of the statute were uniform in offering assurances that no employer would be required to hire, promote, or retain an incompetent employee. But unlike the situation with at will contracts, a huge percentage of cases squarely raise the question of whether competence dominated illicit motive or the reverse. Resolving the standard dual motive dispute necessarily taxes the capacity of the trier of fact in any administrative, judicial, or informal setting. In light of the need to prevent a coverup of a bad motive, the plaintiff must be given a leg up on matters of proof.

But how? In *Price Waterhouse,* for example, the Supreme Court adopted a rule which stated that first the plaintiff had to show that the employer took race or gender into account in making its decision. The decision is "because of" race or sex as long as either is a factor in how that decision came about. Thereafter the interest in the "employer's remaining freedom of choice" (the faint but audible echo to a world of freedom of contract) is said to justify a rule that "means an employer shall not be liable if it can prove that, even if it had not taken gender [or race] into account, it would have come to the same decision regarding a particular person."[30] Proof here is by a preponderance of the evidence.

The question of burdens of proof can easily consume a treatise of its own.[31] Yet these intramural disputes only gloss over the basic problem

---

29. *Dillon v. Twin State Gas & Electric Co.,* 85 N.H. 449, 163 A. 111 (1932) (denying liability to the utility company because of the short expected life of the plaintiff, who was electrocuted in the course of a fall that would have killed him anyway).

30. *Price Waterhouse,* 490 U.S. at 242.

31. The preponderance of evidence rule embraced by the Supreme Court has two plausible rivals. The first, followed in the decision of the First Circuit in *Price Waterhouse* is that the employer had to carry this burden of proof by "clear and convincing" evidence—a more stringent standard than the preponderance of evidence eventually adopted by the

with any formulation, which is that each decision requires one not only to identify the existence of these two types of considerations but also to determine their precise relative magnitudes. Under the Court's preponderance of the evidence standard, the initial question is whether race or sex was a relevant factor. Then the employer shows that some legitimate consideration—say, job competence—is a relevant factor as well. Thereafter, there is no way to combine these two pieces of information into a yes-no decision without more information. If the business decision, independent of race or sex, was close, then it seems that a showing of some modest influence of race or sex pushes the case over the line. But if the decision on the business merits of the case was clear, then that same showing of limited bias renders it likely that the decision was closer to the line; it does not establish that the decision would have come out the other way. The causal link is not established. Similarly, if powerful race or sex motives are involved in a case that was also clear on its merits the other way, the final conclusion is again uncertain because two powerful sets of considerations work to cancel each other out. There are likely to be many cases that cluster around the point of decision, making settlement difficult and litigation expensive and uncertain.[32]

Oftentimes cases are more complex than even this summary suggests. Thus the most common situation is one in which the weight of the evidence gathered is (honestly) expressed only in probabilistic terms. To see the point we need only consider a simple case in which there are two possible outcomes on each variable. There may be a 50 percent chance that the employee was regarded as wholly unqualified and a 50 percent chance that the employee was only modestly unqualified. Similarly, it may be that there was a 50 percent chance that race or sex played a strong part in the decision, and a 50 percent chance that it had only a weak effect. There are now four separate cells to be evaluated before we can reach any overall conclusion. The case seems roughly in equipoise if a strong bias is offset by the employer's honest determination that the employee was wholly unqualified, or a finding of weak bias is offset by the employer's determination that the employee was

---

Supreme Court. Id. at 1790. The second, a somewhat more proemployer rule that is consistent with the pretext cases, keeps the burden of proof for the whole case on the plaintiff throughout the trial. Id. at 1806.

32. See George L. Priest and Benjamin Klein, "The Selection of Disputes for Litigation," 13 *J. Legal Stud.* 1 (1984).

only marginally unqualified. But there are clear decisions only for the other two cells, that is, cases of weak bias and wholly unqualified employees on the one hand or marginally unqualified employees and strong bias on the other. The issue does not get any easier where there are continuous probability distributions on both sets of underlying variables.

In light of the large number of hotly contested cases, it is understandable why trial lawyers battle as hard over burdens of proof under the antidiscrimination laws as they do under tort law. One might have thought that the burden of proof should be placed squarely on the employee, for it is not normally in an employer's interest to fire competent workers, especially when there is the additional threat of money damages for improper dismissal. But the level of suspicion about motive is so high that the judicial interpretation of the cases only compounds the problem by setting the presumption of law against the likely probabilities in the cases. The Court's formulation in *Price Waterhouse* places the burden on the employer. But no matter how the burden of proof is assigned, the *systemwide* costs are apt to be high. The relative advantages of the various rules examined in *Price Waterhouse* for handling joint motive cases depend on the types of errors they generate and the costs of their administration. Yet those questions were not addressed in any systematic way in the opinion.

Under present law it remains unfortunately clear that any and all rules on joint motive cases are far more costly and less reliable than the common law rule that allows hiring and firing, accepting and quitting to be done at will. As is so often the case, the soundness of a legal system rests not on how it decides its marginal cases but on the basic choice of which ones lie close to the margin. Burdens of proof are utterly immaterial in an at will world. The key choice, then, is the movement from the at will to the for cause decision, with its inescapable logic of good reasons and hollow pretexts. Once the first wrong step has been made, the solution of the intractable joint causation and burden of proof questions is a second-order issue on which we should (and do) expect to find little consensus.

It is possible to invent legal schemes that finesse the causation question in disparate treatment cases. A proposal to achieve just that result was incorporated into the Civil Rights Act of 1990 vetoed by President George Bush. The key relevant provisions were two. First, the bill provided that "the discriminatory practice need not be the sole motivating factor" but only "a motivating factor, even though other factors also motivated such practice."[33] The section went beyond existing law, which required proof of a "substantial" motivating factor. Second, in its critical innovation the companion section provided that if the defendant discharges the burden of proof on causation and "demonstrates that it would have taken the same action in the absence of discrimination," the court "may grant declaratory relief, injunctive relief, attorney's fees and costs, and it shall not award damages."[34] Attorney's fees are defined to include "expert fees and other litigation expenses." The scope of the court's discretion is not clear, save for the general aid to construction that says that the act "shall be broadly construed to effectuate the purpose of such laws and to provide equal opportunity and provide effective remedies." It is possible, therefore, that the bill, taken as a whole, would have created a presumption allowing the recovery of attorney's fees, broadly defined, if the discriminatory motive had even the slightest effect on the probability of dismissal, but no one can say for sure. The elimination of the causation question would be a massive invitation for new suits even in cases where legitimate motives were strong and discriminatory factors weak, for the quantum of proof required to trigger the (one-way) prospect of relief from legal fees seems very low. The bill thus created the (uncertain) prospect of overdeterrence in disparate treatment cases, for the causation requirement would no longer weed out those in which the wrongful conduct did not make a (sufficient) difference.[35] It is as if contingent fee lawyers were told that they could recover their legal fees if they proved that a defendant was a negligent driver, even though they could not recover actual damages. This proposed modification of the civil rights law is a mischievous device, but one that is likely to appear in some future civil rights bill.

The Pressures for Formality

The effect of the dual motive cases is not felt only at the time of litigation but extends before it. Under a contract at will, a pink slip beats back a charge of contractual liability. With the motive cases, however, *every* adverse decision with regard to every worker becomes a potential source

33. See proposed Civil Rights Act of 1990 (S. 2104) §5(a).

34. Id. §5(b).

35. For a discussion of these issues in the context of disparate impact cases, see Chapter 11.

of liability, given the reach of the basic statute and the muddiness of the rules on motive and proof.

Nor are these cases easy to defend. As the general test I have outlined suggests, the evidence has to be relatively complete, given the suspicion of pretext and the superior access the employer has to the information concerning its decisions. The motive test of the antidiscrimination laws becomes relevant before trial, where it exerts a pervasive influence on the internal patterns and practices of the firm. Under common law the firm could choose that level of formality necessary to function with a minimum of record keeping and documentation. But once all employment decisions are justiciable, the external pressures for formality become far stronger. The Civil Rights Act routinely requires employers to make and maintain relevant and voluminous records, and to keep them available for government inspection.[36] The effort to trace subtle and illicit motives thus leads to an inexorable .expansion of government control, given the need to ferret out covert discrimination. Wholly lost in the process is the argument that free mobility of labor provides better protection for all workers than any system of judicial or administrative review of employment decisions.

From Color-Blind to Protected Classes

McDonnell Douglas also marks a subtle shift in the basic orientation of the antidiscrimination laws. On its face the statutory language falls within the tradition of color-blind laws. It is illegal to discriminate against *any* individual because of race, color, religion, sex, or national origin. But the verbal formula in *McDonnell Douglas* changes the substantive rule, for it is geared solely toward workers from a "racial minority." (Parallel arguments apply to sex discrimination.) On textual grounds there is no reason to shift from the color-blind statutory language to the race-specific protected class in articulating the cause of action. It is perfectly consistent with both the language and purpose of Title VII to make the first element of the prima facie case outlined in *McDonnell Douglas* that the plaintiff, *any* plaintiff, was "qualified" but nonetheless was passed over for someone of a different race. This formulation of the basic test is consistent with the language of the statutory text and its application to "all

36. The applicable section is 709, which (1) allows the Equal Employment Opportunity Commission (EEOC) access to employer records; (2) allows cooperation with state and local agencies; and (3) requires employer record keeping.

individuals," and it should also supply extra protection to members of minority groups *if* they have in fact been the victims of racial discrimination.

This neutral rule on discrimination need not promise equal benefits for all persons in light of the historical patterns of discrimination. If the historical discrimination ran all in one direction, then its elimination would (subject to the complex distributional issues raised by the statute) run in the opposite direction. The color-blind statute could well transform the basic patterns of life in the workplace, which is what the proponents of the Civil Rights Act supposed when they defended the bill as a way to root out past discrimination and also to ensure a prejudice-free workplace, with hiring based on merit and ability. In that context there was no room for protected classes. As Senator Harrison Williams said in support of the bill:

> Some people charge that [the bill] favors the Negro, at the expense of the white majority. But how can the language of equality favor one race or one religion over another? Equality can have only one meaning, and that meaning is self-evident to reasonable men. Those who say that equality means favoritism do violence to common sense.[37]

There is no room for protected classes under this account. Nonetheless, the original view of the statute was rejected without argument in *McDonnell Douglas.* Indeed, the case is silent on the question of whether disparate treatment claims could be raised by whites, and if so whether they would be governed by the same sort of rules. But its silence on that critical question speaks volumes. *McDonnell Douglas* is therefore best understood in the way in which it has come to be read, as replacing the older color-blind state with a protected-class limitation, all without explicit discussion or analysis. The reasons for this dramatic shift in orientation may have been partly prudential. The mere assertion that a plaintiff was qualified vastly broadens the scope of disparate treatment cases. The statute uses the same rules for internal decisions on salary, jobs, and promotion as it does with regard to hiring decisions, and the same logic applies not only to race but also to color, sex, religion, and national origin. *McDonnell Douglas* narrows the reach of the statute, but at the considerable expense of shifting it away from its color-blind orientation. Yet even here questions remain that are unresolved to this day. The stan-

---

37. 110 *Cong. Rec.* 8921 (1964).

dards that are applicable for disparate treatment cases brought by members of the nonprotected group are not resolved explicitly by *McDonnell Douglas,* or for that matter by subsequent law, which generally allows firms to engage in voluntary affirmative action. Similarly, genuine condundrums arise when persons of one protected group are passed over in favor of individuals of a second protected group, as in the Daniel Lamp case, where all the positions were taken by blacks or Hispanics.[38]

Searching for "Qualified" Applicants

Finally, the disparate treatment cases depend on a showing that the rejected applicant is not qualified for the position at hand. Again, there is a vast cleavage between what the statute requires and the operation of unregulated markets. The basic point can be illustrated with the initial selection process discussed in *McDonnell Douglas,* but the economics of search, which explains these cases, extends as well to all other aspects of the employment relationship covered by the statute: promotion, demotion, layoff, change in work conditions, reverse discrimination, and the like. Consider the decision confronting the employer looking to expand its work force. That employer assigns some expected value to hiring the first applicant who presents himself for a job. The business question is whether the expected gain from considering a second applicant (who may be no better or worse than the first) is sufficiently large to justify the additional costs imposed by delay and by a second round of interviews and tests. That decision is often close; it depends on several factors.

Let us start with the benefit side. One key element concerns the variation in the quality of the applicant pool. The greater the variance, the greater the gains from search. Consider first the limiting case in which the employer knows that all workers are identical in all relevant respects. Here the only rational strategy is to take the first worker who walks through the door. A search has a positive cost, however small, but it cannot generate any additional benefits, given the assumption of perfect identity among workers. If the variation among workers is small, so most are concentrated around the median, then the prospects of finding a better worker are positive but limited. The first worker may be at the low end of the distribution, and the costs of delay are not large. But the likelihood of making real gains is greatest where differences in quality are perceived to be substantial. Then

38. See Chapter 3 at 60–72, under the heading "Relational Contracts and Governance Costs."

a second, third, or even fourth inquiry could yield a worker who is far better than those screened in the initial phases of the search.

The theory is borne out by common practice; the search for key employees is often protracted and expensive, with extensive reliance on hiring committees and headhunters. The anticipated gain from getting the right person justifies these expenses. Search, therefore, is driven not by a single yes-no, on-off evaluation as to whether the applicant is qualified, like that posited by the *McDonnell Douglas* formula. Within a business context any rigid, bifurcated preconception about qualified applicants wholly ignores the desire of the firm to *maximize* its gain from search, given the variations in its applicant pool. Qualified and unqualified are matters of degree. Candidates do not fall into sharply discontinuous classes, as the *McDonnell Douglas* formula presupposes.

Let us look next at the cost side of the equation. *McDonnell Douglas* contains no account of how long it pays to search for new applicants, but the decision is again critical in the business context. The screening of additional candidates imposes costs on the firm, both directly, in the expenses of the search, and indirectly, in the form of lost business opportunities resulting from delay. These costs need not be constant across different business settings, and indeed may vary as the firm expands the size of the candidate list. Setting up a search committee or hiring a headhunter is a front-end cost whose effect is to reduce the marginal cost of looking at additional applicants. The marginal costs of search are critical to the decision of how long to look after a qualified candidate appears. If these costs are low, then the next look may be worth taking. But if they are high, then it may not.

This brief discussion of the benefits and costs of search thus yields an equilibrium. Over time the gains from additional search will decrease, while the costs of running the search will trend upward. The search will reach closure when the inequality reverses to the extent that the costs of additional search are greater than the expected yield from the search. The employer who has some sense of what the market will bring at the price it is prepared to pay can guess with reasonable certainty, and will live with the faulty consequences of either hasty or tardy action in the event that searches are not carried out when needed, or are carried out when redundant. No system of markets guarantees that the right choices are made for any given applicant. Nonetheless, the market does not create incentive structures that distort the employer's choices.

Title VII, as construed in *McDonnell Douglas*, necessarily places a crimp in the rational search strategy of the employer. If the first worker interviewed is black and meets some standard of qualification—for example, the firm would hire her if after looking at five candidates none better appeared—the firm would face the difficult decision of whether to pursue additional candidates, black or white. Without the statute, the benefits of search might outweigh the future costs, and the search would continue. But the statute imposes some risk that further search will, without more, create a prima facie case of liability, which itself is the prelude to rugged litigation: a qualified black candidate has been passed over. The firm is therefore under pressure to curtail the search in order to minimize the sum of its future search costs and the risk of liability from searching.

On balance, pressures are thus created to hire (protected) candidates whose qualifications are lower than those that would lead the employer to call off or limit the search in an unregulated market. The employer, moreover, may decide to adopt other strategies to minimize the risks posed by the *McDonnell Douglas* formula. It may be possible to interview the white candidates before the black ones in order to reduce the risks inherent in passing over a qualified black candidate while searching for a better-qualified white one. But the logistical problems quickly become acute when large numbers of persons are considered for many different positions over an extended period of time. "Before" and "after" are far less well defined when candidate A is contacted before candidate B, who in turn is interviewed before candidate A.

To be sure, there are offsetting factors that may afford the employer some refuge. At the second stage of the case the firm could show that there was some legitimate nondiscriminatory reason for it to continue the search. The legal standard here, it should be stressed, is not particularly strict, at least in disparate treatment cases. The Supreme Court, for example, has held that a construction firm that does not maintain a permanent staff of bricklayers may hire only on the strength of personal references, without having to examine candidates who simply show up at the gate. The dangers of getting bad workers are too severe, given the delays and damage they can cause to an ongoing project.[39] Similarly, the New York Transit Authority need not consider for safety-sensitive positions any person who has been in a methadone treatment program.[40] But these reasons are not infinitely plastic and are in all cases subject to challenge as pretexts for racial discrimination. An employer may well be able to continue with a search after it has found a qualified applicant in a protected class if it makes clear at the outset its

39. See *Furnco Construction Corp. v. Waters*, 438 U.S. 567 (1978).
40. *New York Transit Authority v. Beazer*, 440 U.S. 568 (1979).

intention to conduct an extensive search. But the simple adoption of this policy, without any showing of the particular failings of the current candidate, still leave the firm exposed to a risk of liability that it would not face in a market regime.

Disparate Treatment as a Practical Compromise

In the end, therefore, the conclusion must be inescapable that the disparate treatment system of Title VII is costlier to operate than the common law rules that allow hiring at will on both sides. How much in dollars and cents it is impossible to say. Even if a firm can prevail at trial, it must nonetheless bear the costs of litigation for winning, and take the risk of losing if the evidence comes in the other way. These costs, moreover, are borne not only by the firms that might, deep down, choose to discriminate against blacks or women, but also by those firms that have had by conventional wisdom the best possible record in race relations. Nor do the rules generate any net benefits for the class of employees as a whole. The time and costs of the overall process impose an implicit tax that is borne in part by all prospective employees, who must wait somewhat longer before they can obtain a job, if a position is available, given the additional costs the employer must incur to fill it. That some workers will be fortunate while others are not is a distributional consequence that comes only at some allocative cost.

The overall picture should be neither overdrawn nor understated. Employers (and employees) may adopt strategies to mitigate the costs of complying with Title VII, and this is all to the good. But mitigation does not restore the market to the status quo ante of the unregulated world. Mitigation costs money, so after the appropriate steps are taken, both employers and employees as a class will be left *worse off* with the regulation than they were in its absence.

Although the costs of trying disparate treatment cases are substantial, on balance I have little doubt that these costs, had they been made explicit in the early debates, would have been regarded as acceptable by the Congress that passed the 1964 act. As a practical compromise, moreover, a limitation of Title VII race cases to individual disparate treatment cases would honor the original intentions of the statute while removing most of its heavy costs. These cases are not especially controversial today, and though greater in number, they may be of lesser significance in the employment context than the major disparate impact cases, which are the subject of the next two chapters.

CHAPTER 10

From Disparate Treatment
to Disparate Impact

A Critical Transition

The disparate treatment cases discussed in the previous chapter represent one effort to make judgments about the elusive issue of discriminatory intent. In some cases the court may have direct evidence on the matter; where it does not, the court looks into the willingness of an employer to continue to search for a qualified applicant after a member of a racial minority has presented himself. The inference is then drawn from the overt behavior to the state of mind that animated that behavior. One innocent way to view the disparate impact cases is as an effort to take this same process of inference one step further. Where the pattern of hiring or promotion shows that different percentages of blacks and whites, or men and women, receive certain types of jobs, then the implication may (but need not) be drawn that these disparate impacts are the result of certain employment practices. The further inference can then be drawn that the challenged practices were undertaken with motives impermissible under Title VII. Statistics thus become a standard tool of the aggrieved employee or the government. But in a disparate treatment case they may in principle be used "only because such imbalance is often a telltale sign of purposeful discrimination."[1] The inference of discrimination, however, remains open to rebuttal. The ultimate question of liability is still phrased in terms of intent of and treatment by the employer, not impact and adverse affects on the employee. A demonstration that the practice was used for legitimate business purposes, without pretext, would thus bring

1. *International Brotherhood of Teamsters v. United States*, 431 U.S. 324, 340 n.20 (1977).

the case back within the fold of the three-stage test developed at length in *McDonnell Douglas*.

Within the conventional disparate treatment framework, therefore, statistics could at most create a rebuttable presumption of discriminatory intent. Modern disparate impact cases have taken the process of inference one step further, and in the process have radically transformed the scope and effect of Title VII. Disparate impact became a wrong in itself justified only by stringent tests of business necessity. The watershed case on this issue is *Griggs v. Duke Power Co.*[2] of 1971, the *first* and single most important Supreme Court decision under Title VII—at least until the 1989 disparate impact decision in *Wards Cove Packing Co., Inc. v. Atonio*,[3] which softened business necessity to the far more compliant standard of "legitimate employer interest," parallel to that in the disparate treatment tests. The present law may not represent a stable status quo, for the most controversial provisions of the vetoed Civil Rights Act of 1990 were those that purported to undo the *Ward's Cove* decision and return to the business necessity standard found in *Griggs*[4] but that may have done far more than this. Similarly, the Bush administration's 1991 proposal calls in so many words for overruling *Ward's Cove* and returning to the business necessity test of *Griggs*.[5] The question of disparate impact, and the issue of quotas with which it is so closely linked, remains in the legislative arena.

It is useful to undertake a careful review of *Griggs*, after which it becomes possible to assess both *Ward's Cove* and some legislative proposals for its overruling.

This chapter chronicles the movement from disparate treatment to disparate impact. That transformation was accomplished largely as a matter of statutory construction of the 1964 Civil Rights Act, although the full story requires some attention to be paid to the 1972 Equal Opportunity Act, which was enacted in a radically different political climate from that

2. 401 U.S. 424 (1971).

3. 490 U.S. 642 (1990).

4. S. 2104 §4, "Restoring the Burden of Proof in Disparate Impact Tests."

5. See letter of Attorney General Richard Thornburgh to House Speaker Thomas Foley (March 15, 1991), 1, which explains the administration bill. Section 4 of that bill provides: "Under this Title, an unlawful employment practice based on disparate impact is established only when a complaining party demonstrates that a particular employment practice causes a disparate impact on the basis of race, color, religion, sex or national origin, and the respondent fails to demonstrate that such practice is justified by business necessity." The inclusion of "religion" on this list is especially unfortunate because it raises the specter of increased religious divisions and strife.

surrounding the earlier statute. The thesis of this chapter is that *Griggs* is fatally misguided as an exercise of statutory construction. By imposing the disparate impact test, the Court seriously misunderstood the text, structure, and purpose of the 1964 act. Chapter 11 will then examine the practical problems of enforcement that arise under *Griggs* and the extent to which the rules of the game have been reshaped, at least for the moment, by the *Ward's Cove* decision.

Statutory Construction of the 1964 Statute

That disparate impact cases are a creature of judicial innovation is reasonably clear from the text of the 1964 Civil Rights Act, and manifestly clear from its legislative history. The general language emphasizes the motivation of the employer for not hiring a worker: "because of race, color, sex, religion and national origin." In connection with section 703(a)(1), which governs hiring, promotion, and discharge, it is apparent that this "because" language refers to the reason for the employer's decision to "discriminate against" the employee. In this context "because" speaks, more concretely, of the reason the employer had for the refusal to deal. It is not enough to prove the counterfactual case that if the employer had thought about the matter further, it might have used a different criterion for its hiring decision that would have proved more advantageous for blacks or for some other protected group. As long as the employer's decision was based on reasons unrelated to race or sex, the decision not to hire or promote was not *because of* race or sex. The effect of a decision is in itself no reason to impose liability under the statute.

Griggs also relied on section 703(a)(2), which is best analyzed side by side with section 703(a)(1).

> Section 703(a)   It shall be an unlawful employment practice for an employer—
>
> (1) to fail or refuse to hire or to discharge any individual, or otherwise to discriminate against any individual with respect to his compensation, terms, conditions, or privileges of employment, because of such individual's race, color, religion, sex or national origin; or
>
> (2) to limit, segregate, or classify his employees in any way which would deprive or tend to deprive any individual of employment opportunities or otherwise adversely affect his status as an employee, because of such individual's race, color, religion, sex or national origin.

The drafting of section 703(a)(2) is the catchall phrase that covers sources of unlawful conduct that fall outside of section 703(a)(1). In consequence, the drafting of section 703(a)(2) is far muddier than the drafting of section 703(a)(1). An argument could be made that (notwithstanding the comma) the final clause in section 703(a)(2) refers only to the adverse effects and not to the reasons for the employment decision itself. On balance that conclusion seems textually incorrect, however, for if the "because" clause refers only to adverse effect, it cannot modify "to limit, segregate, or classify," which defines the set of practices to which the prohibition in section 703(a)(2) applies. The best reading of the statute therefore treats "because" as modifying these prior words as well, such that the middle phrase—"which would deprive or tend to deprive any individual of employment opportunities or otherwise adversely affect his status as an employee"—refers solely to the damage consequent upon any improper decision "to limit, segregate, or classify." With respect to this damage, there is no requirement that the employer must intend it to flow from his wrongful practices. As is common in the law of tort, the unintended consequences of intentional wrongs are actionable just as if they were intended. The issue of damages is relevant only after liability has been established; and liability still requires proof of the requisite state of mind.

This reading of the clause also seems preferable because it provides more congruence between section 703(a)(1) and section 703(a)(2). The "because" language in section 703(a)(1) plainly covers any decision "to fail or refuse to hire or to discharge," for otherwise the section would require an employer to hire and grant lifetime tenure to every prospective employee who walks through the door. There is no reason to assume that there are radical differences in the underlying theories of liability of the two subsections, which were written to complement each other. To preserve the internal coherence of the section as a whole, the basis of liability under both halves should be the same in the absence of some clear signal that different rules were intended. It seems quite inconceivable as a structural matter that Congress should choose to adopt two very different conceptions of the basic wrongful conduct without giving any explanation of how the two different sections should be coordinated. There is some obvious overlap between a decision "to discriminate against" an employee because of race or sex and a decision to "limit, segregate, or classify" an employee. With some truth it could be said that the wrongs set out in section 703(a)(2) are specific illustrations of the wrongs that are identified in section 703(a)(1). It would be odd indeed for the same section to adopt wholly different theories of the underlying wrong, and to embark on that course by using the same key phrase, "because of." It follows that under both subsections, once the evidence on motive is clear, then the question of effects is wholly beside the point. Statistical evidence is relevant, if at all, in a limited way solely to resolve the ultimate issue of discriminatory intent, as is now allowed under disparate treatment cases.[6]

Legislative History

This view of the textual construction is strongly confirmed by any fair reading of the extensive commentary on the statute. During the course of that history the structural distinction between disparate treatment and disparate impact was nowhere in evidence. The failure to articulate the distinction between these two now current theories of discrimination was, in retrospect, an enormous boon to the supporters of the bill. They were able to take the position that Title VII attacked only "discrimination," and were never forced to confront the argument that discrimination could be proved solely by its impact. Instead the debate was shifted from the as yet unformed disparate impact theory to the legality under Title VII of quotas along racial, ethnic, and religious lines. The southern states' position was that Title VII invited the use of quotas in employment. Their argument was *not* that there was any explicit language in the statute that mandated the use of quota. Rather it was that the imprecision of the term *discrimination* allowed courts to impose quotas under the guise of implementing the substantive provisions of the statute. Although they groped toward the disparate impact handle, they were never able to pin that label on their concerns. Thus Senator Absalom Robertson said:

> What does "discrimination" mean? If it means what I think it does, and which it could mean, it means that a man could be required to have a quota or he would be discriminating. The question comes down to what is meant by "discrimination" and the framers of the bill will not tell us.[7]

6. For a contemporary account of the "limit, segregate, or classify" language, see, *The Civil Rights Act of 1964: Text, Analysis, Legislative History* 33–34 (1964): "Under this provision [703(a)(2)], such practices as separate seniority rosters for male and female or white and Negro employees presumably would be violations. The same would appear to be true with respect to the designation of certain jobs as 'male' or 'white' jobs or 'female' or 'Negro' jobs." There is no hint of the disparate impact test anywhere in the manual.

7. 110 *Cong. Rec.* 7419 (1964).

Elsewhere Senator George Smathers echoed the same theme:

It is not written in the bill that there must be a quota system, but the net effect of the adoption of the proposed law would be that employers, in order to keep themselves from being charged with having discriminated, would, in time, have certain people working for them to meet the color qualifications, the religious qualifications, the creed qualifications, and so on.[8]

The basic response of the supporters of the bill was that the meaning of the term *discrimination* was perfectly clear. Senator Joseph Clark inserted into the *Congressional Record* some of the more common objections to Title VII and his answers to them:

Objection: The language of the statute is vague and unclear. It may interfere with the employer's right to select on the basis of qualifications. Answer: Discrimination is a word which has been used in State FEPC [Fair Employment Practices Commission] statutes for at least 20 years, and has been used in Federal statutes, such as the National Labor Relations Act and the Fair Labor Standards Act, for even a longer period. To discriminate is to make distinctions or differences in the treatment of employees, and are prohibited only if they are based on any of the five forbidden criteria (race, color, religion, sex, or national origin): any other criteria or qualification is untouched by this bill.[9]

The entire question of disparate impact was never addressed. Throughout Title VII was defended as limited in scope on the ground that the absence of any reference to quotas was sufficient to show that employers would not have to adopt this defensive tactic in order to comply with the bill.[10] The defenders of Title VII did not have to justify using disparate impact theory because it had not been crystalized by its opponents or captured in a magic phrase. The defenders of Title VII were free to wax indignant at the set of outrageous hypotheticals that were launched against this unambiguous bill. At one point Senator Humphrey grew so exasperated that he responded to Senator Robertson by saying:

8. 110 *Cong. Rec.* 8500 (1964).

9. 110 *Cong. Rec.* 7218 (1964).

10. See, e.g., 110 *Cong. Rec.* 8500 (1964) (remarks of Senator Allott); 110 *Cong. Rec.* 8618 (1964) (remarks of Senator Keating); 110 *Cong. Rec.* 7418–20 (1964) (remarks of Senator Humphrey).

I would like to make an offer to [the Senator]. If the Senator can find in title VII . . . any language which provided that an employer will have to hire on the basis of percentage or quota related to color, race, religion, or national origin, I will start eating the pages one after another, because it is not in there.[11]

The same message came through in the exhaustive memo prepared by Senators Case and Clark in their role as bipartisan captains for the bill while it was being debated on the Senate floor.[12] In line with the basic position that the proposed legislation represented only a "mild and moderate" (their phrase, not mine) interference with the market, both senators took pains to emphasize the extensive sphere of employment decision making that was left to the complete discretion of the firm. Thus they prepared a lengthy memo defending the statute against charges of overreaching, which contained this language:

There is no requirement in title VII that an employer maintain a racial balance in his work force. On the contrary, any deliberate attempt to maintain a racial balance, whatever such a balance may be, would involve a violation of title VII because maintaining a balance would require an employer to hire or to refuse to hire on the basis of race.[13]

Similarly:

Title VII would not require, and no court could read title VII as requiring, an employer to lower or change the occupational qualifications he sets for his employees simply because proportionately fewer Negroes than whites are able to meet them . . . Title VII says merely that a covered employer cannot refuse to hire someone simply because of his color; that is, because he is a Negro. But it expressly protects the employer's right to insist that any prospective applicant, Negro or white, must meet the applicable job qualifications.[14]

Under Title VII, even a Federal court could not order an employer to lower or change job qualifications simply because proportionately fewer Negroes than whites are able to meet them. Title VII says only that the

11. 110 *Cong. Rec.* 7420 (1964).

12. Senator James O. Eastland of Mississippi was in control of the Senate Judiciary Committee and had refused to hold hearings on the bill.

13. 110 *Cong. Rec.* 7213 (1964).

14. Id. at 7246–47 (1964).

covered employers cannot refuse to hire someone simply because of his color.[15]

Finally, it has been asserted title VII would impose a requirement for "racial balance." That is incorrect. There is no provision, either in title VII or in any other part of this bill, that requires or authorizes any Federal agency or Federal court to require preferential treatment for any individual or any group for the purpose of achieving racial balance. No employer is required to hire an individual because that individual is a Negro. No employer is required to maintain any ratio of Negroes to whites, Jews to gentiles, Italians to English, or women to men. The same is true of labor organizations. On the contrary, any deliberate attempt to maintain a given balance would almost certainly run afoul of title VII because it would involve a failure or refusal to hire some individual because of his race, color, religion, sex, or national origin. What title VII seeks to accomplish, what the civil rights bill seeks to accomplish is equal treatment for all.[16]

Other provisions of the statute seem to confirm this repudiation of effect-based tests. Thus section 703(h) provides:

Notwithstanding any other provision of this title, it shall not be an unlawful employment practice for an employer to apply different standards of compensation, or different terms, conditions, or privileges of employment pursuant to a bona fide seniority or merit system, or a system which measures earnings by quantity or quality of production or to employees who work in different locations, provided that such differences are not the result of an intention to discriminate because of race, color, religion, sex, or national origin; nor shall it be an unlawful employment practice for an employer to give and act upon the results of any professionally developed ability test provided that such test, its use or action upon the results is not designed, intended, or used to discriminate because of race, color, religion, sex or national origin.

As drafted the statute seems, to the untutored eye, to preserve the ability of the employer to make bona fide decisions connected with seniority and with merit, and to use professional tests, as long as these are not resorted to as a disguise or pretext for discriminating on the grounds prohibited by the statute. That interpretation is borne out again by the legislative history, this time by Senators Clark and Case, who wrote:

15. Id. at 7246 (remarks of Senator Case).
16. Id. at 7246.

There is no requirement in Title VII that employers abandon bona fide qualification tests where, because of differences in background and education, members of some groups are able to perform better on these tests than members of other groups. An employer may set his qualifications as high as he likes, he may test to determine which applicants have these qualifications, and he may hire, assign, and promote on the basis of test performance.[17]

There were strong political reasons to write about this issue in such clear terms. During the debates over Title VII, Senator John Tower brought to the attention of the Senate an episode under the Illinois Fair Employment Practices Code. There an Illinois hearing examiner had held a standard ability test that Motorola had used since 1949 to be illegal because the test was "unfair to culturally deprived and disadvantaged groups."[18] That incident raised something of a furor and was explicitly addressed by Senators Case and Humphrey, who sought to distance themselves from the examiner's decision. They had plainly been placed on the defensive, and were working to keep Title VII part of the overall statute. Senator Humphrey downplayed *Motorola* by noting that it was only the decision of a single hearing examiner, which had not been affirmed by a full board or by the court. Senator Case gave his explicit avowal that *Motorola* was a "red herring" and that "the Attorney General and his office and the leadership concerned with civil rights organizations have all worked diligently to avoid any possibility of such abuse," and therefore had produced "here a mild title dealing with unemployment practices."[19] Elsewhere Senator Case observed that Title VII "is completely different from the law which the commission in Illinois was asked to administer, and from the decision adopted by the hearing examiner in the Motorola case."[20] No supporter of Title VII defended the hearing examiner's decision in *Motorola* as a desirable outcome. Everyone sought to explain why it could not happen under Title VII.

At the time it was generally thought that the statute did what it set out to do. Strong evidence of this point comes from a contemporaneous (1966) account of the testing provisions authored by Michael Sovern (now president of Columbia University), who was then, as now, an

17. Id. at 7213.
18. Id. at 7246.
19. Id. at 13082.
20. Id. at 7246.

unstinting champion of the Civil Rights Act.[21] Sovern first noted that section 703(h) is for the most part "a reassuring redundancy."[22] He then spelled out the implications of the section in detail.

> Many tests obviously place those with inferior formal educations at a serious disadvantage. If the tests separate those who can do the job from those who cannot, so be it; employers cannot be asked to settle for unqualified workers. But many ability tests require a high degree of literacy when the job being tested for does not. A common example is the written examination for a job requiring manual skills. The marginally literate applicant is likely to lose the job to a better educated competitor who may not be as good at the job itself. That Title VII permits employers to use such examinations, provided that they are "not designed, intended or used to discriminate because of race," etc. should not prevent those administering the act from seeking to educate and persuade employers to use tests better suited to their needs and less likely to heap an additional disadvantage on the Negro product of a segregated school system.[23]

The gist of Sovern's position is that testing is subject to the same motive-based standards that are applicable generally under section 703(a). In all cases it was necessary for any plaintiff to go through the entire three-part system of proof, developed in *McDonnell Douglas,* and applicable in disparate treatment cases generally, to attack the seniority, merit, or testing system imposed by the employer. Simply put, the words *because of* in section 703(h) consciously echo the same term in section 703(a), and should be read in the same fashion. Therefore, as long as these tests related in any ordinary sense to the business purposes of the employer, liability based on their use would be foreclosed, *unless* it could be shown that the system in question was used as a pretext for further discrimina-

21. See Michael I. Sovern, *Legal Restraints on Racial Discrimination in Employment* (1966). At the time the book was published, Sovern was a professor of law specializing in labor law. Chapter 4 of the book, in which the quotation cited in the text appears, is entitled "Congress at Last: The Civil Rights Act of 1964." His careful and balanced account of the statute is not that of a southern opponent but that of a staunch supporter and is entitled to special weight on that account alone. It is also noteworthy that his book was written not solely to state his own views but as a study for the Twentieth Century Fund, and it thus carries with it an institutional imprimatur as well.

22. Id. at 70.

23. Id. at 73.

tion. As these various ability tests have long been in use, the burden of proof on the plaintiff would be very heavy, typically requiring some individuated evidence of improper bias in the administration of the test. These standard management tools would face only rare challenges precisely because they were commonly used not only by firms that had a history of racial bias but also by those that did not. The individual plaintiff would have strong extrajudicial protections because he or she would know that large numbers of other firms use the same test or a similar one. Standardized tests effectively counter the risk of being singled out for special and invidious treatment.

Any analyst who predicted that Title VII would follow the guarded lines outlined in the Senate memos or the Sovern explication has been proved with hindsight a bad prophet. In the subsequent litigation practice many major suits have relied heavily or exclusively on disparate impact theories. Ironically, the fears of the diehard opponents of the statue have proved correct. As Senator Tower protested: "I feel that the regulations, lawsuits, and Federal pressures placed upon private business by this title are utterly unacceptable in a free economy, particularly since these pressures can be placed upon any firm at any time in presuming the firm guilty until it proves itself innocent."[24] He turned out to be right in the wake of *Griggs,* whose disparate impact hurdle is easily overcome in most cases. *Griggs* is an unqualified boon to economists, statisticians, and social scientists of all persuasions. It is also a travesty of statutory construction.

Griggs v. Duke Power

These were the facts in *Griggs.* The Duke Power Company divided its power plant employees into five divisions: labor, coal handling, operations, maintenance, and laboratory and testing. Before the passage of the Civil Rights Act the plant was rigidly segregated by race, with black workers being allowed to apply only for jobs in the lowest classification, the labor department, but not in the other four operations departments. In 1955 the company instituted a policy of requiring a high school diploma for workers who were to take positions in any operations department, or who, having started in coal handling, wanted internal transfers to higher departments. This requirement for the upper divisions was obviously not instituted as a ploy to bar promotions for blacks, for at the time they were already explicitly barred on racial grounds.

24. 110 *Cong. Rec.* 9024 (1964).

The passage of the 1964 Civil Rights Act led Duke Power to dismantle its old system of racial classification. On the day Title VII of the 1964 act went into effect (July 2, 1965) the company imposed the high school equivalence program on all workers who wanted to transfer out of the labor department. Previously, before the equivalence program was instituted, some white workers had transferred out of labor into higher departments, and they had done satisfactory work in their new operations jobs. No black workers hired prior to 1965 had been afforded this opportunity, owing to the rigid racial ban.

Under the new plant rules, the workers seeking promotion from the labor department could establish the high school equivalence requirement by achieving prescribed scores on certain widely used tests, namely the Wonderlic general intelligence test and the Bennett AA general mechanical test. (It should be noted that the tests in the *Motorola* case were general intelligence tests as well.) The minimum scores on these tests were set at a level that corresponded roughly to the scores of the average high school graduate.[25] Before introducing the test, Duke Power had hired an outside consultant to determine whether the tests were necessary, given the increased complexity of its own internal operations. After the Civil Rights Act became law, the company introduced a program, open to all members of the labor department regardless of race, to pay for two-thirds of the cost of education for employees who did not have the credentials required to advance. The company had, "by plaintiffs' own admission, discontinued the use of discriminatory tactics in employment, promotions and transfers."[26] In a sense it was an appropriate occasion for the supporters of the Civil Rights Act to declare victory, given the enormous changes wrought by the statute.

The majority opinion in the Fourth Circuit took this approach by treating *Griggs* as a transitional case between the old and the new legal order. Accordingly, it distinguished between two classes of black complainants. The first group contained workers in the labor department who had been hired before 1965. Under the company's rules they were required to pass the high school equivalence test in order to transfer out of that department. With respect to them, the Fourth Circuit held the test requirement invalid because white workers hired at the same time had

---

25. For an account, see the opinion of Judge Herbert Boreman in *Griggs v. Duke Power Co.*, 420 F.2d 1225, 1229–33 (4th Cir. 1970). There is a dissent by Judge Simon Sobeloff, id. at 1237, taking the position eventually adopted by the Supreme Court.

26. Id. at 1233.

been able to advance without taking the test. In essence the decision placed these black workers in a position of rough parity with white workers in the labor department who had been hired at the same time. The solution was not perfect because the black workers had less seniority than white workers hired before 1965, a defect that could have been remedied by adjustments in their seniority status to secure them their rightful place in the hierarchy.[27] The decision invalidating the tests in this context seems correct under the statute, but its general applicability is strictly limited. Some cases were plainly caught in the transition between the old and new legal regimes. But by definition these cases would diminish sharply over time. And indeed, more than twenty-five years after the passage of the act, these transitional issues are no longer of significance.

The second class of black workers had been hired after the high school equivalence requirement had been imposed for all employees. For these workers there was no argument of transitional inequity. The Fourth Circuit held that they had not received any disparate treatment, and hence refused to afford them any relief. In its reading of the statute the Fourth Circuit, relying on the language and the legislative history just described, rejected the plaintiff's claim that the two intelligence tests used by Duke Power had to be "job related" in addition to being "professionally developed," as the statute provided. In reaching its conclusion, the court refused to follow the lead of the EEOC that all tests had to be validated to the particular job, given that the EEOC's interpretation was "clearly contrary to compelling legislative history."[28]

That history, some of which I have already cited, was not based on abstract speculation. Rather, the strictures section 703(h) placed on bona fide seniority and testing requirements had been inserted specifically to allay concerns, largely expressed by Senator Tower, that the EEOC would follow the logic of the Illinois Fair Employment Practices Commission in the *Motorola* case. The circuit court concluded, therefore, that Duke Power was within its rights to administer these tests to all its workers,

---

27. See, e.g., *International Brotherhood of Teamsters v. United States,* 431 U.S. 324 (1977), which held that discrimination prior to the act could be remedied only by allowing blacks their rightful place in filling future vacancies without displacing current white workers from their jobs. Displacement was possible for discrimination subsequent to the act. The decision is consistent with the text of section 703(h) and the legislative history. See, e.g., 110 *Cong. Rec.* 7207, 7213 (1964).

28. *Griggs,* 420 F.2d at 1234.

even if a significantly larger proportion of whites than blacks passed. In the Fourth Circuit's view, the purpose of the statute was not to redress whatever inequalities existed in the larger social system, a theme that is also apparent in Sovern's own conclusion that the act did not seek to correct the injustices of segregated schools by altering the rules governing the employment market.[29] Rather, the court concluded that the statute was meant only to ensure that all applicants for jobs would be subject to similar treatment, which in this context meant that they were to be given the same battery of tests scored in the same way, a nontrivial innovation in light of past practices. Disparate treatment, not disparate impact, was the key.

Great puzzles of statutory construction often arise when the language of a statute conflicts with its legislative history. But no such conflict arose in *Griggs,* for the very issue of testing raised in the case had been expressly debated and resolved by the statute. In this instance there are no mysteries of statutory construction: the act said what it meant, and it meant what it said. It was therefore something of an unexpected tour de force that a *unanimous* Supreme Court reversed *Griggs* and imposed the "job related" requirement on all hiring tests with a disparate impact in its initial Title VII case. Chief Justice Warren Burger began his opinion by emphasizing both the transitional and the analytical points:

> We granted the writ in this case to resolve the question whether an employer is prohibited by the Civil Rights Act of 1964, Title VII, from requiring a high school education or passing of a standardized general intelligence test as a condition of employment in or transfer to jobs when (a) neither standard is shown to be significantly related to successful job performance, (b) both requirements operate to disqualify Negroes at a substantially higher rate than white applicants, and (c) the jobs in question formerly had been filled only by white employees as part of a longstanding practice of giving preference to whites.[30]

29. "In a southern school district, for example, training in metal trades may be available in the white, but not in the Negro, vocational school; as a result, when a local metal-working shop advertises for high school seniors with metal-trades training, there is a sense in which it is discriminating against Negroes. But section 703(h) makes it clear that this is not the sense in which Title VII uses the word 'discriminate.' To violate Title VII, one must treat differently because of race itself and not merely because of an applicant's lack of qualification which he was prevented from acquiring because of his race." Sovern, *Legal Restraints* at 71. Scribbled in the margin of my library copy is the phrase "not so after *Griggs.*"

30. *Griggs,* 401 U.S. at 425–426.

As the opinion progressed, however, the transitional elements referred to in (c) quickly disappeared when the Court laid down the basic propositions that have long been central to the entire corpus of antidiscrimination law. It is necessary to quote the relevant passages extensively.

> Congress did not intend by Title VII, however, to guarantee a job to every person regardless of qualifications. In short, the Act does not command that any person be hired simply because he was formerly the subject of discrimination, or because he is a member of a minority group. Discriminatory preference for any group, minority or majority, is precisely and only what Congress has proscribed. What is required by Congress is the removal of artificial, arbitrary, and unnecessary barriers to employment when the barriers operate invidiously to discriminate on the basis of racial or other impermissible classification.
>
> Congress has now provided that tests or criteria for employment or promotion may not provide equality of opportunity merely in the sense of the fabled offer of milk to the stork and the fox. On the contrary, Congress has now required that the posture and condition of the job-seeker be taken into account. It has—to resort again to the fable—provided that the vessel in which the milk is preferred be one all seekers can use. The Act proscribes not only overt discrimination but also practices that are fair in form, but discriminatory in operation. The touchstone is business necessity. If an employment practice which operates to exclude Negroes cannot be shown to be related to job performance, the practice is prohibited.
>
> On the record before us, neither the high school completion requirement nor the general intelligence test is shown to bear a demonstrable relationship to successful performance of the jobs for which it was used. Both were adopted, as the Court of Appeals noted, without meaningful study of their relationship to job-performance ability . . .
>
> In the context of this case, it is unnecessary to reach the question whether testing requirements that take into account capability for the next succeeding position or related future promotion might be utilized upon a showing that such long-range requirements fulfill a genuine business need. In the present case the Company has made no such showing . . .
>
> The Company's lack of discriminatory intent is suggested by special efforts to help the undereducated employees through Company financing of two-thirds the costs of tuition for high school training. But Congress directed the thrust of the Act to the *consequences* of employment prac-

tices, not simply the motivation. More than that, Congress has placed on the employer the burden of showing that any given requirement must have a manifest relationship to the employment in question.[31]

With that general prelude it took the Court little time to dispose of the argument based on section 703(h) of the statute. It first italicized the word *used* in the phrase "any professionally developed test" that is not "designed, intended *or used* to discriminate because of race."[32] Its argument was in essence that "used" refers to consequences, not intention. The Court then disposed of the legislative history. The language of the Clark-Case interpretative amendment was held irrelevant because it referred only to the right of an employer to set *qualifications* as high as it liked, but did not expressly state that the employer could choose how to test or measure them, a proposition that the legislative history flatly contradicts.[33] Qualifications were thus construed to refer to ultimate abilities, not to the actual standards that employers set to accept or reject workers, such as the tests or high school diplomas at issue here.

The Supreme Court in *Griggs* perverted both the language and the legislative history of the act. As a general matter it overstated the intention of the statute by insisting that it was designed to allow all persons to compete equally in the workplace regardless of differences in their prior training. Nothing in the statute or its history speaks of "the removal of artificial, arbitrary, and unnecessary barriers to employment" referred to in *Griggs.* Quite the contrary. By design and effect the act eliminates only decisions based on certain forbidden motives, and thereafter it lets the chips fall where they may, as Sovern's account of the statute makes clear.[34] If in 1964 any sponsor of the Civil Rights Act had admitted Title VII on the ground that it adopted the disparate impact test read into it by the Supreme Court in *Griggs,* Title VII would have gone down to thundering defeat, and perhaps brought the rest of the act down with it. Senators Clark and Case were well aware of the weakness at their flanks, and whatever their private preferences, they said nothing that supports the extravagant statement of purpose used in *Griggs* to usher in the disparate impact test.

31. Id. at 430–432.
32. Id. at 433; emphasis in original.
33. See interpretative memorandum of Title VII of H.R. 7152, submitted jointly by Senator Joseph S. Clark and Senator Clifford P. Case, floor managers, 88th Cong., 2nd sess., 110 *Cong. Rec.* 7213 (1964); see note 13, supra.
34. See Sovern, *Legal Restraints.*

Chief Justice Burger's opinion is also far off the mark in its construction of section 703(h). His infelicitous use of italics for the word *used* distorts the sense of the full sentence. Initially it suppresses the obvious point that section 703(h) was designed to legitimate and preserve testing, not to ban it. The word therefore appears in a phrase that states the exception under the basic rule. Within that context "used" should be read as part of the phrase "intended, designed or used." The words are in parallel construction, so "used" refers to tests prepared by third parties with proper motive but applied by the defendant in order to discriminate because of race or other unacceptable criteria. The word *used* in the statute has the same meaning here that it has in the phrase "Smith used his position at the firm to feather his own nest," or "Jones is an unscrupulous opportunist who uses her friends." The word refers not to effects or inadvertent consequences but to artifice or manipulation bordering on deceit. In other words, the proper construction of the statutory language precludes the argument that *simple knowledge* that one or another test produces better results for whites than blacks invalidates the test. That knowledge is a background condition that is known by all personnel in charge of testing, now as in 1964. It is impossible to claim that this knowledge invalidates the use of virtually all professional tests, especially since the statute was drafted to preserve them. A single word in a limited exception should not be used to gut an entire statutory provision.

An alternative construction avoids these difficulties. What is needed, therefore, is evidence that the employer picked *a particular* test that promised to give the lowest passing rate to blacks (or, for that matter, whites) even though it believed that some other test was better suited for the legitimate purpose in question. The judicial inquiry could be sharpened by asking, if the test population were all white (or all black), which test would the employer choose to adopt? If the answer is test A, but test B was chosen because the passing rate for blacks (or whites) is lower than it would be on test A, then there is a violation of the statute, because a professionally developed test has been "used" to discriminate. There is now evidence that the employer sacrificed its own business needs to advance its racial prejudice. This reading of the statute preserves the continuity of the phrase "designed, intended or used" and keeps the exception within boundaries that are both sensible and principled. By stressing the intention of the employer, it invalidates the test if its use is prejudicial to any individual employee. Since the employer has already sacrificed business needs on the altar of racial prejudice, the business necessity exception is wholly irrelevant to the case. The statute for testing can be fit into the general pattern adopted by section 703(a) with its "because of" language.

In contrast, the construction adopted by the Court rewrote the phrase to read "intended or designed to discriminate or has the effect of discriminating" because of race. Its reading of "used" renders the first two terms of the phrase redundant. It also requires a court to read into the statute both the "job related" and the "business necessity" exceptions, which appear nowhere in the original statute, and which are discussed nowhere in the legislative history.[35] The Clark-Case memo defends the use of "bona fide qualification tests," but it never uses the words *job related* or *business necessity*. The term *bona fide* itself ordinarily refers to tests that are used honestly and in good faith by an employer, which again returns the inquiry to matters of disparate treatment and away from any stricter effects test, under which bona fides are irrelevant, even as a defense. For its part, business necessity is the far more rigid and unyielding standard, one that lies at the opposite edge of the intellectual spectrum. The Supreme Court in its interpretation of the critical passages from the Clark-Case memo never explains away the force of the "bona fide" language. More dramatically, the Court does not choose to mention, let alone discuss, the controversial Motorola incident,[36] which prompted the specific statutory language of section 703(h). The savings clause in the statute is written to prevent testing from becoming a clever trick for circumventing the statute, and to ensure that section 703(h) meshes with the basic command of section 703(a). It was not inserted into the act to place insuperable obstacles in the way of standard professional tests introduced for ordinary business purposes.

Given the sensible interpretation of the exception in section 703(h), it might be possible to defend the outcome, but not the reasoning, in *Griggs*. Tying the test requirement to the effective date of Title VII might be taken to suggest that the test was "used" for illegitimate purposes, and thus falls outside the protection of section 703(h). At this stage *Griggs* should then be analyzed as a disparate treatment case, where it looks like a sure loser for the employee, at least if the transi-

---

35. On which see also Michael Gold, "The Similarity of Congressional and Judicial Lawmaking under Title VII of the Civil Rights Act of 1964," 18 *U. C. Davis. L. Rev.* 721, 737 (1985), noting that the reference to professionally developed tests in Title VII was solely to distinguish the use of "home-grown" tests and not job-related tests.

36. See notes 18–20 and the discussion earlier in this chapter, at 190.

tional issues are left to one side. Initially, his inability to pass the required tests would make it difficult for the plaintiff to prove that he was "qualified" under the terms of *McDonnell Douglas.* Even if that hurdle could be overcome, there would surely be some business reason for adopting the test, given the evidence that the company wanted to upgrade the caliber of its work force to improve both safety and efficiency within the plant, and even hired a consultant to figure out how to accomplish these goals. The issue would therefore have to shift to the matter of pretext, where the plaintiff's case would depend, as before, on whether the effective date of the new policy overrode the company's decision to pay two-thirds of the cost of acquiring a high school diploma, its use of the same tests elsewhere in its business as of 1955, and the present color-blind policy of its overall operation. The ultimate finding of no discriminatory intent, accepted in the Fourth Circuit, seems clearly defensible and probably unassailable.

Against this backdrop *Griggs* worked an ironic inversion of legal doctrine. Disparate impact opens up a far wider vista of potential liability than disparate treatment, given that disparate impact is a virtually universal consequence of most standardized tests, and of many other employment practices as well. Even if these cases were seen as a separate kind of liability, we should have expected them to be handled gingerly. But until *Ward's Cove* (temporarily?) reversed the trend, the opposite happened. The disparate treatment cases create some limited liability under Title VII, for which a significant defense is provided by allowing proof of any reasonable nondiscriminatory motive for the practice. The disparate impact cases after *Griggs* often read and applied the business necessity defense in a hard and uncompromising fashion.

Until *Ward's Cove* the case law under Title VII revealed this irony. Where a plaintiff can show that he has been passed over when he meets the relevant qualifications, then the defendant's burden of justification is low: any nondiscriminatory reason will do. But let a plaintiff be passed over because he does *not* meet the defendant's stated qualifications—that is, because he cannot pass the test—and the burden of justification becomes quite high: "The touchstone is business necessity." The weaker the plaintiff's prima facie case, the more obstacles are placed in the path of a defendant who seeks to rebut it—exactly the opposite of what any sensible system of law should require. This one-two punch has revolutionized the "mild and moderate" statute of Senators Humphrey, Clark, and Case.

The Equal Opportunity Employment Act of 1972

Griggs, then, marked a systematic distortion of the language and outlook of the 1964 act. Nonetheless, that shift in orientation was perhaps endorsed (but at most in a backhanded way) by the different Congress (both in years and in mood) that passed the Equal Opportunity Act of 1972,[37] which contained key amendments to the 1964 statute. The substantive provisions of the statute construed by the Court in *Griggs* were not amended in any relevant fashion: the language of section 703(a)(2) was merely extended to cover applicants for original employment.[38] Instead, the main statutory changes in the 1972 act took place in two other areas. First, the act expanded the coverage of the statute to include, for example, firms with more than eight employees (down from twenty five), employees of the federal, state, and local governments, and employees of educational institutions.[39] Second, it increased the enforcement powers of the EEOC beyond those of mediation and conciliation by allowing the EEOC its own direct enforcement power.[40] Nonetheless, the Congress refused to repeal or amend section 703(h), with its protection for professionally developed tests, or section 706(g), which required a court to find intentional discrimination before ordering various sorts of relief.[41]

The relevant amendments are significant but not earth-shattering, for the continuity between the two acts has more weight than the changes on collateral points. Nonetheless, the legislative history of the 1972 act reflects a consensus moral certitude about social rights and wrongs that stands in stark contrast to the closely fought, tightly reasoned struggle over the 1964 act. In a sense it offers powerful evidence that *Griggs* anticipated the mood of the 1972 Congress. There are explicit approving references to *Griggs,*[42] and the Senate report even discusses the change in orientation from the 1964 debates.

37. Equal Employment Opportunity Act of 1972, 72 U.S.C. §2000 et seq. (1982).

38. The Equal Opportunity Employment Act of 1972, Pub. L. no. 92–261, 86 Stat. 103 (1972).

39. Id. §701(b)

40. Id. §706.

41. For a careful discussion of these points, see U.S. Department of Justice, *Office of Legal Policy Report to the Attorney General, Redefining Discrimination: Disparate Impact and the Institutionalization of Affirmative Action* 74–76 (1987), which notes that the 1964 act and its legislative history control on those issues not explicitly amended by the 1972 act.

42. *Legislative History of the 1972 Equal Opportunity Employment Act* 163, 175–176 (House), 238 (Senate). *Report to the Attorney General* at 74–75 contains some powerful

In 1964, employment discrimination tended to be viewed as a series of isolated and distinguishable events, for the most part due to the ill-will on the part of some identifiable individual or organization. It was thought that a scheme which stressed conciliation rather than compulsory processes would be most appropriate for the resolution of this essentially "human" problem, and that litigation would be necessary only on an occasional basis. Experience has shown this view to be false.

Employment discrimination as viewed today is a far more complex and pervasive phenomenon. Experts familiar with the subject now generally describe the problem in terms of "systems" and "effects" rather than simply intentional wrongs, and the literature on the subject is replete with discussion of, for example, the mechanics of seniority and lines of progression, perpetuation of the present effect of pre-Act discriminatory practices through various institutional devices, and testing and validation requirements.[43]

Thereafter the legislative history provides its evidence of the level of discrimination. Even though the statute speaks in terms of employment opportunities, the evidence marshaled in support of the newly discovered problems in employment does not mention any explicit discriminatory practices (the overt ones, such as those found in *Griggs,* were halted shortly after 1965) but is exclusively couched in the language of disparate impact, not of employment practices but of general wage and income levels, and thus fails to take into account Gary Becker's critical distinction between voluntary segregation and differences in income levels.[44] The legislative history, for example, noted that the median income of black families in 1970 was $6,279, while that of white families for the same period was $10,236. Whereas blacks held 10 percent of all jobs, they accounted for "only 3 percent of all jobs in the high-paying professional, technical, and managerial positions."[45] There was no effort to adjust these figures to take into account conflating factors: levels of education are not discussed, and more subtle factors are similarly ignored. For instance, since parents in the average black family are younger than parents in the

---

arguments against the use of the legislative history adopted by the Supreme Court, in *Connecticut v. Teal,* 457 U.S. 440, 447 n.8 (1982), by noting that the Supreme Court relies on approving references to *Griggs* made in support of proposed amendments to the 1964 act that were not passed.

43. *Legislative History* at 229.
44. See Chapter 2 at 41–42, under the heading "Natural Limits on Discrimination."
45. *Legislative History* at 230.

average white family, we should expect to see an income differential that would be corrected if we looked at the family sample by cohort instead of in the aggregate.[46]

The most striking feature of the 1971 legislative report, however, is the way in which it reinterprets the underlying social approach to the 1964 amendments. In 1964 the broad moral attack on racial discrimination stemmed from the formally and explicitly required discrimination practiced by states, private employers, and unions. It was widely understood that these practices were pervasive; indeed there were extensive enforcement efforts to strike down formal barriers in the years immediately following the passage of the statute. Only in retrospect could the 1972 Senate report rewrite history to trivialize Jim Crow by calling the systematic patterns of government-sponsored and government-protected discrimination "isolated and distinguishable events." The supporters of the 1964 act also believed that the statute would eliminate the occurrence of such "events" without disrupting the operation of the private marketplace. By the standards of those who passed the 1964 act, its enforcement was a smashing success, not a failure. The barriers to public accommodation of blacks came tumbling down instantly, and the formal programs of discrimination in employment disappeared overnight, as on the facts of *Griggs,* leaving only the vexing but short-term problems of selecting the right set of transitional rules which the 1964 act had addressed, for example on seniority.[47] The evidence of differential income and success

46. For an excellent discussion of these points, see Thomas Sowell, *Civil Rights: Rhetoric or Reality?* 42–43 (1984), noting that black and Hispanic parents in the United States are on average younger than Jewish and Japanese-Americans parents, who have higher income levels. It is important, however, not to attribute all the differences to demographics, for the relevant question is whether, age held constant, we can observe differences in income and educational attainment for members of different ethnic groups. It is clear, nonetheless, that the legislative history to the 1972 Civil Rights Act made no effort to control for any relevant factors but relied on gross uncorrected figures.

47. Section 703(h). Note, in reference to seniority, that there was a similarly cautious view of the reach of the statute, as with professional tests. Sovern, for example, took the position that any bona fide seniority system instituted prior to passage of the statute was protected, even if blacks had been unable to obtain positions that would give them seniority. In his view the tough case arose where prior to the statute both blacks and whites were hired, but blacks were allowed to work only one hour for every three allotted to the white workers. The question in his mind was whether the seniority accumulated under this system would survive in the post-1964 world. He acknowledged first that this issue had not been addressed in the drafting of section 703(h) but surmised that "when new systems are created to replace such arrangements, section 703(h) may well induce courts to ignore what

rates of whites and blacks, without evidence of intentional discrimination by someone, may well have been thought to be a social problem, but it was not the problem that was addressed by the Civil Rights Act.

Judged on its own terms, the 1964 act had succeeded in all its major objectives by 1972. With its success, the so-called March of Dimes problem (what does the foundation do once an effective vaccine for polio is found?) has come to bedevil the civil rights movement. Once the earlier objectives were achieved, a new set of problems far more daunting than the old had to be put in their place. By 1972 the agenda had been changed from the logic of no discriminatory intent to the more aggressive logic of no disparate impact. The latter agenda depends critically on the success of the disparate impact formula announced in *Griggs,* which allowed the enforcement of Title VII to go beyond disparate treatment cases without running into the groundswell of objections that quotas attract. The soundness of this formula is the subject of the next chapter.

---

went before and to permit continued Negro subordination for years to come." Sovern, *Legal Restraints* at 73.

The Supreme Court's interpretation of seniority provisions is far more restrained than its parallel construction of testing. See, e.g., *International Brotherhood of Teamsters v. United States,* 431 U.S. 324 (1977), which upheld the separation of two pre-act seniority systems. Under the plan, workers on the less desirable city routes could not transfer their credit to the more desirable intercity routes. Prior to passage of the statute, workers had been directed to one position or another on the basis of race. Yet the Court held that the legislative history precluded the possibility of attacking any racially motivated pre-act seniority. The Court has never faced a seniority system quite as stark as that discussed by Sovern.

CHAPTER 11

Disparate Impact

In the preceding chapter I articulated the case against the soundness of *Griggs*, viewed exclusively as a question of statutory construction. But on any view *Griggs* deserves the label of a transformative case, one that ushered in a new age of institutional litigation under Title VII. With *Griggs* the object is no longer to redress the particular grievances of individual employees. To give an analogy, *Griggs* is to the run-of-the-mill disparate treatment case as complex toxic tort litigation is to the ordinary intersection collision. Disparate treatment cases have to be tried one at a time, given their fact-specific content. The statistical basis of the disparate impact case, the focus on the firm by the business necessity defense, and the irrelevance of pretext reduce the individual plaintiff to a condition of relative invisibility. This facelessness allows consolidated disparate impact cases to be brought against institutional defendants by unnamed plaintiffs, often by the EEOC itself. Although disparate treatment cases arise more frequently than disparate impact cases, weighted by the number of potential plaintiffs and the size of the stakes, these cases have come to overshadow, both in the courtroom and in the newspaper headlines, the more prosaic cases of individual disparate treatment.

Within this setting it is critical to examine the internal logic of the modern disparate impact case to see how it operates and why it is so often counterproductive. There are two prongs to the basic analysis. The first points toward the standards by which disparate impact is measured, the second toward the business necessity defense. On both the rules of the game set out in *Griggs* appear to have been altered, at least provisionally, by the 1989 *Ward's Cove* decision. But a discussion of the extent of these changes must be postponed until we have understood disparate impact litigation under *Griggs*. That topic is a vast one that cuts across cases of both race and sex discrimination. This chapter is devoted to those issues that arise predominantly but not exclusively in the race cases.

Related issues on disparate impact in connection with cases of sex discrimination are considered in Chapter 18.

Dismantling the House of Cards

Testing

Griggs itself dealt with disparate impact in testing, and that area is an appropriate one in which to begin the basic analysis. The initial stage in any disparate impact case is, predictably, for the plaintiff to show that the test used by the employer has a disparate impact on the passing rates of blacks and whites. The issue is somewhat technical, and both sides resort freely to statistical techniques to prove their claims. But beneath the technical issues lurks a broader social question: Does the law make it too easy or too hard to prove the prima facie case of disparate impact? The short answer is, too easy. The longer answer requires a more complete exposition of the problem of disparate impact generally.

Choosing the proper baseline. The threshold inquiry is how to identify cases of disparate impact. Intuitively it seems clear that if the same percentage of blacks and whites pass a given test, then the test has no disparate impact. But this intuition is naive, if not wrong. It may well be, and indeed seems highly likely, that with a true test of merit the passing rates would be different for different groups, given their varying backgrounds and levels of preparation. Thus the uniformity of results represents an implicit but unwarranted benefit to the group that would have had the poorer test results in a world of perfect measurement. The analysis of a test's impact cannot take as the implicit baseline equal passing rates for different groups. For example, if equal numbers of blacks and whites pass a test despite the fact that members of one group have a higher average level of education, then in principle it seems likely that the test has an implicit racial bias that neutralizes the differences in test performance that would normally be predicted on the strength of years of education alone. The possibilities for complication are not limited to this particular example, but indeed embrace any difference in objective characteristics between the two classes. In principle the correct analytical approach requires a court first to normalize any test with respect to the relevant background information, and only thereafter to decide the disparate impact question.

Nothing of this sort is ever even attempted in disparate impact cases, and it is easy enough to see why. Taking that approach would mean that any set of test results could be attacked from any quarter, thus creating the potential for a frenzy of litigation that would make even government administrators, ever eager to control the agenda, wary. Driven by a powerful set of aspirations, the law makes the false but convenient simplifying assumption that an unbiased test yields an equal percentage of passing grades across all racial groups. Unless differential passing rates triggered legal inquiry, disparate impact litigation would in all likelihood cease. Today the question of illegality arises only where a significant difference in the passing rates of individuals is correlated with race. In the absence of further information it is impossible to determine whether too many or too few disparate impact cases are brought, or, even if the overall level of suits is correct, and whether the right cases are being selected. In principle, the EEOC should first validate statistically *its* view that an equal percentage of passing grades is the proper baseline against which all tests should be judged. But if validation must meet the EEOC's own demanding testing criteria, then the EEOC could not, as shall become clear, justify the extensive resources that it commits to disparate impact litigation, which it frequently initiates in its institutional role. We start today with an undefended baseline of equal success, all deviations from which must be justified.

What impact is disparate? Even if an equal success rate sets the appropriate baseline, it then becomes necessary to define the degree of difference sufficient to warrant legal interference. In answering this question the EEOC has taken the position that the issue should be governed by the so-called 80 percent rule:

> A selection rate for any race, sex, or ethnic group which is less than four-fifths (4/5) or (eighty percent) of the rate for the group with the highest rate will generally be regarded by the Federal enforcement agencies as evidence of adverse impact, while a greater than four-fifths rate will generally not be regarded by Federal enforcement agencies as evidence of adverse impact.[1]

The guidelines then go on to state that where smaller differences have statistical significance, the government may undertake enforcement proceedings, and that the failure to satisfy the 80 percent rule "may not

---

1. Uniform Guidelines on Employee Selection Procedures (1978) 29 C.F.R. §1607.4D (1989) (hereafter cited as 1989 Uniform Guidelines). For a qualified defense of the rule, see Paul Meier, Jerome Sacks, and Sandy L. Zabell, "What Happened in *Hazelwood*: Statistics, Employment Discrimination, and the 80% Rule," 1984 *Am. Bar Found. Res. J.* 139, 166–170.

constitute adverse impact where the differences are based on small numbers and are not statistically significant."[2] In general, the 80 percent rule and its qualifications correlate tolerably well with the usual 5 percent significance test normally regarded as appropriate for dealing with statistical matters.[3] By this test the null hypothesis (that is, a presumption of no discrimination by the employer) can be rejected only if there is less than a 5 percent chance that the observed distribution could have been achieved from the underlying sample by random (that is, race-neutral) practices.[4] Generally the strength of that inference depends both on the ratio between the percentage of successful workers chosen from the two groups and on the size of the total sample. Where only five workers are involved, the likelihood of sustaining a false charge of discrimination tends to be about 50 percent, depending on the relative size of the two populations.[5] In a group as large as 50 workers, the applicable statistical rate of error is over 20 percent, far in excess of the 5 percent normally

2. 1989 Uniform Guidelines, 29 C.F.R. §1607.4D.

3. See Anthony E. Boardman and Aidan R. Vining, "The Role of Probative Statistics in Employment Discrimination Cases," 46 *Law & Contemp. Prob.* 189, 211–217 (Autumn 1983).

4. Defining randomness in social settings is often very difficult, given the interdependence of various factors and the difficulty in controlling for certain practices, See, for discussion, Meier, Sacks, and Zabell, "What Happened in *Hazelwood*" at 139, 152–158. The authors identify "clustering" (for example, advertising patterns), which, while ostensibly unrelated to hiring practices, influences the mix of applicants, and hence the success and failure rates of different groups, and "stratification," which arises when employees in different functional slots (say, carpenters and electricians) are grouped together under one umbrella rubric (craft workers) that conceals the relevant differences among the constituent parts.

5. The probability that the 80 percent rule would permit a claim of discrimination when in fact none exists is calculated in Anthony E. Boardman, "Another Analysis of the EEOC 'Four-Fifths' Rule," 25 *Mgmt. Sci.* 770, 773 (1979):

Relative group size	Total number selected ($n = 4$)					
	5	10	15	20	25	50
$n_1 = (3/7)n_2$	.528	.383	.297	.416	.341	.223
$n_1 = n_2$	.500	.377	.304	.252	.345	.240
$n_1 = (7/3)n_2$	.472	.350	.278	.392	.323	.218

Note that n_1 refers to the size of the protected group and n_2 to the size of the unprotected group. The differences in the table indicate that the reliability of the EEOC's 80 percent test depends not only on the total size of the sample but on the mix of the two groups as well.

tolerated in statistical work.[6] Only when the size of the group reaches 100 workers does the four-fifths rule begin to converge with standard statistical tests. A result is fully attained only when there are between 200 and 400 workers in the group. Indeed, as the size of the work force increases, the four-fifths test actually gives the firm slightly more leeway than ordinary tests of statistical significance, for the greater sample size allows rejection of the null hypothesis with smaller deviations from the purported baseline of equal passing rates. In this sense the 80 percent test works best in the massive litigation that is so characteristic of disparate impact suits. Given its mechanical simplicity, many advocates of *Griggs* have championed its use.[7]

The 80 percent test works best in cases where there are only two classes of workers—black (or protected) and white (unprotected). That test will raise difficult problems in several settings. One setting is that in which there are differential passing rates between two different groups both of which are entitled to protected status under the current interpretation of Title VII. Thus it is quite possible to have two workplaces in which the passing rate in one is 80 percent for black applicants and 50 percent for Hispanic and vice versa in the second. The differential rates in both cases could lead to a finding of disparate impact against both employers, even if there were no disparate impact in the market overall.[8] To impose heavy financial penalties on both employers is justified only if one of two conclusions is true: either that the distribution of black and Hispanic workers within firms is critical, even when there is no diminution in their overall welfare,[9] or that the society would be better off if both employers shut down and *all* these workers were denied their jobs.

In addition, the 80 percent test works only with difficulty where there are three or more distinct racial or ethnic groups. The likelihood that the employment test will fail the 80 percent criterion substantially increases. The larger the number of discrete groups, the more likely it is that one group will migrate to the top and another to the bottom of the distribution. These deviations are driven only by the general nature of all proba-

6. Id.

7. See Alfred W. Blumrosen, "The Bottom Line Concept in Equal Employment Opportunity Law," 12 *N.C. Cent. L. J.* 1 (1980).

8. See the discussion of the Daniel Lamp case in Chapter 3 at 70–72, under the heading "Relational Contracts and Governing Costs."

9. Indeed, if the two firms operate more efficiently because of the ethnic sorting, then statistical parity comes at the cost of real wages. See Chapters 2 and 3.

bility distributions; they are unconnected with the substance or design of the tests. If, for example, in a sample of ten groups, eight separate groups cluster about the mean, then the disparity between the best and the worst group—the benchmark stated in the federal guidelines—would presumptively invalidate the test for all groups in the middle. As a general statistical truth the expected gap between the highest and lowest observation will always increase with the number of observations (for example, of separate groups). The increase in the number of groups could well result in an increase in the height of the bell-shaped curve—a sign of the fair test—while at the same time the presence of a single outlier group could condemn the use of the test. A single 80 percent measure is a very bad proxy for the amount of variation in a statistical sample, which could be calculated by the more traditional tests of statistical significance. None of the caveats in the EEOC guidelines addresses this problem.

Selection biases. Taken by itself the 80 percent test does not overcome the baseline problem as I have discussed it, but, given a proper baseline, it does offer a workable statistical measure for large groups (although not for small ones). In practice, however, an additional set of strategic factors is at work that undermines the statistical power of the test. The EEOC guidelines do not offer a natural definition of what counts as "any" race, sex, or ethnic group. The question of group definition has to arise, therefore, in the course of litigation or government investigation. As matters now stand in Title VII cases, the plaintiffs have an enormous advantage because they have first crack at specifying the relevant group to which the 80 percent test (or indeed any other test) of disparate impact is to be applied. It is thus possible for plaintiffs, or the EEOC in its institutional role, to ignore all those groups in which the disparate impact is small and to concentrate solely on those in which it is large. Nonetheless, there is no obvious way to reconfigure the "appropriate group" in order to nullify the consequences of the initial selection bias.

This point has enormous consequences in the way any statistical test operates, as is forcefully developed by Robert Follett and Finis Welch in their critique of statistical testing for employment discrimination.[10] The initial step is for the EEOC or any private champion to break down a work force into small components, and then to select that subgroup showing the greatest disparity and to target it for litigation. As Follett and Welch point out, with a large number of separate units it becomes rela-

---

10. See Robert Follett and Finis Welch, "Testing for Discrimination in Employment Practices," 46 *Law & Contemp. Prob.* 172 (1983).

tively easy to establish that the testing in *some* unit is in violation even if the underlying test is perfectly fair. As I have noted, the distribution necessarily gets wider as the number of groups grows. Thus, if there are two possible groups within a plant, then the chance that one of them will fail the 5 percent significance test is close to 10 percent. As Follett and Welch observe: "If the 0.05 rule were applied to fourteen independent practices, the chance is about 50–50 that one or more would fail, even with neutral treatment."[11] As long as no formal procedures guard against this selection bias,[12] well-honed litigation will be directed toward the group that fails and will ignore those that succeed.

The incentive effects of the selective attack on hiring practices are dramatic for the firm. One possible approach is for it to defend itself by introducing the full results of testing across all separate groups. That evidence, however, would not serve today as a complete defense for the employer, even if it were admissible. In any event, the costs of defending and *winning* a single suit may easily exceed the firm's cost of forgoing any system of testing. The safe strategy may thus be to do without the information that testing provides in order to obtain some safe harbor against litigation. It is of course impossible to find hard data that confirm the extent to which testing has been abandoned because of fears of liability. But the baseline and selection effect problems taken together inflate the likelihood that firms will improperly be held responsible for discriminatory practices.

Baselines in Other Disparate Impact Cases

The problem of disparate impact need not arise only in connection with testing. Other practices adopted within a firm might well be attacked on the same ground, along other possible baselines. Thus, in *Wards Cove Packing Co., Inc. v. Atonio*[13] the issue of statistical disparity arose in the treatment of cannery and noncannery workers who were employed at the defendant's remote Alaskan site during the summer months. The majority of the cannery workers, members of Local 37 of the Longshoremen's Union, were Filipinos and Alaskan Natives. The more skilled noncannery workers were predominantly white and had been hired the previous

11. Id. at 175.

12. The problem is pervasive in all litigation. See, generally, George L. Priest and Benjamin Klein, "The Selection of Disputes for Litigation," 13 *J. Legal Stud.* 1 (1984).

13. 490 U.S. 642 (1989).

winter at the company's offices in Washington and Oregon.[14] The district court rejected all disparate treatment attacks on the hiring process; after extensive maneuvers the Court of Appeals held that the statistical disparity in the racial balance of the two components of the work force established a disparate impact case under *Griggs*.[15] The Supreme Court reversed the decision on this point on the ground that the relevant statistics were "nonsensical" largely because the two sets of workers were drawn from very different labor pools, a fact that precluded any possibility of the cannery workers' having the slightest qualifications for the noncannery jobs. A disparate impact case requires that one identify comparable classes of applicants and hired workers. Where the hiring takes place through different methods (union versus nonunion) and at different locations (locally versus in Oregon and Washington), the numbers prove nothing because they bear no relation to the qualifications that individual applicants bring to the job. The insistence on proper baselines seems almost too obvious for comment, save that it was overlooked by the Court of Appeals.

The Business Necessity Defense

The Costs of Demanding Perfection

In most cases, showing a disparate impact of a test is a relatively straightforward issue. Once the disparate impact qualification had been satisfied, the inquiry under *Griggs* moved to business necessity. The words *business necessity* were not casually chosen, for they have real bite in practice. They have been strictly construed in the EEOC guidelines on the subject,[16] which have received a general acceptance in the courts.[17] Although there is some variation in the level of rigor found in various cases,[18] one common formulation of the concept provides that "the practice must be essential, the purpose compelling."[19] On this view it is not enough that a

14. Id. at 647.

15. *Atonio v. Wards Cove Packing Co., Inc.*, 827 F.2d 439 (9th Cir. 1987).

16. See, for the current guidelines, 29 C.F.R. pt. 1607 discussed later in this chapter.

17. See Barbara Schlei and Paul Grossman, *Employment Discrimination Law* 38–39 and cases cited there (2nd ed., five-year cumulative supp., D. Cathcart and R. Ashe eds. 1989).

18. See discussion of *Clady v. County of Los Angeles*, 770 F.2d 1421 (9th Cir. 1985) later in this chapter.

19. *Williams v. Colorado Springs, Colo. Sch. Dist.*, 641 F.2d 835, 842 (10th Cir. 1981), followed by the Ninth Circuit in *Wards Cove*. The 1991 administration bill reads: "§3 (n)

test is perfectly reasonable and plausible, in the sense of cost effective: virtually any test in common use meets this standard. More must be shown, not to meet any sensible social objective but only to ensure that the statistical power of the prima facie case is not undone by the accommodating nature of the available defenses. Business necessity is a close cousin to the "private necessity" defense at common law, and it conjures up the image of a criterion test designed to avoid imminent peril of bankruptcy or death. Rarely is there any necessity to use personnel tests. Firms are generally in the business of making profits. There is no business necessity to use testing to keep a plant in operation; after all, workers who have been promoted without taking the test have often done satisfactory work, as was seen in *Griggs* itself.

The intellectual case for the business necessity criterion, however, is weak even if disparate impact cases are allowed. The Supreme Court's initial hostility to testing, evidenced in *Griggs* and reinforced in the subsequent decision of *Albemarle Paper Co. v. Moody*,[20] requires some deviation from established widespread practices that were not driven by any desire to discriminate. In *Griggs*, employee testing was first adopted in 1955, a time when the company overtly discriminated on grounds of race. The tests therefore were not a cloak for discrimination, which was openly practiced. Rather, they were used because they gave the firm some information about the prospective performance of employees that was worth more than the cost of obtaining it. The same tests would have been used even if all workers were of the same race, sex, or national origin, and for the same reasons. Stating that workers are qualified misses enormous variations in the level of anticipated performance, which can affect the profits of the firm, the safety of workers, and the prices charged to the consumer. By analogy, there are enormous differences in quality among physicians who are not guilty of medical malpractice. No one expects patients to patronize the first doctor they encounter solely because he or she meets some minimum competency standard set by the tort law.

A firm in this respect has as much incentive to search for good workers as a customer has to search for good firms. The employer has

---

The term 'justified by business necessity' means that the challenged practice has a manifest relationship to the employment in question or that the respondent's legitimate employment goals are significantly served by, even if they do not require, the challenged practice." The standard is somewhat weaker than the stronger judicial renderings of business necessity, and are obviously ripe for litigation.

20. 422 U.S. 405 (1975).

every reason to test to determine relative abilities: testing is indeed one of the best ways to reduce the risk of statistical discrimination and to combat the lemons problem.[21] But testing will be undertaken by the firm only to the extent that the familiar requirements for rational behavior are met. The analogy to the costs of search is complete.[22] Tests provide benefits in the form of reliable information about worker aptitude and performance. But they cost money to administer. Infinite testing is clearly too costly, but forgoing testing may deprive the firm of imperfect but valuable information. The efficient solution therefore is testing in limited amounts. By raising the costs of testing to prohibitive levels under the rubric of business necessity, *Griggs* and its progeny deprive all employers, good and bad, virtuous and corrupt, of a valuable tool for improving the quality of their internal operations. Workers, too, both black and white, will have less information about their fitness for particular jobs, and, more critically, about their prospects over the long haul for advancement within the firm. The term *job related,* as it is used in the context of Title VII, is tied to entry-level positions, not to possible promotion two or three years down the road. Professionally developed tests have worked well because they were used so widely that it was possible to devise very strong statistical checks across firms and over time to make sure that they were internally consistent and reliably applied.[23] They tested (the past tense is all too appropriate) skills that are doubtless related in some positive way to success on the job. The whole movement to increase the educational level of young people rested, and perhaps still rests, on a global social perception that education, like good personal habits, is always job related.[24] Why, then, do we behave as though education, and the basic

21. See Chapter 2 at 31-41, under the heading "To the Urn."

22. See Chapter 8.

23. See, on this process of validity generalization, John E. Hunter, Frank L. Schmidt, and Gregg B. Jackson, *Meta-Analysis: Cumulating Research Findings across Studies* (1982). *Fairness in Employment Testing: Validity Generalization, Minority Issues, and the General Aptitude Test Battery,* ch. 6 (J. A. Hartigan and Alexandra Wigdor eds. 1989) (hereafter cited as Fairness). For an early and able defense of testing, see also Barbara Lerner, "*Washington v. Davis*: Quantity, Quality, and Equality in Employment Testing," 1976 *Sup. Ct. Rev.* 263.

24. "There has now been enough judicial and professional experience with educational requirements in law enforcement to establish a presumption in civil rights cases that a high school education is an appropriate requirement for anyone who is going to be a policeman, or, we add, a corrections officer (jail or prison guard), and therefore to excuse civil rights defendants from having to prove, over and over again, that such requirements really are necessary for such jobs." *Aguilera v. Cook County Police and Corrections Merit Board,* 760

knowledge and skills that it produces, is irrelevant in each individual case when we generally think otherwise? By demanding very nearly perfect correlations between tests and performance, *Griggs*, as well as the EEOC guidelines and the cases that followed, shows a preference for less information rather than more. And by reducing the returns on education, it removes one of the incentives that young people have to expend money, time, and effort on acquiring an education.

The burdens imposed in the wake of *Griggs* are often very substantial. Once disparate impact is established, the law, as outlined in the EEOC guidelines, requires an extensive validation of any test with a disproportionate impact on the passing rates of whites and blacks. This validation cannot be taken wholesale. Indeed, the EEOC guidelines warn test users that "they are responsible for compliance with these guidelines." The official rules convey the unmistakable impression that individual users can at most place limited reliance on the validity studies undertaken by the test's publishers. At the very least, the results must be shown to be applicable to the special circumstances of the employer.[25] The routine use of the Wunderlic and Bennett tests, condemned in *Griggs*, is today a thing of the past; employers are now required to mount the extensive research and preclearance programs necessary to validate a test tailor-made to their own situation.

The constant drumbeat of the EEOC guidelines is that job testing requires heavy expenditures in verification. What is so perverse about the situation is that the EEOC has never verified the relevance of its own strict standards. Critical to the EEOC's entire stance is the proposition that general tests do not predict job success as well as tests that meet the EEOC standards. That proposition is an empirical one, and it should itself be capable of being tested. At the very least, the EEOC should commission its own cadre of independent experts to run studies that compare performance on standard tests rejected by the agency with the narrowly defined tests that have received agency approval. The betting here (by one singularly ill suited to conduct such studies) is that the correlation between performance on allowable and impermissible tests will be higher than the normal 0.2 to 0.5 correlation coefficients that are found in these

F.2d 844 (7th Cir.) (per Posner, J.). Judge Posner also noted that "the exacting criteria [of the EEOC guidelines] are more applicable to tests than to educational requirements. Tests are made and scored by the employer, and hence easily misused." Id. at 847. His criticism does not seem applicable to standardized tests scored by independent agencies.

25. 29 C.F.R. §1607.7A.

tests generally.[26] If the correlation between the permitted and the nonpermitted tests should be high, then the insistence on the elaborate individuated validation would turn out to be an expensive and unnecessary mistake, given the costs of preparing and validating a test. If that prediction is wrong, then the EEOC will (at least within a universe that approves of *Griggs* on substantive grounds) have shown some justification for maintaining its current standards, as there will be some apparent benefit from the costs of validation. But if my prediction is right, the whole testing apparatus is just another costly piece of bureaucratic activity. The insistence on ad hoc testing can only increase costs and reduce the reliability of a firm's personnel decisions.

EEOC Guidelines: Forgotten Objectives and Unavailable Data

The point on costs is made clear if we look at the three ways that employers may validate tests under the EEOC guidelines: content studies, construct studies, and criterion validity studies. In each case the guidelines are full of mine fields that inhibit the widespread, routine use of any standard test.

Content studies aim to isolate individual features of the job and to develop tests that measure performance with respect to those features. The welder can be tested on the ability to weld, the typist on the ability to type. The firefighter can be tested on the ability to lift hoses and climb ladders.[27] The advantage of this form of testing is that its relation to the job is so close that statistical validation is not required. Nonetheless, content tests, especially pencil and paper tests, frequently cannot duplicate situations encountered in the field; at the very least they can reach only a small segment of the relevant work experience, and this may be insufficient to allow the tests to serve as a useful measure of overall job performance. These tests are by definition limited to narrow job classifications, and it is very expensive to justify their start-up costs, for their use can be challenged every inch of the way.

Construct studies are closely related to content tests, but at present

---

26. See, e.g., John Hunter, *Validity Generalization for 12,000 Jobs: An Application of Synthetic Validity and Validity Generalization to the General Aptitude Test Battery (GATB)* (1980) (validity of about 0.56 with technical, managerial, and professional jobs, but only 0.23 for unskilled labor). See also *Fairness*, ch. 8.

27. Held valid in *Evans v. City of Evanston,* 881 F.2d 382 (7th Cir. 1989) (disparate impact sex case).

they serve no practical purpose. The employer selects certain traits that are thought to be relevant to a job—leadership for policeman, patience for teachers—and seeks to establish that connection and then show that the test measures a construct whose relevance has been independently demonstrated. The three sets of variables that have to be connected are so difficult to control that no one resorts to this method at all.

The final form of testing, the so-called criterion validity study, seeks to relate the use of the selection device with success on the job, and by nature requires extensive statistical validation. On this matter the EEOC guidelines contain six pages of densely worded standards, ostensibly to protect against every possible form of bias, overt and hidden.[28] The guidelines show a sustained distaste for any written test: "Criterion measures consisting of paper and pencil tests will be closely reviewed for job relevance."[29] Validation is forced into the field, and thus necessarily depends on reports of supervisors and personnel officials, whose subjectivity can easily be attacked in hiring and promotion disputes. In addition, the guidelines on field testing consist largely of identifying obstacles to be overcome. Separate job classifications can be grouped only with caution. The reports of supervisors and personnel officers have to be scrutinized for bias. Statistical significance has to be clearly established. Although the guidelines heap requirement on requirement, they do not provide the one thing that would make this form of testing feasible: safe-harbor rules that ensure the validity of those tests that do comply with certain standards.

These criterion studies, moreover, are subject to a bias of their own, known as range restriction, which makes the relevant correlations unlikely to be observed.[30] A strong statistical test does its job when it keeps weak candidates from getting the jobs in the first instance. The predictive power of the test may therefore largely be exhausted in selecting the proper people for the job. In principle some predictive power will remain where there is a wide variation in passing scores. But in practice we should not expect to see many candidates who do exceptionally well on a given test relative to the cohort of other candidates who

28. See 28 C.F.R. §1607.14.

29. 16 C.F.R. §1607.14B(3).

30. See *Fairness* at 166: "If the test standard deviation is smaller in the study sample than in the applicant pool, then the validity coefficient for workers will be reduced due to range restriction and will be an underestimate of the true validity of the test for applicants." Correcting for the error is often difficult because the standard deviation for test takers is not often known, and can be assumed only arbitrarily to be equal to that of the entire United States work force. Id.

simply pass. People who know they can score high on the tests will not be taking them in large numbers because they usually have better opportunities elsewhere. Candidates who do get high scores may reevaluate their prospects and choose to move on. The range of passing candidates might be narrower than expected because the giver of the test cannot determine by fiat the pool of candidates. As long as these candidates have any prior information about their own abilities, they will self-select in ways that maximize their job opportunities. The extreme ends of the distribution will tend to melt away.

To give a parallel example, if the Scholastic Aptitude Tests used for college admission predict accurately, then the class members at an elite college should all be drawn from the top 2 or 3 percent of the test sample. There may be little doubt that this class will be far better than one drawn from students who have scored between the fortieth and sixtieth percentiles on the SAT, but this result is not validated by a positive correlation between test scores and school performance of the elite *after* their admission to a top-ranked college. What is needed is a test that compares the performance levels of those who were admitted and those who were rejected from the class. In the labor context what is required is a way to measure the work performance of people who were *not* hired or promoted against those who were. But workers who are not hired cannot be evaluated. The relevant data are just not available.

Criterion Testing Confounded

One well-known case illustrates the difficulties of validating tests with disproportionate impact. The New York City Police Department made several notable and sustained efforts to develop a test for entry-level officers that was predictive on the one hand and job related on the other. Its first attempt was successfully challenged in *Guardians Association of New York City v. Civil Service*.[31] There the city wanted to hire 400 trainees; it received 36,000 applications for the available places. Trainees for the New York City Police Department are selected in a thorough hiring process that includes a medical examination, an agility test, a psychological test, a character investigation, and a general written test. Pass-fail scores are used for the first four components, but not for the written test. The use of that test was attacked by black and Hispanic police offers on disparate impact grounds. In litigation the

31. 630 F.2nd 79 (2d Cir. 1980).

test's disparate impact was easy to establish. Candidates identified as black, for example, accounted for 16.7 percent of the pool but only 7.6 percent of the passing grades. Those identified as Hispanic constituted 14.2 percent of the test takers but only 7.8 percent of the passing group. Whites made up 53.8 percent of the applicant pool and 66 percent of the passing group. The 80 percent standard of the EEOC was met, as well as any ordinary standard of statistical significance.

The question therefore quickly shifted to test validation. The city had worked hard to construct a "second-generation" test, one that would meet the standards set out in *Griggs, Albemarle Paper*, and the EEOC guidelines. To that end the city sought to justify its test by content analysis. It introduced evidence that broke down police performance into some forty-two categories, such as "checks the condition of personal and department equipment," "performs foot patrol," and "attends training meetings." Next it tried to develop a list of the abilities (skills in human relations, remembering details, filling out forms, applying general principles to particular cases) needed for each of these separate tasks. But, as might be expected in light of the delicacy of its mission, the city slipped up, for it assumed that the same set of abilities was required across the board. It then used its in-house staff to develop tests for each of the abilities in each subject area, and it devised a test for the purpose, without the aid of any outside expert—a step, which Judge Jon Newman noted, the city took "at [its] peril."[32] The questions themselves were not produced in a systematic fashion, nor were they pretested before being put into general use. The court tolerated the tests as being reasonably representative of the tasks involved, although it was somewhat troubled by the attempt to measure human relations skills through testing devices.

In the end, however, the test foundered because it adopted a rank order and a cutoff score. The EEOC guidelines on these matters are a marvel of opacity which defy summarization; they are (if only out of self-defense) duly set out in the margin.[33] The persons who attained the highest scores received the highest ranking for entry into the training

32. Id. at 96.

33. "*Cutoff Scores*. Where cutoff scores are used, they should normally be set so as to be reasonable and consistent with normal expectations of acceptable proficiency within the workforce. Where applicants are ranked on the basis of properly validated selection procedures and those applicants scoring below a higher cutoff score than appropriate in light of such expectations have little or no chance of being selected for employment, the higher cutoff score may be appropriate, but the degree of adverse impact should be considered." 29 C.F.R. §1607.5H.

program, even though there was no strong correspondence between test rank and job performance. Judge Newman, while troubled by this feature of the system, did not invalidate the test on that ground. Every test must use some ranking function. To be sure, it is always possible to choose randomly among job applicants who pass the test at some prespecified level, but there is no obvious reason why this would be preferable.

In Newman's view the fatal objection to the test was its arbitrary cutoff at the score of 94, given that around 8,900, or about two-thirds, of the applicants who passed received scores between 94 and 97, and another 4,000 applicants received scores of 93 and 92. Initially there does appear to be something very odd about a cutoff point that yields a group of candidates twenty times the number of available positions.[34] As Judge Newman wrote: "Selecting a cutoff score in the middle of the range in which the test scores were closely bunched meant that the inevitable error of measurement led to a much higher number of mistaken passes and failures than would have otherwise occurred."[35]

The judge was quite right to note that the rate of error is apt to be high when a large number of scores cluster around the cutoff point. But he was wrong to conclude that *any* sound test will be able to overcome this bunching problem. As I have noted, one important function of a test is to give information in advance to people who are thinking of applying for the job. If those people know they cannot pass the test, they will tend not to apply. If they know they can excel on the test, they may also not apply, realizing that they have a good chance of obtaining better positions elsewhere. The very sorting function of the test therefore induces large numbers of people not to take it, given their private knowledge of their own background and skills. This selection bias ensures that those who remain are likely to be close to the line. If the test is changed or eliminated, the composition of the applicant pool will change in response; weaker candidates are more likely to apply if their chances of passing improve. As long as any test is used, bunching at the cutoff point will always occur, wholly

---

34. A similar pattern is found in *Evans v. City of Evanston,* 881 F.2d 382 (7th Cir.), a sex discrimination case in which 85 percent of the women applicants but only 7 percent of the males failed a physical agility test whose relevance to firefighting was conceded. The nub of contention in that case was that the city accepted a standard deviation of 1.0 in this instance, whereas in earlier runs of the test it had used higher standard deviations (1.7 and 2.8) and was unable to justify the difference. Note that only 1.2 percent of the group that passed the test were hired, and it appears that for passing candidates the ranking on the test was treated as irrelevant. Id. at 385–386.

35. 630 F.2d at 105.

without regard to the content of the test. Judge Newman failed to take into account the dynamic responses of potential candidates.

At first blush *Guardians Association* seems to contradict the sorting proposition, since 8,900 candidates passed a test when there were only 400 positions available. But the explanation doubtless lies in the politics surrounding the selection of applicants for public office once a test has been passed. The very large list of potential applicants preserves the prospects of wheeling and dealing that might have been eliminated under a more selective testing procedure. Once the passing rate for the other four tests was known (say, 80 percent), then the first 500 candidates could have been told that they remained in a pool, with another 100 or so on the waiting list, just in case the failure rate in other parts of the hiring process was high. At this point the cutoff score could have been moved up to 101 on the test to avoid the large bulge in the middle (125 candidates got a score of 101, and 823 got a score of 100). But if that cutoff procedure had been announced in advance, the number of applicants would not have been 36,000 but rather a small fraction of that number, with the bulge reappearing near the new cutoff point. As a rule the composition of the applicant pool is heavily influenced by the choice of a cutoff point.

In light of this analysis, the decisive question should *never* be whether test scores bunch at some arbitrary cutoff. *All* tests do that. Instead, it should be whether a group of policemen taken from the pool that passed the test will do better on the job than a group of policeman taken from the pool that failed. To the extent that any test has that anticipated result, it has served its function, even if it fails to make perfect selections. If (as seems to be the case) there is a high correlation between the results on one test and the results on another, then very little further information is gained by insisting on the baroque validation procedures required by the EEOC guidelines and ratified by the Second Circuit. Judge Newman tried to be sensible and sensitive to the law as construed in the guidelines and the Supreme Court cases. He refused, for example, to accept the remedy awarded by the trial judge (a 50 percent quota for blacks and Hispanics), and he authorized the construction of a new test, subject, of course, to judicial supervision. But for reasons wholly unrelated to Title VII, matters would have been far better if he had simply raised the passing score from 94 to 101. Still, in light of his decision the inescapable message is that no test can quite do the job, given the number of hurdles it must cross.

This conclusion about *Guardians Association* does not rest solely on abstract speculation. After the invalidation of the first test in *Guardians,*

New York City went back to the drawing boards to prepare a second version of its second-generation test. Elaborate precautions were taken to select an independent testing firm; the city even obtained the approval of the plaintiff groups. The test cost $500,000 to develop, and it yielded a passing rate for blacks of 1.6 percent, for Hispanics of 4.4 percent, and for whites of about 11 percent, far lower than those on the first round of tests but disparate in their impact nonetheless. Since this test was presumptively invalid, New York City did not even attempt to defend it in court. The requirements of business necessity and job relatedness were adjudged too stringent.[36]

So, then, as long as high business necessity standards are imposed, it will be difficult if not impossible to validate tests that have useful but imperfect predictive ability. Indeed, those cases in which tests have been upheld have taken a fundamentally different approach to the problem from that taken by the court in *Guardians.* Thus in *Clady v. County of Los Angeles*[37] the Ninth Circuit upheld the selection procedures for the Los Angeles County Fire Department against a disparate impact challenge. The opinion first began by refusing (rightly) to treat the EEOC guidelines as dispositive on the question of disparate impact. More significant, it then eschewed the very detailed analysis of the written examination undertaken in *Guardians* in favor of a much more deferential approach to job relatedness, which, far from stressing business necessity as articulated in *Griggs,* noted that the test was acceptable provided there was no nondiscriminatory alternative test that would promise equal reliability in measuring job fitness without loss of predictability. The difference in tone between *Guardians* and *Clady* is the difference between night and day; it was the difference in fact between disparate treatment and disparate impact. Much turns on the attitude that is taken toward the business necessity defense.

Type I and Type II Errors

The major role of the EEOC in the testing area invests its guidelines with enormous importance. Its misguided forays into the area stem, I believe, in large measure from a common error that too often infects government decisions. A statute is passed that is directed against a certain social ill.

---

36. See, generally, Mark Snyderman and Stanley Rothman, *The IQ Controversy* 11–29 (1988), which contains an excellent account of the history of IQ testing.
37. 770 F.2d 1421 (9th Cir. 1985).

Those in charge of enforcing the statute then define their mission in heroic terms: to root out *all* instances of the illegal practice with a series of stringent rules. The question of overbreadth is suppressed in the articulation of statistical rules. This cycle is at work with testing, since no disparate treatment test will catch all forms of subtle or even unconscious discrimination.[38] Disparate impact suits provide the fallback protection against firms that escape detection on the less exacting motive-based criteria.

This stance exacts a high social price. In statistical language the entire thrust of the disparate impact rules is to minimize what statisticians call a Type II error—the chance that the employer's illegal practice will be held to be legal.[39] But any sensible legal system must also concern itself with Type I error—the chance that an employer will be found to have discriminated illegally when its conduct has been perfectly legal. Usually the two types of error vary in an inverse relationship: as one goes up the other goes down. In principle it is possible to reduce both types of error to an acceptable level by increasing the sample size. But that course of action is often not available in litigation, where the aggrieved employee is able to select the department of the employer to which the disparate impact test will apply. In practice the effort to drive the incidence of Type II errors down to zero requires the legal system to tolerate very large amounts of Type I error.

The central analytical point is that the *sum* of the two types of error is never constant. On the contrary, the relationship between these two types of error is strikingly nonlinear over large portions of the total domain. Toward the middle of a distribution, where the two types of error are about equal in frequency, small decreases in one type will generally result in small increases in the other. The reduction in one will roughly offset the increase in the other. That is the usual result in ordinary civil litiga-

38. See, on the theme of unconscious discrimination, Charles Lawrence, "The Id, the Ego, and Equal Protection: Reckoning with Unconscious Racism," 39 *Stan. L. Rev.* 317 (1987).

39. "The risk of an erroneous rejection of the hypothesis that the disparity was caused by change is considered 'Type I' error, i.e. rejecting the null hypothesis when it should have been accepted. An alternative form of error, known as 'Type II' error, is the erroneous acceptance of the chance hypothesis when it should have been rejected. As the risk of Type I error rises the risk of Type II error declines and vice versa." David C. Baldus and James W. L. Cole, *Statistical Proof of Discrimination* 291–292 n.5 (1980). For further discussion of the two types of error, see Daniel L. Rubinfeld, "Econometrics in the Courtroom," 85 *Colum. L. Rev.* 1048, 1051 (1985).

tion, where the plaintiff prevails on the preponderance of evidence, that is, where the probability that the plaintiff's case is true is greater than 50 percent. In the middle range the sum of the two errors will be roughly constant. But that relationship ceases to be approximately linear the further one moves toward elimination of all error in one direction or the other. Thus, reducing the amount of Type II error in race discrimination cases from 1 percent to 0.1 percent will require increases in Type I error far greater than 0.9 percent. It may be that the rate of erroneous plaintiff's verdicts will jump from 20 to 50 percent. Or it may be less. But one thing is certain: the increase in Type I error will be far greater than the 0.9 percent needed to keep the sum of the two errors constant. The law of diminishing returns shows its full force at both tails of the distribution.

The hard question throughout, therefore, is how to minimize a total cost, equal to the sum of the two types of error, plus the enforcement costs of their correction. In this regard it becomes necessary to make one additional refinement. It is critical to know not only the *probability* of Type I and Type II error but also the severity of loss associated with each type. The simplest and most naive assumption weights the two kinds of error equally, so minimizing the sum of the two types of error is a first approximation of the minimization of the whole loss. Moreover, since the costs of detecting and wrongly holding defendants liable are always positive, Type I errors, for which enforcement costs are positive, are presumptively more severe than Type II errors, which involve the less costly alternative of wrongful underenforcement (that is, letting the guilty defendant go). In measuring social losses by the traditional analysis, we err in favor of the plaintiff in an antidiscrimination case, and in favor of the EEOC rules, by assuming that the ideal system places equal weight on the two types of error.

In response it may be urged that this analysis is incomplete because the two types of errors do not possess equal dignity. If escaping punishment (Type II error) is regarded as a more serious miscarriage than being wrongfully punished (Type I error), then errors of underenforcement count more than errors of overenforcement. It becomes proper, therefore, to minimize an expression of the sort

Cost of Type I error + n (Cost of Type II Error) + Cost of Enforcement

for some n greater than 1. Accordingly, the higher the value of n, the more resources should be brought into the fray to deter and correct discrimination. But how does one establish the greater weight of Type II errors? The obvious argument is that the moral centrality of the antidiscrimination norm requires that the multiplier of Type II error be large. To that contention there are two answers. First, the antidiscrimination law is not that central: even its defenders do not consider it as central as the libertarian prohibitions against assault and battery, rape, and murder.

Even if we pass that point by, the second objection remains: Why should the (assumed) importance of the antidiscrimination laws require us to slight the errors of overenforcement? The consensus that murder is a grave wrong, punishable under the criminal laws, has never been regarded as a reason to make life easy for prosecutors: they do not get convictions on mere suspicion alone, or even on proof by a preponderance of the evidence. Quite the opposite. The severity and centrality of murder has generated a procedural code that affords the criminal defendant *extra* forms of protection, including conviction only upon proof beyond a reasonable doubt of each element of the crime. The loss of liberty is rated as so weighty that two, three, five, or ten guilty persons *do* go free so that one innocent person is not falsely convicted.

In the civil rights context there is always a risk that cases won on disparate impact alone will be trumpeted as instances of conscious discrimination unmasked by astute methods of proof. The loss of reputation from a false accusation of discrimination similarly suggests that civil rights defendants, like criminal defendants, should, if anything, receive higher levels of protection than defendants in ordinary tort litigation, where issues of bad faith (for example, illicit motive) do not apply. At the very least, any analogy with deliberate wrongs points to a rule that weights the two forms of error equally just as is done, for example, in ordinary medical malpractice or breach of contract cases. By this standard the rules on Title VII fail, as the present law skews matters two ways. First, it allows effects to do the work of intent; and second, it biases the inquiry on effects. Even within the world of Title VII, the social goal should not be the *maximum* enforcement of the antidiscrimination laws but instead their *optimal* enforcement, given both the frequency and severity of errors of overenforcement and underenforcement.

Beyond Griggs

The question of the disparate impact test does not end with the mandate of *Griggs* and the EEOC guidelines used to implement it. Three subsequent cases merit special attention: *Connecticut v. Teal,*[40] *Watson v. Fort Worth Bank and Trust,*[41] and *Ward's Cove.* These cases illustrate something of the shift in attitudes since *Griggs.* Initially *Teal* continued the expansive view of disparate impact and the continued judicial assault on testing. *Watson* showed a tendency toward uneasiness with the disparate impact tests in the area of interviews and subjective evaluations of workers. For the moment *Ward's Cove* has largely undercut the business necessity defense that lies at the heart of the *Griggs* edifice, with implications that extend far beyond the testing area.

Teal: *The Demise of the Bottom Line Defense*

Teal is a disparate impact case with both a twist and a vengeance. The plaintiff, Winnie Teal, applied for a promotion in the Connecticut Department of Income Maintenance, which required her to pass a written test. Of the 48 candidates who identified themselves as black, about 54 percent passed; of the 259 candidates who identified themselves as white, about 80 percent passed. Since the passing rate for blacks was only 68 percent of the white rate, Connecticut's written test flunked the EEOC's 80 percent rule. In this case, however, Connecticut did not seek to validate the test but argued instead that the disparate impact of the test should be disregarded as an intermediate way station in a total selection process, for in the end about 23 percent of the black candidates were promoted as against 11 percent of the white candidates. The explanation for the difference lies in the disparate treatment of those candidates who did pass the written test: nearly one-quarter of the blacks were promoted (11 of 48), wheras only about 13.5 percent (35 out of 259) of the whites received comparable promotions.

The question in *Teal* was whether Connecticut could avail itself of the favorable "bottom line" for blacks as a defense against a disparate impact charge based on the test results. The Supreme Court, speaking through Justice William J. Brennan, Jr., rejected this defense, stressing that each individual must "achieve equality of employment *opportunities.*"[42] The test was regarded as a barrier to this particular plaintiff which could be

40. 457 U.S. 440 (1982). For an excellent analysis of *Teal,* see Michael W. McConnell, "A New Twist on Affirmative Action?" 38 Regulation (March–April 1983).

41. 487 U.S. 977 (1988).

42. 457 U.S. at 448. "Opportunities" is italicized in the original. Indeed the word is italicized eight times in three pages.

eliminated only by its invalidation. Brennan thus rejected an argument that the post-test procedures could function as a stepladder for climbing over the barrier. Accordingly, each stage has to be evaluated separately and in isolation for its discriminatory effect. If it fails, then the entire selection process must be thrown out. Is this approach sound?

The first point to note is that the question of individual opportunity cuts in both directions. In this case large numbers of white persons did not receive promotions even though they had passed the test. If one looks at the ratio of employees who made it to the second stage, it is evident that the promotion rate for whites, at around 55 percent, was far less than 80 percent of the promotion rate for blacks. If, therefore, section 703(a) (2) does apply to "any individual," then a disparate impact attack could be successfully launched against *both* ends of the promotion procedure. On balance, it would be found to discriminate against *everyone*. Indeed, the claim of the disappointed white workers would appear to be stronger, given their lower success rate (55 percent of the black rate) at the second stage than that of blacks (68 percent of the white rate) at the first stage. It is, moreover, not possible to defend this result on the ground that some preconceived distribution is desirable in the workplace, because that is inconsistent with Justice Brennan's stress on equality of individual *opportunity,* which is a far cry from racial equality in the hiring process. By opening the components up to separate examination, we therefore create the possibility that any multistage employee selection procedure discriminates against applicants of all groups simultaneously—the legal equivalent of squaring the circle.

Justice Brennan's protestations to one side, *Teal* is of course not an equal opportunity case: if it were, then the whole disparate impact test would have been rejected out of hand, given the force of the color-blind norm. *Teal* must therefore be understood as a disguised affirmative action case, and an inefficient one at that. Suppose that the state decided that it wanted to run an overt affirmative action program.[43] The sensible approach (notwithstanding the universal opposition to quotas in 1964) would have been to set a goal or target for whites and blacks to be promoted within the organization. With the explicit measure of discrimination thereby established, the rest becomes technique, for the next task is to be sure that within each cohort, black and white, the best available

43. A more exhaustive analysis of the constitutionality of affirmative action, its legality under Title VII, and its general desirability in private and public institutions follows in Chapters 19 and 20.

workers are chosen for the jobs. It follows, therefore, that the tests should be used, taking the best *starting from the top* in each category, black or white. There is, to be sure, some perhaps significant efficiency loss if, by standards of the tests, better qualified white workers are passed over in favor of less qualified black workers, or vice versa. But we can assume for the moment that this is one cost that the state is prepared and entitled to bear.

There is precedent for adopting this approach from the *Guardians* case. Thus, in the wake of the futile effort to construct a reliable job-related test in *Guardians,* all sides, including a hostile Mayor Edward Koch, wearily but sensibly accepted just this compromise three years after *Teal* was decided.[44] Although it is a rational outcome, it does expose the weakness of the underlying substantive complaint—that the tests are bad because they are not job related. Worthless tests cannot lay the groundwork for acceptable settlements. What was at stake in *Guardians* and *Teal* was not the validity of the test; rather, it was the question of power, and of the division of valuable social spoils. The very test whose validity was rejected in litigation was explicitly relied on in settlement to hire new employees within racial and ethnic cohorts.

The lingering question is why this shrewd political solution should not be, in the rough world of second best, the correct legal solution as well. Why should *Teal* replace a system of dual-line selection with a system that allows weaker black candidates to obtain positions at the expense of stronger black candidates? Using the tests, the state made an effort to select the best candidates within the black applicant pool, to whom it then gave a systematic advantage in the rest of the selection process relative to whites. After the invalidation of the test, the employer can still obtain exactly the same ratio of blacks to whites, but average quality will be lower than when the written test was used. Invalidating the test improves the prospects of Ms. Teal: she had no chance of promotion, having flunked the test, but now she has some chance of promotion under any other selection criteria. But if the black-to-white promotion ratio is kept constant, then other individual blacks who scored higher on the test now have reduced chances of success, and are deprived of opportunities that they would have enjoyed under a system that mixed merit promotion and affirmative action through an overt dual tracking system. If the concern of the Civil Rights Act is to help all individuals obtain equal oppor-

44. See Patrick Fenton, "The Way Police Exams Used to Be," *N.Y. Times,* July 27, 1985, at 23.

tunity, then it becomes idle to act as if the only persons who matter are those persons, black or white, who flunked the test. Only if one regards testing as some kind of farce should such results be welcomed.[45] The vice of *Teal* is that it dashes any effort to maintain quality while simultaneously increasing the percentage of black promotions. *Teal* thus displays that same relentless preference for universal ignorance over partial knowledge that characterizes the Supreme Court's approach to testing in *Griggs*. It is one of those rare decisions that should be condemned by supporters and opponents of affirmative action alike. Its myopic protection of particular black candidates makes it ever harder to run a decent civil service with workers able to perform their jobs. Neither Title VII nor *Griggs* mandates such perverse results.

Watson: *The Role of Subjective Judgment*

Thus far the analysis has been confined to the use of the disparate impact rule as applied to objective forms of testing. Both hiring and promotions often rely on subjective information, either alone or in combination with objective tests, as was the case, for example, in both *Teal* and *Guardians Association*. In principle these subjective measures of job performance are fair grist for the mill of disparate treatment cases, where the plaintiff must overcome two major obstacles: the difficulties of accumulating the relevant evidence on mental state, and the broad class of legitimate nondiscriminatory reasons for making employment decisions.

Watson asked whether the apparatus of the disparate impact cases could be carried over to interview and subjective evaluation processes. The plaintiff was employed by the defendant bank first as a telephone operator and then as a teller in the bank's drive-in facility. She then applied for several supervisory positions, but was turned down each time. In some cases the position was taken by a white male, in others by a white female. There were about eighty employees in the bank, which did not rely on "precise and formal criteria" for promotion but instead depended "on the subjective judgment of supervisors who were acquainted with the

45. See, e.g., Mark Kelman, "Concepts of Discrimination in 'General Ability' Job Testing," 104 *Harv. L. Rev.* 1158, 1169 (1991): "The Supreme Court's refusal to allow the 'bottom-line' defense in [*Teal*] frees each successful black applicant from the stigmatizing insult that she was hired 'politically' rather than 'meritocratically' and vindicates each unsuccessful black individual's right to be evaluated through an unbigoted lens." See also D. Don Welch, "Superficially Neutral Classifications: Extended Disparate Impact to Individual," 63 *N.C. L. Rev.* 849 (1985).

candidates and with the nature of the jobs to be filled."[46] Thereafter she filed a case urging that she had been discriminated against on the ground of race. The District Court held that she had made out a prima facie case of race discrimination by showing the disproportionately small number of blacks hired or promoted, but it then concluded that her case nonetheless failed because the bank gave nondiscriminatory reasons for its decisions which were not shown to be pretextual. In effect the case was handled as a hybrid of disparate impact and disparate treatment, without the enormous sting of the business necessity test.

The question before the Supreme Court was whether, and if so how, disparate impact should be applied to subjective techniques such as interviewing. The obvious difficulty with using this approach is that the hard data are insufficient for running the statistical analysis on which the disparate impact approach necessarily depends. Nonetheless, a plurality of the Supreme Court, speaking through Justice Sandra Day O'Connor, was prepared to endorse this approach out of fear that *Griggs* would be "nullified if disparate impact analysis were applied only to standardized selection practices."[47]

> Thus, for example, if the employer in *Griggs* had consistently preferred applicants who had a high school diploma and who passed the company's general aptitude test, its selection system could nonetheless have been considered "subjective" if it also included brief interviews with the candidates. So long as an employer refrained from making standardized criteria absolutely determinative, it would remain free to give such tests almost as much weight as it chose without risking a disparate impact challenge. If we announced a rule that allowed employers so easily to insulate themselves from liability under *Griggs*, disparate impact analysis might be effectively abolished.[48]

Would that it were! But the fears expressed by Justice O'Connor seem quite beside the point under current law. If *Teal* is good law, the absence of the bottom line defense means that the disparate impact of the tests remains subject to collateral attack even if the second-round selection favors blacks or other minorities who passed the tests. But even if *Teal* were overturned or ignored, it does not follow that the disparate impact test could be easily circumvented by the use of interviews. Thus, if the

46. 487 U.S. 982.
47. Id. at 989.
48. Id. at 989–990.

interview portion of the hiring process preserved or increased the disparate impact of a questionable test, then the entire process could be attacked on a disparate impact theory. Even though the bottom line defense remains by assumption allowable in principle, it would be unavailable on the facts of a particular case, given the overall level of disparate impact. The only cases, therefore, that could not be caught by the *Griggs* analysis would be those in which blacks fared *better* in the subjective phases of the process, and these are hardly likely to be the situations rife with subtle and unconscious discrimination. In addition, the disparate treatment line of attack remains open at all phases of the employment process, and may well have been appropriate in *Watson* itself, since Watson "was apparently told at one point that the teller position was a big responsibility with 'a lot of money . . . for blacks to have to count.' "[49]

The Supreme Court therefore overstated the need to extend *Griggs* as a prophylactic against further abuse—at least if Type I and Type II error are accorded equal weight. But it is at just this point that the Supreme Court's opinion reveals its weaknesses:

> It does not follow, however, that the particular supervisors to whom this discretion [over promotion] is delegated always act without discriminatory intent. Furthermore, even if one assumed that any such discrimination can be adequately policed through disparate treatment analysis, the problem of subconscious stereotypes and prejudices would remain.[50]

In essence the Court has again set its face against Type II error without even considering Type I error at this stage of analysis: that is, cases where the disparate impact theory yields an incorrect finding of liability that reverses the correct no liability decision under the disparate treatment analysis. No one should want a rule that *always* captures employers who act with discriminatory intent, or that blocks every unconscious stereotype. As ever, there is some reason to stop the inquiry under Title VII once the benefits of further enforcement are outweighed, indeed overwhelmed, by their costs. Here the problem is simple and persistent. Even in an environment in which all workers are of the same race (or sex), subjective impressions of employers and fellow employees must be critical in judgments about promotion. Internal to the firm, labor is not impersonal, and transaction costs are always positive. People who do not get

49. Id. at 990.
50. Id. at 990.

along impose costs on others and on the firm and its owners, and subjective impressions are perhaps the best way to sort out the employees who conform to the implicit norms of the establishment from those who do not. In the absence of any discrimination law, these methods would be relied on extensively. These techniques therefore cannot be regarded as wholly out of place simply because any given work force has a mixed racial or sexual composition.

The creation of an external antidiscrimination norm, however, creates a genuine impasse, because it is so difficult for outsiders to the firm and its culture to review and monitor its internal decisions. In order, therefore, to make it possible to regulate, it is necessary to bend the internal practices of the firm to fit the demands of the regulators. One extreme technique, which the Court did not entertain in *Watson,* would be to prohibit the use of informal evaluation techniques or soft data that are otherwise viable. But why throw the baby out with the bathwater? Alternatively, courts could try to find some (expensive) way to overcome informational deficits. It is just this desire to preserve the structure of the statute that led Justice O'Connor to push a disparate impact test where it is least useful and welcome, to wit, in the evaluation of subjective impressions. But to her credit she did so in ways that left just about everyone unhappy with her solution. In *Watson* the employer had argued that unless the disparate impact analysis were relaxed, all employers would be forced to move toward quotas in order to escape the clutches of a disparate impact analysis. That policy in turn runs against the explicit command of the 1964 act, which provides that

> nothing contained in this title shall be interpreted to require any employer . . . to grant preferential treatment to any individual or group because of the race, color, religion, sex or national origin of such individual or group on account of any imbalance which may exist with respect to the total number of percentages of persons of any race, color, religion, sex, or national origin.[51]

The employer's argument is simple enough. Given the insuperable difficulties attendant in showing job relatedness, the employer can avert a finding of disparate impact only by resorting to preferential hiring, if not outright quotas. It is exactly the same argument that was made by Senators Smathers and Robertson in the 1964 Senate debates over the statute,

51. See section 703(j), on which still more is discussed in Chapter 18 at 397, 402–403.

and was derided by Senator Humphrey: the bad guys have proved to be the good prophets.[52] And it was the issue that brought forth the greatest wrath in the debates over the 1990 Civil Rights Act.[53] The business necessity test, in other words, poses a threat to the use of the ordinary interview.

The Supreme Court did not appreciate being cast on the horns of a dilemma between quotas and the explicit abandonment of disparate impact. It therefore tried to steer a middle course between the two extremes by reducing the burdens that the employer needs to meet to make out the defense to the disparate impact claim. First, the Court stressed the various lines of attack that the defendant could make on a disparate impact finding, including a showing that the plaintiffs did not take the tests "seriously"; that there was no causal connection between "the challenged employment practice (testing) and discrimination in the work force";[54] or that the EEOC guidelines were inappropriate for the case at hand. Most critical, it used language that blurred the powerful difference between the stark business necessity language of *Griggs* and the softer nondiscriminatory reason language of disparate treatment cases such as *McDonnell Douglas*. Thus Justice O'Connor stated: "When a plaintiff has made out a prima facie case of disparate impact, and when the defendant has met its burden of producing evidence that its employment practices are based on legitimate business reasons, the plaintiff must 'show that other tests or selection devices, without a similarly undesirable racial effect, would also serve the employer's legitimate interest in efficient and trustworthy workmanship.'"[55] Her choice of words—"legitimate business reasons"—was not an inadvertent slip, but represented a conscious retreat from the business necessity rigors of *Griggs*.

Ward's Cove: *Quotas and Legitimate Business Purpose*

The question left unresolved in *Watkins* was the scope of the Court's modified vision of the disparate impact test, and the next year in *Ward's*

---

52. See Chapter 10 at 187–188.

53. Compare, e.g., Lane Kirkland, "Veto of Civil Rights Bill Is Nonsense," *Chicago Tribune,* November 3, 1990, §1 at 19, noting that the claim that the bill would force businesses to resort to quotas was "nothing less than the sheerest nonsense" with Charles Fried, "Hands in the Quota Cookie Jar," *Wall Street Journal,* May 17, 1990, 18A.

54. *Watson,* 487 U.S. at 997, quoting *Carroll v. Sears, Roebuck & Co.,* 708 F.2d 183, 189 (5th Cir. 1983).

55. 487 U.S. at 998.

Cove the Court extended the legitimate business purpose test to all types of disparate impact cases by announcing a two-step process. The first step is to determine "whether the legitimate employment goals of the employer" justify the practices that led to the disparate impact. If the defendant prevails on that point, the plaintiff must then show "the availability of alternate practices to achieve the same business ends, with less racial impact."[56] "The touchstone of this inquiry is a reasoned review of the employer's justification for his use of the challenged practice."[57] The *Griggs* touchstone of business necessity no longer applies. To live by the sword is to die by the sword. Business necessity was first smuggled into these cases by judicial legerdemain, and its demise (if such there comes to be) proceeds, it appears, by the same dubious technique. There is no defensible construction of the 1964 act that yields the *Griggs* result. By the same token, there is no defensible construction of *Griggs* that supports its wholesale reinterpretation in *Ward's Cove.*

At one level the question is no longer one of statutory construction but rather one of social policy. Thus, in rejecting the business necessity test, the Court raised the now familiar contention that the test,

> at the very least, would mean that any employer who had a segment of his work force that was—for some reason—racially imbalanced, could be haled into court and forced to engage in the expensive and time-consuming task of defending the "business necessity" of the methods used to select the other members of his work force. The only practicable option for many employers will be to adopt racial quotas, insuring that no portion of his work force deviates in racial composition from the other portions thereof; this is a result that Congress expressly rejected in drafting Title VII.[58]

It was just this proposition that was the source of the major debate over the vetoed Civil Rights Act of 1990. Since the issue continues to recur, it is worth discussing at least briefly. The first point to note is that there is no formal or explicit requirement of quotas in the original 1964 act or in the 1990 bill.[59] But that is not what the opponents of the statute (themselves strong defenders of the antidiscrimination principle) objected to. Rather, their point was that the *incentive structure* created by the act

56. *Ward's Cove,* 490 U.S. at 658–659.
57. Id. at 659.
58. Id. at 652.
59. For a discussion of why quotas might be right or wrong, see Chapter 20 at 412–420.

would induce employers to adopt quotas on their own in order to minimize liability under the disparate impact rules. To be sure, most firms would not adopt formal and explicit quotas, if only because of their fear of potential suits for reverse discrimination. But in their personnel reviews and hiring and promotion practices they would always cast a wary eye on the numbers, knowing that if they strayed too far from the norm implicit in the 80 percent rule, they could be subject to a disparate impact suit. The absence, therefore, of a formal system of quotas does little to protect an employer from the risks of litigation.

The key dispute over the merits of the 1990 bill concerned whether the statute did anything to blunt the incentives toward race-conscious hiring. On this score it is clear that the bill did not. If anything, the pressure toward implicit quotas was made stronger. Although it was promoted as a restoration of *Griggs,* the bill imposed more stringent standards of liability, for two reasons.

First, the scope of a disparate impact test was extended beyond those cases attacking a discrete employment practice (for example, requiring a test or a high school diploma) to cover those cases where "a group of employment practices," defined as "a combination of one or more decisions with respect to employment, employment referral," are challenged as well.[60] Under the bill there was no requirement that the plaintiff had to identify *which* employment practice within the group had the disparate impact.[61] The employer therefore would have been left to raise the business necessity test with respect to a broad constellation of practices, save those that it could show (do not ask how) did not contribute to the disparate impact. The scope of basic liability would thus be enlarged.

Second, under the 1990 bill the expected damages for violating the disparate impact norm seemed to increase as well, although the statute was not fully clear on this point. Section 8 of the bill provided that compensatory damages could be obtained from an employer for cases of "intentional discrimination," and that punitive damages could be recovered from a defendant who "engaged in the unlawful employment practice with reckless or callous indifference to the federally protected rights of others."[62] There are no definitions of the critical terms "intentional," "reckless," or "callous," with the first of these being exceptionally slip-

---

60. Civil Rights Act of 1990 (S. 2104) §3(m). None of these features are part of the 1991 Bush administration bill. See note 19 at 212–213.

61. Id. §4, amending §703 (k)(B)(i).

62. S. 2104 §8.

pery. Nor did the 1990 bill provide categorically that disparate impact cases were never cases of intentional or reckless discrimination; nor did it classify as unintentional those mixed cases brought under both disparate treatment and disparate impact theories. In sum, it appears that the potential under *Griggs* was expanded in both key dimensions: liability and damages.

The proponents of the Civil Rights Act have urged that since *Griggs* did not lead to quotas (narrowly defined, of course), its restoration could not lead to quotas either.[63] But the difference in potential payoffs makes it treacherous to argue from any reading of employer practices under *Griggs* to a prediction of future employment practices should the 1990 bill become law at some future time. The incentive arguments articulated by the Supreme Court in *Ward's Cove* will be all the more relevant given that the exposure to disparate impact suits can only increase.

Testing after *Griggs*

Validity Generalization

Whether or not *Griggs* has led to quotas, it is apparent that the decision has had a profound impact on the way in which testing is done at all levels of the employment process, an influence that will persist no matter what the future direction of the law may be. The source of the problem is simple enough to state. Notwithstanding their embattled status under Title VII, there is a widespread belief on the part of those who design and use general employment tests that these provide accurate and essential predictions of job success for individual workers and should therefore be regarded as an important, indeed an indispensable, aid in hiring and promotion decisions.[64] Although it is impossible to review even a tiny fraction of the literature here, it is sufficient to say that the professionals in

63. See, e.g., debate between Richard A. Epstein and Antonio J. Califa, *Resolved: The Civil Rights Act of 1990 Is a Threat to Our Civil Rights* 33 (1990) (remarks of Antonio Califa) (Cato Institute).

64. There is a vast literature on this subject. Some of the places in which to dip into it include the symposium "The g Factor in Employment," 29 *J. Vocational Behavior* (1986), which includes these articles: Arthur R. Jensen, "g: Artifact or Reality?" at 301; John E. Hunter, "Cognitive Ability, Cognitive Aptitudes, Job Knowledge, and Job Performance" at 340; Linda S. Gottfredson, "Societal Consequences of the g Factor in Employment" at 379. See also *Fairness,* chs. 4–9; and Frank L. Schmidt, "The Problem of Group Differences in Ability Test Scores in Employment Selection," 33 *J. Vocational Behavior* 272 (1988). For an

the field all agree that there is a positive correlation between test performance and job success; they debate only its extent. The relative doubters place the correlation coefficient at around 0.3, while those who are more supportive of the practice tend to place it at around 0.5.[65] In addition, extensive work has been done in "validity generalization" techniques, which allow for an assessment of the validity of various tests without any need to pretest them in some narrow or particular environment.[66] The entire thrust of this research cuts against the implicit empirical claim in *Griggs* that tests will be valid only to the extent that they can be shown to be job related. Rather, the greater their range and use, the more likely it is that investigators will be able to assemble a large number of data points that will establish the significance of the test in question.

The acceptance of the validity generalization approach within the psychological literature led to an effort to increase the use of testing as an aid to employment. Most concretely, the United States Employment Service (USES) administers a standard test, the General Aptitude Test Battery (GATB), "to screen many of the 19 million people who pass through the system annually in search of private- and public-sector jobs."[67] In order to promote the competitiveness of American business, the Department of Labor advocated an expanded use of this test during the 1980s. Indeed, one estimate (for which I will not vouch) claims that the systematic and rigorous use of testing could increase productivity in the order of $80 billion (1983), a staggering sum even if overstated.[68] The standard test,

---

exhaustive and dismissive evaluation of all testing, see Kelman, "Concepts of Discrimination" at 46. All these references contain extensive citation to this vast literature.

65. See Jan H. Blits and Linda S. Gottfredson, "Employment Testing and Job Performance," 98 *The Public Interest* 18, 22 (Winter 1990).

66. The major study is Hunter, Schmidt, and Jackson, *Meta-Analysis.* Crudely stated, the intuition behind their basic strategy is to unpack the aggregate data, which are usually presented in an abbreviated form as "significant" or "no significant" correlation (at the 0.05 level), and to look at the confidence intervals on which that conclusion is based. Thus, if there are two studies, one of which purports to find a significant correlation and the other which does not, the results will seem weak if they are reported as holding that "only 50 percent of the studies confirm the hypothesis." They will seem (and be) far more powerful if the combined data points in the two studies can be integrated, since, taken jointly, they will support the hypothesis. To put it another way, where one test easily exceeds the 0.05 threshold and the other just misses it, the two taken together should be reinterpreted to support the asserted connection. For a rigorous explanation of the practice and illustrations that motivate it, see id., chs. 1–3.

67. *Fairness* at vii.

68. Id. at 19. The estimates are John Hunter's.

however, has a manifest disparate impact between blacks and whites that would generally disqualify its use under *Griggs*.[69] "A raw score that would place a candidate at the 50th percentile among whites would place him at the 84th percentile among blacks."[70]

Race Norming

One question was whether the test could be relied on, given its disparate impact. The issue turned not only on *Griggs* but also on the political situation inside the Labor Department. The compromise approach that was adopted by the department, and later endorsed by the National Research Council (NRC) study that reviewed it,[71] is a practice known as race norming, whereby the scores for any individual are reported only as the percentile relative to that individual's own race, not to the tested population as a whole. Thus, under the revised procedures, the same fraction of blacks as whites will score in the ninety-ninth percentile, even though there will be different underlying raw scores. The entire practice was challenged in November 1986 by William Bradford Reynolds, then Assistant Attorney General for Civil Rights, who claimed that this race norming system was "an unlawful and unconstitutional violation of an applicant's rights to be free from racial discrimination because the within-group scoring procedure not only classifies Employment Service regis-trants by race or national origin, but also 'requires job service offices to prefer some and disadvantage other individuals based on their member-ship in racial or ethnic groups. Such a procedure constitutes intentional racial discrimination.' "[72] Wholly apart from the statute another question can be raised, given that race norming looks like a systematic conceal-ment of relevant information. All things considered, how could the prac-tice be justified?

The NRC's study was organized in order to respond to Reynolds' charges. It sought to justify the practice at a number of different levels. In the first place, the NRC insists that the long history of discrimination in the United States justifies some preferential treatment. But even if that were true, the correct procedure should be to supply the raw scores and all relevant distributions (black, white, and combined) so that public and

69. Id. at 41–43.
70. Blits and Gottfredson, "Employment Testing" at 20.
71. See *Fairness*, ch. 13.
72. Id. at 21. The internal quotation is from Reynolds' letter.

private employers could make whatever adjustment they saw proper. The NRC also argued that the race-conscious adjustments were necessary to eliminate discrimination and not to foster it. But again, an explicit revelation of the differences coupled with a conscious top-down hiring policy within each class could achieve the same result, as in *Guardians,* once the practice was brought to light.

The NRC's second justification for race norming is more technical. Although there is no evidence that any individual tested suffers from race bias, it is clear that there are more blacks than whites in the lower tail of the combined distribution.[73] From this fact the NRC concludes that race norming is justified to lift the relatively heavier burdens that the testing system has imposed on blacks as a class (since more are located below the median for the distribution as a whole).

This rationale is flawed for two reasons. First, even if it is conceded that some compensatory adjustment should be made for persons located below the median, the extent of the adjustment still has to be fixed. To use the identical distributions for both blacks and whites is to say that the expected performance level of both groups, taken as a whole, is the same. If that is the case, however, then it is difficult to see how there is any positive correlation between testing and work performance at all: yet the test predicts as well for blacks as it does for whites. Saying that whites and blacks have the same expected level of success is to say that there is no principled way to account for the systematic discrepancies in scores between the two groups. But if so, then why should tests that have reliable predictive abilities within the groups have no predictive abilities across the groups?

Second, stating that more blacks are below the median than above it assumes, contrary to what the test establishes, that there is a single distribution for both blacks and whites. Yet the two distributions differ by the standard deviation, so the error calculations cannot be made on the assumption that all applicants are drawn from the same distribution. Thus, if the median score for blacks is 100 and the median score for whites is 150, then how should black and white candidates each of whom scores 125 be evaluated? (To simplify the analysis, assume that equal numbers in both groups have taken the tests, and the median for the total is 125). If there were only one distribution for blacks and whites, neither score would require correction. But if there are two separate distribu-

---

73. Id. at 254–260, criticized in Blits and Gottfredson, "Employment Testing" at 21–23, and defended in a response.

tions, one with a median of 100 and one with a median of 150, then presumably both scores could be in error, and some correction would be required for each. At this juncture the proper procedure is to invoke Bayes's theorem,[74] which allows the combination of general base rate information with the results of specific tests. Stated otherwise, the accurate prediction would lie somewhere between the score received by the individual *and* the background distribution. Given the two separate distributions, it follows that the tests, taken alone, should overpredict black success relative to white success, and to some slight extent it appears that they do.[75] If this is correct, then it follows that the NRC has run its corrections for error in the *wrong* direction by assuming for this purpose only (contrary to the overall data base) that blacks and whites are drawn to the same distribution.

There is, I think, no way in which the release of less information can be justified in preference to more. The only approach that might make sense is one that praises the blurring of the testing signal on the ground that the tests themselves are of no value, against the consensus among professional testers that they are.[76] On this score the key element is often the level of correlation between the test results on the one hand and supervisory reports on the other hand, where there is obvious room for bias or error in one direction or the other. A striking finding of the NRC is that the predictive ability of the tests seems to have been much higher before 1972 than since.[77] How should this information be interpreted?

The first point is that there may be more than coincidence between the pre- and post-1972 findings and the decision in *Griggs,* but it is difficult to know how to interpret it. Initially, it is clear that the response time of employers to the decision should be far more rapid than any litigation of its effects, so it is likely that the case exerted some influence over the process. But there are two explanations, which are not mutually exclusive, as to how that influence was exerted. On the one hand, it is possible to argue that white supervisors before *Griggs* were biased in their evaluation of black workers and hence understated their value. On the other hand, it

74. See Chapter 2 under the heading "To the Urn" and note 11.

75. Blits and Gottfredson, "Employment Testing" at 21.

76. See, e.g., Alexandra K. Widgor, "Fairness in Employment Testing," *Issues in Science and Technology* 54, 55 (Spring 1990).

77. "The average validity (corrected for criterion unreliability) of GATB aptitude composites in studies conducted since 1972 is about .25, whereas corresponding adjustments for the older studies produce an average validity of .35." *Fairness* at 5. See also Chapter 7.

is possible that the pressure of liability under *Griggs* has led supervisors to rate black employees *too highly* in order to forestall liability under Title VII. If it is seen that any disparate promotion levels can expose an employer to a lawsuit, the signal that comes from the top may be to flatten out all the evaluations so that overall promotion levels are within the 80 percent safe-harbor rules under *Griggs*. On this view the supervisors respond less to their biases, conscious or unconscious, than to the business demands of the firm.

It is very hard to know how to resolve the debate in the abstract, given the institutional setting. The main problem here is that the employment discrimination laws have made the question of whether tests may be used into a collective decision instead of a firm decision. But if the statute (or even the disparate impact doctrine) were wholly repealed, then each individual firm could decide whether to use the tests and how to interpret the results. If the tests are worthless in some settings, they will be abandoned regardless of their ostensible appeal. But if they have value, they will be kept and used. The learned debates over their effectiveness can then be transferred to other forums, so it will no longer be necessary to have government decisions on matters that are best left to a firm's choice. The debate over testing and disparate impact again illustrates the central insight regarding Title VII: the question of *who* decides is in the long run more important than the question of *what* will be decided.

CHAPTER 12

The Effects of Title VII

In this chapter I turn from the analysis of the doctrinal apparatus that has grown up around Title VII to the question that was raised in its more theoretical form in Chapters 1, 2, and 3: What are the effects of the antidiscrimination laws on workers, black and white, in the workplace? This is an inquiry that necessarily blends history with doctrine, theory with practice, and law with economics. The data are often difficult to gather and even more difficult to disentangle and evaluate. At best it is necessary to be diffident about the conclusions. But it is equally important to be sure that the right questions are being asked and answered. In answering the questions, one must take two different types of evidence into account. The first examines the shifts in the composition of the work force over time, and then relates these shifts to the passage of the Civil Rights Act of 1964. The second seeks to draw inferences about the effects of Title VII, usually through a comparison of the wage levels of blacks and whites, but occasionally by other more indirect forms of measurement.

With some unavoidable selectivity, I shall look at both sorts of evidence. History, however, is often unkind to empirical investigations. In principle the types of questions that are most accessible are those that make comparisons between pure types of social and economic institutions. Thus the critical analytical issue for Title VII is whether pure competitive markets function better with an antidiscrimination law than they do without it, given the costs of enforcement. The theory works best where the facts are the cleanest.

This historical inquiry is clouded, however, because neither of these systems in its pure type has existed anywhere in the United States. For much of the period before 1965, segregation pursuant to statute, the very antithesis of a market system, was dominant in the South, and to a lesser extent elsewhere throughout the country. In addition, labor markets have long been a favorite target of regulation by government at all levels. And there is good theoretical reason to believe that both the minimum wage laws and the collective bargaining statutes work to the disadvantage of black workers, who frequently have lower levels of educational and specialized skills to bring to the employment markets, and who often risk being relegated to minority status under collective bargaining arrangements.[1] Any comparisons, therefore, between the periods before and after 1965 are not comparisons between markets and regulation; they are comparisons between mixed systems, both of which include substantial, and different, components of government regulation. Any evidence that supports a conclusion of some improvement in the income and employment prospects of black workers relative to those of whites since 1965 need not support the more universal proposition that the antidiscrimination laws correct some market failure. It may only be evidence of a more modest variety, heavily bound by time, place, and circumstance, showing simply that the distortions in labor markets prior to the passage of the Civil Rights Act of 1964 exceeded the distortions that the act created.

There has been a rash of detailed investigations of the effects of the Civil Rights Act on black and white workers. These studies for the most part have concentrated on aggregate data gathered from around the United States, sometimes classified by region or by industry.[2] The conclusions are summarized by James Heckman and J. Hoult Verkerke:

> The basic facts of black economic progress are well known. Since 1940, black wages and occupational status have improved, approaching the higher levels that whites enjoy. Beginning in 1965, the rate of improvement in black relative wages and occupational status accelerated. However, since 1975, relative black economic status has not

1. "In the covered labor markets, the minimum wage will likely encourage discrimination against the very young and the very old, blacks and Hispanics, women, and any particular religious group that might be in current disfavor." Richard B. McKenzie, *The American Job Machine* 204 (1988). See also Walter Williams, *The State against Blacks,* ch. 3 (1982).

2. See, e.g., John J. Donohue III and James Heckman, "Continuous versus Episodic Change: The Impact of Civil Rights Policy on the Economic Status of Blacks," 29 *J. Econ. Lit.* 1603 (1991); James J. Heckman and J. Hoult Verkerke, "Racial Disparity and Employment Discrimination Law: An Economic Perspective," 8 *Yale Law & Pol. Rev.* 276 (1990); James Smith and Finis Welch, "Black Economic Progress after Myrdal," 27 *J. Econ. Lit.* 519 (1989). For my comments on this literature, see Richard A. Epstein, "The Paradox of Civil Rights," 8 *Yale Law & Pol. Rev.* 299 (1990).

advanced and may have deteriorated slightly. The South is the region of the United States where blacks have made the most dramatic gains in relative wages and occupational status.[3]

It is impossible to analyze each of the many studies that buttress this conclusion, but it is instructive to look closely at one study which has a narrower institutional focus, and for that reason allows the use of particular historical and institutional data, and which yields the same basic conclusion as the more general studies.

Title VII as Deregulation

Heckman and Brook S. Payner have published an excellent and exhaustive study of the textile industry in South Carolina.[4] At the outset they note that the earlier studies showing the favorable effects of the Civil Rights Act have generally been inconclusive because their "highly aggregated" data do not allow for the meaningful separation of the influences on the supply and demand sides of the labor markets.[5] In order to overcome the situation in which "numerous plausible explanations compete for scarce degrees of freedom,"[6] Heckman and Payner sought a relatively well developed and well defined market where it was possible to isolate the separate influences that bear on supply and demand. Their study thus focuses on the rates of employment and wage levels in the textile industry in South Carolina during the period between roughly 1940 and 1970.[7] The purpose of their study is to disentangle several rival explanations that could be offered to explain the systematic low level of black employment

3. Heckman and Verkerke, "Racial Disparity" at 276; footnotes omitted.

4. James J. Heckman and Brook S. Payner, "Determining the Impact of Federal Antidiscrimination Policy on the Economic Status of Blacks: A Study of South Carolina," 79 *Am. Econ. Rev.* 138 (1989).

5. Id.

6. Id.

7. Some of the disaggregated data in the study run through 1980, but a large portion of the material presented on statewide data begins in 1940 and ends in 1970, some five years after the passage of the Civil Rights Act. See, e.g., figures 1–5. For the data most relevant here, their collection stops at 1970. The absence of post-1970 data is noteworthy because it makes it quite impossible to determine the effects that the disparate impact theory of *Griggs* had on employment and wage levels. The subsequent studies that carry the data forward into the 1980s generally reveal a very mixed picture with no discernible trend line even on the ratio between corrected black-white wage gaps, as reported by Heckman and Verkerke in "Racial Disparity."

in the textile industry until 1965. Proceeding by elimination, they conclude that the key factor accounting for the rising black employment levels after that time was the active and energetic enforcement efforts of the civil rights statute, an effort that included "more than 140 charges of wage and employment discrimination [that] were filed against textile firms in North and South Carolina in 1965."[8]

> Alternative explanations of the black breakthrough in textiles appear to be much less cogent. A supply shift story attributing the black improvement to the decline in agriculture cannot account for the timing of the black breakthrough in textiles. The human capital story of improvement in black skill also cannot account for the timing. Increases in black human capital between 1960 and 1970 should have reduced black employment because textiles is a low skill industry. By 1960, there were plenty of blacks with skill levels adequate to perform textile jobs.[9]

Heckman and Payner note that the "labor tightness" explanation for the decline in discrimination is somewhat harder to dismiss.[10] That explanation holds that in a tight economy blacks are most vulnerable to dismissal, and correspondingly in good economic times blacks will tend to be hired in large numbers after available sources of white labor have dried up. A boom around 1965 to 1970 in the South Carolina textile industry leads Heckman and Payner to conclude that the explanation cannot be ruled out of hand. Nonetheless, they are rightly skeptical of the labor tightness explanation if only because the level of black employment in the textile market remained at uniformly low levels before 1965, notwithstanding similar cycles of expansion and contraction.

Their analysis ignores what I believe is the strongest explanation for the post-1965 changes in employment levels, namely the concerted action of the federal government to counter the effects of Jim Crow regulation in the South. Indeed, their numbers support that revised interpretation of their data. For the pre-1965 period the employment of blacks in the textile industry is remarkably constant, hovering for long periods of time around 5 percent for black males and around 1 percent for black females—and this in a state with (at least in the earlier years of the study) a labor force that is 40 percent black. After 1965 the number of black males and females employed in the textile industry rose sharply, until by

8. Heckman and Payner, "Determining the Impact" at 143.
9. Id.
10. See Milton Friedman, *Capitalism and Freedom* (1962).

the early 1970s the percentage of black males was around 15 percent and of black females around 10 percent, even in the face of a decline in the percentage of blacks in the total South Carolina work force (attributable largely to migration) from 1940 to 1970. Heckman and Payner write: "Our evidence confirms the wisdom of Gavin Wright's (1986) emphasis on the role of institutions in explaining southern economic history. Our analysis also provides evidence against the widely held belief espoused by Charles Murray (1984) and other conservatives that federal government policy has not contributed to the elevation of black economic status."[11]

Yet it is at just the institutional level stressed by Wright that the explanatory work of Heckman and Payner misfires. They have failed to take into account two factors: first, the various legal restrictions on entry into the labor markets that were in place prior to 1965, and second, a public choice explanation of the applicable state laws. The nature and form of the legal restrictions could be either direct or indirect. The direct restrictions are those that regulate the hiring and firing of labor as such; the indirect ones are collateral restrictions (taxes, zoning permits, health inspections) that could be brought to bear on firms that did not toe the line set by Jim Crow. In the end, it is necessary to make some educated guess as to the relative significance of these dual constraints. But for the moment it is useful to begin with a piece of direct regulation of labor markets under Jim Crow. Heckman and Payner observe: "The strongest evidence of federal impact is found in the traditional manufacturing sectors of the state that were already thriving when Jim Crow law formalized racial segregation in employment in 1915."[12] But here they leave out a critical institutional detail, for although they refer to the South Carolina statute, they do not quote it in all its chilling detail:

> Criminal Code (167) §45.   *Separation of Employees of Different Races in Cotton Textile Factories—Penalties.*—That it shall be unlawful for any person, firm or corporation engaged in the business of cotton textile manufacturing in this State to allow or permit operatives, help and labor of different races to labor and work together within the same room, or to use the same doors of entrance and exit at the same time, or to use and occupy the same pay ticket windows or doors for paying off its operatives and laborers at the same time, or to use the same stairway and

---

11. Heckman and Payner, "Determining the Impact" at 139. The references are to Gavin Wright, *Old South, New South* (1986), and Charles Murray, *Losing Ground: American Social Policy, 1950–1980* (1984).

12. Heckman and Payner, "Determining the Impact."

windows at the same time, or to use at any time the same lavatories, toilets, drinking water buckets, pails, cups, dippers or glasses: *Provided,* Equal accommodations shall be supplied and furnished to all persons employed by said person, firm or corporation engaged in the business of cotton textile manufacturing as aforesaid, without distinction to race, color or previous conditions. [The statute then provides for fines of up to $100 and thirty days' imprisonment at hard labor for each violation.] This section shall not apply to employment of firemen as subordinates in boiler rooms, or to floor scrubbers and those persons employed in keeping in proper condition lavatories and toilets, and carpenters, mechanics and others engaged in the repair or erection of buildings.[13]

Several elements of this statute bear on the interpretation of the data gathered by Heckman and Payner. Initially the statute on its face applies only to employees who work in any "cotton textile factory." A cursory look at the South Carolina Criminal Code, moreover, reveals no comparable statutory provision regulating employment in this manner in any other line of work. Instead, the other provisions of the Jim Crow system were directed toward segregation in eating places,[14] public transportation,[15] and entranceways for tent shows.[16] The legal environment associated with segregation thus differed across different industries. In principle we should be able to ask the question of whether the level of black penetration into other businesses and professions showed the same stunted growth as in the textile industries. Fortunately, Heckman and Payner supply the necessary information.

Prior to 1960, we find that adjusting for qualifications black males are not underrepresented in *any* industry except textiles. In fact, black males are overrepresented in agriculture and professional services as of 1960. It is important to note that in 1960 blacks are underrepresented in the nontraditional manufacturing industries in relation to their share in the population and the labor force. However, controlling for individual characteristics, . . . black males are not underrepresented in these industries.[17]

13. *S. Carolina Crim. Code* §45 (1922).

14. Id. at §41.

15. Id. at §42.

16. Id. at §44. Before and after this section are unrelated provisions dealing with the defacing of public monuments and destruction and mutilation of the flag (some things never change). Id. at §40 (public monuments); §47 (destruction of flag).

17. Heckman and Payner, "Determining the Impact" at 158.

These differences are not easily attributable to any general cultural or social explanation. If the general power of segregated institutions could thwart all black advancement, then we should expect to see the same profile of black underrepresentation in the professions (which operate at the high end of the skill spectrum) that we see at the low end. The differential results are fully consistent, however, with the pattern of segregationist legislation. The direct Jim Crow laws applied only to the cotton textile industry, not to other industries and professions.

The same evidence cuts powerfully against the various arguments that unaided markets cannot overcome the prejudices and biases of their individual members. The passage and retention of the Jim Crow legislation speaks volumes about the dominant racial attitudes in South Carolina. If social pressures made it impossible for any single firm to deal with black workers as long as other firms refused to do so, we should expect to see the same level of black disadvantage outside the textile industry as within it, or at least the same level of relative deprivation. Similarly, if cognitive bias, endogenous preferences, or calculation error were the source of the problem, the effects of segregation on economic performance should have been more widespread than Heckman and Payner found. But again their data lend support to a different conclusion. The formal industry-specific restraints on entry offer the most cogent explanation for the constant picture prior to 1965. Remove those constraints on employer freedom, and there is a pronounced change in the employment mix. The sudden upsurge in black workers' participation in the cotton textile industry is indeed explained by the Civil Rights Act of 1964, for it was that statute which negated the effectiveness of the local Jim Crow restrictions on freedom of contract. The earlier repudiation of separate but equal in *Brown v. Board of Education*[18] applied to more than public schools, but that decision did not of itself transform the legal system of South Carolina. The key issue was always enforcement, not doctrine,[19] that depended

18. 347 U.S. 483 (1954).

19. A particularly graphic illustration of the point is provided in Gerald Rosenberg, *The Hollow Hope: Courts and Social Reform*, ch. 4 (1990), which recounts the working history of the National Association for the Advancement of Colored People (NAACP) in Alabama. In *N.A.A.C.P. v. Alabama*, 357 U.S. 449 (1958), Justice Harlan wrote a powerful and cogent opinion which held that the NAACP had the right to refuse to turn over its membership lists to the state. The forced disclosure was an obvious means whereby the state could place effective pressure on the political activities of those who wished in concert to oppose standard government policy. In response the Supreme Court interpreted the First Amendment as protecting associational efforts to advance speech as well as the speech

on the vigorous enforcement of the Civil Rights Act in the years that immediately followed its passage. The radical change in legal environment permitted the quick market responses. The orthodox neoclassical model explains the transformation in the South without any subtle refinements that fill the world with exotic types of market failure.

It is, moreover, relatively easy to come up with a powerful public choice explanation for why a statute with these provisions could be passed. As Heckman and Payner note, the textile industry was by far the biggest in South Carolina, and relied on large supplies of unskilled labor. In a market economy whites could expect to find stiff competition from blacks. Given the large number of white employees and the powerful restrictions on black voting rights at the time, the state legislature could easily be induced to pass a statute for the benefit of its most visible and vocal political constituency, even if these restrictions were opposed by firms that might seek to tap black labor sources. In economic markets the preferences of individuals and firms at the margin can always be registered; but in political markets the locus of power switches from the marginal entrant to the median voter. There were more workers who wanted this statute than employers (especially prospective employers from out of state) who were in a position to oppose it. In addition, some employers, who were committed to all-white firms, supported the statute for its anticompetitive effects. The exact composition of the winning coalition is difficult to identify in the abstract. But no amount of uncertainty about the process can falsify the outcome of the political struggle.

Any such restrictive legislation still had to overcome two obstacles. First, if the fixed requirement of segregation were applied to all industries across the board, the statute might meet strong opposition from other interest groups that opposed the separate but equal regime. An industry-specific statute forestalls those difficulties. In this regard the situation is not unlike that which existed in *Lochner v. New York,* where the ten-hour maximum hours law applied only to bakers in certain lines of business, namely "a biscuit, bread or cake bakery or confectionary establish-

---

itself. Nonetheless, even with this stirring victory for the NAACP, the state of Alabama was able to keep the pressure on the local chapter through a variety of other legal maneuvers, thus depressing sharply its total membership and cash contributions. Occasional Supreme Court intervention is not enough to remake the world, be it for better or worse. What is required is sustained administrative interference which places the ongoing executive and administrative power of the government at the disposal of an interest group. Rosenberg's book contains an exhaustive documentation of this central thesis.

ment," since other segments of the bakery industry might have resisted passage of the statute had it applied to them.[20] Tailoring a statute is an effective way of neutralizing some of the opposition to it.

Second, the statute did not totally prohibit the use of black labor in the textile industry, even though that outcome might have been sought by the white interest groups that championed the statute. Here the explanation has less to do with interest group politics than with constitutional constraint: *Plessy v. Ferguson* did have some constitutional teeth.[21] Its standard of separate but equal would have invalidated a total ban on black workers in the textile industry. Given this legal constraint, a separate but equal statute was all that the political process could deliver. In principle this statute allowed both blacks and whites to work together at the same plant, but it increased the costs of running such a business. It is hard to imagine how any plant could operate if blacks and whites could not use the same stairs and rooms at the same time. It is costly to erect two sets of toilet facilities (which could *never* be shared, even at different times, under the statute). Any plant that adopted an all-white work force (save, perhaps, for the exception of janitorial help) would thus have an enormous economic advantage over a firm that did not. To run an all-black plant required having sufficient numbers of employees to fill all the slots, an end that might have been difficult to achieve if there were critical shortages of certain management or technical personnel. Similarly, no firm could call on white outsiders to advise or teach its black workers. The statute thus imposed strong constraints on internal organization, and led in practice to an industry dominated by all-white firms.

The difficult question is whether this industry-specific norm was sufficient to account for all patterns of development. A point against that argument is that rigid employment segregation was adopted in other southern states without the explicit statute found in South Carolina.[22] This evidence suggests that the South Carolina statute was not indispens-

20. See section 110 of the labor law of the State of New York, reprinted in *Lochner v. New York,* 198 U.S. 45, 46 (1905). It is also worth noting that the classification involved under the statute led the plaintiff to mount an equal protection challenge against the statute, "which singles out a certain number of men employing bakers, and permits all others similarly situated, including many who are competitors in business, to work their employees as long as they choose." Id. at 48.

21. 163 U.S. 537 (1896). For a discussion of the case, see Chapter 5 at 99–103, under the heading "The Plessy Case."

22. See James Heckman and J. Hoult Verkerke, "Response to Epstein," 8 *Yale Law & Pol. Rev.* 324, 326 (1990).

able for the maintenance of segregation, although it is hard to tell how important its industry-specific restrictions were without closer study of the composition of the work force and of the network of state, county, and local regulations in effect in other states. But the observation does not show that custom and culture alone are sufficient to maintain segregated practices in the face of new entry.

Why, then, did outside entrepreneurs not move into the South before the 1964 act? The best explanation, again, is that the elaborate set of indirect legal sanctions could have made entry by an outsider exceedingly treacherous. Any firm that maintained integrated or all-black work forces would have been forced to do business with a political establishment which at the state and local level was under the exclusive control of white supremacists sympathetic to rival white workers and firms. It is all too easy for an all-white town board to lose an application for a building permit, to postpone a meeting on a sewage connection line, or to harass unwelcome businesses into bankruptcy. The same political forces that put the separate but equal statutes on the books were doubtless capable of using their power in the underworld of administrative discretion to ensure that no separate but equal firm would emerge.

Whatever laws accounted for the rigidity in the southern labor markets, Title VII was heaven-sent, if only in the short run, especially for a libertarian. Even if it is not possible to disentangle the effects of general and particular regulation, it is possible to attack them both simultaneously with the same broad-based statute. The Civil Rights Act in its early days therefore countered the totalitarian influences at the state and local levels. It established a federal system of enforcement, which was not dependent on the powerful grip of local politics. Heckman and Payner write: "What cannot be dismissed and indeed seems quite plausible is that in 1965 entrepreneurs seized on the new federal legislation and decrees to do what they wanted to do anyway."[23] Stated otherwise, the 1964 act made free entry possible.

What must be added, however, is that this hypothesis (which seems to be indubitably correct) is in no sense inconsistent with their main conclusion that the Civil Rights Act of 1964 played an enormous role in the advancement of black economic interests by knocking out Jim Crow restrictions and changed political markets by securing black voting rights. Some federal enforcement shock to the system was no doubt necessary. The Jim Crow laws were all unconstitutional after *Brown* was decided in

23. Heckman and Payner, "Determining the Impact" at 174.

1954. Yet the Heckman and Payner data show that the logjam itself was not broken until ten years later. The Civil Rights Act protected those firms that wanted to compete in open markets and gave a needed short-term jolt that helped upset the segregated practices that had flourished under Jim Crow.

This early history shows the beneficial effects of the act in combating prior racial discrimination imposed by law. Yet in this context it becomes critical to identify the different ways in which the antidiscrimination statute operates, and to determine which of these ways is responsible for the increase in black participation in the labor market. First, Title VII overturned all formal barriers imposed by law, such as those found in the 1915 South Carolina statute. Second, it proscribed formal modes of discrimination that private firms might have imposed even after the Jim Crow statutes had been repealed. Third, it introduced bad motive cases covered by the theory of disparate treatment. Fourth, it led to the development of the disparate impact theory after the 1971 *Griggs* decision. It is instructive to line the theories up against the rates of change in the South Carolina mills.

Initially it seems apparent that the substantial increase in black participation in the labor force followed quickly on the heels of the introduction of Title VII. Virtually all of that increase is attributable to the removal of formal barriers to entry, both public and private. The early enforcement efforts were relatively easy. Federal officials took on the most obvious targets which offered the greatest civil rights gains through direct administrative attacks on explicit discriminatory practices, public and private. Here the illegality of the conduct was so patent that most firms would desist without a real fight, seeing that it was one they could not win. Even in *Griggs* the defendant, the Duke Power Company, had dismantled its formal programs of racial segregation the day the statute was put into effect. Large employers (here in a regulated industry) whose formal rules were in violation of Title VII were the first to comply, for they offered big targets and had the resources to pay any fines and back pay orders that might be entered against them.

Other forms of enforcement necessarily lagged behind. To be sure, disparate treatment was patently actionable from the outset under the 1964 act, but its enforcement potential was sharply limited in the early years. Title VII litigation is necessarily based on the facts and circumstances of specific cases. The pre-1965 record of discrimination could not, however, be made part of the evidence in these cases, given the general prohibition against retroactive legislation, which the statute respected. It takes time, therefore, for violations to occur after the passage of the statute, and still more time for these violations to become the focus of litigation. In my view it is no accident that the cases dealing with allocating the burden of proof in disparate treatment suits[24] did not reach the Supreme Court until the mid-1970s, given the substantial delays in both finding suitable claims and running them through the legal system. It is likely that the disparate treatment rules contributed only a tiny fraction of the total change in black labor force participation found in the Heckman and Payner study.

It is even more obvious that the disparate impact cases had little or no influence on the Heckman and Payner data. The theory itself was first announced in the Supreme Court in 1971. Disparate impact theory might have played some role in the earlier activities if any lower court had developed and applied it: firms do respond to the probability as well as to the certainty of loss. Nonetheless, that result is not remotely plausible in this context because the lower court decision in *Griggs* had flatly rejected the entire apparatus of the disparate impact test and the business necessity defense; nor was the theory in evidence, much less in vogue, anywhere else. The Supreme Court decision in *Griggs* came very much as a bolt out of the blue.

Even after the *Griggs* decision was handed down, it had to work itself into the legal culture. The exact magnitude of this lag, however, is hard to measure. Unlike with the disparate treatment cases, astute plaintiffs did not have to wait for violations to occur after *Griggs* was decided. To the contrary, by 1971 there was plenty of post-1965 conduct that could retroactively constitute grist for the legal mill once the disparate impact test burst onto the legal scene. In the wake of the stunning reversal of expectations that *Griggs* worked, thousands of employers, public and private, North and South, found themselves in arguable noncompliance with the 1964 statute precisely because they had used tests or other practices that appeared lawful under the 1964 act. But even if these practices afforded grist for the mill, it still had to be ground. Therefore several years passed before these cases were ready to be processed in large numbers. The effect of disparate impact could not have been felt until at the earliest 1974 or 1975,[25] in other words after the period in which the Heckman and Payner

24. See the discussion in Chapter 8.

25. For suggestive parallels, see the data in John J. Donohue III and Peter Siegelman, "The Changing Nature of Employment Discrimination Litigation," 43 *Stan. L. Rev.* 983 (1991). This report details a sharp rise in the incidence of employment litigation after 1972. But the data are not disaggregated. They cover all types of violations, including age and sex violations,

data, and the findings in other studies,[26] show that blacks reached rough parity in the textile industry. The most costly form of litigation seems, therefore, to have had the lowest possible yield.

It is vital to draw the right conclusions from the Heckman and Payner study. The primary feature of the Civil Rights Act was the removal of the formal barriers to entry that had been erected by the Jim Crow legislation. At this point the historical evidence tells a libertarian story, not a government intervention story. The "conservative" arguments of Charles Murray can now be recast in a way that is both more precise and more forceful.[27] Government intervention did not help blacks (or anyone else) when it functioned to override private contractual choice. But it did help most blacks and most whites by increasing the scope of market activities. The successes of the civil rights movement derived from the shrinkage, not the expansion, of total government power, both state and federal.

Relative Wage Levels

My analysis of the Heckman and Payner data focuses on the changes in black participation in labor markets in consequence of the 1964 act. There are of course other ways to try to measure these levels of advancement. One method is to compare the percentage of blacks and whites in certain broadly defined occupational categories; and indeed such studies have revealed that the percentage of black workers in these categories has increased since 1964.[28] But the findings overstate the ostensible level of

---

and are not theory specific. The point is important here because one large disparate impact case can use up far more consumer resources than many single-person disparate treatment cases.

26. See studies cited at note 2.

27. Indeed this is more or less the way that Murray himself tells it. The pattern of improvement in the income level of blacks is tied closely to the fortunes of whites, and is shown (with some persuasiveness) to be largely independent of the legislative programs for redistribution that were introduced during the Lyndon Johnson administration. Thus, even though a considerable drop in the percentage of the population living below the poverty line was registered during those years, this occurred at a time when the funding of the poverty programs was in its low initial stages. As funding increased in the 1970s, the decline in poverty rates did not accelerate but themselves slowed or even reversed. See, e.g., Charles Murray, *Losing Ground,* 61–63 (1984).

28. See Alfred W. Blumrosen, "Society in Transition I: A Broader Agenda for Equal Employment—The Peace Dividend, Leapfrogging, and Other Matters," 8 *Yale Law & Pol. Rev.* 257, 260–263 (1990).

parity if the occupational categories are broadly defined and blacks occupy the bottom rungs in each niche.

A more profitable and more common way to approach the matter is to look not so much at crude occupational categories as at relative wage levels. That very approach has been taken in many articles dealing with the subject, and these tend to yield the conclusion of Heckman and Verkerke cited at the beginning of this chapter. One early study of this sort is Richard Freeman's highly influential 1978 paper analyzing the effects of the antidiscrimination laws on the wage prospects of black workers.[29] Freeman compares the relative wage levels of blacks and whites before and after the passage of the civil rights statute. He notes that the ratio of black to white income across all classes increased after the passage of the 1964 act in many (but by no means all) instances more rapidly than in the prior period.[30] As was the case with the Heckman and Payner study, Freeman sought various explanations for the shifts, and concluded that the Civil Rights Act of 1964 was a critical variable. "Detailed investigation of the National Longitudinal Survey has found the occupational position of young black men entering the market after 1964 to be essentially the same as the characteristics of young whites with similar premarket background characteristics."[31]

All his evidence, however, is consistent with the hypothesis that the major gain from the civil rights statute was its removal of the separate but equal barriers associated with segregation in the South—or (a factor not relevant in Heckman and Payner's nonunion South Carolina environment) the elimination of the formal exclusionary practices of northern unions that were still in widespread use around the country. Freeman's data also offers some evidence against the tight labor market theory because it indicates that the relative position of black workers did *not* erode through the severe recession of the mid-1970s. He is able to report similar advances in the position of black workers in the labor force when he measures relative occupational position rather than income[32] and finds a parallel increase in the penetration of blacks to desirable positions in the overall labor force.[33]

---

29. Richard Freeman, "Black Economic Progress after 1964: Who Has Gained and Why?" in *Studies in Labor Markets* (S. Rosen ed. 1978).

30. See id., table 8.1 at 251.

31. Id. at 249.

32. Id. at 253.

33. Id. at 253.

Interpreting his data, however, raises the same hard questions that can be directed against Heckman and Payner's conclusions. The antidiscrimination laws are a variegated collection of distinct and inconsistent theories of individual rights. To say simply that the advances are attributable to the enforcement of the antidiscrimination laws is to ignore the very different strategies that have been adopted in different cases and different eras. In addition, Freeman's own data highlight the sharp increase in the number of cases coming before the EEOC, which took place relatively late in the process (the mid-1970s), well after the initial surge of institutional desegregation in 1965. At this point, moreover, the aggregate data become hopelessly complex because much of the gain in black income may be attributable not to the color-blind proscriptions of the 1964 act but to the explicit and aggressive affirmative action programs (a topic to which I return later) that were well in place by the late 1960s and the early 1970s,[34] and which were, if anything, proscribed by the act. Again, the improvements in the position of blacks may, as I have argued, be attributable largely to the removal of formal barriers, especially those imposed by government. Indeed, as Freeman himself notes, the level of progress flattens out significantly in the last few years of his sample,[35] a pattern that has become quite permanent in the years since. As Heckman and Verkerke concluded in 1990, there were no similar advances anywhere after 1975 and no reason to expect any through the 1990s.[36]

34. Id. at 254. "Among Ph.D.'s and faculty blacks earned roughly as much as comparable whites in 1973, which contrasts sharply to long-standing patterns of market discrimination." His data do not disaggregate southern from northern or public from private prior to 1964. Id. at 269.

35. Freeman himself is aware of some of the shifts in the legal environment. He writes: "The changed attitude of courts toward affirmative action is evidenced in several successful reverse discrimination suits by those injured by affirmative action and in changing burdens of proof in showing discrimination." Id. at 290, n.21. There are no citations for either part of the proposition. The first half overstates the boomlet for reverse discrimination cases, and of course does not take into account the dominant influence of *Steelworkers v. Weber,* 443 U.S. 193 (1979), decided shortly before the volume was published but probably after Freeman's paper was written. The shifts in proof in *Burdine* and similar cases are not important enough to account for any significant change in the aggregate data. The key elements were the one-two punch of disparate impact and affirmative action, which are not incorporated into his formal analysis.

36. "The influence of federal pressure was most pronounced between 1965 and 1975, and in the South where black wages and integration improved most rapidly. However, it is unlikely that the success of the first decade of enforcement will be repeated in the 1990s." Heckman and Verkerke, "Racial Disparity" at 279–280. There is no Jim Crow to demolish.

Taken on their own terms, the relative wage rate studies offer a cautious message about civil rights enforcement in a market economy. But there are good reasons to question whether narrowing the wage gap is a good proxy for the overall improvement of the economic system, reasons which, if correct, cast further doubt on the effectiveness of civil rights enforcement. Two ways exist to narrow the wage gap between white and black workers, provided other aspects of work quality are held constant. One is to raise the wage level of black workers relative to whites, and the other is to lower the wages of white workers relative to blacks. To make matters more difficult, accurate analytical procedures require that the question of comparison be made not with historical data but with the wage levels that would have been achieved during the period in question if the world had been otherwise. In other words, it becomes critical that some component in the analysis looks less at wage parity and more at the overall level of wages and productivity.

Suppose that in 1965 the ratio of black salaries to white was 0.7. If in 1970 that gap narrows to 0.75, what should be made of the shift? The gap could be attributable to a reduction in white wages without a corresponding increase in black wages; or an increase in black wages and shrinkage of white wages; or an increase in black wages and a smaller increase in white wages. To state this more generally, the wage gap could well narrow at the same time that aggregate wages for whites and blacks fall. Thus, if white wages were $100 and black wages $70 in the initial period, a closing of the wage ratio to 0.75 is consistent with data that report white wages of $80 and black wages of $60, or white wages of $120 and black wages of $90. Indeed, black wages might show far larger real increases when the gap widens than when it narrows.

The nub of the problem is that any ratio between black and white wage levels tells only a very small part of the overall story. It focuses on the *distributive* consequences of the civil rights legislation between blacks and whites. But it ignores the *allocative* gains or losses that flow from the legislation, which are captured only by some measure of the overall growth rate.

In addition, the relative wage data do not take into account the position of potential workers, often at the low end of the wage and skill distribution, who are excluded from the workplace by Title VII, a point that was recognized early on.[37] In this regard the picture is far more

37. See William M. Landes, "The Economics of Fair Employment Laws," 76 *J. Pol. Econ.* 507, 544–545 and n.32 (1968), noting that the gains that black labor received in

discouraging, for the level of participation of black males in the labor force "has fallen significantly since the mid-1960s."[38] The unemployment level for blacks remains at twice the level for whites, and there are greater concentrations (and increases) in black than in white male unemployment in the same post-1965 period.[39] Heckman himself has estimated that perhaps 15 to 25 percent of the improvement in relative black wages results from the decline in black participation at the lower end of the market.[40] Again, any wage convergence of employed workers offers a poor proxy for overall social welfare.

It is necessary, therefore, to look beyond the relative wage data to other considerations. In the first place, enforcement costs are always positive. A second point is that bringing a disparate impact case is wildly expensive compared to stripping a Jim Crow law from the statute book. Once these enforcement costs are taken into account, then the right question to be asked for each additional unit of administrative effort is whether that extra unit is justified in terms of the favorable allocative or distributive consequences that it achieves, when measured by any standard test of social welfare.

Where the statute is used to remove formal restrictions on entry and the mandatory separate but equal regime, it seems clear that the social gains justify the additional social costs. That question probably still receives an affirmative answer, even if the removal of the separate but equal restrictions is accompanied by the imposition of a formal prohibition against explicit forms of private discrimination. But the application of the statute to private discrimination in competitive markets generates not only administrative costs but allocative losses as well. The real private gains, shared by blacks and whites alike, that flow from the ability of all individuals to choose their trading partners without state interference are diminished when private choices are subjected to systematic state scrutiny. In practice, positive administrative costs generate negative allocative

---

wages were in part offset by reduced opportunities for employment. It is difficult to determine whether this was a consequence of the Civil Rights Act or of increases in the level of the minimum wage.

38. Heckman and Verkerke, "Racial Disparity" at 278 n.7.

39. Id. The levels of black participation in labor markets, especially for workers aged sixteen to twenty-four, are sharply lower since 1964 than they were, for instance, in 1955. For the data, see Murray, *Losing Ground,* fig. 5.2 at 73.

40. James Heckman, "The Impact of Government on the Economic Status of Black Americans," in *The Question of Discrimination: Racial Inequality in the U.S. Labor Market* 50 (1989).

consequences. The application of the antidiscrimination law to private competitive markets looks like a bad social investment. Nothing in the findings on relative wage levels contradicts that conclusion.

The dominant position of administrative costs could be contested by those who think that Title VII produces some allocative benefits, as John Donohue urges.[41] But even if his conclusion is correct, and some allocative benefits do exist, a certain asymmetry must nonetheless be observed. If regulation yields better outcomes than the market, there is still the question of whether the administrative costs necessary to run the system are smaller than the allocative gain otherwise achieved. Donohue recognizes this problem but makes assumptions about the administrative costs that seem to understate matters substantially.[42] He notes that about six thousand suits per year are brought, and he estimates the costs of servicing those suits in the area of $300 million per year. But the estimate ignores all the indirect costs in response to the prospect of litigation: firms must bring their policies into compliance with Title VII, and plaintiffs' lawyers must expend resources with an eye toward future suits. That estimate also ignores the administrative costs of running the EEOC, the constant political jousting over the reform of the statute, and even the heavy educational costs of training new generations of lawyers and employers and keeping them all up to date on employment discrimination law. As litigation is only the tip of the iceberg, Donohue's numbers may be off by as much as an order of magnitude, although no one can say for sure.

Redistributive Effects of the Antidiscrimination Laws

This discussion of relative earnings offers a convenient jumping-off point for examining yet another issue raised by the antidiscrimination laws: the redistributive gains that might be thought (along with some perceived allocative benefits) to justify the administrative costs under the statute. At one level the redistributive argument is appealing: blacks have long been the victims of government-mandated discrimination. It is now their turn to be made whole within a system that has treated them badly. But here too the argument is far more tenuous than is commonly supposed. There

41. I have already criticized his reasoning; see Chapter 3 at 76–78, under the heading "Is Title VII Efficient?"

42. John J. Donohue III, "Further Thoughts on Employment Discrimination Legislation: A Reply to Judge Posner," 136 *U. Pa. L. Rev.* 523, 524 (1987).

is only an imperfect correlation between wealth and race. Poverty, not race, is a more desirable ground for redistribution, because the diminishing marginal utility of wealth holds across different individuals regardless of race. The effort to redistribute wealth along racial lines runs into the obvious objection to having poorer whites subsidize richer blacks. It is largely for the purpose of meeting these concerns that arguments in favor of an antidiscrimination statute are rarely couched in redistributive terms. References to the victims of discrimination and the wrongful conduct of discriminators are meant to invoke notions of corrective justice, which are so dominant in the ordinary perception of common law torts and crimes against persons and property.[43]

There is a second response to the argument that the statute works any redistribution in favor of blacks. The problem here is the classic one of the unanticipated consequences of purposive action. The goals sought by any regulatory statute are often frustrated by its passage. The statute that is designed to benefit blacks may hurt them, or, more to the point, it may hurt *some* blacks while benefiting others.

Let us assume that a civil rights statute has as its sole objective to eliminate Jim Crow restrictions. There is little doubt that blacks as a group will tend to gain substantially from increased opportunities to trade with whites. It is also clear that many whites will gain as well from the opportunity to trade with blacks. But net gains to most persons within the group is not the same as net gains to all. There were doubtless some blacks in the South and elsewhere who stood to profit from continuing segregation. A self-interested black owner of a baseball team in the Negro League in 1947 would have been quite ambivalent about Jackie Robinson and the integration of major league baseball. Overcoming the white barrier may well have increased the value of players held under long-term contract, but it also spelled the end of the separate Negro League and the destruction of the capital value of its franchises. The same position surely holds for teachers and administrators who had positions of power within the segregated educational establishments in the South, and for the owners of the countless businesses that catered to black consumers or depended on large sources of black labor.

None of these points begins to justify the maintenance of segregation or the limitation of civil capacity. Viewed from the lofty perspective of the original position, the overall levels of wealth, happiness, and utility ex ante are all severely compromised by the restraints on trade imposed in

43. On which see Chapter 1.

the name of Jim Crow. Nonetheless, once the flawed system has been allowed to operate for many years, it generates some winners, black as well as white, even if it produces many more losers. Escaping an old and oppressive system is far more costly than avoiding it in the first place; in some cases (Jim Crow is not one) the effort may not be worthwhile.

Redistribution within racial groups remains an issue in current contexts as well. In this area there is an instructive parallel to the minimum wage, which has powerful redistributive effects among the class of workers it is designed to protect. The workers who are laid off or not hired are not chosen at random. Here we find powerful evidence that black workers, who have low levels of education and skills, tend to be hurt most by the minimum wage laws because a larger fraction of that group has value productivity below the wage level set by the statute.[44]

As Marvin Kosters and Finis Welch have noted:

As expected, minimum wages are estimated to have a destabilizing effect upon teenagers and a stabilizing effect on adults. In a sense, minimum wages seem to shift much of the burden of variation in aggregate employment from adults to teenagers, from males to females, from whites to nonwhites; in each case the destabilizing effect is upon those with lower average wages.[45]

In the simplest form, these workers are required to take a lesser chance of getting a job (with less attractive terms) in exchange for a chance of a higher wage. The situation is of course more complicated, for those who lose their positions are surely worse off than before, and those who retain them may not be better off on balance than before.[46] What is easily over-

---

44. See Marvin Kosters and Finis Welch, "The Effects of Minimum Wages by Age and Sex," in *Racial Discrimination in Economic Life* 103 (Anthony H. Pascal ed. 1972). McKenzie, *The American Job Machine*, ch. 9.

45. Kosters and Welch, "The Effects of Minimum Wages" at 112–113. They note that the elasticities may seem small in that an increase of 1 percent in the minimum wage increases the "marginality coefficients" by only 0.19 percent. But they also note that these changes become substantial when the minimum wage increases are themselves substantial, as was the case, for example, in 1956, when the wage increased from seventy-five cents to one dollar.

46. The empirical evidence here is somewhat complicated. In general most studies have estimated that for each 1 percent increase in minimum wage, the loss of jobs is between 0.15 and 0.25 percent. But other terms in the contract may change as well, to the detriment of the workers who remain behind. "Granted, minimum-wage workers often have few conventional fringe benefits, but they are also paid in terms of working conditions, on-the-

looked, however, is that the minimum wage law also has adverse distributional consequences *within* the class of black workers. Its effects are
disproportionately heavy at the bottom of the skill pyramid, so there is an
implicit transfer from unskilled to skilled black laborers. If one assumes a
diminishing marginal utility to money that carries over between persons,
these implicit transfer payments run in the wrong direction, both within
and across races. The minimum wage increases the gap between the two
cultures, between the haves and the have-nots, between the middle class
and the underclass, which is made larger by a law that is designed to
diminish that difference.

The antidiscrimination law also works transfers within races, and for
the same reason that the minimum wage does. Changes in the legal environment are not met with simple compliance, in the absence of other
changes. Firms seek to maximize their profits subject to the constraints
imposed by law. The modern antidiscrimination law provides that at the
very least blacks must receive the same wages as whites for comparable
positions, and to avoid evasion it regulates the other terms and conditions
of employment as well. Its comprehensiveness is in part its undoing. If
black labor is perceived as having lower value than white labor (for the
same human capital reasons applicable to the minimum wage), then
employers will seek ways to comply with the statute and evade its sting.

The methods available are legion. The critical point is that the
responses to the statute are not invoked only at the hiring gate. Quite the
opposite. Virtually every facet of firm life can be influenced by the possible effect of the antidiscrimination laws. One key decision is the location of a firm's new plants and facilities.[47] A decision on plant location is

---

job training, rest periods, promises of college educations, courtesy of employers and supervisors, scheduling of work hours, time off, company discounts, recommendations, credit,
and opportunities for advancement." McKenzie, *The American Job Machine* at 206. These
benefits can be reduced to offset the increase in wages so on balance the losses to workers
exceed their gains. Only a fraction of employee losses are measured in lost jobs. The rest
come in reduced worker surplus from retained positions.

47. The point is made in Richard A. Posner, "The Efficiency and Efficacy of Title VII,"
136 *U. Pa. L. Rev.* 513, 519 (1987), noting that the threat of a disparate impact suit "makes
it more costly for a firm to operate in an area where the labor pool contains a high
percentage of blacks, by enlarging the firm's legal exposure. There, when deciding where to
locate a new plant or whether to expand an existing one, a firm will be attracted (other
things being equal) to areas that have only small percentages of blacks in their labor force."
Posner then refers to *Terry Properties, Inc. v. Standard Oil Co. (Ind.),* 799 F.2d 1523, 1527
(11th Cir. 1986), in which the defendant wished to build a plant in a location with fewer
than 35 percent minority workers "because it had previously experienced difficulty meeting

not reached by any theory under Title VII, but it has enormous effects on the prospects of black workers. If the antidiscrimination law induces firms to open their plants in the suburbs and not in the inner city, the transportation barriers are sufficient to lock out large numbers of black workers who are unable or unwilling to make the long daily commute. Yet no tough local ordinance can do anything except exacerbate the flight to the suburbs or beyond. Similarly, the types of jobs made available in the plant or office can well be influenced by the antidiscrimination laws. The firm might adopt a more capital-intensive strategy to minimize reliance on the local labor force, or it can use job classifications for which the applicant pool of black labor is small.

More generally, no set of decisions is fixed, independent of the hiring rules. If blacks bring lower levels of education into the job market, the best way for them to compete is by offering their services at lower wages. They should be willing, indeed eager, to take jobs on an at will basis in order to get a chance to show their abilities and to develop the skills and habits they need to go further. In this regard they are in identical positions with low-skilled whites. The goal is to overcome the natural reluctance to hire. Equal opportunity ex ante requires unequal contract terms.

On this model the right response is to repeal the antidiscrimination laws insofar as they restrict private contracts. The gains recorded under the statute are only the gains received by blacks who are skillful enough or lucky enough to remain in the hiring market. The figures on relative wages do not reflect the increased unemployment rates for black labor, which can plainly be tied to the minimum wage law, and probably to the antidiscrimination law as well, as the data on the decreases in black labor force participation illustrate.[48] The chief effect of Title VII is to make highly skilled black labor more desirable relative to low-skilled black labor. As with the minimum wage, Title VII works a redistribution from worse-off to better-off blacks, which is surely far from what its principled supporters intended.

The evidence for this proposition can be found in many places. The antidiscrimination laws increase the relative advantage of privilege. At the most general level, the sociologist William Julius Wilson has noted that race-specific civil rights initiatives do not seem to work, and that the gaps

---

affirmative action goals in communities with proportionately larger minority populations." Posner, "Efficiency and Efficacy" at 519 n.27.

48. See the discussion earlier in this chapter.

between rich and poor within the races have only increased with time.[49] His major concern is the elimination of a large black underclass that is trapped in poverty, with low occupational skills and high levels of illegitimacy. This problem has increased in intensity since 1964, although it would be irresponsible to assert that the Civil Rights Act is its major cause, in light of the weaknesses in the structure of family, school, and church. But apart from the lifting of Jim Crow, the 1964 act could have done nothing to ameliorate the situation, given its tendency to increase the gap between top and bottom. The more precise economic measurements tell much the same story. Thus, most studies tend to confirm that "Blacks employed in higher level managerial and professional jobs experienced the *greatest advances in relative wages*."[50] "In contrast to the relative deterioration of the position of unskilled black workers, highly educated Blacks now appear to earn salaries comparable to Whites with equal education and experience."[51] These results are often described as progress, but like other relative wage studies they treat a narrowing of black-white differentials as signs of social improvement, even though it is perfectly consistent with overall productivity losses and a new set of economic inequities within racial groups. Finally, there is evidence that the Civil Rights Act increases the dispersion in income by class across generations, which itself poses a threat to social mobility. As Freeman writes:

> The principal finding is that, in contrast to the pattern of social mobility before 1964, when family background was found to have relatively small effects on black achievement and when only a modest fraction of black-white economic differences could be attributed to the "burden of background," in the late 1960s background factors became an important determinant of black socioeconomic achievement and the

49. William Julius Wilson, *The Truly Disadvantaged: The Inner City, the Underclass, and Public Policy* (1987). Wilson himself is committed to liberal programs, such as the minimum wage, which I think are destructive of the ends he seeks. But it is his perception of the problem, not his proposed cures, that is relevant to this point in the argument.

50. Heckman and Verkerke, "Racial Disparity" at 284 (emphasis in original). The studies cited include Richard Freeman, "Changes in the Labor Market for Black Americans, 1948–1972," 1 *Brookings Papers on Economic Activities* 67 (1973); Freeman, "Black Economic Progress after 1964"; James. P. Smith and Finis Welch, "Affirmative Action and Labor Markets," 2 *J. Lab. Econ.* 269 (1984). Much of this change took place early on, and part of it is doubtless attributable, as Heckman and Verkerke observe, to the " 'pro-skill bias' of affirmative action pressure." Heckman and Verkerke, "Racial Disparity" at 284 n.36.

51. Heckman and Verkerke, "Racial Disparity" at 285.

major cause of difference between black and white young men. The implication is that *blacks from more advantaged backgrounds made greater gains in the market than those from less advantaged backgrounds*."[52]

The explanation for this last finding seems clear enough. One effect of an antidiscrimination law is to make high-quality black labor better able to compete in the market than low-quality black labor. As long as there is any correlation between family background and overall education and skill levels, we should expect to see these differences mount. The Jim Crow laws prior to 1964 would not have had this effect because of their systematic exclusion of all blacks from key social institutions. But the antidiscrimination norm of Title VII does. The net effect gives new meaning to the convergence of wage levels between blacks and whites. It registers in the social calculation only those blacks who win from the system ex post. It wholly overlooks the losses to blacks for whom Title VII serves as a barrier to entry ex ante.[53] Income profiles on the survivors completely ignore the plight of those who drop out of the contest.

The key problem with black unemployment and underemployment, especially at low skill levels, cannot be solved by an antidiscrimination statute that increases the costs to firms of hiring black labor. In order to stem the flight of business to the suburbs, the ideal social policy should allow them to offer jobs to whomever they choose at whatever wages they wish. Competitive pressures will do the rest. The implicit tax that the antidiscrimination law imposes on a firm is paid in part by the black workers who are shut out of the labor market as a consequence thereof. Nothing in Heckman and Payner's South Carolina textile study or in the relative wage data presented by Freeman contradicts that conclusion, and

52. Freeman, "Black Economic Progress" at 255; emphasis in original.

53. The point applies not only to the antidiscrimination laws but also to the gains attributed in other contexts to unionization. See Richard B. Freeman and James L. Medoff, *What Do Unions Do?* (1984); Charles Brown and James L. Medoff, "Trade Unions in the Production Process," 86 *J. Pol. Econ.* 355 (1978). Both works argue that unions serve a useful social function because they are able to maintain high wage levels for their members even in competition with nonunion labor. The error in the argument is pointed out in Morgan O. Reynolds, "Trade Unions in the Production Process Reconsidered," 94 *J. Pol. Econ.* 443 (1986), where Reynolds notes: "If all firms maximize profits and trade unions impose higher than competitive wage rates on unionized firms, then the marginal productivity of unionized labor is necessarily greater than that of nonunion labor." The key question, ignored in these arguments, concerns the welfare loss of those firms that could have survived in a competitive environment but not in a union one.

Freeman's own evidence about the increased dispersion between rich and poor after 1965 tends to support it. Rightly interpreted, then, the empirical data on race and employment support the need for limited government and open markets. The findings do nothing to make the case for Title VII.

In essence the case for repeal with regard to private employers is clear enough. Labor markets are generally competitive, so the preferences of individual firms do little to alter the overall shape of the market or the prospects of workers within it. There are good reasons to believe, moreover, that some (not all, but some) firms may be better able to operate if they select their workers by race rather than by some race-neutral criterion. We should not expect race to be irrelevant in markets, and neither whites nor blacks should desire it to be so. Yet there is a vast difference between segregation by choice and segregation by public command, for in the former case we should expect the choices to be driven by efforts to improve output, whereas in the latter we should expect the impulse for redistribution to drive the effort, with the usual consequences: the diminution of long-term freedom, wealth, and utility, and an increase in government power, planning, and control. There is a vast difference in motivation between the passage of Jim Crow legislation and the 1964 statute. The latter can claim an appeal to high principle that the former cannot. But the political pressures and the partisan politics of race legislation were in a sense released anew after 1964, as within a short time the question of color-blind treatment was displaced by an explicit demand for equality of results and, if necessary, for race-conscious affirmative action programs. The evaluation of affirmative action is thus an indispensable element of the overall picture, but it is best deferred until after a fuller examination of sex discrimination, for on that issue at least there is much in common between the treatment of race and of sex under Title VII.

PART IV

Sex Discrimination

CHAPTER 13

Separate but Equal

Race and Sex Discrimination: A Misleading Parallel

The basic provisions of the Civil Rights Act link race and sex as parallel grounds on which it is impermissible to discriminate against employees. This statutory parallelism could easily lead to the belief that the same basic issues are at stake in the two types of cases, and that the received learning in race cases explains what happens in sex cases as well. The substantive theories developed by the courts reinforce this apparent basic symmetry. Disparate treatment and disparate impact theories apply to cases of both sex and race discrimination, and their similarity could lead to the mistaken conclusion that the two can easily be yoked into a single harness.

A moment's reflection, however, should reveal that the differences between the cases are as great as their similarities, and in some ways even come to dominate the comparison. The simplest way to capture the distinction is to note that the phrase "separate but equal" rightfully carries with it odious connotations in race cases, but it generates far more ambivalent responses when carried over to sex cases. In both the public and the private sphere there is a sense that systematic differences between the sexes matter in a way that differences among races do not. Wholly apart from the commands of Title VII, many employers have no use for policies that take race into account in any way, shape, or form, but they regard it as vitally necessary to take sex differences into account in making certain employment decisions. Pregnancy, parenthood, medical coverage, rest room facilities, and job descriptions and classifications are all areas in which some differentiation of contract terms by sex is routinely considered and routinely practiced. The demand for separate treatment need not come from men; in fact it often comes from women, who rightly understand that, just as women need different diet, exercise, and medical services, they often require a package of employment benefits different from that demanded by men. Making the total compensation package equal in light of these differences is never an easy task. But there is no viable alternative: any employer who decided in an unregulated market to exclude women workers across the board would doubtless be committing a form of hara-kiri, for reasons too obvious to belabor.

The differences in sex roles are so important that no one can ignore them, and their effects are not cordoned off into any limited domain of human experience. What goes on outside the workplace heavily influences what takes place within it. Thus, the large percentage of women who plan to devote a substantial proportion of their adult lives to raising children and managing a family should be expected on average to make relatively low levels of investment in skills that would yield high returns on the job. Since they have fewer years to work in the market, they will have a smaller return on any given investment in market skills, which translates into a lower level of demand for those skills. Rather than turn to the market, many married women may well maximize their total utility by relying on a mix of earned income from their husbands and imputed income derived from their own labor at home. Accordingly, any diminution of men's prospects in the workplace reduces for many women their total expected income and welfare.[1] The utilities of married men and women exhibit a heavy and permanent interdependence as each partner relies on the labor of the other, and each often takes the welfare of the other into account in assessing the desirability of his or her own situation.

The pervasive importance of sex roles can be stated even more strongly: durable marriages often depend on a conscious division of labor within the family whereby both partners realize gains from specialization and trade, just as people do in ordinary economic markets.[2] Decisions about marriage and child rearing thus create very different incentives for men and women (or at least some men and some women), and these incentives influence enormously the patterns of interaction and the job decisions of men and women in the workplace. Historically these forces were quite strong, especially when women's work was needed to raise children and run a household in the days before laborsaving devices and improved contraception.[3] But even

---

1. This point is stressed at length in Richard A. Posner, "An Economic Analysis of Sex Discrimination Laws," 56 *U. Chi. L. Rev.* 1311 (1989).

2. See, generally, Gary S. Becker, *A Treatise on the Family* (enlarged ed. 1991).

3. Victor R. Fuchs, *Women's Quest for Economic Equality,* ch. 2 (1988).

today many asymmetries still remain in the form of male and female work patterns, and there is no question that choices in the job market differ much more by sex than they do by race.[4] Given the underlying asymmetry in incentives and opportunities, we should not expect to see any identity of job roles in the marketplace. The proposition that like cases should be treated alike has little relevance in this context. If anything, the converse proposition—that unlike cases should be treated differently—appears to be far more salient. The differences between the sexes do matter.

The conventional wisdom and the traditional practices on sex differences have come under heavy assault in recent years. It has become fashionable to assert that historical accident and cultural conditioning explain much, perhaps all, of this differentiation in sex roles.[5] Some radical feminists have taken the view that androgyny—the elimination of all sex-specific roles—is appropriate not only for the workplace but for the greater society at large.[6] In so doing they commit the sin of hubris by insisting that they can, through law and coercion, transform the behavior and preferences of ordinary women and men. There is of course a wide-ranging debate as to whether the observed differences in human behavior are attributable to socialization patterns, to biology, or to some mixture of the two. I incline to the view that the biology of sex differences is profound, and influences not only the activities immediately related to courtship, reproduction, and child rearing, but also virtually every other

4. Id. at ch. 3.

5. "Liberal feminists have been concerned to prove that women are as capable as men of being fully rational agents. This concern has inspired much recent feminist research, which has demonstrated conclusively that most if not all of the cognitive and emotional differences between the sexes can be attributed to the different experiences of males and females, especially in their early years." Alison Jagger, *Feminist Politics and Human Nature* 42 (1983) (citing no sources).

The hormonal basis for differences in sexual behavior has been long established. See, e.g., John Money and Anke A. Ehrhardt, *Man and Woman, Boy and Girl: The Differentiation and Dimorphism of Gender Identity from Conception to Maturity* (1972), noting that young girls exposed to large doses of testosterone and other male hormones during the early stages in the womb developed pronounced tomboy characteristics. See also Eleanor Maccoby and Carol Jacklin, *The Psychology of Sex Differences* (1974), noting that differences in aggressiveness by sex cut across all societies, and that they begin early in life before social influences can be exerted.

6. For variations on the radical feminist themes, see, e.g., Jagger, *Feminist Politics*; Catharine MacKinnon, *Toward a Feminist Theory of the State* (1989); Robin West, "Jurisprudence and Gender," 55 *U. Chi. L. Rev.* 1 (1988).

aspect of human conduct.[7] Whether one thinks that hormones (say, differences in testosterone levels) and innate drives or socialization dominates, however, is quite beside the point for this discussion. Any analysis of the employment market has to take as a given the stock of workers who are available for different positions. No market can operate on the assumption that it should be organized *as if* the tastes and preferences of the work force were wholly uncorrelated with sex, when the correlations are there. If biological forces are dominant, then these can be changed only with enormous difficulty, if at all, and only over the resistance of both men and women. If social forces are dominant, the situation differs to only a small degree, for rooting out sex differences in the workplace requires a systematic effort to override the influence of parents, siblings, teachers, religion, play, and courtship.

It is possible, moreover, to place a more positive light on the pattern of sex differences. This pattern should be regarded not with suspicion but with approval because it raises the prospect of systematic gains from trade between men and women. Even though we may not know enough from biology, sociology, and intuition to infer exactly which trades will take place under what circumstances, we do know enough to predict that some of these trades will be profitable precisely because they exploit differences in sex-linked abilities and strengths. If women as a rule are better at one task (say, affective personal relations) and men are better at another task (working mechanical equipment, for instance, or military combat), then we should expect to see more female nurses and social workers and more male construction workers and soldiers. Within the firm, both men and women specialize in those jobs that give greatest scope to their natural talents by gravitating toward areas of comparative strength. As a matter of principle, a society with a proportionate number of men and women in all job, trade, and professional groups is one that is likely to suffer from insufficient occupational specialization. Constant and rigid proportions of men and women across occupational categories are a clear sign that state regulation has unduly prevented mutually advantageous trades between men and women.

General theory, biology, and sociology all have a lot to say about the proper division of labor within society. Nonetheless, their proper use in political discourse is cautious and defensive, not assertive and controlling.

---

7. See, for an extended defense of the biological origins of sex differences, Donald Symons, *The Evolution of Human Sexuality* (1979). For my views, see Richard A. Epstein, "The Varieties of Self-Interest," 8 *Soc. Phil. & Pol.* 102 (1990).

A wide confluence of biological and social forces explains why the asymmetrical patterns that emerge in markets may be productive and useful. Most decidedly, none of them offers *any* support for the view that natural differences between the sexes justify state restrictions limiting freedom of contract in the job market, for example, a ban on women as lawyers,[8] or for that matter on men as midwives. There is no case for banning anyone from choosing any line of employment, as long as an employer is willing to offer a job. Quite the contrary, we know that there are sufficient variations in relevant characteristics *within* each sex, and sufficient overlaps in the distribution of tastes between men and women, to make that kind of centralized social planning as mischievous and unwarranted as any other.

My argument about the significance of sex differences is meant to demonstrate only that we should expect differential proportions of men and women across occupational lines, as is indeed the case. It in no way suggests that within a market system all occupational categories should be rigorously divided by sex, although some might be and indeed are. In this light the theoretical insights are also in manifest tension with the antidiscrimination laws, to the extent that these erect or rely on a presumption that men and women bring the same set of preferences and abilities into the job market, when there is biological, sociological, historical, and economic evidence that they do not.[9] The appreciation of sex differences, some of which are biologically based, should caution us against imposing any centralized and comprehensive world view of employment markets. There is enough that we do understand, and too much that we do not, to allow any single vision of just and proper social sex roles to dominate the workplace or any other area of life. The biological arguments play a corrective role in limiting the demands for social engineering. There are sensible ways to account for the persistence of sex differences in job markets that do not depend on a story of domination and exploitation.

The modern champions of Title VII take a different and more dangerous view. They recognize that its scope would be sharply diminished if

---

8. See, e.g., *Bradwell v. State,* 83 U.S. 130 (1873), which sustained a legal bar against the practice of law by women, with its distinctive mix of biological and theological justifications. "The paramount destiny and mission of woman are to fulfill the noble and benign offices of wife and mother. This is the law of the Creator." Id. at 141.

9. See the discussion in Chapter 17 of *EEOC v. Sears, Roebuck & Co.,* 839 F.2d 302 (7th Cir. 1988), where these issues are critical.

existing preference structures were taken as given for the operation of the law,[10] and frequently advocate various forms of restructuring, or "dynamic discrimination,"[11] whereby the reach of the antidiscrimination law requires firms to alter their existing employment practices where these have an adverse impact on women or blacks. The demands that the antidiscrimination law could place on the market are not self-defining. These laws could be expanded into a complete code of socialization, and still they would fail if legal innovations outstripped either the ability or the desire of all persons to change their own behavior or personality. Even if human nature can be changed by collective social action, it need not be changed for the better. It is a mistake, as Christina Sommers has written, "to conflate mutability with corrigibility."[12] The risks of major social dislocation are all the more severe because the reform is instituted from without, by coercive organizations, and not from within by persons who have intimate local knowledge of the institutions within which they work.

Responding to Sex Differences in Practice

The differences between sex discrimination and race discrimination enter into the law in many contexts that exist wholly independently of Title VII. Historically as well as analytically one sees the constant tension between race and sex discrimination cases. The distinction between race and sex runs through the length and breadth of the law,[13] and becomes especially vivid on the critical issue of separate but equal accommodations. In race relations the label "separate but equal" carries with it the heavy opprobrium of segregated washrooms and drinking fountains, of being sent to the back of the bus. Yet in the area of male-female relations, separate but equal captures a large portion of what is desired by the champions of the antidiscrimination principle, and of feminists more generally. The goal is not unisex bathrooms in airports or single-sex locker rooms. Rather, the goal, never seriously contested, is to ensure that men

10. See Cass R. Sunstein, "Why Markets Don't Stop Discrimination," 8 *Soc. Phil. & Pol.* 22 (1991).

11. The term is Mark Kelman's. See his "Concepts of Discrimination in 'General Ability' Job Testing," 104 *Harv. L. Rev.* 1157, 1170–73 (1991).

12. Christina Sommers, "The Feminist Revelation," 8 *Soc. Phil. & Pol.* 141, 147 (1990).

13. For a perceptive discussion, see George Rutherglen, "Sexual Equality in Fringe Benefit Plans," 65 *Va. L. Rev.* 199, 205–212 (1979), justifying differential standards of review for race and sex discrimination under the equal protection clause.

and women have access to accommodations that offer equal quality and comfort. In this context the reason for the shift is quite clear. Providing separate but equal public accommodations is a strategy that advances the welfare of men and women simultaneously. There are no separate water fountains or restaurants because single accommodations serve everyone well enough. But where separate accommodations do exist, it is because these are widely if not universally preferred by people of both sexes. The "separate" thus works to the advantage of members of both sexes, while the "equal" ensures that members of either sex can obtain the same level of financial support and public services. In the case of race, the "separate" was a guise for rigid segregation, and the "equal" was a transparent fig leaf when whites had a monopoly on government power which allowed them to arrange collections and expenditures for their own benefit. The point is borne out by the radically different origins of separate accommodations on railroads during the nineteenth century, where, in the instance of race, the discrimination was often invidious as to the quality of service provided, whereas on matters of sex it was not.[14] There are ample economic differences in the operation of the separate but equal principle in the two realms.

If the public accommodation question seems easy, the program of separate but equal faces more complex tasks in other settings—from athletics, dance, and gambling to business, mathematics, and the arts—where again differences between men and women, such as those related to risk taking, do matter, and are likely to remain critical no matter what government policy is introduced. The hard problem is to disentangle the relative effects of social and biological influences. But often it seems best to make peace with natural differences instead of railing against them. No program of weightlifting or socialization will ever make women equal in strength with men, and there is no reason to try. Nor is there any possibility that a set of adroit exercises will allow men to dance on pointe, and no reason why ballet should forfeit its charm by forbidding women to do so as well. And there is no reason to ban boxing or football for women, because women on the whole do not choose to participate in those sports.

The sources of the differences between men and women, however, do not have to be sorted out with precision to prove that they count. With athletic facilities, separate but equal is widely regarded as unacceptable on grounds of race, but at some level it is virtually required on grounds of sex. Feminist authors such as Catharine MacKinnon will at least broach

14. See Chapter 5 at 105–108, under the heading "Understanding the Police Power."

the subject, even if MacKinnon provides no insight on how to respond to it.[15] And judges are overtly hostile toward efforts by men to invoke constitutional principles of equal protection to secure male plaintiffs a place on women's volleyball teams.[16] It is difficult to insist that any university, for example, should field only one tennis or basketball team whose membership is determined by open competition without regard to sex. That formula would be a recipe for all-male teams in a large number of sports, or for mixed teams run by quotas. Either way, athletic programs would be impoverished. Unisex competition would distort the dynamics in other sports such as gymnastics, where men and women participate in different events, again to the benefit of neither women nor men. The separation of the two sexes in competitive sports is therefore rightly understood as a way to advance the welfare of both men and women.

The hard questions, accordingly, go not to the issue of separation but to the issue of equality, both in access to facilities and in financing. The problem is a difficult one because the revenues generated for universities by men's and women's sports are typically not equal, given the differences in spectator interest. Football is the most obvious example, but the point is true to lesser, but still substantial, degrees for basketball and other sports as well. Equality can turn on the question of whether each program should be required to stand on its own, or whether funds should be diverted from profitable (or even marginally profitable) programs to subsidize those that are not, where men's and women's programs are equal recipients of the subsidy. Matters are made no less difficult if there are different levels of participation by male and female students in intramural sports. These thorny issues are quite beyond the scope of this book, and my own view, to no one's surprise, is that each school and each university should work them out internally as best it can, free of any government interference. The variations between schools and universities make it unlikely that any single solution will suit all.

Military service offers yet another context in which sex differences do

15. See, e.g., for endless repetition of the theme of differences, Catherine MacKinnon, *Feminism Unmodified* 123 (1986): "Given what I have said about women's physicality, women's point of view on athletics, and its connections with sexuality and the subordination of women generally, *now* let's ask, what about separate teams? what about separate programs? what about separate institutions?" MacKinnon does not answer the questions she raises, but surely they could not even be asked today in the context of race.

16. *Clark v. Arizona Interscholastic Association*, 886 F.2d 1191 (9th Cir. 1989), noting that "due to physiological differences, males would displace females to a substantial extent if they were allowed to compete for positions on the volleyball team." Id. at 1193.

and should matter. An extensive portion of the military (about 10 percent in the early 1990s) is female, and there is still some formal restriction against women in combat, narrowly defined, however, to allow women to be part of certain units (for example, engineering and reconnaissance) that are in combat areas but not engaged in actual fighting. There is also an extensive commitment to enroll women (although far short of equal numbers) in the three military academies. But again equality is in large measure a fig leaf, because of both the differences in job assignments and the differences in qualifications for various tasks. The blunt truth is that women as a group cannot begin to match the levels of physical performance expected of and achieved by the subset of men fit for military service. There are double standards on all tests of strength and endurance for both running and lifting, and the injury rate for women is far higher than it is for men.[17] Although it is said to be strictly against military policy to invoke this evidence to oppose the current practices,[18] skeptical civil-

17. For an account, see Brian Mitchell, *Weak Link: The Feminization of the American Military* 54, 158 (1989). He writes of women introduced into the Air Force Academy: "They fell out of group runs, lagged behind in road marches, failed to negotiate obstacles on the assault course (later modified to make them easier), and could not climb a rope, sometimes breaking down in tears when confronted with their own limitations. The rate at which the female cadets sought medical attention could hardly have allowed them to keep up the pace of training . . . On the average, women suffered nine times as many shin splints as men, five times as many stress fractures, and more than five times as many cases of tendonitis."

The consequences of the differential performance, however, led not to a reassessment of the basic policy to admit women to the service academies but to a reduction in the applicable standards. Mitchell writes: "All the services have double standards for men and women on all events of their regular fitness tests. Young male marines must perform at least 3 push-ups to pass the test, but women marines must only hang from the bar with arms flexed for 16 seconds. In the Army, the youngest women are given an extra three minutes to complete a two-mile run. All the services require men to perform more situps than women, despite the much-vaunted strength of the female midsection."

The same differential rates are reported on physical tests for firefighters; see, e.g., *Evans v. City of Evanston*, 881 F.2d 382 (7th Cir. 1989), where the men far outperformed the women.

18. See Mitchell, *Weak Link* at 223, who details the role of the Defense Advisory Committee on Women in the Services and the powerful influence that the organization has on the internal operations of the military: "Personnel are required to attend equal opportunity training, during which EO officers preach the sanctity of sexual equality and the folly and immorality of belief in traditional sex roles. The definition of sexual harassment has expanded to include the one expression of opposition to women in the military. Officers and senior enlisted are kept in check by their performance reports; a 'ding' in the block that reads 'Supports Equal Opportunity' can have career-ending consequences."

ians are still free to object. The effort toward full integration in military affairs marks a preference for ideology over experience and common sense. The stunning victory of American and Allied forces in the Persian Gulf war should not blind us to the long-term risks of the present policies. Where the military conflict is more evenly balanced, and its outcome less certain, our forces may be in retreat, and women close to the front lines may be drawn into actual combat, at unnecessary cost to their own lives and the safety of the country.

The sex differences between men and women are too large to be ignored. It is entirely proper to note that on a wide range of issues women speak "in a different voice."[19] But this dialogue on the question of difference is a two-way street. Some of those differences support explicit distinctions in the treatment of men and women that reinforce traditional practices and policies rather than undermining them. A categorical sex-blind policy does not work in many of the countless domains to which it is applied.

Sex Differences and Title VII

The relevance of biological differences has influenced the development of Title VII, a statute deriving its moral force from the consensus on the question of race. Sex discrimination was almost an afterthought. The statutory prohibition was added to Title VII while the bill was on the floor of the House of Representatives as a ploy by the bill's opponents, who hoped to make the entire bill unpalatable to some of its wavering supporters.[20] The clear message of the amenders was that discrimination on grounds of sex was a common everyday occurrence, north, south, east, and west. Accordingly, any practice that was universal was surely permissible, perhaps necessary, and even desirable. If the antidiscrimination principle was powerful enough to reach sex cases with undiminished rigor, then surely something was amiss with the principle as it applied to race.

In political terms, the opponents of the Civil Rights Act made a fatal miscalculation: the dare was taken up, and the statute passed with its broader coverage. But the legislative maneuvers show at the very least the

19. See Carol Gilligan, *In a Different Voice* (1982), stressing the differences in male and female responses to different kinds of social situations.

20. See, e.g., Francis J. Vaas, "Title VII: Legislative History," 7 *Bost. C. Ind. & Comm. L. Rev.* 431, 441 (1966).

wholly different social histories that lie behind the two prohibitions. Whatever the source and extent of sexual inequality in this country, women were never slaves, and they have never been subjected to invidious discrimination in public accommodations.[21] The earlier battles over women's rights were in connection, first, with ordinary civil capacity, typically after marriage, to hold property, to contract, to dispose of property, and to make wills. With the married women's property acts of the late nineteenth century, any civil disabilities were removed; that battle was won, and won cleanly. The second major women's issue was the vote, and that too was put to rest in 1920 with the passage of the Nineteenth Amendment.

The driving force behind the 1964 Civil Rights Act was racial segregation and racial oppression, period. It was around that one issue that the forces of support and opposition coalesced. Title I on voting rights and Title II on public accommodations, the most dramatic parts of the act, had no sex-linked component beforehand, nor have they generated sex-related issues in the years since its passage. There have never been separate drinking fountains for men and women, separate voting booths and ballots, or geographical separation of the sexes.

Once sex discrimination was covered under Title VII, however, it generated a new source of legal obligation to which first the disparate treatment and then, eventually, the disparate impact theory applied. But from the first, the antidiscrimination principle was more contestable and more ambiguous in matters of sex than of race. The disparate treatment cases illustrate the difference. Within the area of racial discrimination Title VII works on an overwhelming, virtually conclusive presumption that disparate treatment is, and ought to be, illegal. The conviction undergirding the act (apart from issues of affirmative action) is that the relevant differ-

---

21. Many ordinances provided separate cars for women on trains during the nineteenth century, but the evidence suggests that these were offered at the request of women, who desired more genteel accommodations. These regulations (unlike those at issue in *Plessy*, discussed in Chapter 5) were imposed by company rule and were upheld against challenges of unreasonableness. See, e.g., *Bass v. The Chicago & Northwestern Railway Co.*, 36 Wis. 450 (1874). The regulation in *Bass* was subject to an examination for reasonableness because the railroad was considered a common carrier with a duty to take on all comers. Id. at 459. The court had no difficulty upholding the rule, noting that "in view of the crowds of men of all sorts and conditions and habits constantly traveling by railroad, it appears to us to be not only a reasonable regulation, but almost if not quite a humane duty, for railroad companies to appropriate a car of each passenger train primarily for women and men accompanying them." Id. at 460.

ences between white and black, for example, are so trivial that they should almost never be the grounds for explicit distinctions in treatment. There are of course extreme cases to test this proposition. A white man would not be a good undercover narcotics agent in a black neighborhood, and a black man could not work as a CIA agent trying to pass himself off as a Swedish businessman vacationing in London. But these extreme cases show how far from ordinary jobs one has to deviate in order to find a viable exception to the rule, once the basic antidiscrimination principle is accepted. On matters of race the dominant inquiry under the Civil Rights Act is instrumental: what steps are best able to root out all forms of disparate treatment at acceptable social cost? The hardest task facing the legal system is to determine whether facially legitimate and race-neutral reasons for passing over blacks in favor of whites are pretexts for some underlying bias.

The disparate treatment cases in regard to sex do not share that logic at all. Again the contrasting responses to the slogan "separate but equal" in race and sex cases hold the key. There are many instances in which employers have defended explicit sex classifications that were in common use before the statute and had been subject to no moral criticism. It is also worth recalling that the bona fide occupational qualification exception to the antidiscrimination principle applies to sex but not to race. It follows, therefore, that when we turn to the specific context of employment, we should expect to see some serious debate over the proper reach of the antidiscrimination principle. More concretely, we should also expect to see a shift in emphasis on matters of relative importance. In race cases few defendants have offered any justification for the disparate treatment of blacks and whites. The race cases thus tend to focus on motives and impact. But with sex cases the dominant question is whether these explicit differences in treatment are justifiable. Within the legal context the issue can arise in two separate ways.

First, disparate treatment issues emerge where outright discrimination between the two sexes is thought in some sense to be *justified*. Typically in these cases members of one sex are told in some particular context that they cannot have a job because they are less fit for it than members of the other sex. There is, of course, no argument that the discrimination works in any way to the immediate advantage of the excluded individuals. Rather, the claim is that the legitimate interests of the employer are so powerful that they justify discrimination that harms particular workers. Within the context of the Civil Rights Act this type of claim translates into the question of whether the employer may rely on some bona fide occupational qualification—the so-called BFOQ—as the ground for refusing to hire either men or women. The statutory recognition does not carry over to race, but is allowed for distinctions made on grounds of religion and national origin, a point of statutory language attributable not to accident but to design.[22] The disparate treatment issues in BFOQ cases can quickly shade into disparate impact cases when formally neutral standards on such matters as height and weight have disparate impact on men and women. The business necessity tests that have been used in race cases therefore come back to complement the discussion of BFOQ issues in ways that often make them difficult to distinguish.[23] The two kinds of cases are treated together in Chapter 14.

Second, the question of disparate treatment may also arise in attempts to sort out the question under Title VII of whether certain conduct is a form of prohibited discrimination at all. Thus the basic provision of the Civil Rights Act speaks of "discrimination against any individual." Certain employment practices are not discrimination *against* women because of their sex but rather discrimination *between* men and women that works ex ante, so it can be argued, to the long-term advantage of both sexes. The most significant cases that fall into this category are those that regulate the benefits that male and female employees receive with respect to pensions (the subject of Chapter 15) and pregnancy (the subject of Chapter 16).

Finally, there are some cases that are hard to classify as either disparate treatment or disparate impact, but which nonetheless play a key role. I refer here to the matter of sexual harassment, about which there has been some uncertainty as to whether such incidents qualify as discrimination at all. This issue is examined in Chapter 17. Finally, in Chapter 18 I look at the use of disparate impact analysis as it applies in sex discrimination cases to both job selection and wage differentials. I have omitted from this book any lengthy discussion of the issue of comparable worth—equal pay for work of equal value—given that claims of this sort, while

22. See Michael I. Sovern, *Legal Restraints on Racial Discrimination in Employment* 67–68 (1966): "The most heartening aspect of these provisions from the Negro's point of view is the limitation of section 703(e)(1)'s general exception to instances in which '*religion, sex, or national origin* is a bona fide occupational qualification . . . ' The omission of the words 'race' and 'color' means that a man's race is never 'a bona fide occupational qualification.' "

23. See the discussion of *International Union, UAW v. Johnson Controls, Inc.,* 111 Sup. Ct. 1196 (1991).

not rejected under Title VII, have received only limited encouragement,[24] and the subject has already benefitted from extensive ventilation and analysis elsewhere.[25] If Title VII is misconceived, so much more is the notion of comparable worth.

It bears stressing again at the outset, however, that the formidable complications of all these issues, including those raised by the idea of comparable worth, are largely obviated under a regime of freedom of contract, which allows contractual matchings to be made when and only when both parties to them regard them as beneficial. Any system that places limitations on voluntary exchanges is expensive to run, and, by forbidding some desired transaction, requires us all to forgo certain social benefits. The hard question that the Civil Rights Act raises in sex discrimination cases is identical to that raised by race discrimination cases: Does the antidiscrimination principle provide benefits that in any sense offset the costs that it imposes? I believe that an examination of the various types of commonly litigated cases shows that the law works only as a source of mischief for ordinary employers and workers in the marketplace, while providing enormous gains in influence, wealth, and arbitrary power for the lawyers and bureaucrats who run the system in both government and private industry. A preoccupation with the details of the present law does not commit one to its defense, but only furnishes additional reasons for its immediate repeal.

24. *County of Washington v. Gunther,* 421 U.S. 161 (1981).

25. For criticism of comparable worth, see Ellen Frankel Paul, *Equity and Gender: The Comparable Worth Debate* (1989), with its extensive bibliography at 134. See also Paul Weiler, "The Wages of Sex," 99 *Harv. L. Rev.* 1728 (1986), which is sympathetic with the program's aspirations but skeptical about its practical success. The chief objections to the notion of comparable worth are that (1) it is an administrative nightmare; (2) it substitutes bureaucratic determinations of value for market evaluations and thus takes no account of scarcity in determining wages; and (3) it leads to major imbalances in labor markets, of chronic oversupply where wages are artificially raised, and chronic shortages where they are depressed.

CHAPTER 14

Bona Fide Occupational Qualifications

Statutory Framework

The Civil Rights Act has, since its inception, contained an exception to the basic antidiscrimination norm that is directed to sex but not to race. The act reads:

> Notwithstanding any other provision of this title, (1) it shall not be an unlawful employment practice for an employer to hire and employ employees . . . on the basis of . . . religion, sex, or national origin in those certain instances where religion, sex, or national origin is a bona fide occupational qualification reasonably necessary to the normal operation of that particular business or enterprise.[1]

To the untutored this provision looks to be a substantial qualification of the basic nondiscrimination principle, one which recognizes that differences in sex (as well as religion and national origin) are matters that people could, and would, on some occasions at least, regard as relevant to private decision making. The exclusion of race from this section reflects the strong intuition that racial discrimination is always impermissible. The difficult question of statutory construction is to determine the extent to which the bona fide occupational qualification (BFOQ) authorizes a deviation from this categorical norm in sex discrimination cases. On this question the standard sources are the language and the legislative history. The evidence does not all speak with one voice, but taken as a whole it does not come close to supporting the exceedingly narrow construction placed

1. Civil Rights Act of 1964 §703(e).

on the exception by both the EEOC and the Supreme Court. Today the BFOQ exception is construed as narrowly as the business necessity defense developed in *Griggs* for disparate impact cases.[2] Recast into its modern EEOC and Supreme Court reformulation the section is read as though it said:

> Notwithstanding any other provision of this title, (1) it shall not be an unlawful employment practice for an employer to hire and employ employees . . . on the basis of their religion, sex, or national origins in those rare or extraordinary instances where discrimination on the basis of religion, sex, or national origin is a manifest business necessity for the economic survival or social authenticity of that particular business or enterprise.[3]

This rendition of the statute does considerable violence to the text, and it receives only modest support from the legislative history. If we look first at the statutory language, the BFOQ exception seems quite deferential to the employer. The term *occupational* appears to cover any work-related issue, including safety and health, just as it does under OSHA, the Occupational Safety and Health Act. The words *bona fide* are part of the statutory provision, and their normative import should not be concealed by the acronym BFOQ, which drains the words of their ordinary meaning. The notion of "good faith" stresses that the honest belief that a person's sex matters in the performance of any given position should be sufficient to incline the scales in the direction of the employer. The parallel is the standard of good faith that is used to judge, for example, whether a corporation director has discharged his duty of loyalty to the shareholders or whether an insurance company has fairly and honestly handled and settled claims for its insured. The dominant image created by the good faith standard envisions a situation in which alternate choices of action are characterized by pitfalls and uncertainty. The bona fide decision is one that conscientiously seeks to minimize the total costs of any such decision without favoring the interests of one's self over those of another person. A good faith judgment cannot be impugned solely on the ground that it turned out to be incorrect after the fact, or even on the ground that a reasonable person, faced with the same choices and armed with the same knowledge, might, or even would, have made a different (and better) decision. The driving idea behind the principle is that of a

---

2. See, e.g., *Chambers v. Omaha Girls Club, Inc.*, 840 F.2d 583 (8th Cir. 1988).

3. The reference to authenticity comes from the EEOC regulations cited at note 8.

subjective and honest desire to conform to the requirements of some fiduciary duty, that is, to treat the welfare of some other person as of equal, but not greater, importance than one's own welfare.[4] Good faith stands in opposition not only to a strict liability standard, where a defendant pays whenever he has made a mistake, however innocent, but also in opposition to a negligence standard, under which good faith errors are actionable if they are found to have been unreasonable. It is often a matter of genuine difficulty even to decide whether a good faith standard should be applicable in any particular context. But once that standard governs, its consequences are reasonably well understood in the legal literature and in ordinary practice.

The proper statutory construction of section 703(e) is somewhat more clouded, however, since the wholly subjective view associated with the idea of good faith occupational qualifications is itself qualified with the phrase "reasonably necessary for the normal operation of the particular business or enterprise." That phrase seems to demand some melding of objective and subjective standards as in self-defense cases where the defendant's privilege, in both tort and criminal law, is allowed only when force was exercised "reasonably and in good faith." It is easy to suggest reasons why this compromise standard might be adopted under Title VII. The BFOQ issue always places the interest of the employer (to maintain control over the ability to hire and fire) in conflict with its duty under law (to honor the statutory requirement). In this conflict of interest situation, a good faith standard is often made somewhat more stringent because it is known that the decision maker cannot be wholly dispassionate. Some extra check against abuse is required.

Viewed as a whole, then, the mixed statutory language does not set the linguistic threshold for scrutiny very high. The statutory phrase is "reasonably necessary"; it is not "absolutely necessary" or "totally indispensable," much less "business necessity." If "necessary and proper" can be construed to mean "appropriate" in the context of constitutional interpretation,[5] then "reasonably necessary" carries roughly the same weight

---

4. There is a parallel duty to settle in good faith on an insurer when there is a potential liability in excess of the policy limits. The basic point of the duty is to make certain that the insurer treats the insured's dollars with the same respect it gives its own, and thus makes the same decision that it would make if the policy contained no limits on coverage. See, e.g., *Crisci v. Security Insurance Co.*, 66 Cal.2d 425, 426 P.2d 173, 58 *Cal. Rptr.* 13 (1967). The conflict of interest rationales are set out with considerable clarity in *Merritt v. Reserve Insurance Co.*, 34 Cal. App. 3d 858, 110 *Cal. Rptr.* 511 (1973).

5. *M'Culloch v. Maryland*, 17 U.S. 316 (1819).

in the Civil Rights Act. The words "normal operation of the particular business or enterprise" reinforce the conclusion that the application of this exception, though not universal, is at least unremarkable. There is no hint in the statutory language that some rare or extraordinary circumstance is required for the exception to take hold. The statute on this point speaks of "certain instances," a phrase that has a calculated ambiguity: it seems very odd for a statute to make its own prediction about the number of cases that are expected to fall within its own explicit exception. But even here the phrase "certain instances" is not a synonym for "extraordinary" or "rare."

Finally, the same cautionary inference is fortified in yet another fashion. The statute speaks of sex, national origin, and religion in the same breath, and presumably applies the same standard of review to all three. It is easy to conceive of reasons why fairly ample protection would be given to demands for religious association, and the same standard carries over to sex cases as well. All in all, the best reading of the proviso is that its standard is somewhat stricter than good faith, but not by much. Perhaps the ubiquitous idea of "legitimate interest" or "good cause" captures the general spirit of the language as well as any other.

This basic analysis of the text receives some modest support from the legislative history. The critical passage comes from the Clark-Case memorandum on the statute:

> This exception is a limited right to discriminate on the basis of religion, sex or national origin where the reason for the discrimination is a bona fide occupational qualification. Examples of such legitimate discrimination would be the preference of a French restaurant for a French cook, the preference of a professional baseball team for male players, and the preference of a business which seeks the patronage of members of particular religious groups for a salesman of that religion.[6]

The passage does not suggest any unduly narrow construction of the section. But more to the point, perhaps, this list of examples is remarkably uninstructive for all hard cases. It contains only a single illustration that probes the sex qualification, one where the lines of sexual division have been absolute and indelible in practice. It does not begin to touch those cases in which members of one sex have the inside track but not an absolute advantage over members of the opposite sex, whether it be for

6. 110 *Cong. Rec.* 7213 (1964).

jobs as ditchdiggers or nurses. It does not state whether a firm that caters to women or men as customers and clients can choose sales representatives only of the same (or opposite) sex as the customers. It does not state whether the legitimate preference for coreligionists in sales positions carries over to cases of national origin or sex. It does not indicate whether the examples given cover the entire scope of the BFOQ or are only representative of how the section may be approached. Indeed, the memo gives no illustration of any context in which the use of sexual classification flunks the BFOQ test. Perhaps the most evident feature of the legislative history is that it suggests that the statute means what it says, and should therefore be construed in just that fashion, without any presumption one way or the other. To read the Clark-Case memorandum as supporting a narrow construction of the statute because it contains the phrase "limited exception" without further elaboration is to strip words from their immediate context. "Legitimate discrimination," also referred to in the passage, is a far less demanding standard than business necessity.

Nonetheless, the "business necessity" construction of the BFOQ provision has swept the boards, first in the circuit courts and later in the the Supreme Court.[7] The EEOC has followed suit and has issued regulations construing the BFOQ exception in the narrowest possible fashion. Although neither the statutory language nor the legislative history establishes any presumption about the application of the statute, the EEOC guidelines begin with this declaration: "The commission believes that the bona fide occupational qualification exception as to sex should be interpreted narrowly." There is no explanation why. The EEOC then elaborates its position with a set of examples that bear little relation to those used in the Clark-Case memorandum. "Labels—'Men's jobs' and 'Women's jobs'—tend to deny employment opportunities unnecessarily to one sex or the other," say the guidelines. The regulations interdict reliance on "assumptions about the comparative employment characteristics of women in general," and refuse to allow the use of "stereotyped characterizations" of the sexes, which include claims that women are less able than men "to assemble intricate equipment" or are "less capable of aggressive salesmanship." The regulations finally announce that the BFOQ cannot justify "the refusal to hire an individual because of the preferences of coworkers, the employer, clients or customers," subject to a very

7. See *International Union, UAW v. Johnson Controls,* 111 S. Ct. 1196 (1991); *Weeks v. Southern Bell Telephone & Telgraph Company,* 408 F.2d 228, 232 n.3 (1969); see also *Dothard v. Rawlinson,* 433 U.S. 321, 332 n.14 (1977).

narrow exception "necessary for the purpose of authenticity or genuineness," as with actors and actresses for male and female roles.[8]

This general position of the EEOC has been fully vindicated by the courts, which look with considerable hostility on any explicit sex classification, save perhaps those that are based on the need to accommodate the personal privacy of clients and customers in certain intimate situations involving bodily functions, hygiene, and the like.[9] Those situations apart, the received wisdom today is that applicant qualifications must always be determined on an individual basis, where the applicant is allowed to show first that she (or he) can meet some sex-neutral standard.

This narrow construction of the statute is consistent with the bureaucratic imperative to expand the scope of government power over private employment relations. In some instances the expansion of power is justified as a protection of freedom against paternalism, even though it substitutes public paternalism for private market decisions. In others the narrow rendering of the BFOQ is justified in terms that are overtly coercive: "Title VII in some cases prohibits employers from making judgments that are economically rational [because it] requires that such considerations be secondary to the perceived need to make employment decisions sex-blind, as well as color-blind."[10] Left unappreciated is the dangerous concentration of public power, and the magnitude of the private costs that must be borne in order to satisfy the "perceived" need for some uniform social standard on the role of sex-based criteria in private employment decisions.

This enormous expansion of government power need not have happened. It surely would not have happened had Title VII never been passed. But even under its provisions the proper approach is (or should have been) to allow the employer to demonstrate by a preponderance of evidence that the use of the sex test reduces costs or increases benefits derived from the employment relation by some substantial amount. De minimis alterations would not be sufficient, and with all reasonableness tests there would a genuine gray area in the middle. No finer precision is attainable, given that the statute contains both the "bona fide" and "reasonably necessary" language.

---

8. 29 C.F.R. §1604.2 (1989).

9. See at note 36 the discussion of *Torres v. Wisconsin Dept. of Health and Social Sciences*, 859 F.2d 1523 (7th Cir. 1988) (en banc).

10. "Developments in the Law: Employment Discrimination and Title VII of the Civil Rights Act of 1964," 84 *Harv. L. Rev.* 1109, 1174–75 (1971).

The sensible application of that statutory test is, in my view, distinctly a second-best solution. The best solution would recognize that employers and employees have all necessary incentives to fix the appropriate employment standards without any antidiscrimination statute at all. There are no bargaining obstacles between the parties or externalities imposed on strangers. There is no market failure to counteract, for the stubborn and unprincipled unwillingness of a firm to hire either males or females only creates a built-in opportunity for new rivals to enter the market with a cost advantage.[11] Ideally no public justification of relevance should *ever* have to be made either to the EEOC or the courts. But once the courts have taken us down the path of business necessity, the social losses generated by the strict scrutiny of BFOQ claims in all likelihood hurt men and women alike.

To some people these losses may be justified by the need for a monolithic social determination to root out sex differences in employment; and perhaps this is a goal that people support in the round even as they oppose it in particular cases. Yet that supposed benefit may be the greatest cost of all, for it shows how quickly well-intentioned desires can turn into authoritarian commands on hard questions on which informed women and men of good faith can and do have violent disagreements. These disputes are best resolved not by instigating pitched legislative battles but by letting people and firms go their separate ways. Central planning does no better in dealing with sex differences than in dealing with any other issue of labor allocation. These restrictions are not confined only to rights of property and contract, for the enforcement of these norms imposes some restriction on how firms may advertise and, more subtly, on what they may think and say about sex differences and performance without fear of liability. The remorseless elimination of the BFOQ defense shows the allure of authoritarian thinking that seems inseparable from public enforcement of any antidiscrimination norm.

In the discussion of principle the question of statutory construction always assumes a back seat. The more fundamental questions go to what the law should provide. In order to analyze both how a BFOQ might work and why neither it nor the basic provisions of Title VII are needed, I shall consider three types of problems that arise under the current interpretation of the BFOQ. The first problem concerns cost differentials. The second asks whether firms should be allowed to take into account the preferences of customers, suppliers, or co-workers. The

11. See Chapters 2 and 3. A parallel case is made in Fuchs, *Women's Quest,* at 35–38.

third involves the interaction between the BFOQ and asserted health justifications for explicit discrimination between male and female employees.

Legitimate Cost Differentials

Voluntarily Adopted Work Rules

Let us begin with work rules adopted voluntarily by firms before the passage of Title VII which were designed to reduce the total set of employer costs, of which wage payments were only one albeit significant part. For example, many employers had rules that restricted women from certain positions that required them to lift heavy objects, weighing, say, over fifty pounds, or to engage in strenuous physical activity. In a world of freedom of contract these terms are as valid as any other. The employer may choose to cut itself off from a certain source of labor. If (but only if) its decision is erroneous, the firm will have to pay the price, since other firms will ignore those self-imposed restrictions and be able to provide goods and services at lower cost. The mechanisms of self-correction are powerful, and the demands on the courts are slight. With freedom of contract, therefore, the legal system judges only those contractual offers that are made and accepted. Thereafter, competition within the economic system, and not government fiat, determines which hiring strategy is superior.

Within the market setting we should expect some sex-specific classifications to endure. The obvious line of defense is that sex-based limitations work at low cost to distinguish those workers who are likely to be injured on the job from those who are not. The fit between the rule and its objective is, of course, not perfect, but the positive correlation is still better than random association. Sex classifications, at least the ones that endure, thus operate like other types of tests or qualifications by providing some useful information for making decisions at reasonable cost. As long as they generate net improvements, they will be used—at least by some firms some of the time.

Under Title VII, however, any reliance on market judgment and self-correction is misplaced, for now there has to be some "objective" showing of the relation of the explicit requirement to the job at hand. The attack on these rough-and-ready classifications is familiar: individual case-by-case judgments about strength are possible, and should therefore be preferred to broad classifications, which may or may not be accurate. But the same reply should be decisive: the object of the firm is not to minimize the costs of error alone, which perfect individuation might do, but to minimize the sum of the twin costs of error and administration. At this point two sets of considerations enter. First, the case-by-case analysis may be less accurate than the per se rule. If only a small percentage of men or women qualify for a certain job, the tests may not be able to identify them. If, for example, under a perfect test 95 out of 100 qualifiers would be women, a test that has a 10 percent error rate is inferior to the per se rule that says hire only women, for the per se rule makes only 5 percent errors. The case-by-case rule, even if it appoints 5 men and 95 women, may cut the wrong 5 women and hire the wrong 5 men. The error costs may not be reduced to an acceptable rate even if the level of precaution taken is very high. The ideal solution to finding the *right* 5 men and the *right* 95 women is unattainable in a world with positive transaction costs.

Second, the costs of administration are relevant to any overall calculation. The use of sex-based rules of thumb is consistent with minimizing the sum of administrative and error costs, so the firm that adopts the so-called stereotype (read: accurate statistical generalization) may well flourish in competition with a firm that chooses to abandon it in favor of tests that are perhaps both more costly and less reliable. In principle, employers should easily be able to demonstrate that case-by-case individuation costs a good deal of money but has little predictive power. After all, the EEOC is the leading skeptic on facially neutral job-related standards for all forms of testing. The relevant trade-off, moreover, is sufficiently pervasive that it seems pointless to require much proof in individual cases. Per se rules are always cheaper to design and administer than complex balancing tests.

The attack on the BFOQ exception does not rest, however, solely on the insufficient ground that sex classifications are imperfect. In addition, there have been arguments based on individual liberty—that the weight and work restrictions, for example, represent a misguided form of paternalism. Perhaps the most influential statement of that position is found in the well-known decision of *Weeks v. Southern Bell Telephone & Telegraph Co.*,[12] where just such weight requirements for a telephone switchman were held not to fall within the BFOQ exception:

12. 408 F.2d 228 (5th Cir. 1969).

Title VII rejects just this type of romantic paternalism as unduly Victorian and instead vests individual women with the power to decide whether or not to take on unromantic tasks. Men have always had the right to determine whether the incremental increase in remuneration for strenuous, dangerous, obnoxious, boring or unromantic tasks is worth the candle. The promise of Title VII is that women are now to be on equal footing.[13]

Thus the language of freedom of choice is pressed into service to justify the narrow construction given to the BFOQ exception. Rhetorically *Weeks* appeals to the market-enforcing impetus behind the antidiscrimination acts by positing an outcome that increases the scope of individual choice and gives women parity in terms of the "rights" long held and enjoyed by men. On matters of contracting choice, Title VII, we are told, enacts Mr. Herbert Spencer's Social Statics after all.

Yet the antipaternalist defense of Title VII is wrong in one vital respect. The ability of men to undertake strenuous, risky, or boring work has always been contingent on the willingness of an employer, male or female, corporate or individual, to offer that work to them. There is nothing paternalistic about a legal rule that says that workers may not take risks for employers who do not wish to hire them or to provide them with the demanded compensation. The market baseline made it perfectly clear that risk-preferring men could not foist themselves on employers, and the same rule does, and should, apply to women now that the nineteenth-century limitations on contractual capacity have happily been lifted. The equal footing of men and women in a marketplace gives both groups the right to *offer* their labor to the highest bidder on whatever terms and conditions they choose. It does not give either group the right to conscript employers to provide them with the identical wages and positions that are offered to members of the opposite sex, regardless of the losses to those employers. *Weeks* did not strike down legally imposed barriers to entry that prevent women from competing with men. It addressed only the case of a private employer who chose not to hire for reasons it found sufficient.

Title VII, of course, is the antithesis of the freedom of contract statute that *Weeks* makes it out to be. The real issue is not whether the state should ban certain employment as dangerous or unfit for women. Rather, it is whether there is some good reason, some BFOQ,

13. Id. at 236.

why an employer might not want to hire a female applicant on account of her sex. In *Weeks* the obvious explanation might be that the natural differences between men and women bulk large not only in matters of physical strength but also in issues of temperament, deportment, and attitude. That a given physical task in general imposes a heavier toll on women than on men is a statistical truth, which is not overridden by the common exceptions of powerful women and frail men that we all encounter in everyday life. But why, it might be asked, should the employer care if the woman is prepared to take the risk in the ways *Weeks* so eloquently describes? It is her life, her backache, and therefore her loss.

This view of the employment relationship is wholly myopic. The differences in strength may be positively correlated with differences in performance, in which the employer has a vital interest. Employer profits will be improved if any simple test is accurate enough in the broad run of cases to sort workers into categories of high and low risk. The positive correlation is not, of course, perfect, but it is far better than any random selection, and it may well be better than any individuating tests that could be administered to determine whether a particular woman has sufficient strength and stamina to perform a particular job. (The test, whether for men or women, may be flawed because it fails to capture endurance, say, or proneness to injury from prolonged work.)

Within the context of the original BFOQ formula, the employer could not simply assert that the differential mattered and prevail on good faith alone. Some reasonableness component would still call for a modest empirical showing—one thinks of an "intermediate scrutiny" standard— that suggests less efficient work by women as a class for the job at hand. If, therefore, there is any performance or cost differential between men and women, the BFOQ is reasonably necessary to the normal operation of the enterprise. When the Robinson-Patman Act imposes a ban on price discrimination for the sale of consumer products, that ban is not absolute but is subject to an exception by which the firm can show that it must lower prices to meet competition or raise prices to cover additional costs.[14] Rightly understood, the BFOQ carries over that same type of exception to a general antidiscrimination norm in labor markets, for if

---

14. See 15 U.S.C. §13(a) (1982). In *Los Angeles Dept. of Water & Power v. Manhart*, 435 U.S. 702, 717, n.31 (1978), Justice John Paul Stephens notes that under the Robinson-Patman Act "proof of cost differences justifies otherwise illegal price discrimination; it does

"reasonably necessary" does not refer to costs, it does not refer to anything at all, and the exception is empty.

The rhetoric in *Weeks* about freedom of choice over accidents hearkens back to the nineteenth-century law of the fellow servant rule (whereby an employee could not sue an employer for the negligence of a co-worker), contributory negligence, and assumption of risk. With some modification these doctrines can, I believe, be defended on their own terms for workplace accidents. In the absence of external harms to third parties, employers and employees will bargain to optimum agreements, which may—but need not—adopt just these rules.[15] But those market arrangements have been rejected historically by legislatures and judges who believed that individual workers were incapable of making intelligent choices about risk because of either imperfect information, limited competence, or superior employer bargaining power. In consequence, workers' compensation programs for accidents "arising out of and in the course of employment" were introduced on a mandatory basis in the first part of this century.[16]

In order to understand the workplace situation, then, it is necessary to understand the interaction of two systems of regulation—workers' compensation and Title VII—on an employer who has consented to neither. Suppose (as happens to be the case) that it turns out that the rate of accidents for women in certain dangerous lines of employment (for example, telephone line repair) is far higher than it is for men. In a market system the differential rate will lead employers to offer a lower wage to women workers on the line than to men, even if other aspects of productivity are undiminished when accident rates increase—itself a doubtful assumption. Given that the workers' compensation system does not provide full compensation for job-related injuries—that is, compensation that renders workers indifferent to being injured or not—the employer must pay the worker a wage premium to offset any uncompensated risk still borne by him or her. Thus one source estimates that the total costs to employers from workers' compensation benefits was about $11.8 billion in 1980, yet the risk premium in wages, attributable to uncompensated

---

not negate the existence of discrimination itself." See, generally, *Federal Trade Commission v. Morton Salt Co.,* 334 U.S. 37 (1948).

15. See Richard A. Epstein, "The Historical Origins and Economic Structure of the Workers' Compensation Law," 16 *Ga. L. Rev.* 775 (1982).

16. See, generally, *New York Central R.R. Co. v. White,* 243 U.S. 188 (1917), for a discussion of the system in a case upholding its constitutionality.

losses, was about $69 billion dollars, a sixfold difference.[17] The situation is unstable. Women workers will require an even larger risk premium to take dangerous jobs because they are subject to a greater risk of injury. Their wage demands will rise. But employers, conscious of the additional workers' compensation premium they incur by hiring women, will be prepared to offer only a low wage, at least in the absence of an explicit government subsidy. If the shifts in both supply and demand are combined, women workers will have to deduct a larger self-insurance premium from a smaller take-home wage to determine their total compensation package. There will of course be some women who have private knowledge that their expected rate of risk is lower than for the class, and they may be willing to accept these dangerous jobs. But even they will have to persuade the employer that its costs will not increase by providing assurances that they are not at any extra risk for injury. In this setting, however, the (Bayesian) employer is likely to trust its own baseline estimate of accident rates more than the prospective employee's, and its assessment may indeed be correct in light of its broader experiential base.

Taking the situation as a whole, we find that there are powerful constraints on both the demand and the supply side of the market. On balance there will not be very many female telephone line repair workers, given this one-two punch. The market itself will reach a stable and efficient equilibrium with mainly male employees, as most women will compete in other markets where they are not subject to such disabilities, and may in fact have powerful advantages over men. Unless Title VII is expanded in totalitarian fashion to impose *duties* on individual women to work at jobs they do not want to take, the imbalance in work force composition in the regulated marketplace should persist.

The question posed by Title VII is whether the law should interfere with the pattern that emerges of male-dominated employment in certain occupations even with workers' compensation statutes in place. The employer could argue that the wage differential is both bona fide and reasonably necessary for the operation of the business. In essence the argument is that there are cost-justified reasons for differential wages or hiring preferences in order to equalize the employer's returns from two

---

17. See W. Kip Viscusi, *Risk by Choice: Regulating Health and Safety in the Workplace* 44 (1983). OSHA fines were about one-three thousandth of the risk premium, or $23 million, although compliance costs are far higher. See Ann P. Bartel and Lacy Glenn Thomas, "Direct and Indirect Effects of Regulation: A New Look at OSHA's Impact," 28 *J.L. & Econ.* 1 (1985).

different classes of labor. The sex-based differences do not give proof of a market dominated by dark and irrational forces, for the wages offered provide powerful and accurate signals as to the appropriateness of certain groups for certain jobs. The employer can show a difference in its costs that justifies the discrimination in employment policy (in the same way that a woman is justified in not taking a job that is riskier for her than it is for a man). In all likelihood that same line of argument would *not* be open to ordinary office work, where any differential in risk of injury between men and women (if it exists at all in either direction) is probably too small to worry about. This sensible reading of the exception does not serve as a mask for what Title VII condemns as idle bigotry or *false* stereotypes about women or men. It captures relevant and important economic information derivable from biological and social differences that long antedate the employment relation. The state does not use this information on sex differences to dictate employment patterns. We all use this information to understand why the differences appear and persist.

Arguments of this sort have never gotten to first base under the BFOQ exception. The EEOC has steadfastly rejected them explicitly from the outset, and the issue has not been renewed in judicial decisions. The bottom line, therefore, is that under Title VII employers are forced to pay the same wage and compensation packages to men and women, a requirement that often results in their making a profit on the one and a loss on the other. The principle is sex neutral only in that it requires the cross-subsidization of women by men in some jobs with the same relentless insistence that it requires cross-subsidization by women of men in other jobs. Within certain job categories, however, this equalization provision does not have its intended results. Thus, a rule that bans discrimination in heavy labor does not lead women to flock to such jobs, since any fixed wage and workers' compensation package does not equalize total *net* return to the worker, given differential injury rates. But as the levels of awards in workers' compensation increase, as they have done since 1964,[18] the number of women who want to take advantage of Title VII has increased modestly, since employers must bear a growing fraction of the residual costs.

The issue can be placed in a somewhat broader perspective. The antidiscrimination statute imposes an implicit tax that employers will try to resist, an observation that explains much of the foot-dragging

18. See, generally, Arthur Larson, *Workmen's Compensation Law*, vol. 2 (1987), for exhaustive compilations of benefit levels and rules.

evasions and ill-concealed hostility that develop when Title VII is invoked to insert women into, say, heavy manufacturing or the construction industry. A law would be regarded as both unfair and inefficient if it enabled a person to make a hapless buyer pay $100 for a good that he values at only $50. The same principle applies when Title VII coerces employers into hiring workers worth on net $50 for $100 in wages. The losing contract forced on an employer by Title VII operates as the thin edge of the wedge for a regime of inefficient state confiscation. Given the evident size of the displacement, the overall efficiency losses are substantial. The total number of employment opportunities for both men and women necessarily *shrinks* as a result of the reduced level of economic activity. The de facto obliteration of the BFOQ requirement thus works synergistically with the mistaken mandatory features of the workers' compensation statute by denying the employer any sensible leeway in selecting workers whose anticipated accident rates are lower than other applicants'.

Weeks, then, badly misfires when it seeks to justify public coercion on antipaternalistic grounds. In practice the case sanctions a massive interference with market forces. Nonetheless, the decision has been widely accepted not only for determining workers' compensation costs but also for setting other costs that may be higher for women than for men or vice versa—for example, when new facilities have to be provided in the switch from a single-sex to a dual-sex work force. As one textbook writer in the field has written: "The thrust of the BFOQ defense is on the inability of an employee to perform. Additional costs cannot be a defense because they do not affect an employee's performance."[19] The law in effect ignores the total level of employer benefit and the total level of employer cost. Title VII systematically disregards those factors most relevant to the operation of a sensible market.

Protective Government Regulations

The foregoing arguments suggest that a far more favorable response should be given when the antipaternalistic impetus of Title VII is directed toward state legislation that provides women with legal protection that is not similarly applied to men. Here the EEOC has urged, and the courts have agreed with, the basic proposition that these state laws should be struck down under the supremacy clause of the Constitution, which

19. Mack A. Player, *Employment Discrimination Law* 288 (1988).

requires state laws to yield to inconsistent federal laws.[20] In this context Title VII does adopt a freedom of contract approach, and in so doing parallels the general reevaluation of protective legislation directed exclusively toward women. During the first part of the twentieth century, legislation of this sort was regarded as the vanguard of enlightened social reform. Thus the decision of the Supreme Court in *Muller v. Oregon,*[21] sustaining the constitutionality of a maximum hours statute for women, was welcomed at the time as an enlightened exception to the general doctrine of *Lochner v. New York,*[22] which generally banned legislation of that sort in occupations dominated by men. Indeed, the 1937 breakthrough that undid the *Lochner* decision—*West Coast Hotel v. Parrish*[23]—upheld a minimum wage statute applicable to women only on the ground that the equal protection clause of the Constitution did not extend to sex discrimination. The judicial view of the legislative process was generally benign, so the stated beneficiaries of the statutory scheme—women—were mistakenly regarded, perhaps conclusively, as its real beneficiaries.

The advent of Title VII brought an overdue change in the area of protective legislation. In ways that are consonant with one strand of modern feminist thought,[24] "protective" legislation is (rightly) viewed with deep suspicion. The political process is no longer regarded as benign. Those statutes are now understood for what they really are: efforts that, under the guise of romantic paternalism, exclude women from competing with men in certain lines of work. The change in the relevant constitutional doctrine is so vast that any maximum hour or minimum wage statute that applies to women only has become unconstitutional without much fanfare or ado.[25] Today's equal protection clause applies some genuine level of scrutiny to any explicit sex-based government distinction.

Ironically, however, just as one level of false protection was unmasked at the constitutional level, a second one was reimposed under Title VII. By failing to distinguish between state restrictions on hiring by sex and

---

20. See *Rosenfeld v. Southern Pacific Company,* 444 F.2d 1219 (9th Cir. 1971).

21. 208 U.S. 412 (1908).

22. 198 U.S. 45 (1905), discussed in Chapter 5.

23. 300 U.S. 379 (1937).

24. See Sylvia A. Law, "Rethinking Sex and the Constitution," 132 *U. Pa. L. Rev.* 955 (1984).

25. See, e.g., *Wengler v. Druggists Mutual Ins. Co.,* 446 U.S. 142 (1980) (striking down law that presumed dependence of wife, but not husband, in workers' compensation context).

private decisions not to hire women, Title VII mandates the same form of "protective" interference practiced by sex-specific state laws that is so readily condemned today. If women workers impose higher costs on the firm than men, they will not be hired voluntarily for wages equal to those paid to male workers, and vice versa. But with regard to these hiring choices, there is no justification for either public concern or legal regulation. Women should be able to compete for positions by accepting lower wages than men.

Customer Preferences and Forgone Benefits

The BFOQ serves double duty. In addition to its potential application to the cost side of the equation, it also has relevance to the benefit side: that is, may the employer rely on the BFOQ to offer men and women different wages and terms of employment when the benefits they provide to the employer differ systematically by sex? A ski resort I visited proudly advertised that it provided male or female instructors at the preference of the customer. Yet any employer that allows women skiers to match themselves with women instructors appears to be in flat violation of Title VII, at least as construed by the EEOC, whose guidelines provide in no uncertain terms that employers cannot take into account "the preferences of coworkers, the employer, clients or customers," save in exceptionally rare cases.[26] Its position is that the only question that matters is the ability to perform a particular job, taken in isolation from the environment in which the work is done, or the value of the performance tendered. In a sense its view is almost preordained. If the employer is not permitted to take into account the collateral costs of hiring certain classes of employees (such as accident or life insurance), there is no particular reason to allow it to take into account preferences of customers or coworkers either. "Reasonably necessary for the normal operation of the business" hardly gives a preferred status to dealing with customers as opposed to controlling internal costs. Indeed, in light of *Weeks* the result here is in a sense inexorable. Once the preferences of other people are taken into account, the BFOQ exception becomes large enough to engulf Title VII's prohibition against sex discrimination, for many, if not all, employers can use this argument to take refuge in the BFOQ and thus gut Title VII's prohibition against sex discrimination.

This argument is, however, a two-edged sword. If the number of cases

26. 29 C.F.R. §1604.2(a)(iii) (1989).

that properly falls within this exception is large, then the basic prohibition against sex-based discrimination is flawed and should be repealed, precisely because there are widely shared social beliefs that differences between the sexes do matter in all sorts of ways. Employers are far more responsive to customer demands than the defenders of the "contract of adhesion" view of the world will admit. But arguments based on the efficiency of market mechanisms are too powerful for interpreting the BFOQ exception, in light of the central purpose of Title VII. Rather, the criticism of the EEOC guidelines in the context of the statute takes another form. Not being able to take customers' and co-workers' preferences into account is wholly inconsistent with the effort to find a middle ground which is characteristic of any statute that relies on the twin tests of "bona fide" and "reasonably necessary." The task, therefore, is to try to find some way in which to distinguish between the informed and honest preferences of the vast majority of well-meaning people and the intensely irrational or invidious preferences of the bigoted few. It is in essence a matter of articulating an objective standard to determine which subjective preferences should prevail.

At this point the inquiry becomes cautious and factually dense. It is very hard to formulate any a priori judgment as to the types of subjective preferences that should be vindicated or the frequency of their occurrence. Instead, the employer should be allowed to introduce proof of the pervasive nature of a given practice, or of the unsuccessful efforts to replace it with a sex-blind policy. Evidence from the EEOC could be used to show that other firms have succeeded without relying on the sex-based practice, or that other low-cost precautions, such as good marketing programs, can reduce the level of consumer dissatisfaction. Of course, all this trouble could be avoided by repealing Title VII. But the problems are only magnified by its remorseless application.

The death knell for this interpretive attitude came early in the litigation under Title VII. The case that best illustrates the now dominant approach is *Diaz v. Pan American World Airways, Inc.*,[27] where the Court of Appeals, in reversing the decision of the district court,[28] held that Pan Am could not justify its practice of hiring only female cabin attendants under the BFOQ exception to the basic statute. The attack against the practice was organized both by the AFL-CIO and the EEOC, so the case should be regarded as an institutional lawsuit, replete with long-term strategic goals.

27. 442 F.2d 385 (5th Cir. 1971).
28. *Diaz v. Pan American World Airways, Inc.*, 311 Supp. 559 (1970).

Pan Am justified its approach by claiming, and the district court found, that female attendants had higher performance ratings than male attendants, and seemed better able to reassure passengers who were anxious about flying. In addition, passengers "overwhelmingly preferred" being served by stewardesses. Pan Am bolstered its evidence with the testimony of a psychiatric witness who stated that the emotional needs of all passengers were better attended to by women than by men. The airline then set out the difficulties for the firm in trying to run a hiring process for both men and women. The plaintiffs, the EEOC, and the AFL-CIO introduced *no* evidence.

The prior decision was reversed on the law because the court applied "a business *necessity* test, not a business *convenience* test."[29] In a sense the extension of the business necessity test into the area of BFOQ was inevitable, for if evidence of business necessity is required to justify disparate impact under formally neutral rules, how could less be required where there was an explicit sex classification? It is not surprising, therefore, that Judge Elbert Tuttle made this explicit linkage between *Griggs* and the BFOQ problem.[30] He then gave his account of how to run an airline:

Discrimination based on sex is valid only when the *essence* of the business operation would be undermined by not hiring members of one sex exclusively.

The primary function of an airline is to transport passengers safely from one point to another. While a pleasant environment, enhanced by the obvious cosmetic effect that female stewardesses provide as well as, according to the finding of the trial court, their apparent ability to perform the non-mechanical functions of the job in a more effective manner than most men, may all be important, they are tangential to the essence of the business involved. No one has suggested that having male stewards will so seriously affect the operation of an airline as to jeopardize or

---

29. *Diaz,* 442 F.2d at 388.

30. Id. *Griggs,* decided earlier that year, was cited with approval in support of the proposition that the EEOC interpretation was entitled to "great deference." 442 F.2d at 389. Note that several years later, in *Dothard v. Rawlinson,* 433 U.S. 321 (1977), the Supreme Court held that disparate impact theories applied in sex discrimination cases. It thus used the business necessity test to invalidate minimum height and weight restrictions for prison guards on a showing that a minimum height of five feet, two inches, excluded about 33 percent of the pool of eligible women from applying but only 1 percent of the men, and a minimum weight requirement of 120 pounds excluded about 40 percent of the women and again only 1 percent of the men.

even minimize its ability to provide safe transportation from one place to another. Indeed the record discloses that many airlines including Pan Am have utilized both men and women flight cabin attendants in the past and Pan Am, even at the time of this suit, has 283 male stewards employed on some of its foreign flights.[31]

The error in his argument is a familiar one. Contracts do not have "essences." They have multiple terms and dimensions, and sensible contracting requires parties to make trade-offs at the margin of these many distinct dimensions. The choice that customers make between airlines depends not only on safety (a factor that may differ by only a tiny degree among the major carriers) but also on price, schedule, ground service, food, and of course in-flight service. Good airline executives could easily expand the list. It is quite clear that if the airlines decided to cartelize the market on any or all of the non–safety-related issues, they would not be able to defend themselves on the ground that their actions did not go to the "essence" of the contract since they still competed on safety. They would rightly be met with the response that vital markets require vigorous competition on all dimensions of consumer service. The judgment in *Diaz* shows once again how business understandings are sacrificed in order to ease the expansion of government innovation. Under the guise of mere regulation, the dominant question in Title VII cases is: Who runs a business, its management or the courts? The skewed view that the Fifth Circuit took of the "tangential" aspects of the airline business points the royal road to inefficiency.

It is possible, moreover, actually to look at the evidence in question and see what it establishes. Pan Am's wish to introduce its own surveys need not legitimate its decision under the statute. It is surely open for the plaintiffs to show that the intensity of the preferences stated in the Pan Am surveys was weak, and that the responses to the changes in business patterns would group at the de minimis level. What people say on surveys may not be the best guide to the way they will respond in practice when they have to pay price differentials to honor their preferences. Nonetheless, Pan Am may have been right (although it is doubtful that any airline today would collect the data needed to make an informed judgment). Its willingness to fight the case perhaps reflected its strong conviction that customers respond to differences in services, and that it needs hiring flexibility to serve its markets efficiently. The per se rule invalidation of the

---

31. *Diaz,* 442 F.2d at 388 (emphasis in original).

distinction is inappropriate, given the reasonableness inquiry that the statute invites.

The outcome in *Diaz* could be defended on the ground that the hiring restriction in question is neither important nor harmful to the business because it is imposed not only on Pan Am but also on all of its competitors. Therefore, as long as the playing field remains level, the argument goes, we can have the benefits of government regulation without any cost to competition within the industry. But the argument rests on misplaced optimism.

First, as within industries, the initial argument is one that should be familiar to defenders of Title VII: the formally neutral rule may have a disparate impact on the firms that are subject to it. If, say, Pan Am had built its claims to service around an all-female flight attendant staff, it would be harder hit than a rival airline that had already made extensive use of male flight attendants. So relative costs would always change, unless all firms had been identically situated prior to the regulation—an unlikely prospect.

Second, even if all firms within the industry were identically situated, the regulation would result in shifts of consumer demand between market sectors. The imposition of the sex-blind flight attendant rule acts as an implicit tax on the airlines. Slightly less desirable service at the same price is scarcely distinguishable from a small increase in the price of a ticket with service quality held constant. Unless demand is perfectly inelastic (that is, it in no way responds to changes in price), it follows that some persons who might otherwise choose to fly will cancel or postpone their trips, reduce the frequency of their travel, change their destination or time of departure, or choose to drive their cars or take the bus. (And if demand is perfectly inelastic, the social loss is measured by the decline in net consumer satisfaction.) It is highly unlikely that a shift in cost structure will exert no influence on primary conduct.

Taken to its extreme, the argument that treats proportionate regulations as benign must hold that there is less of a threat to firms within an industry from a 100 percent tax than there is from a differential tax, which hits some firms with a 1 percent levy and others with a 2 percent levy. Yet all firms would prefer to be hit with a discriminatory 2 percent tax than a nondiscriminatory 100 percent tax. The relationship between explicit discrimination and facial neutrality is thus more complex than is commonly understood. The explicit distinction calls out for justification, and thus is easily detected and rectified. The mischief that *may* be caused by formally neutral rules is far more difficult to expose precisely because there is no convenient handle that allows for judicial review, and permits one to distinguish between those neutral rules (for example, flat taxes on income) that are justified and those that create genuine resource dislocations. Only if one knows the domain of the neutral rule, and works through the probable effects of a formally neutral rule on overall output, can one decide whether or not the rule leads to a social improvement. But formal neutrality in and of itself is consistent with both prudent and unwise government interventions.

The case for uniform government intervention, then, cannot be made by showing that it causes no economic harm. But it may be justified in the alternative by the idea that the job of a business is to ignore if not mold the preferences of its customers to accord with the general views of Title VII. Indeed, Title VII is often justified because of its capacity to alter preferences.[32] The basic idea, often associated with the notion of "adaptive" or "endogenous" preferences, is that once the legal rule changes, people learn to prefer the new situation to the one that displaced it. If these preference shifts do take place, there is no real cost in social utility. Under the usual analysis of regulation, preferences are treated as if they were constant, so the only relevant questions involve the behavioral shifts along *existing* supply or demand curves. The social loss thus comes from the forgone trades that would have worked to the mutual benefit of buyers and sellers. The theory of exogenous preferences says in essence that the demand curves *as a whole* shift upward and to the right, or the supply curves downward and to the left, as buyers and sellers change their world view (that is, the demand and supply schedules) instead of merely responding to the incentives generated by the regulatory regime. If that fundamental shift in preferences left markets in perfect equilibrium, no trades would be forgone, and the regulation could be justified on the ground that it allowed people to achieve higher (or equal) levels of satisfaction through coercion than they could obtain otherwise. It is yet another modern refinement on the bad old idea that people can be forced to be free and profit from the experience.

Alternatively it could be argued that these individual preferences may not be transformed by the law but should nonetheless be ignored by it. Only "legitimate" preferences count; all others should be disregarded.

---

32. See Cass R. Sunstein, "Legal Interference with Private Preferences," 53 *U. Chi. L. Rev.* 1135 (1986); Jon Elster, *Sour Grapes: Studies in the Subversion of Rationality* (1983). I have criticized these two works in Richard A. Epstein, "Two Conceptions of Civil Rights," 8 *Soc. Phil. & Pol.* 38 (1991).

The ambition thus becomes far broader than it is under the traditional common law approach, which sought only to identify a perimeter of rights within which individuals could exercise their preferences as they saw fit. Now the state must decide *which* private preferences it will ignore in formulating social policy. Every political system makes such decisions to the extent that it restrains the use of force, but it does so on the ground that the general exercise of force leads to the ruin of all concerned. The collective suppression of force is meant to expand the domain of private preferences, not to classify some as legitimate and others as not. In the context of consensual contracts it is possible for persons to go their separate ways if they cannot agree to work together, so the imposition of public force requires a far higher degree of justification. Given the efficiency losses (shared by all) of antidiscrimination rules, very powerful justifications have to be found for one group to announce that another group's preferences just do not matter and they will be forced to do business with others on terms they find disadvantageous. None of substance is offered.

The dangers of rigid political orthodoxy are easily overlooked when we concern ourselves with the psychological determinants of behavior. In First Amendment law the dominant view is that as many different forms of expression as possible should be allowed into the marketplace so that no single agency becomes endowed with the power to determine truth or mold preferences for us all. Orthodoxy is a danger, not a goal. As the protracted struggle over the 1989 flag-burning case proved, the greater the offensiveness of the conduct, the greater its constitutional protection.[33] Yet the dangers of government tyranny are systematically underestimated when the statute tells a firm that it cannot provide its customers with the service they want and instead tells the customers to like the services that are provided. There is no assurance that the power in question will be turned to good ends instead of evil ones, nor is there any way to refute the argument that the transformation of preferences has been a success once the coercion has been applied. One trembles at the thought that the argument for adaptive or endogenous preferences could be enlisted to justify Jim Crow laws, to which in principle it is equally applicable.

No one can deny, or should want to deny, that preferences shift as a result of new opportunities and new demands. Changes in information are changes in opportunities, and hence should be understood as changes in costs, at least for preferences for particular goods as opposed to prefer-

33. See, e.g., *Texas v. Johnson*, 491 U.S. 397 (1989).

ences for underlying happiness and welfare, where natural and biological factors impose powerful constraints. But the issue is not whether preferences are malleable; rather it is *who* should mold them. With markets, the preferences of any single person are influenced by many different individuals, none of whom wields coercive power. Under Title VII, the staffing decisions at the EEOC, with its own heavy institutional biases, mold preferences.

The old joke about preferences is still applicable, and still pointed:

Comrade I: Think of the Revolution. When it comes we shall all eat strawberries.
Comrade II: But I don't like strawberries.
Comrade I: Come the Revolution, you'll like strawberries.

It may well be that the preference of most passengers for female flight attendants is outdated. It may be that the changes in social tastes since 1964, or since 1970, are so vast that Pan Am's practices would now be regarded as laughable by the vast majority of passengers that the airlines serve. But it is a risky business indeed to argue that the government should take it upon itself to hasten the day when these attitudes are shared by the public at large. Even if the government has by chance anticipated a shift in preferences on flight attendants, its coercion deprives us of the only evidence that allows us to document the proposition that the changes have been adopted voluntarily and, perhaps, universally. But greater dangers still lurk, for it may be the case that the practices required under the statute would not have been adopted at all, or not by very many parties, at which point the state is making people concede to practices that they do not agree with. Indeed, if Title VII were repealed tomorrow without any chance of reenactment, just how would airline hiring policies change?

Perhaps the risk of totalitarian excess is overdrawn. The question of who works as a flight attendant is small potatoes, one way or the other. But even if this industrywide decision is regarded as unimportant, there is still no reason to get it wrong. If it is important as a symbol for those who believe that employers (and passengers) should be sex-blind, then it is of equal importance for those who believe that each person should be allowed to make up his or her mind about the kind of service he or she prefers on airplanes or anywhere else. No one is indifferent to small incursions of freedom of speech; the same attitude should carry over to freedom of contract as well.

The issue, moreover, is hardly restricted to the hiring of flight attendants: Indeed, the litigation on the BFOQ has gone much further. One common question is whether a same-sex rule is appropriate in far trickier prison guard situations, where the arguments on the merits (that is, without regard to the statute) are weighty on either side. In the context of maximum security prisons for men, the Supreme Court has held it permissible for a state to prohibit the use of female guards in situations where they come in contact with prisoners.[34] In the Seventh Circuit case of *Torres v. Wisconsin Department of Health and Social Services*,[35] the superintendent of the only maximum security prison for women in Wisconsin decided that the rehabilitation of prisoners within her department would be "enhanced" if the prison hired only women as correctional officers. The trial judge struck down the superintendent's decision on the ground of the need to show a business necessity. A panel of the Seventh Circuit affirmed the decision, saying that there was no rigorous empirical evidence that justified the prohibition against male guards. The panel decision was in turn reversed by a divided en banc proceeding holding that the demand for rigorous justification was wholly unrealistic, given the scattered empirical evidence available in a case of this sort.[36] Judge Frank Easterbrook pointed out in a powerful dissent that under the business necessity test the absence of evidence is the death knell for the employer's case. "Even-handed skepticism implies that the party with the burden [of proof] loses."[37]

The hardest question is not what decision is right under the statute, but why the statute should apply at all. I have no idea whether on balance the Wisconsin policy is wise or not, but it is fairly easy to glean the relevant pros and cons from the arguments in the case. In favor of the use of female guards is the perception that many women inmates have previously been abused by men at home or elsewhere and would therefore be unable to relate effectively to men in a position of authority. On the other side is the argument that women prisoners must learn to deal with men in all sorts of situations if they are to succeed outside the prison walls after

---

34. *Dothard v. Rawlinson*, 433 U.S. (1977).

35. 838 F.2d 944 (7th Cir. 1988), overturned en banc, 859 F.2d 1523 (7th Cir. 1988).

36. "As the district court and one of the plaintiffs' own witnesses quite candidly acknowledged, the same historical and empirical evidence that might guide the administrator of a similar institution for males simply is not available with respect to this environment." *Torres*, 859 F.2d at 1529 (footnote omitted).

37. Id. at 1538 (Easterbrook, J., dissenting).

their release. There are in addition some important privacy questions: Would male guards be as effective as women in providing security if they were required to allow their female prisoners privacy inside their cells or in washrooms and showers?

In a world without Title VII the superintendent's decision would pass muster even if the equal protection clause required public officials to make some reasonable showing of why they had adopted a same-sex policy.[38] When the decision in separate prisons is made by different superintendents, some consensus may (or may not) emerge over time about which set of practices is best. But the new sources of information will be kept open if prison superintendents are allowed to experiment in deciding what mix they think appropriate. The decentralized employment practices in various prisons and states are a far cry from any single policy enforced by the EEOC or the courts based on rigid conceptions of right and wrong conduct. It is hard to believe that any net social gain is to be achieved from construing the BFOQ so narrowly as to preclude all honest disagreements among government officials.

Yet it is in this context that the expansive and coercive nature of the antidiscrimination law surges to the fore. It is no longer sufficient to treat the job as though it were a given and then to ask what its qualifications are. Instead, the employer is always told by degrees that some internal adjustment to the business must be undertaken in order to make jobs equally available to men and women. A small amount of inefficiency is necessary to obviate some greater level of discrimination. Mark Kelman writes: "It is a 'bfoq' for those who guard male prisoners to be male, because guards perform body searches that strongly invade personal privacy. If, however, the guard duties are reassigned so that only a subset of guards perform all body searches, women could be guards in the reorganized workplace."[39] But the doctrine of coerced trade-offs knows no natural stopping point. Neither I nor Kelman has the slightest knowledge about when and why body searches are performed. If these must be done under unanticipated circumstances, then the reorganization could impose serious costs on the operation of the prisons, which are always run on limited budgets, thus making them more dangerous places for all. With

---

38. The contrast between the strict standards of Title VII and the more forgiving standards of the equal protection clause is stressed by Judge Easterbrook in his dissenting opinion in *Torres*, 859 F.2d at 1535.

39. See Mark Kelman, "Concepts of Discrimination in 'General Ability' Job Testing," 104 *Harv. L. Rev.* 1158, 1178–79 (1991).

BFOQs there is a strong tendency to "flatten" the efficiency losses to make it appear as though the asserted gains of an antidiscrimination norm come at a far lower price than is doubtless the case, for outsiders always are less able to fine-tune a business than insiders. The creeping coercion offers further confirmation of a more general proposition: that those who are willing to force others to be free care far more about coercion than they ever could care about freedom.

Safety Concerns as a Justification for Disparate Treatment

The legislative debates over Title VII did not anticipate the most controversial question about the BFOQ: To what extent must the business necessity test be bent in order to take into account concerns, ostensible or real, about the safety of employees? That issue came to a head in the critical 1991 Supreme Court decision, *International Union, UAW v. Johnson Controls, Inc.,*[40] on the vexing question of fetal vulnerability. The relevant company rule applied to the battery division of Johnson Controls, whose work necessarily exposes employees to levels of lead high enough to cause potentially serious damage to unborn children. In response to this risk, Johnson Controls (actually a predecessor company) in the late 1960s instituted internal tests to monitor workers for lead exposure and installed an extensive $15 million control system to minimize that exposure. In 1977 the company issued a warning to women that they should not work in the battery division, citing the cumulative evidence of the impact of lead poisoning in the early stages of fetal development. But it stopped short of excluding women from taking jobs in the division. By 1982 the company had concluded that it was "medically necessary" to bar women from working in the battery division except for those whose inability to bear children was "medically documented." It was this last decision that was challenged under Title VII and defended successfully as a BFOQ when the Seventh Circuit, sitting en banc, affirmed the defendant's motion for summary judgment by a seven-to-four-vote.

The majority in the Seventh Circuit took the view that the broad prohibition adopted by Johnson Controls was justified as a BFOQ. In its view, the risk to the offspring of women was greater than the parallel risk to men, and no lesser restriction could be certain to contain it. As long as there was a "definite possibility" that a woman could learn of the risk

40. 886 F.2d 871 (7th Cir. 1989), rev'd., 111 Sup. Ct. 1196 (1991).

only after her pregnancy, it concluded that the restriction was justified.[41] Judge Richard Posner in dissent believed that it was premature to grant summary judgment for the defendant, and thought it relevant to examine the policies adopted by similarly situated firms as well as the company's exposure to tort liability if women were to continue to work in the battery division.[42] Only Judge Frank Easterbrook would have granted summary judgment for the plaintiff. He concluded that the company's restriction was manifestly overbroad in that it applied to women with either a small or a nonexistent chance of bearing children and, further, that it bore no relation to a woman's ability to do her assigned work.[43]

The Supreme Court unanimously reversed the decision of the Seventh Circuit and awarded the summary judgment for the plaintiff.[44] The first step in its analysis is uncontroversial; Johnson Controls adopted a policy that did discriminate on its face between men and women. The entire case therefore turns on the issue of justification. On this second issue the Court is on far weaker ground when it construes the business necessity standard so narrowly that it becomes *always* improper for employers for reasons of sex to take into account the risks to employees or their off-spring, wholly apart from the question of overbreadth. The firm could not impose a fetal vulnerability policy even if *all* women (or their off-spring) were exposed to a manifest risk of injury when *no* men were subject to that risk. Overbreadth does not matter. All that matters is the work that women do, not the risks to which they are exposed.

The Court initially reaches this conclusion by statutory construction. Here it places primary emphasis not on the words "reasonably necessary" or "certain instances"—which in ordinary language are antonyms, not synonyms, for strict necessity,[45] but on the word "occupational," which it construes as referring only to "qualifications that affect an employee's ability to do the job,"[46] wholly apart from the additional costs that doing that job may inflict on the employer. The narrow reading of "occupational" has no support in the legislative history or the prior case law, and it represents something of a tour de force on statutory language. By placing employee qualifications and employee risks in separate domains,

---

41. Id. at 878–883.
42. Id. at 903.
43. Id. at 914.
44. *International Union, UAW v. Johnson Controls,* 111 S.C. 1196 (1991).
45. See under the heading "Statutory Framework," this chapter.
46. *Johnson Controls,* 111 S.Ct. at 1205.

the Court relegates matters of occupational health and safety, which are unquestionably occupational under OSHA, to an irrelevancy under Title VII. It is yet another illustration of the perverse perception of the employment discrimination laws (which once were thought to cleanse market mechanisms) that costs are, and should be, irrelevant to the firm. "The extra cost of employing members of one sex, however, does not provide an affirmative Title VII defense for a discriminatory refusal to hire members of that gender."[47] The "essence of the business" test receives the same narrow interpretation that it received in earlier cases, and any element of paternalism that influences safety regulation generally is displaced by the employment discrimination laws. "Decisions about the welfare of future children must be left to the parents who conceive, bear, support, and raise them rather than to the employers who hire those parents"[48]— even if it appears that parental behavior is foolhardy enough to constitute abuse or neglect. In addition, the Court declined, at least for the moment, to create the appropriate tort immunities against the risks that do remain. Instead it wrote: "Without negligence, it would be difficult for a court to find liability on the part of the employer. If, under general tort principles, Title VII bans sex-specific fetal-protection policies, the employer fully informs the woman of the risk, and the employer has not acted negligently, the basis for holding an employer not liable seems remote at best."[49]

The basic argument here should have a familiar ring. First, the employment discrimination laws sweep away all protective regulation with sex-specific orientation, no matter what the magnitude of the risk. If women were certain to die from a class of exposures harmless to men, Title VII would preclude any state intervention by the employer. The same Court that is suspicious of freedom of choice in a thousand other industrial contexts adopts it here, but for only one side of the contractual relationship. In addition, the Court notes that there is still some residual risk— small in probability but potentially large in magnitude. That risk follows the usual pattern under Title VII: firms must take the residual losses, which the Court then proceeds to understate. Initially the Court ignores the possible claims of its female employees under the workers' compensation laws, in which recovery depends not on proof of negligence but on accidents or occupational diseases arising out of and in the scope of

47. Id. at 1209.
48. Id. at 1207.
49. Id. at 1208.

employment. It then understates the relevant tort exposure to suits by offspring. It is often unnecessary to show negligence under modern products liability law.[50] In addition, it is far more difficult to protect oneself by warnings than the Court perceives. "Full disclosure" in products cases is a term of art, and state courts often impose disclosure requirements that are far stricter than those that the reassuring words "full disclosure" might suggest.[51] Even if warnings were found adequate, the offspring of a worker might well maintain a tort action on the ground that the defendant should have taken steps to reduce the level of exposure below what it in fact was, even if it already met the stringent standards imposed by OSHA.

It is hard to know whether these risks of liability were what motivated Johnson Controls to progressively tighten its fetal vulnerability policy. But it is a plausible guess that the firm would have been more willing to allow women in their battery division if the law had made clear what was not resolved in the case: that the Court's own robust account of individual choice penetrates into every corner of the legal system, immunizing the firm from all liability risks under state law. But the Court, although pressed by the concurrence, refused to address the issue because the speculation about liability "appears unfounded as well as premature."[52] Similarly, it did not indicate whether women protected by Title VII are sufficiently competent to sign waivers that bind both themselves and their offspring. Injured or helpless infants make attractive plaintiffs. It is possible, if not likely, that state courts either will hold any waiver unenforceable as a matter of first principle, given the incapability of consent by unborn children, or will find it inapplicable in the particular case because the woman lacked sufficient information to make an informed judgment.

It is a familiar story. Costs that are speculative and uncertain may also be large. But whether large or small, they are now borne by an employer. The implicit subsidies worked by the employment discrimination laws are again explicitly ratified by the Supreme Court. There are surely many delicate judgments that must be made about sex roles in the workplace, but a decent respect for differences in judgment and taste, both of employers and employees, makes it imperative that these judgments be made *in* the workplace, and not in the halls of Congress or the courts.

50. See Restatement (Second) of Torts §402A (1965).

51. See, e.g., *MacDonald v. Ortho Pharmaceutical Corp.*, 394 Mass. 131, 475 N.E.2d 65 (1985).

52. *Johnson Controls* at 1209.

CHAPTER 15

Pensions

What Counts as Discrimination?

In this chapter the analysis of sex discrimination cases leaves the explicit statutory haven of the BFOQ and turns to a more discrete problem under the basic antidiscrimination norm of Title VII: What is the proper treatment of pension plans that use sex-based rules to allocate contributions and distributions? As a matter of first principle, there is no reason why the allocation of pension or insurance benefits should not be governed wholly by the principle of freedom of contract. There are no systematic difficulties with contract formation and no externalities. The job of the courts should be solely to ensure that all contracts are enforced in accordance with their stated terms. Under the operation of normal market pressures, pensions and insurance benefits across firms should tend to converge, with the result that work of equal value is rewarded with equal fringe benefits, if wages are held constant. But, owing to this last condition, it may be difficult to verify the point by looking at a particular set of employment contracts if one group of workers wishes to take a larger fraction of compensation in cash and a second group wishes to take it in fringe benefits. The real difficulties are in the internal structure of plan design, a business problem for the firm and its employees, not for the courts and the legislatures. If first principles governed, the legal analysis of pensions and insurance could end right here, where the business decisions begin.

That course of action, however, is not possible with Title VII on the books, since its general prohibition against discrimination extends to all the terms and conditions of the contract, including pensions and insurance. Under the statute, it is possible to take two different approaches to the question of what it means to "discriminate against" women (or men) because of their sex. By the first, some discrimination *between* the sexes is permissible if it responds to differences in the cost of providing the specified benefit and compensation packages of men and women. In effect the statute is read as roughly consistent with standard market practices in that it seeks to prevent rather than foster redistribution of income and wealth across the many employees of a single employer. The applicable standard says that if men and women in the same position, performing work of equal value, receive total compensation packages of *equal present value* from the employer, there is no sex discrimination, regardless of any differences in the timing and amount of the individual payments that make up the whole. The prohibition of the statute might invalidate market practices in some isolated cases, but the congruence between business requirements and permitted practices under Title VII would be nearly complete.

The second, more aggressive interpretation of the antidiscrimination statutes does not allow the employer to escape potential liability under Title VII because it has equalized total benefit packages in exchange for (as we can assume for the moment) work of equal value. Indeed, the equalization of the total benefit packages becomes a reason to impose liability. From this viewpoint Title VII mandates redistribution of income across the sexes. This aggressive reading requires the employer to make each part of the compensation package "identical" in some formal respect, even though it may cost the employer more to fund the total package received by women (or by men).

What counts as discrimination? Taking a leaf from the bona fide occupational qualification (BFOQ) cases, the Supreme Court has emphatically rejected any cost-based interpretation of Title VII. The issue is, moreover, of enormous structural significance for the entire American economy. Under any view the use of sex-based classifications for work performance would apply to at most a significant minority of jobs within the economy. Accordingly the BFOQ defense, even sensibly read, is available in only a relatively small fraction of the relevant cases. For most of the workaday world, therefore, the asserted cost justifications cannot be made out, and no one will try.

Using sex-based distinctions for life insurance, health insurance, and pensions is a different kettle of fish entirely. Those distinctions have been a standard part of American business practice since long before the passage of Title VII. Once these practices are called into question under the statute, *every* worker and *every* business covered by Title VII is affected. The claims for efficiency of Title VII, pro and con, cannot be evaluated solely in the context of the individual disparate treatment cases that are the subject of most routine litigation. They must be evaluated in the context of the structural reforms that Title VII, as construed, applies.[1]

It is therefore essential to trace the evolution of the law as it touches pensions. In so doing we find that the historical pattern takes a familiar course. Initially it was clear that the sponsors of the 1964 statute had no desire to interfere with sex-based calculations of insurance and other fringe benefits.[2] But the dam did not hold. By 1978, in *Los Angeles Department of Water and Power v. Manhart*,[3] the Supreme Court held that it was a violation of Title VII to take into account the sex of an employee in determining contribution levels into a standard defined benefit pension plan.

The effects of *Manhart* and similar cases have followed a pattern of case law development similar to that for BFOQs. The modest purposes of the original statute have been displaced by a far more interventionist objective: to make an employer's costs irrelevant in the provision of benefits. The antidiscrimination statutes have thus been converted from a system that demands that employers treat like cases alike into one that demands that unlike cases be funded alike: workers who impose unequal costs on the firm are required by law to receive equal benefits.

The possible impact of Title VII on pension plans was foreseen and understood by the defenders of the original 1964 act. As part of their effort to preserve Title VII in the statute, they inserted the so-called Bennett amendment, which provided: "It shall not be an unlawful employment practice under this title for any employer to differentiate upon the basis of sex in determining the amount of the wages or compensation paid to employees of such employer if such differential is authorized by the provisions of Section 6(d) of the Fair Labor Standards Act of 1938, as amended."[4]

As drafted, this provision unquestionably contemplates that some differences in compensation packages may be allowable on the grounds of sex, but it does not specify what they are. Instead, it refers the reader to section 6(d) of the Fair Labor Standards Act, which contains the provi-

---

1. See, for example, the exchange between Richard A. Posner, "An Economic Analysis of Sex Discrimination Laws," *56 U. Chi. L. Rev.* 1311 (1989), and John J. Donohue III, "Prohibiting Sex Discrimination in the Workplace: An Economic Perspective," *56 U. Chi. L. Rev.* 1337 (1989), both of which ignore the structural features of Title VII, where the inefficiencies are in some sense most extreme.

2. See the discussion in this section.

3. 435 U.S. 702 (1978).

4. Section 703(h) (last sentence).

sions of the Equal Pay Act of 1963. That statute in turn sets a presumption that equal wages should be paid for equal work and then proceeds to recognize four exceptions to that basic rule: "(i) a seniority system; (ii) a merit system; (iii) a system which measures earnings by quantity or quality of production; or (iv) a differential based on any factor other than sex."[5] The relevant exception is the last one. The differences in insurance and pensions are based on a "factor other than sex" because they are tied to a distinct compensable event—longevity for life insurance, and frequency and severity of illness for health insurance. Nonetheless, the statutory drafting approach can be faulted for taking inherent and unnecessary risks in that it seeks to dispose of a question of principle by the slipperiest technique of all—incorporation by reference to another statute—a flaw compounded in this instance by the fact that the cross-reference is to another statute, passed just the year before, which itself had not received any authoritative construction by any court. The two provisions in sequence do *not* say that it is, or is not, a form of sex discrimination to take into account cost factors that are highly correlated with sex but that in individual cases might deviate from it. They do not say in so many words that any employer who sets aside equal amounts of money to fund the pensions for men and women has not engaged in sex discrimination under the act. Reading the statute alone, therefore, does not answer the question, what becomes of pensions under Title VII? It only directs one to an all-purpose savings clause of the Equal Pay Act, which, like the Civil Rights Act itself, has been construed more narrowly than its own legislative history might suggest.[6]

---

5. 29 U.S.C.A. §206(d) (1990). The section contains a proviso that reads: "*Provided,* That an employer who is paying a wage rate differential in violation of this subsection shall not, in order to comply with the provisions of this subsection, reduce the wage rate of any employee."

6. See Committee on Education and Labor, *Legislative History of the Equal Pay Act of 1963* at 25, in connection with the so-called Findley Amendment, rejected in the House. The amendment added a new defense to the statute: "a differential which does not exceed ascertainable and specific added cost resulting from employment of the opposite sex." The amendment was introduced to protect women in the belief that on an accounting basis, "The cost of employing women is higher than the cost of employing men. If the effect of this bill is to force them into a wage policy that will deny them the opportunity to make a wage differential, then it will surely follow that they will tend to employ men instead of women. It might then have the effect of destroying job opportunities for women rather than improving these opportunities."

The response to this amendment was that these cost concerns were already caught by the "factors other than sex" defense. But the response was evasive: "We feel if there are

The legislative history therefore has a larger role to play here than in most cases since the statute contains no substantive commands. And the history behind the Bennett amendment is, or at least was, far clearer than the statute itself. Senator Foster Bennett announced that his amendment was necessary to prevent any conflict from arising between Title VII and the Equal Pay Act; he thought that it would coordinate the two sections and preserve the exceptions of the Equal Pay Act in Title VII litigation. As Senator Everett Dirksen said: "All recognize that the pending amendment does recognize those exceptions that are carried in the basic act."[7] Thereafter the question arose about the relationship between this provision and the differential treatment for men and women under social security and other retirement plans. Here the dialogue (between Senators Jennings Randolph and Hubert Humphrey) is both short enough and clear enough to set out in full:

Mr. Randolph: Mr. President, I wish to ask of the Senator from Minnesota [Hubert Humphrey], who is the effective manager of the pending bill, a clarifying question on the provisions of Title VII.

I have in mind that the social security system in certain respects treats men and women differently. For example widows' benefits are paid automatically, but a widower qualifies only if he is disabled or if he was actually supported by his deceased wife. Also, the wife of a retired employee entitled to social security receives an additional old age benefit; but the husband of such an employee does not. These differences in treatment as I recall are of long standing.

Am I correct, I ask the Senator from Minnesota, in assuming that similar differences of treatment in industrial benefit plans, including earlier retirement options for women, may continue in operation under this bill if it becomes law.

Mr. Humphrey: Yes. That point was made unmistakably clear earlier today by the adoption of the Bennett amendment; so there can be no doubt about it.[8]

---

specific and ascertainable additional costs as to certain employees, if the employer sets up a differential in pay which applies equally to men and women, that those specific and ascertainable costs may very well be valid exceptions to this bill." Remarks of Congressman Charles Goodell, at 26. But "may very well" is not the same as "are," and "a differential in pay which applies equally to men and women" does not refer to cost differentials, if it has any meaning at all.

7. 110 *Cong. Rec.* 13, 663–664 (1964).
8. Id. at 13, 664.

One message comes through. Whether we are dealing with government-run social security programs or with private industrial retirement plans, explicit sex differences are permissible. Indeed, the editor's note to the exchange tells us in italics that the result of Senator Randolph's query was that "the Bennett amendment makes clear that the law does not forbid early retirement for women or other differences of treatment under industrial retirement plans or the Social Security Act."[9] There was of course no legal analysis as to why or how the Bennett amendment achieved that desired effect; but on a point on which there was no disagreement, no detailed argumentation can be expected. It was generally assumed that wide differences in treatment were tolerable because they were sanctioned by common practice, which the statute was intended to accommodate. The possibility that Title VII was designed to restructure the workplace or American society may be a fashionable thought today, but it would have been greeted with incomprehension in 1964.

The social consensus behind the statute proved fragile over the long run. When put to the test in *Manhart,* the legislative history was regarded as at best irrelevant. Even if "Senator Humphrey apparently assumed that the 1964 Act would have little, if any impact on existing pension plans,"[10] the result was otherwise. As the *Manhart* decision reads: "We conclude that Senator Humphrey's isolated comment on the Senate floor cannot change the effect of the plain language of the statute itself."[11] It seems that the more staged the dialogue, the greater the authority of the spokesman (Humphrey was expressly referred to as "the effective manager of the pending bill" in Randolph's query, and was enormously respected for his role in advancing the statute), and the clearer the history, the less its relevance. Humphrey was not a foggy thinker who "apparently assumed" anything. He knew exactly the end the Bennett amendment was designed to achieve. *Manhart* is sheer judicial legislation, and its consequences are scarcely better than its illegitimate pedigree.

The Basic Economics of Sex-Linked Annuities

The manifest deconstruction of Title VII's response to pension plans was driven by the same attitudes that gutted the BFOQ exception in the basic statute: relevant cost differences were ignored because they rested on

9. *Legislative History of Titles VII and IX of the Civil Rights Act of 1964,* at 3234.
10. *Manhart,* 435 U.S. 702, 714 (1978).
11. Id. at 714.

statistical information that was dismissed as being based on little more than invidious stereotypes. The basic statistical information is indisputable. Women in the work force have substantially longer life expectancy than men.[12] It is not that every woman lives longer than every man. Rather, the distribution of life expectancy for women is to the right of that for men. In other words, it is possible to establish a one-to-one correspondence whereby virtually every women is matched up with a man whose life expectancy is shorter than her own. Any system of pensions must come to grips with this inescapable truth.

One possible response is to sidestep that basic fact by providing lump sum pensions, pegged to salaries, which would allow all employees to use the money as they pleased. The chief advantage of such a plan is that it does not violate Title VII. But the disadvantages must be noted as well. Before Title VII the lump sum alternative was available to workers, but it was chosen only rarely. Instead, an overwhelming fraction of men and women—in excess of 95 percent—opted for annuities, measured either against their own life or the joint lives of themselves and their spouses. This wholesale preference for life-based annuities made, and continues to make, good sense, because it allows everyone to insure against his or her own mortality risk. No one knows for certain whether he or she will live for one year or for twenty-five. It thus becomes very difficult for any retiree to determine the optimal rate of consumption of any lump sum or fixed-benefit payment.[13] If too much money is consumed in the early years, the principal will disappear, and long-lived persons will have to endure poverty or public assistance in their last years. But by the same token, if retired employees die relatively young, large amounts of the money will go unexpended, to be left to children who may already be well provided for. The purchase of the annuity allows all employees to have a predictable sum of money on an annual basis tied to their living needs. The price they pay for this convenience is that they take their chances on whether they will live long or die soon. If the overwhelming preference of men and women for lifetime annuities is any indication, the

12. Note that there is no similar problem for race, for with blacks and whites there is no appreciable difference in life expectancy at pension age. See "Brief for the Society of Actuaries" at 11 n.10, filed in *Manhart*.

13. As a matter of basic finance theory, any fixed flow of periodic income payments can be converted into a lump sum as long as the proper discount rate is known. Hence, for these purposes a twenty-year certain pension works the same as a single lump sum payment obtainable on retirement, which can be used to purchase that twenty-year annuity.

certainty of preserving one's living standard over an uncertain life span seems to make that price well worth paying.

Once employees opt for a system of lifetime annuities in a world without Title VII, employers must do something that they need not do with lump sum or fixed-period payments: they must estimate the total expected number of payments to each recipient in order to be able to estimate the costs of running a pension plan. In order to offer a fair annuity, the employer must know the expected life span of each person in the plan. It then takes those individual numbers and sums them up in order to find the expected costs for operating the plan as a whole. By virtue of the large number of persons in any annuity pool, the employer and annuity carrier bear only a small residual level of uncertainty. Within this system sex is a powerful predictor of longevity. Every person is either male or female, so there are none of the borderline questions that would arise, for example, in efforts to classify pension recipients by race or national origin. The sex classification is also cheap to employ and almost impossible to manipulate for strategic advantage. There was no voluntary insurance or annuity market that did not take sex into account—at least before Title VII.

Under proper actuarial techniques men received larger payouts for a smaller number of expected periods so that the *present value* of the annuity at retirement was equal for men and for women, as (ironically) one might have thought was required under the Equal Pay Act. (I would gladly give up my extra annual payments in exchange for the expectation of extra years in good health, but that is a separate matter.) The insurance pool thus created was stable because all interested parties were better off with the system than without it. Women and men both got coverage worth more to them than its cost. The employer was able to structure a more desirable benefit package for all workers without any increase in the level of its own contribution. There was one good business reason for the universal use of sex-linked annuities: everyone gained.

For that reason, perhaps, it was branded illegal sex discrimination in *Los Angeles Department of Water and Power v. Manhart*.[14] According to

14. 435 U.S. (1978). The decision and the underlying issue have generated a massive amount of comment and discussion. See, for some notable contributions, Spencer Kimball, "Reverse Sex Discrimination: *Manhart*," 1979 *Am. Bar Found. Res. J.* 83; Lea Brilmayer et al., "Sex Discrimination in Employer-Sponsored Insurance Plans," 47 *U. Chi. L. Rev.* 505 (1980); George Benston, "The Economics of Gender Discrimination in Employee Fringe Benefits: *Manhart* Revisited," 49 *U. Chi. L. Rev.* 489 (1982). Kimball and Benston are

Justice John Paul Stevens, the alleged vice was that the plans placed the emphasis on the group instead of the individual: "The statute makes it unlawful 'to discriminate against any *individual* with respect to his compensation, terms, conditions, or privileges of employment, because of such *individual's* race, color, religion, sex or national origin.' The statute's focus on the individual is unambiguous."[15] The Court then explained why the language was congruent with the purpose of the statute:

> The basic policy of the statute requires that we focus on fairness to individuals rather than fairness to classes. Practices that classify employees in terms of religion, race, or sex tend to preserve traditional assumptions about groups rather than thoughtful scrutiny of individuals. The generalization involved in this case illustrates the point. Separate mortality tables are easily interpreted as reflecting innate differences between the sexes; but a significant part of the longevity differential may be explained by the social fact that men are heavier smokers than women.[16]

This focus on the individual, however, proves absolutely nothing, unless *all* group pensions and life insurance systems are to be banned under Title VII. If sex-based classifications do not involve a "thoughtful scrutiny" of individuals, then any mortality arrangement that ignores sex cannot be thoughtful either, since it lumps all individuals together without any consideration of their particular worth or prospects. The only proper approach would be to hold that any system of life-based insurance is corrupt under Title VII because it always involves the antithesis of individuation even when all the persons are of the same sex. Yet that extreme position was not taken because its consequences are ruinous enough for all to see. Instead, the Court opted for a more limited approach that forced all persons into the same mortality pool, notwithstanding the systematic differences among them.

Ironically, however, it is not possible to avoid essential sex-based calculations even if the annual benefits payable to men and women are made equal by judicial fiat. The mandated equality only removes the require-

---

critical of *Manhart,* and I am much indebted to their work. Brilmayer et al. support it. I have attacked the *Manhart* decision on constitutional grounds in Richard A. Epstein, *Takings: Private Property and the Power of Eminent Domain* 312–314 (1985).

15. 435 U.S. at 708 (emphasis in original).

16. Id. at 709–710 (footnote omitted).

ment that each person obtain fair insurance, that is, insurance whose expected value (expenses aside) equals his or her total contribution. Unisex insurance does not eliminate the need to take sex into account in order to ensure the financial balance of the plan. Even after *Manhart* some actuary still has to determine the contributions and benefits for each person. That task cannot be done on a sex-blind basis, and *Manhart* (in a footnote, of course) carefully allowed employers to take into account the composition of the pool by sex in setting the rates.[17] Justice Stevens understood the indispensable nature of insurance principles in calculating overall benefit levels even as he repudiated their use in calculating individual shares.

To see why some continued use of mortality tables by sex is critical, suppose that sex-based generalizations are ruled out of order anywhere in the process. It is still necessary to estimate the total expected payout from the plan. Accordingly, some estimate of life expectation is required. For calculating the benefits, free of "stereotyped" prejudices, the only possible measure is the *average* life expectancy of all persons in the general population, both male and female, at retirement. That sex-blind approach is a recipe for financial disaster, however, save for the happenstance of a particular work force whose proportion of men and women is identical to that in the general population. In *Manhart,* for example, the Department of Water and Power employed roughly ten thousand men and two thousand women. To set payout schedules on the assumption that the work force is half male and half female leads to the unwanted accumulation of a surplus in the fund. Since more men than women are covered by the plan, the expected life of plan members is lower than that of the general population (or the general work force). Excess cash will accumulate, to the prejudice of all contributors. Similarly, if the proportions are reversed (that is, if the Department employed ten thousand women and two thousand men), the use of national or work force averages leads inexorably to systematic over-payments to all plan members in the early years, followed by bankruptcy of the fund in subsequent years, by which time women would constitute the majority of recipients.

The only way to achieve a balanced budget, therefore, is to use the sex-specific information, the so-called forbidden stereotype, to determine the total level of plan obligations. Under *Manhart* that number is far closer to

---

17. Id. at 718 n.34. The argument is that as long as the wage is equal for both sexes, the employer can use any method to determine its funding requirements.

the male life expectancy than to the female life expectancy. Justice Stevens notwithstanding, it does not matter whether the differences in life expectancy are attributable to nature or nurture, to stress or smoking. It matters only that these differences in expectations exist. Indeed, as the life expectancy data change, the payouts can be revised, for no benefit calculations need be made before payouts begin. Far from reinforcing silly stereotypes, accurate generalizations provide the information needed for any thoughtful treatment of sex differences. But without information there is only one indubitable truth: to a moral certainty the women covered by the plan will take more money from it than they put in, here on the order of 6 to 12 percent more.[18] As George Benston has noted: "Male mortality rates at all relevant ages and time periods are greater than female rates. The magnitudes are such that, if they are not accounted for and if the relative numbers of females in the group are other than trivial, predicted mortality is likely to differ considerably from actual."[19] Again, if each person in a group of a thousand males and a thousand females of age sixty-five were given a dollar for each year he or she continued to live, "the total annuity payments to the cohort of 1,000 females over their lifetimes would exceed the payments to the 1,000 males by 23.5 percent. In no way can it be asserted that the excess number of payments is financially inconsequential."[20] Finally, "the expected life remaining at age

18. See Benston, "The Economics of Gender Discrimination" at 515. This last figure is especially critical if pensions are payable starting at age sixty-five. The difference in the number of years pensions are payable is about 32 percent, but the difference in current dollars to fund annuities is a smaller figure, depending on the rate of return on investment. But even so, the levels of net transfer from men to women are very considerable, ranging between 12 and 22 percent. Under the prior system of sex-linked annuities, both men and women received annuities with $100,000 present value for their investment of $100,000. With the unisex table the capital value of a man's contribution is reduced by $11,802 if the money can be invested at 2 percent, and the woman's contribution is increased in value by the same amount, creating nearly a $24,000 difference in values. As the rate of return on the investment increases, these differences decrease because the distant years count for less in terms of present value. Nonetheless, the disparities are still high. Benston calculates a value difference of $10,027, or a 20 percent swing for an investment rate of 4 percent; $8,470, or about a 17 percent swing on an investment rate of 6 percent; $7,134, or about a 14.25 percent swing on an investment rate of 8 percent; and $5,984, or about a 12 percent swing on an investment rate of 10 percent. These differences are not adjusted for inflation.

19. Id. at 515.

20. Id. at 517 n.72, quoting Robert J. Johansen, "The Equity of Equality," *The Actuary* (June 1977).

65 was estimated in 1975 to be 18.1 years for females and 13.7 years for males."[21]

Although the antidiscrimination laws may choose to ignore these sex-linked differences in mortality, private parties governed by the statutes will not. Plan participants will take strategic advantage of the relevant data in their choice of benefit packages. In *Manhart* the Court required the plan operator to assume that sex does not matter on the level of pension benefits even though everyone knows that it does. Since plan participants are not bound by the commands of Title VII, they can use this information to maximize their private returns. The choices available to single women and single men before the Title VII dislocations were limited. If they had private knowledge of their own state of health, they could choose annuities if they thought they would live long but not otherwise. The rates charged for these annuities reflected this selection effect.[22] Title VII, however, offers additional opportunities for participants to play the system, especially when both husband and wife are entitled to pension benefits. The optimal strategy may be for the husband to take the self-and-survivor annuity and the wife to take an annuity on her own life alone. By adopting this package, they can receive on average a higher rate of return than if each took self-only annuities or both took self-and-survivor annuities. Quite simply, a larger fraction of their pension benefits is tied to the life of the wife, who has a greater life expectancy than her husband.

In some cases, of course, the parties will not adopt this strategy, for it introduces an additional element of risk which may prove costly if the wife suffers from a known disease or condition. But these parties have private knowledge that allows them to avoid this costly error. Nonetheless, for some couples the increase in total dollar payments may be worth taking, especially if some of the money received in the early years can be set aside to cover the possibility of the early death of the wife. Whenever these strategies are adopted, there is an implicit wealth transfer of uncertain extent from married women who do not work to married women

21. Id. at 516.

22. See Benston, "The Economics of Gender Discrimination" at 519 n.79, quoting Janice E. Greider & William T. Beadles, *Principles of Life Insurance* 296–299 (rev. ed., 1972), for the proposition that "death rates at the various ages are generally lower for annuitants than for insured lives and . . . different mortality tables are used for computing annuity rates and payments than are used for life insurance purposes."

who do, in addition to the transfer from unmarried men to unmarried women effected by the statute. As ever, the unintended consequences of regulation loom large.

The effects of *Manhart,* however, are more than distributional. There are negative allocative consequences as well.[23] The first point is that unisex annuities increase the gaming possibilities and hence raise the costs of selecting coverage and designing plans. Although these costs are not likely to be large, they will be positive, and they are costs for which there is no offsetting benefit. More important, however, the *Manhart* rule creates net transfers of large magnitude, ranging, as I have noted, from about 12 to 24 percent in present value terms.[24] These swings necessarily influence the primary conduct of market participants. Women will be more eager to obtain jobs that offer hefty pension benefits, and employers will (rationally) prefer not to hire them, even though they cannot publicly voice their preference. Although their reluctance to hire women will not be unshakable, they should at the margin become less willing to hire women and more willing to fire them. Fellow employees (male and female) may be subject to the same incentives, for the hiring of any additional female worker will reduce the expected pension of all other workers in the firm, both male and female.

In other settings the response may be still more extreme. One answer is simply to stop using lifetime annuities, as occurred in *Arizona Governing Committee v. Norris.*[25] The plan in *Norris* differed from that in *Manhart* in that the contributions were both equal and optional, but the benefits paid to men were larger than those paid to women. The Court rightly held that it did not matter whether the sex-based adjustments were made on the benefit side (as in *Norris*) or the contribution side (as in *Manhart*).[26] It further held that the voluntary nature of the contribution did not take the plan out of the scope of Title VII because the employer designated the choice of plan carriers even if it did not require the contribution.[27] But unlike in *Manhart,* we know that in *Norris* the failure to make sex-based adjustments had significant negative allocative conse-

---

23. This argument bears against Donohue's claim in "Prohibiting Sex Discrimination" that Title VII is efficient in the area of sex discrimination.

24. See note 18.

25. 463 U.S. 1073 (1983).

26. Id. at 1081–83.

27. Id. at 1087–91.

quences, since there is evidence in the record that the employer removed the life annuities from the approved list. The dissenting opinion of Justice Lewis Powell put the point forcefully:

> If the cost to employers of offering unisex annuities is prohibitive or if insurance carriers choose not to write such annuities, employees will be denied the opportunity to purchase life annuities—concededly the most advantageous pension plan at lower cost.

He then continued in a footnote:

> This is precisely what happened in this case. Faced with the liabilities resulting from the Court of Appeals' judgment, the State of Arizona discontinued making life annuities available to its employees . . . Any employee who now wishes to have the security provided by a life annuity must withdraw his or her accrued retirement savings from the state pension plan, pay federal income tax on the amount withdrawn, and then use the remainder to purchase an annuity on the open market.[28]

The result is all too familiar. The private responses to the *Manhart* decision leave *everyone* worse off than before, the classic Pareto pessimal result of legislative action. As long as women know that they can secure lifetime annuities, they prefer having more money to less. But if the employer responds to the change by shifting to a fixed payment schedule, they will not obtain any more money from the pension plan after *Manhart* than they were able to obtain before it. But now both women and men will be required to take their benefits in a form that leaves them worse off than they were before *Manhart* was handed down. Let us use numbers to illustrate the principle. Before *Manhart*, men and women making equal pension contributions each received a life annuity with a present value to them of 10. *Manhart* purported to shift the present value of the life annuities to 11 for women and 9 for men, a simple wealth transfer of a single unit. But the distortions in pensions induced employers to shift to fixed annuities, funded by the same monies, worth only 9.5 (or perhaps less) to both men and women alike. Everyone loses.

The same type of result occurs in reverse where life insurance rather than pensions are at stake. As a business matter, life insurance should be cheaper for women because of their longer life expectancy. But once

28. Id. at 1098 n.4. See Rev. Rule. 72-35, 1972-1 *Cum. Bull.* 127. Note that the open market annuity will be sex linked.

insurance carriers reached by Title VII have to shift to unisex tables, the unisex insurance policies will create a greater incentive for men to purchase insurance relative to women. Just this change was introduced in 1984 by Teachers Insurance and Annuity Association (TIAA) after it was forced by judicial decision to adopt unisex tables.[29] The response was to price its unisex policy to reflect the relative proportion of males and females, so that its blended rate was equal to three-fourths the previous male rate and one-fourth the previous female rate, yielding a new rate that was three times closer to the previous male rates than to the previous female rates. That shift in relative prices should, other factors held constant, reduce women's demand for policies. Similarly, the shift created an increased risk of moral hazard for men, one that TIAA counters by maintaining strict underwriting controls. Since 1984 the percentage of insurance purchased by women has increased, so the ratio is now closer to 60 percent male and 40 percent female. That shift runs against the change in relative prices, and it is doubtless largely accounted for by the changes in the composition of the academic marketplace since 1984, which now contains a larger proportion of women, including more in the higher income brackets.[30] As ever it is very difficult to trace the consequences of a single change in pricing on the overall pattern of market purchases.

There is an obvious moral to the entire discussion of insurance and pension coverage. First, a market system without any form of government regulation will tolerate none of the dislocations that occur under the current rules for disability, life, and pension insurance. There is a powerful tendency for all rates to become actuarially fair over both the long and the short run. Second, a sensible version of the antidiscrimination law need not require massive revision of common practice. Instead, where like pay is required by statute for like work, the antidiscrimination principle need be read to insist only that the present value payable to men and women must be the same. Plans that violate that requirement have been found; indeed, the death benefit provisions of the plan in *Manhart* appear to have violated that constraint.[31] There is no reason, however, to require an implicit transfer from men to women for pensions, or from women to men for life insurance. In each instance the antidiscrimination laws are used to require an implicit subsidy, difficult to defend if made overtly.

29. See *Spirt v. Teachers Insurance & Annuity Association,* 691 F.2d 1054 (2d Cir. 1982).
30. My thanks to Neil Gordon of TIAA, who supplied the information about the pricing changes in TIAA by telephone interview, May 22, 1991.
31. 435 U.S. at 710 n.19.

The ostensible goal of the antidiscrimination laws is to make sex irrelevant in employment relations. But the goal is incoherent and mischievous as a universal proposition. The differences between men and women do matter to both men and women. To speak of these undeniable differences as stereotypes is to use Title VII to reject information not because it is false but because it does not meet an ideological preconception of what is desirable in human relations or true in human affairs. These ideological arguments find it far more difficult to take hold in markets because the price is paid directly by the party who hews to the belief. Let any company try to price its insurance in ways that provide net benefits to one group and net losses to another group and its market will disintegrate under its feet. The persons who would receive net benefits will remain with the company. Those who would bear net burdens will acquire their insurance elsewhere. The effort to force men or women to purchase losing insurance contracts is destined to fail, so it is not even attempted.

The *Manhart* decision allowed these ideological arguments to flourish under Title VII because it refused to apply normal actuarial techniques to insurance questions that are fully amenable to them. *Manhart* could have prevented the disruption of the pension market by holding that Title VII required employers to follow sound actuarial provisions, not to abandon them—that is, by insisting that pensions satisfy a test of present value equivalence between men and women. But even that measured intervention, although required under Title VII, suffers from two nagging disadvantages, which point out how difficult it is to get things right under regulation. First, there is the necessary evidentiary burden of showing that a complex set of pension or insurance arrangements is of equal value to another. It is easy to make mistakes when imperfect knowledge in general is coupled with the stunning lack of expertise by judges and the normal pressures of litigation. Second, and more important, the centralized control of the system eliminates the prospects for incremental self-correction. Let five justices of the Supreme Court mangle the principles of pensions and there is nowhere to go but to Congress, which can hardly be expected to do better. The dislocations are large enough to influence economic welfare but not so large as to generate a legislative response.

CHAPTER 16

Pregnancy

The antidiscrimination principle of Title VII, so visible with BFOQ and pensions, has also exerted a powerful influence over the legal treatment of pregnancy benefits for employees. The basic problem concerns the application of a nondiscrimination principle, or more generally of a rule treating like cases alike, to situations where the initial positions of men and women are fundamentally different. Only a woman can bear children; and only a woman must incur the additional costs associated with caring for herself and her child during pregnancy. Within private markets these differences in initial position are reflected in the final bargaining position, for employers and workers explicitly take pregnancy into account in determining the nature and scope of their respective contractual obligations as they relate to salary, work assignments, leave time, insurance benefits, and a thousand other matters, both large and small. Under Title VII the central inquiry is whether those voluntary arrangements, and the systematic asymmetries they contain, can or should survive the application of the nondiscrimination principle. As was the case with BFOQs and pensions, it has become clear that standard insurance practices cannot coexist in the same legal world as Title VII.

The development of the law governing pregnancy benefits in an important sense duplicates that for BFOQs and pension laws. Originally the question of pregnancy was regarded, rightly in my view, as unique to women and therefore subject to the special treatment they received as a matter of course. Normally pregnancy is regarded as a voluntary and welcome event, easily distinguished from any disability for which insurance is usually sought and extended. Because pregnancy is desired, and because women largely control whether and when to become pregnant, the evident moral hazard makes pregnancy a poor candidate for any form of insurance. Before Title VII there were no special rules on the subject either under the Constitution or by statute, so the usual contractual response was the predicted one: pregnancy was a risk or benefit borne by the woman and not by the firm. Over time the understandings have changed sharply. Pregnancy has by degrees become a subject for public regulation, and is conceptualized more as a disability and less as a blessed event. The transition has taken place in two distinct phases. Accordingly, the first section of this chapter examines the relevant constitutional setting for sex discrimination; the next looks more closely at the litigation under Title VII and the legislative responses to it.

Constitutional and Historical Preliminaries

Early Equal Protection Cases

The Equal Pay Act and Title VII were passed in 1963 and 1964 respectively, at a time when there were, both in theory and in practice, no constitutional prohibitions against sex-based classifications. In fact, the great progressive decisions of earlier years had sustained various forms of protective legislation for women on the ground that piecemeal intervention was often the enlightened response to complex social issues. Thus minimum wage and maximum hour legislation applicable to women only was sustained against constitutional attack in *West Coast Hotel Co. v. Parrish*.[1] Nonetheless, the same impulses that led to the passage of Title VII and the Equal Pay Act quickly spilled over into constitutional law, and sex-based classifications became subject to constitutional scrutiny starting in the early 1970s.

The original forays had little to do with sex discrimination in employment. In *Reed v. Reed*[2] the Court held that the Equal Protection Clause prohibited the use of an explicit statutory sex classification for choosing the administrator of the decedent's estate. The Idaho statute in *Reed* provided that for persons within the same entitlement class (for example, parents of the intestate with no closer relatives), the male was to be conclusively preferred to the female. The scheme was justified on grounds of cost: it is cheaper to have an arbitrary rule than to have fitness hearings between a father and mother who are antagonistic to each other. This justification is subject to two lines of attack. The first, and more modest, concedes that costs of administration are relevant to the decision, but then insists that the sex-based rule is not necessary to control cost. A choice by lottery would do as well. To be sure, a lottery does not adjust

1. 300 U.S. 379 (1937).
2. 404 U.S 71 (1971).

for possible competence, but the same is true of the automatic sex-based choice.

A second and more expansive attack insists that costs are irrelevant. Although costs were of little practical consequence in *Reed*, they could be of far greater moment in other contexts where the simple adjustments available in *Reed* are not feasible. Shortly after *Reed*, *Frontiero v. Richardson*[3] examined the same dependence benefits rules that the amendment had been designed to preserve under Title VII. The question posed here was, could the United States provide a system of military benefits by which female spouses were presumed to be dependents of their husbands without an actual showing of dependency, while male spouses had to prove dependency? The basis for the distinction was doubtless the (then more) common differences in marriage roles. Many wives did not work, but only the occasional husband did not. In addition, since the military was then about 99 percent male, the automatic rule for female dependents saved substantial costs. But these arguments are far from overpowering, and they were rejected by the Supreme Court. Justice Brennan, for example, made the obvious and sensible point that the benefits for dependent wives may well have been overstated, since many were doubtless gainfully employed. In his opinion the inability to provide differential treatment only allowed the government to presume dependence in all cases or none, or (perhaps) to adopt some intermediate sex-neutral position, such as presuming dependence where the spouse is unemployed, but not otherwise.

The invalidation of the benefits scheme in *Frontiero*, though a stunning reversal of the assumptions about constitutional law uniformly shared in 1964, did not work a major revision in either the financing or the operations of the military. In practice it may only have expedited changes that would soon have taken place in the political arena.[4] The key question therefore concerned not the outcome, which was correct, but the constitutional standard used to bring about invalidation. Justice Brennan's plurality opinion in *Frontiero* hinted at a high level of scrutiny for sex-based classifications: "When we enter the realm of 'strict judicial scrutiny,' there can be no doubt that 'administrative convenience' is not a shibboleth, the

---

3. 411 U.S. 677 (1973).

4. See Brian Mitchell, *Weak Link: The Feminization of the American Military*, ch. 3 (1989), noting the close connection between the increased role for women in the military and the movement toward a volunteer army.

mere recitation of which dictates constitutionality."[5] Left unresolved was whether this strict scrutiny standard would ever be adopted by a clear majority of the Court, and if so how it would apply to sex discrimination cases.

Geduldig v. Aiello: *Right Result, Wrong Reasons*

The answers to Brennan's questions came quickly. *Geduldig v. Aiello*[6] raised a direct equal protection challenge to the California Unemployment Compensation Disability Fund, which administered a system of mandatory disability insurance for private employees whose short-term disabilities were not covered by the state workers' compensation plans. Under the statutory scheme each worker contributed to the plan 1 percent of salary up to a maximum of $85 per annum. The plan covered a wide range of disabilities. After some wrangling, the administrators adopted a two-part rule for pregnancy: (1) the pregnancy itself was not regarded as a disability covered by the statute; but (2) any complications arising from the pregnancy were covered. As administered, the plan was financially stable and solvent. The question was whether it was constitutionally deficient, given its explicit exclusion of normal pregnancy from coverage.

As often happens in constitutional litigation, the choice of the standard of judicial scrutiny foreordained the outcome of the case. Justice Potter Stewart, speaking for a majority of the Court, held that the applicable standard of review was the same low standard of rational basis review applicable to economic regulation generally. "This Court has held that, consistently with the Equal Protection Clause, a State 'may take one step at a time, addressing itself to the phase of the problem which seems most acute to the legislative mind . . . The legislature may select one phase of one field and apply a remedy there, neglecting the others.' "[7] The Court then treated the case essentially as one involving social welfare programs and *not* sex discrimination as such, since women received every bit as much coverage as men.[8] California, it determined, could properly worry about the total costs of the expanded coverage and the soundness of its

5. Id. at 690.

6. 417 U.S. 484 (1974).

7. Id. at 495, citing *Williamson v. Lee Optical Co.*, 348 U.S. 483, 489 (1955), arguably the most lenient of the substantive due process and equal protection cases.

8. Id. at 495.

independent program. *Frontiero's* invitation to adopt a strict scrutiny standard to review sex classifications was rebuffed, and the California plan was saved from attack.

Justice Brennan in dissent adhered to the strict scrutiny standard he had proposed in *Frontiero*.[9] In light of the wide range of conditions covered by the statute, he said, to single out normal pregnancy for special treatment was a form of sex discrimination that required a high level of justification to withstand constitutional attack. As long as the need for disability payments was the same, Justice Brennan could not see how pregnancy could be excluded when every other condition—from voluntary cosmetic surgery to sterilization to single-sex illnesses—was covered. The obvious financial dislocations were not sufficient to save the statute: the same pie could be sliced into thinner pieces in order to release the funds needed to cover pregnancy, or the total size of the pie could be increased through larger premiums in order to keep constant existing levels of compensation. Justice Brennan concluded that the Constitution required California to use the same set of rules for pregnancy coverage that the EEOC guidelines specified for Title VII: although an employer is under no obligation to provide health coverage, once health coverage is provided, it must extend to pregnancy.[10]

The outcome in *Geduldig* is right, but not for the reasons advanced by the Court. Justice Brennan's strict scrutiny test should apply, but the statute passes muster nonetheless for reasons hinted at in Justice Stewart's opinion.[11] Initially there is no reason why a low level of scrutiny should be applied to the operation of a mandatory state insurance pool. The accommodating "rational basis" test applied in *Geduldig* has long shielded from constitutional scrutiny countless legislative excesses driven by special interest politics. To allow the legislature to proceed one step at a time all too often issues an open invitation to impose unprincipled taxation and regulation, all of which move us further from viable and robust competitive markets.[12]

Nonetheless, a powerful defense of the California statute is possible

9. Id. at 497.

10. Id. at 502. The regulations, 29 C.F.R. §1604.10(b) (1989), are still in place today.

11. For a parallel approach to mine, see George Rutherglen, "Sexual Equality in Fringe-Benefit Plans," 65 *Va. L. Rev.* 199, 217–223 (1979).

12. Thus, the law contested in *Williamson v. Lee Optical Co.,* 348 U.S. 483 (1955), forbade opticians from fixing broken glasses or fitting them to a patient without a prescription from a licensed optometrist or ophthalmologist. The statute protected more skilled eye doctors from their lower-skilled competitors for no good social reason.

under the strict scrutiny standard championed but misapplied in Justice Brennan's dissent. The correct analysis starts with an understanding of how any insurance pool works.[13] As manager of an economic institution, the operator of an insurance plan has to guard against the private strategic behavior of participants that threatens to undermine the plan's viability. Special issues arise in *Geduldig,* since participation in the California pool was mandatory for anyone taking up employment in a covered industry. The basic insurance insights, however, are better understood if one first looks to the way in which disability insurance, indeed insurance generally, functions in a voluntary market.

Initially, to be stable, a voluntary insurance system must provide each participant a benefit (in the form of expected disability payments) that exceeds his or her costs of joining the program. Unless that condition is satisfied, the entire plan will unravel. The best risks will leave the plan, which then will be unable to collect premiums sufficient to cover its total obligations from the remaining high-risk pool members. In private situations a variety of factors helps to achieve plan stability. Most persons are risk averse (that is, they will pay some price to be rid of uncertainty). In terms of disability, then, they want insurance, as a rough first approximation, to equalize the stream of income that they would obtain both working and unable to work. Even if the insurance system is not totally fair (that is, it does not charge persons exactly in proportion with their risk), it may be stable if the resulting imbalances are small enough to provide all participants with some net gain once risk aversion is taken into account. As long as everyone prospers, the gains do not have to be equal for all participants for the pool to remain stable. So constructed, a sound insurance program has an obvious advantage over private saving for the same class of covered disabilities. Payment of a small premium replaces the need to put aside a large cash reserve, which may never be called on if the anticipated contingency does not occur. Insurance obviates the need for large cash accumulations for disability as much as for death.

There is an obverse side to this analysis. Any voluntary insurance plan will disintegrate if some individuals find that they have to pay more in coverage than they expect to receive in benefits. That risk is substantial unless certain conditions are attached to participation. Two major villains are at work in all insurance markets: moral hazard and adverse selection. The first term refers to situations in which the proba-

13. This understanding is essential for many areas of law; see, generally, Richard A. Epstein, "Products Liability as an Insurance Market," 14 *J. Legal Stud.* 645 (1985).

bility that a certain event will occur is increased by virtue of its being rendered compensable under the insurance policy. Originally moral hazard referred, as the term suggests, only to deliberate acts of destruction, such as when an owner commits arson on his own property in order to collect fire insurance. But in modern discussions it refers to *any* increase in the likelihood that the insured event will occur owing to the awareness that the risk of loss is covered and thus not fully borne by the insured. The problem is all-pervasive: people are likely to be less careful in securing their valuables if they are insured; they are more likely to seek out medical attention for small complaints if they have health insurance; they are more likely to drive carelessly if they have medical or liability insurance; they are more likely to lend money without consideration of the borrower's solvency if repayment of the loan is guaranteed by a third party. And women are more likely to choose to become pregnant if they can receive disability payments for an outcome they regard as beneficial.

Adverse selection refers to the common practice whereby the individuals who know (or have reason to believe) that they are likely to suffer a compensable event are the ones who are most willing to join an insurance plan. If the premium is held constant for all covered persons, those who have the greatest likelihood of collecting will receive an implicit subsidy from those who do not. These high-risk people will gravitate toward the plan while the low-risk people will stay away. Risky drivers are more eager to join an auto insurance pool if every customer is charged the same rate regardless of age, sex, marital status, or driving record. Accurate rate differentials and risk classifications are necessary to counter the problem, but these safeguards are both costly to implement and necessarily imperfect in design. Nonetheless, even though perfection is not obtainable, certain elementary cost-effective steps, such as classification by age and sex, are usually taken, at least when they are not prohibited by regulation.

Every system of private insurance contains eligibility requirements, policy limits and deductibles, and a raft of other specially tailored terms and conditions, all designed to combat these two persistent threats to a plan's viability. Fire insurance will not pay for arson; this exclusion is a means of controlling moral hazard. Individuals do better under group medical insurance than with individual coverage at far higher rates, for group insurance has exemptions for preexisting conditions to control for adverse selection. Insurance is therefore far more than a system for the distribution of benefits ex post. It is designed to maximize ex ante the gains from the pooling of risk in a world where all insured parties have systematic incentives to reduce their contributions to, and to increase their payouts from, the plan.

Justice Brennan in *Geduldig* writes as though moral hazard and adverse selection posed no risk to the viability of any disability plan, voluntary or mandatory. But of course they do. The point is not that the total dollar cost of a program will rise as coverage is increased. That is true whenever coverage is expanded; in and of itself that expansion is neither good nor bad. Rather, the critical issue is whether there is reason to believe that the inclusion of normal pregnancy as a disability leads to a rise in costs that exceeds the associated rise in benefits.

In order to see why this concern is warranted, consider the question of insuring for pregnancy outside the employment context, where no issue of discrimination between men and women arises. Assume that there is a pool of one thousand married women, all of childbearing age, who might seek coverage for normal pregnancy. How would one sell insurance to members of that group? If a company sold policies on an individual basis, we can guess who would buy the policies and who would not: the women who planned to have children would purchase insurance; women who did not want (or could not have) children would not. Many others would face harder decisions because of their uncertainty about their prospects or desires. The insurer therefore could not calculate the rates by assuming that the women who signed on to its plan were a random sample of the entire class of women, even of similar age and marital status. Using average birth rates for that subset of the population would understate the frequency of claims and the total number of claim dollars. The plan would go broke. Instead, a far higher premium would have to be charged to offset the bias in participation.

Alternatively, all women in the group could be required to purchase insurance against the risk of normal pregnancy. That solution would prevent the adverse selection affecting a voluntary plan, but at the cost of creating two other problems of equal or greater severity. First, those women who did not want to become pregnant would be asked to subsidize those who did; and second, the frequency of pregnancy across the class of insured women would increase beyond the expected level in a world without insurance since part of the cost would be socialized through the fund. The only question here is the extent of the increase, which could be small if the costs of pregnancy were small relative to the total costs of raising a child. But any compulsory plan clearly increases moral hazard as part of the price of controlling adverse selection.

The California disability system sought to cope with these conflicting pressures. Recall that the plan placed at least some constraint on adverse selection. But more serious complications arise when normal pregnancy is added to the list of compensable events. The inclusion of pregnancy so skews the mix of contributions and payouts that the pool becomes unstable in that some workers are made to pay more in premiums than they receive (subjectively) in benefits. In the California plan at issue in *Geduldig,* even before pregnancy benefits were included, women made 28 percent of the contributions to the plan but received 33 percent of the benefits. The addition of pregnancy benefits boosted their receipts to 45 percent of plan payouts.[14]

Nonetheless, even with this skew, dissolution need not take place as a matter of course. With private plans the other benefits received by the workers who do not want pregnancy coverage may be sufficient that they still find it worth their while to remain in the pool. Say, when pregnancy was not covered, the recipients paid in $100 and received $120. Once it was covered, they still paid in $100 but received $105 in exchange; hence they did not exit, although they were allowed to by law. When membership in the insurance pool is required by state law, the political calculations are somewhat different. Certain workers may find that they are forced to make contributions in excess of benefits; yet they will be unable to exit. The political coalition will survive as long as a majority of workers continues to derive net benefits from the pool and hence are able (under very simple legislative choice models) to block repeal of the total plan.

There is, however, a second question that is more relevant to overall social analysis. If the mandatory plan is modified to cover the expenses of normal pregnancy, will the total net gains of all participants (whether measured in dollars or utility) increase or decrease? On the foregoing analysis the answer is clear: it will decrease. Some plan members will, in effect, be required to subsidize the pregnancies of others. No subsidy is a simple transfer from one group to another. All subsidies have negative allocative consequences as well, in this case by inducing additional pregnancies that women would not choose to undergo if they had to bear the full cost themselves.[15] In addition, employers will surely have some additional incentive to avoid hiring women likely to bear children, given the

14. Figures cited in Rutherglen, "Sexual Equality" at 220 n.98. These calculations were doubtless static in that they did not take into account any increases in on-the-job pregnancies in response to the change in coverage rules.

15. More formally any system of pregnancy coverage means that to receive benefits (B), the covered woman pays out of her own pocket only some fraction, p, of the total

additional costs in excess of premiums that they will have to pay. Other potential workers, both men and women, whose total compensation package is reduced by the payment they make to the pregnancy fund, will also be less willing to accept jobs than before.[16] Workers already employed may lobby in subtle ways against hiring women likely to become pregnant.

The only real question, then, concerns the magnitude of the negative effects. There is no reason to assume that they will be small. The decisions are not all-or-nothing choices. Individuals can temporize. At the margin some women will decide to have babies sooner than otherwise, or to increase family size. Other workers may choose to remain self-employed, to return to work later, or to retire sooner. The decision to provide pregnancy coverage has a powerful influence on primary conduct which cannot be ignored in any constitutional analysis.

Under this analysis it should now be clear why *Geduldig* is *not* a situation where the Court should say that if the state wants a system of disability insurance, it must include pregnancy in the pool of covered events. There are too many instances in which the extension of coverage to pregnancy results in an overall social welfare loss. As I have argued elsewhere,[17] the function of the doctrine of unconstitutional conditions (the state need not do X but if it does do X, then it cannot do it on condition Y) is to prevent the state from exploiting its monopoly position in order to extract some disproportionate share of the cooperative gains of any government project for the benefit of some select group of individuals. Behind the argument is the all-too-familiar proposition that any effort ex ante to shift gains among persons results ex post in a net total loss for everyone concerned. To say that women cannot be allowed on the public highway unless they pay license fees twice that of men, or vice versa, given that there are no cost differences in processing their applications, is unconstitutional.

Justice Brennan invokes the unconstitutional condition argument for the disability plan in *Geduldig:* although the state need not have a dis-

---

costs (C). Where pC < B < C, her private benefits are greater than her private costs, so she will have the baby. But there will be a social loss equal to C − B.

16. See Richard A. Posner, "An Economic Analysis of Discrimination," 56 *U. Chi. L. Rev.* 1311, 1332–34 (1989), noting the redistribution to married couples with children from married couples without.

17. Richard A. Epstein, "Foreword: Unconstitutional Conditions, State Power, and the Limits of Consent," 102 *Harv. L. Rev.* 4 (1988). See also Chapter 5 at 108–112, under the heading "Unconstitutional Conditions."

ability plan, if it does have one, pregnancy must be covered. In making this claim he implicitly assumes that the state has moved to deprive future pregnant women of their proportionate gains from the disability program. But that conclusion is wrong, first, because there is reason to believe that the total amount of gain will shrink if normal pregnancy is included in coverage, and second, because including normal pregnancy under the plan gives some women a *higher* rate of return from their participation dollars than is received by other plan members, male or female. If anything, the exclusion of pregnancy from the pool might be constitutionally *required* in order to equalize benefits for other participants, both male and female.[18]

Two other errors in Brennan's analysis should now be apparent. First, he argues that it is unprincipled to exclude pregnancy while offering coverage for a large number of other conditions, voluntary and involuntary. But the right question is whether offering coverage for any of these events significantly alters the ratio of benefits to costs for all contributors; these critical numbers may be in balance whether the coverage is extensive or limited. It is a mistake in analyzing insurance to focus on the need for coverage only after an event occurs. Most of the other voluntary events are low-cost operations that occur only infrequently, without a large moral hazard component. Their inclusion or exclusion from coverage is of supreme indifference to this constitutional equal protection challenge, provided women gain in proportion with men under the programs already in place.

Second, pregnancy need not be included simply because the plan has other features that may not comport with the strict insurance objective of equalizing the ratio of contributions to benefits for all plan participants. Some imperfections are not large enough to matter. For example, the decision to cover the complications of pregnancy will surely work to skew the distribution of plan benefits, for only those women who become pregnant will face this class of risk. But the percentage of cases within this class is far smaller than the number of normal pregnancies. It is therefore

---

18. That conclusion rests on the assumption that the other benefits and burdens are roughly equally distributed across the pool. If pregnant women have lower costs of other kinds, inclusion of pregnancy coverage may be warranted to offset those risks. But the case was never put on this ground, which demands sound actuarial accounting for all losses. In addition, the evidence suggests that women have higher health costs than men, independent of pregnancy. See note 21 and accompanying text. For further discussion of the parallel issues in unemployment insurance in religion cases, see Richard A. Epstein, "Foreword: Unconstitutional Conditions" at 79–89.

understandable why the plan administrator in *Geduldig* first sought to exclude the complications of pregnancy from plan coverage but then relented on that issue after litigation.[19] But even without that modification the plan in *Geduldig* should meet Justice Brennan's standard of strict scrutiny under the equal protection clause. As long as the feature of the plan does not work any redistribution of wealth from women to men or vice versa, the constitutional inquiry is at an end.

Title VII Analysis

General Electric v. Gilbert

Geduldig set the stage for the next pregnancy coverage case, *General Electric Co. v. Gilbert*,[20] in which General Electric's exclusion of medical benefits for normal pregnancy was challenged not under the equal protection clause but under Title VII. In sustaining the plan against a charge of sex discrimination, the Court, speaking through Justice Rehnquist, reiterated its analysis in *Geduldig*, noting that there was no risk covered for men that was not covered for women, and that adding pregnancy coverage would materially increase the cost of the plan. The Court presented evidence of plan experience for both 1970 and 1971 which suggested that, even without pregnancy benefits, General Electric's cost in funding the plan for women workers was nearly twice that for funding the same coverage for men—$82.57 for women as opposed to $45.76 for men in 1970, and $112.91 for women to $62.08 for men in 1971.[21] The Court thus hewed to the outcome in *Geduldig* under the stricter disparate treatment and disparate impact analysis of Title VII. As long as the overall distribution of benefits under its plan favored women, General Electric could not be held to have discriminated against them. If anything, men

19. 417 U.S. 484 at 490–491.

20. 429 U.S. 125 (1976).

21. Id. at 130–131 n.9. These figures are not unrepresentative of the overall situation. See, e.g., *State of New York Insurance Department, Disability Income Insurance Cost Differentials between Men and Women* (1976). Note that this conclusion is consistent with the general observation that women receive smaller payments than men from the system because men have somewhat higher rates of absenteeism and sickness. As Rutherglen notes: "These statistics fail to take account of the distribution of men in more hazardous occupations, which while increasing the aggregate rate of disability and sickness of men relative to women, does not affect the higher rate of women within equally hazardous occupations." Rutherglen, "Sexual Equality" at 239 n.181.

might be able to complain. Adding pregnancy benefits only increased the overall redistribution from men to women, and from those women unlikely to become pregnant to those who were. The Court's own economic analysis thus led it to reject the 1972 EEOC guidelines on the subject.[22] The prohibition against sex discrimination does not require a subsidy for pregnancy and childbirth.

Justice Brennan in dissent never confronted the Court's evidence that the current plan, even with its pregnancy exclusion, worked a modest redistribution in wealth toward women employees. Instead, he noted that the only conditions excluded were solely and explicitly female, and hence the program had to be discriminatory. He further suggested that the list could be expanded to exclude other procedures (such as mastectomies) that are required only by females without offending the Court's logic. In so arguing he wrote as if Title VII necessarily would be reduced to toothless formalism by the Court's upholding the G.E. plan. He overlooked the powerful economic constraint that still remained: the present value of the benefits for women must still equal that of the benefits for men. Any systematic exclusion of female-related conditions would change the benefit-to-contribution ratio for both male and female employees and could lead to a violation of Title VII's basic constraint, which is similar to the equal present value constraint for pensions. This ratio provides powerful protection against insurance programs that would cover prostate surgery but exclude mastectomies, or vice versa.

Accordingly, the correct reading of Title VII is supportive of the prosaic and common practices of the insurance industry. Title VII can be applied intelligently to insurance benefit plans without setting that world upside down, and without abandoning the use of the "neutral actuarial principles" on which, as Justice Brennan recognizes, they necessarily depend.[23] Insurance is a term or condition of employment whereby, ceteris paribus, neither men nor women can obtain a preferred deal. The prohibition against implicit redistribution is thus identical to that demanded by the constitutional standards of strict scrutiny. If anything, standard actuarial techniques are *required* by Title VII, not prohibited by it.

So construed, Title VII deviates from the market solution in only one respect. The market system allows the employer to provide packages of

22. Id. at 142. The 1966 opinion letters by the general counsel at the EEOC had in fact held that the pregnancy exclusion did not violate Title VII. Id. at 142–143.

23. Id. at 149 (Brennan, J., dissenting).

employment benefits with different values. This added flexibility is a virtue. The basket of fringe benefits demanded by women may differ systematically from that demanded by men. Before Title VII the employer merely had to respond to the differences without having to justify them to an external government authority suspicious of its motives. Now there is a risk that the justifications offered will be rejected. Even so, allowing the employer under Title VII to defend by showing that the present value of the total fringe benefit package is identical for men and for women is not too onerous, for the law compels persons to do only what they (roughly speaking) want to do.

Gilbert then reflects the view that Title VII allows the employer to respond to differences in basic positions between men and women. It thus follows the original legislative understanding that the employer was under no duty to make adjustments internal to the firm to offset the imbalance of fortunes, prospects, and endowments that workers bring to their jobs. Just as Title VII does not require the employer to correct for differences in education, job training, or personal aptitudes,[24] so too it does not require the firm to correct for differences in insurance risks that arise outside the employment relationship.

The attack on *Gilbert* rejects this view and rests heavily on an expanded vision of Title VII: the employer is under the obligation to correct imbalances that are not created by the employment relationship. Pregnancy constitutes a major asymmetry in the initial position between men and women. Women are subject to this risk of interruption of employment whereas men are not. Women bear the costs of pregnancy and its medical complications and men (at least directly) do not. The law, it is said, should do something about this skewed distribution of original endowments. This criticism of *Gilbert* thus resonates closely with the writings of John Rawls, who has constantly attacked "natural differences" as arbitrary and not worthy of social respect.[25] *Gilbert,* by enshrining the dominance of biology, is said to have far more unfortunate consequences for women than it does for men.

The message has been applied to the area of sex discrimination. Catharine MacKinnon condemns *Gilbert* in these terms: "Women thus buy less employment security for the same insurance contributions."[26] Her state-

---

24. See the excerpts from Michael I. Sovern, *Legal Restraints on Racial Discrimination in Employment* (1966), in Chapter 9.

25. John Rawls, *A Theory of Justice* (1971).

26. Catharine A. MacKinnon, *Sexual Harassment of Working Women* 114 (1979).

ment has a plausible ring, but she is wrong on the economics. Women have bought *as much* insurance protection as men for *the same* insurance contributions; indeed, according to the facts of *Gilbert,* they have bought more. If women's security needs are 100 and men's needs are 50, then any insurance plan that reduces men's needs to 0 and women's to 40 provides *more* insurance protection (60 versus 50) for women than it does for men. It is wholly irrelevant to the question of *what* has been bought that the residual risk of women is now 40 and that of men is 0. The insurance contracts work to everyone's benefit even though women have an additional exposure to risk ex post, just as they did ex ante. The critical question is the level of risk reduction achievable for the same dollar, and by that standard the women in *Gilbert* fared better than the men. The insurance *transaction,* therefore, is hard to condemn in and of itself on equity grounds, even if the original distribution of natural endowments is thought indefensible.

MacKinnon's argument is not only wrong, it is counterproductive. The antidiscrimination law does not require that any health insurance be provided at all. It is therefore permissible to leave women with 100 units of exposure as long as men are required to bear 50. Why then place a barrier in the path of women who seek to obtain some protection? Her expectation must be that the insistence on complete coverage for all conditions will induce employers to provide women with 100 units of benefits in order to provide men with 50. But in some cases the invitation will be declined, so both sides will be worse off, as was the case with pension benefits.[27] In other cases the full coverage will be provided to all women, but those likely to become pregnant will be that much less likely to be hired in the first instance. One cannot look at the soundness of mandatory pregnancy benefits solely from the perspective of pregnant women who are covered after the fact. The larger incentive structure is critical, and again it is not possible to identify any social benefits from this disruption of voluntary contracts.

All this is not to say that the special position of pregnant women should be ignored as a matter of social policy. It is only that the attack on *Gilbert,* with its Rawlsian skepticism about natural differences, takes a wrong turn when it spills over into Title VII. It may well be that someone should do something about the problems that women face in the workplace. But if so, the question should be faced head on for what it is—one of public subsidy for child rearing as a desirable social activity. There is

27. See discussion of *Norris* in Chapter 15 at 325–326.

no discrimination against women from insurance plans that work to their net advantage relative to men. It may be appropriate, however, to provide tax relief for pregnant women, or even to set up a program of family allowances that become payable during pregnancy. On balance I oppose such subsidies on the ground that, like other forms of subsidy, they distort resource allocation. But at least if any subsidy is made, it should be done openly as a charge against the public fisc, and not covertly through the fashionable but costly off-budget system of mandated benefits.[28]

To use Title VII to provide financial aid to pregnant women thus fails on three counts. First, it injects the element of employer wrong into a situation where none has been committed. Second, it distorts the operation of the system of employee benefits by inducing some employers to drop or reduce coverage in order to minimize the impact of Title VII. Third, it uses a system of mandated benefits to pass on to particular employers costs that are better borne through social insurance; here the costs are made explicit and are incorporated into the tax base, where they can be subject to political scrutiny and review.

The Aftermath of Gilbert

The position reached in *Gilbert,* though sound on the merits, did not endure judicially or politically under the avalanche of criticism directed against it. Instead it was quickly gutted, first by judicial and then by legislative action. *Nashville Gas Company v. Satty*[29] involved both medical expenses and leave privileges for pregnancy. Justice Rehnquist, speaking for a majority of the Court, upheld under *Gilbert* the policy that denied sick leave for pregnancy when it was allowed for other conditions. But writing for a unanimous Court, he struck down the employer's leave policy. It was held to be a violation of Title VII to require female employees to sacrifice all employment seniority (on which priority for new assignments depended) when they took a pregnancy leave, although seniority was preserved for employees who took work leaves for other

---

28. The attack on the use of off-budget devices in lieu of direct subsidies has direct application to all forms of regulation that are in effect implicit wealth transfers. The point has surfaced in constitutional law in connection with rent control. See *Pennell v. City of San Jose,* 485 U.S. 1, 21–23 (1988) (Scalia, J., dissenting), which is discussed in Richard A. Epstein, "Rent Control and the Theory of Efficient Regulation," 54 *Brooklyn L. Rev.* 741, 753–755 (1988). The issue becomes manifest in connection with the handicap discrimination laws. See Chapter 22.

29. 434 U.S. 136 (1977).

nonoccupational disabilities. The case was distinguished from *Gilbert* on these grounds:

> Here, by comparison [to *Gilbert*], petitioner has not merely refused to extend to women a benefit that men cannot and do not receive [i.e., medical expenses for pregnancy], but has imposed on women a substantial burden that men need not suffer. The distinction between benefits and burdens is more than one of semantics. We held in *Gilbert* that §703(a)(1) did not require that greater economic benefits be paid to one sex or the other "because of their differing roles in 'the scheme of human existence,' " 429 U.S., at 139 n.17. But that holding does not allow us to read §703(a)(2) to permit an employer to burden female employees in such a way as to deprive them of employment opportunities because of their different role.[30]

The proposed distinction rightly leaves no one happy. The critics of *Gilbert* regard the decision as something of a sop to women employees. As MacKinnon writes: "It is hard to avoid the impression that the real distinction here is that granting seniority credit is a cheap concession which mainly benefits some workers over others, while paying disability benefits is expensive for employers."[31] The economics of the situation are more complex than this, however, because the shift in seniority influences both the relative income and position of employees and the overall success of the firm, for otherwise the firm would be indifferent as to whether the policy were retained or discarded. Nonetheless, MacKinnon's point does have force in that there is little in the logic of sex discrimination and pregnancy that permits cash benefits to be treated in one fashion and in-kind benefits such as sick leave in another. Her argument, however, is a two-edged sword, because if *Gilbert* is correct in its refusal to require under Title VII a cash subsidy for pregnant women, it becomes indefensible to bury the subsidy even deeper in the guise of an in-kind mandated benefit.

The thinness of the distinction between *Gilbert* and *Satty,* moreover, is evident on the face of *Satty* itself. Justice Rehnquist's verbal gymnastics to one side, the Court offers us no explanation why the failure to provide leave privileges was "imposing a burden" and "not extending a benefit." That distinction makes some good sense in "stranger cases," where there is a difference between killing a person and choosing not to rescue him.

30. Id. at 142.
31. MacKinnon, *Sexual Harassment* at 113.

The baseline against which conduct is judged normally is individual autonomy against physical invasion; thus hitting people is actionable but not helping them is not. Both *Satty* and *Gilbert,* however, arise in the context of an ongoing employment relation, replete with affirmative actions of all sorts, in which the stark dichotomy between harming and not benefiting is wholly useless. All cases involve the withholding of benefits, or, if it matters, imposing burdens. If the initial baseline is work without leave, then leave is a benefit that is conferred by the employer. The only distinction between *Gilbert* and *Satty* is between the types of benefits that the employer chooses to give or withhold.

Within the framework of Title VII, moreover, the same inquiry made in *Gilbert* should, and could, be undertaken in *Satty* to determine whether the leave privilege under the existing plan provided greater benefits to men than to women or vice versa. It could then have been asked whether extending the leave privilege to women would increase the extent of the redistribution in their favor. But unlike *Gilbert, Satty* made no effort to quantify the frequency of leaves for men and women, or to estimate the employer's costs in keeping their places open, evidence of a sort that might well have hurt the plaintiff's case. Instead, the argument that prevailed was that if the risk of lost privileges for men is reduced to zero, it must also be reduced to zero for women, even at far higher cost—the very same argument rightly rejected in *Gilbert.* After *Satty,* the only way to avoid a violation of Title VII is to provide an implicit subsidy to pregnant women.

The ease with which *Satty* bypassed *Gilbert* marked the latter case as ripe for overruling, an action I suspect would have come within a few years at most. But this prediction was never put to the test. *Gilbert* provoked an instantaneous and sustained outcry. One quotation among countless others captures the dominant mood:

It [*Gilbert*] may go down as the most cost-conscious decision the Supreme Court has made since Dred Scott was forcibly returned to his masters after escaping to free territory.

The Supreme Court ruled then that Scott was somebody's property no matter where he was located. So much for the interpretation of human rights when big money and economic systems are at stake.[32]

32. Bernice Malamud, "Sick Pay-Pregnancy Rule Hit," *New York Journal of Commerce,* December 14, 1976, reprinted in *Legislative History of the Pregnancy Discrimination Act of 1978,* Pub. Law 95–555, at 4.

Compulsion and freedom thus become indistinguishable, as market solutions sanctioned by *Gilbert* are denounced as being tantamount to slavery. The irresistible tide resulted in the Pregnancy Discrimination Act of 1978, which added section 701(k) to Title VII. The major arguments for the new statute were two. It was first argued that the exclusion of a sex-specific condition violated Title VII because it left women at greater risk than men once the disability program was introduced. The answer, of course, is identical to that developed in the discussion of *Gilbert*. The attack on the employer's insurance program again proves too much because these women were at greater risk before employment and would have been at greater risk had they been employed by a firm with no disability program at all. Yet even under Title VII there is no obligation to provide any coverage at all. Therefore the failure to provide pregnancy coverage must be sex discrimination even if no other coverage is provided. How else is it possible to equalize the uninsured risks for men and women in the context of employment?

The second argument ties into the first, and shows the confusion between antidiscrimination and general welfare rights arguments. The legislative report emphasizes repeatedly that the want of pregnancy benefits hits poor women hardest. "Thirty-five million women are working or seeking work. And 25 million of these are working because they must, either because they are the sole support of their families or because their husbands earn less than $7,000 per year."[33] Yet if that is the concern, on this point the statute is misguided, if only because it will surely induce some firms to avoid all disability coverage if the costs of pregnancy coverage are too high. If any program is appropriate, the question of subsidy should be faced outright as a question of general appropriations, not by an amendment to Title VII. The decision to use the antidiscrimination laws as a heavyhanded effort to evade the subsidy problem is but one illustration of the massive transformation that overtook the civil rights laws during the 1970s. The modest goal of removing irrational prejudices from employment decisions had long since been attained, to the extent that legal doctrines could obtain them. What was at stake was a perceived imperfect wealth distribution attributable to other social causes. In line with its new expanded objective, the 1978 act provided:

The terms "because of sex" or "on the basis of sex" include, but are not limited to, because of or on the basis of pregnancy, childbirth, or

---

33. Statement of Senator Edward Brooke, *Legislative History* at 7.

related medical conditions; and women affected by pregnancy, child-birth, or related conditions shall be treated the same for all employment purposes, including receipt of benefits under fringe benefit programs, as other persons not so affected but similar in their ability or inability to work, and nothing in section 703(h) [regulating seniority and merit systems] shall be interpreted to permit otherwise.[34]

There are several notable features about the statutory treatment of pregnancy. First, the subject is not regarded as a sui generis problem that demands unique handling. Instead, pregnancy discrimination is dealt with in the definition section of the act, where it is deemed to be a form of sex discrimination, an analysis that furthers the confusion between welfare benefits and the antidiscrimination laws. The implicit sleight of hand of the statute is revealed by the interpretation given to the statute under the EEOC's "Questions and Answers on the Pregnancy Discrimination Act":

Q. If an employer has an all female workforce or job classification, must benefits be provided for pregnancy-related conditions?

A. Yes. If benefits are provided for other conditions, they must also be provided for pregnancy-related conditions.

The questions and answers then set out in detail the exact equivalence that is demanded between pregnancy and other disabilities on matters of payment, leave, promotion, reinstatement, and the like. No longer does anyone think that there is a viable distinction between *Gilbert* and *Satty*. There is no need to analyze the EEOC responses in depth because they all stem from the more general premise of section 701(k): "It shall not be a defense under title VII to a charge of sex discrimination in benefits that the cost of such benefits is greater with respect to one sex than the other."[35] The major ongoing debate about the Pregnancy Discrimination Act is whether it affords relief only for disparate treatment claims or whether it covers disparate impact claims as well, and thus allows employees to attack facially neutral policies that have a larger impact on pregnant women.[36] The matter could have been clarified by Congress if it

34. The Pregnancy Discrimination Act of 1978, Pub. L. 95–555, now found in section 701(k), as amended.

35. 29 C.F.R. §1604.9 (1989).

36. See, e.g., *Scherr v. Woodland School Community Consolidated District No. 50*, 867 F.2d 974 (7th Cir. 1988). There are also questions under the statute as to whether the pregnancy benefits for female spouses and dependents must be the same as pregnancy benefits for female employees. See *Newport News Shipbuilding & Dry Dock Co. v. EEOC*,

had stopped to consider the issue one way or the other. There are also delicate questions of how and whether the BFOQ exception to the basic statute should be applied to employers who dismiss workers on account of pregnancy.[37] On the face of matters, it appears that the full apparatus of disparate impact and the BFOQ would apply to pregnancy cases under the statute, as it does to ordinary cases of sex discrimination, even though there has been some judicial uneasiness about pushing the statute that far. But if the basic pattern of the statute is a mistake, then, in theory, its extension cannot be a good thing.

The variations do not affect the key principle. The Pregnancy Discrimination Act illustrates the use of the antidiscrimination norm as a tool for redistributive ends. The implications of that strategy are as clear here as elsewhere. Every impulse of the market system is designed to ensure that all persons and firms internalize all their relevant costs; in this way market decisions advance social welfare by preventing people from making others pay for their own personal consumption. Most modern systems of tort law and environmental regulation regard cost internalization as central to their own coherence and success: where costs are partially externalized and benefits are fully internalized, there will be too much of the underlying activity. It is impossible to imagine, therefore, how any collective decisions could be justified or defended when these costs are explicitly ignored. But the antidiscrimination laws receive a different response because of their ostensibly preferred status within the legal order. The legislative and judicial insistence on their special status, however, cannot obscure the social losses incurred by their implementation, with pregnancy as elsewhere.

462 U.S. 669 (1983), which held that the differential treatment discriminated against male employees by offering them a less inclusive benefit package than it offered female employees. Note that there is at least this asymmetry in the underlying situation: medical benefits are at issue for both spouses and dependents, but leave time and promotions apply only to employees.

37. See, e.g., *Chambers v. Omaha Girls Club, Inc.,* 834 F.2d 697 (8th Cir. 1988), rehearing denied, 840 F.2d 583 (8th Cir. 1988), upholding (over three dissenting judges) the dismissal of an unmarried pregnant worker on the ground that she could not provide "a positive role model" in the Girls Club in which she worked.

CHAPTER 17

Sexual Harassment

A Tort in Disguise?

Harassment comes in all forms and shapes; yet it is notoriously difficult to define. It plainly includes all forms of conduct designed to vex, annoy, or bother another person by means that fall short of serious and permanent physical injury or threats thereof. Its status as a source of intermediate harm creates a persistent dilemma for the legal system. As a general matter, the class of punishable offenses includes those behaviors that generate social losses that exceed the costs of preventing them by public enforcement. Although preventing murder, rape, burglary, and theft is expensive, the protection to the integrity of the person and the stability of property clearly justify the social expense. The only hard questions remaining are those of incremental enforcement: How many resources should be devoted to each category of offense, and how should they be spent?

Harassment, by contrast, introduces genuine difficulties on both the benefit and the cost sides of the social equation. The losses from harassment are not as severe as those from murder and rape and, in some instances at least, perhaps not even as serious as those attributable to burglary and theft. (Harassment by definition excludes the commission of more serious offenses such as molestation and forcible rape.) But to say that the harms inflicted by harassment are smaller than those caused by other forms of criminal conduct is not to say that these losses are small or insignificant. Harassment is anything but trivial.

The cost side of harassment is also problematic. Harassment is, or often may be, a diffuse offense, taking place in an irregular pattern over a long period of time. The parties to the dispute usually have some prior or ongoing relationship, a fact that raises the issue of consent, express or implied, which is difficult to prove or disprove. Enforcement costs are thus far higher than those associated with the major criminal offenses or tortious actions against strangers. On the whole, the question becomes a very difficult empirical one of whether the reduced benefits from enforcing norms against harassment (relative, say, to those for murder or rape) outweigh the increased costs and difficulties of putting that system into operation. Until relatively recently there was no strong social consensus on the question of legal prohibition against these antisocial practices. Do the benefits of eliminating harassment outweigh the costs of controlling it? The social problem arises because we must determine the *relative* importance when both costs are large.

Given the uneasy theoretical situation, how do harassment cases fit into the common law and the general antidiscrimination norm of Title VII? The brief account of harassment just given contains nothing to link harassment to the prohibition against sex discrimination. The legal issues surrounding BFOQs or sex-linked pension and insurance plans are solely artifacts of Title VII. But sexual harassment is not. Nonetheless, starting with Catharine MacKinnon's 1979 book on sexual harassment,[1] most modern case law and scholarship on the subject posit an ever closer connection between harassment and discrimination, in view of the sexual motives behind the overt behavior and the sexual vulnerabilities on which it preys. Sexual harassment and sex discrimination have become linked under Title VII.

It is at this initial juncture, however, that the basic analysis goes astray. As a matter of first principle I have argued that all previously discussed forms of discrimination by private parties are not wrongs requiring state intervention or correction: the norms of ordinary contract law are adequate to deal with the problems that arise in the employment context. Where there is solely a failure or refusal to deal, there should be no remedy in contract or tort. So, too, when contractual terms differ by race or sex it is a private matter, best handled by individual choice and consent. Those who believe, for example, that they are worth more than they have been offered can search elsewhere. Those who regard taking lower wages as an opportunity to break into a market can accept the offer tendered. No uniform rule need determine which offers may be made or accepted.

Sexual harassment is an entirely different matter. Contractual principles

---

1. Catharine MacKinnon, *Sexual Harassment of Working Women: A Case of Sex Discrimination* (1979). For an exception to the dominant view, see Ellen Paul, "Sexual Harassment as Sex Discrimination: A Defective Paradigm," 8 *Yale Law & Pol. Rev.* 33 (1990). Paul's views and my own are highly congruent, and I owe much to her exposition of the problem.

play a leading role, and significant common law tort liability for both individual and firm would, and should, remain even if the antidiscrimination laws were erased from the statute books tomorrow. With harassment cases, the elimination of the antidiscrimination law does not return us to a world of properly functioning competitive markets. If it did, the firms in these competitive markets most likely would (and do) choose to check problems of sexual harassment in the workplace.[2] In order to show how these contract and tort principles work, and where they tend to break down, I examine the structure of common law rules that govern sexual harassment cases, for both the primary liability of the fellow workers who harass and the vicarious liability of the employer. I then move on to an examination of the advantages and disadvantages of treating sexual harassment cases under Title VII.

It is useful to set out the definition of sexual harassment contained in the EEOC's guidelines on discrimination because of sex, which offer a valuable counterpoint to my own analysis:

> Unwelcome sexual advances, requests for sexual favors, and other verbal or physical conduct of a sexual nature constitute sexual harassment when (1) submission to such conduct is made either explicitly or implicitly a term or condition of an individual's employment, (2) submission to or rejection of such conduct by an individual is used as the basis for employment decisions affecting such individual, or (3) such conduct has the purpose or effect of unreasonably interfering with an individual's work performance or creating an intimidating, hostile or offensive working environment.[3]

The first and second are commonly called quid pro quo harassment, and the third hostile environment harassment.[4]

Common Law Action for Sexual Harassment

The Prima Facie Case

The common law does not take harassment lightly. Consider the many possible causes of action that can support a charge of harassment on the

---

2. Thus most universities, including the University of Chicago, have introduced detailed codes to regulate the question of sexual and racial harassment.

3. 29 C.F.R. §1604.11(a) (1980).

4. For the differences between the two, see the discussion in this chapter.

job: assault and battery, insult, offensive battery, intentional infliction of emotional distress by extreme and outrageous conduct, invasion of privacy. Catharine MacKinnon observes that before the term *sexual harassment* was used, no one was aware of the problem because the language to describe it did not exist. "Sexual harassment has been not only legally allowed; it has been legally unthinkable."[5] In her view a new terminology was necessary to force the issue to the fore. But her own powerful depictions of workplace harassment, not to say brutalization, provide a powerful refutation of her phenomenological or linguistic point.[6] The words *assault, insult, intimidation, coercion,* and *emotional distress* all capture the scenes that she powerfully describes, and they are all part of an ancient common law lexicon. If the harasser engaged in touching without consent, he committed a battery.[7] If the touching was only threatened but not consummated, he committed an assault.[8] If the threat was for future physical harm, he committed the tort of intentional infliction of emotional distress.[9] If the challenged conduct involved shadowing or following a person, he committed the tort of invasion of privacy,[10] an action recognized long before Ron Gallela hounded Jacqueline Onassis.[11] Common law protection does not begin or end with rape or the infliction of serious bodily harm.

One notable feature of the common law rules is that they dispense with proof of motive for the assault, battery, or insult. It did not matter why the harassment took place or whether it was directed toward men, women, or children for reasons of race, sex, or national origin. Any motive will do. But this legal point does not show that *sexual* harassment is a side issue. It shows only that in one relevant dimension the common law rules of liability are *broader* than the analogous rules of Title VII,

5. See MacKinnon, *Sexual Harassment* at xi.
6. Id. at 57–99.
7. See Restatement (Second) of Torts §18 (1965), imposing liability for intentional offensive contact with another person.
8. See Restatement (Second) of Torts §21 (1965), subjecting a defendant to liability if "he acts intending to cause a harmful or offensive contact with the person of the other."
9. See Restatement (Second) of Torts §46 (1965), governing "outrageous conduct causing severe emotional distress."
10. See Restatement (Second) of Torts §652B (1965), governing intrusion upon seclusion. *DeMay v. Roberts,* 46 Mich. 160, 9 N.W. 146 (1881); *Nader v. General Motors Corp.,* 25 N.Y.2d 560, 255 N.E.2d 765, 307 N.Y.S.2d 647 (1970).
11. See, e.g., *Gallela v. Onassis,* 487 F.2d 986 (2d Cir. 1973).

which are unnecessarily limited by an antidiscrimination norm to certain motive-based forms of conduct.

Consent: Express and (Sometimes) Implied

The second broad class of relevant rules allows the defense of consent, express or implied, to any prima facie charge of harassment. Physical touching, including intimate sexual contact, for which there is consent is not tortious. In principle this line between consent and coercion is central to the maintenance of a free society. Precisely because the basic structural distinction is so powerful and enduring, there can be no thought of eliminating it altogether either by equating coercion with consent or consent with coercion. It makes as little sense to say that all sexual relations are rape as it is to say that none of them are. Because both analytical end points, naked coercion and eager consent, are so secure, the legal system faces the daunting task of sorting out the bewildering array of implied consent cases that occupy a significant middle portion of the spectrum. The consent issue is thus one unavoidable battleground in all harassment cases.

These consent and contract issues are never far from the surface in harassment cases arising in the employment setting. Indeed, the most troublesome cases analytically are the quid pro quo cases under the EEOC's guidelines, whereby the employer or supervisor simply says that a person will be hired or promoted only upon agreeing to have sexual relations. Within the standard model of contract, if the offer is made without complication it can be accepted or rejected. The *content* of the offer alone does not convert it into a form of harassment. It is the manner in which the advances are made, and the persistence with which they are pushed. At one level the complete private response is just to say no.

Nonetheless, it seems clear that offers of this sort are wholly unacceptable in virtually all work settings, to both employer and employee alike. Where that is the case, the logic of consent can be used not to excuse physical contact or personal behavior that would otherwise be regarded as tortious, but to render as improper certain forms of conduct that would otherwise be legal. The firm could therefore establish a set of rules, for the benefit of applicants as well as employees, that make certain specified forms of sexual conduct a violation. That violation can then become the basis of a private contract right of action against the offending party, an action to which that party consents as a condition for obtaining his or her job. To the extent that the EEOC definition of harassment tracks the standard expectations within the workplace, it offers a suitable set of implied terms that confer both benefits and burdens on all interested parties. But to the extent that it imposes *mandatory* terms, it may well impose solutions to this contracting problem that deviate from those that would be reached in a voluntary market transaction.

Problems of Proof

At this juncture the key issue is likely to be not one of principle but one of proof under any definition of harassment. If proof of consent is made too easy, then serious misbehavior may well escape punishment. But if proof of consent is made too difficult, then all sorts of levity, flirtation, and courtship are, de facto, banned from the workplace. It is pointless to go into the enormous factual problems that arise in individual cases, for hard definitional problems are often tested against an endless series of battles over evidence and credibility. It is enough to say that no matter how the common law sets its presumptions and organizes the evidence, there will always be serious and correct charges of a miscarriage of justice in individual cases, in both directions. It is as necessary to protect defendants against false accusations that can destroy family and career as it is to protect plaintiffs from forced advances with the same devastating effects. The right set of rules therefore is that which minimizes both sorts of error. No enforcement regime will eliminate them all.

Employer Liability, Contracting Out, and Contracting In

The common law, moreover, contains rules that hold employers vicariously liable for the torts of their employees within the scope of their employment. Harassment in the workplace is covered by these vicarious liability rules. But what form should they take? Here the possibilities are legion.[12] The employer could be held liable only if it authorized or ratified the particular act of the employee. At the opposite extreme, the employer could be strictly liable for the wrongs of the employee committed within the scope of employment, even if the conduct was explicitly forbidden by the employer, and even if the employer took all possible care to ensure that the harassment not take place. The only exception to this strict

12. For one explication of the general doctrine, see Alan O. Sykes, "The Economics of Vicarious Liability," 93 *Yale L. J.* 1231 (1984).

liability rule is for the frolic and detour of the employee.[13] In between, liability could be predicated on a theory of negligence—namely that the employer failed to institute certain safeguards, either in the selection or in the supervision of employees, necessary to prevent the harassment.

It is difficult to make a choice among these various rules at an abstract level. But there is no reason to attempt the task, for the use of contract responses to tort issues is as essential to establishing vicarious liability as it is for defining within a firm setting the direct liability of the harasser. Although there are powerful reasons to apply the strict tort rule of vicarious liability to protect *strangers* to the business, there is far less reason to do so when victim and harasser were contractually related to each other before the occurrence of the incident.[14] Potential employer liability for the harasser's misconduct is a proper subject of bargaining between the employer and employee, as the compensation for the position can be adjusted to take into account the residual risks that are left after various risks and precautions are assigned to each party. By abandoning tort rules of vicarious liability, we may craft superior rules that leave both sides better by contract than they are under the tort law.

The agreement need not cast all risk of liability on the employee, and it will not do so where the employer is in a better position to avoid the loss. The early workmen's compensation plans in the mid-nineteenth century, for example, displaced the tort rules and voluntarily *expanded* liability by a system of broader coverage for accidents with lower payments and more informal administrative procedures.[15] That solution may not be ideal in this case, but it may be advisable for the firm to mete out strong administrative sanctions in harassment cases without itself being subject to any tort liability. From an outside perch it is impossible to say. But since employers and employees are the best judges of their own self-interest, their agreements about the proper treatment of sexual harass-

13. Young B. Smith, "Frolic and Detour," 23 *Colum. L. Rev.* 44 (1923); Alan O. Sykes, "The Boundaries of Vicarious Liability: An Economic Analysis of the Scope of Employment Rule and Related Legal Doctrines," 101 *Harv. L. Rev.* 563 (1988). A frolic and detour is a diversion that an employee takes for his own benefit, and thus removes him from the course of his employment, thereby defeating any vicarious liability of the employer.

14. The distinction between vicarious liability to strangers and liability to contracting parties was recognized as long ago as *Farwell v. Boston & Worcester Railroad*, 45 Mass. (4 Met.) 49 (1842).

15. See, e.g., the terms of the plan set out in *Griffiths v. Earl of Dudley*, 9 Q.B.D. 357 (1882), discussed at length in Richard A. Epstein, "The Historical Origins and Economic Structure of Workers' Compensation Law," 16 *Ga. L. Rev.* 775, 789–797 (1982).

ment should be honored unless there is some breakdown in the bargaining process. In some instances—say, if false charges of harassment became rampant—it might be appropriate to contract out of tort liability for *both* the employer and the employee. Again, the outsider cannot say.

The Title VII Alternative

The early cases under Title VII did not regard sexual harassment as a form of sex discrimination because acts of harassment did not reflect official firm policy but were only the individual actions of company personnel exercised for their own benefit.[16] Cases of harassment were instances of employee frolic and detour, and hence were outside the scope of employment. No support for their inclusion is found in the legislative history of Title VII, which was silent on the subject.[17] These points have been brushed aside in more recent treatments of the subject, and the Supreme Court has endorsed the view, first made fashionable by MacKinnon, that sexual harassment is actionable under Title VII.[18]

There seems to be something of a stretch on the matter of statutory construction, but the point made little difference, for if the Supreme Court had held that sexual harassment fell outside Title VII, it is quite likely that Congress would have reversed that decision with great fanfare in a matter of months. The important and difficult question, therefore, is that of principle: Does Title VII offer a regime for regulating sexual harassment better than its common law alternative? The analytical contrast between these two systems is stark. Title VII stresses the harasser's motive, while the common law ties liability to the use or threat of force that results in emotional distress to its victim. Which basic approach do we prefer, and why?

Bisexual Harassment

One way to compare these two approaches conceptually is to consider the hypothetical case of the bisexual harasser, a person whose preferences run equally toward victimizing male and female employees.[19] The bisexual

---

16. See, e.g., *Corne v. Bausch & Lomb,* 390 F. Supp. 161 (D. Ariz. 1975).
17. See Paul, "Defective Paradigm" at 339.
18. See, for example, *Meritor Savings Bank v. Vinson,* 477 U.S. 57, 64–66 (1986).
19. A theme developed in *Corne,* 390 F. Supp. at 163, and Paul, "Defective Paradigm" at 339.

harasser is perfectly willing to alter the mix of his targets to satisfy any nondiscrimination norm that the law wishes to impose. Thus, if the work force is 40 percent male and 60 percent female, he will guarantee that 40 percent of his harassment victims are male and 60 percent are female. If randomization of victims, and not proportionate representation, is desired, he will follow the dictates of any lottery or random computer generator. As long as the only constraint on his conduct is a norm of equal treatment, he will allow the state to decide *who* his victims will be. The rub, of course, is that the bisexual harasser cannot be enjoined from harassing as much or as little as he wants. At most the antidiscrimination laws reduce the total level of harassment if the ratios forced on the harasser are different from those he would choose if left to his own devices. But enormous amounts of harassment could be practiced in perfect conformity with the nondiscrimination principle. As MacKinnon recognizes: "If both sexes are [harassed], under this argument [of equal rights] the treatment would probably not be considered gender-based, hence not sex discriminatory."[20]

She does not, however, appreciate the significance of this observation. This hypothetical case of bisexual harassment illustrates anew the primacy of the autonomy norm over the antidiscrimination norm in setting up the basic substantive provisions of the legal system.[21] Just as equal treatment by sex or race does nothing whatsoever to justify or excuse murder, so too it does nothing to justify or excuse harassment. The antidiscrimination norm has a limited office in any comprehensive social welfare theory. It makes sense only where equal treatment between men and women, whites and blacks, serves to advance the welfare of *both* classes by providing them with a higher level of satisfaction than could be obtained if interest group politics were allowed to skew the benefits of public coercion from one side to the other. It is a way of seeing that all parties get their just desserts when government regulation upsets ordinary common law property rights. But when both men and women lose equally from any antidiscrimination norm, then its continued use can make no sense. Why should everyone be made worse off in equal measure? There are too many cases where perfect compliance with the antidiscrimination norm allows unpardonable excesses of antisocial behavior.

Understood systemically, the antidiscrimination norm makes sense only as a qualification on the more powerful background norm of individual

---

20. MacKinnon, *Sexual Harassment* at 6.
21. See Chapter 1.

autonomy. Unlike the antidiscrimination norm, the autonomy norm takes from the would-be harasser the option of continuing his practice by alternating the objects of his abuse. In moral terms it calls for a total prohibition against harassment, tempered only by the costs of enforcement. Sexual harassment is best understood as a libertarian wrong based on utilitarian considerations of overall social welfare. The common law system, with its combined tort and contract approach, is for all its flaws the preferred way of combatting harassment. The best that the law of sex discrimination can do is imitate that approach. But the downside cannot be ignored, for the law of sex discrimination can confuse, and has confused, matters with institutional or statutory imperfections.

Consent, Proof, and Employer Liability Revisited

The dominance of the common law approach is confirmed by a closer look at the law of sexual harassment as it has evolved under Title VII. Even if the gist of the action is said to turn on the motive of the harasser, the outcomes in particular cases under Title VII turn on the same questions of consent, proof, and vicarious liability that cause so much difficulty within a common law framework. The antidiscrimination law may change the name of the action, and the court in which it is brought, but it cannot evade the fundamental issues of principle that determine right and wrong. The fragile accommodations at common law on consent, proof, and employer liability must also be made under Title VII. But the change in context adds the additional vexed inquiry and statutory overlay that can at best only muddy the legal waters and complicate litigation. And the use of contractual solutions (which has some faint chance of survival under state common law) is more surely doomed, given the general anticontractual bias of Title VII.[22]

The Case Law Response

The inability to formulate superior, or even different, liability rules for harassment cases under Title VII is well revealed in the decided cases. Here the sexual motivation is the easiest point to establish: normally it is apparent when a woman charges harassment by a man. Thereafter the prima facie case, consent, and vicarious liability arise just as they would at

---

22. See, e.g., *Sparks v. Pilot Freight Carriers, Inc.,* 830 F.2d 1554, 1558–59 (11th Cir. 1987), relying on the Restatement (Second) of Agency, §§219–237 (1958).

common law. Yet Title VII, and the EEOC regulations on harassment,[23] do nothing to clarify these familiar issues.

In *Meritor Savings Bank v. Vinson*[24] the Supreme Court held that sexual harassment cases were covered by Title VII. The conclusion is odd (not wrong, but odd) in light of the deafening silence in the legislative history. But the Court reached that conclusion on two grounds.[25] First, it held that the language of the statute, which covers all "terms, conditions, and privileges" of the employment relationship, is sufficient to reach harassment as a matter of linguistic construction, divorced from any knowledge of the legislative history. Second, it held that the Court should defer to EEOC, which in 1980 had issued its own regulations concerning harassment in the workplace.[26] The Court also noted that a uniform line of circuit court decisions had accepted the EEOC's guidelines.

The difficulties are substantial if Title VII reaches sexual harassment cases, for its substantive provisions give not a single hint as to how these cases should be treated. *Vinson* itself offers a replay of all the standard problems that arise under the common law analysis. The plaintiff, Michelle Vinson, was hired as a bank teller trainee by the defendant, Sidney Taylor, a vice president of the bank and one of its branch managers. Over the next four years she was promoted in stages to assistant branch manager, which position she held when she was fired, allegedly for demanding too much time off for sick leave. After she was fired, she claimed sexual harassment, asserting that although Taylor had originally treated her in a fatherly way, he had thereafter invited her out to dinner and suggested that they have sexual relations at a nearby hotel. Vinson alleged that she and Taylor had had relations some forty or fifty times. "In addition, respondent testified that Taylor fondled her in front of other employees, followed her into the women's restroom when she went there alone, exposed himself to her, and even forcibly raped her on several occasions. These activities ceased after 1977, [Vinson] stated, when she started going with a steady boyfriend."[27] The dismissal followed in November 1978.

The response was predictable. Taylor denied all charges and insisted that he had never had sexual relations with Vinson and had never propo-

23. See 29 C.F.R. §1604.11 (1989).
24. 477 U.S. 57 (1986).
25. Id. at 64–65.
26. See discussion in this chapter at 350–352.
27. 477 U.S. at 60.

sitioned her. He further charged that her accusations were made "in response to a business-related suit."[28] After an eleven-day bench trial the district court denied relief without deciding whether Taylor and Vinson had had sexual intercourse, noting that, if they had, "that relationship was a voluntary one having nothing to do with her continued employment at [the bank] or her advancement or promotions at that institution."[29] Thereafter the district court addressed the question of the bank's liability. "After noting the bank's express policy against discrimination, and finding that neither [Vinson] nor any other employee had ever lodged a complaint about sexual harassment by Taylor, the court ultimately concluded that 'the bank was without notice and cannot be held liable for the alleged actions of Taylor.' "[30]

On appeal this decision was reversed and remanded by the Court of Appeals, which relied on a now standard distinction in sexual harassment cases under Title VII.[31] In the view of the Appeals Court, the case had been tried as a "quid pro quo" case, since the supervisor had demanded sexual favors in return for hiring, retention, or promotion. In its view *Vinson* had to be retried as a "hostile environment" case, wherein the general working conditions at the bank, and not any particular request, demand, or offer, constituted the relevant form of institutional harassment. It then (apparently) reversed field and noted that even if the consent to sexual relations had been voluntary, there was still a violation of Title VII if "Taylor made Vinson's toleration of sexual harassment a condition of her employment."[32] With that said, the Court of Appeals noted that "the District Court's finding of voluntariness might have been based on 'the voluminous testimony regarding respondent's dress and personal fantasies,' " testimony that the Court of Appeals believed "had no place in this litigation."[33] On the bank's liability the court took the position that Taylor, although a supervisor, had to be treated as an employer, given the statutory definition, which, in contrast to the usual common law rule, defined an employer to include "any agent of such a person,"[34] wholly without regard to his capacity to hire or fire or promote.

28. Id. at 61.
29. Id. at 61, quoting *Vinson v. Taylor*, 22 EPD §30,708, p. 14,692, 23 FEP Cases 37, 42 (D.C. 1980).
30. Id. at 62, quoting 23 FEP Cases at 42.
31. See 29 C.F.R. §1611(a) (1989).
32. *Vinson*, 477 U.S. at 62, quoting *Vinson v. Taylor*, 753 F.2d 141, 146 (D.C. Cir. 1985).
33. Id. at 63, quoting 753 F.2d at 146 n.36.
34. See 42 *U.S.C.* §2000e(b) (1982).

The Supreme Court, speaking through Justice Rehnquist, then added its own separate account of sexual harassment. It endorsed the EEOC guidelines and held that the critical test was not whether the consent was "voluntary" but whether the overtures were themselves "unwelcome." On this point both reviewing courts appeared to read the district court's opinion too narrowly by taking the word *voluntary* in isolation, for its finding—that the relations were voluntary and had nothing to do with business—seems to preclude the element of illicit exchange of sexual favors for professional advancement that the EEOC's use of the word *unwelcome* is designed to capture. But again it remanded on the facts to deal with the question of "hostile environment," although the hostility of the environment stemmed, if at all, from the actions of a single man. Finally, Rehnquist noted that the question of "whether particular conduct was indeed unwelcome presents difficult problems of proof and turns largely on credibility determinations committed to the trier of fact."[35]

Only on the question of vicarious liability did the Supreme Court split. Justice Rehnquist, speaking for four others, simply postponed the day of reckoning. The EEOC guidelines held employers strictly liable for the torts of their supervisors "regardless of whether the specific acts complained of were authorized or even forbidden by the employer and regardless of whether the employer knew or should have known of their occurrence."[36] Justice Rehnquist rejected that rule because it "automatically" held the employer vicariously liable under Title VII, but by the same token he held that "absence of notice to an employer does not necessarily insulate that employer from liability."[37] In particular, he noted that the internal procedures of the bank were flawed in that they did not explicitly cover sexual harassment and required that the grievance be made to the supervisor, who in this instance was the source of the problem. Every hard question of fact and law is evaded in a case that does not advance the common law analysis one whit.

A large number of subsequent decisions have sought to make sense out of the debris of *Vinson,* but with, at best, mixed results.[38] In *Steele v. Offshore Shipbuilding, Inc.*[39] the court wrote:

35. *Vinson,* 477 U.S. at 68.
36. 29 C.F.R. §1604.11(c) (1989).
37. *Vinson,* 477 U.S. at 72.
38. See, e.g., *Sparks v. Pilot Freight Carriers, Inc.,* 830 F.2d 1554 (11th Cir. 1987); *Huddleston v. Roger Dean Chevrolet, Inc.,* 845 F.2d 900 (11th Cir. 1988); *Steele v. Offshore Shipbuilding Inc.,* 867 F.2d 1311 (11th Cir. 1989). The most notable pre-*Vinson* case on the subject is *Henson v. City of Dundee,* 682 F.2d 897 (11th Cir. 1982).
39. 867 F.2d 1311 (11th Cir. 1989).

The standard for determining corporate liability due to a supervisor's sexual harassment depends on the type of sexual harassment that occurs. In a *quid pro quo* case, the corporate defendant is strictly liable for the supervisor's harassment . . . This is logical. When a supervisor requires sexual favors as *quid pro quo* for job benefits, the supervisor, by definition, acts as the company . . .

Strict liability is illogical in a pure hostile environment setting. In a hostile environment case, no *quid pro quo* exists. The supervisor does not act as the company; the supervisor acts outside "the scope of actual or apparent authority to hire, fire, discipline or promote." Corporate liability, therefore, exists only through *respondeat superior;* liability exists where the corporate defendant knew or should have known of the harassment and failed to take prompt remedial action against the supervisor.[40]

This analysis of the problem is inadequate and backward. At the most elementary level it mistakenly equates the principle of respondeat superior (let the superior be responsible) with the employer's liability for negligence; under ordinary common law usage it points toward the strict vicarious liability of the employer.[41] But the defects in the analysis go far beyond definitional errors, for the court also misapplied the relevant agency principles. First, a supervisor who requests sexual favors "does not act as the company," but acts only to convert wealth for the company into pleasure for himself. Since there is a frolic and detour, there is no corporate liability respondeat superior. The only relevant issue is whether there is corporate negligence in supervision or selection that justifies the imposition of tort liability. The court's argument from "logic" therefore proves nothing. The right question to ask is which rule produces optimal deterrence, given the risks of overdeterrence and underdeterrence.

The hostile environment cases are stronger candidates for ordinary vicarious liability treatment, because any hostility in the workplace occurs as part of the routine business of the firm. But here too the harassed employee may know that a supervisor or fellow employee has over-

40. Id. at 1316.

41. See W. Page Keeton et al., *Prosser and Keeton on the Law of Torts* 499 (5th ed., 1984): "A is negligent, B is not. Imputed negligence means that, by reason of some relation existing between A and B, the negligence of A is to be charged against B, although B has played no part in it, has done nothing whatever to aid and encourage it, or indeed has done all that he possibly can to prevent it . . . The result may be that B, in C's action against him, becomes liable as a defendant for C's injuries, on the basis of A's negligence. This is sometimes called imputed negligence. More often it is called vicarious liability, or the principle is given the Latin name of *respondeat superior*."

stepped his bounds. Again, the right question is which liability rule provides optimal deterrence, if we take into account errors of over-enforcement and underenforcement.

The answers to these questions are hard to come by. Initially it appears as though the court in *Steele* got the distinction between the two kinds of harassment backwards on functional grounds. The problem with quid pro quo harassment is that it is secret and concealed. The employee has all the relevant information; the firm has none. In this instance a notice rule seems to make good sense, for it enlists employee cooperation to start the process, but once the notice is given, the aggrieved employee does not have to battle her case out toe to toe with her supervisor. She is able to appeal to executives within the firm who have strong incentives for making the right finding. The upshot is a negligence rule that holds the firm liable only after it receives notice of the wrong and fails to correct it.

Secrecy, however, is much less a problem in hostile environment cases. Presumably if one employee is harassed in this manner, her fellow employees are being harassed as well. The open and notorious nature of the wrong makes it highly likely that the firm has notice of the wrong. If anything, a strict liability rule here has a modest advantage of eliminating from the case an issue on which the plaintiff is likely to prevail in any event, given the notoriety of the practices. Again, no definitions are at stake but only questions of relative convenience, and these are not discussed in *Steele*.

With all this said, it is unclear that any split in the rules of corporate responsibility is desirable in harassment cases. Distinctions always cost money to administer, and elements of quid pro quo and hostile environment may be blended into a single dispute, as was the case in *Vinson*. If forced to state one unifying principle, I should adopt the general rule of notice. That notice in turn can be satisfied in either of two ways. First, where the conditions are pervasive throughout the workplace, the corporate employer should generally be treated as having known the obvious and should be charged accordingly. Second, where there is secret harassment, an employer should be charged with knowledge only where he has been informed by the employee. Where formal grievance or mediation processes are available, they should be used. If not, the worker should be able to seek out some disinterested senior official to whom to present the case. That last path is very tricky, but at least among large firms (especially in today's environment) it is doubtful that any company would leave the lines of authority unspecified.

Common Law and Title VII: Does Detail Matter?

What, then, is the net effect of making Title VII the dominant source of law in sexual harassment cases? At one level it seems to be relatively small, for the Supreme Court, the circuit courts, and the EEOC have all been more or less driven to adopt some variant of the common law rules on primary and vicarious liability. But a closer look reveals some more significant differences between the two approaches.

First, the shift in forum introduces into the area an administrative process that would not otherwise be available. The EEOC, for example, has championed strict employer liability even in quid pro quo cases, where the basic analysis suggests that the notice requirement, adopted by the district court in *Vinson,* makes better sense. As long as the EEOC operates under the usual bureaucratic incentives, it will tend to expand liability for harassment further than a sound set of principles indicates. Common law courts without specialized jurisdiction will tend to see these problems through a different lens. They will not defer to EEOC rules, they will have no special institutional bias, and they will be more likely to weigh the errors of false charges of harassment equally with errors that allow true cases of harassment to escape undetected. How strong these tendencies are is difficult to say in the abstract. Much may depend on whether a liberal Democrat or conservative Republican appoints key personnel to the EEOC, or to the courts.

There is a second advantage to the common law rules: they have been tried and tested in many different contexts over the generations, and they are in a relatively mature state of development. The rules under Title VII are much more fluid. At one level there is some risk that the entire question of liability will be determined by the general views of litigation under Title VII. Thus one common formulation of sexual harassment cases under Title VII provides that the plaintiff must prove, in addition to the other elements of a sexual harassment claim, that the "employee belongs to a protected group."[42] In some contexts that phrase may seem innocent enough, but the statute's terms do apply to "any individual," and it seems that principles of quid pro quo harassment, and especially hostile environment harassment, should be available to men who can show that their female superiors have, for example, propositioned them. At a guess, common law judges, who search for more general principles, are inher-

---

42. See *Sparks v. Pilot Freight Carriers, Inc.,* 830 F.2d 1554, 1564 (11th Cir. 1987)

ently less likely to make this mistake than the administrators under Title VII.

Similarly, I would predict that common law judges would show some greater willingness to accept contractual provisions and institutional safeguards that made notice of secret advances a prerequisite to an action against the firm. But Title VII starts with a far stronger hostility to freedom of contract than the common law, so again there is some weak reason to think that state courts will be more receptive to private solutions than either the EEOC or the federal courts.

All in all, therefore, there are a number of second-order reasons to be uneasy about the development of sexual harassment theories under Title VII. But these are *only* second-order objections, precisely because the basic wrong is a tort actionable at common law. The law of employment discrimination works best when it imitates the common law principles that it is said to displace.

CHAPTER 18

Empirical Evidence of Disparate Impact

In this chapter I explore the role of disparate impact theory in sex discrimination cases. Much of the material relevant to this branch of the law has already been canvased in connection with race discrimination cases and need not be reviewed in depth here.[1] Thus, as I noted earlier, the disparate impact theory has generally been defended on the ground of practical necessity: it allows the plaintiff to prevail even without "smoking gun" evidence of disparate treatment, which employers, knowing of the heavy sanctions they face, will keep off the formal record. The disparate impact theory is said to detect these subterranean abuses through statistical proof of discrimination. This argument is subject to the same rejoinder that is raised in cases of racial discrimination: it shows excessive preoccupation with one type of error, undiscovered illegality, while ignoring the second, the erroneous punishment of lawful behavior.

As a matter of theory, within the framework of Title VII disparate impact theory can be justified only if the incremental gains from eliminating discrimination exceed the administrative and error costs of resorting to statistical inference. A look at the full range of consideration suggests that the costs of disparate impact outweigh its benefits, in sex as well as race cases. Under Title VII proof of discriminatory intent should be strictly required, especially in the pattern and practice cases that are grist for the disparate impact mill. If discrimination plays such a large role in hiring and promotion, it must (like affirmative action programs) be implemented by explicit and formal procedures. Finding proof of the illegality of these pervasive practices should not be difficult, given the many modern discovery techniques available to the plaintiff.

In this chapter I examine the problems involved in using statistical evidence to establish the prima facie case of discrimination in both hiring and promotion and wage and salary cases. I then discuss the extent to

1. See Chapter 11.

which biological, sociological, and historical evidence of sex differences can be used to explain or justify whatever disparities in impact are found, with special reference to two important sex discrimination cases that have received extensive appellate review.

Finding Disparate Impact

Hiring and Promotion

In the area of race, testing bore perhaps the heaviest brunt of the disparate impact theory. The prima facie case of disparate impact depended largely on a showing of the differential passing rates of black and white candidates, a relatively straightfoward matter. The tricky question had to do with test validation, given disparate impact, under the narrow business necessity criterion. With cases of sex discrimination, the dominant question revolves around differentials in positions within the work force or in salary paid for the same or similar jobs. Proof of these differentials establishes a prima facie case of sex discrimination under the disparate impact theory. These cases present a fresh set of difficulties because there is no litmus test that places men and women in wholly different categories. It is not as though women work only in some fields but not in others, or that in any given field women are paid zero wages for the same jobs for which men are paid infinite ones. Rather, there is some gross difference by sex in the positions assumed or the wages or salaries paid. It is that difference that calls out for explanation.

In the case of new hirings, the threshold question is to identify the available pool of workers for the job in question. The task is far from straightforward. On the employer's side there is no reason why formal qualifications, easily measured, should represent the sole or even the best way to choose or promote workers. Similarly, from the worker's side there is no reason to assume that men and women of identical formal qualifications have the same propensity to apply for any given job. Any assumption of homogeneity across the sexes is likely to be erroneous, in light of the enormous differences in natural preferences and socialization of all people before they enter the job market. Controlling for these factors is, moreover, exceedingly difficult, for although the existence of such sex-linked preferences may be clear, the same cannot be said about either their magnitude or persistence over time.

Identical difficulties arise in determining the geographic boundaries of the relevant applicant pool. It is not possible simply to identify regions in which workers live, and then to compare the percentage of eligible workers hired from one region with the percentage hired from another, with any significant difference attributed to disparate impact.[2] The problems here go far beyond those of assigning relevant burdens of proof. The willingness of any worker to choose any particular employer is a function of at least three variables: opportunity costs, out-of-pocket costs, and the worker's perception of the employer's discriminatory intent. The first two must be controlled if we are to isolate the last. The entire enterprise is fraught with serious difficulties. Initially the problem arises because an employee seeks to maximize not the wage from a position but the total net return from employment. In that calculation the wage paid is only the starting point. A wide range of costs and benefits associated with the job must also be taken into account, including the nonwage benefits (work experience, possibilities for promotion or advancement) and burdens of the job (work environment, burnout, risk of injury, fatigue, declining interest level). Working these additional factors into the general account is a perilous process even for a knowledgeable employee. The problems become exceptionally acute with any judicial effort to model the hiring process, for the matters most critical to choice are often least amenable to external observation and quantification. The subjective theory of value takes a heavy toll on any public effort under Title VII to scrutinize the hiring process from without and after the fact. One of the costs of any resort to statistical methods is that it requires the quantifiable to assume a larger significance in the legal analysis that it does or should in the ordinary business calculus. Note the complications that arise.

First, it is necessary to account for any opportunities to obtain employment elsewhere that promise a total higher net return. In principle there is no reason why these alternatives should be valued equally by men and women. The effective choice for any given woman may well be between the job offered by a defendant and position X. The effective choice for any given man may well be between the same job offered by the defendant and position Y. There may be no persons who choose between positions X and Y directly. Nonetheless, any changes in the relative wages or fringe benefits for either (or both) of these two alternative positions will change the probabilities that a man or woman will apply for the defendant's job, or accept it if it is offered. These opportunities, infinitely

2. On which see, generally, David C. Baldus and James W. L. Cole, *Statistical Proof of Discrimination,* ch. 4 (1980), and cumulative supplement, ch. 4 (1987).

varied across different workers, are likely to influence the number and quality of applications along sex-based lines. If they do, a differential hiring rate for men and women should not only be allowable under Title VII but (if theory is the master) should plainly be required by it. After all, it is a violation to pass up a superior woman in order to hire an inferior man, even if he ranks in the top 10 percent of the male pool and she ranks only in the top 20 percent of the female pool. As with race, there can be, in principle, no automatic presumption that having equal percentages of men and women in any job category represents the no-discrimination position.

It is far easier to state these complications than it is to account for them in individual cases. As a brute matter of fact, it is plainly impossible for the legal system to determine the set of viable job alternatives open to each person within the overall pool. The difficulties are only compounded since there are hundreds of potential applicants for any given set of positions, each with his or her distinctive set of preferences and alternatives. Any static analysis that rests on broad demographic data necessarily ignores the dynamic behavior of employment markets and drastically simplifies the data solely to salvage the antidiscrimination laws. Using broad availability pools thus represents a conscious decision to apply an unreliable test in order to avoid the insuperable empirical and measurement difficulties that a more precise test imposes. Simple tests are thus unreliable, and reliable tests are wholly invalid and unworkable. Nothing in Title VII compels a choice between two unappealing alternatives. When the administrative and error costs are taken into account, the entire disparate impact game is not worth the candle.

Second, members of any applicant pool must incur certain direct out-of-pocket costs in order to get to work. As the cases have recognized,[3] these may be a function of both distance and ease of access to the job site. A trip of ten miles to the plant gate may be easier and cheaper to make by using the freeway or subway than by changing buses on surface streets. Distance therefore is at best an imperfect proxy for accessibility,

---

3. See, e.g., *Markey v. Tenneco Oil Co.*, 635 F.2d 497, 500–501 (5th Cir. 1981), ordering a new trial to determine discriminating impact by attempts to "assign a statistical weight to the percentage of blacks in each parish based on that parish's contribution to the applicant pool." The changes were introduced because of the realization that public transportation was not equally available from all points in town. That study did not reveal any disparate impact, so the plaintiff's case was eventually dismissed on appeal. See *Markey v. Tenneco Oil Co.*, 707 F.2d 172 (5th Cir. 1983). Note that Tenneco's stated policy was to eliminate all possibility of discrimination in employment. Id. at 174.

commuting time, or the cost of getting to work. Distance is also unlikely to be invariable across all potential workers. Those who travel by car may have a great deal more freedom in choosing where they live and work than those who are dependent on public transportation. As long as applicants' decisions are based on their net private return to labor, these differential transportation costs must be taken into account. Under a market system the levels of self-selection are so powerful that there is no reason to superintend the process. Workers will gravitate toward convenient jobs without external prodding, relocating, if necessary, to maximize the net gains from employment. Only Title VII places these decisions under a judicial microscope. As ever, reasonably reliable data, if available at all, are always costly to obtain.[4]

The third possible explanation for disparate impact—discrimination by employers—has under Title VII radically different consequences from those of the first two. If a woman does not apply for a job, her decision may well reflect a rational determination that she will not be hired precisely because of the rampant and explicit discrimination in certain all-male enclaves, whether a surgical team or a construction or maintenance crew.[5] As along as this possibility is a valid one, there is no obvious inference that workers who did not apply did not want the job. Rather, they chose to avoid the costs of an unpleasant and pointless application process. In some cases these problems are difficult to attack with quantitative data; but where the attitudes are widespread enough for potential applicants to learn of them, it is doubtful that one need rely on a disparate impact theory at all. A disparate treatment approach is sufficient.

The same problems exist if we abandon the search for potential applicants and turn our attention toward the actual applicant flow. In one sense these data, if available, should be somewhat more reliable than geographic data, given that simply filing applications allows persons to select themselves out for certain positions. But again, the process of selection is sufficiently complex that there is no reason to suppose that all the

4. See, e.g., the careful examination of the evidence by Judge Frank Easterbrook, in *Mister v. Illinois Central Gulf Railroad Co.*, 832 F.2d 1427 (7th Cir. 1987), where the railroad defended itself against a disparate impact race claim on the ground that it wished to hire workers locally, close to the site where they were needed. But the argument had little merit, given that the white workers who were hired tended to live about twice as far from their job sites as black workers. Id. at 1432.

5. See, e.g., *Catlett v. Missouri Highway and Transportation Commission*, 828 F.2d 1260, 1265 (8th Cir. 1987), where the hostility toward women workers was manifest in the interviews that were conducted.

workers within the applicant pool are uniform in quality relative to the jobs in question, or that they have the same objectives in mind. Subjective preferences continue to exert their influence at every stage of the hiring process. The question may be rendered more problematic since candidates often do not apply for single positions but consider and are considered for several different openings within the firm at one time. The process of normalization requires a close examination of both the qualifications and the preference structures of the applicants at hand.

The problem is only made more difficult when other factors intrude into the basic analysis. Thus a firm may have an affirmative action program in place during the same period in which it is charged with discrimination,[6] and that plan could well influence the composition of the applicant pool by inducing less qualified members of a protected class to apply for a position. In addition, the sex-linked treatment of fringe benefits—pensions and health and workers' compensation insurance, for example—under Title VII is unresponsive to the private costs of employers. The implicit subsidy to women may induce a disproportionately large number of them to apply.[7] Although it may be possible to correct for each error separately, the cumulative difficulties can easily overwhelm the entire process.

Even more vexing are the problems that arise from the issue of separate but equal with which this section on sex discrimination was introduced. It is possible to start with the assumption that men and women both seek to maximize their individual welfare, given their natural endowments, and subject to their external constraints. There is no reason to assume a priori that they will make the same set of business and personal decisions to achieve that common end. Again, there are two types of differences that have to be taken into account. The differences within the class of men or within the class of women are as important as the differences between the sexes. Under a disparate impact theory, the overall differences between the two distributions are as important as differences within each distribution. In order to show that there is some disparate impact, it is not necessary to identify the cause of the differential preference (although the existence of some biological distinctions makes it credible that these dif-

---

6. See, e.g., *Davis v. City of Dallas,* 483 F. Supp. 54 (N.D. Texas 1979), where the court placed the burden on the defendant employer to show that "the strong recruitment efforts were directed at an applicant pool less well qualified than the applicant pool it would have had without the strong recruitment." Id. at 58.

7. See Chapters 13–15.

ferences are both substantial and persistent); nor is it necessary to show that on some key variable every woman is to the right (or left) of every man in some preference distribution. It is sufficient to show that there is some nontrivial difference in the medians of the two distributions, even if there is still some substantial overlap as well. Nor is it possible to assume that the two groups have the same variance when they have different medians. Thus, when two normal distributions have different medians, it is still possible for one to be flatter than the other.

Ultimately, given the possible sources of difference, all that matters is that a different percentage of men than of women, and vice versa, is likely to want some particular type of employment. The trade-offs having to do with raising families or working in jobs that demand strength and stamina as opposed to those that involve care and nurturing, or in jobs that are financially risky as opposed to those that are nonrisky, are part and parcel of every employment situation. It is not credible to think that these differences will fail to lead to some skewing, indeed some powerful skewing, in the occupational choices of men and women. What is required is not perfect correspondence but significant correlation.[8] If one found the same percentage of women as men in heavy construction or in nursery school teaching, that would be powerful evidence of sex discrimination (or affirmative action) by employers in both markets, in the first case against men and in the second against women. The impact is likely to be far from trivial. Enormous differences in male-to-female employment ratios are commonplace, far in excess of the 20 percent variation needed to trigger a disparate impact inquiry under the EEOC guidelines.[9] Why then should it

8. According to the biological theories of natural selection, it is not necessary for there to be a perfect correlation between a given trait and the purpose for which it is adapted. It is quite possible for nature to develop "quick and dirty" solutions that work better than the more precise responses that can be envisioned. "In its culling of these properties that bear indirectly on fitness, natural selection puts a premium on quick and dirty solutions to the problem of fitness-maximization. It prefers these cheap, imperfect solutions to slow but sweet ones that may do the job better but take a long time to emerge." Alexander Rosenberg, "The Biological Justification of Ethics: A Best-Case Scenario," 8 *Soc. Phil. & Pol.* 86, 91 (1990).

9. See Victor R. Fuchs, *Women's Quest for Economic Equality* 32–57 (1988), which documents much larger differences by recourse to the so-called Duncan index, which is "calculated by summing the absolute differences between the percent of all men and percent of all women in different occupations and dividing by two." Id. at 33. By this index a measure of 100 is total segregation, and lesser measures are calculated accordingly. Fuchs then confines his analysis to persons in full-time employment markets and calculates a general Duncan index of 57 percent, which means that over half the workers (men or

raise suspicion under the standard disparate impact tests championed by the EEOC?

There is a large theme at work here. Any system of discrimination laws that blends, as ours seeks to blend, free choice for workers with an antidiscrimination norm for employers must take these *employee* selection biases into account, both in setting its basic rules and in evaluating individual cases. It may try to postpone the inevitable by setting the burden of proof against the probable outcome, or by requiring employers to show how the selection effects influence the actual hiring patterns. But only by *mandating* a system of proportionate representation can the law eliminate the profound influence of sex differences on employment status. Yet in order to do that, it must radically recast Title VII to place an obligation on *employees* to accept positions they do not want to take, and thereby to complete the coercive reorientation of employment law begun on the employer side by Title VII itself.

Of course, within a market system the preferences of workers not to have female or male co-workers would be respected, and one should not (even at this late date) dismiss them solely as irrational forms of bigotry. It is very clear that these attitudes are far stronger in some lines of business—say, blue-collar trades involving heavy physical labor—than in others, including teaching, medicine, law, and many areas of business. The difference may well be attributable to the free-rider effects within the firm. That is, as more women are hired for road crews, male co-workers will not ignore any resulting increase in their own burdens when they are required to take up the slack from female workers who cannot shoulder as much of the load. The resentments are apt to run deep if the hiring decisions are set outside the firm or department, and if individual protests or sentiment can do nothing to alter the outcome. The change in co-workers could be perceived by many as a unilateral increase in the burdens of the job—one that only outsiders find it easy to deprecate or ignore.

Notwithstanding all the specific explanations for sex discrimination in

women) "have to change occupations in order for them to have the same distribution as men (women)." Id. at 33. In fact, Fuchs understates the enormity of the change because the Duncan index will vary only if the men change to an occupation dominated by women and vice versa. It will not alter the Duncan index for female secretaries to become nurses or male mechanics to become construction workers. The comparable indexes by race are much narrower: 28 percent for black to white women and 33 percent for black to white men. Id. at 34.

labor markets, it is common today to attribute the sharp skews in the market to the effects of prior discrimination. But the explanation rings hollow, for the shift in relative percentages has remained small in the years since the passage of Title VII, in a world in which employers often clamor to hire, as it were, against the grain. The more powerful explanation for the persistence of these differences in employment patterns is that they are desired by employees and employers alike. The problem of selection bias by employees dominates this area as it does no other.

Wage and Salary Differentials

The problems associated with the disparate impact theory extend also to differences in wages and salaries, especially in regard to promotion, where again there is no all-or-nothing solution to the problem. As a matter of theory, the same pressures toward selection bias should again dominate. Success on the job often requires sacrifice of interests outside the job, and for women who are concerned with balancing home and career, the "fast track" option, even if they are encouraged by the firm to take it, may nonetheless be unappealing. Similarly, any differential taste for risk will influence the type of assignments and projects undertaken by male and female workers and their resulting performance. Yet the relevant variables may be obscured from public view.

It is at this point that the hidden costs of the disparate impact theory are highest, because, in policing the private practice, the law emphasizes the very attributes that in business count the least. The law flattens perceived differences in quality and fitness in order to make its own task more manageable, and thus places an exceedingly low weight on what Friedrich Hayek has called local knowledge, that is, the situation sense developed within a trade or profession that is difficult to articulate to the outsider.[10] Where evidence of this sort is essential for running any business, the advocate who can win the rational argument about what should be done is likely to be the failed entrepreneur who would run the business into the ground by following the course of action plotted by the winning argument. The internal complexity of any business is hard to verbalize to oneself and even harder to communicate to an outsider.

Notwithstanding these pervasive limitations, the case law under Title VII makes a determined effort to use statistical methods to prove discrim-

10. See John Gray, *Hayek on Liberty* 28, 36–37 (2nd. ed., 1986), for a discussion of spontaneous social order.

ination. The standard practice in these cases is to run a multiple regression analysis, whereby the plaintiff seeks to take into account the permissible factors that might account for variation in salary and then to show that there remains some residual effect that is unexplained by the permissible reasons.[11] The implication is that the unexplained variation in behavior is attributable to discrimination, which, if significant, the employer must redress either by changing the future pattern of hiring employees and setting their salary, or by awarding damages to the members of the aggrieved class. This approach presents a number of problems. One concerns the relationship between omitted terms and subjective impressions. Another concerns the form of the regression equation or equations. And a third involves the so-called reverse regression.

Omitted terms and subjective impressions. Within this framework defendants often try to show that the plaintiff has miscalculated or misclassified the underlying data, or has omitted additional legitimate factors bearing on performance. If the plaintiff's regression takes into account the years of experience and the most advanced professional degree, the defendant may introduce the number of publications to explain residual wage difference between the sexes which the plaintiff seeks to assign to discriminatory practices. Often the defendant will also seek to introduce certain other elements, such as supervisors' evaluations or ranking of workers, that are left out of the plaintiff's presentation.[12] Many analysts regard these variables as "tainted" because they treat as valid independent variables the very discriminatory practices that the plaintiff seeks to isolate and identify by statistical means. If unfair supervisory evaluations have held back a given class of workers, an employer cannot legitimate the resulting wage differentials by citing the judgment of the same supervisors whose impartiality has been challenged.

Nonetheless, a high price is paid in excluding these subjective elements

11. For detailed accounts of the procedure, see Baldus and Cole, *Statistical Proof of Discrimination*, ch. 8. See also, for a criticism of the standard models used in discrimination cases, Thomas J. Campbell, "Regression Analysis in Title VII Cases: Minimum Standards, Comparable Worth, and Other Issues Where Law and Statistics Meet," 36 *Stan. L. Rev.* 1299 (1984). (Campbell, a former professor, is a Republican congressman from California.)

12. For a readable account of this problem, see Michael O. Finkelstein, "The Judicial Reception of Multiple Regression Studies in Race and Sex Discrimination Cases," 80 *Colum. L. Rev.* 737 (1980). For the cases analyzed, see *James v. Stockham Valves & Fittings Co.*, 559 F.2d 310 (5th Cir. 1977); *Stastny v. Southern Bell Telephone & Telegraph Co.*, 458 F. Supp. 314 (W.D. N.C. 1978).

from consideration. Often these variables do measure something of importance, since subjective impressions normally play a critical role even in firms where no discrimination is suspected or possible. This mode of evaluation has been used where the work force is all male or all female, and it was used long before Title VII became law. If these evaluations do in fact offer honest, accurate, and up-to-date assessments of the work in question, then, as evidence of performance, they may be more probative than any objective factor (highest degree, years of experience) traditionally included as an independent variable in the plaintiff's standard regression. The problems with the tainted variables therefore run in two directions. To admit the evidence is to bias the inquiry against the plaintiff where the subjective evaluations have been used to shield the firm against valid charges of discrimination. But to exclude the evidence is to bias the inquiry in favor of the plaintiff where the evaluations were an accurate and perhaps indispensable part of a qualitative analysis of performance. The modern practice assumes illegal conduct is so pervasive (even within firms that are committed to affirmative action policies) that all hard data must be evaluated from a presumption of distrust. "Unconscious discrimination" by whites and by men is used as a benchmark for analysis in a world that often contains pervasive conscious discrimination running the other way, by men and women alike.

Once the objective data are regarded as tainted, the die is cast. The only way to resolve the impasse is to conduct a hands-on examination of the subjective portions of the case, employee by employee and supervisor by supervisor. Undertaking that review makes it clear that the technical objection to multiple regression studies conceals a much larger flaw in the entire enterprise, namely that the worth of the regression depends on the motive and bias of the employer's supervisory personnel. Yet once that fact is independently established, the regression itself becomes largely redundant. Where supervisors have misbehaved, there is direct evidence of discrimination to support a disparate treatment case. Where the supervisors have not misbehaved, the defendant's evidence is sufficient, first, to knock out the disparate treatment case, and second, to be incorporated into the regression, where it now operates to defeat any disparate impact case as well. The moral of the story is clear. On either view the regression is irrelevant, and so too is the disparate impact theory.

The lurking difficulties of omitted variables give rise to other technical problems inherent in multiple regression analysis. Thus it is highly doubtful that any regression will be able to account for the complete operation of *any* labor market. In normal statistical parlance, a key variable is the so-called R^2 figure, which is a rough measure of the percentage of variation in the data that is explained by the terms that have been included in the regression relative to the total variance.[13] The unattainable R^2 of 1 means that the variables included in the regression fully explain all the variation in the dependent variable. An R^2 of 0 means that the elements in the regression explain none of the variation in that same variable. In most empirical studies the R^2 figure lies somewhere between the two extremes, which means that large portions of the variation (often more than half) are not accounted for by the independent variables. Studies of this sort may still have some value if they identify the significance of some variable that had been previously ignored. But there is nonetheless an enormous difference between a study that purports to show the significance of a single variable, such as age, as a determinant of salaries or promotions and a study that purports to supply a comprehensive account of all the determinants of salary sufficient to preclude any possibility of discrimination.

This difference in focus and objective is of special interest in discrimination cases, where the issue is often how the residual, unexplained variation in salaries should be treated. One possibility is to argue that the variation, or some significant part of it, is explained by factors that have not been included in the regression. Their exclusion could be explained by a number of powerful reasons. The data available may not have covered the trait in question at all. There may be a strong element of subjective judgment which made a widely recognized vital trait ("get-up-and-go," leadership potential) difficult to quantify. Again, the basic theories that explain success or failure within the firm are sufficiently undeveloped that we are unable to identify certain underlying considerations. It is impossible to measure the extent of an unknown variable.

Notwithstanding this range of possibilities, there is of course one other, namely that the differences in dependent variables are attributable to discrimination on the ground of a forbidden category such as sex. The question then arises, *what* should be assumed about that portion of the

13. The relevant definitions are given in Baldus and Cole, *Statistical Proof of Discrimination,* ch. 19 n.11, at 356–357, 351. "R^2: The square of the multiple correlation coefficient between the dependent and independent variables in a multiple regression model, or equivalently the proportion of the total variance in the dependent variable that is associated with variations in the independent variable or variables found in the model. In a bivariate regression, R^2 equals r^2, the square of the *correlation coefficient.*

"*Correlation coefficient:* A measure of the strength of the association or linear correlation between two quantities measured on a collection of observed units."

unexplained variance? Treating it as simply unknown makes proof of discrimination by statistical methods impossible in most situations. If the R^2 is 0.60, it cannot be blithely assumed that only, say, 30 percent of the residual is explained by unidentified economic factors and the rest is attributable to discrimination. One might as well conclude that if any unknown set of variables can explain 30 percent of the residual, it can easily explain some larger fraction. To be sure, there are forms of voluntary discrimination that may be rational in this setting and would persist in the absence of Title VII. Therefore, one cannot dismiss out of hand the possibility that discrimination is present in a given workplace. But in view of the major risk of liability, it seems unlikely that any firm would be prepared to pay the heavy price of explicitly continuing these practices even if they were efficient. Treating any unexplained residual in the R^2 as resulting from discrimination systematically overstates the employer's level of misconduct.

The choice thus boils down to the familiar one between Type I and Type II error encountered in the disparate impact race discrimination cases.[14] Are we more worried about cases of discrimination that escape detection (Type II error) than cases of nondiscrimination that are treated as discriminatory (Type I error)? As with race, the dominant tendency in sex cases is to tolerate massive amounts of Type I error. Even where the defendant shows some significant gap or omission in the plaintiff's regression, that showing typically (but not always) goes to the probative value of the study, not to its admissibility into evidence. Justice Brennan, writing for the full Court in *Bazemore v. Friday*,[15] articulated the general approach:

> While the omission of variables from a regression analysis may render the analysis less probative than it otherwise might be, it can hardly be said, absent some other infirmity, that an analysis which accounts for the major factors "must be considered unacceptable as evidence of discrimination" . . . Normally, failure to include variables will affect the analysis' probativeness, not its admissibility.
>
> Importantly, it is clear that a regression analysis that includes less than "all measurable variables" may serve to prove a plaintiff's case. A plaintiff in a Title VII action need not prove discrimination with scientific certainty; rather, his or her burden is to prove discrimination by a prepon-

---

14. See Chapter 11.
15. 478 U.S. 385 (1986).

derance of the evidence . . . Whether, in fact, such a regression analysis does carry the plaintiffs' ultimate burden will depend in a given case on the factual context of each case in light of all the evidence presented by both the plaintiff and the defendant. However, as long as the court may fairly conclude, in light of all the evidence, that it is more likely than not that impermissible discrimination exists, the plaintiff is entitled to prevail.[16]

The Court's footnote 10 then states the exception to the basic rule: "There may, of course, be some regressions so incomplete as to be inadmissible as irrelevant; but such was clearly not the case here"—largely, one might add, because the record was replete with evidence of overt official discrimination.[17] In effect Brennan's full position, in text and footnote, establishes a presumption in favor of the admissibility of the regression, which can be overridden in cases of severe incompleteness. By characterizing the issue as one of burden of proof, he neatly sidesteps the central question: What level of R^2 is sufficient to protect the regression analysis from charges of irrelevance?

By using the presumption, *Bazemore* forces the defendant to run his own regressions even where the plaintiff's regression has no real probative value. The decision thus bends the normal rules of evidence in order to facilitate the bringing of disparate impact cases. Ordinarily the defendant need only deny an unproved prima facie case without introducing any affirmative evidence of his own. Thus, if the plaintiff's negligence action depends on the evidence of an eyewitness whose testimony is discredited, the defendant is not obliged to develop an alternative account of the accident that does not involve its own culpability. The same principle should apply a fortiori to cases based on statistical evidence, where the

16. Id. at 400. This language has been extensively quoted in circuit court opinions that have sought to apply the rule. See, e.g., *Catlett v. Missouri Highway and Transportation Commission*, 828 F.2d 1260, 1265 (8th Cir. 1987); *Palmer v. Shultz*, 815 F.2d 84, 99–100 (D.C. Cir. 1987); *Penk v. Oregon State Bd. of Higher Education*, 816 F.2d 458, 465 (9th Cir. 1987).

17. Indeed, on its facts *Bazemore* is an easy case on just this ground. The case involved differences in salaries between black and white workers in North Carolina's Agricultural Extension Service, which had been segregated before the 1964 Civil Rights Act and integrated thereafter. North Carolina sought to justify the salary differentials after the passage of the act as a continuation of the earlier salary scales of the separated services. That argument itself should be sufficient to support the disparate treatment case against the state, without recourse to the statistical argument. See *Bazemore*, 478 U.S. at 395–396 (Brennan, J., concurring).

proof is suspect to begin with, especially in pattern and practice cases in which explicit evidence of discriminatory intention should be easy to find if it exists, given the large number of discrete encounters between employers and employees. Yet so effective are the Civil Rights Acts (or the societal norms) in stopping conscious employer discrimination that it is rare to find any solid evidence of improper practice. Commonly the evidence of discriminatory intent shows not discrete misbehavior by the employer but only "attitudes" and "traditions," which are said to influence decisions but are not linked to the particular decisions that were made.[18] In these cases the silence speaks loudly. No firm can recruit or promote without detailed internal guidelines or practices.[19] A pattern of discrimination requires explicit direction from the center. One reason why it may be difficult to prove discrimination is that it may not be present.

More generally, it is dangerous to evaluate the disparate treatment and disparate impact aspects of a suit in separate compartments, for the weak-

---

18. *Palmer v. Schultz*, 815 F.2d 84 (D.C. Cir. 1987), where the plaintiff's class action relied heavily on the testimony of Benjamin Reid, undersecretary of state for management between 1977 and 1981 in the Carter administration. In the court's words, Reid (as a defense witness) stated that the Foreign Service, as a result of being traditionally "white, male, and Ivy League," had "set ways of doing things," and although during his tenure the Foreign Service "had come a long way," it nevertheless "still had a long way to go" in eliminating bias when he left. Id. at 102. The court did not link his testimony with any particular promotion decision. Rather, it found discrimination in the higher rate of promotion of men relative to women from Class 5 to Class 4 (that is, competitive performance) because, while "there was no significant difference in the *performance* ratings of men and women, . . . the disparity between men and women [in their *potential* ratings] measured 2.49 standard deviations." Id. at 102, quoting the lower court opinion, 616 F. Supp. 1540, 1549 (D.D.C. 1985).

In principle, however, the two different ratings may both be correct. If success at higher levels involves different attributes (such as the ability to handle risk, pressure, or stress), present success and future performance need not perfectly correlate. The variations could take place both for individual candidates of the same sex and for male and female candidates as groups.

19. At the top of an employment application at Tenneco Oil Company this statement appears: "NOTICE: This information will not be used for the purpose of discrimination. Any item on this form which you feel tends to be discriminatory need not be completed. Employment and advancement in Tenneco and its Associated Companies is determined by a person's qualifications and abilities without regard to race, color, age, religion, sex, national origin, physical & mental handicap[s] or veterans [status]. It is our policy to treat each individual who applies for work and those subsequently hired in a fair and equitable manner." *Markey v. Tenneco Oil Co.,* 707 F.2d 172, 174 (5th Cir. 1983).

ness on the first type of liability is not taken into account in evaluating the second. In other cases, if the evidence of disparate treatment is not sufficient on its own, the tendency is to use that evidence to bolster up a weak disparate impact charge.[20] But in principle the proper chain of inference should run in the reverse direction. If proof of disparate treatment has failed, then greater doubt should be cast on the disparate impact aspects of the case, and vice versa. The right question to ask is not how it helps a plaintiff in a disparate impact case to establish a 20 percent probability of disparate treatment but rather what likelihood there is of making out disparate impact where the evidence on disparate treatment suggests an 80 percent possibility that the defendant did no wrong.

Choosing the form of the regression equation. The technical difficulties with proof of discrimination should also be mentioned briefly. These fall into two separate categories. The first deals with the question of whether, when wage is regressed on salary, proper procedures call for one equation or two. The second involves the choice between the regression and the reverse regression, that is, whether wage should be regressed on qualifications or qualifications on wages.

First, as Thomas Campbell has pointed out,[21] most multiple regression cases take the form:

$$\text{Wage} = A + Bx_1 + Cx_2 + Nx_{n-1} \pm K \; (- \text{ for female})$$

In this equation the wage is estimated by taking some constant, A (the place where the best-fitting line intercepts the Y axis), and then determining the relative weights of other variables to define the linear relationship. K represents in dollars the difference between the wages of male and female employees and thus picks up the discriminatory impact, assuming that each of the factors (age, length of service, and so on) has the same effect on the wages of males and females. In principle, however, a more complex mathematical form (such as taking logarithms or squares) gives a better fit and reduces the size of K. In principle a court should see *all* the various forms of regressions that both sides run, for otherwise each side will selectively present that version it finds most beneficial.

It is also in principle possible to develop a refinement on the estimation procedure that uses two separate equations, one for male workers and the

20. See, e.g., *Palmer v. Shultz,* 815 F.2d 84, 102 (D.C. Cir. 1987).

21. See Campbell, "Regression Analysis" at 1305–8, 1313–19.

other for female workers, which does not seek to measure the difference (K) by indirection.

$$\text{Wage (female)} = A + B^f x_1 + C^f x_2 + N^f x_{n-1}$$
$$\text{Wage (male)} = A + B^m x_1 + C^m x_2 + N^m x_{n-1}$$

In these two equations, the As refer to the y-intercept of their respective regression lines, while the Bs, Cs, and so forth are the coefficients for the variables that are used to explain the dependent wage variable. Using the two separate equations gives rise to additional complications, for it is possible that the coefficients for any given variable, such as age or years of experience, may have different values in the male and the female equations (that is, B^f is not equal to B^m). If one could show that all coefficients were higher for the males than for the females, it would be tantamount to an assertion that men were advanced more quickly, even when all other things were equal, and there would be, within the framework of Title VII, powerful evidence of discrimination, if we assume that the disparate impact theory makes sense in the first place. But where the coefficients flip-flop, so that some are greater for males and others are greater for females, there is genuine confusion, because the evidence cuts both ways on the ostensible discrimination questions. Does an employer prefer educated females and experienced males to experienced females and educated males? The reasons for these distinctions may elude everyone, but it seems odd in the extreme to allow both least-preferred classes (educated females and experienced males) to maintain actions against the employer under Title VII. Campbell's proposal for two equations increases the number of quandaries and reduces (as the number of variables increases) the likelihood that discrimination will be found, relative to a system that asks, from a single equation, whether some coefficient (K) is significantly negative. But perhaps, even within the framework of Title VII, this element of caution is appropriate. Heavy liabilities should not be imposed on the strength of unexplained data.

Second, as to the choice between regression and reverse regression, perhaps a more fundamental difficulty in proving sex discrimination arises in connection with the latter. The situation has been extensively ventilated in the statistical literature, most notably by Arthur Dempster,[22] who explains the difference between "direct" and "reverse" regressions:

22. See Arthur P. Dempster, "Employment Discrimination and Statistical Science," 3 *Stat. Science* 149 (1988). Dempster's article is followed by the contributions and com-

Both approaches agree that each employee should be paid exactly what he or she deserves, and then ask for a substitute principle to be used in the real world where such perfection is not achievable. In the first [direct] approach, the principle is to require that, given equal qualifications, males and females should be paid the same on average. Ordinary, or direct, regression . . . is seen as the means to obtain a suitable qualifications measure to be used as a practical standard for judging such equality of pay averages over gender groups . . . The second [reverse] approach [the reverse regression] reverses the roles of pay and qualifications and suggests that the criterion for no discrimination should be that males and females with given pay should on average have equal qualifications measure . . .

The key point is that direct and reverse regressions often give conflicting messages. In situations where males are on average more qualified than females, it often happens that the average male salary exceeds the average female salary among employees with a given qualifications measure, suggesting discrimination against females, whereas simultaneously among employees with a given salary the average qualification measure of males exceeds the average qualification measure of females, suggesting discrimination against males.[23]

The precise technical reasons for this anomaly are quite beside the point for this discussion.[24] But the size of the effects can be quite striking; for example, a statistically significant differential of 14 percent on the direct regression yields statistically insignificant differences of 3 percent on the reverse regression.[25] It is of course difficult to decide which, if either, of these regression forms should be given pride of place in the

---

ments of other analysts. Additional notable contributions to this literature are Michael H. Birnbaum, "Procedures for the Detection and Correction of Salary Inequities," in *Salary Inequities* (T. R. Pezzullo and B. E. Brittingham eds. 1979); Dolores Conway and Harry Roberts, "Reverse Regression, Fairness, and Employment Discrimination," 1 *J. Bus. Econ. Statist.* 75 (1983); Arthur S. Goldberger, "Reverse Regression and Salary Discrimination," 19 *J. Human Resources* 293 (1984).

23. Dempster, "Employment Discrimination," n.22 at 156–157.

24. Basically, when the salary is regressed on the qualifications, women will tend to congregate closer to the origin than will men, given that they tend to be younger and have fewer years of experience. Running the regression line through both men and women, therefore, could produce evidence of discrimination. When salary is held constant, these separate groups disappear, so the regression line could show discrimination the other way, with a greater error term as the data points are not bunched so tightly around the regression line.

25. See Dolores Conway, "Comment on Dempster," 3 *Stat. Science* 171–172 (1988).

analysis. My own (weak) preference would be for the reverse regression, because the direct choice faced by the employer is usually between two persons of roughly the same qualifications who are competing for a single job. The extrapolations across different jobs are more difficult and need not assume any obvious linear form. But it is a mistake to dwell too long on the wrong question. Where the statistical measures provide mixed messages, it should be remembered that the entire problem of legal proof can be avoided by eliminating statistical inference altogether, and of course by repealing Title VII. It should leave the defenders of Title VII most uneasy that liabilities, expenses, and loss of reputation should rest so heavily on such weak statistical foundations.

Disparate Impact in Action: *Sears*

A noteworthy example of the dangers inherent when the disparate impact theory is used in practice is provided by *EEOC v. Sears, Roebuck & Co.*,[26] in which Sears prevailed after a bitter and protracted confrontation with the EEOC. The case generated academic controversy perhaps more bitter than the lawsuit itself. The EEOC sought to establish that Sears was guilty of discrimination with respect to its handling of men and women for commissioned sales in the period between March 1973 and December 1980. The district court in a lengthy opinion entered a judgment for Sears on all counts after a ten-month trial in 1984,[27] and its judgment was upheld on appeal against a variety of challenges in the Seventh Circuit by a two-to-one vote. Any effort to give an accurate summary of the highways and byways of the underlying case is doomed to at least partial inaccuracy, so extensive is the web of charges and countercharges in a case whose trial record ran over 19,000 pages. Indeed, the sheer mass of data in the case offers one of the strongest reasons against hearing disparate impact cases at all. Nonetheless, the main issues command attention.[28]

The EEOC's basic contention was that Sears had engaged in a pattern and practice of discrimination against women in commissioned sales. At

---

26. 839 F.2d 302 (7th Cir. 1988).

27. *EEOC v. Sears, Roebuck & Co.*, 628 F. Supp. 1264 (N.D. Ill. 1986).

28. I omit a discussion of other complex points, such as the relationship between the hiring patterns in the early years, at the inception of the litigation or just before, and the impact of Sears's affirmative action program for women instituted after the inception of the litigation. See, for discussion, *EEOC v. Sears, Roebuck & Co.*, 839 F.2d 302, 312–318.

issue in the case were approximately 47,000 instances of hiring and promotion. Notwithstanding the mass of individual cases, the EEOC chose to rely wholly on statistical evidence. Accordingly, it offered *no* instances in which individual women employees had complained or protested about discriminatory treatment by the firm. In fashioning its statistical case the EEOC had to deal with two separate problems. First, it had to identify the correct pool of applicants in order to show that there was in fact a differential rate of acceptance for women and men for these positions.

Next it had to combat evidence offered by the defendant's expert witness, Rosalind Rosenberg of the Barnard College history department, that any such differential could be explained, at least in part, by the simple fact that women were more likely than men to prefer noncommissioned work. Rosenberg's attitudinal testimony tended to show that the disparate outcome in Sears's work force was attributable to employee preferences, not to discrimination. On this last point the EEOC countered with its own historical expert, Alice Kessler-Harris of Temple University, who testified that workplace preferences and attitudes did not differ *at all* by sex. If Kessler-Harris was correct, then Sears could not overcome any presumption created by disparate impact.

Throughout the case the sharpest controversy centered on the composition of the relevant applicant pools. At the practical level one critical difficulty was that the Sears application form did not distinguish between applicants for commissioned and noncommissioned jobs. It differentiated only between sales and nonsales positions. The EEOC included in the applicant pool for noncommissioned jobs any person who had expressed an interest in sales, regardless of any expressed preference for commissioned, or for that matter noncommissioned, sales.[29] The courts regarded the lack of differentiation among members of the broader applicant pool as a pervasive failure that undermined the EEOC's statistical analysis. By lumping all applicants together, the EEOC failed to take into account the differences in interests and qualifications of men and women. Even though the EEOC adjusted for certain objective measures (six in this case: job applied for, age, education, job experience, product line experience, and commissioned sales experience),[30] its regressions did not seek to control for interest and aptitude, the issues that Sears regarded as critical to

29. Id. at 324.

30. Id. at 324. The EEOC used similar multiple regression techniques and also a more complex multivariate cross-cell variation whereby each cell containing the various combi-

its own case. Nor did the EEOC study seek to quantify certain other variables such as physical appearance, assertiveness, the ability to communicate, friendliness, and economic motivation.

The uncertainties in the basic statistical proof were compounded by the hotly contested expert testimony on sex preferences for commissioned jobs. Given basic sexual differences, both biological and social, one should expect that there would be *some* differences that might influence the propensity of men and women to take the relatively riskier commissioned sales jobs. We should anticipate some overlap between the male and female distributions, and indeed there were a large number of women in commissioned sales. The evidence is thus consistent with two basic propositions: first, that some women have a greater taste for risk than some men, and second, that other factors apart from the taste for risk influence one's willingness to engage in commissioned sales. In this connection, however, the evidence of Rosalind Rosenberg, who relied heavily on the feminism of "differences," is especially powerful because it shows that the social patterns of behavior are more or less consistent with what the biological model predicts. (Neither Rosenberg nor Sears, it should be noted, relied at all on biological evidence, but it lurks constantly in the background nonetheless.) It therefore is relevant that commissioned selling requires work outside regular hours, and in the customer's home, especially if women (say, because they have children at home) prefer to work regular hours. Sears needed to rely on Rosenberg's testimony to explain only why some sex differences should be expected. It did not have to establish any categorical difference between men and women in order to deflect the charge of discrimination. The EEOC, through Kessler-Harris, had the far more daunting task of proving that sex differences play *no* role whatsoever in the occupational choices of men and women.[31]

---

nations of the six variables was analyzed separately for both men and women; the disparities were somewhat reduced. Id. at 325.

31. The point here is made forcefully in Thomas Haskell and Sanford Levinson, "Academic Freedom and Expert Witnessing: Historians and the Sears Case," 66 *Texas L. Rev.* 1629, 1634–35 (1988), criticizing Alice Kessler-Harris for urging in her written testimony that "failure to find women in so-called nontraditional jobs can thus *only* be interpreted as a consequence of employers' unexamined attitudes or preferences, which phenomenon is the essence of discrimination." Not only does this passage show the mistaken all-or-nothing attitude, but also it raises discrimination from the quintessential motive case into the area of "false consciousness." For her response, see Alice Kessler-Harris, "Academic Freedom and Expert Witnessing: A Response to Haskell and Levinson," 67 *Texas L. Rev.* 429 (1988), and the inevitable rejoinder, Thomas Haskell and Sanford Levinson, "On

That tour-de-force cannot be performed unless we ignore the entire matrix of biology and culture that works on men and women alike.

Sears squarely raises all the difficulties evaded in *Bazemore v. Friday*.[32] The plaintiff's case depends on a regression that includes some relevant variables but omits other critical ones, provided Rosenberg's testimony about differences in applicants' tastes and interests is correct. So, then, should a court regard the EEOC's regression as admissible into evidence? As presumptive even if admitted? Should the rebuttal testimony on attitude differences be regarded as powerful enough to exclude the regressions from evidence? Or should it be allowed to override the evidence to the extent that it is admitted? (The differences between these two views are hard to articulate in a world of bench trials.) The problem here is acute, for there was no way that *Sears* could have run its own regressions to quantify the soft evidence of attitude and behavior differences on which its case rested. The "tainted" variable thus dominates this case. The question has to be faced head-on: Do the numbers dominate the theory, or the theory the numbers?

Under Title VII two factors seemed to tilt the balance: first, the utter absence of any evidence of individual cases of discrimination,[33] and second, Sears's decision (doubtless in anticipation of suit) to institute its own internal affirmative action program and to make extensive efforts to boost the number of women in its commissioned sales departments.[34] It is of course possible to downplay the first element and to deprecate the second, as the EEOC did. The want of testimonial evidence of discriminatory practices arises because applicants are (said to be) afraid to speak for fear of losing their jobs, or because the evidence would be too scattered to be persuasive. Yet surely there is substantial turnover in Sears employees, and ex-workers could testify about the employment policies

---

Academic Freedom and Hypothetical Pools: A Reply to Alice Kessler-Harris," 67 *Texas L. Rev.* 1591 (1989).

32. 478 U.S. 385 (1986) (analyzed in *Sears* 839 F.2d at 327). Note that *Sears* has been rejected on its view of regressions, and *Bazemore* was otherwise interpreted in *EEOC v. General Telephone Co. of Northwest*, 885 F.2d 575, 579–558 (9th Cir. 1989).

33. See *Sears*, 839 F.2d at 310–312, where the court rejected the EEOC's claim that "such evidence would be 'inappropriate' because 'where 47,000 hires and promotions were at issue . . . it would have been impossible to present enough individual demonstrations of discrimination to fully reflect the statistics." Id. at 311. But the problem was that the EEOC did not have *any* instances at all. It is hard to accept the claim that no applicant came forward because she "would not know if she had been discriminated against." Id. at 312.

34. Id. at 314–318.

that induced them to leave. In this context a *single* piece of evidence on inappropriate behavior would likely have had devastating effects.

Consider as a reference point one documented case of racial discrimination during an interview. A University of Chicago law student who was asked abusive, tasteless, and vulgar questions at a single interview at the large international law firm of Baker & McKenzie had only to write a short, direct letter to the head of the firm, and all hell broke loose. Massive investigations were conducted within the firm and at the law school. The offending partner at Baker & McKenzie was forced to resign his position. Other partners were grilled by law students, and the firm was thereafter suspended from interviewing at the University of Chicago for a year and was subjected to similar restrictions at other law schools that had no connection with the underlying incident. The newspaper publicity was relentless. Yet it is likely that there was *no* violation of Title VII, for even though the candidate did not receive an offer, the offending partner was in favor of hiring the student. Here the short-term market response was so powerful that it was clear that any possible legal action would drag on, a pointless footnote to history. The story has its moral here. If any evidence of this sort had been available to the EEOC, it would have been admissible and it would have been used, to great effect. The difficulty of course is not with the characterization of the conduct but with its probative force in a pattern and practice suit. An isolated incident, no matter how inappropriate, does not call into question the basic hiring practices of an entire firm.

Similarly, the affirmative action program implemented by Sears could be portrayed as a cynical effort to forestall the lawsuit that followed. But there are other ways to interpret the situation. One possibility is that the discrimination problems that this lawsuit was designed to handle had been largely dealt with in any event, if they even existed in the first place. Why then engage dubious statistics and worse sociology to make a point? Another possibility is that the affirmative action program was counterproductive and forced Sears to abandon the most efficient mode of selling, to the detriment of both its customers and its shareholders, while introducing explicit sex classifications into its business. The cynicism about litigation thus runs both ways. Sears's affirmative action program may therefore be attacked from both sides.

In the end the absence of hard evidence meant that the case against Sears rested on the proposition that the firm practiced extensive subterranean discrimination that somehow escaped the attention of all the women hurt by it. If evidence of that sort is allowed to prevail, then there is an inexhaustible (if unprovable) class of Title VII violations that neces-sarily call for strong legal medicine. But enthusiasm outruns evidence. The better explanation may be that unconscious discrimination in the modern corporation is like the "ether" to the nineteenth-century physi-cist. It does not exist at all, or it is overridden by conscious discrimination that cuts the other way, whether for sound business reasons or out of fear of Title VII liability, or, as seems most likely, from some combination of the two. Surely there must be a better way to run a railroad. The social pressures for affirmative action will survive the repeal of Title VII.

This conclusion does not sit well with the strong defenders of an aggressive use of Title VII in sex cases. Rosalind Rosenberg has been subjected to savage criticism for agreeing to work for Sears as an expert witness,[35] and the case itself has been denounced as an effort to use relational feminism, the feminism of sex differences, to perpetuate the worst stereotypes that Title VII is designed to eliminate. But the basic point leads us in the opposite direction. If there are differences in the basic composition of the applicant pool, one should expect to see some sorting equilibrium in the positions that men and women accept. The existence of sex differences increases the gains from trade for all persons through specialization in the market. Since sex differences continue to matter to applicants as well as to firms, the decision and reasoning of the Seventh Circuit was correct.

In closing I should note that the issues raised in *Sears* will of necessity dominate all sex discrimination cases that are brought to make institu-tional changes in the pattern of hiring and promotion. These suits con-sume enormous resources, but to what end? The market constraints of

35. See, e.g., Joan C. Williams, "Deconstructing Gender," 87 *Mich. L. Rev.* 797 (1989). See also Haskell and Levinson, "Academic Freedom" at 1630–31, setting out the strong denunciations of Rosenberg: "Articles in such publications as *The Nation, Radical History Review, The Chronicle of Higher Education,* and *Ms.* have quoted Rosenberg's critics as calling her 'immoral' and 'unprofessional.' Her critics claim that she has 'betrayed' femi-nism and launched 'an attack on working women and sexual equality, an attack on the whole concept of affirmative action.' They have called her decision to testify 'stupid' and have attributed it to 'class bias.' They have accused her of 'red-baiting.' They have written even worse things in letters that have been widely circulated within the community of professional historians" (footnotes omitted).

In particular, the Coordinating Committee of Women in the Historical Profession and the Conference Group on Women's History passed a resolution that condemned Rosen-berg for testifying. It concluded with the declaration: "As feminist scholars we have a responsibility not to allow our scholarship to be used against the interests of women struggling for equity in our society." Id. at 1631.

reputation and survival are powerful checks against any firmwide effort to engage in sex discrimination. In the few cases of actual discrimination, there is usually some evidence of disparate treatment that renders the statistics unnecessary in any event. The constant refrain behind these suits is that discrimination is hidden and covert, that it is unconscious in the minds of those who practice it, and that it is pervasive in and destructive to the American way of life. The reality seems altogether different. The suits that are successful often create a crisis atmosphere where none should exist, for the success of class action and disparate impact suits only creates the false impression that there is more discrimination against women than any theory of rational behavior could predict. These successes are then used to urge ever greater public scrutiny of market decisions, which feeds the cycle once again. Decisions such as *Sears* represent a welcome reversal of the dominant trend, but it is far from clear that the approach in *Sears* will survive review by the Supreme Court or that its principle will be adopted by other circuits.

In the meantime there is this irony: vast amounts of discrimination are evident on the face of the record, but most of it takes place in the form of affirmative action programs that are tied to race and sex. Here proof of discrimination is as easily found as it was in the cases of formal discrimination against blacks in the years just after the passage of the Civil Rights Act. The hard issues go only to the question of justification, both under Title VII and as a matter of first principle. It is to those issues that the next part of this book is devoted.

PART V

Affirmative Action

CHAPTER 19

Protected Groups under Title VII

The Two-Pronged Attack

The antidiscrimination law regulating both race and sex has evolved in two directions simultaneously. First, the courts have crafted out of the basic language of Title VII an enormous commitment to rooting out all possible forms of discrimination against members of protected classes, most notably blacks and women. Toward that end they have undertaken wholesale attacks on standard industry practices such as the use of sex-linked mortality tables for pensions and insurance; they have given a narrow reading to any appeal on a sex-linked BFOQ; and they have aggressively applied disparate impact tests, complete with their statistical apparatus and narrow business necessity exceptions, in cases where there is no evidence of any overt or conscious discrimination on the employer's part. With a few notable exceptions, such as the 1989 *Ward's Cove* decision, the courts have been far more assiduous in ferreting out possible cases of discrimination than in protecting employers against false charges.

A second side to the antidiscrimination statutes, however, bespeaks a very different attitude. Early on there was much talk about the importance of color-blind and sex-blind rules for all employment decisions. Stress was placed on merit and the irrelevance of color and sex in terms of all the explicit assumptions about the independence of the former from the latter. Many of these concerns hearkened back to the famous remark of Martin Luther King, Jr., that all persons should be judged "not by the color of their skin, but by the content of their character." Yet the ink was scarcely dry on the Civil Rights Act of 1964 when a very different set of goals and objectives came to dominate the civil rights movement: affirmative action for protected groups. In essence the program of the civil rights movement has become the creation of two very different sets of rules. The first imposes harsh sanctions on employers, public and private, that discriminate against blacks and women; the second gives large (if not total) immunity to those employers, again public and private, that explicitly take race or sex into account in making their hiring and promotion decisions. The purpose of this chapter is to examine the case for affirmative action under the Civil Rights Act of 1964.

In this regard I should state my conclusions baldly at the outset. First, there is no credible case that any comprehensive affirmative action program is authorized under Title VII. At most there may be some suggestions that certain race-conscious remedies might be used to correct persistent patterns of prior discrimination measured by the color-blind or sex-blind standard. Second, as a matter of first principle the categorical statutory conclusion is surely wrong. There should be no legal obstacle against the practice, no matter how extensive or overt, of affirmative action by private institutions if they are willing to pay the costs of implementing any such programs, whether these costs are large or small.

Public institutions are another matter. Precisely because the distinction between merit on the one hand and race and sex on the other breaks down, there is a creditable case for some affirmative action, but to a far lesser degree than political pressures that drive in that direction. It is easy to state the arguments for and against affirmative action in the public sector, but it is very hard to come to any resolution of the matter that is both principled and comprehensive. Affirmative action offers yet another reason to shrink the size of government at all levels: there are few intelligent ways to configure the applicable set of rules that delineate the permissible scope of government hiring practices.

Does Title VII Allow Affirmative Action?

An examination of the legality of affirmative action under Title VII was the subject of extensive and learned debates illustrating the simple truth that a statute may mean exactly what it says. The basic prohibitions in Title VII speak clearly to its color-blind and sex-blind status. The basic provision, section 703(a)(1), provides that "it shall be an unlawful employment practice for an employer (1) to fail or refuse to hire, or discharge or otherwise discriminate against any individual with respect to his compensation terms, conditions or privileges of employment, because of such individual's race, color, sex or national origin." That same line is reinforced in connection with training programs in section 703(d), which reads:

> It shall be an unlawful employment practice for any employer, labor organization, or joint labor-management committee controlling apprenticeship or other training or retraining, including on-the-job training programs to discriminate against any individual because of his race, color, religion, sex or national origin in admission to, or employment in, any program established to provide apprenticeship or other training.

Finally, section 703(j), on which the defenders of affirmative action under Title VII rely, states:

> Nothing contained in this title shall be interpreted to require any employer, employment agency, labor organization, or joint labor-management committee subject to this title to grant preferential treatment to any individual or to any group because of the race, color, religion, sex or national origin of such individual or group on account of any imbalance which may exist with respect to the total number or percentages of persons of any race, color, religion or sex, or national origin employed by any employer.

Extensive statements in the legislative history take pains to indicate that the words "any individual" mean just that, and do not refer to "any individual contained in some preferred and protected class."[1] One passage among many indicates the uninterrupted run of the debate. In their joint memo Senators Clark and Case addressed this problem:

> Title VII would have no effect on established seniority rights. Its effect is prospective and not retrospective. Thus, for example, if a business has been discriminating in the past and as a result has an all-white working force, when the title comes into effect the employer's obligation would be simply to fill future vacancies on a nondiscriminatory basis. He would not be obliged—or indeed, permitted—to fire whites in order to hire Negroes, or to prefer Negroes for future vacancies, or, once Negroes are

---

1. In addition to the quoted passages, see also 110 *Cong. Rec.* 1518 (1964) (Rep. Cellar) ("The Bill would do more than prevent . . . employers from discriminating against or in favor of workers because because of their race, religion, or national origin"); 110 *Cong. Rec.* 1540 (Rep. Lindsay); 110 *Cong. Rec.* 8291 (Sen. Williams); 110 *Cong. Rec.* 11,848 (Sen. Humphrey) (Title VII "would prohibit preferential treatment for any particular group").

hired, to give them special seniority rights at the expense of the white workers hired earlier.[2]

And further:

There is no requirement in title VII that an employer maintain a racial balance in his work force. On the contrary, any deliberate attempt to maintain a racial balance, whatever such a balance may be, would involve a violation of title VII because maintaining such a balance would require an employer to hire or to refuse to hire on the basis of race.

There is, moreover, little doubt that Title VII and perhaps the entire statute would have been shipwrecked had it not expressed this wholly consistent attitude toward the question of color-blindness. Everyone knew, as the quotation from the Clark-Case memo explicitly states, that the Civil Rights Act would in the future render illegal practices that had been commonplace and legal for years. The only way to get the 1964 Civil Rights Act through a divided and uneasy Congress was to insulate those prior practices from the sting of retroactive liability under the new law.[3] As the second quoted paragraph indicates, the support of organized labor, so critical for the passage of the bill could not have been obtained if unions and their rank-and-file membership were to be held subject to serious exposure for their acts prior to 1964 or the subsequent consequences of those acts. The politics of the day dictated the basic structure of the protections afforded unions under the act.[4] There was to be a clean slate in law even if there could be none in practice. Conduct prior to the passage of the statute could not, therefore, be used to establish the illegality of what came after the statute, or as a reason to deviate from the color-blind (and, by parity of reasoning, sex-blind) norms that the statute implemented.

2. 110 *Cong. Rec.* 7213 (1964). Reams of this material are collected in Justice Rehnquist's dissent in *Steelworkers v. Weber,* 443 U.S. 193 (1979).

3. See William Eskridge, "Dynamic Statutory Interpretation," 135 *U. Pa. L. Rev.* 1479, 1491 n.46 (1987): "The Civil Rights Act barely beat back the Southern Democratic filibuster in the Senate (by a vote of 71 to 29, four votes more than the required two-thirds majority), and only with the support of Senator Dirksen and about a dozen other Republican conservatives." Eskridge, who has staunchly defended affirmative action under the statute on other grounds, notes that it is "inconceivable" that that these senators would have voted for cloture if the bill had "tolerated, or even encouraged affirmative action plans." Id. at n.46.

4. See 42 *U.S.C.* §703(h), as construed in *Int'l Brotherhood of Teamsters v. United States,* 431 U.S. 324 (1977).

The bias against freedom of contract within the statute carried over to discrimination against whites and men as much as it did to discrimination against blacks and women. The price of eliminating the pattern of past discrimination was an explicit promise not to use new forms of discrimination in reverse. The *Bipartisan Civil Rights Newsletter* showed that more recent attitudes on deconstruction, indeterminacy, and statutory interpretation were not yet in vogue in 1964: "There is no sound basis for uncertainty about the meaning of discrimination in the context of the civil rights bill. It means a distinction in treatment given to different individuals because of their different race, religion, or national origin."[5] Discrimination (not the disparate impact of neutral standards) was what the statute prohibited. The motive for the discrimination, whether benevolent or malevolent, was quite beside the point.

It is the genius of statutory construction to recognize that fundamental questions are often easy. In this case the critical question is whether the words "any individual" mean what they say or mean "certain individuals who fall into a protected class." As a semantic question this point answers itself. The legislative history only confirms that the Civil Rights Act means what it says and says what it means. The size of the stakes and the starkness of the issue precluded any ambiguity on this central point of principle.

Nonetheless, the pattern of illegitimate statutory construction so common with the Civil Rights Act on other issues reached its zenith here. *Steelworkers v. Weber*[6] was an action brought by a disappointed white male who had sought admission to a training program from which he was excluded on racial grounds. Justice Brennan, speaking for five members of the Court, held that the categorical language of the Civil Rights Act did not prohibit a voluntary affirmative action program, such as that undertaken by the Steelworkers Union and Kaiser Steel pursuant to their collective bargaining agreement, which "reserves for black employees 50% of the openings in an in-plant craft training program until the percentage of black craftworkers in the plant is commensurate with the percentage of blacks in the local labor force."[7] As a matter of statutory construction his opinion rests largely on quicksand. Its numerous defects were exposed in a powerful dissent by Justice Rehnquist[8] and have been well pointed

5. 110 *Cong. Rec.* 7477 (1964).
6. 443 U.S. 193 (1979).
7. Id. at 197.
8. *Weber*, 443 U.S. at 219–255.

out by others.[9] But as Justice Brennan's decision seems to attract new defenders,[10] it is necessary to reexamine some of the basic points here.

Justice Brennan takes two separate tacks—one purposive and one textual—to confront the color-blind command of the operative provisions of Title VII, including section 703(d), explicitly applicable to training programs. He thus begins with the familiar, if overused, rule of statutory construction that "a thing may be within the letter of the statute and yet not within the statute, because not within its spirit, nor within the intention of its makers."[11] But here the repudiation of all voluntary affirmative action was within both the intent and the spirit of the act, as the legislative history and political circumstances plentifully revealed. Congress may not have anticipated the determination with which affirmative action programs have been pursued in the last decade, but it was aware of that possibility, and constructed language to defeat it.

In order, therefore, to deflect the obvious conclusion, Justice Brennan flees to higher levels of abstraction. He first culls from the legislative history the most general statements of purpose. He refers to an observed decline in the employment prospects of blacks before the passage of the statute, and to statements such as "What good does it do a Negro to be able to eat in a fine restaurant if he cannot afford to pay the bill?"[12]—a point, of course, that is true of poor whites as well. He also quotes some language, equally general, about the role of good will and voluntary action in settling disputes under the statute.[13] At no point does he ever quote or discuss any of the specific material in the legislative history that

9. See especially Bernard D. Meltzer, "The Weber Case: The Judicial Abrogation of the Antidiscrimination Standard in Employment," 47 *U. Chi. L. Rev.* 423 (1980), which concludes: "The net result is an opinion that, with respect, is a profound disappointment, whether tested by its depth, its clarity, its candor, or its power to convince." Id. at 465.

10. See, e.g., Richard A. Posner, *The Problems of Jurisprudence* 283–285 (1989), and Cass R. Sunstein, *After the Rights Revolution* 201–205 (1990).

11. *Weber,* 443 U.S. at 201, quoting *Holy Trinity Church v. United States,* 143 U.S. 457, 459 (1892).

12. *Weber,* 443 U.S. at 203, quoting 110 *Cong. Rec.* 6547 (1964) (remarks of Senator Humphrey dealing with the general problem of racial discrimination in employment).

13. "No bill can or should lay claim to eliminating all of the causes and consequences of racial and other types of discrimination against minorities. There is reason to believe, however, that national leadership provided by the enactment of Federal legislation dealing with the most troublesome problems *will create an atmosphere conducive to voluntary or local resolution of other forms of discrimination.*" H.R. Rep. BH. 914, 88th Cong. 1st sess., pt. 1, p. 18 (1963) (emphasis added). *Weber,* 443 U.S. at 203–204. But the quote has to do

deals with the precise sections on which Weber based his complaint, most notably section 703(d),[14] even though these are set out at length in Justice Rehnquist's dissent. Instead, Brennan quickly moves to his own restatement of purpose for the entire complex grid of Title VII in what is rhetorically the most powerful sentence in his opinion: "It would be ironic indeed if a law triggered by a Nation's concern over centuries of racial injustice and intended to improve the lot of those who had 'been excluded from the American dream for so long' . . . constituted the first legislative prohibition of all voluntary, private, race-conscious efforts to abolish traditional patterns of racial segregation and hierarchy."[15]

This argument for statutory purpose constitutes a radical oversimplification. The Civil Rights Act did not have any single purpose. It was an elaborate compromise born of conflicting desires and interests. The vision that prevailed was of color-blindness, not favoritism for blacks. That vision was, moreover, perfectly consistent with the idea that the statute would be of vast help to blacks in getting the jobs that would allow them to participate in the good life. No one was under any illusions that whites as a class had been subjected to systematic discrimination before 1964. In the view of Congress, the movement to a color-blind standard would eliminate the chief impediments to black equality by refusing to allow *anyone* to take race into account in hiring, promotion, or discharge. A neutral, color-blind principle can, and will, have the desired disparate impact precisely because of the unequal historical position of the various groups whose employment prospects the statute covers. But sharp limitations were placed on the permissible *means* for achieving the desired end.

---

only with voluntary measures to enter into compliance with the law. It does not even address affirmative action, let alone the employment context.

14. One of the many ironies in this area is found in the brief for the United Steelworkers of America at 25, where section 703(d) is dismissed as indeterminate: "Section 703(d) standing alone does little to advance the inquiry since its operative words are 'discriminate against any individual . . . in admission to . . . any [training] program,' and 'the concept of discrimination is susceptible to varying interpretations.' "

The meaning of the term *discrimination* was crystal clear when the statute was proposed. See note 5.

15. *Weber,* 443 U.S. at 204. Brennan's inspiration was again from the Steelworkers brief at 84: "But it would be ironic if a law triggered by a Nation's guilt over centuries of racial injustice constituted the first prohibition of private endeavors to accelerate the elimination of the vestiges of that injustice. And it would be particularly ironic if that result were predicated upon isolated remarks of Senators Humphrey, Case, and Clark, whose anguish over the present consequences of historical discrimination was eloquently stated during the debates on Title VII."

The fear of exclusion and special partisan favor for blacks pushed Congress to the race- and sex-neutral language of the statute. There was no support or sentiment whatsoever for rules that introduced or tolerated overt racial and sexual preferences in the opposite direction. To the contrary, one purpose of the statute was to block the possibility, both in the context of unions and more generally, that future employment decisions would be used to compensate for the injustices of past ones. There is nothing whatsoever in the general pronouncements about the beneficial effects of the statute that committed the 1964 Congress to embrace or tolerate affirmative action.

The second half of Justice Brennan's argument turns on the strict textual construction of section 703(j), which he claims supports his basic position by negative inference. The language of the provision says only that "nothing contained in this title shall be interpreted to require any employer . . . [or] labor organization . . . to grant preferential treatment to any individual or to any group because of race, color, religion, sex, or national origin." The fatal gap in this provision, so we are told, was that the word "permit" was not included after the words "to require." This absence was in Brennan's view fatal to any argument that Title VII prohibited all forms of race-conscious relief. "The section does *not* state that 'nothing in Title VII shall be interpreted to *permit*' voluntary affirmative efforts to correct racial imbalances. The natural inference is that Congress chose not to forbid all voluntary race-conscious affirmative action."[16]

Initially there is no question that one of the weakest canons of statutory construction is *expressio unius, exclusio alterius*—the explicit mention of one thing is the exclusion of another. Silence by itself is normally a weak guide to interpretation, one that at most creates ambiguity but does not resolve it. It thus becomes appropriate to read section 703(j) alongside other relevant provisions. Sections 703(a) and 703(d) in explicitly color-blind language refer to "any individual." The ostensible silence of section 703(j) is thus consistent with a uniform color-blind norm. It is difficult to infer the legality of some race-conscious behavior from silence, when any inference to that effect must overcome express textual language that cuts in the opposite direction. Since section 703(j) is, moreover, by its own terms only an aid to interpretation, it does not contain any statutory command to deflect or override the color-blind principle contained else-

---

16. *Weber*, 443 U.S. at 206 (emphasis in original). This part of the argument is also endorsed in Ronald Dworkin, "How to Read the Civil Rights Act," *New York Review of Books*, December 19, 1979, p. 37.

where in the statute. Indeed, this was just the view taken by Senator Humphrey, who stated that this section was added to remove doubts on the question of whether Title VII requires an employer to maintain a balanced work force: "This subsection does not represent any change in the substance of the title. It does state clearly and accurately what we have maintained all along about the bill's intent and meaning."[17] It is for this reason that the section begins with the words "nothing contained in this title shall be *interpreted* to require . . ."

The case against Brennan's view, however, does not rest solely on the relation of section 703(j) to the remainder of the section. His view is wrong just in terms of the internal construction of section 703(j) itself. Brennan's key error is that he truncates the quotation after the insertion of the words "to *permit*" and then adds his own description of what is permitted, namely "voluntary affirmative efforts to correct racial imbalances." Section 703(j) does not continue with his free-standing embellishment, but rather carries on with the same color-blind theme that dominates elsewhere in the statute. The negative inference flips the section around so that it would have to read: "This title shall be interpreted to *permit* any employer [or labor organization] . . . to grant preferential treatment to *any* individual or to any group because of race . . ." The ostensible opposition between *permit* and *require* thus becomes a statutory sleight of hand sufficient to repeal the *entire* color-blind civil rights statute by allowing any voluntary preference to any person, regardless of race, color, and so on, or for any other reason. The only way to wriggle out of this problem is to argue that the color-blind language of section 703(j) simply introduces a one-directional test in favor of protected classes. But since this interpretive section takes exactly the same neutral line as section 703(a), one has to find in a coherent statutory draft wildly contradictory policy orientations. Nowhere in the legislative history of section 703, however, can anyone find explicit recognition of the affirmative action exception to Title VII. Indeed, it is not possible to find in that history any reference to, let alone explicit endorsement of, the idea that women and minorities fall into protected classes entitled to a special place under Title VII. Quite simply, no one thought that Title VII either required or permitted any use of race-conscious standards. Section 703(d) means just what it says. The 1964 act was in its inception, design, and execution both a repudiation of freedom of contract and an endorsement of the ideal of a color-blind workplace.

17. 110 *Cong. Rec.* 12,723 (1964).

The modern efforts to resurrect Justice Brennan's opinions fare no better than the opinion itself. Thus both Richard Posner and Cass Sunstein, who normally find so much on which to disagree, insist that it is a "myth" to believe that the ordinary canons of statutory interpretation can yield a determinate answer to the question of whether affirmative action programs are consistent with the language and legislative history of Title VII. Sunstein writes:

> It was clear that Congress had not foreseen or focused on the possibility that employers would voluntarily engage in affirmative action in favor of blacks, whether to fend off litigation, to overcome societal discrimination or to improve the efficacy of the workplace, or for some other reason. In the racial setting, Congress understood the term "discrimination" in reference to race-conscious members harming blacks.[18]

Posner for his part makes much the same argument:

> The problem with all this [textual] evidence in favor of Weber is that it can be sidestepped by observing that Congress in 1964 never considered the possible application of the statute to voluntary private efforts by white employers (or employers controlled by white people, as Kaiser surely was and is) to promote employment of blacks. The problem at that time was discrimination against blacks, not in favor of them.[19]

Their common argument seems wrong at every turn. Historically the possibility of affirmative action was considered, and rejected, in the 1964 debates. The Clark-Case memo covers this possibility; and it can be sidestepped only if it is not quoted or analyzed. It is no mere coincidence that both Posner and Sunstein pass over that history in silence. It is of course possible that the members of the 1964 Congress would have changed their minds about affirmative action in light of subsequent history. To say, however, that they had not "considered" or "foreseen or focused on" the possibility of affirmative action is to make an incorrect leap of faith. At most the 1964 Congress did not anticipate all the novel arguments that resourceful academics and determined politicians of the next generation would make for affirmative action—or for that matter against it.

Likewise the textual arguments in support of *Weber* fail. The word "discrimination" does not appear in isolation in the text. It is followed by

18. Sunstein, *After the Rights Revolution* at 203.
19. Posner, *The Problems of Jurisprudence* at 284.

the words "against any individual." To say that its meaning is limited to race-conscious measures is to pluck the word out of context and assign to it one meaning for race while leaving open the possibility that it has the "blind" meaning for color, sex, or national origin. Under Posner's and Sunstein's view of the world it is always possible (if never strictly required) to take refuge behind a myriad of general purposes and contemporary public policy arguments (contemporary, that is, to the current debate and not the original statute) to defeat the combined force of text and legislative history. At this point there is nothing left to the distinctive task of statutory interpretation, which only requires us to do what others think rather than what we wish to do on our own. On their view, interpretation becomes indistinguishable from determining whether to pass the statute in the first instance, or to repeal it when it is no longer to our liking. There are surely cases in which plain meaning or ordinary language fails to give a clear and unambiguous answer, although I believe that these are fewer and less important that either Posner or Sunstein would acknowledge. But *Weber* is not one of those cases. One can disagree, as I surely do, with the basic premise and logic of Title VII, and still recognize that the statute was driven by someone else's view of the world and not my own.

Affirmative Remedial Action

The second major interpretive issue under the statute arises with respect to its remedial provisions as to whether race-conscious or sex-conscious action should be allowed under Title VII to remedy acts of discrimination that the statute itself renders unlawful. In this context the statutory provisions speak with a far less authoritative voice than they do on the question of underlying statutory liability. The operative section is 706(g), which reads:

> If the court finds that the respondent has intentionally engaged in or is intentionally engaging in an unlawful employment practice charged in the complaint, the court may enjoin the respondent from engaging in such unlawful employment practice, and order such affirmative action as may be appropriate, which may include, [but is not limited to,] reinstatement or hiring of employees, with or without back pay . . . , [or any other equitable relief as the court deems appropriate] . . . No order of the court shall require the admission or reinstatement of an individual as a member of a union, or the hiring, reinstatement, or promotion of an

individual as an employee, or the payment to him of any back pay, if such individual was refused admission, suspended, or expelled, or was refused employment or advancement or was suspended or discharged for any reason other than discrimination on account of race, color, religion, sex or national origin.[20]

"Affirmative action" is written across the face of the statute. The question arises, then, as to how the term fits into the overall scheme. In order to answer this question as a matter of statutory construction it is first necessary to note how this remedial provision squares with the basic provisions on liability. In modern cases this question is answered on the assumption that the disparate impact cases (regardless of the viability of the business necessity defense) are part of the basic system to which remedial relief can be attached. Since the scope for potential violation is large, it follows that the remedial provisions have a large scope as well. It seems, therefore, that there is some authorization for the use of affirmative action remedies, where the narrowest possible construction allows such remedies in favor of the individuals against whom the discrimination is practiced, but only against the employer (or labor organization) that practiced that discrimination.

Nonetheless, this narrow interpretation is by no means secure. There is some question under the statutory language whether the affirmative action remedy allows the hiring of employees who were not themselves the victims of discrimination. A further question exists as to whether the scope of "appropriate relief" could encompass broader action, such as the imposition of goals or even quotas. There is no doubt that the text of this statutory provision raises as many questions as it answers. By way of analogy, there is far less clarity at common law in stating the choice of remedy (damages, specific performance, restitution, injunction) than there is in articulating the general provision that a defendant in breach of contract should be held liable.

It is just this confusion that is reflected in the cases decided under the basic provision. The first of the relevant cases, *Franks v. Bowman Transportation Co.*,[21] involves a class action brought by a group of black employees against both their employer and certain labor unions. The suit alleged that these black drivers were systematically denied access to preferred open-road routes and were confined to the less desirable city

20. Section 706(g).
21. 424 U.S. 747 (1976).

routes. After the finding of discrimination, the question became whether the courts had authority under section 706(g) to award seniority to the black workers, calculated from the date that their applications had been wrongfully refused, even though that decision would give these black workers more seniority than white workers, themselves guilty of no discrimination, who were hired after the black workers had been turned down but before the suit was initiated. The Court, speaking through Justice Brennan, held that the broad remedial purposes of the civil rights statute should not be read to exclude a race-conscious "make whole" remedy, even one that prejudiced the position of innocent white workers hired in the interim. A fairly solid legislative history supports his overall conclusion about the broad scope of discretion, especially in the 1972 amendments,[22] but none addresses the precise problem raised in the case. In any event, the debate over the scope of section 706(g) is surely far more delicate than the issue of voluntary affirmative action, which *Weber* decided some two years after *Franks*.[23]

Three subsequent decisions are worthy of some brief comment. In *Sheet Metal Workers v. EEOC*[24] the Court, with Justice Brennan again taking the lead, held that *Franks* did not bar affirmative action relief for

22. See section-by-section analysis of H.R. 1746, accompanying the Equal Employment Opportunity Act of 1972 conference report, 118 *Cong. Rec.* 7166, 7168 (1972), cited in *Franks,* 424 U.S. at 764.

23. On a parallel issue, *Franks* held that the protection of bona fide seniority provisions under section 703(h) insulated seniority systems from challenges based on discrimination prior to 1964 and not thereafter. 424 U.S. at 761–762. See also *International Brotherhood of Teamsters v. United States,* 431 U.S. 324 (1977); *Firefighters Local Union No. 1784 v. Stotts,* 467 U.S. 561, 575 (1984). In *Stotts,* the Court refused to read a consent decree, which by its language was directed only toward affirmative action in new hirings, to override a seniority system on the question of layoffs, which were not explicitly governed by the agreement. The decision thus left new affirmative action employees at the same risk of layoff as all other workers on the last-to-hire, first-to-go regime.

Of all the explicit provisions of the 1964 act, section 703(h) seems to have best weathered the storm of statutory construction. See *Lorance v. AT&T Technologies, Inc.,* 490 U.S. 900 (1989), where the Court held that the statute of limitations for challenges to seniority systems start to run at the moment the allegedly discriminatory system was put into place, not when a woman was laid off in consequence of its operation. To start the statute running from the moment the plan is put into effect quickly insulates the system from all charges. But to start the statute from the time of layoff renders it subject to perpetual challenge. Both periods are inapposite. The decision in *Lorance* would have been overturned by section 7 of the Civil Rights Bill of 1990.

24. *Local 28 of the Sheet Metal Workers' International Association v. EEOC,* 478 U.S. 421 (1986).

black workers who had not been discriminated against by a union in its membership program. The argument exploited a glitch in the last phrase of section 706(g). As drafted that sentence precludes using hiring or reinstatement remedies only for workers who had been refused admission to a union "for any reason other than race." By its own terms the restrictions on hiring and reinstatement do not apply to workers who never sought a job in the first instance.[25] As construed by Justice Brennan, therefore, the provision imposes *no* limitations on affirmative action orders "appropriate" to new workers.

The counterargument is that the first section of the statute, which does authorize affirmative action, including the "reinstatement or hiring of employees," could (indeed probably should) be read as being limited to employees who had worked for the firm or who had applied for jobs in the first place, on the ground that private remedies are normally vested in the victim of the wrong. Coupling the statutory *re*instatement remedy with the question of back pay ("reinstatement or hiring, with or without back pay") seems to imply that the affirmative action remedy is limited only to employees who are eligible for back pay, and that class includes only the actual or prospective employees of the firm. Even the allowance of broad equitable relief is satisfied by fashioning conditional decrees ordering specific performance for the benefit of the underlying victims in the case alone. By this reading it follows that strangers to the discrimination are entitled to *no* special remedial protection. Accordingly, there is no general authority under the section to award relief for strangers in the first instance.

This "victims only" approach seeks to fit Title VII into the standard corrective justice mode of adjudication. Only victims can initiate actions against wrongdoers. The substantive provisions state who is entitled to recover. The remedial provisions then address the relief to be granted to the class in question. Brennan's broad construction of the remedial provisions undertaken in *Sheet Metal Workers* is a self-conscious effort to transform that mission of Title VII into something far broader, namely a restructuring of society that takes into account the interests of nonparties to the litigation in fashioning remedies for breach. Under this broader conception of the statute Justice Brennan upheld an order that required the union to meet a 29 percent membership goal for black workers. That program did not remove any given worker from his job, and thus its burdens were diffused over future white workers, not concentrated on

25. *Bazemore v. Friday*, 478 U.S. 385, 446–447 (1986) (Brennan, J., concurring).

present ones. In the companion case of *Firefighters v. Cleveland*,[26] Justice Brennan dubiously held that it was equally permissible to allow the use of race-conscious remedies under a consent decree over the objection of the union, even if it was impermissible to use race-conscious remedies by judicial decree. Here again Title VII is used to restructure large-scale institutions, not to redress individual wrongs.

The next (but hardly final) stage in the evolution was not long in coming. In *Johnson v. Transportation Agency, Santa Clara County, Calif.*,[27] the Court, again speaking through Justice Brennan, completely unhitched affirmative action remedies from any prior wrong of the defendant. *Johnson* held that it was no violation of Title VII for the county to promote a female employee to road dispatcher over a male worker who had scored higher on a test. The action was protected against illegality by the county's intention to remedy the underrepresentation of female workers in certain job classifications. The action was said to lose its sting because men were not absolutely excluded from competing for these positions.

Johnson is hard to understand because it speaks with two voices. On the one hand, the Santa Clara program had very broad objectives, including the attainment of a county work force "whose composition in all job levels and major job classifications approximates the distribution of women, minority and handicapped persons in the Santa Clara area workforce."[28] The basic program thus looks like a mandate for proportional representation in all areas of life, which is as far from a color-blind or sex-blind world as one can imagine. Yet, on the other hand, the action

---

26. *Firefighters v. Cleveland*, 478 U.S. 501 (1986). One difficult aspect of this case is that it allowed the consent decree to bind a union that did not have full rights to participate in its decision. The implicit due process arguments of *Firefighters* received judicial expression in *Martin v. Wilks*, 490 U.S. 955 (1989), which refused to bind the union to any decree to which it was not a full-fledged party, and placed the obligation on the participants of the lawsuit to join the union in the dispute, and not on the union to intervene in order to preserve its rights. Given that the civil rights statutes preserve for all persons protection against discrimination, it is not persuasive to argue that the white union need not be joined in the suit solely because it has no explicit contract right that was violated by a consent decree. The requirement of equal treatment is imposed by statute independent of contract, and its violation should be sufficient to require a party's full participation in the case before it is bound. Only in a common law regime would an economic loss, without breach of contract, be an unprotected loss.

27. 480 U.S. 616 (1987).

28. Id. at 1466 (Scalia, J., dissenting), quoting from the affirmative action program adopted by the County in 1979.

taken under the decision involved a single worker whose score was only two points lower (73 as opposed to 75) than that of the man who was passed over for the position, and in a setting in which *none* of the 238 relevant skill positions was occupied by a woman. Moreover, the county made no effort to use this particular piece of information to establish its own prior discrimination against women, even by a disparate impact theory, in order to defend its present discriminatory decision. Whatever the facts might have been, the case as argued did not fall within the remedial contours of section 706(g). Justice Antonin Scalia, writing in dissent, therefore stressed the obvious when he said that here was a sex-conscious decision for affirmative action that was manifestly at cross-purposes with the basic statutory provision and that could not be salvaged by any resort to the remedial provisions of section 706(g).[29]

There is no question but that affirmative action remedial decisions have resulted in an erosion of the color-blind and race-blind standards. What is unclear is whether *Johnson* will be read to validate comprehensive programs of proportionate representation that generate not isolated employment decisions but wide-scale changes in hiring and promotion practices, all in the service of forward-looking goals that are regarded as far more compelling in today's political environment than they were in 1964.[30]

Even from this brief review it is apparent that the Supreme Court has read Title VII's remedial provisions as reinforcing its pervasive institutional double standard on discrimination. *Weber* in effect allows voluntary discrimination in favor of certain protected groups; cases such as *Firefighters* add the explicit use of affirmative action on the remedial side for the same groups. All the while the disparate impact test under *Griggs* leads to exaggerated findings of discrimination against protected groups. The magnitude of these shifts, moreover, can be made evident by an unconventional thought experiment. What would be the forensic position of Justice Brennan on the remedial provisions of section 706(g) if both *Weber* and *Griggs* had been (correctly) decided the other way?

In this original-intent Title-VII world, liability for discrimination extends only as far as the disparate treatment cases, and one never has to address the question of whether maintaining a system with known dispa-

---

29. 480 U.S. at 666.

30. For two very different responses to *Johnson,* see *Hammon v. Barry,* 826 F.2d 73 (D.C. Cir. 1987) (striking down an affirmative action plan for the District of Columbia fire department, notwithstanding *Johnson,* and over strong dissent); *Higgins v. City of Vallejo,* 823 F.2d 351 (9th Cir. 1987) (upholding affirmative action plan).

rate impact is a form of intentional discrimination. Without *Griggs,* the potential scope for affirmative action remedies under section 706(g) is truncated because the class of underlying violations is itself sharply limited. Without *Weber,* race-conscious admission standards for training and promotion programs are self-evidently both illegal and intentional. Justice Brennan's broad reading of section 706(g) would therefore allow, and perhaps require, a court to issue affirmative action orders that would reinstate workers such as Brian Weber under the "make whole" doctrine, even to the prejudice of innocent black workers. In addition, section 706(g) would permit, or perhaps compel, courts to establish explicit goals and timetables that would *benefit* white or male workers who were the victims of discrimination under the race-conscious or sex-conscious plans so common today. The whole world would be turned topsy-turvy, especially if *Weber* were overruled retroactively. Those who embrace the broad reading of the remedial provisions of section 706(g) should pause to ask whether they would hold to that view if liability under section 703(a) had been confined to its original race-blind and sex-blind contours.

CHAPTER 20

First Principles

A Fresh Start

The legitimacy of affirmative action within the contemporary American debate has always been posed as an exception to the basic antidiscrimination norm. Within the legal context the case for this exception is inescapably discussed in connection with the initial color-blind and sex-blind norm that permeates Title VII. The question of principle, however, should be wholly divorced from the textual interpretation or the legislative history of a statute enacted over a quarter of a century ago. Senators Humphrey, Case, and Clark are not our floor leaders, even if they were the able leaders for their own generation. It is now both possible and necessary to begin with a blank slate. The question becomes, what should any future legal regime provide? Given this new-found freedom, some people could argue that employers are bound to follow the basic anti-discrimination norm for men and for whites but can adopt affirmative action programs for women and blacks. Others could say that any employer can run an affirmative action program for whomever it wants. Drafting a statute is easy; drafting no statute, as with a return to freedom of contract, is even easier. The question is, what should the law provide?

In undertaking a fresh look at affirmative action, I start with a traditional distinction that was obliterated by Title VII of the 1964 act, and which has remained obscure in the more recent general debate over affirmative action. It is the distinction between public and private conduct. In my view affirmative action poses serious difficulties only in the context of public employment. By contrast, in the context of private employment those who want to practice affirmative action should be free to do so, for whatever reason, and for the benefit of whichever groups they choose. The first part of this chapter offers a libertarian, market-oriented defense of affirmative action for all. I then proceed to a much more limited, guarded, and anxious endorsement of some forms of race-conscious and sex-conscious decision making, which might pass for affirmative action in the public sphere. In working out the cases where race and sex are permissible criteria, I try to make a first cut at a hopeless tangle: to distinguish between those cases in which explicit racial or sexual preferences represent a policy for the public good and not the outgrowth of private factional pressures.

The Private Sphere: Affirmative Action for All

Most normative accounts today seek to justify affirmative action for favored groups as a principled exception to an otherwise unshakable general antidiscrimination norm. Since I believe, however, that Title VII should in principle be repealed for all private employment relationships, I start from an initial premise that stresses the dominance of freedom of contract and voluntary market transactions. In a competitive private market every employer should have the right to offer employment to whomever it chooses on whatever terms and conditions it sees fit, for the reasons set out extensively earlier in this book.[1] Within that framework affirmative action in the private sphere ceases to be either a difficult or a novel question of legal principle, or even a recognizable category of analysis.

One central part of the argument against Title VII was that there is no independent conception of which characteristics count as "merit" characteristics and which are invidious. Under a rigorous theory that regards all valuations as subjective, any private conception of merit will do as well as any other, but only to the extent that the employer or employee chooses to attach any weight to that conception. Productivity, if that is what is desired, could be measured by counting widgets, or taking into account the interactive effects between workers or anything else. There is no external measure of value that allows the legal system or the public at large to impose its preferences on the parties in their own relationship. There is thus no reason to have to decide whether we should weigh the need for merit in employment decisions against the need for diversity in workers. Both excellence and diversity are relevant features for the employers that wish to consider them. With regard to a principled public opposition to private affirmative action, I am happily hoist with my own petard. Surely a general theory that allows firms to engage in explicit

1. See Chapters 1–3.

discrimination against blacks or women must take the identical attitude toward affirmative action on behalf of those same groups, or indeed any other group. Since there is no prima facie legal wrong in taking race and sex into account in hiring whites and males, there is none either in hiring blacks and females on the ground of race or sex. Formal equality and substantive soundness thus work in perfect harmony.

The same approach should be taken to the divisive issue of quotas, which sparked so much controversy both at the passage of the 1964 Civil Rights Act[2] and during the endless battles over the proposed 1990 Civil Rights Act as well. Throughout that debate *everyone* at both ends of the political spectrum believed that quotas were bad, and their unanimity on the subject spared them the obligation to explain why their self-evident conclusion was correct. In principle, the proper analysis of quotas fits to a 'T' the analysis of affirmative action. The central issue here is not whether quotas are a good or a bad thing but who decides whether they should be used. When that decision is made by the state, there is evident interference with freedom of contract, and the welfare losses are measured by the extent to which employers and employees are forced to alter their conduct in order to comply with the dictates of the state.

Yet once it is clear that Title VII is the law, it becomes hard to denounce quotas in any categorical way. The deviation from market principles that quotas require may be *less* demanding than the deviation required by a disparate impact rule. For example, a quota might impose an explicit directive that, say, 10 percent of the work force be drawn from a particular racial or ethnic group, whereas a disparate treatment ruling might create a powerful incentive to hire twice that percentage of workers from the same group, in accordance with the composition of the available pool. In addition, quotas could be defended, relative to disparate impact standards, on the ground that they give clear notice to firms whether they are or are not in compliance with the law, and hence reduce their exposure to damage actions and the attendant costs of litigation. One cannot decide whether the explicit quota is better or worse in the abstract. The comparison has to be made relative to some alternative scheme of coercion.

If Title VII is repealed, however, the only quotas that will be adopted are those that are voluntary, where voluntary is not a term of art subject to the evident taint in *Weber* of referring to an action undertaken only as an effort to forestall some anticipated lawsuit under Title VII. Therefore, if firms choose to adopt a quota, it will be because they are responding to some element of internal pressure or market demand. The fear that

2. See Chapter 10.

quotas will sweep the land and relegate certain groups (such as white males) to second-class citizenship should no longer be regarded as serious, and for the same familiar reasons that explain why free entry can check the invidious effects of private discrimination. The larger the number of firms that choose to adopt quotas, the greater the opportunity for new entrants to hire the superior workers who are passed over in the process. Remove the coercive power of Title VII (or, for that matter, state and professional accreditation societies), and the quota issue ceases to be a matter for urgent public debate; instead it becomes just another consideration to be taken into account by the firm.

The only limitations on employer choice involve either defects in the contracting process or the risk of external harm. Since misrepresentation and duress are not involved when some persons receive favored treatment, the contracts formed should stand between the parties. There is, moreover, no reason to take into account the so-called negative externalities of the practice, for with ordinary two-party contracts the only externalities of any legal relevance are the threat of force against strangers and the use of monopolistic practices, both of which are as remote from affirmative action programs or quotas as from any other form of employer choice. The other kinds of externalities, namely distaste for the decisions made, are as real in this case as in any other, and no one should make light of them. But not all externalities should be subject to legal redress. Rather, there should be a calculated and general social reason to exclude *all* instances of mere offense born of moral outrage or bruised sensibilities from the class of actionable harms, however deeply felt the hurt.

There are thousands of contractual arrangements (just as there are thousands of speech or sexual acts) that give offense to others. If the performance of these contracts, speech, or actions can be stopped because others object to what is done or said, or to the reasons the parties have for acting as they do, then it follows that *every* program of contract is necessarily at the mercy of outsiders to the transaction. The question of offense cannot be treated one way for persons who object to contracts that favor men or whites and another way for persons who object to contracts that favor blacks or women. Whether we speak of external or internal preferences, no one person is entitled to elevate his or her beliefs about how others should act above those of anyone else.[3]

3. The distinction is from Ronald Dworkin, *Taking Rights Seriously*, ch. 9 (1977). But the distinction cannot occupy the central place that he attaches to it, for virtually everyone can find some reason to explain why his or her preferences depend on the private impact of some policy point. On this at least I agree with Richard Posner, who rightly takes Dworkin

Whether we speak in the domain of contract or of externality, the basic subjective value condition holds. The sole choice, then, for the legal system is to decide whether *all* contracts may be blocked because of the objections of outsiders to the terms on which they are conducted, or whether *none* should be so blocked.

The first of these alternatives results in stalemate and political confusion as rival factions seek to determine whose preferences are legitimate and whose are not. There is no possible or principled way to sort out which forms of offense are strong enough or pervasive enough to warrant condemnation. The libertarian thinkers were surely wrong when they argued that offense was not a category of harm, when it so clearly is. But they were right when they concluded that this was a form of harm that for good social reasons should not be subject to redress. The common law, in dealing with offense and competitive harms, adopted the Roman category *damnum absque iniuria*—harm without legal injury. Although there is ample room for common law protection against various forms of personal abuse, as the law of sexual harassment shows, there is no place for a rule that says that simple objection to ordinary commercial conduct transforms a private contract into some form of mass tort. The level of affirmative action or the extent of quotas should be regarded as an internal affair of the firm, and never as the affair of the public at large or the state. Implementing quotas or an affirmative action program is thus an exercise of an ordinary contractual liberty, not a justified exception to some grander antidiscrimination norm. The size of the public domain mercifully shrinks.

The change in the nature of the inquiry should have important consequences in the tone of the overall debate about the legitimacy of race-conscious hiring practices. No one is willing to take up the battle for quotas; but affirmative action, as these words are written, remains at center stage. In the present political climate some *public* justification for affirmative action in employment becomes strictly required because of the perceived tenacity of the basic antidiscrimination norm. That need for justification typically evokes several kinds of responses, some backward-looking and some forward-looking.[4]

---

to task for his rendition of *Weber* without offering "the political and ethical judgment" that he thinks necessary to resolve the case correctly. See Richard A. Posner, *The Problems of Jurisprudence* 286–288 (1990).

4. See, for a convenient summary of the arguments, Kathleen M. Sullivan, "Sins of Discrimination: Last Term's Affirmative Action Cases," 100 *Harv. L. Rev.* 78 (1986).

Many people will argue that affirmative action is justified in order to counter past discrimination, both public and private, against blacks and women in society. In order to support their claim, they have a systematic incentive to overstate the degree of discrimination that has taken place; to dwell at length on the idea of unconscious discrimination; to attribute the discrimination that did exist to the marketplace and not to invidious forms of state action; to assert that prior remedial programs have been woefully inadequate to undo the corrosive effects of past discrimination; and to claim that the pervasive dominance of racist or sexist attitudes in the larger society justifies the affirmative action programs undertaken by courageous private firms and government agencies. The list goes on. In essence the dominant strategy is to show that one-way affirmative action is proper because there has been, and continues to be, one-way discrimination in employment markets. The condemnation of the status quo in America as a total society must be made out in the strongest possible terms in order to justify a principled exception to the basic anti-discrimination norm. Affirmative action is a principled, voluntary response to an otherwise corrupt society. Remove the corruption and the public justifications for affirmative actions vanish.

The opponents of affirmative action are similarly driven to make extreme public justifications for their opposition to the practice. Thus they argue that many successful people have made it to the top notwithstanding the extensive amounts of discrimination practiced against them in all phases of life. They will cite the successes of Armenian, Chinese, Italian, Japanese, Jewish, Korean, and Vietnamese immigrants in the face of pervasive patterns of overt discrimination. They point to the political instability of any public law that authorizes some level of affirmative action without limiting its extent. They stress the adverse consequences of affirmative action on innocent whites and males (most notably innocent white males), who have seen their progress blocked by the overt exclusion and differential hiring criteria that bring back chilling memories of the Jim Crow era in the Old South. They scoff at the claim that affirmative action is acceptable because it is meant not to "stigmatize" whites or males but only to help blacks and women. They insist that the nation must lose its way in metaphysical subtleties when its leading spokesmen claim that they can distinguish between invidious and acceptable forms of discrimination. They speak of the risk of perpetual double standards under the law and point to the dangers of introducing ugly forms of reverse discrimination in the guise of affirmative action. They stress the subtle corruption of discourse when people insist that affirmative action be allowed and then turn around and claim that everyone in their firm meets the ordinary standards of merit. They assert an implicit reduction in the level of quality in the marketplace that must follow in the wake of passing over well-qualified men and whites for less-qualified women and blacks. They insist that affirmative action works to the prejudice of able blacks and women, since outsiders (in yet another version of the "lemons" argument) think that they received their advancement solely or largely because of their race or sex and not on their merits. The useful signals that are normally generated by title, position, and responsibility become muffled.

The opponents of affirmative action can condemn it roundly as a short-term fix that introduces more abuse than it eliminates. They point to the distinguished blacks who oppose, or at least are skeptical of, affirmative action.[5] They claim that affirmative action leads to a certain level of dissembling within the firm as it seeks to move slowly in implementing the affirmative action programs that it announced with such glorious fanfare. At bottom they claim that affirmative action is generosity gone astray, or, more ominously, that it arises from the same dark impulses of favoritism that led to the dominance of separate but equal in the Old South. This list also goes on. In a word, the strategy in opposition to affirmative action is to paint it as just another cleverly crafted violation of the antidiscrimination norm, as another social *wrong* of the very sort that the 1964 Civil Rights Act (how quickly we forget!) was designed to prevent.

It should be evident that the rhetoric on both sides is necessarily inflamed by one common need: to justify a position for or against affirmative action on the basis of some comprehensive social theory of right and wrong. But once we recognize that freedom of contract should be the basic social norm, then the need for inflamed public rhetoric is reduced, since there are no longer any collective decisions to tear at and sear our collective conscience. Some firms may well decide to engage in an affirmative action program anyway: it is only a matter of following the internal decision-making procedures adopted by the firm. Any organization can opt for a little bit of affirmative action or a lot. It can decide to hire only women or blacks or anyone else. It can grant broad discretion to managers or write a rule book that is no more comprehensible than the dreaded EEOC regulations under Title VII. The absence of any need for external justification allows the firm to decide whether diversity is, as it

---

5. See, e.g., Glenn C. Loury, "Why Should We Care about Group Inequality?" 5 *Soc. Phil. & Pol.* 249 (1987).

were, a good it values, and if so to what extent. Once it has made its contractual promises, it will, of course, be bound by them. Once it makes its public announcements, it will bear the reputational consequences, for good or ill. The possibility of heavy liabilities or serious loss of reputation should exert the same sobering effect on affirmative action programs as on any other aspect of internal policy. If prudence fails, the firm suffers the loss and in the limit goes bankrupt.

Firms with affirmative action programs do not, of course, have any monopoly on wisdom. Whatever their grounds for choice, the key element remains: if markets are to decentralize and move decision-making power to private firms, the level of rhetoric cannot escalate to the fever pitch it reaches when the proper pattern of employment decisions is instead considered, as it so commonly is today, a public or collective function for the state to discharge. The way to resolve the fundamental social disagreement is not to have a knock-down, drag-out moral fight in which both sides are wrong. It is to allow people to go their separate ways.

What will happen in practice if the law allows an employer to practice affirmative action toward everyone or no one? One possibility is that some firms will decide to hire only whites or only men. But what of it? My guess is that the sample will be relatively small. All the intrafirm hiring disputes that I have ever encountered or heard of *anywhere* pit claims for affirmative action for blacks and women against claims for a color-blind or sex-blind policy. Were discrimination allowed as a matter of course, the greatest victory for the civil rights movement would be to see its own position prevail in an atmosphere wholly free from any threat of government coercion. Why should anyone be uneasy about winning 90 percent of the battles? Why in the name of diversity must we exclude a few all-male or all-white enclaves for those who want them, for whatever reason? Once the question of affirmative action is privatized, we will all enjoy some modest gain from the relative lack of tension and from the cost savings as litigation ceases.

How much affirmative action will survive? It is hard to say exactly, given that many affirmative action programs were adopted or expanded to minimize the sting of disparate impact liability from claims available solely to women or minorities. The *Sears* case is an instance of an affirmative action program that was adopted in an unsuccessful effort to stave off an impending government suit of monstrous proportions. Nonetheless, at this juncture the inquiry should be turned on its head. In what sense does the present level of affirmative action programs represent any social consensus, given the specter of enormous government coercion that lurks in the wings? Affirmative action would have far more legitimacy if these programs were adopted after the stick is removed and only the carrot remains.

In a sense I think that in large measure this is exactly what would happen. In universities the pressure for affirmative action, for both students and faculty, is not driven solely, or even largely, by Title VII, but rather arises from an enormous internal constituency that flattens all opposition. Affirmative action would not disappear if Title VII were repealed tomorrow; the political support for the current status quo would still exert extensive power within private firms. It is very doubtful that Sears—to take a nonrandom example—would ever choose to adopt a hiring policy that excludes blacks or women, or that formally or practically relegates them to inferior status. I doubt that they would find it in their interest to eliminate their affirmative action program, either, even though they might choose to reduce its scope and scale. When that result comes about by the decisions of free individuals, then it is all for the good. The job of the legal analyst is to articulate the legal rules under which persons make responsible choices, the circumstances that require them to bear the costs of their decisions and to reap the benefits free from external compulsion and control. Their own views (and my own views) on the proper level of affirmative action within a firm are of no consequence whatsoever on the question of legal rights.

One final point: it should be clear that the substantive position I adopt differs in at least one key respect from that urged by Justice Brennan. His decision spoke of the case for affirmative action in isolation from the rest of Title VII. At no point did it evaluate affirmative action as part of a comprehensive system of social control that also incorporates a strong antidiscrimination norm in favor of protected classes. Brennan's system-wide view is that there should be extensive use of both the stick of *Griggs* and the carrot of *Weber*. That position is, I suppose, superior to one that allows disparate impact theories to be invoked by any individual, for it seems unlikely that any employer could survive the constant exposure to liability on all fronts. But Brennan's position is, I think, inferior to a world in which the stick of Title VII, and especially *Griggs,* is removed, while the possibility of affirmative action remains. To the extent that present affirmative action programs do owe their vitality to the fear of Title VII suits, they are coerced, and for that reason alone suspect, if not illegitimate. To the extent that they respond to the internal demands of employers and employees, they are voluntary, and for that reason legitimate. At present it is hard to decide which programs fall into which category, and to what extent. Only the repeal of Title VII will give the definitive answer.

Discrimination in the Public Sphere

The Problem of Cost Minimization

The use of affirmative action programs in the public sphere raises far more delicate and balanced issues. Initially one could start with the assumption that any government agency is simply another prospective employer entitled to the same degree of discretion in hiring and promotion as any other employer, and constrained only by the same set of market forces. If, therefore, private employers may pick and choose the objects of their affections, then public employers should be afforded the same degree of latitude. That theory, of course, is too powerful because it allows the adoption of both an affirmative action program and the reversion to an employment system of Jim Crow, if that could be implemented by a political majority. Unbounded contractual freedom does not sit nearly as well for public officials, subject to some fiduciary duties, as it does for private parties. To make this point, however, is not to end the inquiry but to begin it. The question remains, what kinds of limitations on state contractual choices should be regarded as appropriate and why?

In order to answer this question one must recall that public officials stand in a dual relationship. At all times they must act both as trustees for the public whom they serve and as contracting partners with employees and other parties. In dealing with possible restrictions on freedom of contract, each side of the relationship is subject to a distinct set of constraints. With regard to potential contracting partners, the question is whether the state enjoys any form of special monopoly position that allows it to extract some disproportionate benefit from trade, an issue already encountered in my discussion of *Berea College*.[6] The hard questions that arise are whether the conditions in question are exploitive (for example, requiring payment of a discriminatory tax by out-of-state firms) or virtuous (for example, ensuring that out-of-state firms will accept service of process for torts committed within the jurisdiction). The central task of the law of unconstitutional conditions is to weave its way between these two extreme positions.

6. See Chapter 5 at 108–112.

The problems of state monopoly power, however, are not acute in the employment context. Employment markets are generally highly competitive, and should be treated as such.[7] There is a huge number of government operations at the state, national, and local levels. Although there may be some unique positions with few equivalents elsewhere in government, or in the private sector, that surely cannot be the rule. The constantly revolving door in and out of government shows how transferable most labor skills are across public and private domains. The party that ran the government bureaucracy may be just the person to advise clients on how to deal with it. The real problems in this area stem from conflicts of interest, including the use of confidential government information for private purposes. The fear of exploitation of a monopoly position is not viable, and the risk of systematic exclusion is not credible. As long as different government employers have distinct preferences, and as long as private firms are able to hire at their pleasure, a government strategy to select employees along racial or sexual lines will not keep disfavored classes from advancing within the market. It is only when the government acts as a regulator of private markets that its role becomes ominous.

The concerns with affirmative action programs, then, come from the reverse side of the government obligation, that is, its obligation to its citizens who foot the bill. The different manifestations of this problem all revolve around a single theme. The diversion of public funds for private gain is a rarefied form of theft that only governments can practice. The problem again runs far beyond employment contexts. Suppose that $1,000 in taxpayer funds is used to purchase an asset worth $1,000. Presumptively the cash of each taxpayer has been transformed into a material asset of equal value. There is a taking, to be sure, but one that is fully compensated. (The analysis here ignores the possibility that the asset may have different values for different taxpayers, all of whom contributed equal sums, and so on). Should the government sell that asset to a single citizen for $600, however, then it has abused its public trust, just as if it had made a simple transfer of $400 in public funds to some private person.[8] To guard against disguised illicit transfers, the law must develop rules that allow someone, be it a private citizen or a public watchdog

7. See Stephen F. Williams, "Liberty and Property: The Problem of Government Benefits," 12 *J. Legal Stud.* 3, 27–31 (1983).

8. See Richard A. Epstein, "The Public Trust Doctrine," 7 *Cato J.* 411 (1987), reprinted in *Public Choice and Constitutional Economics* 315 (J. Gwartney and R. Wagner eds. 1988).

group, to police transactions to prevent the implicit diversion of resources.

This same overriding concern with diversion of public assets arises when government officials dispense employment contracts to their friends. If a local politician hires a crony for $1,000 and receives in exchange services known at the outset to be worth $600, then $400 has fled the public fisc, just as in the case of a bargain sale or an outright gift. The only difference among these cases is practical: it is somewhat easier to monitor a straight cash handout, or even a bargain sale of property, than a one-sided employment contract with persons on the public payroll.

Government policies that assign jobs on the basis of race and gender raise the same issue of diversion of public assets for private gain. Affirmative action and old-style racial preferences may involve these familiar considerations. At one level both types of programs take money from the public at large and use it to line the pockets of favored individuals. But this is too simple, for there is a second side to the problem, beyond controlling the diversion of assets, that makes it too easy to endorse what many have endorsed—a straight color-blind and sex-blind policy of hiring in the public sector. That prophylactic rule neatly cuts out all diversion from the public trough because of race and sex but introduces other distortions in its stead. The uncompromising color-blind, sex-blind model dominates only if there is no *legitimate* reason for the state as employer to take race and sex into account. That condition seems to be true over a broad range of cases. I am hard-pressed to see why most policy and clerical positions should, for example, be better performed by women or men, by blacks or whites, at least to the point where we should want to adopt an affirmative action program to advance one group over the other.

In the age of the extended welfare state, however, government acts as an employer in an enormous number of businesses and it undertakes tasks that private firms (if there were no legal restrictions) would routinely practice with some limited forms of discrimination on matters of both sex and race. If private hospitals would (without Title VII) generally restrict their hiring of nurses to women only, why should a public hospital, which operates in competition with private ones, be forced to incur the costs of considering men for positions that its managers think women are as a rule better able to fill? If pregnant women prefer to have female obstetricians, who should insist on hiring male doctors? But the shoe is sometimes on the other foot: if street cleaning, sanitation, and maintenance work are male occupations in a world without Title VII, why should we render government services less efficient than they might otherwise be by forcing government to hire women, perhaps under the threat of a disparate impact suit?

Many cases of race-conscious hiring make sense as well, even if we are suspicious of affirmative action promoted as mere favoritism. If I were running a program designed to help ghetto youth escape the terrors of drugs in the housing projects, I would be sure to hire some black staff: identification and role model arguments do count for something, although it is difficult to say how much. If I were running a Head-Start program in a Hispanic neighborhood, I would insist that some Spanish-speaking staff be part of the program. The basic theory of the private law—that there is nothing that makes merit necessarily independent of race, ethnicity, or sex—does not lose its relevance solely because the government is an employer. "Blind" hiring in some instances is in the interest of the public at large, but in other cases it is not. Where there is a positive correlation between race, ethnicity, or sex and job performance, we should not duplicate in the public sector the same mistakes of tunnel vision that Title VII has wrought in the private sector. Being "blind" in the role of the state is inconsistent with exercising normal prudence and foresight in the role of employer.

In other cases race-conscious hiring by government employers makes sense for institutional reasons. Many positions in government are avenues for the transmission of political power from the government to the electorate and back again. Government employees often shuttle back and forth as intermediaries between public officials and their constituents, with the mission of softening tensions between government bureaucracy and individual citizens. These public employees must command the trust of the citizens they represent—citizens who are usually organized along racial or religious lines. If the city of Chicago seeks community acceptance of some program to improve police relations, or to fund neighborhood parks, no race-blind liaison will yield the optimal results. Black citizens will not trust white political operatives in the infighting at City Hall, nor will whites trust their interests to blacks. Hispanics will demand their own representatives, and so on down the line. Similarly, organizing a police force along racial lines may make some sense as well; public acceptance of the force would be at a low ebb if only white officers patrolled the streets or ran the drug busts in black neighborhoods. Insisting on some racial balance in public employment need not be a cynical way to institute rigid quotas or a systematic division of spoils. It helps build legitimacy on the streets and elsewhere. Race, religion, and national origin are useful proxies, if not defining characteristics, for affinity in public contexts. The strong persistence of racial politics may be abstractly regrettable but socially unavoidable until human nature can be made over, if anyone should commit so delicate a task to public bodies.

One piece of the picture therefore is clear. Within vast portions of the public sphere, there will be some carryover of the arguments for rational discrimination along racial or sexual lines. The freedom of public officials to choose employees by racial or sexual criteria is not fairly subject to any blanket condemnation based on a color-blind or sex-blind principle that should itself have no applicability in setting the legal rules governing private employment relations. But there is a second, sobering part of the picture that cuts in exactly the opposite direction. Public officials are only imperfectly constrained by the electoral process. In the absence of further constitutional limitations, some substantial fraction of them will succumb as a matter of course to the temptation to turn public office to private gain for themselves and their friends. If X percentage of blacks on the police force will help to promote effective police work, X + Y percentage may well diminish the effectiveness of the force. Although the suspicions blacks feel toward public authority may be allayed by having some representation on the force, the suspicions of whites may be increased if that percentage becomes too high. Yet nothing in the political theory suggests that public officials would gravitate toward the ideal percentages, even if they knew what these were. Every political group—white or black—will tend to push any short-term advantage to the limit, whether or not its proposed division of political spoils is wholly adverse to the public interest, defined here as getting a dollar's worth of services for a dollar paid in taxes. Curbing one difficulty of legitimation may invite more significant mistakes on the other side.

The race-conscious and sex-conscious issues in public employment thus impale us on the horns of a troublesome dilemma. To ignore questions of race and sex is to ignore issues that people have traditionally regarded as important in ordering their own lives. Yet to allow these differences to be taken into account in the public arena is to open the door to mediocrity and cronyism. Either solution ignores one large set of risks to obtain a second large set of benefits. An all-white police force might be a disaster in an urban setting, but a perfectly racially balanced force may be little better. There is surely room for some intermediate position, one that by default must be monitored from without by the courts, typically in their constitutional role. But to raise that intermediate possibility is to pose the additional question of whether any system of judicial review can be devised that will minimize the joint costs of these alternative perils. At this point the inquiry becomes one of working the right trade-offs. The relevant questions are highly empirical and contingent, since there seems to be no way to quantify the relevant costs and benefits of alternate policies. One must proceed in increments, and what follows is only the barest hint of groping toward a solution to minimize the sum of three sets of costs: the costs of running and supervising the system (which increase with the complexity of the governing rules); the costs of favoritism and abuse; and the costs of not hiring along lines of race and sex when there is good reason to do so. The case provides a haunting parallel with the basic problem of the tort system, which Guido Calabresi's famous formulation summarizes as: How do we minimize (the sum of) the costs of accidents, the costs of their prevention, and the costs of their administration, when a reduction in one cost comes only at the expense of an increase in another?[9]

Splitting the Difference

The initial presumption. My first cut into the problem is to establish a presumption. In this case it should be set against the expansion of government discretion, which is always costly for courts to monitor. That basic presumption is that the state should make its hiring decision on race-blind and sex-blind criteria unless it can show clearly why some deviation is justified by the circumstances of a particular case or class of cases. The presumption should be set in this way for two reasons. First, there will always be some slippage in the system of external monitoring, since public officials have control over hiring in the first instance. To set the presumption in favor of explicit racial or sexual classifications is likely to make it too hard for outsiders to challenge any explicit race-conscious or sex-

9. See Guido Calabresi, *The Costs of Accidents* (1970). In the original version of the book, Calabresi sought to answer this question within an additional side constraint, the principle of justice. But it has been very difficult for me (or anyone else) to locate the primitive conception of justice which alters an analysis that considers the other three questions alone. Principles of corrective justice presuppose a system of property rights and personal liberties, and can (I believe) be deduced by taking into account the various difficulties of Calabresi's formulation. One glaring omission in Calabresi's work, and in much of the other law and economics literature, is that it has no public choice dimension. It is far more difficult to formulate the ideal set of rules when it is necessary to constrain both the governors and the governed. The constitutional inquiry clearly contains both elements, especially in the context of affirmative action by government.

conscious practice. Second, the risk of abuse is considerable, given the enormous gains from controlling political patronage. Public officials simply do not work unswervingly according to some virtuous conception of the public good. An inescapable set of temptations accompanies participation in political life, and these are on balance too strong to permit tolerance of any broad presumption in favor of race- and sex-conscious classifications.

Overriding the presumption. The second cut addresses the types of justifications that override the initial presumption. These should not include some abstract desire, however intense, to see a work force of a certain racial and sexual composition. It seems quite clear that the outcome would reflect only a portion of the public, mainly that which benefited from the rule. Instead, a demonstration should be required at the workplace level to show the connection between the race- and sex-conscious norm on the one hand and the particular requirements of the job or the needs of ordinary citizens on the other. One obvious source of information would be the strategies that private employers adopt in the same or similar occupations, or (better) that they would adopt in a world devoid of Title VII. Taking this approach shows the difficulty of trying to identify objectively a set of contractual merits or essences. There is a certain unavoidable irony here, for the strongest objections to Title VII arise precisely from attacking the application of the objective theory of value to private exchanges.[10] Yet within the public sector the *only* way to check misconduct by public officials is to draw just that tenuous distinction between meritorious and nonmeritorious practices. Otherwise any form of race preference, however motivated, is as good as any other. It thus becomes necessary to elevate the default terms normally used in cases of contractual silence to the status of binding legal constraints.

In making these calculations about permissible discrimination, the government should not be in the business of reshaping the preferences of its citizens, any more than it should undertake that risky enterprise by regulating private employment relations under Title VII. Instead, the state (itself a set of individuals with their own skewed preferences) should take the preferences of its citizens (warts and all) as given and then seek to satisfy them as best it can within the budget constraints imposed on it. The posture is purely defensive. Each of us gives up the political right to reform our neighbors in order to be protected in turn against their

---

10. See Chapter 9 at 163–167 for a discussion on the merits in disparate treatment cases, and Chapter 14 at 299–309 on the BFOQ cases.

reformist zeal. Removing the issue of race or sex from the playing field is apt to reduce political turmoil and administrative expense, leaving all persons free to use their private resources to change any popular conception of racial or sexual relations in ways they believe appropriate. But none of us has a monopoly on moral wisdom that elevates our preferences above everybody else's.

Government as supplier and government as purchaser. In trying to demonstrate the connection between jobs and the need for racial, ethnic, or sexual classifications, courts should make a rough and ready distinction between two roles of government: as provider of direct services to individual citizens, and as purchaser of goods and services needed to discharge ordinary government functions, including obtaining supplies for public bureaus, maintaining existing facilities, constructing new public works, and the like. In this broad class of cases the government typically is not the employer but the general contractor, and the choice of that relationship is not accidental. What the government typically wants (like what the typical airline passenger wants, and so on) is to acquire a standardized product of a specified quality. Contracting is used instead of internal production because profit-maximizing firms, who obtain business by competitive bid, are cheaper providers of those services than are government agencies.[11] Likewise, there is no political risk (such as that which might arise from the delegation of control of the police force to a private firm) to cloud the overall picture.

In light of this general pattern of employment, there is at best a weak case for any preference based on race or sex when the question is which firms should provide city stationery, repair the city, streets, or issue bonds in the capital markets.[12] The key elements are the quality and price of the goods or services supplied; *who* supplies these services seems (if one is committed to a theory of objective merit) largely irrelevant to the taxpayers who have to pay for smudged stationery, cracked concrete, or excessive borrowing. To be sure, there may well be some personal element helpful in the discharge of these contracts, which is why a ban against race-conscious or sex-conscious decisions is not unproblematic. But

11. See, e.g., Robert L. Bish, "Federalism: A Market Economics Perspective," 7 *Cato J.* 377 (1987). Note that federalism introduces an additional element of competition because the exit (or nonentrance) threat, while not perfect, does limit the scope of a government monopoly.

12. See, on abuses in these areas, Red Suspenders, "Minority Interest: Affirmative Action in the Bond Underwriting Business," *New Republic*, November 7, 1988, p. 23. (The author chose to use a nom de plume.)

those gains are slender relative to the manifest risk of abuse. Race and sex should not count at all in most situations where the government purchases some specific product, even if they do matter when the mayor's office is hiring a community liaison official or the manager of a neighborhood drug clinic. Contracting work is a different kettle of fish entirely.

The Upshot

Minority Set-Asides

It follows from the foregoing analysis that we can make short shrift of two important Supreme Court cases that addressed constitutional challenges to minority set-aside programs for government contracts—*Fullilove v. Klutznick*[13] and *City of Richmond v. J. A. Croson Co.*[14] *Fullilove* involved a federal program that required a 10 percent set-aside of all government construction contracts for minority-owned enterprises. *Croson* involved the validity of a local program that set aside some 30 percent of local contracts to minority-owned businesses. In *Fullilove* the applicable provision on minority business enterprises (MBEs) reads:

> For purposes of this paragraph the term "minority business enterprise" means a business at least 50 per centum of which is owned by minority group members or, in the case of a publicly owned business, at least 51 per centum of the stock of which is owned by minority group members. For the purposes of the preceding sentence, minority group members are citizens of the United States who are Negroes, Spanish-speaking, Orientals, Indians, Eskimos, and Aleuts.[15]

In the debates in Congress the program was justified strictly on disparate impact grounds: only 1 percent of federal contract dollars went to minority-owned businesses, even though members of minorities constituted some 15 to 18 percent of the population.[16] The set-aside program was defended on the grounds that its absence would "perpetuate the historic practices that have precluded minority business from effective participation in public contracting opportunities."[17] The statute did not

13. 448 U.S. 448 (1980).
14. 488 U.S. 469 (1989).
15. 42 *U.S.C.* §6705(f)(2) (1989).
16. 448 U.S. at 459.
17. Id. at 461.

mark a novel departure in the federal awards of grants and contracts, as set-asides had been routinely adopted at the administrative level prior to the passage of the statute.

The Court, speaking through Chief Justice Warren Burger, upheld the statutory set-aside program against both equal protection and due process clause challenges, largely on the ground that it was a remedial statute designed to counteract the abuses of past discrimination. This function was critical to the analysis of the case under the Fourteenth Amendment, since the prior decisions of the Court gave Congress increased power to enact race-conscious legislation to correct for past abuses. But the showing of past discrimination was weak, consisting entirely of statements by members of Congress that the low rate of minority contracts could be attributable only to past local discrimination. There was no independent substantiation of the charges—not even anecdotal evidence of better minority contractors being passed over for more established white contractors. Nor was there any recognition of the simple point that if such abuses did exist, a system of penalties imposed on local governments who engaged in them could stop the practice in its tracks. Instead, a far broader remedy—a 10 percent nationwide set-aside—was regarded as the appropriate response to a record devoid of any evidence of nationwide abuse. How can the set-aside legislation be regarded as remedial when it identifies neither the victim nor the wrongdoer?

Fullilove went so far astray in sustaining the set-aside program because the Court implicitly assumed that Congress was acting in its public interest mode; its findings about the frequency of past discrimination were given characteristically broad deference, and the statute was seen as an act of largess by the white majority which had decided voluntarily to cede some of its power to minorities that had been excluded from the field. But the account reflects an enormous oversimplification of the political process, starting with the naive assumption that all whites together constitute a single cohesive interest group, all of whose members are similarly situated with respect to the state. A closer look at who the individual players are would surely bring the specter of interest group politics back to center stage by asking what quids were exchanged for what quos in forging the winning political coalition. As long as some key votes for set-asides could have been obtained by payoffs to critical groups of whites, the naive model of voluntary cession by high-minded white politicians, so critical to *Fullilove's* outcome, loses its credibility. Thus, if some white firms hope to gain as joint venturers with minority-owned firms, or if some white politicians hope to obtain minority interests in MBEs, the entire political picture is transformed. If support for set-asides is traded for defense contracts or public highways, the calculations become more complex still. None of these machinations will appear on the record, which will always be replete with the usual banalities about legislative purpose to which the Court paid such deference in *Fullilove*. Gifts in politics are not the norm, and we should not presume that they were made here.

Nor does *Fullilove* attend to the abuses of the program once it is in place. The definition of a minority-owned business is simply one with 50 percent or more of its ownership or stock in minority hands. The statute does not begin to cope with the complex capital structures that might be used to comply with the letter if not the spirit of the statute. What, then, should be done if the statute gives white businessmen 55 percent of the voting stock and black shareholders 60 percent of non-voting preferred? In evaluating the capital structure of the firm, should one pay any attention to the long-term contracts that the owners of the business may make with its white managers, who then siphon off some of the profits? It is wholly naive to think that the structure of the firm will remain constant regardless of the regulation. On the contrary, we should expect to see inefficient capital and contract structures adopted in order to allow a firm to take advantage of being an MBE, not to mention cases of outright fraud in the documentation of status. The minority ownership rules are satisfied if well-connected minority businessmen and lawyers take shares in specially created firms; as a result, businessmen of all races and creeds can rip off taxpayers of more modest means by charging higher prices than their competitors, secure in the knowledge that their own high costs will be chalked up to pervasive, but invisible, past discrimination and not to their current inefficiency and greed. One does not need to be naively devoted to a color-blind constitution to stop this misguided program in its tracks.

The Supreme Court showed a far higher level of realism some nine years later in *Croson* by striking down the 30 percent minority set-aside program adopted by Richmond, Virginia. One does not have to envision an elaborate system of side contracts and coalitions to see here the special interest model of politics in operation. Blacks occupied many dominant positions on the city council. They could easily generate the same broad statements of purpose that in *Fullilove* were allowed to explain why the imbalance in contracting was properly attributable to past discrimination.[18] The only intellectual difficulty posed by the case was to distinguish it from *Fullilove,* which the Court did neatly enough by noting that Congress had more power to use race-conscious remedies under the Fourteenth Amendment than the cities and states had under state law.[19] Congress, it concluded, should be accorded a level of deference denied the states.

Neat, but unpersuasive, for it is very hard to see why a grant of jurisdiction to the federal government should be read to exclude the same right of self-correction at the local level. Certainly one would not want to argue that states had less power than Congress to eliminate mandated forms of racial discrimination at the local level before 1965 because their legislative initiatives were not authorized by the Fourteenth Amendment. Surely the state legislatures could enforce any state constitutional requirement for a color-blind government. There is good reason to adopt a strict scrutiny standard for race-conscious statutes at both the federal and the state level. But Justice O'Connor, speaking for the plurality, adopted this standard only for the state statute challenged here, noting "the purpose of strict scrutiny is to 'smoke out' illegitimate uses of race by assuring that the legislative body is pursuing a goal important enough to warrant use of a highly suspect tool."[20] Since Richmond had been lulled into complacency by *Fullilove,* it was easy to poke holes in the impressionistic evidence used to justify its massive 30 percent set-aside.

It is important, however, to recognize the flaws as well as the strengths of Justice O'Connor's strict scrutiny analysis. As she applied the test, the critical question was whether there was a decent fit between the 30 percent set-aside remedy and the patterns of past dis-

---

18. Indeed, the level of self-interest involved in *Croson* was even greater than the Court recognized. Set-aside programs normally do not require MBEs to be the prime contractors. Rather, they are enforced by the requirement that some portion of the subcontracts be let to MBEs. Under the Richmond statute an exception from the set-aside program was crafted, but only for prime contractors who were themselves MBEs. See *Croson,* 488 U.S. at 713. But there is no reason for the exemption. A 30 percent rule could apply to all prime contractors if the minority ownership of such a contractor were counted against the 30 percent requirement for the contract as a whole. By excusing the prime contractor from the requirement, however, the Richmond plan gave local minority contractors an enormous competitive advantage over their white rivals, for they could assemble whatever subsidiary bids organized the lowest possible price. The statute thus pitted minority prime contractors against minority subcontractors, where the former were likely to exercise greater political influence.

19. *Croson,* 488 U.S. at 490–493.

20. Id at 493.

crimination. Finding none, she struck down the plan. But even if there were pervasive patterns of discrimination that were flatly illegal under the equal protection clause, the proper remedy is always a cash payment to the victims in compensation for the deprivations they suffered. Those wrongs could be redressed once and for all without resort to a set-aside remedy that necessarily piles one social loss upon another. In the first transaction the city paid a useless premium to a white contractor. Now it has to pay a useless premium to a minority contractor. For the taxpayers the wrongs are cumulative, not offsetting, even if the second contracting decision leaves the aggrieved contractor whole. (The muddy process of calculating the size of gains and losses creates another opportunity for political intrigue.) The damage action for the aggrieved contractor avoids the second half of the social loss, because it mandates only a transfer payment and not an inefficient contract, and it still leaves the aggrieved party an opportunity to bid in any contracting process that remains.

More generally, any effort to tie minority set-aside programs to past wrongful conduct of the local government underwrites the new cottage industry of encouraging present city governments to dredge up all sorts of evidence of their own past wrongdoing in order to justify a second generation of political deals. This strategy entails the obvious political risk that it will fail, leaving local governments exposed to damage suits by disappointed contractors. But this check is far from perfect, for the tab will be paid by taxpayers and not the political entrepreneurs who structured the program. The goal, therefore, is to stop the abuse in its tracks, which only a flat and unequivocal per se prohibition can do. The proper remedy for past discrimination is damage suits brought by aggrieved parties, who have every incentive to do so if the evidence exists. But at that point local governments have a strong incentive not to flaunt the prejudices of their predecessors but to dig in their heels and fight the suit. Decisions based on race and sex are, and should remain, a part (a diminishing part, we can hope) of American public life. But there is no occasion to turn them into big business.

Federal Contracting

Throughout this discussion on set-asides I have drawn a strong distinction between public employees (who provide direct services to citizens) and public independent contractors (who provide standardized goods and services to government), and I have argued that some latitude for race-conscious and sex-conscious hiring should be allowed in the former case but not in the latter. Indeed, one advantage of independent contracting is that it allows government to transform an employment relationship into a more impersonal sale or franchise relationship. The government then must monitor only the output of a firm and not the behavior of large numbers of individual employees, much less the racial or sexual composition of the work force. This is one reason why the federal government should buy missiles from defense contractors instead of manufacturing them itself.

Once some race-conscious or sex-conscious hiring is justified in limited circumstances, an added benefit accrues from contracting out. After the production function of government has been partially privatized, the firm can, and should, be able to decide the racial or sexual composition of its own work force. It is no longer necessary to subject employment decisions to arcane reviews under standards that are at best murky. Even though this opportunity has been available, it has not been seized, given the counterproductive policy of the affirmative action rules routinely applied to federal contractors. The applicable regulations are set out at length in the *Federal Register*.[21] The regulations show the usual divided sentiment in that section 60-1.1 boldly begins with the pronouncement that the purpose of the regulations is "for the promotion and insuring of equal opportunity for all persons, without regard to race, color, religion, sex or national origin."[22] The mandate is enforced by a series of contract clauses, the first of which provides: "The contractor will not discriminate against any employee or applicant for employment because of race, color, religion, sex or national origin."[23] "Subpart B: Required Contents of Affirmative Action Programs" then launches into a lengthy exposition of the affirmative action requirements imposed on all contractors in order to promote equal employment opportunity. The applicable regulations require firms to undertake expensive and extensive utilization review to determine whether "minority groups are being underutilized in various job groups." It is thus necessary to undertake an examination of "the minority population in the labor area surrounding the facility," "the percentage of minority unemployment force" located within that region, "the availability of minorities having requisite skills," including "promotable and transferable minorities," the "existence of training institu-

---

21. See 41 C.F.R. §60(1984); the section runs nearly two hundred pages.
22. Id. at §60.1-1.
23. Id. at §60-1.4, implementing Executive Order 11,246.

tions," and the "degree of training" that the contractor can undertake, and so on.[24]

The list of relevant issues is long, and for major contractors the requirements are costly. But for these purposes the critical question is not what the mechanics or procedures are under the regulations but whether there is any justification for the program at all. In a universe that accepts the two-sided standard of Title VII—strict scrutiny of discrimination against protected classes, and unlimited voluntary affirmative action in their favor—the federal regulations make a certain grim sense. The government is just one of those market actors that has decided to engage in an extensive affirmative action program, albeit under the transparent fig leaf of equal opportunity.

Yet the social calculus looks very different if Title VII is repealed for private employers, while the government (because of its control of the public fisc) is subject to stringent obligations to avoid favoritism in awarding its contracts. The government has no interest in the employment practices of private firms generally: that is why Title VII should be repealed for private firms. So why should it have an interest in keeping certain lawful bidders from making low price offers for the goods and services they provide directly to the government? All citizens, women and minorities included, should benefit from the reduction in paperwork necessary to comply with government contracts and from the improved productivity that comes with low price.

But the same cannot be said when a system of implicit subsidies reduces the overall efficiency of government operations. The current system of affirmative obligations, however, makes it very difficult to trace winners and losers. It is not as though all women and minorities profit from the system, for many do not seek or are not eligible for the preferences built into the government system. Yet by the same token white men and others who are ineligible for benefits apparently lose in at least two ways: they will also have to bear the costs of higher taxes—or, what amounts to the same thing, the receipt of fewer services—and they will be cut out of employment opportunities that they might otherwise have obtained. Yet even here the patterns are clouded: a man whose wife is eligible for the preferential system may count himself a winner because of the preference, as might the white worker whose employer lands a lucrative government contract because of its affirmative action program. The precise distribu-

24. 41 C.F.R. §60–2.11(b), "Required Utilization Analysis," listing eight factors for minorities and the analogous eight factors for women.

tional consequences are, here as in general, a second-order effect. It is far better to have an increase in overall wealth that is generally distributed across society than a decrease in wealth that is justified by an appeal to partisan gains, or to symbolic values that not everyone shares.

The current system is of course firmly entrenched, and its defense rests in large part on the proposition that discrimination is bad in all public and private areas of life, and in part on an ironic appeal to freedom of contract as the reason why the government can impose whatever restrictions it deems appropriate when *its* wealth is at stake. But that conventional analysis overlooks the fact that the government is a fiduciary for *all* members of the public, both those who support its nondiscrimination and affirmative action policies and those who oppose them. It therefore is unwise to impose these restrictions on government grants because "we" (with sufficient outrage) do not want "our" money to support parties who discriminate or who fail to engage in some form of affirmative action. There is no viable we-they opposition. "They" are also taxpayers and citizens, and it is far from clear why "their" preferences should be shut out in determining how the government spends "our" money. Why should the majority squelch a minority?

Price and quality terms are a different matter. No citizen has an interest in paying more rather than less for any given good or service. If we insist that the government search out the lowest price (provided quality is held constant), the aims of one citizen-taxpayer are not placed in conflict with those of another: all share in better goods, lower taxes, or both. But once the government imposes an expensive bureaucratic apparatus on contracts that is unrelated and unresponsive to either price or quality, it acts as a partisan of those citizens who support affirmative action and race-conscious or sex-conscious policies and as an enemy of those who oppose them. Taking sides would be appropriate if certain parties had engaged in illegal conduct prior to the bidding process: thus there is good reason to exclude firms willing to lower prices by using stolen property. But as long as there is no case for making private discrimination illegal, the government should not condition its taking of bids on compliance with its nondiscrimination or affirmative action dictates.

On this point more than a matter of prudence is at stake. There is also a matter of high constitutional principle. The true meaning of equal protection is not that it forces all persons to organize their business in accordance with some government standard. It is quite the opposite. For all persons to enjoy enjoy equal protection of the laws, the government has to treat *all* those firms that choose to discriminate one way or the other equally with those firms that adopt color-blind or sex-blind policies. States should be stripped of the power to decide how any bidder organizes its internal work force; they should look only at what state government gets for the tax dollars it spends. I believe that the same result applies to the federal government, even if it is not bound by the equal protection clause.[25] Since taxes are takings, the federal government is under a strict obligation to see that all citizens receive equal benefits from the moneys so raised. Otherwise there is an implicit wealth transfer among citizens, in that those who are hampered in their patterns of business by the restriction do not receive just compensation in the public services provided by the government.[26] In essence, therefore, the principle of neutrality applies to the government both as a purchaser of general services and as a supplier of government services. There is never an easy collective solution to the optimal employment practices of the state and the individual. Using independent contractors allows us to avoid making difficult distinctions on employment practices, and to narrow the area in which the weakest legal doctrines must be given sway. Insisting on government neutrality toward independent contractors therefore represents the best accommodation of the desire to preserve individual freedom with the government provision of necessary public services. It is in this direction that true affirmative action lies.

25. The cases hold, of course, that there is some equal protection dimension to the due process clause of the Fifth Amendment. See *Bolling v. Sharpe,* 347 U.S. 497 (1954), ordering the integration of the public school system of Washington, D.C.

26. See Richard A. Epstein, *Takings: Private Property and the Power of Eminent Domain* 195–215 (1985), which examines the relationship between the just compensation requirement and the disproportionate impact test. The ability of the state to dispense disproportionate benefits is a way for it to make disguised transfers between parties. Thus, if two persons are taxed the same but A receives twice as many benefits as B, there is good reason to believe that B is left worse off by the combination of tax and expenditures than he was before. The restriction on the ability to obtain government contracts counts as a differential treatment that could result in such an imbalance.

PART VI

Newer Forbidden Grounds

CHAPTER 21

Age Discrimination

A Statutory Reprise

The original Civil Rights Act of 1964 applied to discrimination against persons because of their race, color, religion, sex, or national origin. Not included on that initial statutory list was discrimination against any person because of age. The appeal of the antidiscrimination principle was such, however, that by 1967 Congress had passed the Age Discrimination in Employment Act (ADEA),[1] which was designed to remedy the perceived gap in the previous law. On the substantive side, the ADEA is tightly modeled on the 1964 act. It has the same basic provisions on discrimination[2] and also has the same basic exception for bona fide occupational qualification,[3] and it includes a somewhat new seniority provision.[4] The existing case law allows proof of violation under a disparate treatment theory, with the tripartite tests (prima facie violation, employer interest, and pretext) first developed in *McDonnell Douglas v. Green*,[5]

1. Pub. L. no. 90-202, 81 Stat. 602 (1967), codified at 29 *U.S.C.* §§621–634 (1982). I shall refer to the provisions not by their code number but by their numbers in the act itself, which run from 1 through 17.

2. Section 4(a), 29 U.S.C. §623(a) (1982), provides that it shall be unlawful for an employer "(1) to fail or refuse to hire or to discharge any individual or otherwise discriminate against any individual with respect to his compensation, terms, conditions, or privileges of employment, because of such individual's age; (2) to limit, segregate, or classify his employees in any way which would deprive or tend to deprive any individual of employment opportunities or otherwise adversely affect his status as an employee, because of such individual's age; or (3) to reduce the wage rate of any employee in order to comply with this chapter."

3. Section 4(f)(1), codified at 29 U.S.C.A. §623(f)(1) (1985).

4. Section 4(f)(2), codified at 29 U.S.C.A. §623(f)(2) (1982).

5. 411 U.S. 792(1973). The test was carried over to the ADEA in *Williams v. Edward Apffels Coffee Co.*, 792 F.2d 1482 (9th Cir. 1986). For criticism of *McDonnell Douglas*, see Chapter 9.

where the relevant burdens of proof are distributed in the same fashion as in sex or race cases.[6] The disparate impact theory of *Griggs v. Duke Power*,[7] subject to the same business necessity exception, has, it appears, also been imported into the ADEA.

The remedial provisions of the statute are, however, more expansive: any person aggrieved may bring a civil action in any court. Whereas Title VII restricts plaintiffs to trial before a court, under the ADEA the plaintiff may request a jury trial. Nonetheless, the right to bring that action must terminate once the secretary of labor files an enforcement action. The damage measures are intimately tied to the enforcement procedures for the minimum wage laws found in the Fair Labor Standards Act (FLSA), and are somewhat convoluted. Under the applicable rules the plaintiff's damages are normally calibrated to back pay, but the plaintiff is entitled to double recovery unless the defendant satisfies the court that its action was undertaken in "good faith." In addition, section 7(b) also provides that "liquidated damages shall be payable only in cases of willful violations of this Act." In this context "liquidated" means that recovery is not reduced to take into account earnings that the displaced plaintiff could have obtained in suitable alternative employment. For nonwillful violations of the statute, damages are reduced to the extent that the plaintiff should have mitigated them. By Supreme Court construction, the employer's conduct is regarded as willful if "the employer either knew or showed reckless disregard for the matter of whether its conduct was prohibited by the ADEA."[8] It is not enough "if the employer simply knew of the potential applicability of the ADEA," or was aware that the application of the statute might be "in the picture."[9] In addition, under the statute a plaintiff cannot recover compensatory damages for pain and suffering, for consequential economic damages such as loss of credit or relocation expenses, or punitive damages.[10]

---

6. *Texas Department of Community Affairs v. Burdine*, 450 U.S. 248 (1981). For an ADEA application, see *Metz v. Transmit Mix, Inc.*, 828 F.2d 1202 (7th Cir. 1987).

7. 401 U.S. 424 (1971), carried over to the ADEA in, for example, *Geller v Markham*, 635 F.2d 1027 (2d Cir. 1980), and *E.E.O.C. v. Westinghouse Electric Corp.*, 725 F.2d 211 (3rd Cir. 1983). It is an open question whether the transformation of the business necessity test in *Wards Cove Packing Co., Inc. v. Atonio*, 490 U.S. (1989), will be read back into the ADEA cases.

8. *Trans World Airlines, Inc. v. Thurston*, 469 U.S. 111, 128(1985), approving the definition of the Court of Appeals.

9. Id. at 125–126.

10. *Pfeiffer v. Essex Wire Corp.*, 682 F.2d 684 (7th Cir. 1982).

Like the 1964 Civil Rights Act, the ADEA harbors a natural tendency for expansion, largely by legislative action. The 1967 statute did not apply to government employees, either state or federal. But the 1974 amendments brought them within its scope.[11] The 1967 act made it unlawful to discriminate against persons between forty and sixty-five years of age. The 1978 amendments extended the maximum protected age to seventy.[12] In 1977 the Supreme Court, in *United Airlines, Inc. v. McMann*,[13] held that an employer was entitled to discharge a worker pursuant to a bona fide seniority plan when he reached age sixty, provided that plan had been instituted prior to the passage of the ADEA, on the ground that an existing plan could not be regarded as a subterfuge to evade the purposes of the act. The 1978 statute overran that line of defense and prohibited mandatory retirement for any workers protected under the act.[14] In 1986 the act was again amended, this time to remove the ceiling on mandatory retirement altogether, except for certain senior officials within the firm whose vested retirement income is above some fixed amount (set at $44,000 as of March 1990).[15] The 1986 act also contains an exception for certain firefighters and law enforcement officers pursuant to laws in effect as of March 1983. In addition, the statute contains a temporary exception, to expire at the end of 1993, that provides that persons under "unlimited tenure contracts" may be subject to compulsory retirement upon reaching the age of seventy.[16] Since the law was passed there has been no significant contraction in its scope. The ADEA edifice is today every bit as complex and formidable as that which surrounds Title VII.

Why?

The initial query about the ADEA statute is simply this: Why? As with the antidiscrimination laws generally, there is very little theoretical work to

11. Pub. L. no. 93-259, 88 Stat. 74 (1974), codified at 29 U.S.C.A. §633a (1985).

12. Pub. L. no. 95-256, 92 Stat. 189 (1978), codified at 29 U.S.C.A. §631 (1985).

13. 434 U.S. 192 (1977).

14. "No such [bona fide] seniority system or employee benefit plan shall require or permit the involuntary retirement of any individual [protected under the act] because of the age of such individual." 29 U.S.C.A. §623(f)(2) (1985).

15. 29 U.S.C.A. §631(c) (1985), applicable to persons "employed in a bona fide executive or high policymaking position" with aggregate pension benefits from the employer in excess of $44,000.

16. Pub. L no. 99-592, 100 Stat. 3342(1986), codified at 29 U.S.C.A. §623(i) (1989). Id. at §631(d).

justify the statute, whose goals are treated as self-evidently correct. The arguments commonly given have often been rehearsed, and they are conveniently set out by Congress in its statement of purpose to the ADEA.

> The Congress hereby finds and declares that—
> (1) in the face of rising productivity and affluence, older workers find themselves disadvantaged in their efforts to retain employment and especially to regain employment when displaced from jobs;
> (2) the setting of arbitrary age limits regardless of potential for job performance has become a common practice, and certain otherwise desirable practices may work to the disadvantage of older persons.[17]

The statutory preamble first asserts that there are serious defects in the way in which private and public firms conduct their business, and then seeks to remedy these defects with the same coercive legal devices that are used in other areas, most notably race and sex. Yet before crafting these words Congress made no effort to understand the business reasons for the practices that it rendered illegal. Instead, without asking why, it offered only the blanket judgment that discrimination on the basis of age is "arbitrary" and should for that reason be forbidden. The upshot of its position is that categorical judgments are thereby rendered illegal, and firms are now required, under a presumption of distrust, to make individualized decisions about ability independent of their knowledge of age. The statute thus treats age discrimination as though it were cut from the same cloth as sex and race discrimination. In one sense this is true, and in another sense it is false. But in neither case are matters nearly as simple as Congress sees them.

Similarities with Race and Sex

The basic congressional theme of parity of treatment for different forms of discrimination carries over to this context: the major implication is that since Title VII is desirable, the ADEA must be desirable as well. But the argument also works in reverse: that is, on its face the ADEA is no more desirable than the other antidiscrimination provisions found under the civil rights laws. If the arguments that favor the repeal of Title VII are in general sound, they call unambiguously for the repeal of the ADEA as well.

17. Section 2(a), 29 *U.S.C.* §621(a) (1982).

Irrational or invidious discrimination on the basis of race or sex will not last in a regime of freedom of contract, since the prospect for new entry will discipline the behavior of all players in the market. The same argument applies to discrimination on grounds of age. The firm that passes over superior older workers in favor of inferior younger ones will find itself at a cost disadvantage that it cannot recoup in the market. To be sure, there may be some firms who for internal reasons will not hire workers above some particular age, but again (as with race and sex) it is important to distinguish between the position of the single firm and the overall structure of the industry. Business decisions may be made for reasons that reduce the internal costs of production, and parallel gains can be obtained by firms that specialize in hiring older workers as well as younger ones. In each case if the workers have equal levels of competence, a voluntary regime of separate but equal should result in equal wages. In addition, both sides are left better off than before because firms in each camp can specialize in the types of programs that cater to their preselected pool of workers. One firm can offer excellent day care, for example, while the other has specialized food services for persons on restricted diets.

Within this general regime individual instances of disappointed expectations are not a condemnation of the marketplace unless they are tied to some structural failure. There is no such failure here. Labor generally tends to move to the jobs where it is most highly valued as long as freedom of entry and exit are preserved. The right policy, therefore, is to keep all barriers as low as possible.

The antidiscrimination laws have precisely the opposite effect: they raise new barriers to entry and keep markets in a state of perpetual disequilibrium. Voluntary contracts are entered into only when they are expected to generate net gains to both sides. But antidiscrimination laws force people to enter into transactions against their will. These laws necessarily create an unstable situation, because one side to the exchange gains while the other loses. This mandated imbalance can be maintained only if the state imposes heavy external pressures on the unwilling party. Even today the law does not guarantee every potential worker a job from the employer of his or her choice at the desired wage. At the minimum, then, the state must monitor the motives of the employer at all stages of the employment relationship.

The process has no logical stopping point. With the move from disparate treatment to disparate impact, the levels of external control quickly become intrusive. Although there are some disputes at the margin, age discrimination law has largely followed the lead of the sex discrimination cases with a vengeance by making it unambiguous that the costs employers bear in hiring older workers are wholly irrelevant to their legal obligations.[18] You must not consider the costs that you pay: that is the dominant message. This position runs wholly counter to the logic of any sound system of social relations, which seeks to create a set of property entitlements that require human action only where it promises some net social gain—net, of course, of social costs. Here, in effect, the law requires the worker to be hired where the employer can expect large net social losses. If a net gain were anticipated between the parties to the employment relationship, they could achieve it through voluntary negotiation in low transaction cost settings. The law thus creates the very deviation between private and social costs that legal rules are generally designed to overcome.

By a process of degree the legal system thus backs itself into a corner. It will never allow any objections on the workability or economic consequences of the antidiscrimination law to lead to a reexamination of the basic rule. That initial decision is engraved in stone for reasons that are said to be moral but are indeed unexamined. Once the commitment to the basic statutory norm is irrevocable, introducing cost differentials into evidence quickly guts the system because that cost evidence (based on standard insurance data) will be decisive in every case. So the law shoots the messenger instead of heeding the message. Rather than realizing the error of its own basic rules, Congress, along with the EEOC and the courts, plunges forward with ever more intrusive rules that expand the reach of the basic norm.

This blunderbuss approach has the same effect as a tax on the employment relationship: the total number of positions available necessarily shrinks, and employers must take long-term evasive action in order to minimize the sting of the antidiscrimination laws. The only interesting question is pathological: to estimate (1) the amount of total social losses, and (2) the redistribution of the gains and losses, which are often *between* persons within the same racial, sex, or age group, and *not* among the various groups themselves. On balance the antidiscrimination laws are a major social and intellectual mistake. What is true for Title VII is true for the ADEA as well.

---

18. "A differentiation based on the average cost of employing older employees as a group is unlawful except with respect to employee benefit plans which qualify for the section 4(f)(2) exception of the Act." 29 C.F.R. §1625.7(f) (1989).

Differences from Race and Sex

Although the general condemnation of the ADEA follows a familiar script, there are certain key differences between the prohibitions that suggest that age is not the same sort of consideration as sex or race. In this regard Congress is again wrong. Even if Title VII were sound, the ADEA should still be rejected because the inability to discriminate on the basis of age is peculiarly destructive to the health of employment markets. In making this general assertion I use the same benchmark of voluntary private contracts that forms the basis for analysis in other areas. It thus becomes clear that, wholly without regard to any statute, there are many areas in which the employer has no rational reason to discriminate on the basis of race or sex; such discrimination will not be found to any systematic or large degree, even if some discrimination will (and should) survive for reasons set out earlier.[19] But discrimination on the basis of age is not an infrequent or marginal occurrence in voluntary markets. As the congressional statement of purpose notes, age discrimination is a common practice, which (before the passage of the statute) was adopted by virtually all major American firms, including those with strong internal policies forbidding any form of racial, ethnic, or sex discrimination.

The decisions made in these firms cannot be explained away on the ground of inequality of bargaining power, for it is quite clear that the age limitations have been enforced with special strictness against the senior officials of the firm, who have been required to relinquish all of their executive responsibility, typically at age sixty or sixty-five. Similar rules for mandatory retirement are common today in various forms of professional partnerships—legal, accounting, and medical—that fall outside the scope of the statute because partners are not employees covered by the ADEA.

In some cases there is good reason to be suspicious of common practice. Slavery may have been common practice, although slaves were rarely given a voice in shaping that peculiar institution. But the common practice here *binds* the very persons who institute it. Age restrictions are not some crude effort by one group of persons to obtain advancement at the expense of strangers. Men will never become women; whites will never become blacks. Racial and sexual groups hence face some temptation to impose (especially through legislation) costs on a group of which they will never be a part: mandated racial segregation was one deplorable conse-

---

19. See Chapter 3 at 60–72, discussing the way in which selection of workers can reduce problems associated with informal bonding within the firm, and with overcoming wide differences in tastes among firm members.

quence of that tendency. But younger employees will become older employees in the ordinary course of life, and they will be bound by the very restrictions that typically are implemented by senior partners in the first place. Even in firms that start life with no old partners, it is common to find restrictions that call for a buyout of interest at some specified age.

Given the dominant nature of the common practice within the firm, what reason is there to believe that all private parties are so irrational on a matter so close to their financial success and survival that Congress (an institution in need of mandatory retirement rules) should intervene with legislation? A rhetorical question, to be sure, to which the short answer is none. All employment contracts have low transaction costs and no externalities. The bargains they produce should not be viewed with the same suspicion that is reserved for contracts to fix prices or to commit murder. The bargains that *do not* occur are the ones that in general *should not* occur, precisely because there are no terms on which a mutually beneficial exchange can be made. There is no market imperfection that justifies the ADEA. There is only a political coalition that supports its passage.

The ADEA, then, in a sense is far more mischievous than the anti-discrimination statutes governing race or sex because it imposes the largest deviation between the contracts that would emerge in an unregulated competitive market and those that emerge under the statutory restriction. The greater the deviation that is imposed, the more serious the intrusion into private affairs, and the larger the social welfare loss attendant on the scheme of regulation. A minimum wage law of one cent per hour is less mischievous than one of ten dollars per hour, even though in the abstract both should be condemned for their interference with voluntary employment markets. In order to understand why the ADEA exercises such a baleful influence on labor markets, one must put aside the inflated congressional rhetoric and examine the logic of long-term relational contracts of employment, all of which necessarily have an age dimension. Only if we understand why contracts work in an unregulated setting can we determine the costs of the regulation of one aspect of a contract that in the end destroys all others.

Relational Labor Contracts and the ADEA

The Legal and the Social Contract

The initial paradox in employment contracts is that they have two faces. They are often terminable at will under the law but nonetheless in practice have a long expected life. Indeed, in those cases where contracts are for a fixed term of years, the anticipated duration of the relationship is often far longer than the contract term. There are reasons for the generally stable nature of employment contracts: both sides stand to gain from the continuation of a long-term arrangement. The employer gets to know the employee, who in turn gets to know the firm. Each side therefore obtains some specific gain from the relationship that cannot be obtained elsewhere. Hand in hand with any long-term relationship, however, comes the risk of exploitation. That point is only half understood by the proponents of the ADEA, who frequently point out that the employer may seek a sharp cut in wages because older workers are less able than younger ones to take their services elsewhere. But there are two sides to this coin, and that second side is often suppressed: the older worker may well demand a sharp increase in wages because his or her particular skills are not replaceable. Advantage-taking runs in both directions. Legal rules, like contract rules, should not be designed to curb employer opportunism when employee opportunism is a problem as well.

The difficulties of long-term contracting are not lost on parties; they can devise ex ante all forms of devices that limit the potential for abuse. Ironically, the contract at will rules are a powerful weapon against opportunism. At will contracts remove only formal legal sanctions. These contracts are not inconsistent with informal social sanctions, since it may make eminently good sense for a particular firm to advertise that it has all sorts of internal "for cause" provisions, even if it explicitly reserves the right to fire at will under the law. The reputational effects are sufficiently powerful with large firms that this disjunction between what the legal agreement allows and what the social contract requires need not doom the arrangement. But be this as it may, at some future time the mutual gain condition of the contract may no longer be satisfied: production ceases at death or incapacitation, and it may well fall before that.

The problem, then, for the worker and the firm is to devise a long-term arrangement that keeps that contract alive only as long as both parties have some reason for maintaining it. Working out those arrangements may be tricky in practice because a firm may agree to keep a worker on even after there has been some decline in production: the longer period of employment could be regarded as a form of deferred compensation for valuable work that was performed earlier, a practice that allows employees to equalize income over all stages of their working life. Yet even here the firm may have an incentive to fire a worker and thus deprive him of that deferred compensation. If there is a sudden downturn in its primary product market, or a threat of a hostile takeover, or the chance for a highly favorable asset sale, the firm may lose its concern with its long-term commitments and choose to default on the informal promises it has made.

The ADEA works on the assumption that regulation minimizes certain risks. But it ignores others that persist. As long as informal monitoring arrangements are imperfect, voluntary markets will yield some bad outcomes; since perfect contract enforcement comes only at infinite cost, the parties must take calculated risks that they will be victimized by some opportunistic behavior. But the size of these risks should not be overestimated. Firms have large numbers of employees. To behave poorly toward those on the edge of retirement sends a message to workers at an earlier stage in their careers: leave now while the going is good. The best way to maintain stability throughout the work force is to keep to a uniform set of rules that evolve only in gradual and predictable ways over time. Nor does reputation provide the only constraint. Pension rights may be vested in whole or in part; employers may enter into contracts that provide for additional severance pay based on years of service with the firm. Cases in which these mechanisms break down are bound to occur, but not often; and when they do occur, legal rules targeted solely at opportunistic behavior can be introduced.

Legal intervention never comes cheap. There is thus a danger that systems of employee protection will open up still greater opportunities for worker abuse. Once workers know that they cannot be fired, demoted, or fined in the ordinary course of business, they have a form of legal protection that allows them to let their production fall further than might otherwise be the case. As always, a comprehensive view of the situation requires both kinds of error to be taken into account, where both cannot be driven to zero simultaneously. The virtually uniform market response that keeps some age-based standards in employment shows how these alternative risks are generally priced across a wide spectrum of firms and employees. To argue that markets are inefficient because they make mistakes with individual workers is to condemn regulation as well, which makes even worse mistakes with firms (and with the other workers who benefit from the firm's decisions).

The ADEA and Hiring

The role of relational contracting begins at the onset of the contract. As a matter of sensible business arrangements the firm that makes its initial employment decisions should look at the projected long-term career path of the worker within the business. Again the key point to understand is that the employment relationship has a dominant temporal dimension. Both employers and employees are required to make expenditures in one period that will not realize benefits until some subsequent period. Thus both employees and employers may have to make an initial investment in firm-specific skills that can be recovered only over the life of the employment contract. Yet there is no reason to believe that these initial expenditures are equal on both sides. Typically the side that gets to perform last will have an advantage relative to the side that is obliged to perform first. In the employment context the balance of advantage on this score often lies with the employee, who will generate benefits to the firm only after some initial training or probation period. The firm's resources have been expended, but its return on its investment is still contingent. In calculating the benefits in question, the firm should necessarily take into account the length of the payback period. To expend $10,000 on a worker who at age sixty-five may have left only an expected five years of productive labor makes little sense if the firm can expend that same resource on a worker of forty-five, whose expected life at the firm is fifteen years.[20] This threefold increase in the period in which to recover the initial investment justifies a smaller yield.

It may be said in reply that the older worker is the better investment because he is less likely to move. True enough; but once that realization becomes clear to the firm, there is no need for the ADEA at all. The firm will make the same calculations as before and, ceteris paribus, will prefer to hire the older worker because of the longer payout period. Unfortunately a selection bias ensures that the litigated cases will only obscure the true industrywide state of affairs.[21] The older worker who is hired because he is unlikely to quit is also unlikely to have an occasion to sue. The older worker who is not hired because she is likely to quit will indeed have occasion to sue. The legal system distorts the long-term investment in human capital by acting as though a firm should be indifferent as to the rates of return that it gets from individual members of its work force. Any hiring decision is dominated by complex contracting problems of falling productivity, differential return periods, moral hazard, and the like. All these are glossed over by

20. See the discussion of *Bartsh v. Northwest Airlines, Inc.,* 831 F.2d 1297(7th Cir. 1987), at note 30.

21. See, generally, George L. Priest and Benjamin Klein, "The Selection of Disputes for Litigation," 13 *J. Legal Stud.* 1 (1984).

a heroic but false pronouncement that age discrimination is arbitrary and that hiring (now assumed to be costless and error free) should be based on ability alone.

The decision to hire a worker of any particular age, then, is dependent not only on what she can do at that age but on what she can do in the years that follow. In making these projections into the future, the firm must rely on probabilistic evidence about general regularities of human conduct. But it is just that process that runs headlong into one of the central tenets of the ADEA: ability must be evaluated on tests wholly independent of age. To be sure, the statute does not contain a categorical prohibition on age discrimination, given the BFOQ exception; but, as is the case with sex, this exception is read by the EEOC as allowing explicit age tests only in cases of business necessity.

> An employer asserting a BFOQ defense has the burden of proving that (1) the age limit is reasonably necessary to the essence of the business, and either (2) that all or substantially all individuals excluded from the job involved are in fact disqualified, or (3) that some of the individuals so excluded possess a disqualifying trait that cannot be ascertained except by reference to age. If the employer's objective in asserting a BFOQ is the goal of public safety, the employer must establish that the challenged practice does indeed effectuate that goal and there is no acceptable alternative which would better advance it or equally advance it with less discriminatory impact.[22]

At one level the standard established in the last sentence is less demanding than the BFOQ for sex, at least in cases of public safety. Nonetheless, it is clear that the very insistence on the BFOQ standard itself necessarily impedes the safety goal in question. A closer look at the standard bears out the basic point. The first condition is rarely the issue, because safety has been generally held to go to the essence of the business.[23] The typical litigated case therefore turns on the second and third elements of the test, which have to be established in the alternative. With regard to the second element, the regulations insist that individuated determinations must be made case by case as long as there is any chance of error: *all* applicants excluded by the age limitation must be unqualified. Taken literally, this requirement will be routinely

---

22. 29 C.F.R. §1625.6(b) (1989).

23. See the discussion in Chapter 14 of the point in connection with *Diaz v. Pan American World Airways, Inc.,* 442 F.2d 385 (5th Cir. 1971).

defeated simply because at least one applicant in any large group is likely to be qualified under any general standard. But even if the requirement is relaxed, as has been done in these cases,[24] to mean "substantially all," the task is formidable. It may not be cost justified to seek out the tiny fraction of eligible persons above the age limit, in light of the intrinsic unreliability of standard tests. Ironically, the errors have had relatively minor consequences, for the fittest person is most likely to succeed at finding desirable work elsewhere, say, in a small firm where such individuation is more feasible. But these considerations are all ignored in construing the BFOQ requirement.

If the EEOC regulations are exceedingly hostile to cost-based justifications, the case law takes only a slightly more accommodating stance by allowing age to be a proxy for safety where obtaining specific proof is "impossible or highly impractical."[25] But even this accommodation is not as generous as might appear at first blush. If medical tests are a perfectly reliable predictor of physical fitness for job performance but cost $500 per applicant, they must be applied across the board to all applicants over the age of forty if they are applied to applicants under the age of forty, even though testing in the under-forty group may find 50 percent of the applicants qualified while the same test applied to the over-forty group may generate only a 10 percent yield. Those cost differentials in any unregulated market might drive some firms to a two-part hiring procedure, with an absolute ban on applicants over forty and a test requirement for applicants under forty. No test in standard use under the present legal rule, however, can be regarded as either "impossible or highly impractical" when it is merely economically wasteful.

There are virtually no ADEA cases where a BFOQ can be established without a struggle. As the costs of testing go up, there will be less testing. As the statute applies with equal force to both the protected over-forty age group and the below-forty group, the changes in behavior will not be confined to letting in some persons over forty. It will instead influence the composition of *both* pools, allowing less qualified workers under forty to become eligible for employment under the less expensive (and less reliable) standards. Even if the statute does not require any direct relaxation in standards, its effect on costs will necessarily lead to some across-the-board decline in employment standards, and thus some increased safety

24. See *Western Airlines, Inc. v. Criswell,* 472 U.S. 400, 414 (1985).
25. See, e.g., id. at 414, quoting from *Usery v. Tamiami Trail Tours, Inc.,* 531 F.2d 224, 235 (1976).

risk. A preoccupation with safety and a stringent antidiscrimination norm cannot cohabit in the same legal universe: something has to give.

The problems with the BFOQ standards are well illustrated by the cases. In *Usery v. Tamiami Trail Tours, Inc.*,[26] the question was whether the firm could insist that all its new employees be below the age of forty. The company's argument was that new workers had no seniority and were in consequence forced to work longer shifts and odd hours on short notice. Older workers were less likely to perform well under such arduous circumstances. The age maximum was therefore justified on grounds of public safety. The firm, of course, had older workers who had been hired earlier, but their accident profile was different. These workers had accumulated experience on the job, and their seniority allowed them to work preferred routes at regular hours.[27] The company thus took into account the long-term profile of the workers in a way in which the EEOC guidelines do not.

The court sustained Tamiami's practice, noting that it could not be required to establish its case to a certainty, "for certainty would require running the risk until a tragic accident would prove that the judgment was sound."[28] But the decision, however sensible, does not provide any form of safe harbor for Tamiami in the next case. On appeal the court refused to overturn a jury verdict for the defendant under the "clearly erroneous" standards used to review questions of fact. It did not hold that the initial age cutoff was a legitimate hiring practice as a matter of law. Other cases therefore could go quite the opposite way, further clouding the relationship between age requirements and public safety.

In this connection it is useful to trace the parallel airline litigation to give some sense of the relative roles of the government and the airlines in running that industry. The first act of the drama was set in *Western Air Lines, Inc. v. Criswell*,[29] which involved a suit under the ADEA by cap-

26. 531 F.2d 224 (5th Cir. 1976).

27. Id. at 237: "Because of the established seniority system, Tamiami argues that older bus drivers can compensate for the decline in physical attributes that is part of the aging process by choosing day shifts and short routes. If older applicants were hired, however, they could not chose [sic] the easier shifts because they would not have seniority."

28. Id. at 238.

29. 472 U.S. 400 (1985). Note also that in *Trans World Airlines v. Thurston*, 469 U.S. 111 (1985), the Supreme Court upheld under the ADEA a direct facial evidence challenge to TWA's rules that required retiring captains to bid for flight engineers' jobs when captains disqualified from service for other reasons were allowed to "bump" flight engineers as of right.

tains and first officers challenging an airline rule of mandatory retirement at age sixty. The distinctive feature in this case was the interaction between company rules and FAA regulation. The regulations applicable to captains and first officers required them to relinquish their positions at age sixty. Again the justification was safety: older pilots have an increased risk of heart attacks and similar on-the-job ailments. That government rationale, however, did not apply to second officers (flight engineers), who have a wholly different set of responsibilities, chiefly to monitor the operating systems on the plane, including those governing fuel management, hydraulics, and cabin pressurization. The claim for age discrimination, upheld in *Criswell,* was that it was improper to dismiss the pilots and first officers without allowing them them to "downbid" for flight engineer positions, for which the FAA proposed no maximum age limitation. The jury verdict in favor of the plaintiff was affirmed by the Supreme Court, in an opinion that seems entirely consistent with the basic structure of the BFOQ exception.

Then came *Bartsh v. Northwest Airlines, Inc.*[30] Even before *Criswell* was decided, Northwest Airlines saw the handwriting on the wall. In June 1983 it negotiated a settlement with its captains and first officers that allowed them the option of applying for second officer positions. Of the thirty-three pilots who elected to join the program, sixteen passed, eight withdrew, and nine had their participation in the program terminated. This last group sued the airline, not for a violation of the statute but for a breach of the settlement decree. Their argument was that they had not been given sufficient time to prove themselves, in part because the instructors sabotaged their training out of resentment over the seniority these former pilots would have had relative to younger flight engineers with years of experience at that particular job. The company defended on the ground that even with extra instruction many of the pilots were unable to grasp the requirements of the new job. On appeal the company's defense prevailed, but the overriding question is, cui bono? The training program for the displaced pilots was doubtless more costly per new recruit than the programs ordinarily undertaken (otherwise the company would have welcomed their participation); it introduced extensive bitterness and discord into the work force; it produced a cadre of flight engineers who were doubtless less competent as a group than those with lower seniority but longer experience; and it gave a huge preference to a group of pilots who already had the benefit of exceedingly favorable union contracts.

30. 831 F.2d 1297 (7th Cir. 1987).

Northwest was required to train as flight engineers individuals who would doubtless have shorter useful careers than the workers they displaced; and some of the workers with reduced seniority were themselves over forty and ostensible beneficiaries of the ADEA.

Northwest may also find itself at a competitive disadvantage to boot, for the law in this area is sufficiently amorphous to resist any industrywide rule on the status of flight engineers. Delta Airlines fought its flight engineers and prevailed in *Iervolino v. Delta Air Lines, Inc.*,[31] in part by introducing evidence that with former captains in the cabin in a subordinate position, "the roles of the crew members may become confused or ambiguous and former captains serving as flight engineers may intimidate other crew members during an emergency."[32] But again there was no blanket rule, only a jury verdict, which could go the other way in the next case.[33] Against this backdrop it is useful to recall the basic common law rule: let there be no specific performance of the employment contract. The ADEA is no way to run an airline, or any other complex business.

Mandatory Retirement

If the hiring cases have generated a certain confusion, there is no question that the mandatory retirement issue is far more controversial still. Within the private setting the age for retirement is a critical part of any negotiation. It is usually specified by contract, and enforced without any inquiry by the firm into the current level of performance by any individual worker. At the outset retirement and poverty are not synonymous. The firm's pension obligations are timed to kick in when the worker's employment ceases, and the worker has the option (subject to covenants against competition that are binding without regard to age) to find a new position in the market to supplement the deferred compensation received from the firm.

The key question is whether termination per se is superior to termination only for cause. The standard argument for the ADEA postulates that the private loss of the worker is a social loss as well. The House report to

31. 796 F.2d 1408 (11th Cir. 1986).

32. Id at 1412.

33. See, e.g., *EEOC v. Wyoming*, 460 U.S. 226 (1983); *Johnson v. Mayor & City Council of Baltimore*, 472 U.S. 353 (1986); *EEOC v. Pennsylvania*, 829 F.2d 392 (3rd Cir. 1987) (rejecting mandatory retirement age of sixty for state police officers); *Williams v. Hughes Helicopters, Inc.*, 806 F.2d 1387 (9th Cir. 1986) (accepting mandatory retirement at fifty-five for test pilots).

the 1978 amendment makes the argument that "Society, as a whole, suffers from mandatory retirement as well. As a result of mandatory retirement, skills and experience are lost from the work force resulting in reduced GNP. Such practices also add a burden to Government income maintenance programs such as social security."[34] The argument founders in its obvious confusion between the firm and the world. Mandatory retirement is separation from the firm. It is not a *legal* prohibition against reentering the work force in some other job—an entry that will be easier to make if the ADEA is off the books. The case against the ADEA on mandatory retirement rests on a showing that individual retirement determinations are far more costly and inefficient than the per se rules that they displace. It is yet another instance of why simple rules are best for a complex world.

Again the key point is cost. Most obviously, case-by-case determinations are expensive to make. Any "for cause" determination works best where there is a smoking gun—stealing from the corporate till, providing proprietary secrets to a competitor—which either is a criminal offense or can be adjudicated as though it were one. For cause standards do not work well, however, when personnel decisions are reviewed from outside the system. Although a misconduct charge is a discrete event, decisions about job productivity are not. It is therefore far harder to subject productivity decisions to external monitoring or judicial review. Productivity is a continuous variable, and any termination decision may well be made less on a judgment that work has faltered than on the judgment that it is likely to falter in the near or not so distant future. The well-intentioned personnel department under a for cause system would have to take into account a wide range of information that requires prying into the medical and personal history of the worker and his or her family, thereby opening up vast vistas for favoritism and preference. Worse still, when many separate decisions must be made in a large organization, some outcomes are certain to be inconsistent with others and with the amorphous guidelines governing the matter. Case-by-case review leads us into a veritable swamp of unwanted complications.

There is, moreover, no reason to suspect that blanket rules are less reliable than ad hoc determinations. In case-by-case hearings individual workers may present special evidence as to why any general statistics

---

34. H. R. Rep. no. 95-527, pt. 1, p. 2 (1977). *Legislative History of Age Discrimination in Employment Act* 362 (1981). The passage is often cited in litigation. See, e.g., *Western Airlines, Inc. v. Criswell,* 472 U.S. 400, 411 (1972).

about production do not apply to them. But that evidence is always apt to be skewed in ways that may easily escape cross-examination. (Workers will suppress private knowledge unfavorable to their case.) It is particularly hard to refute without resort to general statistical information of the sort that the ADEA spurns as an inaccurate stereotype of older people. But the basic economic and institutional logic is quite the opposite. Accurate application of decision theory makes it clear beyond a doubt that using particular case evidence to the exclusion of *base rate* evidence on performance follows the royal road to error. Everyone cannot be the exception. To make each retirement case a one-of-a-kind extravaganza as the ADEA does is likely to introduce an increased rate of error in personnel decisions at a higher administrative cost.

It may be said in reply that these automatic rules work to the advantage of the firm but not to the worker. Not so. Using the basic probability judgment to generate the bright line rule means that the employee need not fear the compiling of a dossier designed to demean him in his own eyes or the eyes of his co-workers. A per se rule means that there is a clear signal as to how long a job will last, which allows a worker to plan retirement alternatives in advance without having to juggle a termination hearing within the firm against any possible outside offers (as long as these have not dried up altogether under the influence of the ADEA). It also means that the worker can rely on the automatic termination rule to tell (truthfully) any new prospective employer that leaving the first job was part of company policy and not a reflection of individual abilities or poor performance in the short run. Finding a new job will be far more difficult after a for cause dismissal than after dismissal pursuant to a mandatory rule.

In addition, the question of benefits to and burdens on the worker cannot be considered solely at the time of retirement or dismissal. It must instead be considered over the full employment cycle. A systematic turnover at the top will make opportunities for advancement available to younger workers in the firm. The workers who are now being asked to retire are likely to be the same workers who at some earlier stage profited from the openings at the top created by the same mandatory retirement policy that they now attack. But even if memories are short, all workers benefit from the absence of any special rules on age discrimination that make it hard for older workers to obtain new jobs in the secondary market. Firms with the absolute power to fire are more willing to exercise their power to hire in favor of high-risk workers. To look at only the cases of retirement, demotion, or disappointment is to look only at the negatives of the system, and to ignore the gains that other workers have obtained from a system that preserves the absolute contractual discretion of both employers and employees.

The labor market thus depends on the ability of employers to make blanket judgments about their workers. It is of course true that the decline in ability (if any) at sixty-five or seventy will vary enormously across workers. But that variation may be best detected by the individual judgments that can, and will, be made in the *next* stage, when workers look for new jobs from employers for whom there is no overlay of the loyalty and hostility that arise in long-term relationships. Facing an external review, workers themselves have an incentive to keep their skills sharp. If they are not able to bully their employers, they must sell themselves to other employers who demand performance. And, since many workers will choose to stay retired, the individual judgments need be made for only a fraction of the retired workers. All in all there is much less recontracting and bluffing without mandatory retirement than with it, and all parties can share in the savings brought on by lower transaction costs. In some cases these benefits may be oversold, but repealing the ADEA does not require mandatory retirement for any firm; it simply allows it. That invitation is one that many firms will accept, because on balance mandatory retirement offers pervasive gains to all interested parties. Here as elsewhere the road to error is paved with legal judgments that presume that all private market practices are based on widespread mistakes in judgment that only Congress can detect and correct.

Tenured University Faculty

Contractual freedom should be the norm in all cases of mandatory retirement. Were that the law today, the subject of mandatory retirement for tenured faculty could be conveniently dismissed as a footnote to the general rule. The principles of contract law applicable to retirement in business and trade would carry over to academic retirements without missing a beat. Accordingly, at the social level there would be no reason to examine the internal structural differences within various kinds of private institutions. The parties to those institutions would perform that task on their own initiative, by choosing, where appropriate, different internal schemes of governance. The academic task would be one of discussion and understanding, not of advocacy.

Once regulation displaces contract, however, the force of the law does not visit its harm on all institutions in equal measure. Just as all forms of discrimination law do not have the same social consequences, so too the same antidiscrimination norm does not have an identical impact on different institutions. The differentiation across classes of institutions, alas, necessarily becomes a collective undertaking; in the process special pleading and astute analysis become ever harder to distinguish. The question of mandatory retirement for tenured faculty is so critical to universities that it is worthwhile to risk charges of special pleading in order to strive for intellectual understanding. The 1986 amendments to the ADEA singled out tenure from the mass of employment relations and allowed universities to retain their own mandatory retirement policies until December 31, 1993. That exception should be made permanent even if the ADEA continues in force. The internal operation of universities (especially the prominent research universities) will suffer if mandatory retirement is eliminated—more, I suspect, than most pessimists fear. In order to understand why, it is necessary to begin not with the ADEA but with the peculiar institution of tenure so common in universities and so absent from ordinary business.

The key question is, who owns the university? That question receives a different answer from the parallel question, who owns the business? With businesses, the shareholders of the firm are the residual claimants on all revenues and losses. Because shareholders have this unique financial position, they usually receive by corporate charter (not public command) full control over the business, including rights to participate in dividends, to sell shares, and to hire and fire the managers of the firm.[35] The firm is in the business of producing private goods, so profits, broadly defined, are an appropriate measure of success. In universities the output is much more difficult to measure because the knowledge and information produced have, and are intended to have, the characteristics of a public good. The output of intellectual inquiry is far harder to monitor by conventional measures of profit and loss than the operations of the usual business corporation. Academic performance is not bought and sold like inventory and stock-in-trade, and the importance of the research is not

35. See, generally, Eugene F. Fama and Michael C. Jensen, "Agency Problems and Residual Claims," 26 *J. Law & Econ.* 327 (1983). See also, on the scope of contractual freedom in corporate law generally, Symposium, Contractual Freedom in Corporate Law, 89 *Colum. L. Rev.* 1395 (1989). Note that in the corporate context the debate over mandatory terms and freedom of contract has a somewhat artificial sense about it, given that some of the mandatory terms (e.g., annual meetings) are those that all firms typically require. But as long as there is no risk to outsiders, I am hard-pressed to see why any restriction on freedom of contract among shareholders and their employees is justified.

measured in any direct sense by the revenues that it generates for the researcher, for much of what is produced falls into the public domain.

The organization of a university (or at least some universities) is profoundly shaped by the nature of its output and by its central mission of transmitting knowledge and culture across the generations. In that environment tenure emerged as a dominant institutional feature long before anyone had to worry about charitable exemptions under the tax code or about the impact of external regulations such as the ADEA. The best explanations for tenure are internal to the university.[36] The system was adopted in part to assure potential donors that their gifts, motivated by the desire to advance education and knowledge, would not be expropriated by the nonacademic managers of the institution. It was also adopted in part to ensure that the worth of a degree received by graduates would not depreciate over time owing to a systematic reduction in standards. And it was adopted in part to give faculty members the freedom to explore and develop ideas with some protection against the prevailing sentiments of the day or pressures for hasty publication. In hard or intolerant times it is an important bulwark of academic freedom generally.

For these and perhaps other reasons, tenure gives academic faculty a permanent lien on the assets of the institution, and it insulates the selection of faculty from the business side of the university. It introduces a system of separation of power and prevents the risky concentration of power in the hands of a single administrator or academic figure. Tenure is as much a system of governance, of divided control, as it is of job security.[37] No such lien on university assets, no such governance structure, has to be provided on the business side of an academic institution, which is run much like any other business. There is no tenure for the registrar, treasurer, or grounds keeper, or even the president, provost, or deans.

In theory a faculty may govern without a system of tenure, for example, through round-robin reviews whereby every faculty member comes up for reconsideration on a five- or ten-year cycle. But that system imposes heavy costs on retention decisions, which must be made by a faculty already deeply engaged in dealing with entry and lateral appoint-

36. The peculiar features of the university also help explain why universities, unlike businesses, tend to build endowments instead of borrowing on their future income flow. See, generally, Henry Hansmann, "Why Do Universities Have Endowments?," 19 *J. Legal Stud.* 3 (1990).

37. See, generally, Eugene F. Fama and Michael C. Jensen, "Separation of Ownership and Control," 26 *J. Law & Econ.* 301 (1983).

ments. Faculties cannot easily respond to the substantial burdens of additional decisions, for they have only so much time and emotional energy for personnel work. Any system of periodic "for cause" review for a faculty as a whole will result either in massive overwork and intrigue if done conscientiously, or purely ceremonial review if not.

Tenure is the mode of avoidance. And it comes at a high price. A system that brings faculty members up for consideration once and for all creates enormous pressure at the time of tenure, and wrong decisions either way can have grievous consequences for departments or entire universities. But there is a relatively clean end to the process, and it nullifies the risk of cycling inherent in periodic review: those who review now will not be reviewed by others later. Tenure may be job security, but it is not everything. Thereafter the system of rewards and sanctions gives rise to a delicate minuet, internal to the university, that involves not only salary but also leave and sabbatical time, research support, space and facilities, course and committee assignments, collegial respect, honors and perquisites, and the like. At the same time there are useful pressures from the outside, in the form of offers for permanent and visiting appointments, editorial positions, lectures, conferences, and so on that provide incentives for productive labor beyond the reach of the tenured faculty member's own university. The system works reasonably well in the round, notwithstanding the frequent cases of "intellectual retirement" after tenure. The high return from the ablest scholars offsets the losses from keeping the unproductive scholars around the academy. The imperfections are such that they cannot be eliminated or reduced, save by the creation of greater imperfections in some unforeseen corner of the university world.

This elaborate system is not without its demands. In order to engage in scholarship, an academic has to think of something, prove something, test something in a way that has not been done before. There is almost no academic return from coming in second or from understanding well what others have already demonstrated. Scholars must work at peak ability, and at some point the benefits of experience are more than offset by the loss of skills brought on by age. There has to be some way to end the lifetime contract in order to preserve the vitality and productivity of the institution. Mandatory retirement is the only possible system that allows that to be done. The *automatic* termination rule avoids the endless evaluations of personnel and scholarship, the invidious and delicate comparisons between colleagues and friends that drove universities to take refuge in tenure in the first place. To require for cause, case-by-case determinations, as the ADEA does, will cement in place older academics who can soldier on at levels of innovation and scholarship far below those that earned them their tenure in the first place.

Of course there are exceptions to the general rule, but those exceptional individuals will be able to obtain teaching positions at other institutions, provided the ADEA does not make other institutions leery of hiring on the sensible theory that violations of the statute are far easier to establish once someone is on staff than before. But even in an unregulated market the ablest of retired professors will not be offered tenure in this secondary market, and for good reason. Governance requires only that a core of faculty has independent power. It does not require that every faculty member participate in it. With age, the risk of rapid decline, even for the ablest academics, is too serious to ignore. The hiring of skilled older academics on short-term contracts would allow them to teach and research as long as they were able without putting them into the governance structure of the institution.

That issue of governance, moreover, is key. Academics assume management roles in appointments and promotions because of the divided ownership structure within universities. The level of genuine institutional control is so vast that faculty members have been held on one occasion *not* to constitute employees who could form a bargaining unit under the National Labor Relations Act.[38] In their area of control they *are* management, with power over internal appointments, curriculum, degrees, and standards. The ability to control the future should not be placed in the hands of the past. The law of property has often railed against "dead hand" control. It is senseless to override the retirement decisions of every university that has entrusted the future to the faculty members who will live with the consequences of their decisions, good and bad. The dramatic shift in power from young to old that is generated by removing mandatory retirement will confer the greatest responsibility on senior faculty, when as a group they have the shortest time horizons and are most likely to have lost touch with the cutting edge of their disciplines. It is only to the eye of the untrained bureaucrat or politician that all professors and scholars are alike. Inside universities the differences between top and bottom are understood to be enormous. Universities are at root collections of scholars. The thousands of fragile interactions that hold them together will be largely disrupted if it is Congress and not universities that decides who should govern. The point was recognized when the ADEA law was written to allow busi-

---

38. See *NLRB v. Yeshiva University*, 444 U.S. 672 (1980).

nesses to retire their key people at age sixty-five. There is equally good reason, indeed an imperative necessity, to allow universities the same degree of authority over their faculty governance structure.

In this regard we should learn the lesson of the earlier Civil Rights Acts, which were initially, if erroneously, billed as modest interferences with the markets. The same capacity for remorseless expansion of federal intervention exists here once personnel practices are placed under the judicial microscope. Compliance with the nondiscrimination norm will be difficult to achieve. If faculty members over seventy are subject to annual review in order to weed them out, it is a per se violation under the statute unless all members of the faculty are subject to similar review. The case-by-case approach therefore invites (with fiendish intensification) the protracted personnel battles that the tenure system helps moderate. Worse still, even if the review process is extended to all faculty members, its outcomes are not invulnerable to attack. The dean must choose the committee. Is it evidence of disparate treatment if a smaller percentage of faculty over seventy are on the committee than of those under seventy? And once the decision of the committee is reached, if younger faculty members do better in the review than older ones, is there a plausible ADEA case on a disparate impact theory? Is the structure of the committee, coupled with the outcome of the case, sufficient on a cumulative basis to support an action, even if each taken alone might be regarded as inconclusive?

The formal system, then, will not render personnel decisions invulnerable to legal attack. There are still subtle ways of making faculty feel unwelcome. Raises can be reduced. Offices can be reassigned. Committee and course assignments can be changed. But even here there is no guarantee that these strategies, especially if undertaken in a systematic and coordinated fashion, are outside the scope of the statute. Regulation of "terms, conditions, and privileges" of employment covers just about everything that happens in the workplace. A faculty member can be retained, given a raise, and still have a viable action under the ADEA. In addition, a convenient doctrine of "constructive discharge" covers the case of the employee who leaves because he or she is not made to feel welcome to stay. The problem here is stunningly simple. The anti-discrimination norm demands like treatment in cases when the rational market response requires radically different treatment. There is no easy way to make the transition from a regime that calls for automatic retirement at age sixty-five or seventy to one that grants a lifetime contract at that age. It is not possible to change one critical feature of an employment contract without upsetting the entire institutional balance. It is just naive to assume that radical jolts to the system on a single contractual term will have no ripple effects. (One might as well say that the only response to the minimum wage is to raise the income levels of workers below the minimum wage.)

There is one further sobering note. It will not take litigation to bring about major changes in university governance structures. Unless the statute is altered, the simple formal requirements of the ADEA will dismantle many university practices and will force major changes in faculty composition and voting power. These structural and personnel changes will in turn have powerful implications for the budget, since any decision to demote or alter the responsibilities of faculty members or change their level of compensation and fringe benefits, if tied to age, will be subject to EEOC scrutiny wholly apart from litigation. Even before any private suits for back pay are brought, the changes in university life will be profound. If suits for back pay are allowed in individual cases, the chilling effect on internal governance will become still more severe. (And the stakes will become even higher if suits are allowed, as proposed in the debates over the Civil Rights Act of 1990, for full compensatory and punitive damages.[39]) Even if individual faculty members are reluctant to expose their entire scholarly career to public scrutiny, universities are equally reluctant to have their own internal files (including those of all similar cases in the last ten years, please) opened up to public scrutiny as well. It can hardly improve relations within the faculty, or between faculty and administration, to have the frequency of suits and the size of settlements determined by who blinks first in the face of threats of unpleasant and unwanted disclosures from the other side. Litigation is the modern version of the medieval ordeal. The automatic retirement rule spares both sides that prospect.

It may be said in reply that there is no need to make special provisions for faculty members. Given the mass of retirements expected throughout the 1990s, there should be a dearth of academics available to fill the empty places. The factual point may be true, but legal changes are made for the duration, not for one year or two or three. Whether true or false, however, the argument has no logical relation to the choice of proper institutional structure. Even if mandatory retirement is retained by private universities, there will be an active market in retired professors to fill the gaps. The teaching will therefore be done, but the governance will pass

39. See Civil Rights Legislation of 1990.

from their hands, as will much of the research. Indeed, if the mandatory retirement rules are abolished, the result will be the opposite of what is intended: the secondary market for senior faculty is likely to dry up and the shortage of qualified teachers may well be worse than projected. The level of employment opportunities in the universities bears no logical relation to their internal contract and governance rules. Faculty governance requires a tenured faculty; and older professors should have no role in that operation except with the consent of the university in question.

There is another argument that might be advanced to explain why universities have so little to fear from lifting the cap on mandatory faculty retirement: the changes in the law have gone into effect in business, and most workers have opted to retire early, so the impact on the firm has been minor indeed. But the argument amounts to a serious oversimplification of the situation. Initially, businesses lobbied hard and successfully to keep their mandatory retirement rules in effect for senior personnel after the basic law had been changed. They well understood that powerful executives might be unwilling to relinquish power at any age, even if assembly-line workers could not wait to escape the tedium of their own jobs. University life (at least at some universities) is an attractive one. Teaching and scholarship in combination are consumption goods for faculty members who produce them. Oftentimes I have asked myself, "What do you plan to do when you grow up?" The temptation to stay on at the University of Chicago is indeed great.

The peculiar attraction of academic institutions, however, does not depend simply on the special nature of the work. Another central ingredient is the structure of university pension programs. The key point here can be traced to the critical distinction between defined benefit and defined contribution plans.[40] In its simplest form, a defined benefit plan keys retirement compensation of employees to some specific financial target, say, 60 percent of the average wages during the last three years of employment with the firm. The employer is responsible for funding the plan, and (in theory at least) is entitled to reap the benefit of prudent investments, but must make additional contributions to the fund if the original moneys were insufficient to fund the obligation. The residual economic risk under a defined benefit plan thus remains with the employer until the pension is drawn down. One chief feature of the defined benefit plan is that it tends (for better or worse) to bind employees to their

---

40. For discussion, see John H. Langbein and Bruce A. Wolk, *Pension and Employee Benefit Law* 40–44 (1990).

original employer, since compensation is payable only for workers who are with the firm at retirement, where its amount is closely tied to years of service. This scheme makes it difficult to change jobs in the years just before retirement.

The second form of pension plan is the defined contribution plan. Under this system, initially put in effect through the TIAA-CREF (Teachers Insurance and Annuity Association and College Retirement Equities Fund, for fixed and equity investments respectively), and now replicated by other investment vehicles as well, all monies paid into the fund by the employer or employee are immediately vested in the employee, even though they cannot be drawn down until retirement age. There is no minimum vesting period, and faculty members may (with the foresight of Andrew Carnegie, who designed the original program) carry their "portable" pensions with them from job to job without loss of benefits. The open market thereby created is in all likelihood one of the major strengths of the American academic system. The pensions themselves vary in size, depending on years of service, the total value of contributions made, and the investment vehicle chosen by faculty members. It is probably not uncommon for faculty members at retirement age to have a pension that exceeds their last annual salary, and most pensions are a substantial fraction (60 percent and more) of final salary. It is not a bad deal, even without the ADEA.

The defined contribution plans were adopted by universities when the mandatory retirement rules were in effect. There was, therefore, no occasion to consider the incentives that would be created once the mandatory retirement rule was abrogated by federal decree. But it is now clear that these defined contribution plans create perverse incentives in a world without mandatory retirement. The comparison with defined benefit plans is instructive. With a defined benefit plan, each year that the employee stays on the job *diminishes* the total value of the pension, at least until age seventy.[41] The obligation of the employer is to fund benefits at a certain level for the retirement period of the worker. The pension obligation is deferred one year by the decision to work, and the period over which the pension has to be paid is reduced by one year as well. In addition, it is the current year of benefits (which need not be discounted to present value) that is sacrificed. Thus the worker who at age sixty-five retires with, say, a

---

41. At age seventy the amount of their annual benefits are frozen whether or not employees continue to work. But by the same token additional contributions need not be made to fund the pension plans, as is the case with defined contribution programs.

sixteen-year life expectancy will have a sixteen-year pension keyed to his last three years of salary. Staying on another year may increase the base level of the salary by a bit, but now there is roughly only a fifteen-year period that has to be funded. In effect, the total compensation benefits to the employee are reduced by the amount of the benefits that are forgone in the year of continued employment. There are strong financial inducements to go elsewhere, so the pension benefit is collected from the university while a full salary is drawn from some other employer.

The incentive structure under the defined contribution plan is far different. If the ADEA stays in effect, then each employee is entitled to (1) a normal salary, with increases; (2) the standard contributions from the university to the defined contribution plan; and (3) withdrawals from the defined contribution plan, which are required to begin as a matter of law at age seventy and one-half.[42] There is in short no implicit loss of pension benefits that operates as an offset against salary, for the value of the pension rights grows, not shrinks, with time. The incentive therefore is to stay on.

There remains of course a critical empirical question: How many faculty members will decide to stay past seventy, and how long will they stay? Within the general population there is a broad movement toward early retirement for both men and women, spurred on in part by special benefits that sweeten the pot.[43] But it is dangerous to generalize from business employment to university faculty, and even to generalize from one university to another. To be sure, one piece of available evidence is the behavior of faculty between the ages of sixty-five and seventy. The mandatory retirement features of the current law ruled out the possibility that faculty members in this age group would decide to keep their positions in order to wring a strategic settlement from their universities. The element of threat was hardly credible, given the mandatory retirement age of seventy. Now, staying on longer gives an option of a favorable buyout, backed by the threat of litigation if termination is made without consent. If the rate of retirement in this age group was low (and it was close to zero at the University of Chicago), there is some reason to believe that it will not be high at age seventy, at least without some university buyout.

42. Internal Revenue Code §401(a)(9): "Defined contribution plans may not cease or reduce allocations to an employee's account because of age." Michael J. Canan, *Qualified Retirement and Other Employee Benefit Plans* 9 (1990 ed.). The book contains exhaustive accounts of the other tax and pension rules regulating the distribution of pensions.

43. See, e.g., James H. Schulz, *The Economics of Aging* 70 (4th ed 1988).

The best one can do, therefore, is to consider a static model (one that ignores changes in bargaining behavior and costs of litigation) to see what the percentage of faculty members over sixty-five or seventy will be. (The first number is significant because it represents the retirement age under voluntary employment contracts.) But the numbers generated offer only a lower boundary for the total dislocation.

The best study of future faculty behavior is the detailed evaluation of the University of Chicago figures prepared by Stephen Stigler.[44] Stigler estimated that in steady state about 10 percent of the university's tenured faculty would be over the age of seventy. In order to make this estimate, Stigler examined the period between 1990 and 2000, and sought to determine the rate of departures from the university through either death or retirement. This procedure was necessary since the full effects of mandatory retirement would be felt only after the program had been in effect for at least ten years. In the first year, for example, no member of the faculty would be over seventy-one, in the second year none over seventy-two, and so on. Even ten years into the program, steady state would not quite be achieved, as there would be some faculty members who could be expected to stay on after that date.

Running estimates of this sort is a chancy business because of the total lack of experience in those institutions that are now required to uncap. The analysis is further complicated because possible modifications in pension plans (as proposed in the Stigler report)[45] may increase the incentive effects that defined contributions plans have on faculty retention, provided these changes could be made applicable to faculty members near or

---

44. Stephen M. Stigler, *Report of the Faculty Committee on Retirement* 4, 20–23 (1991).

45. Id. at 7–9. In essence the report suggests that the university make contributions to a faculty pension plan until the faculty member has accumulated an amount sufficient to allow receipt at age sixty-eight of a pension equal to 75 percent of his or her final policy if annuitized at that time. That financial target remains in effect even if faculty members stay on after that age, and hence have fewer years over which to draw down the pensions. In order to prevent faculty members from adopting risky investment strategies that take advantage of the university guarantee, the report proposes that the value of the faculty portfolio be calculated as if the contributions were invested half in equity and half in debt. The report also proposes transitional rules for previous accumulations. Id. at 9. It is difficult to predict where the dislocations and disappointments will lie, but the institutional shifts are of such magnitude and uncertainty that some must arise. Two faculty members who have made equal contributions to private pension plans are likely to have holdings of different value, depending on when, and to what extent, they have followed risky or cautious investment strategies. Any new rule is likely to have a differential effect objectionable to one or the other.

over the age of seventy when they are introduced. Finally, Stigler's estimation might have come out somewhat differently if he had chosen, for example, to investigate the ten-year period between 1994 and 2004, given that the faculty members within a single institution are not, year by year, uniformly distributed by age. But even with these caveats Stigler's conclusions are significant: "A change in the average length of service of the magnitude we expect would, even with a constant faculty size and no change in tenure ratio, imply a reduction in the number of newly tenured faculty of about 10 percent. If we assume a constant faculty budget instead of constant faculty size, then this would translate into either a more severe cut in the number of newly tenured positions (perhaps 20%), or perhaps into a 10% cut in faculty salaries coupled with a 10% reduction in newly tenured faculty."[46] Given that government regulation under the present ADEA is in part responsible for raising retirement age from sixty-five to seventy, it seems clear that closer to 20 percent of faculty, and over 30 percent of the university's instructional budget, is constrained, if not commandeered, by external regulation.

Stigler's results contrast sharply with the major cross-university study by Albert Rees and Sharon Smith, *Faculty Retirement in the Arts and Sciences*,[47] which reports that in the public and private universities in which mandatory retirement has been abolished, the increase in the median age of retirement is only 0.2 years.[48] Smith has observed elsewhere that "uncapping has had no perceptible effect on the mean age of retirement in selective liberal arts colleges and prominent public universities. Whether behavior might be different for private elite research universities or change over time in liberal arts colleges and public universities remains an open question."[49]

The differences in the two sets of results are quite striking, and deserve at least this short comment. Rees and Smith focus on a group of universities whose internal characteristics are such that people tended to retire well before the mandatory age limit when it was in effect, typically in their mid-sixties.[50] There is little reason to expect that this class of professors

46. Id. at 4–5.
47. Albert Rees and Sharon P. Smith, *Faculty Retirement in the Arts and Sciences* (1991).
48. Id. at ch. 4.
49. Sharon P. Smith, "Ending Mandatory Retirement in the Arts and Sciences," 81 *Am. Econ. Rev.* 106, 109 (1991).
50. "Mean retirement age at 66.8 is highest in private universities and lowest in liberal arts colleges and 65.3 for capped colleges and 64.3 for uncapped colleges—with public universities in between. There is generally little difference by discipline. In both public and

would alter their conduct to avail themselves of the option to stay on longer after the mandatory retirement limit was raised. Indeed, the finding that retirement ages are *lower* at uncapped institutions shows that some selection effect is clearly at work: either the university lifts the mandatory retirement rule because the change in policy will have little or no effect, or there is some belief that only the strongest professors in a particular institution will choose to stay on. But the critical feature of any system of regulation is that it treats all entities that fall within the regulated class as though they were identical, notwithstanding the major differences among them—differences evidenced by the divergent practices of older faculty across universities. The great research universities deviate in many ways from the median, and yet they, in an age increasingly skeptical about claims of excellence, are powerless to protect themselves politically. It may well be that some universities would be better off by removing their mandatory retirement policies. If so, they can be counted on to do it for themselves. But there is no warrant for *imposing* this policy from without in light of the harms that it can impose on some portions of the regulated class. Here too the antidiscrimination laws are a form of centralized planning that is wholly inconsistent with institutional diversity.

Within those institutions where mandatory retirement does matter, the changes in the age distribution of faculty will have deleterious effects that go beyond the decline in academic creativity and productivity. In particular it will influence the governance structure of the university. It will change the nature of the appointments that are made in favor of persons who are likely to be older and to work in traditional fields. There will of course be some offsetting gains from productive faculty members (higher for those under seventy as a group than for those over it as a group), but on balance this one federal mandate will effectively dictate to some universities how roughly 25 percent of its academic and instructional budget should be spent. These calculations will vary from university to university, and (as I have suggested) the impact of uncapping mandatory retirement may be felt most severely at the major research institutions. In addition, the outcome at any university will be influenced by buyouts (the subject of the next section), which will reduce available cash for new positions, and by the threat of litigation, a total social loss. Even if the effects are scaled down by perhaps 50 percent, in my view the full set of changes, both

---

private institutions, the mean age at retirement is generally slightly lower in the uncapped type." Id. at 108.

qualitative and quantitative, make this issue a critical one for the continued vitality of universities as we know them.

Ideally the current rule allowing universities to keep their mandatory retirement provisions in place should be continued. But if not, at least some intermediate measures to dampen the impact of the shift should be adopted to cushion the blow to the new regime. Three of these deserve some brief mention.

First, universities should be allowed to reduce salaries by some fraction of the pension benefits that faculty members draw down at age seventy. This credit against salary in effect replicates the payment structure that routinely exists today under defined benefit plans, and it eliminates the obvious unfairness of paying senior faculty members, in their declining years of productivity, salaries that dwarf those of their younger colleagues (whose base salaries will decline owing to the budgetary claims of faculty over seventy). It is sure to be objected that any such change in the pension program represents a form of "theft," given that these pension benefits have been vested in employees, just like their houses and private pension funds. But the vesting was contingent on the enforcement of the mandatory retirement provisions, which were so central to the original contractual design. It is surely odd to insist on the sanctity of contract with respect to the receipt of benefits while systematically rejecting it with respect to retirement. The intervention by government to outlaw mandatory retirement is as much a frustrating event as any that is imaginable. If one part of the equation has been changed by brute government force, other portions of the contract should not be immune from offsetting changes. A faculty member's house or private pension fund was not part of the comprehensive contract and should remain untouched. But there is no reason why a university that has paid in advance for the retirement years should be required to pay in full once again for services that it does not want at the price it is forced to pay for them.

Second, on the model of the senior executive exemption currently built into the law, universities should be allowed to keep on faculty members over seventy (or perhaps over sixty-five) outside the governance structure. The key decisions on hiring and policy should pass to the younger generations, whose longer expected association with the university should lead to decisions more likely to increase its future prospects and success.

Third, it should be made clear (as it is not today) that it is possible to offer term contracts to faculty members over seventy without running afoul of the ADEA. At present there will be no aftermarket in senior faculty members if a contract to stay for a year or more is transformed by law into a lifetime contract, subject only to dismissal for cause. If opportunities for faculty members to go elsewhere are opened up, the pressures of mandatory retirement can be somewhat relaxed.

On balance I doubt that these devices, or others that might be suggested, will counteract most of the harm that universities will suffer when the ADEA removes the mandatory retirement clause from tenure contracts. There is, however, little that universities can do by altering their internal constitutions that will respond to this problem without creating worse problems in its wake. A shift, for example, to defined benefit pension plans will have no immediate effect on vested benefits of senior faculty members, and will undermine the portability of pensions, which has been so helpful in keeping the academic marketplace competitive. In addition, monstrous bookkeeping problems will be created when individual faculty members take on successive jobs with different universities. Likewise, efforts to preserve the defined contribution system subject to guarantees of minimum pensions will be difficult to administer because they require the introduction of complicated safeguards to prevent faculty members from adopting risky investment strategies, and they face in any event an uncertain future under the ADEA because of the disparate impact by age on the total compensation packages of faculty members. Nor do these pension adjustments, even if perfectly successful, do anything to ease the scholarly, governance, or other financial costs associated with uncapping. More radical approaches, such as the elimination of tenure, or major changes in salary policies (for example, explicit reductions for poor performance) will permeate every aspect of university life, and are apt to be bitter and divisive as well. Here is yet another instance where doing nothing is doing good. Let us hope that Congress in its ignorance does not engage in the gratuitous crippling of American universities, one of our last few areas of competitive advantage in world markets.[51]

Buyouts

The discussion of mandatory retirement, both generally and within universities, concentrates on the enormous dichotomy whereby age is critical to the marketplace but deemed irrelevant under the ADEA. Like all

---

51. See, e.g., Henry Rosovsky, *The University: An Owner's Manual* 29–37 (1990), estimating that two-thirds of the world's great universities are located in the United States.

antidiscrimination laws, the ADEA requires employers to enter into losing contracts, or contracts that cost more than they are worth. The gap between money spent and benefit obtained is in practice so large, and the inefficiencies generated by the statute so extensive, that one should expect recontracting within the market, that is, efforts by firms to buy their way out of compliance with the basic antidiscrimination law. And so they do, in droves. At root the problem is no different from that which arises in any business or commercial situation when legal rights are lodged in the hands of the party who values them least. If transaction costs can be controlled, a voluntary transfer can shift them to someone who values them more at a price that leaves both sides better off than they were.

To make the point concrete, assume that there is a one-year employment contract that costs the employer $100,000 per year but generates return benefits to the employer of only $40,000. Assume that the worker has retirement benefits and alternative employment opportunities totaling $75,000 if he retires from the firm. At this point the familiar result of the Coase theorem holds. Any annual payment between $25,000 and $60,000 ($100,000 less $40,000) from the employer to the worker makes both sides better off for the year. If, say, $40,000 is paid to the worker to buy back the contract, the employer is able to reduce a $60,000 loss by $20,000. By the same token, the worker increases his total yield by $15,000, from $100,000 to $115,000 ($75,000 plus $40,000). The size of the stakes is determined by the sharp cleavage between the private wage rate and that mandated under the statute, which even for a single year may be large enough to make renegotiation possible. Indeed, once mandatory retirement is outlawed, even more money is at stake, for the contract itself may run for several years, while the gap between wages and return benefits for the firm increases steadily with the age of the employee. The $60,000 spread in one year may be increased fivefold or more if the employment contract has an expected length of ten years.

The economic question then is whether the two sides can agree on a renegotiation of the deal by purchasing a release from employment rights. Universities, for example, will be able to stave off faculty governance by emeritus professors by buying them off; firms may promote able young employees by buying off their elders. But the buyout option only mitigates an existing problem. It does not return us to the sensible status quo ante, in which mandatory retirement rules were permissible as a matter of course. Far from keeping productive people in the labor force, renegotiation allows unproductive people to receive a second unearned pension, which comes straight from the capital accounts of the shareholders of a firm or the endowment of a university. The distributional consequences are themselves wholly perverse, for they often provide huge bonuses to people who are very well provided for in the first place. The sorry tale of successful renegotiation only reconfirms the general proposition: all antidiscrimination laws are at best no more than ill-disguised systems of transfer payments. But they generate no allocative benefits at all.

This, alas, is the optimistic scenario. It assumes that the bargaining can take place at a relatively costless level, so that all that is accomplished is a raid on the capital account or the endowment. The pessimistic view takes into account the inevitable fact that these bargains will be costly to negotiate, if they can be negotiated at all. Consider some of the crucial complications.

First, there is no single dominant strategy of renegotiation for the employer, or for that matter the employee. Firms and universities do not deal with a single employee at any one time. There are many persons who are eligible for retirement in a given year. Which workers should receive the offer? And for how much? One simple approach is to make a blanket offer of the form that says, anyone who leaves at age sixty is paid some multiple (say, threefold) of his or her last annual salary above and beyond ordinary pension rights. (Recall that within universities that lump sum payment would be equal to enough money to fund two or three entry-level positions.) One virtue of this strategy is that it economizes on administrative costs. Another is that it allows the firm to make a strong advance commitment, which helps prevent haggling by individual employees who seek a better offer than that made available to their peers.

The flaws of this simple strategy, however, are perhaps greater than its benefits. The strategy creates the risk of a selection bias against the firm. Ask just one question: Who will accept the offer? Those employees who have the worst employment prospects in the secondary market and the healthiest constitutions will decide to stay put. The most competent employees at age seventy will take the money and test their luck in the secondary market. Sick employees who may not live out the year will be happy to accept the offer to increase their bequests. Healthy employees will not. The fixed offer commits the employer to a given figure and then allows the employees to engage in unconstrained strategies that guarantee that the wrong people will accept this offer.

So the fixed offer may not be worthwhile. The only alternative is individual buyouts, which are costly to negotiate because the bargaining range is so wide that the contract price becomes difficult to determine. In this setting the ablest employees may get relatively little because they are a smaller net drain on the firm. The weaker employees could get more, although an employer has to fear that making unattractive offers to good people will create an incentive for everyone to slack off. In each case the bargaining range is large and the entire negotiation is complicated because the carrot of buyout and the stick of dismissal for cause are both possibilities. Each case is typically complicated by factors undreamed of in simple examples (within universities, for instance, these include grants, joint appointments, laboratory and office space, medical coverage, internal parallels, and precedents). Mandatory retirement with buyouts promises a transactional nightmare. The transaction cost gains from automatic termination coupled with new contracting in an open market are far lower.

Matters are still more complicated than even this short survey suggests, for it is unsettled whether employers and employees can contract out of the ADEA without either litigation or government approval. The legal complications here arise over the question of "waiver."[52] The problem is one that cannot arise where mandatory retirement is allowed because there is no negotiation of termination of employment. But, given the bilateral monopoly game that the ADEA creates, both firms and employees have incentives to behave strategically—yet another cost to the ADEA. The offer is designed to leave no room for bargaining: you will get extra severance pay, but only on condition that you release all rights of action under the ADEA. There is no warning of what was in the works. It is hard to test the waters elsewhere. You have two weeks to decide before the offer lapses. And you work up a sweat deciding what to do.[53] You take the offer. The question is whether you can now turn around and sue the firm on the ground that the waiver was coerced, and that the early dismissal (although compensated) was a violation of the ADEA.

Within this context the argument of the worker runs like this: the ADEA itself is a protective statute, which presupposes that workers are unable to protect themselves by contract against discrimination. Why then should they be any better able to protect themselves against buyouts, especially after tense negotiations? If the one form of contract is illegal, then why should the second kind of contract (which involves the cashing

52. See, generally, Deborah Jacobs, "The Growing Legal Battle over Employee Waivers," *New York Times,* October 29, 1989, section 3, p. 12.

53. See id., describing an employee response to a Xerox retirement offer: "He had 11 days to make a decision. 'You're in a total sweat. You're not thinking straight. You don't know which way to turn.'"

out of the first) be any better? Settlements cannot be allowed. The most likely alternatives are (1) to have government supervise the buyout (which will necessarily change the terms of trade), or (2) to insist that every case go to litigation before settlement is possible.[54]

For the most part the courts that have passed on this question have upheld the waiver.[55] The legal decisions have not been as straightforward as might be expected because the ADEA does not contain any internal provisions governing waiver, but instead incorporates by reference the waiver rules set out under the FLSA (Fair Labor Standards Act, a euphemism) that establishes, among other things, the minimum wage.[56] That section is silent on the question of whether the damages available under the act may be waived by an employee by way of settlement. The Supreme Court held early on that with respect to *liquidated* claims in which coverage under the statute was not in issue, waiver was not permitted on grounds that such waivers "would nullify the purposes of the Act."[57] That decision was then extended to prevent waiver even where there was a bona fide dispute over coverage under the act,[58] even though a compromise of the claim benefits both sides by eliminating uncertainty and the costs of litigation. If this legal hammerlock is imposed under the FLSA, why should matters be different under the ADEA? The answer to date has come from the simple perception that minimum wage workers are drawn from the lowest rung of society (which is why they are most constrained), whereas plaintiffs in age discrimination cases are usually successful and sophisticated, and thus well able to take care of themselves— an argument that is sufficient to allow not only for voluntary waivers of claims but for repeal of the statute as well. As long, therefore, as there are

54. In favor of allowing the buyouts under the ADEA as an additional benefit to retiring employees is the opinion of Judge Richard Posner in *Karlen v. City Colleges of Chicago,* 837 F.2d 314 (7th Cir. 1987); against it on the ground that it fosters "ageist" stereotypes is Richard G. Kass, "Early Retirement Incentives and the Age Discrimination in Employment Act," 4 *Hofstra Labor L. J.* 63, 66 (1986).

55. See, e.g., *Runyan v. National Cash Register Corp.,* 787 F.2d 1039 (6th Cir 1986).

56. See 29 U.S.C.A. §626(b) (1985), incorporating by reference, the FLSA, 29 U.S.C. §216(b) (1982). "Any employer who violates the provisions . . . of this title shall be liable to the employee or employees affected in the amount of their unpaid minimum wages, or their unpaid overtime compensation, as the case may be, and an additional amount as liquidated damages."

57. *Brooklyn Savings Bank v. O'Neil,* 324 U.S. 697, 707 (1945).

58. See *Schulte Co. v. Gangi,* 328 U.S. 108 (1946).

"factual" disputes over coverage, violation, and damages, settlements are allowable.

But matters may yet change tomorrow, for the question is ripe for legislative reform.[59] It is still possible that the law will be amended to require EEOC or court approval for employee waivers, or even that some lawsuit be filed, internal procedures followed, or EEOC complaint made. For future disputes it is not clear in whose interests these protective modifications are made. There is surely no reason to protect private parties who are quite able to protect themselves by contract, notwithstanding the rhetoric surrounding the ADEA. Since there is under present law no serious constitutional obstacle against retroactive invalidation of existing contracts (under the police power, of course),[60] the political picture is more clouded, and the stakes are correspondingly higher.

The issue of waiver illustrates the imperial nature of the antidiscrimination laws in general. In any sensible system waiver problems would not arise. But our system is not sensible. The rules of property and contract have been displaced in principle by an antidiscrimination norm that has run amok. In a sense the progression should be expected. Once the basic wall of freedom of contract, of individual and firm autonomy, has been breached, there is no obvious reason why contractual freedom should survive in the context of waiver any more than it does in the context of initial employment. There is no principled hard-edged argument that explains why some forms of discrimination are legitimate and others are not. Statutes that are passed with an eye toward invidious discrimination seek to prevent the occasional miscarriages of justice that are present in any major social institution. It is doubtful that they can eliminate them. But it is clear that they can do things that are both more dangerous and more insidious. They destroy established and sensible patterns of doing business, and impose a regime of centralized planning that can only sap the strength and vitality of an economy already under siege from a thou-

---

59. Older Workers Protection Act, P.L. no. 101-433, 29 *U.S.C.* §201 adds a new section 7 to the ADEA which provides that waivers of rights under the ADEA shall be regarded as "knowing and voluntary" only if they are in writing and specifically refer to the rights and claims that arise under the ADEA. In addition, the waiver cannot waive future claims, must afford new consideration for the waiver, and, most important, must allow the worker at least twenty-one days to consider the waiver agreement.

60. See, e.g., *Pension Benefit Guaranty Corp. v. R.A. Gray & Co.*, 467 U.S. 717 (1984); *Connolly v. Pension Benefit Guaranty Corp.*, 475 U.S. 211 (1986).

sand different government incursions. We may legislate in the name of human dignity. But by ignoring the constraints of scarcity and the problem of cost, we end up with a system of brokered political deals which in the long run impoverish us all and strip us of our dignity. The ADEA is a serious social mistake that should be repealed forthwith.

CHAPTER 22

Disability Discrimination

In this chapter I conclude my examination of the various forms of anti-discrimination laws by considering the desirability of restrictions and prohibitions on discrimination against disabled persons. The subject is one on which Congress has provided a major piece of legislation with the Americans with Disabilities Act of 1990 (ADA),[1] which ushers in an era of extensive regulation of both public accommodations and facilities (whether publicly or privately owned) and of the employment relationship.

The scope of the legislative initiative is somewhat difficult to determine because the exhaustive preliminary regulations issued under the statute do little to clarify the operative provisions of the statute, leaving its costs largely concealed from public view.[2] It seems clear, however, that the ADA will rescue the public accommodations component of the anti-discrimination laws from the sleepy fate they now enjoy under Title II of the 1964 act. Whereas there is normally little if any private reason for a common carrier or a public accommodation to *want* to discriminate on grounds of race or (subject to familiar limitations) sex, the same cannot be said of the ADA, which requires major expenditures with respect to trains, buses, airports, and all other forms of public facilities, to be financed out of general revenues rather than specific charges levied on disabled persons.[3]

1. Pub. Law. no. 101-336, 104 Stat. 327 (hereafter cited as ADA).

2. 29 C.F.R. 1630 (Equal Employment Opportunity for Individuals with Disabilities) (February 28, 1991). The regulations also contain an extensive effort to justify the statute in economic terms, citing the literature to Arrow, Becker, and others, much of which was discussed in Chapters 2 and 3. The regulations assume (wrongly) that all discrimination cuts in one direction and that there are no economic gains associated with various discriminatory practice. Also, it does not discuss the role of free entry in restraining limiting discrimination, and of course it contains no public choice analysis of the limitations of the legislative or administrative process and the ways in which these could go awry.

3. ADA, Title II, Public Services, and Title III, Public Services and Accommodations Operated by Private Entities.

The public accommodation obligations under the ADA lie outside the scope of this book, but the parallel provisions, regulating the employment relationship, go quickly to its core.[4] The statute imposes both general and specific obligations on employers in terms of the "reasonable accommodations" that must be made for persons with disabilities, and then sets out a limited defense based on the "undue hardship" associated with compliance.[5] The details of the statute require some particular comment, but analytically the first question is the same as that raised throughout this book: Why have an antidiscrimination provision with respect to disabilities at all?

A Problem for People of Two Minds

A sensible analytical approach to the question of disability discrimination is in one sense different from that in all the other forms of discrimination previously considered. With race and sex everyone knows his or her role at the outset. With age, one knows that although he is young today, he will (if he lives) be old tomorrow. With disabled persons, however, some people know that they are handicapped today; but, no matter how healthy we may be, we all know that through misfortune or ill health we could become handicapped tomorrow. There is thus a powerful insurance feature that leads everyone to think that some assistance for the disabled may not be solely an act of disinterested benevolence but one of prudent self-interest as well.

Given these dual motivations, the right analytical approach asks all persons to be of two minds behind the familiar veil of ignorance. In putting people behind the veil, we should not expect to see the same set of outcomes that arise when people *already* know whether they or their close relations suffer from some sort of disability. The world thus pits some people who know their interests against others who are uncertain as to their future needs. The pressure from the political arena leads to more public support for the handicapped than would occur if persons could take a disinterested attitude toward the subject. Suppose, for example, all members of society are healthy today, but that every person knows that he or she faces some chance of disability tomorrow. Would people as a class support societal assistance for the disabled, and (as a distinct question) would that aid include an antidiscrimination

4. ADA, Title I, Employment.
5. ADA, §101(9) (reasonable accommodation), and §101(10) (undue hardship).

norm that governs employment and other relations? Putting the two-part inquiry into that fashion requires each person to come face to face with four points that are frequently ignored. The neutral participant (that is, one ignorant of his future status) must consider at least these four factors:

First, the *probability* that any person will become disabled. The lower the chance of using the benefit, the weaker the case for having it. Prudent insurance for the individual depends on how common as well as how severe the risk is.

Second, the *alternative uses* of the same resources. Perhaps some resources are better spent in the *prevention* of handicaps than in palliating their effects once they occur. If we assume scarcity and limited budgets, no individual is able to purchase both prevention and palliation in unlimited quantities. The choice may be whether an individual wants, for example, a combined accident and disease rate of one in one thousand, with lots of care once disability occurs, or a risk rate of one in ten thousand, with less care if the disability occurs.

Third, the *correct level of support* once a person is disabled. In some cases small expenditures for the handicapped yield enormous benefits. But in other situations comparable expenditures produce only small net gains. Behind the veil of ignorance the prudent individual in the second kind of situation may choose to allocate the lion's share of resources for expenditures in the heathy state. The point is true even though overall utility is lower in the disabled state than it is in the healthy state, as long as the *marginal* benefit from any given expenditure is greater for persons who are healthy.[6] Thus, if welfare in the handicapped state is 10 and in the healthy state is 1,000, X dollars will be invested in the healthy state if it improves individual welfare by ten units provided that those same dol-

---

6. For a demonstration of the point in connection with damage actions for personal injury or wrongful death, see David D. Friedman, "What Is 'Fair Compensation' for Death or Injury?" 2 *Int'l. Rev. of Law & Econ.* 81 (1982). Friedman's point is that if the marginal value of money after injury is lower than it is before injury, the individual would never choose to spend money should sickness occur as long as he could spend it when well. That observation does not, however, call for the elimination of the tort system, given its deterrence function. To allow for optimal compensation and optimal deterrence, Friedman suggests allowing persons to *sell* their future tort claims to a third party. Whatever the practical and administrative objections to his proposal, his basic point remains correct. A healthy person today would not invest any of his own resources in care after injury *if* the marginal benefit from the first dollar in the injured state is lower than the marginal benefit of the last dollar in the healthy state.

lars would advance welfare in the handicapped state by only nine units, assuming that the two states have an equal probability of occurrence.[7]

The allocation of resources, therefore, between healthy and disabled states will not take place on an all-or-nothing basis, for the individual tradeoffs involved are quite difficult. Matters are of course made even harder when collective decisions must be reached when we know that different persons will attach different weights to the benefits and costs of being in these two states. No matter what the ultimate allocation decision, the total level of expenditures on the disabled would turn not on the terrible plight of being disabled, but on the improvement in their position that these expenditures can bring about. Even in the collective situation, small improvements from a very low base will be rejected in favor of far larger improvements from a higher base, at least by rational decision makers behind the veil.

Fourth, *the potential gains* from public regulation. Here the calculations are far from straightforward, for the baseline level of assistance in a voluntary market includes some private aid to the disabled. Most people know in their bones that they can and should make accommodations in their daily life to assist the handicapped. Indeed, I suspect that there are few if any businesses that on a voluntary basis have steadfastly refused as a matter of principle to make *any* accommodation for the disabled, either before or after the passage of the Rehabilitation Act of 1973, the initial federal legislative foray in this area. A helping hand or a kind word can go a long way in many contexts. It is false, therefore, to assume that disabled people will routinely meet uniform and stony hostility in all workplace situations. The very fact that most people have disabled friends and relatives generates a substantial level of empathy in its own right. In principle, everyone acknowledges the gains in terms of dignity if disabled people are able to participate in social life and occupy positions as useful and productive members of society. The only serious empirical question concerns the level of voluntary support relative to some social ideal, which has to take into account cost as well as benefit, scarcity as well as dignity. Everyone is involved in making that assessment, and the demands of the disabled as voiced in the political arena cannot be accepted as the appro-

---

7. Once the difference in probabilities is taken into account, the investments that must be made ex ante will be still more heavily inclined to the healthy state because the expected return is weighted by the probability of occurrence. Risk aversion will tend to work the balance back in the other direction, but it probably has a smaller effect on the overall decision.

priate benchmark of analysis. The antidiscrimination norm must generate an improvement over the preexisting state of affairs, not over an imaginary world in which disabled persons are always left to fend unsuccessfully for themselves.

When these four factors are taken into account, it is far from clear that a legally enforceable voluntary antidiscrimination norm would form *any* part of a comprehensive strategy. Enforcement costs money, and successful enforcement under the guise of "reasonable accommodation" necessarily impedes the operation and efficiency of firms. Since there must be a fixed budget for aiding the handicapped, the better strategy might well be to concentrate on programs that deal with rehabilitation, training, and counseling and direct assistance, rather than with coercion and litigation. Or alternatively, as I shall argue, it may be far better for the government to make *grants* to certain firms to allow them to offer employment to particular classes of disabled workers. There is nothing ironclad about these judgments, since much depends not only on the ends of the program but also on the details of its institutional design. But the closer look at the institutional framework of the antidiscrimination norm suggests that in this area it is singularly ill applied. My position at bottom is the same as elsewhere. The entire statutory scheme should be scrapped, even if expenditures for disabled persons under other programs remain constant or are increased.[8]

My opposition to the Americans with Disabilities Act, and to the Rehabilitation Act of 1973 before it, should not be construed to imply that disabled persons have not been subject to unfair treatment in the marketplace. They have been and are; but often the source of the unfairness does not lie in the inability of the handicapped to receive subsidies for work but in government interference with the control of their labor. Like everyone else, the disabled should be allowed to sell their labor at whatever price, and on whatever terms, they see fit. At this point disabled persons have just criticisms of the whole array of supposedly protective legislation that in fact limits their ability to negotiate on their own behalf: the minimum wage laws and various kinds of ostensible safety and health regulations can impose a greater burden on them than on others. Repeal

8. The 1989 figures revealed that about 30 billion dollars of public funds were spent on the disabled through disability insurance and supplemental social insurance, and a like figure through Medicare and Medicaid. See Carolyn Weaver, "Cross-Currents in Federal Disability Policy: Incentives vs. Controls," in *Disability and Work: Incentives, Rights, and Opportunities*, 95 n.2 (1991).

those laws as well. And beware of other forms of intervention. Some time ago I was called by a friend for some informal advice on aid to the disabled. He was on the board of an organization that worked with the handicapped on bidding for contracts from both public and private sources. His group's problems had arisen because rival unionized firms, who had lost some contracts, were pulling the various legal levers of the welfare state in order to defeat the "unfair" competition from his organization. His questions concerned the possible ways to combat those initiatives from within the system.

The exact nature of the problems are really not to the point, but the larger issue is of direct relevance. The American system works on the assumption that the only correction for one market imperfection is yet another market imperfection. Thus, if the disabled are not allowed to underbid their competition, they should be protected by an antidiscrimination law. But the two wrongs do not cancel; they cumulate. The same lesson that should have been learned from Jim Crow applies here: disguised subsidies do not cancel out explicit prohibitions. The best solution is always to repeal all legislation that interferes with market operations.

The dominant social view today rejects out of hand any return to a market solution. It treats all existing antidiscrimination regulation as sacrosanct and then demands that parallel protections be extended to the disabled, notwithstanding the far higher costs of compliance. The statutory scheme has never been effectively justified by an argument that starts from behind the veil of ignorance. Rather, the political debate usually begins with the assumption that Congress should do something to neutralize unthinking prejudice, archaic attitudes, arbitrary sentiments, and irrational preferences and perceptions.[9] To state the problem in this

9. See, e.g., ADA §2(a), Findings and Purposes: "Historically, society has tended to isolate and segregate individuals with disabilities, and, despite some improvements, such forms of discrimination against individuals with disabilities continue to be a serious and pervasive social problem.

"Individuals with disabilities are a discrete and insular minority who have been faced with restrictions and limitations, subject to a history of purposeful unequal treatment, and relegated to a position of political powerlessness in our society, based on characteristics that are beyond the control of such individuals and resulting from stereotypic assumptions not truly indicative of the individual ability of such individuals to participate in, and contribute to, society."

Similar attitudes influenced the adoption of the 1973 rehabilitations statute. "The amended definition [of a handicapped individual] reflected Congress's concern with pro-

fashion makes the solution apparent. If the practices attacked are irrational and arbitrary, then their defenders are little better. Why exhibit caution in the face of foolishness? Although this attitude has large political payoffs, it ignores all the complexities, outlined earlier, of formulating the optimal social response to the question of handicap. There is in fact another way, consistent with the veil of ignorance, to look at disability legislation that does not require us to adopt so harsh a judgment about common attitudes and common states of mind.

Having a disability is the source of an enormous level of personal loss. It requires extra effort just to tread water, and still more extraordinary effort to succeed against built-in deprivations The sympathies of most people go out to those with limitations. If it were just a question of whether one wishes success to those who labor under disability, the popular sentiment seems clear: their exploits are the source of admiration and amazement, and the subject of plays, stories, and movies that tug knowingly at the heartstrings. There are good reasons to read Ron Kovic's *Born on the Fourth of July* and to see Daniel Day Lewis as Christy Brown in *My Left Foot*. The entire apparatus of charitable giving and charitable service would be unintelligible if public attitudes were as harsh and archaic as Congress and the commentators so easily assume.

The losses that disabilities impose, however, are not restricted to people with handicaps. They also extend to those persons who have, or might have had, ongoing relationships, legal or social, with them. No comprehensive analysis can ignore those losses. Yet the rhetoric of the debate over the ADA sidestepped all these issues by calling this common sentiment irrational or arbitrary, effectively ignoring the unmistakable costs that other people bear in doing business with the disabled. Even if no one is at fault for X's disability, having to deal with X, given that disability, is costlier than having to deal with Y, who lacks that disability. Business is harder to conduct as the pace of transaction slows. Customers may find it inconvenient, unpleasant, or awkward to deal with persons who are deaf, blind, or palsied, or who have disfiguring marks or speech

---

tecting the handicapped against discrimination stemming not only from simple prejudice, but from 'archaic attitudes and laws' and from 'the fact that the American people are simply unfamiliar with and insensitive to the difficulties confront[ing] individuals with handicaps.'" Sen. Rep. no. 93-1297 at 50 (1974), quoted in *School Board of Nassau County, Florida v. Arline*, 480 U.S. 273, 279 (1987). The same theme is picked up in the academic literature as well. See, e.g., Judith Welch Wegner, "The Antidiscrimination Model Reconsidered: Ensuring Equal Opportunity without Respect to Handicap under Section 504 of the Rehabilitation Act of 1973," 69 *Cornell L. Rev.* 401 (1989).

impairments. Their preferences should not be blithely condemned as irrational, for in their own personal life they may have to cope with difficult emotional or family problems, face powerful time and budgetary constraints, or even cope with disabilities of their own. It is wishful idealization to assume that anyone who is not disabled has an infinite store of emotional energy available for public consumption. In some cases—many cases—it may still be worth doing business with the disabled, but the terms of trade may change; in other cases no deal will be possible. Even without legal controls it is hard to decide whether or not to go forward, whether to seek some voluntary accommodation, and if so, how to structure it.

In light of the business realities of the situation, the popular treatment of the disabled cannot simply be dismissed as prejudice or bigotry. There is no contradiction between refusing to hire disabled persons for certain jobs, while offering them others at lower wages, and simultaneously making generous gifts to a charitable organization that specializes in the rehabilitation of seriously handicapped children. In some contexts at least it is perfectly rational for someone to separate her charitable from her business affairs. That separation of functions has, moreover, at least this desirable social consequence: one can choose the object of her charitable ambitions by directing the gifts to those organizations for which she has the greatest affinity. It is a commonplace observation that most charity is not truly disinterested. If a family member suffers from multiple sclerosis, one is more likely to support an MS society than a cancer society.

The administrative costs of state coercion are always high, and promise to be especially so under the ADA. Freedom of association works because it means that both sides stand to gain from the transaction. Insisting that disabled individuals be accorded job opportunities that cost more than they are worth means that the mutual gain condition of voluntary contracts is no longer satisfied. If a plant is not already equipped with ramps and elevators, it may prove too costly to hire workers who can navigate only with motorized wheelchairs. But as long as there are other places for such people to work, why force the relationship? The basic logic against the antidiscrimination laws still holds: all persons can seek out those who promise them the best deals. They do not have to make do with the worst. But once coercion replaces informal accommodation, we should expect employers to take steps to minimize their losses, and public agencies to take steps to counteract that tendency, and for the cycle of evasion, resentment, and regulation to continue without closure. Whether we speak of race, sex, age, or disability, the antidiscrimination norm is simply another way of seizing partial control of a business from its firm managers and of forcing a redistribution of wealth off the public balance sheet. The risk of excessive enforcement is large when the associated costs are ignored or understated. It is simply not a sufficient condition for aid to the disabled to show that the benefits they (or some subgroup) derive from any social expenditure is positive. These benefits must also be larger than the associated costs, and these costs are ignored or systematically belittled under the ADA. Without cost there is no system of constraint, and no limit on natural ambition. The mismatch of cost and benefit is a fatal flaw of any antidiscrimination law for the handicapped.

The Statutory Scheme of Reasonable Accommodation

It is now useful to take a closer look at the basic statutory scheme under the ADA. Its key provision is patterned on Title VII and provides:

> No covered entity shall discriminate against a qualified individual with a disability because of the disability of such individual in regard to job application procedures, the hiring, advance, or discharge of employees, employee compensation, job training, and other terms, conditions, and privileges of employment.[10]

A "qualified" individual in turn is defined as "an individual with a disability who, with or without reasonable accommodation, can perform the essential functions of the employment position that such individual holds or desires."[11]

Unlike the earlier statutes on discrimination, the ADA does not leave the scope of its general antidiscrimination provision to chance or interpretation. Instead, its basic injunction is followed by detailed provisions that indicate the kinds of activities that should be regarded as discriminatory. The key features are difficult to summarize with precision, but they cover at least these situations: improper classification of jobs; improper utilization of standards, criteria, or methods of administration that have the effect of discriminating against disabled persons; taking into account the disabilities of persons who are related to the employee in deciding whether or not to offer a job or job benefits to any applicant; not making "reasonable" accommodations to workers who are "otherwise qualified" except where the employer can demonstrate that making the accommo-

10. ADA §102(a).
11. ADA §101(8).

dation imposes some "undue hardship" on the firm; using any employment standard, test, or other selection criterion that discriminates against the disabled persons unless that standard, test, or criterion "is shown to be job-related for the position in question and is consistent with business necessity"; and administering any medical examination or inquiry into the question of whether an applicant has a disability, or the extent of the disability that he or she has.

Central to this statutory scheme are two recurring core concepts—reasonable accommodation and undue hardship—and the definition of neither is left to chance in the statute. The actions covered by reasonable accommodation include:

(A) making existing facilities used by employees readily accessible to and usable by individuals with disabilities; and

(B) job restructuring, part-time or modified work schedules, reassignment to a vacant position, acquisition or modifications of equipment or devices, appropriate adjustment or modification of examinations, training materials or policies, the provision of qualified readers or interpreters, and other similar accommodations for individuals with disabilities.[12]

The definition of undue hardship is provided in similar fashion to cover "an action requiring significant difficulty or expense" in light of a list of enumerated factors that looks to the overall financial resources of both the particular facility and the firm that operates it, the costs of the adjustments made, and the nature and the type of operations that are conducted, and the impact of the expenditure on the operations of the facility in question.[13]

Several features of these companion provisions should be noted at the outset. First, precision and comprehensiveness move in only one direction—to list the factors that are relevant in making any particular determination. There is no effort to indicate the interrelations among the various factors, or to quantify the influence that any or all of them should have on the operation of the firm as a whole. Nor is there any explicit effort to coordinate the responses required in one case with those required in another. Given the basic structure of the statute, the increase in the number of factors only increases the uncertainty as to whether or not there is compliance in any individual case. Obviously the relevant

12. ADA §101(9).
13. ADA §101(10).

considerations on cost and accommodation cannot be be reduced to a formula of the sort that says "stop at red lights" or "pay your taxes in accordance with the rate structure found in Schedule X." But the utter want of precision is not treated, as it should be, as a reason for jettisoning the system altogether. Instead, it becomes a reason for committing enormous amounts of discretion within the system to the EEOC, to the attorney general, or to any private person with a grievance who wishes to bring an action for damages or an injunction under the statute.[14]

The difficulties involved in generating standards cannot be cured by issuing regulations, which will only hammer home a point implicit in the basic statutory structure—that larger and wealthier firms will be required to make more substantial accommodations than smaller operations[15]—an outcome that tracks the regulations issued to federal contractors under the Rehabilitation Act.[16] The Supreme Court learning under the Rehabilitation Act is scarcely more helpful, for it is confined to broad platitudes that only postpone the ultimate day of reckoning: "While a grantee need not be required to make 'fundamental' or 'substantial' modifications to accommodate the handicapped, it may be required to make 'reasonable' ones." The proper balance "requires that an otherwise qualified handicapped individual must be provided with meaningful access to the benefit that the grantee offers."[17] But beyond that point the harvest is scanty. Under the Rehabilitation Act the state may cut back its Medicaid coverage from twenty to fourteen days without running afoul of the statute.[18] A community college need not provide at its expense, and at the cost of the disruption of its teaching programs, a special personal assistant to a hearing-impaired person seeking to become a registered nurse if she could not satisfy licensing requirements for the position even with a degree.[19] If the easy cases, carefully selected, seem clear, thousands of harder cases will follow in their wake, virtually none of which will reach the august chambers of the Supreme Court.

The apparent guise of reasonableness in these intermediate cases can, however, conceal the steep social costs of mandated accommodation.

---

14. ADA §107(a). Section 107(b) calls for a coordination of remedies under this statute with those under the Rehabilitation Act of 1973.

15. Section 106 requires the EEOC to issue regulations to enforce the act, which goes into effect twenty-four months from the date of its passage, July 26, 1992.

16. See 5 C.F.R.

17. See *Alexander v. Choate*, 469 U.S. 287, 301 (1985).

18. Id. at 287.

19. *Southeastern Community College v. Davis*, 442 U.S. 397 (1979).

Suppose there are two positions available for a clerk, one of which involves working in a dangerous area, and the other of which allows work in a modern, safe office. If the ADA requires the employer of the first facility to modernize for handicapped clerks, then it requires social expenditures that could be avoided if the firm refused to hire the handicapped worker, who could always (perhaps at a somewhat lower wage) work at the other facility. It is far cheaper for workers to change positions than it is for every employer to redesign its workplace. The use of market forces therefore leads to some selection, specialization, and concentration of firms that hire handicapped workers. It is just those forms of economy that would appeal to people behind the veil of ignorance, so the market order once again promotes the public good. If there are a few firms that specialize in hiring workers with certain kinds of handicaps, the heavy front-end costs of designing and constructing specialized facilities and of providing specialized services can be spread over a large number of workers, which reduces the cost per individual worker and helps increase the wages that the firm is willing to pay. By this standard the proposed regime of mandated, universal access, however ardently championed by advocates of the disabled, represents unwise and indefensible social policy: by insisting that all businesses be open to all workers save in cases of exceptional expense or business necessity, the law again does its best to cripple the operation of employment markets. And by driving up the prices of finished goods, it hurts all persons, able and disabled alike, in their role as consumers. The irony here is especially broad, for in the effort to aid disabled persons who are able to work, the ADA necessarily increases the costs to those disabled persons (and their families) who are too impaired to work at all. These people will bear the costs of the statute while reaping none of its benefits. As with the other forms of the antidiscrimination laws, the ADA redistributes *within* the class of disabled persons as well as between the healthy and the disabled. The more stringent its commands, the greater its capricious effects.

The argument against the ADA is perfectly general. The explicit rejection of all market solutions means that the ADA imposes losses in dollar terms on employers that are greater than the gains received by the workers involved. Within this framework, "undue hardship" provisions of the ADA can be interpreted only as a vague injunction which says that the implicit subsidy need not continue when it becomes too expensive by a measure that it is impossible for anyone to articulate in advance of the fact. The actual interpretation and enforcement of the statute will determine the extent of the economic losses, but given the broad purposes of the act, and the concentration of enforcement powers in the EEOC, it is likely that the basic provisions will be broadly enforced and the limited exceptions to it narrowly construed. The only arguments are over the dimensions of the hidden subsidy and its incidence. There can be none over its existence.

One illustration should be sufficient to indicate the size of the implicit subsidies that are required under the ADA. As I have noted, the ADA makes it clear that an employer is not allowed to conduct any medical examination or make any inquiry into an applicant's medical condition in deciding whether to provide certain benefits to an insured. The ADA thus conclusively resolves a debate over whether an employer or its health insurer can ask a prospective job applicant whether he or she has AIDS (or indeed any other preexisting medical condition). The risk of AIDS, however, dominates any analysis of health or life insurance. By conventional analysis there is roughly a twenty-fivefold increase in mortality risk for any thirty-five-year-old carrier of the AIDS virus, which translates into a far higher multiple for health insurance.[20] It is thus simply ruinous to require any employer, as the ADA stipulates, to issue life and health insurance to HIV-positive workers (or even workers likely to become HIV-positive) on the same terms and conditions under which it issues insurance coverage to the rest of its work force. The magnitude of the risk is such that the premiums required to cover HIV-positive workers may well exceed the salaries they earn.

To insist on nondiscrimination forces the firm to adopt one of several unpalatable alternatives. First, it might decide to dispense with the insurance coverage altogether, which will disadvantage ordinary employees whose own risks are at satisfactory levels, and who prefer to receive insurance coverage (which is purchased more cheaply by a group than by the individual) to additional wages. Or the firm may seek to change its internal structure so that it needs to hire fewer workers from the high-risk groups; or it may seek to find new business locations where the work

---

20. See Russel P. Iuculano, *Life Insurance Issues in AIDS: Legal Complexities of a National Crisis,* 105, 107 (1987). Iuculano's estimates presuppose that only 25 percent of the antibody-positive carriers will develop the disease, but the percentage may well be higher, for there is no obvious sign yet that the AIDS virus loses its virulence with the passage of time. The Center for Disease Control has estimated a 50 percent conversion rate. In addition, the health costs for treating AIDS continue to rise with the increased medical expertise in prolonging life, which means that the medical expenses associated with the condition are likely to have above-average severity; thus the twenty-fivefold multiple is low for purposes of health insurance.

force has a low incidence of AIDS; or it may have to go out of business altogether. In the end, this pattern of antidiscrimination law may prove ruinous not only to the firms subject to the surcharges but also to the persons with AIDS who need assistance. If they were free to offer their services while waiving the right to health and life insurance, they would improve their prospects of getting a job without having to call into play the coercive power of the state. To be sure, a job without the insurance is far less desirable than a job with the insurance. But in many cases the use of the antidiscrimination law means that some AIDS carriers will have no job, with *no* pay and *no* insurance. As with minimum wage and other discrimination laws, the antidiscrimination rules are highly beneficial to some members of the protected class, but not to all.

The Grant Alternative

The drawbacks associated with the ADA should lead to a reconsideration of our ways of responding to the condition of the disabled. Even if a subsidy is to be provided, it ought to be provided in a way that allows its cost to be specified in advance, and that ensures the efficient expenditure of the money that is so provided. If some form of government intervention is required because disabled persons cannot afford to bear the full costs of their employment, federal *grants* can be made to particular firms, to be spent in making their facilities accessible to certain classes of disabled persons. Some plants could be made accessible to wheelchairs, others to the blind. But the political dynamics of the process under the grant system are wholly different from those under the system of regulation that is now in place. Under the ADA, Congress mandates a set of off-budget subsidies that are not explicitly taken into account in setting federal policy. The expenditures are borne by private firms and state and local governments, which are left to scramble for resources as best they can. By working through the regulatory mode Congress ensures the fatal separation of the right to order changes from the duty to pay for them.

In contrast, resorting to a system of federal grants undoes that fatal division. The government is then in the position of having to pick and choose the expenditures that it wants to make, while facing an explicit budget limitation at every step of the way. It must contend with many of the same constraints that are operative in ordinary markets. It will no longer insist that all facilities be accessible to all classes of disabled persons. Instead it will choose to concentrate its own resources in the places where they are apt to do the greatest amount of good. The concentration of workers with specific disabilities, far from being seen as handicap ghettoization, will be regarded as a sensible effort to economize on public funds. It will no longer be possible, moreover, to maintain the happy illusion that all disabled workers benefit from the operation of the grant program. Money that is spent on wheelchair access cannot be spent on the blind, and so on down the line. It will therefore become necessary to decide on how the pie, once allocated from general tax revenues, will be divided, a task that should test the diplomatic skills even of the most committed.

As applied to the AIDS illustration, the system of grants would work like this. Workers and employers could first price the health and/or life insurance plans for people with AIDS. Thereafter the employer picks up costs equal to those of similarly situated workers without the disease, and the rest of the coverage is paid for by the state out of general revenues, if it is appropriated under the grant program. At this point the social costs of caring for people with AIDS become explicit, and some hard choices will have to be confronted in a socially responsible way. Even if some support is given, it will be for more limited benefits than are obtainable under the current regulatory system, whereby Congress determines what others pay. The levels of care provided will have to be scaled down, given the public unwillingness to foot the bill. But that outcome is surely preferable to the present system, in which the costs associated with AIDS reform (like the hidden costs associated with price and rent controls) are left off the balance sheet, and as a result people vote for benefits without fully considering the associated costs.

The ADA contributes to that unsound public opinion by making it appear that all questions of cost, and all forms of opposition to aid for the disabled, are irrational. But the charge can be lodged more powerfully in the opposite direction. AIDS plays out the antidiscrimination game to its end. At bottom are only two pure forms of legislation—productive and redistributive. Antidiscrimination legislation is always of the second kind. The form of the redistribution is covert; it is capricious, it is expensive, and it is wasteful. The ADA fares no better than other forms of antidiscrimination laws, and perhaps worse. It too should be repealed, whether or not some subsidy for disabled persons is retained.

Conclusion:
Symbols and Substance

There seems to be little doubt that the civil rights movement is one of the most powerful political and social movements to surface in modern times. From its modest aspirations with the 1964 Civil Rights Act, it has continued to redefine its roles and to expand its goals, until today it represents a complete and consistent world view that permeates all areas of our collective social life. The imperialism of the movement is such that there is no issue within the realm of employment, and indeed within the larger realm of social endeavor, on which the civil rights laws do not exert a heavy, and baleful, influence. A movement with this power and this influence does not arise and flourish on the strength of political power or legal coercion alone. At some level it responds to deep-seated social conditions and powerful social symbols. In this short concluding chapter I draw together recurrent themes from the detailed critiques of the earlier chapters, and speak briefly of some of the verbal symbols that have been used to capture the spirit of the civil rights movement.

If there is one image that drives the movement it is the specter of exclusion on grounds of race and sex. It is the image of "no blacks or women allowed" prominently displayed in businesses and firms throughout the nation. There is a powerful belief that these practices are so odious and their consequences so devastating that we as a nation should be willing to pay a very high price for their elimination, and should not be reluctant to use state force in order to achieve that collective goal. Does a rejection of Title VII mean that whites should be allowed to refuse to deal with blacks and men with women? As stated, the question captures part of the issue but misses other aspects of equal importance. Thus the verb *mean* has two separate meanings. First, it could suggest that the two assertions are identical, and that only whites can discriminate against blacks and only men against women. But the repudiation of the antidiscrimination norm for private affairs does not carry that meaning. A second implication of the general rule is that blacks may refuse to deal with whites (or with other blacks), and women may refuse to deal with men (or with other women). The principle of formal equality of all persons is respected fully when the antidiscrimination principle is accepted. There is of course no *duty* on the part of any person to discriminate against any other person, and there are many situations in which the discrimination will not occur, if only because it is against the interests of the party that might engage in it.

It would be a mistake to insist that all forms of discrimination would disappear in a competitive marketplace. Nonetheless, the antidiscrimination law does not satisfy any condition of formal equality because some forms of discrimination are allowed while others are forbidden. It is possible for organizations to post signs that say "no whites admitted," or "no males admitted," and there is no question that the groups that post such signs believe themselves better able to achieve their collective goals and missions if those policies are observed. The nature of interactions among individuals depends heavily on who is present. The women and blacks who post these signs do not necessarily wish to cut off all contacts with men and with whites, but they do want to have a sanctuary of their own where they can discuss their common concerns about "them" with a level of candor they do not believe to be possible in mixed company. There are gains from having certain groups with select criteria for admission. But there is no reason to believe that people who join one exclusive group thereby insist that *all* groups in which they participate must operate under identical rules of selection.

Once we can see the benefits of exclusion for ourselves, we should be prepared to recognize that these could exist for other people as well, for they too have desires and needs that cannot always be satisfied in mixed groups. Coherence is necessary for the perpetuation and success of voluntary organizations. And exclusion underlies the success of most religious organizations, clubs, and businesses, indeed any organization that has criteria for admission that mark them off from common carriers. Given their ubiquity, the fear of exclusion should lose some of its sting, when it is recognized that the option should be available to all private groups, with no questions asked, and that the freedom to form additional groups leads to a broader range of opportunities across the board. It is not possible to create a world in which all people simultaneously have the right to join any organization that they choose and the right to keep others out of any organization that they form. The key question worth asking about the right to exclude in private settings is whether we are better off with its generalization or its repudiation. I can see no strong case for the latter.

The right to exclude, and the correlative rejection of the antidiscrimination principle, is not a license to kill or an invitation for abuse, insult, or defamation. It is part of the right to be left alone with the people of one's choice.

It will be argued that there are strong externalities from exclusion. Some will say, "I don't wish to live in a society in which other people practice exclusion on grounds of race or sex." But when that claim is made by those who are opposed to the current pattern of state-supported discrimination, they are told that the justifications for the existing practices outweigh any private regret they might feel. It is never explained why one set of needs may be fully satisfied while the other must go completely unanswered. It is very easy to develop rules that give us exactly what we want if the only preferences and desires that are taken into account are those of people with whom we agree on moral or political grounds. The problem of social governance, however, requires that we make peace not with our friends but with our enemies, and that can be done only if we show some respect for their preferences even when we detest them. Using the principle of exclusion allows both groups to go their separate ways side by side. The antidiscrimination laws force them into constant undesired interaction. The totalitarian implications become clear only when one realizes the excessive steps that must be taken to enforce the antidiscrimination principle in favor of some groups while it is overtly ignored relative to other groups. It is not the least of the ironies of the study of Title VII that it has brought in its wake more discrimination (and for less good purpose) than would exist in an unregulated system.

In part the explanation rests on the substantial weight often attached to symbols relative to other forms of gains and losses both for society as a whole and for the individuals who compose it. Thus it is frequently said that even if the employment discrimination laws do bring in their wake major economic dislocations, these costs should be cheerfully borne because they are more than offset by the substantial social and symbolic gains to the larger society. The initial difficulty with this position is that its defenders are no more skillful than its opponents in trading off symbolic losses against economic gains. How much of a symbolic gain is necessary to offset any economic loss? The paralysis induced by the broader analysis is one that infects both the supporters and the critics of the employment discrimination laws. If this were all that there was to the matter, then the best we could say was that there is some unfortunate standoff that advances the case for, even if it does not fully justify, the employment discrimination laws.

This ostensible tension between symbolic gains and economic losses itself seriously understates the difficulty of formulating any intelligent social policy based on the symbolic values of a society writ large. The major breakthrough of the economic analysis of social welfare rests mainly on the insight that the gains and losses to a society can be determined only by first calculating and then combining the gains and losses to its individual members. There are no shortcuts to the social interest that allows any analyst to avoid the inevitable difficulties that arise in implementing the enterprise. Does one measure wealth or utility? Can the gains to one person offset the losses to the next? Do sentiments of empathy or envy count? And so on. None of these difficulties with the aggregation problem are avoided when symbolic issues dominate the agenda. Just as with economic goods, determining social preferences from individual ones is easy only where there is *unanimous* agreement as to what the symbolic values are; and should that improbable state of affairs be achieved, it is likely that we could forge an equally strong consensus on the other economic and moral issues within the employment discrimination laws.

The critical problem, however, is that symbols also speak with many voices. To some an employment discrimination law that speaks of protected classes and affirmative action represents a strong social commitment to rectify the sins of the past, or a special solicitude for the concerns of the weakest and most disadvantaged among us. To those who are excluded or hurt by this body of rules, it could speak in a different voice—that of partisan politics and ordinary special-interest lobbying. To some who benefit economically by it, these policies are regarded as a backhanded insult, as an implicit statement by persons in power that women and minorities cannot today (and will not ever in the future) make it on their own. The civil rights law thus speaks of a perpetual state of dependence, of a group of people who need constant state intervention to redress what would otherwise be their permanent inferior status in the marketplace.

These variations can easily be expanded, and the richer the mosaic, the greater the difficulties. Symbols therefore offer no trump to normative analysis, for the national divisions on economic issues carry over to the symbolic realm as well. If there is no way to trade off symbolic issues against economic ones, neither is there any easy way to trade off symbol against symbol, or different symbolic views of the same legal rules against one another. Given the limits of our own knowledge, I believe that the best way to take into account the full range of symbols, good and bad, noble and vain, is for the legal system to *ignore* them all—mine and yours alike. The symbols that then will prevail are those that can garner the highest level of support in the population at large. No one's symbolic aspirations can be achieved by passing laws that force others to adhere to a set of symbolic meanings and understandings they do not accept. Our strong tradition of freedom of speech, which allows persons to say thoughtless and hurtful things about the symbols held dear by others— think only of the flag-burning cases—is eminently defensible even though these hurts are real to the persons who bear them. The decision to keep off represents a profound social judgment that the business of weighing and trading symbolic meanings is one in which the state should never inject its collective judgment. What is true about speech itself should carry over to other laws, even those with manifest symbolic import. Their adoption or rejection should depend on their capacity to allow individuals to develop a sphere of personal control in which they can lead their own lives. Symbols are, in a sense, too important and too volatile to be either the subject of, or the justification for, direct government regulation.

This position leaves me securely outside the mainstream. The success and dangers of the modern civil rights movement rest in part on the elaborate set of social symbols and meanings that have allowed it to achieve its current dominance. Identifying these symbols reveals, however, a persistent ironic pattern. The most powerful symbols of the civil rights movement often make an implicit appeal to the libertarian tradition of private property and limited government that is in reality the polar opposite of its substantive positions. The dominant language of the modern civil rights movement allows it to draw its symbolic strength from the very principles of the legal order that it has come to undermine.

The first of the critical terms here is of course *civil rights* itself. In its original conception the term referred to civil capacity to contract, to own property, to make wills, to give evidence, and to sue and be sued. These are rights all individuals can enjoy simultaneously against the state and against one another. Their accurate definition and faithful protection is indispensable for any regime of limited government and individual freedom, and for all persons regardless of race, creed, religion, sex, or national origin. The great tragedy of the American experience with segregation was that our nation lost sight of that principle, and substituted an expansive regime of government activity, constitutionally sanctioned under the police power, which injected government influence and government favoritism into every transaction. Private markets respond to the external structures within which they operate; often in the past they took the path of least resistance and adopted explicit discriminatory practices that reflected these external constraints. To the extent that the civil rights movement is dedicated to the elimination of these formal and coercive barriers to entry, there is no conflict between civil rights in its traditional sense and civil rights in its modern incarnation.

Victory on this front was slow in coming, but it was achieved during the period culminating in passage of the Civil Rights Act of 1964. At that time, however, the movement changed its objectives, and civil rights changed its meaning. In the modern context it has become become a term that refers to limits on freedom of association. It has thus repeated the fundamental official mistake of earlier generations by sanctioning active and extensive government interference in private markets. Civil rights quickly assumed an imperial air. It now allows the state (or some group within the state) to force others to enter into private arrangements that they would prefer to avoid. Although the traditional use of the police power allowed certain associations and exchanges to be forced, as with innkeepers and common carriers, it was always understood that this limitation on liberty was a way to diffuse the exercise of monopoly power, and it was subject to quid pro quo in that the party so regulated remained entitled, even as a matter of constitutional principle, to earn a just rate of return on its investment after the imposition of government restraint.

The modern civil rights movement cares little about the overall allocative consequences of its intervention, and often proceeds as if the misallocations that it brings about simply did not exist at all. It redescribes the patterns of routine business operations. If one assumes that firms are not moderately rational in the way in which they make their employment decisions, there is little efficiency cost to government interference that forces firms to restructure the way in which they do business. Similarly, if all firms are more or less homogeneous in their internal composition and identical in their internal modes of operation, then all firms can adapt equally well to a single and rigid system of external regulation, such as that propounded under modern civil rights legislation. Reliable enforcement of a system can then come at reasonably low cost. Finally, if quality differences between employees are, regardless of circumstances and roles, regarded as trivial, there is little net loss to the firm from the legislative limitation on its common law power to hire and fire. The gains from substituting one worker for another are thought to be small enough that productivity will not suffer. It is as though all choices were between productivity differentials of one or two points rather than large magnitudes and there were no high costs from subjecting all personnel decisions to external review.

This approach to business does have its high costs. Progress in business often comes from the cumulation of small edges and incremental advantages brought about by persons with extensive local knowledge. Imperfect information—hunch, intuition, experience—is often all that we have, and it is surely better than no information at all. But it is the kind of information that is greeted with scorn and hostility in the enforcement of a civil rights law that demands the highest level of proof to justify existing business practices that have survived in the market, while offering no proof that its own prescriptions will have their desired effects, or will do so at reasonable cost. Modern civil rights enforcement is thus legitimated because its defenders have flattened the world in order to reduce the apparent costs of regulation.

The civil rights movement has also changed its measures of social success and failure. Its mission today is defined not in terms of any overall standard of social welfare that takes into account the preferences and desires of all persons within society, but solely in terms of the various classes of protected parties. The refusal to take into account wide ranges of consumer preference is but one illustration of how certain individual losses are simply written off the ledger in the name of civil rights enforcement. Although the movement speaks in terms of rights, it suppresses the question of correlative duties, and of overall economic effect. In practice the antidiscrimination laws impose an elaborate set of disguised subsidies, and these distort resource allocation just like any other sort of subsidies. The civil rights statutes are not exempt from the usual critiques of wage and price regulation that point out their unresponsiveness to changes in supply, demand, and external circumstances. There is no reason to believe that in this area, unlike any other, we can be confident that the wisdom and self-restraint of government administrators will limit the excesses of the law. To the contrary, aggressive enforcement is the norm, a norm that is encouraged by the belief that certain losses do not count because they are borne by persons whose preferences do not count.

Civil rights is not the only term that has been ripped from its original libertarian moorings. We are often told that the goal of the civil rights movement is *diversity*. Diversity as it is traditionally understood means that no one should put all his or her eggs into a single basket. Invest in a broad-based fund and not in a single stock in order to diversify your losses and gains. The very term speaks of a toleration of differences and of a willingness to allow other individuals, or other institutions, to go their separate ways when they do not agree with you. With respect to government, diversity speaks of the importance of decentralization in the control of decision-making power, and necessarily directs us to limitations on government authority.

Within the modern civil rights discourse, however, diversity does not have that defensive orientation. Instead, it becomes yet another buzzword in the campaign for political conformity to a state-imposed ideal. Institutions that do not hire the right number of women or minorities are deemed to be not politically correct; therefore they should be exposed to government action, be it by private suit for discrimination, by enforcement actions from the EEOC, or by being hauled before accreditation committees. Unpacked, diversity today amounts to little more than a call for race-conscious and sex-conscious hiring, and in some circumstances even the more extreme position of proportionate representation by race and by sex. In the name of diversity all institutions have to follow the same policies or face the wrath of the state. A true sense of diversity would allow different institutions to explore different policies with respect to race and sex, including a color-blind and sex-blind policy, so often dismissed as a naive anachronism championed only by those who are ignorant of the sordid truth of the American past. But institutional diversity is not what is meant. Institutional rigidity is what is required in the name of diversity.

The call for diversity rests in large measure on the capacity of a new elite to tell the difference between invidious and benevolent forms of discrimination. Whereas the older common law rules stressed the need to set fixed and clear boundaries that established a perimeter of rights within which individuals could create their own autonomous systems, the newer rules make the *motive* from which acts are performed critical in the assessment of their legality. Yet we should always beware of claims of benevolence made in the political context. Even if certain practices are introduced from benevolent motives, the forces of individual self-interest and political action are never far from the scene, and these can easily become dominant no matter how lofty and disinterested the rationale of some defenders of the new practice. The durability of political institutions rests on their ability to resist domination by a few, and no test of good and motive is likely to prove strong enough over the long haul to resist the ravages of self-interest. The claims for diversity may properly be taken into account within private institutions, which can give them great weight if they so choose. But they offer no justification for any system of external coercion or state control. The presumption of distrust should always accompany the use of coercion, and that lesson too has been forgotten in the enforcement of the civil rights laws.

The drive for institutional conformity is further buttressed by pointing to practices of unconscious racism or sexism, which it is said must be rooted out at all costs. But there is scant recognition that much of today's underground resentment of the civil rights movement arises from the conscious racism and sexism that is so visible, powerful, and formalized in modern institutions. Freudian sophistication and Freudian naiveté go hand in hand. People who are quick to impugn the motives and the integrity of others, to find racial or sexual innuendo in innocent and everyday actions and speech, find it all too easy to make race and sex the dominant if not the sole determinants of their institutional decisions. It is as though unconscious racism and sexism were said to justify the formal, explicit, and conscious racism and sexism that so often run the other way. Anyone who works in academic circles, and I dare say elsewhere, knows full well that *all* the overt and institutional discrimination comes from those who claim to be the victims of discrimination imposed by others. It is a sad day when any effort to defend the traditional norms of a discipline, profession, trade, or craft exposes the defender to withering political attack for a covert form of discrimination under the guise of excellence and neutral standards. In all too many cases honorable people are attacked as racist or sexist when the charges often apply with far greater truth to the persons who make these charges than to the persons about whom they are made.

The appeal to unconscious racism is backed up by other powerful notions, which have no libertarian underpinnings. One of these is the condemnation of racial and sexual stereotypes. But the definition of *stereotype* does not refer solely to *false* generalizations about any group of persons. It refers as well to *true* generalizations. But lest one learn to accept and to live with the important differences between groups and individuals, we must dismantle other features of our common social life. The antidiscrimination laws thus play havoc with the use of any standard insurance principles, whether they deal with longevity or health, or any other aspect of human behavior. In a similar vein the antidiscrimination laws lead to a systematic Orwellian campaign of disinformation. One is not allowed to ask about age, about prior disability or handicap, about marital status, about individual abilities. Tests that have modest predictive value are rejected in favor of universal generalizations that have no predictive value at all. And this systematic campaign to discredit accurate statistical generalizations is punctuated by the self-congratulatory pronouncement that we have done all this not for our benefit but for yours. The current legislative view is that perfect information may be used (precisely because it can never be acquired), but nothing less will do.

This constant attack on statistical methods and insurance rests on a larger view of culture that is doubtless false as well. We are constantly instructed that differences between the sexes and among the various races are always *socially constructed*. The use of the term *gender* instead of *sex* is an effort to make it appear as though the differences between the sexes were mere accidents of biology that have no social relevance in employment settings and no long-term consequences for the welfare of either men or women. Similarly, differences along racial, ethnic, or religious lines are regarded as superficial and transient, so persons are to be treated as perfectly fungible with one another—unless, of course, the appeal to these same differences is made on behalf of, if not by, persons who fall into the appropriate protected categories. Then the differences are always relevant if not decisive.

It is difficult to see how discourse can go on in the present circumstances, when the use of language so constrains the nature of the debate that it is quite impossible to have an honest dialogue about the costs and benefits that derive from the present civil rights law. In the civil rights literature there is but scant, passing reference to intellectual excellence, personal dedication, effort, entrepreneurial zeal. It is as though all benefits were a result of luck or impersonal social forces, and none the result of intelligence, initiative, creativity, or plain hard work. One hears only constant complaints about why it is that some vague set of external forces, far short of state coercion and power, holds large classes of persons in its thrall. There is a pervasive ethos of victimology, and an eagerness to destroy standards, to make excuses. Taken together, the defeatist attitude and the lack of self-esteem sap the individual self-reliance that is necessary to ensure the safety and prosperity of a free and self-reliant nation.

A strong undercurrent today suggests that something has gone badly amiss with the civil rights law, that a great cause has become diverted from its central mission, that its excesses have overwhelmed its virtues. People are uneasy about the reach of the disparate impact tests in race and sex cases; they are troubled by the impact of the law on pensions and insurance; they think that a kind word could be said for mandatory retirement; they fret over the high costs associated with complying with rules for disabled employees. But they insist on finding small causes for their uneasiness. They seek errors in application, some explanation of how it is that sound principles have somehow gone awry.

My own examination of the subject has convinced me that the difficulties are far more fundamental. The root difficulty of the statute is that it maintains that a qualified norm of forced association is better than a strong norm of freedom of association. It is dangerous to assume that whatever conduct is thought to be wise or enlightened can and should be forced on society by the public speaking with one voice. There is little understanding of why the proscribed differences might matter, and little appreciation of the enormous political risks that come with concentrating power over employment decisions in the hands of a bureaucracy that operates under its own set of expansionist imperatives. There is also a failure to understand that the first question that should be asked in any public debate is *who* shall decide, not *what* should be decided. On the question of association, the right answer is the private persons who may (or may not) wish to associate, and not the government or the public at large. But having given the wrong collective answer to the "who" question, we find the "what" question receiving an extended elaboration that has resulted in the extensive and disruptive coercive structure that is civil rights enforcement today. More than I had anticipated, my study of the employment discrimination laws has persuaded me of the bedrock social importance of the principles of individual autonomy and freedom of association. Their negation through the modern civil rights law has led to a dangerous form of government coercion that in the end threatens to do more than strangle the operation of labor and employment markets. The modern civil rights laws are a new form of imperialism that threatens the political liberty and intellectual freedom of us all.

Appendix of Statutory Excerpts

Equal Pay Act (1963)

29 U.S.C.A. §206(d)

§206(d) Prohibition of Sex Discrimination

(1) No employer having employees subject to any provisions of this section shall discriminate, within any establishment in which such employees are employed, between employees on the basis of sex by paying wages to employees in such establishment at a rate less than the rate at which he pays wages to employees of the opposite sex in such establishment for equal work on jobs the performance of which requires equal skill, effort, and responsibility, and which are performed under similar working conditions, except where such payment is made pursuant to (i) a seniority system; (ii) a merit system; (iii) a system which measures earnings by quantity or quality of work; or (iv) a differential based on any other factor other than sex; *Provided*, That an employer who is paying a rate differential in violation of this subsection shall not, in order to comply with the provisions of this subsection, reduce the wage rate of any employee.

(3) For Purposes of Administration and enforcement, any amounts owing to any employee which have been withheld in violation of this subsection shall be deemed to be unpaid minimum wages or unpaid overtime compensation under this Act.

29 U.S.C. §216 Remedies [§16(b) of Fair Labor Standards Act of 1938, as Amended]

(b) Any employer who violates the provisions of section 206 or section 207 of this title shall be liable to the employee or employees affected in the amount of their unpaid minimum wages, or their unpaid overtime compensation, as the case may be, and in an additional equal amount as liquidated damages.

Civil Rights Act of 1964

42 U.S.C. §2003 et seq.

§701 Definitions

(k) The terms "because of sex" or "on the basis of sex" include, but are not limited to, because of or on the basis of pregnancy, childbirth, or related medical conditions; and women affected by pregnancy, childbirth, or related medical conditions shall be treated the same for all employment-related purposes, including receipt of benefits of fringe benefit programs, as other persons not so affected but similar in their ability or inability to work, and nothing in section 703(h) shall be interpreted to permit otherwise.

§703 Discrimination Because of Race, Color, Religion, Sex, or National Origin

(a) Employers. It shall be an unlawful employment practice for an employer—
   (1) to fail or refuse to hire or to discharge any individual, or otherwise to discriminate against any individual with respect to his compensation, terms, conditions, or privileges of employment, because of such individual's race, color, religion, sex, or national origin; or
   (2) to limit, segregate, or classify his employees or applicants for employment in any way which would deprive or tend to deprive any individual of employment opportunities or otherwise adversely affect his status as an

employee, because of such individual's race, color, religion, sex, or national origin.

(c) Labor organization. It shall be an unlawful employment practice for a labor organization—

(1) to exclude or to expel from its membership, or otherwise to discriminate against, any individual because of his race, color, religion, sex, or national origin;

(2) to limit, segregate, or classify its membership or applicants for membership, or to classify or fail or refuse to refer for employment any individual, in any way which would deprive or tend to deprive any individual of employment opportunities, or would limit such employment opportunities or otherwise adversely affect his status as an employee or as an applicant for employment, because of such individual's race, color, religion, sex, or national origin; or

(3) to cause or attempt to cause an employer to discriminate against an individual in violation of this section.

(d) Training programs. It shall be an unlawful employment practice for any employer, labor organization, or joint labor-management committee controlling apprenticeship or other training or retraining, including on-the-job training programs, to discriminate against any individual because of his race, color, religion, sex, or national origin in admission to, or employment in, any program established to provide apprenticeship or other training.

(e) Religion, sex, or national origin as bona fide occupational qualification; educational institutions with employees of particular religions. Notwithstanding any other provision of this title (1) it shall not be an unlawful employment practice for an employer to hire and employ employees, for an employment agency to classify, or refer for employment any individual, for a labor organization to classify its membership or to classify or refer for employment any individual, or for an employer, labor organization, or joint labor-management committee controlling apprenticeship or other training or retraining programs to admit or employ any individual in any such program, on the basis of his religion, sex, or national origin in those certain instances where religion, sex, or national origin is a bona fide occupational qualification reasonably necessary to the normal operation of that particular business or enterprise . . .

(h) Seniority or merit system; ability tests. Notwithstanding any other provision of this title it shall not be an unlawful employment practice for an employer to apply different standards of compensation, or different terms, conditions, or privileges of employment pursuant to a bona fide

seniority or merit system, or a system which measures earnings by quantity or quality of production or to employees who work in different locations, provided that such differences are not the result of an intention to discriminate because of race, color, religion, sex, or national origin, nor shall it be an unlawful employment practice for an employer to give and to act upon the results of any professionally developed ability test provided that such test, its administration or action upon the results is not designed, intended or used to discriminate because of race, color, religion, sex or national origin. It shall not be an unlawful employment practice under this title for any employer to differentiate upon the basis of sex in determining the amount of the wages or compensation paid or to be paid to employees of such employer if such differentiation is authorized by the provisions of section 6(d) of the Fair Labor Standards Act of 1938, as amended.

(j) Preferential treatment not required on account of numerical or percentage imbalance. Nothing contained in this title shall be interpreted to require any employer, employment agency, labor organization, or joint labor-management committee subject to this title to grant preferential treatment to any individual or to any group because of the race, color, religion, sex, or national origin of such individual or group on account of an imbalance which may exist with respect to the total number or percentage of persons of any race, color, religion, sex, or national origin employed by an employer, referred or classified for employment by any employment agency or labor organization, admitted to membership or classified by any labor organization, or admitted to, or employed in, any apprenticeship or other training program, in comparison with the total number or percentage of persons of such race, color, religion, sex, or national origin in any community, State, section, or other area, or in the available work force in any community, State, section, or other area.

(k)(1)(A) An unlawful employment practice based on disparate impact is established under this title only if—

> (i) a complaining party demonstrates that a respondent uses a particular employment practice that causes a disparate impact on the basis of race, color, religion, sex, or national origin and the respondent fails to demonstrate that the challenged practice is job related for the position in question and consistent with business necessity; or

> (ii) the complaining party makes the demonstration described in subparagraph (C) with respect to an alternative employment practice and the respondent refuses to adopt such alternative employment practice.

(B)(i) With respect to demonstrating that a particular employment practice causes a disparate impact as described in subparagraph (A)(i), the complaining party shall demonstrate that each particular challenged employment practice causes a disparate impact, except that if the complaining party can demonstrate to the court that the elements of respondent's decisionmaking process are not capable of separation for analysis, the decisionmaking process may be analyzed as one employment practice.

(ii) If the respondent demonstrates that a specific employment practice does not cause the disparate impact, the respondent shall not be required to demonstrate that such practice is required by business necessity.

(C) The demonstration referred to by subparagraph (A)(ii) shall be in accordance with the law as it existed on June 4, 1989, with respect to the concept of alternative employment practice .

(2) A demonstration that an employment practice is required by business necessity may not be used as a defense against a claim of intentional discrimination under this title.

(*l*) It shall be an unlawful employment practice for a respondent, in connection with the selection or referral of applicants or candidates for employment or promotion, to adjust the scores of, use different cutoff scores for, or otherwise alter the results of, employment related tests on the basis of race, color, religion, sex, or national origin.

(*m*) Except as otherwise provided in this title, an unlawful employment practice is established when the complaining party demonstrates that race, color, religion, sex, or national origin was a motivating factor for any employment practice, even though other factors also motivated the practice.

§706 Enforcement Provisions

(g)(1) If the court finds that the respondent has intentionally engaged in or is intentionally engaging in an unlawful employment practice charged in the complaint, the court may enjoin the respondent from engaging in such unlawful employment practice, and order such affirmative action as may be appropriate, which may include, but is not limited to, reinstatement or hiring of employees, with or without back pay . . . or any other equitable relief as the court deems appropriate. Back pay liability shall not accrue from a date more than two years prior to the filing of a charge with the Commission. Interim earnings or amounts earnable with reasonable diligence by the person or persons discriminated against shall operate to reduce the back pay otherwise allowable.

(2)(A) No order of the court shall require the admission or reinstatement of an individual as a member of a union, or the hiring, reinstatement, or promotion of an individual as an employee, or the payment to him of any back pay, if such individual was refused admission, suspended, or expelled, or was refused employment or other advancement or was suspended or discharged for any reason other than discrimination on account of race, color, religion, sex, or national origin.

(B) On a claim in which an individual proves a violation under section 703(m) and a respondent demonstrates that the respondent would have taken the same action in the absence of the impermissible motivating factor, the court—

(i) may grant declaratory relief, injunctive relief (except as provided in clause (ii)), and attorney's fees and costs demonstrated to be directed attributable only to the pursuit of a claim under section 703(m); and

(ii) shall not award damages or issue an order requiring any admission, reinstatement, hiring, promotion or payment, described in subparagraph (A).

Age Discrimination in Employment Act of 1967

29 U.S.C. §621 et seq.

§2 Congressional Statement of Findings and Purpose

(a) The Congress hereby finds and declares that—

(1) in the face of rising productivity and affluence, older workers find themselves disadvantaged in their efforts to retain employment, and especially to regain employment when displaced from jobs;

(2) the setting of arbitrary age limits regardless of potential for job performance has become a common practice, and certain otherwise desirable practices may work to the disadvantage of older persons;

(3) the incidence of unemployment, especially long-term unemployment with resultant deterioration of skill, morale, and employer acceptability is,

relative to the younger ages, high among older workers; their numbers are great and growing; and their employment problems grave;

(4) the existence in industries affecting commerce, of arbitrary discrimination in employment because of age, burdens commerce and the free flow of goods in commerce.

(b) It is therefore the purpose of this Act to promote employment of older persons based on their ability rather than age; to prohibit arbitrary age discrimination in employment; to help employers and workers find ways of meeting problems arising from the impact of age on employment.

§4 Prohibition of Age Discrimination

(a) Employer practices. It shall be unlawful for an employer—

(1) to fail or refuse to hire or to discharge any individual or otherwise discriminate against any individual with respect to his compensation, terms, conditions, or privileges of employment, because of such individual's age;

(2) to limit, segregate, or classify his employees in any way which would deprive or tend to deprive any individual of employment opportunities or otherwise adversely affect his status as an employee, because of such individual's age; or

(3) to reduce the wage rate of any employee in order to comply with this Act.

(f) Lawful practices; age an occupational qualification; other reasonable factors; seniority system; employee benefit plans; discharge or discipline for good cause. It shall not be unlawful for an employer, employment agency, or labor organization—

(1) to take any action otherwise prohibited under subsections (a), (b), (c), or (e) of this section where age is a bona fide occupational qualification reasonably necessary to the normal operation of the particular business, or where the differentiation is based on reasonable factors other than age, or . . .

(2) to take any action otherwise prohibited under subsection (a), (b), (c), or (e) of this section—

(A) to observe the terms of a bona fide seniority system that is not intended to evade the purposes of this Act, except that no such seniority system shall require or permit the involuntary retirement of any individual specified by section 12(a) because of the age of such individual; or

(B) to observe the terms of a bona fide employee benefit plan—

(i) where, for each benefit or benefit package, the actual amount of payment made or cost incurred on behalf of an older worker is no less than that made or incurred on behalf of a younger worker, as permissible under section 1625.10, title 29, Code of Federal Regulations (as in effect on June 22, 1989); or

(ii) that is a voluntary early retirement incentive plan consistent with the relevant purpose or purposes of this Act. Notwithstanding clause (i) or (ii) of subparagraph (B), no such employee benefit plan or voluntary early retirement incentive plan shall excuse the failure to hire any individual, and no such employee benefit plan shall require or permit the involuntary retirement of any individual specified by section 12(a).

§12 Age Limits

(a) The prohibitions in this chapter shall be limited to individuals who are at least 40 years of age.

(c) (1) Nothing in this chapter shall be construed to prohibit compulsory retirement of any employee who has attained 65 years of age and who, for the 2-year period immediately before retirement, is employed in a bona fide executive or high policymaking position, if such employee is entitled to an immediate nonforfeitable annual retirement benefit from a pension, profit-sharing, savings, or deferred compensation plan, or any combination of such plans, of the employer of such employee, which equals in the aggregate, at least $44,000.

(d) Nothing in this chapter shall be construed to prohibit compulsory retirement of any employee who has attained 70 years of age, and who is serving under a contract of unlimited tenure (or similar arrangement provided for unlimited tenure) at an institution of higher education. [Effective until December 31, 1993.]

Americans with Disabilities Act of 1990

42 U.S.C. 12101 et seq.

§2 Findings and Purposes

(a) Findings.—The Congress finds that—

(1) some 43,000,000 Americans have one or more physical or mental disabilities, and this number is increasing as the population as a whole is growing older;

(2) historically, society has tended to isolate and segregate individuals with disabilities, and, despite some improvements, such forms of discrimination against individuals with disabilities continue to be a serious and pervasive social problem;

(3) discrimination against individuals with disabilities persists in such critical areas as employment, housing, public accommodations, education, transportation, communication, recreation, institutionalization, health services, voting, and access to public services;

(4) unlike individuals who have experienced discrimination on the basis of race, color, sex, national origin, religion, or age, individuals who have experienced discrimination on the basis of disability have often had no legal recourse to redress such discrimination;

(5) individuals with disabilities continually encounter various forms of discrimination, including outright intentional exclusion, the discriminatory effects of architectural, transportation, and communication barriers, overprotective rules and policies, failure to make modifications to existing facilities and practices, exclusionary qualification standards and criteria, segregation, and relegation to lesser services, programs, activities, benefits, jobs, or other opportunities;

(6) census data, national polls, and other studies have documented that people with disabilities, as a group, occupy an inferior status in our society, and are severely disadvantaged socially, vocationally, economically, and educationally;

(7) individuals with disabilities are a discrete and insular minority who have been faced with restrictions and limitations, subjected to a history of purposeful unequal treatment, and relegated to a position of political powerlessness in our society, based on characteristics that are beyond the control of such individuals and resulting from stereotypic assumptions not truly indicative of the individual ability of such individuals to participate in, and contribute to, society;

(8) the Nation's proper goals regarding individuals with disabilities are to assure equality of opportunity, full participation, independent living, and economic self-sufficiency for such individuals; and

(9) the continuing existence of unfair and unnecessary discrimination and prejudice denies people with disabilities the opportunity to compete on an equal basis and to pursue those opportunities for which our free society is justifiably famous, and costs the United States billions of dollars in unnecessary expenses resulting from dependency and nonproductivity.

(b) Purpose.—It is the purpose of this Act—

(1) to provide a clear and comprehensive national mandate for the elimination of discrimination against individuals with disabilities;

(2) to provide clear, strong, consistent, enforceable standards addressing discrimination against individuals with disabilities;

(3) to ensure that the Federal Government plays a central role in enforcing the standards established in this Act on behalf of individuals with disabilities; and

(4) to invoke the sweep of congressional authority, including the power to enforce the fourteenth amendment and to regulate commerce, in order to address the major areas of discrimination faced day-to-day by people with disabilities.

Title I—Employment

Section 101. Definitions.

As used in this title:

(8) Qualified Individual with a Disability.—The term "qualified individual with a disability" means an individual with a disability who, with or without reasonable accommodation, can perform the essential functions of the employment position that such individual holds or desires. For the purposes of this title, consideration shall be given to the employer's judgment as to what functions of a job are essential, and if an employer has prepared a written description before advertising or interviewing applicants for the job, this description shall be considered evidence of the essential functions of the job.

(9) Reasonable Accommodation.—The term "reasonable accommodation" may include

(A) making existing facilities used by employees readily accessible to and usable by individuals with disabilities; and

(B) job restructuring, part-time or modified work schedules, reassignment to a vacant position, acquisition or modification of equipment or devices, appropriate adjustment or modifications of examinations, training materials or policies, the provision of qualified readers or interpreters, and other similar accommodations for individuals with disabilities.

(10) Undue Hardship.—

(A) In General.—The term "undue hardship" means an action requiring significant difficulty or expense, when considered in light of the factors set forth in subparagraph (B).

(B) Factors to be Considered.—In determining whether an accommoda-

tion would impose an undue hardship on a covered entity, factors to be considered include—

(i) the nature and cost of the accommodation needed under this Act;

(ii) the overall financial resources of the facility or facilities involved in the provision of the reasonable accommodation; the number of persons employed at such facility; the effect on expenses and resources, or the impact otherwise of such accommodation upon the operation of the facility;

(iii) the overall financial resources of the covered entity; the overall size of the business of a covered entity with respect to the number of its employees; the number, type, and location of its facilities; and

(iv) the type of operation or operations of the covered entity, including the composition, structure, and functions of the workforce of such entity; the geographic separateness, administrative, or fiscal relationship of the facility or facilities in question to the covered entity.

Section 102. Discrimination.

(a) General Rule.—No covered entity shall discriminate against a qualified individual with a disability because of the disability of such individual in regard to job application procedures, the hiring, advancement, or discharge of employees, employee compensation, job training, and other terms, conditions, and privileges of employment.

(b) Construction.—As used in subsection (a), the term "discriminate" includes—

(1) limiting, segregating, or classifying a job applicant or employee in a way that adversely affects the opportunities or status of such applicant or employee because of the disability of such applicant or employee;

(2) participating in a contractual or other arrangement or relationship that has the effect of subjecting a covered entity's qualified applicant or employee with a disability to the discrimination prohibited by this title (such relationship includes a relationship with an employment or referral agency, labor union, an organization providing fringe benefits to an employee of the covered entity, or an organization providing training and apprenticeship programs);

(3) utilizing standards, criteria, or methods of administration—

(A) that have the effect of discrimination on the basis of disability; or

(B) that perpetuate the discrimination of others who are subject to common administrative control;

(4) excluding or otherwise denying equal jobs or benefits to a qualified individual because of the known disability of an individual with whom the qualified individual is known to have a relationship or association;

(5) (A) not making reasonable accommodations to the known physical or mental limitations of an otherwise qualified individual with a disability who is an applicant or employee, unless such covered entity can demonstrate that the accommodation would impose an undue hardship on the operation of the business of such covered entity; or

(B) denying employment opportunities to a job applicant or employee who is an otherwise qualified individual with a disability, if such denial is based on the need of such covered entity to make reasonable accommodation to the physical or mental impairments of the employee or applicant;

(6) using qualification standards, employment tests or other selection criteria that screen out or tend to screen out an individual with a disability or a class of individuals with disabilities unless the standard, test or other selection criteria, as used by the covered entity, is shown to be job-related for the position in question and is consistent with business necessity; and

(7) failing to select and administer tests concerning employment in the most effective manner to ensure that, when such test is administered to a job applicant or employee who has a disability that impairs sensory, manual, or speaking skills, such test results accurately reflect the skills, aptitude, or whatever other factor of such applicant or employee that such test purports to measure, rather than reflecting the impaired sensory, manual, or speaking skills of such employee or applicant (except where such skills are the factors that the test purports to measure).

(c) Medical Examinations and Inquiries.—

(1) In General.—The prohibition against discrimination as referred to in subsection (a) shall include medical examinations and inquiries.

Section 103. Defenses.

(a) In General.—It may be a defense to a charge of discrimination under this Act that an alleged application of qualification standards, tests, or selection criteria that screen out or tend to screen out or otherwise deny a job or benefit to an individual with a disability has been shown to be job-related and consistent with business necessity, and such performance cannot be accomplished by reasonable accommodation, as required under this title.

Table of Cases

Author Index

General Index

Americans with Disabilities (ADA), 481–484; administrative costs, 487; evasions, 492–493; justifications for ADA, 485–486; medical exams, 492; reasonable accommodation, 484–485, 488–491; "undue hardships," 485–488

Affirmative action, 95, 227–228, 255, 256, 388–389, 395–437; desirability of, 417–419; federal contracting, 433–437; libertarian view of, 413–415; market survival of, 419–420; minority set-asides, 429–433; private, 413–421; proportionate representation 409–410; public sphere, 421–437; remedial relief, 405–410; taxpayer support of, 422–423; unconstitutional conditions, 421–422; victims only 408–409; *Weber* case, 399–405; welfare state, 423–424

Age Discrimination in Employment Act (ADEA), 441–479; BFOQ, 452–456; coverage, 442–445; hiring, 450–456; mandatory retirement, 456–476; pensions, 466–469, 473; purposes, 443–444; senior executives, 464

Age discrimination, 441–479; administrative controls, 465; common practice of, 447–448; comparisons to race and sex, 444–448; relational contracts, 448–450

AIDS, 492–494

Antidiscrimination principle, 1–6, 24–27, 232, 464–465, 496–497

Antimiscegenation laws, 114

At-will contracts, 42, 60, 148–158

Autonomy: corrective justice, and, 20; role of, 503; sexual harassment, 357–359

BFOQ, 281, 283–312; age, 452–456; airline attendants, 300–303; business necessity, 285–287, 301–302; cost differentials, 290–297; customer preferences, 299–309; disparate impact, 303–304; legislative history, 286–287; pensions, 314; pregnancy, 329; prison guards, 307–308; protective legislation, 297–299; safety justifications, 309–312; statutory construction, 283–286

Back pay, 405–410

Baseball cards, 48–51

Bayes theorem, 40–41, 240

Biology, 271–272, 342–343, 372–373

Business necessity, 212–221; age, 442; BFOQs, 285–287, 301–302; construct studies, 216–217; content studies, 216; criterion validity, 217, 218–222; legitimate business purpose, 233–234

Car sales, 51–54

Carolene Products, footnote 4, 117–118

Citizenship, 133–134

Civil capacity, 134–135

Civil rights, meanings of, 499–500

Civil Rights Bill, 1990, 3, 174–175, 234–236, 465

Civil War amendments, 130–135

Coercion, 15–18, 307–308

Collective bargaining, 118–125, 139–140

Collective choice, 60–69, 94–95

Color-blind norm, 176–178, 227–229, 288, 395–398, 401–405, 424–425

Commerce power, 135–140; 1875 act under, 136–137; 1964 act under, 139–140

Common carriers, 83–86